The BOOK *of* ROAST

THE CRAFT OF COFFEE ROASTING
FROM BEAN TO BUSINESS

PRESENTED AND PUBLISHED BY

roast

MAGAZINE

First Edition
ISBN-10: 0-9987717-0-8
ISBN-13: 978-0-9987717-0-0

Printed in the United States of America
Library of Congress Control Number: 2017903128

The Book of Roast

Publisher: Connie Blumhardt
Art Director: Jeremy Leff
Editor: Emily Puro

Roast magazine is published bi-monthly by JC Publishing. One-year subscriptions are $35 for subscribers with mailing addresses within the United States; $55 US for Canada; and $65 US for all other countries.

Roast magazine, 1631 NE Broadway, No. 125, Portland, Oregon 97232-1425

COVER PHOTO | Roasting at Stoked Roasters, Hood River, Oregon. | *Photo by Mark Shimahara*

Dedicated to those about to roast;
we salute you.

TABLE OF CONTENTS

PART I | An Introduction to Specialty Coffee Roasting

The History of Coffee Roasting

Roasting Through the Ages
Exploring the Roots of American Craft Roasting **18**

Machinery, Ingenuity, Discovery
A History of Roasting Equipment **24**

Saying Coffee
The Naming Revolution **32**

PART II | Origin & Green Coffee

Coffee Production & Processing

A Family Album
Getting to the Roots of Coffee's Plant Heritage **42**

Cultivating Taste
Coffee Growing 101 .... **50**

Handling the Cherry
The Risks and Rewards of Processing Methods
Origin Case Study: Hawaii **54**

Making Sense of Certifications
A Guide to Green Coffee Certifications **60**

Green Coffee Buying

Signed, Sealed Delivered
A Guide to Green Buying, Parts 1 & 2 68

Talk the Talk
Understanding Commodity Market Lingo 78

Green Coffee Storage & Transportation

Banking Your Green
Proper Storage and Handling of Green Beans. 86

Storage Woes
The Pros and Cons of Third-Party Warehousing 90

Green Coffee Defects

Detecting Defects: Plants & Quakers 100

Detecting Defects:
Overferment / Sour and Stinker Beans 104

Detecting Defects: Defects Created in the Dry Mill 109

Detecting Defects: Storage and Transportation Defects 114

Detecting Defects & Celebrating Gems
The Search for the Perfect Green Bean. 120

Cracking the Phenol Code
Uncovering the Mystery Behind This Taste Defect 126

A Focus on Flaws
Do You Use the SCA's Green Arabica Coffee Classification System? 130

PART III | Roasting

Roasting Equipment

In Hot Pursuit
What Every Business Owner Needs to Know
Before Purchasing a Coffee Roaster 140

Grounds Maintenance
Care and Feeding of Your Roasters 148

The Science of Coffee & Coffee Roasting

The Science of Coffee Roasting
A Brief Overview of Chemical Changes **154**

The Science of Browning Reactions **160**

Roasting Science
Looking Closely at Your Curves **166**

The Heat Is On
A Roaster's Guide to Heat Transfer **172**

Heat Wave
The Way Heat Transfers Your Beans from Green to Brown **178**

Turning Up the Heat on Acrylamide **186**

Alchemy in the Roasting Lab
Discovering Organic Acids, Parts 1 & 2 .... **190**

The Science Behind Coffee Aroma **198**

The Chemisty of Brewing
How Coffee Transforms, from Bean to Brew **202**

The Bitter End
Making a Case for Chlorogenic Acid **208**

Roasting Styles & Techniques

Coffee Roasting
Fine-Tuning Your Technique **218**

Reflections on Roasting Fundamentals **226**

Unwinding the Sample Roasting Thread
How Roasters Manage Quality in Small Doses **230**

Logged In
*How to Use a Roast Log to Improve Your
Coffee and Streamline Your Business* **236**

The Naked Bean
Roasting to Perfection **242**

To Have and Have Not
The Struggle With Sample Roasting **246**

Roast Right the First Time
How to Prevent Inconsistencies, Deficiencies and Errors **253**

How to Be Cool
Cooling Methods and Their Impact from Roast to Cup **256**

Fire Fighters
Prevent Your Beans from Going Up in Smoke **260**

On Good Terms—A Roaster's Dictionary
Green Bean, Roasting and Cupping Terminology **266**

Cupping & Sensory Evaluation

Craft of Cupping
The Art and Science of the Silver Spoon **282**

Cupping Revisited
A Primer for Advanced Coffee Testing **296**

Unbottling the Aromas of Coffee
Improving Sensory Skills with Le Nez Du Café **302**

Quality Control

Lab Report
*How to Set Up an In-House Coffee Lab for
Quality Control and Training* **310**

The Color of Coffee
Using Color Analysis in Quality Control **316**

Blending

Blending the Rules
The Art and Science of Combining Coffees **326**

The Art of the Blend
Channeling Inspiration Into the Cup **332**

Make Your Mark
Creating and Successful Signature Blend **340**

Blending for Espresso: Parts 1 & 2 .... **344**

Flavor, Magnified
Roasting Strategies for Espresso **356**

Finding Beauty in the Blend
What's the Appeal for Today's Specialty Roasters? **362**

Decaffeinated Coffee

Deconstructing Decaf
Decaffeinated Processes Explained **370**

Packaging

Only the Essentials
Advances in Coffee Packaging Equipment **380**

PART IV | Operating a Specialty Coffee Roasting Business

Business Basics

The Importance of a Business Plan
and Business Planning **388**

Flow Chart
How to Plan an Efficient Layout in a Small Production Plan **396**

Leasing 101 for Roasters **402**

The Devil Is in the Details
Production Control and Inventory Management **406**

Write It Up
A Practical Guide to Documenting Business Procedures **410**

Coffee Counts
Accounting and Finance for Coffee Roasters **418**

Marketing Deconstructed
A Guide for Specialty Coffee Roasters and Retailers **424**

Weak Link
*Balancing the Synergy Between Product Development,
Quality Control and Supply Chain Management* **430**

Matter of Appearance
What Trademark Infringement Can Mean for a Brand **436**

Rules & Regulations

Smoke in the Air
An Update on Emissions and Air-Quality Regulations **444**

The Food Safety Modernization Act
Are You in Compliance? **448**

Index **455**

When *Roast* magazine first started publishing in 2004, there were virtually no references for coffee roasters. The Roasters Guild was just finding its legs, coffee consultants were few and far between, and the Specialty Coffee Association of America was toying around with the idea of creating certifications. *Roast* introduced readers to the intricacies of roasting coffee.

Over the years we have covered numerous topics in detail—coffee production and processing, green coffee buying and storage, green coffee defects, roasting equipment, the science of roasting, roasting styles and techniques, cupping and sensory evaluation, and roasting business basics. We want to share with you all the knowledge we've collected in the pages of *Roast*. While many articles in this book were originally published between 2004 and 2016, we believe these selections are just as relevant today for aspiring and professional coffee roasters. We updated information that was out of date and, when possible, we

Photo by Mark Shimahara

updated titles and company affiliations for sources cited in these articles. The original publication date is noted on the first page of each article, and we added some new articles that are exclusive to this book.

From the history of roasting to writing a business plan, *The Book of Roast* will fully engage you in the world of coffee roasting. We hope this collection motivates you to begin roasting or helps you cement your current roasting technique and move to the next level of roasting. ■

ACKNOWLEDGEMENTS

I am eternally grateful for all the passionate roasters who light the torch every day to roast coffee. Without them, I would not have this amazing career in coffee. Thank you for your drive, your commitment, and for providing me with fuel every morning.

Special thanks to the amazing *Roast* magazine team—Jeremy Leff, Emily Puro, Claire Harriman, Beth Winburne and Mark Shimhara. Without their efforts, this book would not have been possible. Thanks also to our past editors and employees, Shanna Germain, Kelsey Klebba, Allyson Marrs and Kelly Stewart, all of whom contributed to this book, and to all the writers who have shared their knowledge and expertise in the pages of *Roast*.

And I would like to express great gratitude for my husband, daughters and family who support me each and every day and drive me to try and make this world a better place.

Connie

Connie Blumhardt
Publisher
Roast magazine

PART I

AN INTRODUCTION TO
SPECIALTY COFFEE ROASTING

HISTORY OF ROASTING

Roasting Through the Ages

Exploring the Roots of American Craft Roasting

by Bruce Mullins

• FROM THE MAY/JUNE 2009 ISSUE OF *ROAST* •

HISTORY, marginalized and reduced for most Americans in school to a mind-numbing exercise of memorizing dates and places, seems largely irrelevant to most working adults, even to many of us in our exceptional careers as specialty coffee professionals. For unlike other time-honored food professions such as artisan baking or fine winemaking, where traditional methods have been cherished and handed down for generations, our predecessors in coffee roasting seldom gave thought to recording and preserving their techniques, recipes, discoveries and innovations—in other words, their shared coffee knowledge and history. Perhaps the methods were too commonplace to warrant recording or were lacking in interest to others, or our forebears thought it too tedious to transcribe the details of running a business. Whatever the reasons, precious little information about the history of craft roasting here or abroad has been preserved.

By drawing on some rare source materials covering the early years of the American coffee industry from the early 19th century through the middle of the 20th century, we can explore the early roots of today's craft roasting, adding depth, color and texture to the more staid technical and scientific aspects of coffee. Such knowledge and appreciation of our common coffee history—we are, after all, nothing more or less than chapters in the middle of an unfinished book—ultimately gives today's craft roasters a better sense of who we are and where we are going, rather than just what we do for a living.

Lost Cause: The Forgotten Coffee Temperance Movement

In the early decades of the 19th century, there was a seldom-remembered movement advocating coffee and tea temperance in the United States. The medical "authorities" behind the movement were convinced that the consumption of coffee and tea was harmful to the body and soul of the imbiber, in much the same way that the misuse of alcoholic beverages is viewed today.

One of the primary voices behind the drive to banish coffee from America was Dr. William Alcott of Boston. In his book *Tea and Coffee*, published in 1839, Alcott states his case clearly and unequivocally: "In regards to the general properties of coffee, and its effects on the human system, there is now, among medical men, so far as we know, but one opinion. It is what may properly be called a narcotic medicine, of more or less power, according to its strength and the quantity used."

Pointing to the greater damage believed done by hot coffee versus cold coffee, the author gives us his proof positive of the deleterious effects of drinking coffee. "Now," Alcott writes, "if we have proved any thing clearly ... it is that the stomach is sooner or later weakened, in a greater or less degree, by the use of both coffee and tea, and especially by the use of these drinks hot." If we harbored doubts about the point, Alcott reminds us, "The condition of the stomach and liver of Napoleon at his decease—who was a great coffee drinker—cannot have escaped the notice of every one who is at all familiar with his history."

Concluding his thoughts regarding the effect of coffee on the human system, Alcott minces no words: "In view of the whole subject, therefore, we are driven to the conclusion, however sweeping it may seem, that no person can be in the habitual use of the smallest quantity of tea or coffee, cold or hot, or in fact of any drink but pure water, without more or less deranging the action of the stomach and liver, and ultimately, these and the nerves and brain, of the whole system. Nay, we are driven to a position stronger still, which is, that no person can take these poisons at all, without, in a greater or less degree, abridging human happiness and human life."

Not surprisingly (and perhaps thankfully), Alcott's ideas found more detractors than admirers, and consumption of his "dreaded coffee"—both hot and cold—continued to increase steadily throughout the rest of the century.

Recollections of a 19th-Century American Craft Roaster

The later years of the 19th century were a time of great growth and opportunity for professional coffee roasters in America. Developments in technology made large-batch roasting economically feasible, while developments in transit made for cost-effective transportation of both green and roasted coffee.

The following first-person transcript was written by Ferdinand Ach, a coffee roaster from Dayton, Ohio, and was published in the

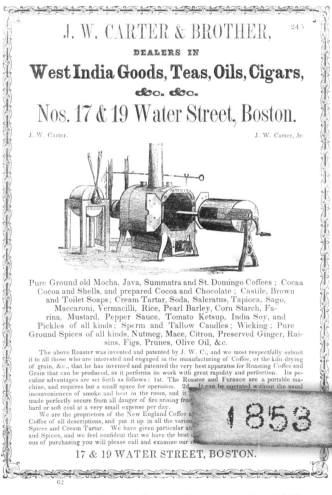

Advertisement for Carter pull-out coffee roasters from 1853. James W. Carter was awarded patent number 4,849 in 1846 for his roaster, one of America's first patented commercial roasters.

Silver Anniversary Issue of William H. Ukers' *Tea & Coffee Trade Journal* in September 1926. It gives an excellent overview of the activities of a typical urban coffee roaster of the 1870s.

Ach notes that he "enlisted" as a bookkeeper at age 15 with one Edward Canby, coffee roaster, in March 1877. As Ach recollected, "My title of bookkeeper was more complimentary than deserved. Office duties (including the sweeping thereof) occupied not more than three or at most four hours daily, except at trial-balance time, and even then interruptions to assist at other functions were frequent and incessant. Every half-hour or so, the head and only roaster, who was also foreman, engineer, and porter, would bawl up the basement hatchway 'All ready!' which meant that the accountant, auditor, house salesman, and general white-collar functionary (myself), was to beat it hastily to said basement, and with a wooden hoe-like implement, rake the discharging coffee into the pan, so that it might be properly cooled."

Without electrical motors to power the roasters or cooling trays, manufacturing enterprises in this period typically relied on a single steam-powered engine for power, using leather belts hanging from overhead pulleys to drive the machinery. As Ach described his employer's setup, "The premises we occupied were known as the 'Wine of Tar' Building [a patent medicine concern that had gone out of business in 1875], a rather ramshackle affair equipped with a very eccentric steam engine, which at periods startled the residential neighborhood by unearthly shrieks, caused by something letting go and releasing the steam. Our entire force of girl operatives would rush into the street, and both remained there until assured that no explosion was imminent. They would be closely followed by yours truly; not out of gallantry, but because he then as now believed in safety first."

Today we enjoy access to a wide assortment of different single origins; however, roasters in the 19th century were limited to only a few—with Brazilian coffees representing more than 75 percent of U.S. imports during the post-Civil War period Ach describes. "A popular blend was Java and Rio," Ach notes, "a singular combination ... Golden Rio was classed with the high grades. There were some really attractive Golden Rios, large yellow bean, bright roasters, and not so heady as the greener Rios of later days. Guatemalas and Maracaibos were pretty well known. Bogatas [sic] came into favor a good bit later. Mexicans were used, but cautiously, as they were likely to run hidey, due as we believed, to their contact in shipment with hides because of imperfect transportation facilities."

During the same period, Java represented an additional 9 percent of U.S. green imports. "The Old Government Java of those days was really Sumatra," Ach explains. "No deception intended in calling it Java, a name recognized as its legitimate designation not only in America, but in its principal market Amsterdam. This technical irregularity was later prohibited in ruling under the national Pure Food Law."

Sea Salt and Skimmings: The Historic Limitations of Green Coffee

For today's craft roasters used to the speed and efficiency of receiving green coffee shipments from origin, it is amazing to consider some of the challenges faced by coffee roasters in the early 20th century.

Published in 1910, the book *History and Reminiscences of Lower Wall Street and Vicinity* is a first-person report about the merchants and traditions of New York's premier coffee and tea street—at the time, the source for nearly all of the nation's green coffee. Written by Abram Wakeman, who started on the street as an office boy earning 50 cents for a six-day workweek (from which was deducted 25 cents for every tasting cup that was broken during washup), the book describes the importation of "old government" Java coffees into New York—which, as Ach mentions, were perhaps actually from Sumatra.

"Prior to the founding of the Coffee Exchange, Java was the coffee of speculation—not only the condition of the market, but also that of the coffee when it arrived being uncertain," Wakeman writes. "It was considered a good gamble, the coffee being bought at the [Java] Government sales, which took place every four months. The coffee of the December sale was thought to have better chance of arriving [in New York] 'brown,' which enhanced its value."

"Let me explain why Java should arrive 'brown,'" Wakeman continues. "When shipped it is very pale, the same color as an ordinary Maracaibo. After being placed in the hold of a vessel, the hatches are battened down as tight as possible. While in the tropical climate the moisture of the coffee evaporates, producing almost a steam in the hold. This moisture condenses on the bottom of the decks and drops on the mats, damaging a portion of the coffee. This damaged coffee is called 'skimmings.' The steam has caused the coffee to become almost parboiled. After the excessive dampness passes away, the heat causes the coffee to 'brown.' The browning process is what gives Java the fine flavor. Any other mild coffee going through the same process will also be greatly improved and closely resemble Java in appearance and taste."

Amazingly, the semi-roasted coffee accidentally produced in the sauna-like conditions that existed below decks was thought by early roasters to be an improvement over the original. Wakeman notes, "As soon as the vessel sailed, float contracts were sold and resold many times before she arrived. As the time drew near for arrival, the anxiety to know as to how her cargo would turn out commenced; if light there would be a loss, if brown a profit."

The situation Wakeman describes with December sailings from what is now Indonesia exists even to this day, as the cooler ocean waters and air hasten the condensation of the coffee's water vapor during the winter months. Most craft roasters have witnessed the changes in many Indonesian coffees' arrival quality as the months

Carter-style pull-out coffee roasters in service at Thurber's in New York, circa 1870. Roasted coffees were dropped into wooden troughs after the drum was pulled from the roaster.

progress, with the potential for damage from condensation and heat feared by today's roasters, rather than anticipated as they once were.

Profession and Confession of an Early New York Roaster

Decades before Ukers crafted his extraordinary *All About Coffee* in the early 1920s, another coffee scholar extensively researched and wrote about the burgeoning American business of roasting coffee. Authoritatively written and first published in 1881 by Francis Thurber, *Coffee: From Plantation to Cup* was dedicated not to Thurber's wife or a professional colleague, but rather amazingly "To The Man At Poughkeepsie, One of the Chosen Few Who Know How To Make A Good Cup Of Coffee." From the coffee-loving author, this dedication was the highest praise possible for an anonymous coffee vendor at Thurber's oft-visited railroad station.

Thurber's lucid and flowing text, written less than 75 years after Alcott's condemnation of coffee, is a celebration of the virtues and beauty of coffee. Barely one lifetime separated Alcott and Thurber, but their profoundly different takes on coffee reveal the effects of America's embrace of technology and scientific learning. Thurber, the head of a prominent New York coffee roasting and grocery distribution operation, deftly mixes his personal coffee knowledge with the latest scientific information on the subject, all flavored with his keen opinions and dry wit. Thurber, without a doubt, would be in his element today with all of the excitement and passion about specialty coffee and craft roasting.

"The most important of all the conditions necessary to be observed in the production of a cup of good coffee is the process of roasting the bean," states Thurber. "The finest quality of coffee unskillfully roasted will give a less satisfactory result in the cup than a poor quality roasted in the best manner." He

Proud owner and staff outside a Harrisburg, Pennsylvania, coffee roastery during the 1880s.

Coffee brokers in Philadelphia in 1895, with samples of their green coffees. Philadelphia and New York were late 19th-century hubs of green coffee suppliers and roasters.

further declares, presumably from firsthand knowledge, "It is no easy matter to acquire the skill in manipulation and accuracy of judgment necessary to roast coffee successfully. Among professional coffee roasters some are bunglers, although their lives have been spent in the occupation, while others seem to be peculiarly adapted to the business, and with much less experience uniformly turn out good work."

With insight that any craft roaster today could appreciate, Thurber describes the potential shortcomings of small-scale retail roasting: "It is with difficulty that uniformly good work can be obtained, and then it is only after repeated failures, necessarily costly to the retailer, because in addition to losing the coffee, his trade is imperiled. Oftentimes a customer, whom it has taken years to secure, has been lost during the experimental effort to acquire sufficient skill to properly roast coffee in a [shop] roaster. Sometimes there will be too much, and then again, too little fire; the attention of the same person cannot always be conveniently given; the turning is not usually as steady and continuous by hand as when done by steam power, while it is manifestly impossible for a person only roasting occasionally to attain the same degree of skill and experience that is acquired by a fit person who makes it a business."

The style of roasters Thurber's roasting business used were Carter patent pull-outs: fire-breathing, "old school" two-bag roasters that discharged their coffee by two operators pulling the drum and coffee out of the fire, and dumping the hot coffee into wooden troughs through a breach in the side of the drum. While the rated capacities of Thurber's roasters were 300 pounds per batch, he found that the results were substantially better when roasting 200-pound batches. The Carter's roast cycle reportedly was 45 minutes per batch (extraordinarily long by today's standards, but typical of the period's technology), with a difference of 30 to 60 seconds between roast levels at the end of the roast. Including dumping, cooling, recharging the drum, and refueling the fire with fresh coal, a roast could be counted on to take a total of 60 minutes.

American Ingenuity Triumphs: Innovations in Coffee Roasting Technology

The more recent evolution of American roasting equipment is well summarized in a rare book written by Payson MacKaye, entitled *The Coffee Man's Manual*, released in 1942 by The Spice Mill Publishing Company in New York.

Spice Mill Publishing was an offshoot of the original Jabez Burns Company in New York, developers of much of the technology still used worldwide for air-cooled drum roasting, and published the famous *The Spice Mill* magazine, covering the coffee trade from the late 19th until the mid-20th century.

The roaster that brought together all of the technological components that we are familiar with today was the Jabez Burns patent 1864 roaster. As MacKaye notes, "The original Burns roaster represented the greatest advance in the art up to that time. An ingenious system of helical flanges (inside the drum) not only served to mix and agitate the coffee, so that it was uniformly heated, but also effected complete discharge of the goods when a door was opened in the front head. This new feature made it unnecessary to remove the cylinder from its position above the firebox—or to stop its rotary motion for charging and discharging. Green coffee was dropped into the cylinder through an opening at the back and a hole through the central shaft provided means for taking small samples for judging the progress of the roast by the color and development of the beans."

Regarding improvements to the basic Burns design, MacKaye writes, "In 1881, the shutter-type discharge door was replaced by a turn-over front head which permitted charging and discharging through the same opening at the front of the machine. This type of bricked-up coal-fired roaster continued in use by the majority of coffee roasting firms in North America until 1914. Its capacity was two Brazil bags (264 pounds green weight) and the roasting time 30 minutes. The average daily output was 30 bags per roaster. Four roasters were operated by one man and 6.6 lbs of coal were required to roast a bag of coffee." Today, of course, those of us who are trained as craft roasters cringe at the idea of 30-minute roasts because of the "baked" damage to the taste of the coffee, especially in the bright top notes. Thankfully, softer Brazilian coffees—then a large share of the coffees imported into the U.S.—would have suffered less from such extended roast cycles.

"Soon after the turn of the century," MacKaye continues, "the quality of the roast and efficiency of heat transfer were much improved by the use of a roasting cylinder with many small perforations—so that the heat was transmitted largely by hot gases, which passed through the perforations and to a lesser degree by contact with the hot metal of the cylinder." Prior to the development of perforated drums, coffee roasting cylinders were solid and constructed of sheet metal, and highly prone to developing hot spots and subsequently scorched or "faced" beans. As MacKaye explains, "The many advantages of gas fuel, in spite of greater cost, resulted in its gradual adoption, beginning about 1900. The first gas-fired machines were standard coal machines, converted to the new fuel by removing the furnace and placing gas burners under the roaster cylinder. There was no change in the roasting time or in general procedure, but some improvement in the uniformity of the product."

As the availability of gas in American cities increased during the years prior to World War I, roasters were designed to take advantage of the inherent qualities that gas offers. MacKaye notes, "The first widely-used machine designed specifically for operation with gas fuel was known as a 'direct-flame' roaster because a mixture of gas and air was burned inside the roasting cylinder and the coffee beans tossed through the flame. The application of heat within the cylinder reduced the roasting time to 15–18 minutes per batch but fuel consumption remained about the same as for converted coal burners because it was necessary to draw a large volume of cold air through the cylinder to temper the flame so the coffee would not burn."

To improve the fuel efficiency and reduce the opportunity for scorching the roast, the next generation of direct-flame American-built roasters was developed. Using an inverted diffusion cover for the gas flame—coupled with an improved series of flanges and baffles to better agitate the green coffee during roasting—the Jabez Burns "Jubilee"-class roasters exemplified this new design, offering reduced fuel consumption by minimizing the need to introduce cool tempering air into the roasting cylinder. According to MacKaye, who evidently had firsthand experience with these roasters, the improved design reduced fuel consumption by 25 percent. At the same time, Jabez Burns' competitors, including Huntley in New York and Lambert in Michigan, were building similar direct-flame roasters.

Conclusion

While many innovations and improvements to coffee and coffee roasters have occurred since World War II, digging deep and discovering the oldest roots of American craft roasting can be an especially interesting and beneficial pastime. If nothing else, it helps put our generation's role in the history of coffee into its proper context as a chapter instead of a conclusion. Our ultimate responsibility to coffee's history is to honor it and all those associated with it, and to never forget that we are not the first, nor will we be the last, people to love coffee with a passion that flows into the rest of our lives. ∎

· ·

BRUCE MULLINS *has been passionate about specialty coffee since the late '70s, after graduating from a private college and landing the prestigious job of unloading sacks of green coffee from trucks. Mullins has served on the board of directors of the Specialty Tea Institute and as a Coffee Corps volunteer in Africa and South America, and currently serves as chair of the Coffee Quality Institute Advisory Council as well as an international cupping judge for Cup of Excellence competitions.*

Lambert one-bag direct-flame roaster, a package deal from 1912.

Photo by Bruce Mullins

Machinery, Ingenuity, Discovery

A History of Roasting Equipment

by Launtia Taylor & Jens Roelofs

• FROM THE MAY/JUNE 2010 ISSUE OF *ROAST* •

We don't know when coffee was first roasted, but it's easy to imagine the scene: A group of inquisitive people gather around a fire where, on top of a stone dish, green coffee beans turn brown as they caramelize. As the beans pop, a heady aroma fills the air.

Roasting equipment originated with a simple container over the fire. Through the ages, coffee lovers have continued to invent new and more efficient ways of roasting beans. Early, rudimentary contraptions gave way to the innovative designs of the industrial age.

Today, roasting companies use fully automated machines that would have boggled coffee drinkers' minds even a century ago. We have invented and created sophisticated computer-controlled machines to accomplish the simple process of roasting coffee beans more consistently and with higher-quality characteristics.

Let's take a trip back in time to discover how coffee-roasting developments unfolded, identify the milestones in the history of roasting, and examine how manufacturers reacted to the demands of the market. A closer look at the history of coffee roasting equipment shows how much expertise and inventive talent have been devoted to the search for an optimal roasting process, both in the past and in the present day.

18th-century coffee roaster.

The Beginnings:
"It Is Certainly The Roasting Which Is Most Important"

Soon after the discovery of coffee, roasting methods began to evolve. In the 15th and 16th centuries, coffee beans were roasted over coals using a perforated clay dish with a handle that looked "something like the modern kitchen skimmer," writes William H. Ukers in his 1922 history book *All About Coffee*. By the year 1600, coffee-obsessed engineers were tinkering with initial roasting machine designs. But apparently roasting was more difficult than it looked. When the French physician François Bernier visited Cairo in the mid-17th century, Ukers noted, "in all the city's thousand-odd coffee houses he found but two persons who understood the art of roasting the bean."

At this point in history, some shops and coffeehouses operated roasting machines designed to accommodate batches of 5 kilograms or less, but those who could afford to purchase green beans were more likely to roast them at home in uncovered pans over charcoal or wood-burning stoves. In the mid-17th century, enterprising coffee roasters developed metal cylinders equipped with cranks for mixing the beans, according to Ukers.

As the coffee trade spread around the globe, early coffee drinkers shared their roasting techniques with people from other cultures. Consequently, as the French coffee historian Hélène Desmet-Grégoire writes, "From Arabia to the Near East, from Maghreb to the Mediterranean countries, the same kind of roaster is found: a metal sheet that is laid directly onto the fire or a drum-shaped container replete with a crank and source of heat."

The initial roasting equipment of the 18th and early 19th century was constructed of metal—sheet metal plates, copper, brass or cast iron. Most roasting contraptions were homemade, though in the 19th century, inventors began to design, patent and manufacture machines. With nearly all models, heat absorption took place through direct contact (conductivity) with the heat source. External heating provided even distribution of heated air to the coffee during roast and a continuous movement of the beans within the roasting drum; it also prevented tipping of the beans. Roasters were designed for fuels like coal, coke and wood—in general, anything that provided a fuel source. Coke burned cleaner than coal, and the least clean fuel source was wood, which also imparted a smoky flavor to the coffee.

The earliest roasters were designed in four different styles:

1) Roasting boxes and roasting pans. The stationary box- or pan-shaped roasting device with a lid was suitable for roasting over open fires. The operator held the long-handled pan over the fire and agitated the beans by shaking the contraption.

2) Saucepan-shaped devices, either open or lidded. These bowl-shaped bins were moveable and designed to handle small amounts of coffee of up to 2 kilograms. Using spoon-shaped rods, the operators were able to stir the beans inside the bin during the roasting process. This allowed relatively consistent heat transfer and roasting.

3) Spheres. Roasting pans and saucepan-shaped devices had shortcomings, as they were open at the top. The more advanced design of spherical "timbal" roasters employed a spindle and a crank to keep the coffee moving. The spheres were easier to operate, and their design accommodated larger amounts of coffee and enabled exhaust air to escape.

4) Cylinders. These precursors of today's drum roasters were, just like spherical roasters, equipped with a spindle and a crank that provided for an even mechanical movement of the roasting product. Also like the spheres, the cylinders were positioned on two fork-like supports over an open fire. After roasting, the beans were added to wooden, clay or stoneware bins and often cooled again with a splash of water. Metal sieves or wire netting, the precursors of today's cooling sieves, were introduced in Europe around 1750. The sieves' movement provided for additional cooling and helped separate the seed coats.

By the late 18th century, coffee knowledge had grown more sophisticated. According to a German encyclopedia published by Dr. Johann Georg Krünitz in 1784, coffee connoisseurs were exploring roasting methods, shrinkage, light and dark roasting, flavored coffee and different cooling techniques. Krünitz pointed to roasting as a major indicator of product quality: "The quality of coffee drink stems not only from the bean, but the former can also be quite poor even if using the best beans. It is certainly the burning or roasting which is most important."

The Industrialization Of Roasting: From Home Roasters To Roasting Plants

Spurred by Europe's economic freedom and the development of the U.S. market, coffee consumption increased markedly between 1824 and 1914. During the industrial revolution, machine manufacturing was born, and the construction of roads, canals and railroads made it easier to transport goods over long distances. Men worked long hours in factories, mills and mines. And competition was fierce among architects and engineers who attempted to outshine each other with ever more awe-inspiring designs.

These years were also a heyday for innovations in roasting technology, as the coffee industry moved away from home-based roasting over the hearth and toward commercial and industrial roasting. A growing group of coffee drinkers preferred the convenience of buying and brewing roasted coffee. Why should you buy green beans and take the time to roast them yourself, when you can just purchase already roasted coffee? In the mid-19th century, Alexius van Gülpen, a German green coffee importer and co-founder of the Emmericher Maschinenfabrik und Eisengiesserei (now called Probat) struck a chord with this assessment of coffee consumers. By adding a refinement step—roasting—the businessman van Gülpen saw the opportunity to enhance his value chain in coffee sales.

But to sell roasted coffee, the necessary technology was needed, so van Gülpen decided to produce the roasting machines as well as procure the beans. A rail link between his factory location in Emmerich, Germany, and the Amsterdam-Basel railway—plus the collaboration with his business partners Johann Heinrich Lensing and Theodor von Gimborn—marked the beginning of the serial production of coffee roasters and, thus, for the increased sales of green coffee and roasting machines.

Free-standing roaster, approximately 1880.

Roasting pan.

Saucepan-shaped roaster.

Spherical roaster.

In 1870, the company produced its spherical, coke-fueled "Lifter" roaster for batch sizes of 2.5 to 120 kilograms. The design allowed the operator to quickly empty the sphere to prevent the beans from overheating.

Using newly available roasting machines, food shops in Europe were advertising "freshly burnt" (aka freshly roasted) coffee, writes C. Hans von Gimborn (Theodor's grandson) in the publication *Nota Bene: Coffee Roasting Machines*. Roasting larger quantities of coffee at once allowed the operator to use less fuel and save time by producing fewer batches.

Elsewhere, other inventors designed roasting prototypes and began to build commercial roasting machines. In 1824, Richard Evans of London patented a commercial-sized cylindrical roaster that is a milestone of industrial production. Evans' device used a hollow axle to discharge steam from the roaster. His design also featured a revolving sampler, turning paddles in the roasting bin and an adjustable fan.

A roaster fire could mean financial ruin for any business, as fire extinguishers and sprinkler systems were not yet in use. To minimize the risk of fire, in the 1840s the enterprising Wright Gillies of New York built a wood-heated outdoor roaster that was situated in the courtyard behind his retail shop. Powered by a horse-drawn pulley, the cylinder-shaped device spun for about 40 minutes to roast each 15- to 20-pound batch.

In 1846, James Carter of Boston was awarded a patent for his cylindrical "pull-out" roaster, which was combined with a furnace. Carter's design was

used for the next two decades in U.S. roasting plants. Machine operators would pull out the cylinder and scatter the roasted coffee on the floor, where it then would be sprinkled with water, according to Ukers. Evans and Carter's designs are early models for the drum roasters used today.

Coffee consumption in the United States began to rise during the 1860s, as Civil War soldiers received coffee in their daily rations. In 1864, Jabez Burns started a New York factory to manufacture his patented roaster with an ingenious interior cylinder design. The 20-year-old Burns reversed the flanges inside the cylinder to allow the roaster to be loaded and unloaded without removing the drum from the heat source. His invention allowed businesses to shorten their production times, which, in turn, made coffee less expensive to produce. For consumers of coffee, this was a boon—roasted beans were no longer a luxury. More than 150 years after Burns filed for his patent, his interior cylinder design is still used in all drum roasters.

The short time frame for the development of a variety of roaster designs signals the increase in demand for commercial roasting technology on both sides of the Atlantic. It was the right time to design and manufacture roasters, which became a business on an industrial scale.

Roaster heating sources shifted—first to coal and later to natural gas. Using coal-fired, perforated roasting cylinders, roasting times decreased from 50 minutes to as little as 20 minutes. Special lids allowed the heat to be regulated—a step that

Carter cylindrical pull-out coffee roaster.

significantly increased the quality of roasted coffee while reducing shrinkage. Natural gas, available in most large cities by the turn of the 20th century, made it possible to position the flame directly under the roasting bin. With a fan, hot air was ducted through the roasting bin to provide convective heat transfer. Gas offered a cleaner burn, convenience and better controlled roast development.

The Emmerich "Quick Roaster"—a coal-fired version was introduced in 1884, and a patented gas model followed in 1889—offered the appeal of greater efficiency. The roaster featured cased worm wheel gearing and an external belt drive. In 1905, Probat introduced a gas roaster with the model name "Perfect," and Burns released the gas model "Jubilee" in 1906. The Jubilee roasters were available in two sizes with a capacity of a two-bag roaster and a four-bag roaster. The new perforated drum design provided for a higher convection compared to previous cylinder designs, which had a significantly higher conductivity. This design also allowed for faster roasting times, down to 16 minutes, and the roasters performed about three roasts per hour. To reduce the impact of tipping due to localized overheating of the perforated roasting cylinder, Probat introduced a double-walled drum. The inner drum or wall was perforated, and the outer wall was solid. The roaster fan drew heated air into the space between the walls and through the perforation of the inner wall into the inside of the roasting drum. This protected the inner perforated wall against clogging and overheating.

An important design improvement in terms of production increase was the option of filling the roaster while the roasting drum was rotating. This allowed the roaster to operate his or her roaster more efficiently. A speedy emptying was also necessary to prevent "subsequent roasting," a problem that had come up due to the higher heat transfer.

Roaster manufacturers also improved the trays for cooling coffee. In the mid-19th century, engineers developed large cooling troughs. Roaster operators poured the hot beans into these troughs and distributed them with rake-like, wooden instruments. Later, manufacturers produced round cooling sieves with paddle-like rotation equipment to stir the coffee. Fans ducted the cooling air through the sieves. Over the years, open-topped cooling sieves were sometimes replaced by closed constructions and cylindrical cooling systems. With the growth of the roasting industry, the dimensions of cooling

1850

A van Gülpen quick roaster.

1870

Spherical, coke-fueled "Lifter" roaster.

systems also grew. These advances in cooling technology limited over-roasting and allowed roaster operators to better control coffee quality.

The Road to High-Tech Roasting

In the past, coffee businesses would send their roastmasters into a steamy hot room filled with roasting machines and beans crunching underfoot. Coffee roasting has come a long way since those days. The sampler and the temperature gauge were introduced and incorporated with the roaster in the early 20th century, and they still remain important tools for many shop roasters, allowing the roaster to control the temperature of the profile and the quality of each roast. After World War II, automatic clean out (known as ACO) systems were introduced to keep the roaster free of deposits. Roasters also were offered thermal afterburners to control emissions from the roasting process.

Twentieth-century engineers continued to investigate new ways to roast. In 1957, Antonio Scolari patented a machine for roasting coffee via infrared lamps, but the concept did not become popular. However, the fluid-bed (hot-air) roaster has stood the test of time. The German company Caasen released a European fluid-bed roaster in 1926. Since then, several fluid-bed roasters have been introduced, including the Australia-made Belaroma Roller Roaster, the Rapido-Nova by Germany's Gothot and, in the United States, the Wolverine and the Sivetz. Michael

Burns Jubilee gas roaster.

Early illustration of a Burns box roaster.

Sivetz patented his fluid-bed roaster design in the 1970s, and makers of small home roasters up to commercial-scale manufacturers like Germany's Neuhaus Neotec continue to model their designs on the Sivetz original.

The purpose of roasting coffee is to produce beans that will create a great-tasting cup of coffee, and advances in technology keep making it easier to produce accurate, repeatable roasts. The computer age has allowed roasters to take advantage of profile roasting technology to measure and graph the internal bean temperature during each roast. Roasters also use laser color and light reflection analyzers, such as Agtron, to measure roast development and ensure consistency. With all of this technology available, many roaster manufacturers continue to service and educate the roasting market on how fresh whole-bean coffee can be offered to the consumer. Today, small roasting shops have the potential to produce great, fresh-roasted beans.

Technological advances in roasting design have continued to focus on improving quality with maximum automation. Today, large-volume roasters use fully automated commercial roasters with high capacities, including features to improve safety and energy consumption. Automation sounds less romantic when compared to the artisan way of eyeballing the roast development and controlling the roast manually based on its aroma development, but in larger commercial

Probat centrifugal roaster.

roasting processes that address the needs of modern roasting companies. Striking a balance between the desired results and the required costs involves finding the ideal compromise between maximum processing performance and reproducible quality. The increase in daily coffee consumption around the world shows that early manufacturers of roasting equipment were on the right track.

Today, roasting businesses have the opportunity to select a roaster with a capacity of 30 grams for sample roasting, a half-bag batch roaster or a large-capacity model that roasts 5,000 kilograms an hour. The future for roasting development will include improvements in environmental controls, automation and operator interface.

At the same time, proving that everything old becomes new again, home coffee roasting is on the rise. Kenneth Davids released his book *Home Coffee Roasting: Romance and Revival* in 1996, spurring a renewed interest in roasting small batches of coffee at home. Through the Internet, home roasters can now purchase equipment and small batches of green beans.

And roasting innovation continues. From the beginning, the partnership between manufacturer and roaster operator was essential and has been the key to developing better roasting technology. Regardless of how customized a technical solution may be, customer feedback to the manufacturer is as essential for keeping roasting technology up to date as it was in the past and as it will be into the future. ■

JENS ROELOFS *is the marketing manager for Probat-Werke.*

roasters, there is a need for more safety and more consistent roasts, considering the amount of coffee to be roasted per batch by the operator.

Probat's tangential roaster (Jupiter), introduced in 1969, offered a closed roasting chamber design that allows for roasting of broken, small, and less-perfect beans, and gives companies who have to deal with frequent bean changes greater flexibility. In 1973, Probat introduced the first centrifugal roaster (Saturn), which consists of a roasting bowl and a specially designed lamella ring and upper housing. The roaster was designed to provide a high percentage of convective heat transfer to the beans, allowing the coffee to travel toroidally inside the bowl for greater roast efficiency and a wider range of roasting times.

Environmental control equipment such as thermal oxidizers, catalytic oxidizers, regenerative thermal oxidizers (RTO), and flameless regenerative thermal oxidizers (FRTO) can be offered with today's roasting systems. Other features, such as preheating of green coffee beans, moisture control for green and roasted beans, carbon monoxide monitors for higher safety, and profile roasting with recipe management are additional improvements than can be incorporated into larger commercial roasting systems.

The development of modern coffee-roasting plants and large industrial roasting companies has continued to speed up. Roaster manufacturers react to growing requirements by developing new

Shop roaster.

Saying Coffee
The Naming Revolution

by Kenneth Davids

• FROM THE NOVEMBER/DECEMBER 2010 ISSUE OF *ROAST* •

anguage is supremely important in the world of coffee. We need it to lead media and consumers alike toward a deeper, more knowing, ultimately more committed relationship with the beverage, and we need it to deepen our own ability to deliver on that relationship.

Which is why I think a review of our collective language about coffee is in order. Both specialty coffee and the language of specialty coffee have undergone an especially dramatic transformation over the past five to seven years. In particular, languages describing roast and green coffee origin are in the throes of change. Older languages overlap with newer languages, while some of the founding terminologies of specialty coffee have disappeared entirely, either to be replaced by new terms or dismissed entirely.

From Heavy to French

Let's start with the evolution of language around darkness or degree of roast.

In the old days, say before cheap robusta took over coffee cans, the language around degree of roast ran something like this:

- Cinnamon (very light brown)
- Light (light end of the traditional American norm)
- Medium
- Medium-high (still preceding the second crack)
- City-high (or just "City"; still preceding the second crack but very close)
- Full city (usually into the second crack; occasional light patches of oil on the surface of the beans)
- Dark (definitely into the second crack; dark brown, sheen of oil)
- Heavy (very dark brown, shiny surface)

Of these terms, light, medium and dark all survive, of course, along with the less obvious descriptor "full city," a term that was taken up enthusiastically by the pioneers of specialty and is still used in some circles. I suppose it survives because the middle of the roast spectrum is so crucial and full city is an attempt to describe the turning moment of the roast cycle—that tantalizing transition at the leading edge of the second crack, neither definitively medium nor dark.

Enter Romance and Europe

The pioneers of specialty had little use for the rest of the hoary, unglamorous language inherited from commercial coffee. Instead, they preferred something that glamorized one of the founding appeals of specialty coffee—more choice for the consumer, more sensory possibilities—and romanticized it with language that evoked the presumed European roots of in-store, small-batch roasting and the old-world artisanry of it all. Consequently, early specialty offered the consumer a whole roast geography: New England (the lightest roast in those days), American (aka medium, regular), Viennese (just into the second crack), and southward in presumed darkness to Italy (Italian or sometimes espresso; solidly into the second crack), farther south darker still—Spanish, Neapolitan or Turkish—with a final bounce back up to northern France for the ultimately dark-roasted French roast.

No wonder dark roasting triumphed over the next 20 years or so of specialty history: Among the romantics and rebels who crowded the early Peet's and Starbucks stores, who wanted to be New English when they could be Italian or French?

Some reality attaches to these names, of course. Certainly in 1950 most American coffee was, well, "American" in roast style, and certainly northern France traditionally roasted coffee darker than anywhere in the world. However, in the 1980s enough specialty coffee namers had actually visited Italy to realize that Italians did not, at least in 1980, roast coffee particularly dark. In fact, Italians roasted their espresso coffee rather light, say somewhere between (using the language of the day) "American" and "Viennese." So to smooth this problem over, some in the industry popularized the idea of a "northern Italian" roast—a phrase describing the middle-of-the-spectrum roast style actually practiced in Italy rather than the very dark styles produced by nostalgic Italian immigrants in New York's Little Italy and San Francisco's North Beach, styles that first gave Americans the idea that dark roasting and Italy went together.

Today most of these romantic European roast descriptors have disappeared from coffee bags and bins. All, that is, except for the ubiquitous "French roast." The extreme nature of this ultra-dark roasted profile, with its thin body and burned pungency, is so polarizing to consumers and so clearly derived from the impact of roast and not from the character of the green coffee that it virtually creates its own product niche. It wears a label that is simultaneously warning to those who find it bitter, shallow and astringent and positive identifier for those 10 percent or so of the coffee drinking population who find its pungency bracingly intense and who won't drink anything else. The "northern Italian" roast descriptor also lives on, though much less prominently, perhaps because it remains a useful way to signal to consumers that the espresso they are about to buy is sweeter and subtler than the robustly pungent espressos that until recently ruled America.

Numbers (in Part) Conquer Romance

What happened to virtually wipe out these early sets of romancing descriptors? Several things, I think. One was the advent of another language to describe roast, a language that comforts us because it rings with such certainty: the language of numbers.

Instrument manufacturers devised ways to read roast color by instrument alone. The instruments report back to us with numbers that describe a continuum of roast color or, more hopefully, changes in sugar chemistry associated with changes in roast color. Carl Staub's Agtron devices have achieved particular success in North America. In my lab, where we regularly use an

Agtron instrument to confirm roast color, we talk about roast not with words, but with numbers based on our instrument readings.

Assuming we keep our Agtron device serviced and calibrated, it gives us quite consistent readings from week to week and month to month. But compare our readings to those generated by another Agtron instrument in another location? The results are considerably less consistent (although still much better than staring at the beans and guessing). Cross-referencing is further complicated by the fact that Agtron proposes two different numerical scales—one set is the original "Commercial" or E10/E20 scale, and the second is the "Gourmet" or M-Basic scale, which Staub devised later in his work to better apply to the specialty practice of 20 years ago, with its emphasis on the dark end of the scale. Our instrument reports in the M-Basic scale.

What about the color readers manufactured by ColorTrack Fresh Roast Systems, Javalytics, Neuhaus-Neotec, Probat and QuantiK? With the exception of Javalytics, these instruments all use their own proprietary scales. (The Javalytics offers the user a choice of four scales, including the two developed by Agtron.) These various scales can roughly be cross-referenced with one another and with the two Agtron versions, but my experience suggests that, regardless of manufacturer or scale, the only way to communicate with any precision between instruments in different locations is to do private instrument-to-instrument calibration by exchanging samples and readings.

From Numbers Back to Words

To return to the theme of language, then, the scales provided by Agtron and various other instruments (all of which invariably read with the *lower* number representing a darker roast and a *higher* number a lighter roast) provide a useful language for describing roast, but a language that remains tricky and ambiguous, almost as tricky as words. Plus, not all small roasting companies have the money to spend on an instrument that costs several thousands of dollars.

The effort to turn Agtron numbers into a usable language accessible to everyone with three hundred bucks to spare came from the Specialty Coffee Association of America (SCAA), which in the early 1990s collaborated with Staub to develop the Agtron/SCAA Roast Classification Color Disk System. The eight reference points in this classification system are identified with rounded numbers in 10-point increments and are matched to eight carefully prepared color disks bearing the most direct possible linguistic descriptors, ranging from "Very Light" to "Very Dark," with "Medium" occupying the midpoint. A sample of roasted coffee, when ground and pressed into a Petri dish, can be matched with a color disk, thus assigning it a number that approximately matches the equivalent number for a ground sample measured on the M-Basic Agtron scale. This system, however ingenious and well-considered, nevertheless appears to have made only a modest impact on the specialty industry.

For one thing, the entire idea of communicating roast color by numbers is thoroughly confusing to consumers (the most frequently asked questions to the editor at *Coffee Review* are puzzled queries about the Agtron numbers that appear with each review). Plus, the high end of the industry appears lately to have re-committed to a more organoleptic and craft approach to determining degree of roast; in other words, more tasting and fewer numbers.

Other Numerical Languages

Numbers figure in other systems for determining and communicating degree of roast. One approach is roughly measuring the internal temperature of the roasting beans by using a probe in the bean bed. Another is measuring the weight loss of the roasted beans—the darker the degree of roast the greater the weight loss. A third is the equipment-relative act of measuring the time of the roast, the favorite starting point of beginning roasters.

The heat probe is particularly useful because it gives us a moving, real-time, on-the-fly numerical measure of roast development or color. Like a thermometer stuck in a turkey, the higher the temperature registered by the probe, the more "done" the roast. I would contend that every roasting installation, however modest, should incorporate such a probe. However, the problem with these simple little devices is, again, consistency across time and place. Even with large, sophisticated, computerized roasting installations, the final call on when to terminate the roast is typically made by the oldest of roast-measurement acts, a human being pulling out a sample of beans with a trier and eyeballing it against a retain sample. The probe and other instrument readings of temperature and airflow supply only a basic framework for this final crucial act (except perhaps in the case of very fast, convection-based "high-yield" roasting machines, where the roast typically develops so quickly that only a machine can act quickly enough to make the call). Certainly formulas have been developed aimed at correcting for variables that impact the variations in probe temperature, like ambient temperature, barometric pressure, bean density and the like, but it appears that, at least with conventional roasting equipment, nothing quite substitutes in that climactic moment of the roast for actually extracting some beans and observing them.

Most of the ways of monitoring roast color and describing it are summed up in a chart on pages 38–39. Note, however, that all of the quantitative values and correspondences proposed in the chart are approximate. Roasting, like so many aspects of coffee production, continues to be difficult to quantify and control with

precision owing to coffee's chemical complexity and variability—a fascinating challenge for some of us and a source of frustration for those who seek quick and certain answers.

Experienced roaster folk also will note that I have simply passed on the much more complex issue of roast profiling, the sequencing and method of transferring heat to the roasting beans and impact on sensory character. Frankly, it was tough enough to get through degree of roast without monopolizing half the magazine.

Dark-Roast Kamikaze and Roast-Color Graphics

Returning to the perhaps more important issue of communicating degree of roast to consumers, a second development appears to have doomed the old geographic-romantic roast-color terminologies: a kind of dark-roast kamikaze that occurred in the '90s. Remember when everybody in the specialty industry except a few East Coast companies roasted *really* dark? By that time Starbucks had managed to define (temporarily, as it turns out) all specialty coffee as dark-roasted coffee, and smaller, newer companies attempted to differentiate themselves from Starbucks by roasting their coffees even darker than Starbucks did. I recall roasters snickering about "Charbucks" when in fact many of their own coffees read several Agtron points darker than the Starbucks norm. For me, the final proof that words had failed us in regard to roast came when I received a sample in the early 2000s that was clearly labeled, on the bag, as a "light" roast. This "light"-roasted coffee was—literally, measured by instrument—considerably darker than a Starbucks espresso roast.

Another thing happened. Consumers began to untangle the impact of roast and the impact of the green coffee, permitting roasters to represent darkness of roast graphically using roast color scales or thermometers. Advances in inexpensive color printing accelerated this graphic approach to communicating roast color. For me, roast color thermometers are an immeasurably better way to communicate roast color than any of the older sets of names. Roast thermometers or scales may not be romantic, but they get the fundamental point across—roast color is relative and exists as a continuum. It cannot be reduced to a series of separate, absolutely defined points on that continuum.

Roast-color thermometers also get the roast-color-communication act out of the way using economical visual means, allowing roasters to allocate more words to the green coffee. And, as it turns out, they needed those words.

Adding the Details

As roast descriptors diminished in importance, green coffee description grew dramatically richer and more complex.

In the '70s, specialty coffee lured converts away from the boring world of supermarket and diner coffee not only with European roast names, but also with the exotic names of the places the coffees came from: Kenya, Guatemala, Sumatra, etc. There was usually a second part to those early names, a qualifier: Kenya was usually Kenya AA, Guatemala usually Guatemala Antigua, Sumatra usually Sumatra Mandheling and so on.

Where did this first wave of names come from? They were, of course, lifted straight off the burlap bags in which the coffee arrived and they reflected the traditional terminology provided by the decades-old system of origins and grades developed by the traditional coffee supply chain. The coolest sounding of these market names migrated right from the bag to specialty coffee menu boards and labels. Much of the Colombia coffee specialty roasters bought in those days came through the rather anonymous channels of the Colombian Coffee Growers Federation, so grade rather than region was the preferred modifier: "Colombia Supremo." Same with Kenya; you didn't want to challenge the newly coffee-energized brains of your novice consumers with a lot of cooperative names that changed by season and auction anyhow, and most Kenya came from the same general region, so grade to the rescue again: Kenya AA. For Guatemala, however, region worked better than grade. Antigua sounded romantic (a few customers may actually have visited there) whereas Strictly Hard Bean (SHB) required too much explanation. Plus, back then, most fine Guatemalas that made it to the United States came from Antigua (or pretended to) anyhow. Hence, "Guatemala Antigua" became the label name of choice.

Traditional Origin and Grade Names as Free Co-Branding

As this regional and grade naming caught on and codified, it brought with it another powerful benefit to the new specialty roasters. These regional and grade names essentially became brands. An impressive and, to me, slightly baffling example of the power of this informal origin-name-branding is Tanzania

Peaberry. True, peaberry is a grade, but Tanzania is the only one of these early specialty green coffee names that regularly added an obligatory reference to bean type. And the connection of Tanzania and peaberry has hung on. Despite the obvious availability of many fine coffees from Tanzania that are not peaberry, it apparently is still difficult for roasters to sell a Tanzania without the peaberry name attached.

Cup Character and Origin/Grade

Along with freebie brands, the specialty industry also inherited from the conventional coffee supply chain an expectation that various origins and grades embody a matching traditional cup character. What people seldom recognized at the time was the fact that the consistent cup character associated with certain origins is not at all natural or inevitable, but the product of human will and cultural practices, hence subject to change.

Allow me to characterize the traditional Costa Rica SHB profile as cleanly acidy, powerful and balanced in structure but relatively straightforward in aromatic nuance. This cup expectation is based on three factors: a Costa Rica tradition of meticulous wet-processing, an almost universal planting of the balanced but aromatically straightforward caturra variety, and high growing altitudes. It also was owing to a supply chain that favored the recognized Costa Rica profile when grading and selecting coffees. Going to the other extreme, we now know that the cup character of the classic Lintong or Mandheling type of Sumatra is mainly owing to a processing wrinkle only recently named wet-hulling, and secondarily to moderate growing elevations. Classic Ethiopia Yirgacheffe coffees mainly owe their unusual cup character to very distinctive local varieties of arabica as influenced by careful wet-processing and moderately high growing elevations.

Readers may disagree with the detail in the preceding paragraph, but the point I am making should be clear: Origin cup character is not inevitable or natural, but the product of culture, history and human will.

At any rate, we know where this story went: jet planes, Internet,

ELEMENTS OF A CONTEMPORARY COFFEE LABEL

- Country of origin
- Region
- Farm or cooperative name
- Growing altitude
- Variety
- Crop year
- Processing method
- Certifications
- Roast level
- Flavor summary
- Grade
- Harvest date, if available
- Roast date

marketing-savvy producers, footloose and curious roasters. And relentless efforts at product differentiation at the green coffee level. Producers and their roaster partners began looking for any differentiator, any edge, something that would allow them to say that their Costa Rica was excitingly different from the usual Costa Rica. For example, today a differentiated Costa Rica could be a "honey" coffee (dried with some mucilage still adhering to the bean) or grown in a special geographical pocket or terroir, or only from trees of the bourbon variety. To the simple region and grade names of specialty tradition the industry first added "estate" names, then an increasingly precise set of identifiers, now routinely including processing methods, botanical variety, farm name and precise growing region.

The old, traditional origin/grade names are still powerful marketing tools among specialty coffee consumers, of course—a fact that has not escaped the attention of some producing country associations and their nongovernmental organization allies. Formal protection of these valuable but heretofore unprotected names perhaps began with the success of the Ethiopian authorities in claiming ownership and licensing rights for the names Yirgacheffe, Sidamo and Harrar.

Green Coffee Descriptors Rule

What is quite apparent in observing communication at the top end of the specialty segment today is that detailed green coffee descriptors have taken precedence over roast descriptors. The implication appears to be that the roaster has chosen the right degree of roast to showcase an often elaborately described green coffee. Rather than ask consumers to first decide which degree of roast they like, the new naming moves directly to extolling the green coffee.

Something similar has happened with mid-tier supermarket blends, those blends that compete on the cusp between true specialty on one hand and cheap blends in plastic cans on the other. I'm thinking of the Starbucks supermarket line of bagged coffees and similar coffee repertoires from companies that compete in the same niche. Here a series of names, probably originating with Starbucks, simultaneously attempts to define both roast style and general green coffee style. "Breakfast Blend" appears to be a code name for a medium-roasted, gently acidy coffee ("Mild" in Starbucks-speak); "House Blend" is a little darker and less acidy—think full-city or Viennese in the old languages. Next darker is espresso, apparently meant more as a descriptor of roast and style rather than recommendation for brewing method. In the supermarket this term appears to describe a blend that

is roast-forward (Starbucks: "Bold"), low in acidity and sweetly pungent. And at the dark end of the spectrum, the inevitable French roast lurks ("Extra bold").

A final curious note on implicit supermarket codes for roast color and green coffee style: "Kona Blend" in supermarket and some food service lineups appears to be more a roast and blend character descriptor than an (albeit phony and deceptive) origin descriptor. In other words, rather than functioning as an origin-oriented descriptor for a coffee made up of 10 percent Kona and 90 percent coffees from anywhere except Kona, it functions as a kind of consumer-oriented code name for a generic low-acid, medium-roasted arabica coffee, a sort of milder version of the supermarket 100-percent Colombias. It represents a carryover of the romance theory of naming. Rather than call your coffee a breakfast blend or a medium-roasted blend, give it a fake geographic association.

More Medium Roasts and Still More Medium Roasts?

The future? At the top end of the market, I predict more medium roasts and more medium roasts as well as more honey-and-flowers super-light roasts. I hope that the tendency to roast control by artisan response to the cup rather than pure quantitative controls continues at the top end of the market, although I feel that heat probes and roast color readers are invaluable for overall contexting and keeping us on track when the shop is busy and palates are blurred. I expect green coffees to continue to be described in detail, with roast color continuing to be pushed into the conceptual background.

By letting the green coffee lead, we doubtless are maximizing opportunities for sensory distinction and quality. On the other hand, if we fall head over heels roasting everything dark or roasting everything light, we will be committing a version of the same mistake we made in the '80s and '90s, a sort of blind adherence to roast-color ideology rather than the expression of a sensitive dialogue among green coffee, roasting machine and roastmaster. ■

. . . .

KENNETH DAVIDS *has observed, documented, described and participated in the specialty coffee movement continuously since its inception more than 40 years ago. He has published three books on coffee, all appearing in multiple editions, and is founding editor and principal writer for the web publication coffeereview.com, which celebrated its 20th anniversary in 2017. He is emeritus professor of critical studies at the California College of Arts in San Francisco.*

ROAST COLOR CHART

Roast Color	Bean Surface (after coffee is rested)	Approximate Bean Temperature at Termination of Roast	Agtron Gourmet Scale Numbers (SCAA Color Tile Number in Italics)	Common Names
Very light brown	Dry	Around 380°F/195°C	95–90 *Tile #95*	Light Cinnamon
Very light brown	Dry	"First crack" Below 400°F/205°C	90–80 *Tile #85*	Light Cinnamon New England
Light brown	Dry	Around 400°F/205°C	80–70 *Tile #75*	Light New England
Medium-light brown	Dry	Between 400°F/205°C and 415°F/215°C	70–60 *Tile #65*	Light Light-Medium American Regular
Medium brown	Dry	Between 415°F/215°C and 435°F/225°C	60–50 *Tile #55*	Light Medium Mild Medium High American Regular City
Medium-dark brown	Dry to tiny droplets or faint patches of oil	"Second crack" Between 435°F/225°C and 445°F/230°C	50–45 *Tile #45*	Full City Mild Viennese Northern Italian Espresso Continental After-Dinner
Moderately dark brown	Faint oily patches to entirely shiny surface	Between 445°F/230°C and 455°F/235°C	45–40	Espresso Bold Dark French European High Continental
Dark brown	Shiny surface	Between 455°F/235°C and 465°F/240°C	40–35 *Tile #35*	French Espresso Italian Dark Turkish
Very dark brown	Very shiny surface	Between 465°F/240°C and 475°F/245°C	35–30	Italian Bold Neapolitan Spanish Heavy
Very dark (nearly black) brown	Shiny surface	Between 475°F/245°C and 480°F/250°C	30–25 *Tile #25*	French (also Dark French) Neapolitan Spanish

Acidity	Body	Aroma	Complexity	Depth	Green Coffee Distinctiveness	Sweetness	Pungency	Comments
3	1	2	2	1	2	1		Roast is barely developed
3	1	2	2	1	2	1		Rare in United States but becoming less so
4	2	3	3	2	4	1		
3	3	3	4	3	4	2		Currently favored by many "Third Wave" roasters
3	3	4	4	4	3	2	1	Traditional American roast style; also currently favored by "Third Wave" roasters
2	4	3	3	4	2	3	2	Least polarizing roast style for American consumers; often used for "one roast fits all" blends and "Third Wave" espressos
1	4	3	3	4	1	4	3	Favorite for lighter American espresso blends
	3	2	2			3	4	Favorite for older-style American espresso blends
	2	2	2	2		2	3	Definitely roast-dominated but still retains generalized body/flavor
	1	2	1	1		1	2	Best known as "French roast." Polarizing for consumers; not much left in the coffee

Thank you to St. Martin's Press, New York, for kind permission to adapt this chart from Kenneth Davids' book *Home Coffee Roasting: Romance & Revival*, 2nd Edition, 2003.

COFFEE PRODUCTION & PROCESSING

Photo courtesy of David Roche

A Family Album

Getting to the Roots of Coffee's Plant Heritage

Research assistance provided by David Roche and Dr. Robert Osgood

• FROM THE NOVEMBER/DECEMBER 2007 ISSUE OF *ROAST* •

You drink it all the time. You roast it daily. You might have picked, pulped and hand-sorted at least a few beans. You can judge the difference between a good coffee and an inferior coffee, and can use taste to determine where a coffee was grown and maybe even how it was processed.

You work with coffee day in and day out. But how well do you really know the heritage behind it? What do you know about where your coffee comes from? Not location-wise or farm-wise, but in the botanical sense. Coffee is a big, extended "family"—from the grandfathers of wild arabica coffee and robusta to today's young new hybrids—and there is a great deal to be learned from the coffee family tree.

First off, to call "coffee" a family is a bit of a misnomer. It is, in fact, a genus (Coffea) that belongs to a large family of plants called the Rubiaceae. Inside the genus are hundreds of species, the best known of which are the two that are grown commercially: arabica and canephora (robusta). There are two other coffees grown on a much smaller scale: Coffea liberica (Liberica coffee) and Coffea dewevrei (Excelsa coffee).

Ancestry

The industry has been keeping scientific track of coffee since the 18th century, when Swedish botanist Carl Linnaeus first described arabica coffee. But, before that, where did it come from? We know that arabica coffee originated somewhere on the plateaus of Ethiopia and was then transported to what is now Yemen, where it's been grown commercially since the sixth century. Later, it was moved to the rest of the tropics, where it has since become one of the most widely traded of all agricultural commodities.

Another coffee, robusta, originated in central Africa. While this coffee is not as widely traded as a commodity, it is nevertheless important for use as a coffee beverage and for blends in espresso. Perhaps even more notably, robusta serves as a source of genes for coffee breeding by providing disease resistance in crossbreeding programs.

BE A GENIUS ABOUT GENUS... OR IS IT FAMILY?

It's been a long time since science class in high school for most of us, but we probably still remember trying to learn the natural order of classification.

Here it is, from larger to smaller, as a reminder:

Photo courtesy of Geoff Watts

Class of the coffee plant: *Dicotyledoneae*

Subclass of the coffee plant: *Sympetalae* or *Metachlamydeae*

Order of the coffee plant: *Rubiales*

Family of the coffee plant: *Rubiaceae*

Genus of the coffee plant: *Coffea*

Species of the coffee plant: *Coffea arabica*, *Coffea canephora*

Varieties of the arabica coffee plant: bourbon and typica*

Cultivars of the coffee plant: bourbon and typica*, caturra, mundo novo, catuai

*You'll notice that bourbon and typica are listed as both varieties and cultivars. This is because they actually are both. There are many cultivars of the bourbon and typica varieties, and these cultivars are often just referred to as bourbon and typica. Just to make things more confusing,

FAMILY, DEFINED

GENUS A category consisting of a group of organisms or species that are closely related and thus exhibit similar characteristics. Coffee is in the genus Coffea, which also includes more than 25 other plant species.

VARIETY VS. VARIETAL Most likely, you've seen these words used interchangeably, or perhaps you've seen them used to describe a location (such as Java). In truth, there are only two generally recognized botanical varieties of arabica coffee: bourbon and typica. The difference between variety and varietal is a grammatical one. Variety is a noun (thus: "This coffee's variety is typica."), while varietal is an adverb ("The differences in bean size are varietal in nature.").

CULTIVAR A cultivated plant that has been selected for its desirable characteristics that distinguish it from other plants of the same species. A cultivar should have a name that conforms to the International Code of Nomenclature for Cultivated Plants (ICNCP, commonly called the "Cultivated Plant Code"). The name must be distinct from other cultivars and when propagated, the plant must retain its desirable and different characteristics. Samples of cultivars include caturra, mundo novo and ruiru 11. Bourbon and typica can be also used as cultivar names, as in red bourbon.

HYBRID A cross between members of the same species (interspecific) or genus (intraspecific). Hybrids can be natural or deliberately made in breeding programs.

MUTATION A sudden departure from the parent plant in one or more characteristics, caused by a change in a chromosome.

SELF POLLINATING When a plant's own pollen is used to produce a fruit, such as in arabica coffee.

CROSS POLLINATING When a plant cannot pollinate itself and requires pollen from another plant to produce a fruit, such as in robusta coffee.

A third coffee—liberica—originated in West Africa. Commonly sold locally, it is also sometimes used as a rootstock for arabica coffee where nematodes (a type of parasite) are a problem.

Characteristics

The arabica plant, which is the one most of us think of when we're talking about coffee, is a large bush with dark-green oval leaves. It's different from other coffee species, having four sets of chromosomes instead of two (technically called a tetraploid). This is one of the attributes that allows current researchers to distinguish whether a cultivar comes from arabica stock or robusta stock. The difference in chromosomes determines coffee traits that affect flavor, body and acidity. These chromosomes also determine how a coffee interacts with the environment to create different characteristics.

There are two scientifically recognized botanical varieties of arabica coffee, typica and bourbon. Additional unclassified varieties are out there but a lot of work remains to be done before they can be categorized as genetically distinct varieties.

Cultivated variations of typica and bourbon are called cultivars. In fact, often when we talk about coffee "varieties," we're not talking about varieties at all, but rather cultivars. There are also a number of coffees, including geisha and other recently rediscovered Ethiopian coffees, which have not yet been determined to be either varieties or cultivars. Future research, much of it based on chromosome studies, will enable us to pinpoint the proper terminologies for these coffees.

Some of the cultivars that occurred naturally as mutations are caturra and pointu. Other cultivars, such as mundo novo and maragogype, originated as a result of crosses in the field.

Still others—namely catuai, pacamara and the catimors—originated as a result of breeding programs. Some of these were created in the hopes of resisting diseases and insects, such as coffee rust, coffee berry disease and the coffee borer. Others were developed in an attempt to decrease the stature of the bushes to facilitate picking and increase yield .

Today a few breeding programs are attempting to modify coffee quality, including caffeine content, acidity, body and flavor. New cultivars are currently being produced especially in Costa Rica, Ethiopia, Brazil and Hawaii.

What about Flavor?

One thing you're likely to notice right off the bat is that in this article we don't talk about flavor. Why not? Because flavor is incredibly subjective, as we all know. And that's not just based on the cupper's palate, but also on where and how a variety or cultivar is grown, processed, shipped and roasted. You'll also notice that we didn't cover all of coffee's many varieties and cultivars in this article; in fact, there's a good chance that you won't find your recent favorite discovery in here. That's not because we're ignoring new or rediscovered coffees, but because we wanted to stick to the facts of coffee's botanical nature and many of these new coffees are still being explored and classified by the scientific community.

arabica coffee tree

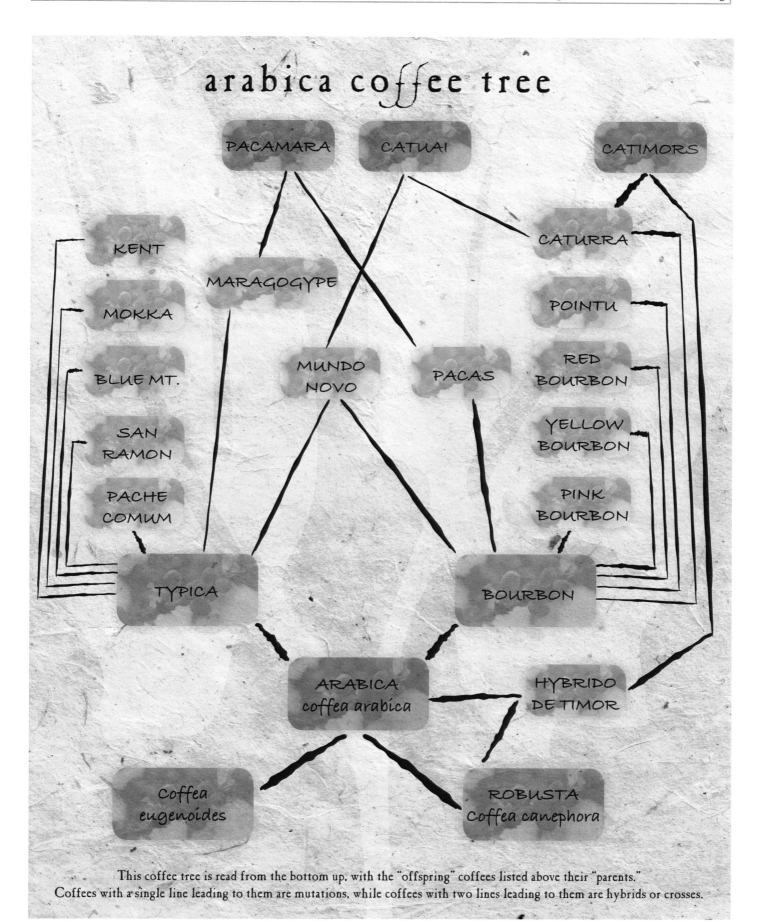

This coffee tree is read from the bottom up, with the "offspring" coffees listed above their "parents."
Coffees with a single line leading to them are mutations, while coffees with two lines leading to them are hybrids or crosses.

COFFEA

The coffee plant was first described by the Swedish botanist Carl Linnaeus. He classified the plant as a member of the Rubiaceae family, which also includes plants such as the gardenia and the quinine tree. Although technically a shrub, the plant can reach more than 12 meters in height. There are a number of coffee species, but the two that are most common, and which are used almost exclusively in the coffee industry, are *Coffea canephora* (robusta) and *Coffea arabica*.

Coffea Canephora

Coffea canephora, or robusta, was discovered in the Congo in 1898 and represents about one-quarter of the total world production. The plant, which is well adapted to warm, humid and low-elevation equatorial climates, is self-sterile and cross-pollinated, which allows for greater variability than arabica. The beans are typically small, rounded and brownish-yellow in appearance. They contain a higher caffeine content, a lower sugar content and significantly higher levels of chlorogenic acid than arabica beans.

photo courtesy of Jeff Taylor

photo courtesy of Josuma Coffee Co.

COFFEA ARABICA

Arabica, also known by its botanical name of *Coffea arabica*, represents three-quarters of the world coffee production. Research at the cellular level shows that arabica is probably a relatively recent cross (possibly around 500 years ago) between *Coffea eugenoides* and *Coffea canephora*. The plant is self-pollinating, which allows it to remain genetically stable. However, spontaneous mutations have occurred, which are then cultivated or crossbred with other mutations and crossbreeds. Typically, the beans are slightly elongated and greenish-blue.

photo courtesy of David Roche

photo courtesy of David Roche

Coffea Liberica is a very tall tree, typically grown in Malaysia and West Africa, which produces large cherries and beans and has large, waxy leaves.

Hybrido de Timor (Hybrid of Timor) is a natural hybrid between robusta and arabica that is best known for its resistance to coffee rust. It has been used extensively as a parent in breeding programs to produce catimors.

CULTIVARS OF ARABICA

The cultivars typica and bourbon, both of which are from arabica, constitute the main genetic base of most of the world's cultivated coffee today. Common bourbon coffees are red, yellow and pink bourbon, pacas and caturra. Typica has given us coffees such as mokka, kent and maragogype. There are also a number of crosses, such as mundo novo and pacamara.

One of the ways to tell the difference between the cultivars is by looking at the leaves: bourbons have green leaf tips and typicas have bronze leaf tips. However, the hybrids of bourbon and typica can have either leaf color following segregation in the second generation and beyond.

Typica is a base from which many coffee cultivars have been developed. Typica plants have a conical shape with a main vertical trunk and many small branches that grow off at a slight upward slant. They can grow up to 14 feet high.

Bourbon trees have less of a conical shape than typica but often have more secondary branches. Green leaf tips are characteristic, as is the arrangement of cherries on the branch—bourbons tend to develop cherries in clusters along the branch with significant internodal spacing between them.

TYPICA-BASED CULTIVARS

Maragogype

Maragogype (or maragogipe) is a mutation of typica. The coffee plant is large, and produces very large beans. There is some controversy over the quality of maragogype beans.

Maragogype (left) and Mokka (right)
photo courtesy of Dr. Robert Osgood

Mokka

Mokka (or moka), usually called tall mokka, is a typica mutation that is commercially grown in Brazil and Hawaii. At one time mokka was thought to be a species but it is clearly an arabica cultivar, as it has four sets of chromosomes.

Blue Mountain

Blue Mountain is a typica that is well known for its ability to thrive in high elevation. Blue Mountain is a location, but it's also used as a cultivar name. There is also a typica cultivar called Guatamala typica in Hawaii which is indistinguishable from Blue Mountain by genetic analysis.

photo courtesy of Dr. Robert Osgood

photo courtesy of Dr. Robert Osgood

Kent

Originally discovered in India, kent is a natural hybrid known for its high yield and partial resistance to coffee rust.

HYBRIDS AND CROSSES

Catimors and Sarchimors

Catimors are the result of crosses between hybrido de Timor and caturra, and sarchimors are the result of crosses between hybrido de Timor and Villa Sarchi. Neither is a distinct variety; they are both groups of many different varieties with similar parentage. Examples of sarchimor varieties include obata, paraneima and cuscatleco; examples of catimor varieties are Costa Rica 95, IHCAFE 90 and Oro Azteca. Production is typically high, especially with proper fertilization and shade, and both groups are resistant to coffee leaf rust. After the coffee leaf rust epidemic in Central America that began in 2012, they have become more prevalent across the region.

Catimor. *Photo courtesy of Dr. Robert Osgood*

Pacamara

Pacamara is the result of breeding pacas and maragogipe. It has characteristics of both parents in the first generation.

Photo courtesy of Jeff Taylor

Catuai

Catuai is the result of a cross between mundo novo and caturra, characterized by either yellow or red cherries (catuai-amarelo or catuai-vermelho). Considered a semi-dwarf, catuai is short and high-yielding, with fruit that does not fall off the branch easily. Typically needs good care and fertilization for best results. There are a number of catuai cultivars.

Photo courtesy of Jeff Taylor

Photo courtesy of Dr. Robert Osgood

Mundo Novo

Mundo novo is a natural hybrid between typica and bourbon that was first discovered in Brazil. This strong, disease-resistant plant has a high production and is a favored cultivar for Brazilian growers.

Photo courtesy of Tom Owen, Sweet Maria's Coffee

FROM ROOTS TO FRUIT

A NEW BEAN IS BORN

ROOTS In addition to having long main vertical roots, coffee trees have taproots and lateral roots. The taproots are usually very close to the soil surface, while the lateral roots can extend more than 6 feet from the trunk. The root systems depend, of course, on the quality of soil, amount of rain, organic matter and concentration of mineral nutrients.

LEAVES Coffee leaves are dark green and waxy, with a high shine. They run 4 to 6 inches in length and are either oval or oblong in shape. Coffee trees have a bilateral leaf arrangement, meaning that two leaves grow from the stem opposite each other.

FLOWER Typically a plant takes two to three years before it begins producing flowers. The flowers, which are most often white or cream in color, grow in clusters in the axils (the location between a leaf and the stem to which it is attached). Arabica coffee is usually self pollinated, and robusta coffee is cross pollinated. The fresh flowers also have an intense jasmine-like aroma.

FRUIT Anywhere from six to eight weeks after the coffee flowers are fertilized, small green berries, called drupes, appear. The first fruit structures to form are called pinheads. These pinheads develop slowly at first, and then grow rapidly into the immature coffee fruits. Depending on the

Photo courtesy of Jeff Taylor

climate, there is usually a four-month period of rapid growth, during which time the outer skin begins to take on the shape of the coffee bean. Inside, the beans are still small, however, as they don't begin to grow until about three months after flowering. By about five months, the beans will almost completely fill the cherry. At this point, the cherry will begin ripening. At about eight or nine months, the cherry is typically full color, ripe and ready to be picked.

FAMILY TRIVIA

The word *cultivar* was coined by Liberty Hyde Bailey, as a combination of "cultivated" and "variety."

Editor's Note

Since this article was published in 2007, the industry has turned more attention to coffee varieties, leading to more widespread attention to many varieties known for high cup quality, such as SL-28, a Kenyan variety developed in the 1920s, and geisha, a "wild-type" coffee from Ethiopia that came to the industry's attention after the 2004 Best of Panama auction, where it broke records for price. New varieties that meet the evolving needs of farmers are also always in the process of being created. Marsellesa is a newer rust-resistant variety in the sarchimor group developed in Central America for better cup quality than previous sarchimors. Centroamericano is one of an entirely new class of F1 hybrid varieties created by crossing established varieties (in this case a rust-resistant sarchimor-type called T5296) with genetically diverse, often wild varieties (in this case Rume Sudan), resulting in new combinations of quality and disease-resistance traits.

To learn more about the remarkable assortment of coffee varieties in production today, explore the World Coffee Research catalog at *varieties.worldcoffeeresearch.org* and the Specialty Coffee Association's list of "Coffee Plants of the World" at *sca.coffee*. ◼

Cultivating Taste

Coffee Growing 101

by Phil Beattie

• FROM THE JULY/AUGUST 2005 ISSUE OF *ROAST* •

Coffee is, without a doubt, my number one interest in life. However, a close second is hot peppers. Each spring, I scour the Internet and flip through page after page in seed catalogs looking for the perfect peppers to grow in my greenhouse.

There are more than 200 varieties of hot peppers. Each has a unique flavor and different level of heat, from common ones like the jalapeño to less common ones, such as the chiltepin pepper, which is the size and shape of a marble but packs an extreme punch when it comes to heat.

Like hot peppers, coffee has a never-ending list of variables that contribute to its flavor characteristics. But the variety of flavors found in peppers is dwarfed by the vast variety found in coffee.

Of course, the roast plays a role in producing this variety— but there is much more to it

than that. Each origin, and each region within it, has a very specific set of circumstances that lead to the flavor of the coffee produced there. As a roaster, it is important to understand what factors go into making coffee taste different from area to area. This will help you to taste coffees and decipher the good from the bad.

Not unlike the coffee industry, gardening also has its "masters." These master gardeners possess three things that are fundamental for mastering anything: passion, knowledge and skill. Passion for the art of growing, knowledge of the environment that their prized plants need and the skill to pull it all together, creating a collage of botanical beauty.

The amount of care and dedication a master gardener puts into creating the perfect rose (or pepper) is equal to that of a coffee farmer. Not only does a coffee farmer attempt to produce the perfect coffee blossom, he tries to cultivate a fruit that can be processed and roasted and brewed to create the gourmet beverage that we all love.

This feat requires what seems to be psychic powers to predict what factors will affect the flavor of the coffee. But in reality there are some simple but crucial cultivation factors that determine how green coffee will taste after being roasted properly.

Just as with any cultivation, the main factors are the location of

the plants, the elements that affect the plants and the varieties of the plants themselves.

LOCATION

We are all aware that to have a successful coffee shop, or roastery for that matter, you have to find the perfect location. This is true for coffee farms too, but for different reasons.

Geography

Coffee is grown between the tropics of Capricorn and Cancer. As you move either north or south of these latitudes, the risk of frost increases. Frost can devastate a coffee plantation by turning the coffee trees' leaves brown, and in severe cases, completely wiping out the trees' foliage.

The microclimate of a location also impacts how well the coffee will grow. Certain areas that have extreme winds are not as suitable for growing coffee, as the winds can hinder the maturation of young trees and knock blossoms and cherries off the tree. If the farm happens to lie in a convergence zone, it will receive too much rain. This will not allow for a predictable harvest cycle.

Elevation

Another factor that plays a role in creating quality coffee is elevation. As you go higher in elevation, the potential for unique-tasting coffees increases. The reason is that coffee grows slower at high altitudes, producing a harder bean. A hard bean generally will possess a crisper, higher level of acidity. For example, a Brazilian Sul Minas, which is grown at around 2,000 feet, can have a mild nutty flavor, but it will not have the high acidity of a coffee grown at higher elevation. Not only does a harder bean increase acidity levels, it also goes through processing with less chance of physical damage.

Coffee flourishes at an average temperature of 68 degrees F. If the average temperature goes much higher or lower, the tree will become unhealthy and produce a sub-par crop. This is the balance that a farm must keep. The trees must be high enough to produce great-tasting coffees, but not so high that they can get frost. The closer you get to the equator, the higher coffee can grow.

In certain areas of Ecuador, coffee is grown as high as 9,500 feet above sea level, but as you move to the southernmost growing regions of Brazil, coffee can only be grown at 2,000 feet due to the frost zone.

ELEMENTS

A balanced diet and exercise are key to a healthy life, right? I am sure you are nodding your head yes, as you drink your 10th cup of coffee. A coffee tree's diet starts when it is a wee little sprout. A coffee tree spends its first year being meticulously cared for in a nursery, after which it is transplanted to the field where it will grow

for three to four years before producing a full yield. Each year a tree will produce 1 to 2 pounds of green coffee, as long as it has the proper elements.

Soil

The foundation of a healthy tree is the soil. The soil must be rich in nutrients, such as potassium and nitrogen, and the correct pH level is also important. Coffee trees prefer a slightly acidic pH level, which is why they do so well in volcanic soil. The soil should allow water to run off during heavy rains but also retain moisture during dry spells.

As the trees grow older they begin to use up the nutrients that the soil has to offer. In order to replace them, some form of fertilizer must be used. The most readily available source of fertilizer is the pulp that is left over after the bean is removed from the cherry. This is put in a compost pile just like what any gardener has pushed in the back corner of their property. This compost can be used in tandem with chicken manure or chemical fertilizers.

Sunlight

Photosynthesis, the envy of every lazy person. If only we could lie out all day soaking up energy from the sun. However, coffee trees prefer sunlight in moderation, which is why shade trees are so important. Shade trees are a key piece of the puzzle for the environment, as they provide rest stops and homes for migratory birds. But they are also crucial to limiting the amount of direct sunlight that the coffee trees receive. Too much sunlight will dry out the root system of the coffee tree, leading to an unhealthy crop.

Another source of shade is the cloud cover that is common in tropical regions. Generally the microclimate in the region of the farm will have predictable cloud cover at certain times of the day. This is a factor in creating the signature coffee development from region to region.

Rain

Rainfall is the top level in the coffee trees' food pyramid. Coffee will flourish with 60 to 80 inches of rain annually. Just as important as the quantity of rain is the timing. Rainfall is like the messenger to the coffee tree telling it what season it is. The seasonal patterns of rainfall trigger the growth of the coffee tree blossoms and ultimately set the schedule for harvest. Not enough rain and the drought will damage production. Too much rain can also negatively affect crops.

VARIETIES

Just like any agricultural product, coffee has many different varieties. Coffee is often compared to wine, and this is one more subject where the comparison is useful. In the wine industry there are many different species of grape: Pinot Noir, Chardonnay, Cabernet Sauvignon, and on and on. Each variety has its own distinct characteristics, everything from how it is grown and processed to its flavor characteristics. Coffee also has many varieties, although they are not as well known. These varieties can be separated into two large categories: originals and hybrids.

Originals

The original varieties are coffees that are naturally occurring. These are coffees that are as old as the trees (pun intended). The most widely known are typica and bourbon which, when grown at high elevation and processed correctly, can produce superb-tasting coffees. But there are two challenges with them. The first is that they have a lower yield potential than other options. The second is that they do not stand up to disease and insects very well.

Hybrids

In the early 1970s, the coffee industry faced major problems with disease in the coffee plantations. Plants everywhere were being afflicted with coffee rust, coffee berry disease and others.

This spawned the beginning of hybrid varieties. These cross-bred varieties had many advantages to growers. Not only did they resist disease, but some, such as caturra, could be grown without the shade requirement of typica and bourbon.

Over the last several decades, a large number of hybrids have been developed. Some, such as catuai, mundo novo and caturra, are capable of producing quality coffees. Others, like catimore, produce a high yield per tree and are very resilient to disease, but do not typically produce great-tasting coffees.

When all of these factors are combined—the elevation, soil, sunlight, rain and variety—you have a formula that creates the

natural flavor characteristics of a coffee. When taking these into consideration as a roaster, it is important to remember that each origin and region will produce a unique result in the cup. Each coffee has a niche that it can fill in the coffee lineup of a roaster.

Not every good coffee will be high in acidity with a crisp clean cup—that would be like having every hot pepper taste like a jalapeño. Instead, the different microclimates and varieties produce such diversity in flavor that there is a coffee for everyone.

Through extensive tasting, you will find that certain growing regions will produce fairly consistent flavor profiles year to year. By possessing knowledge of these profiles, you will be better equipped to purchase and roast consistent quality coffee. And, of course, you'll know just where to find the beans that will give you the sweet, floral, or even spicy, note that you desire. ▪

· ·

PHIL BEATTIE *is the director of coffee for Dillanos Coffee Roasters in Sumner, Washington. Beattie is a veteran roaster, cupper and an all-around coffee enthusiast. He has been an integral piece of the Dillanos success story through his coffee sourcing and relationships across the globe. He has also served as chair of the Roasters Guild Executive Council and a member of many cupping juries. You can find photos of his coffee travels under the alias @justroaster on Instagram.*

Handling the Cherry

The Risks and Rewards of Processing Methods
Origin Case Study: Hawaii

by Shawn Steiman | *photos taken at Kona Earth Coffee Farm*

• FROM THE JULY/AUGUST 2011 ISSUE OF *ROAST* •

Before the notion of specialty coffee made it to Hawaii coffee farms, the industry was fairly simple. For nearly a century, only one region had a significant amount of commercial coffee production: Kona (though there were others in the 1800s). For all that time, only a few processing mills handled nearly all the coffee. The coffee that came out was a blend of many farms. This homogeneity led to the creation of the Kona cup profile: simple, low to medium acidity, and no bitterness.

In the 1990s, some farmers began to realize there was a new model to be followed. They split with tradition and converted into small estate farms—farms that maintain ownership of the coffee until it is sold to the consumer, often as roasted product. They began processing the coffee themselves or contracting someone else to do it. They designed labels, launched websites and operated as individual units within an established industry. Following the national trend, they roasted their coffee on the darker side of the spectrum but kept the traditional wet method for cherry processing that had helped define the Kona cup profile. When other growing regions in Hawaii appeared or were resurrected, nearly all the farms kept entirely with wet processing. At the time, the only exceptions were the large, mechanically harvested operations.

Much like everywhere else, in the last few years the cutting edge of specialty coffee has reached Hawaii. Some farms, no longer content with the cup profile their (typically) one-variety and one-cherry processing style produce, have begun experimenting with cherry processing methods to diversify their offerings. Why exactly are they doing this? What are the benefits? Is it worth it?

This article will take place in two sections. The first section will be a short journey through coffee cherry processing—what it is, how it is done, and what is it doing to the coffee. The second section will explore the current scene in Hawaii and delve into the minds of farmers who've taken up the challenge of creating new and exciting coffees by playing with cherry processing.

Basics of Cherry Processing

A conversation about cherry processing must start with the cherry itself. "Cherry" refers to the ripe fruit of the coffee plant, so named because most varieties have fruits that, when ripe, are the color and size (more or less) of a cherry fruit (*Prunus avium*). The visible, outer layer of the fruit (botanically, the exocarp) is attached to the moist, sugary, fleshy pulp (mesocarp). Beneath the pulp is the mucilage, a sugary and, as the name suggests, sticky goop that strongly adheres to the layer beneath it. That layer is the parchment (endocarp), a thick, rough, papery material. Just beneath the parchment is a thin film called silverskin (testa, which eventually becomes chaff in the roaster). Finally, buried beneath of all of those layers are (typically) two coffee seeds.

The purpose of cherry processing is to extract the seeds from the fruit and prepare them for roasting. All of those layers must be removed and the seeds dried to the standard 9 to 12 percent moisture content. How that happens exactly is less important than doing it well. The pulp and mucilage are high in water and sugar content—two attractive resources to microorganisms whose overabundant presence during drying is suspected of negatively impacting the cup quality of the coffee. Minimizing or eliminating their growth is a key aspect of cherry processing. The farmer decides how to process the cherries depending on the available resources, the climate at the time of processing and the desired taste outcome.

There are three common methods of cherry processing: natural, pulped natural and washed. There are other variations not discussed here.

The natural process, also known as the full natural or the dry process, keeps the entire fruit intact while drying the seeds. The seeds are not removed until every layer, including the seeds, has been dried. On farms where coffee is harvested mechanically, many cherries are already dry when the coffee is harvested. These cherries, sometimes called raisins, can be separated and sold as natural coffee.

The pulped natural process is one step removed from the natural process. The cherries are pulped (the skin and fleshy pulp removed) and the seeds, still covered by the parchment and mucilage, are dried. This process sometimes goes by alternate names, but "honey" is the most common.

The washed process (otherwise known as the wet process) removes not only the skin and pulp but also the mucilage before drying the coffee. There are several ways of doing this. Traditionally, the mucilage is removed by fermentation, either by covering the coffee with water until the mucilage is degraded or simply leaving the coffee to sit and ferment without water (known as dry fermentation). The term "fermentation" is used because microorganisms, naturally occurring on the coffee or in the environment, consume the mucilage and degrade it

via metabolic fermentation processes. When the mucilage is completely removed, we deem the fermentation process complete. The fermentation process takes as few as six hours and as many as 24 to complete. The time required is dependent on the volume of coffee, ambient air temperature, and temperature of the water (if present) used for soaking.

An alternative method uses a demucilager/demucilator to mechanically remove the mucilage just after pulping, eliminating the need for any kind of fermentation before drying. A demucilager forces the coffee into a small space, causing the seeds to rub and push against each other and the container they are in. The pressure liquefies the mucilage, allowing it to be washed away in a few minutes by the small amount of water added to the process. Since water is used to rinse the coffee seeds upon completion, we call these coffees "washed coffees." Whether a washed coffee is fermented or demucilaged, the cup quality is the same.

It is well accepted by both the industry and scientists that processing affects the cup profile. A generality on perfectly pampered and accomplished processing on hand-harvested farms is that going from washed to pulped naturals to full naturals creates an increasing intensity of sweetness, fruitiness (ferment to some), acidity and body. Some suggest that the coffees become increasingly complex through this progression.

On mechanically harvested farms, the results of perfect dry processing on cup quality aren't as predictable. Natural-processed coffees from these farms can be more acidy and fruity than washed coffees, or they can be earthy and spicy.

A big question that is largely unanswered is, how does cherry processing affect coffee quality? What is happening, biochemically, to create such organoleptically noticeable changes in the same batch of seeds? Many people in the coffee industry proffer that the sugars and "fruitness" of the mucilage and pulp diffuse into the seed. Unfortunately, this hypothesis lacks any scientific data to support it. Rather, researchers have demonstrated that some sugars, including sucrose, don't differ in content between different cherry processing methods, suggesting no diffusion into the seed is occurring. Some sugars, like fructose and glucose, do differ in content based upon processing method; however, this is a result of seed metabolism and not sugar infusion. Whether anything else migrates into the seed is anyone's guess.

Scientists have only recently begun to address the questions brought up by the current specialty coffee industry. Thus, there is not much data to address the processing question. Moreover, there is as yet no data linking specific coffee chemistry (green or roasted) to organoleptic quality. So, even when changes in coffee bean chemistry are demonstrated, there is no evidence to support that those differences are causing the tastes we experience.

The same coffee processed by different methods will present different amounts of some cellular molecules, dependent upon the processing method. Also, differences in coffee bean metabolism have conclusively been shown between washed and full-natural coffees. It is not unreasonable to hypothesize that pulped naturals might fall somewhere in the middle of these differences.

Two metabolic responses have been demonstrated. One is that the seed begins its germination sequence almost immediately after being picked. If the presence of germination-specific molecules (isocitrate lyase and β-tubulin) is measured in coffee shortly after picking and daily until the seeds reach 12 percent moisture, differences are seen between seeds that are fermented and seeds that are naturally processed. In washed coffees, the number of these molecules peaks a couple of days after harvesting and drops significantly in about a week, whereas in natural coffees, the quantity of those molecules peak a week after harvesting and slowly decline for another week or so. Two factors explain these patterns. The first is that coffee pulp likely has inhibitors that slow down the germination process (which, incidentally, supports the idea that compounds move into the seed from the fruit). Second, washed coffees dry quickly and, consequently, quickly reach a state of cellular quiescence. Full naturals, with greater mass and higher water content, require more time to dry down to that quiescent state.

The second response is related to water stress. Natural-processed coffees accumulate a much larger amount of γ-aminobutyric acid (GABA), a molecule known to occur in water-stressed plant cells. As above, this disparity exists because the natural-processed coffees have a longer time to be metabolically active than the washed coffees.

These responses indicate a significant amount of metabolic activity that is captured by just a few molecules. Certainly, other molecular differences related to these phenomena exist. While it is possible that these differences in coffee metabolism influence the cup quality of the coffee, until more research is done, we can only hypothesize.

Rising to the Challenge of Processing

Relative to its small size, the Hawaii coffee industry boasts a surprisingly large number of coffee farms (830). Of these, only a handful of farms intentionally plays around with cherry processing, and most of those have been experimenting with it for less than five years.

One reason farmers have been shy to experiment is the risk involved in ruining the coffee with a failed experiment. Losing even a small batch of coffee translates into hundreds, and probably thousands, of dollars of lost potential revenue. Producing pulped naturals and naturals requires a dry climate while the coffees are drying. Without low humidity conditions, the high moisture and sugar content of the mucilage and pulp will promote the growth of molds whose presence seems to result in tainted or foul cup quality. As most farms in Hawaii harvest during part of the rainy season, experimentation is a great financial risk.

Even with the risk, some farmers take on the challenge. They

want to delve into the potential of their coffee and create new and exciting experiences. From small, hand-harvested operations to the large, mechanically harvested ones, farms have begun experimenting.

Four farms in Hawaii harvest mechanically. They have produced both wet- and natural-process coffees since their inceptions in the early 1990s. Mechanical coffee harvesting works by shaking the fruits free of the trees. As cherries of different ripeness levels require similar removal forces, all types of cherries tend to fall off together. To ensure the production of high-quality coffee, the harvested cherries are subjected to a great deal of separation in the wet mill. It is here that the overripes/raisins/naturals are separated from the ripes and underripes. Thus, by the very nature of this type of farming operation, these farms all produce natural coffees.

Unfortunately, it isn't as simple as it sounds. "Natural-processed coffees are by nature exposed to mold spores, and it is one of the primary challenges in processing," says Derek Lanter, manager for Waialua Estate Coffee and Cacao on Oahu. "The drier the harvest season, the lower the incidence of mold, whereas the more rain, the higher the mold. There is nothing that can be done to control this in the field. In the wet milling, water is used to separate the ripe, raisin and immature cherries. Wetting the raisin promotes the environment that spawns mold. The weather conditions and drying capacity are the keys to managing this process."

This challenge aside, being relegated to multiple processes is a huge benefit for the farm. For every variety planted, the number of coffees that can be offered doubles since the raisins taste different. Kimo Falconer, president of MauiGrown Coffee, another mechanically harvested farm, recognizes that his natural coffees are the gems of his operation because "the washed coffees are less distinctive, complex and interesting." With such an array of cup profiles to offer, his farm can satisfy a greater number of customers. After all, different people want different tastes, and having more choices is always beneficial to a business.

Waialua Estate Coffee and Cacao and MauiGrown Coffee are two of the largest coffee farms in Hawaii. They were born out of the crop diversification programs of the large, corporate sugar and pineapple growers when those crops became less viable in Hawaii. While both operations had shaky, uncertain starts, both are now successful and well regarded.

The importance of drying the coffee properly cannot be understated. Every farmer interviewed stressed that this was the key to processing coffee. Lee Patterson, owner of Hula Daddy Coffee, whose coffee consistently receives high scores from *The Coffee Review*, is unequivocal. "In Kona, these processes are subject to mold and fungus if not dried correctly."

There's another problem that can arise from poor drying, particularly with naturals. The problem is at the heart of a debate about coffees processed this way: Do the coffees taste good? Natural-processed coffees can be sweet and fermented berry-fruit flavored (sweet ferment) or they can taste like fermented rotten fruit, sour or alcoholic (sour ferment). Some argue that there isn't an empirical difference in the cup, rather individuals respond differently to an experience and they have a preference for it or not (and give it a commensurate positive or negative descriptor). However, others think that these two taste outcomes arise from the quality of the cherry processing. Patterson believes that

poor drying of naturals leads to the production of the negatively associated fermented taste. Greater attention to drying can push the coffees toward sweet ferment and eliminate sour ferment.

Hula Daddy is a fairly recent addition to the Hawaii coffee scene, and it was one of the first small, hand-harvested farms to begin experimenting with cherry processing. Hoping to find more body and a more complex flavor, the farm gave free reign to its then-roaster Miguel Meza to tinker with processing methods. With an array of offerings of various processes and blends of those processes, Hula Daddy was able to increase demand for its coffee.

The fear of mold and sour ferment has kept Gary Strawn, computer game programmer turned farmer and owner of Kona Earth Coffee Farm, away from experimenting until this past year. "I work so hard to avoid over-fermenting my coffee. I've learned to associate it as a defect," he says. "I think pulped naturals are a nice balance between the washed and naturals. So, I went with that," adds Strawn. However, even losing a small batch of coffee would be a significant loss to his farm's revenue. To minimize the chance of loss, Strawn explains, "I waited until the very end of the harvest season, when it was hot and dry out, to try even a small lot of coffee. I was worried right up until we milled it."

The production of moldy coffee during drying isn't the only risk involved. Less often discussed is the risk of uneven drying. This can add an extra challenge to storing the coffee but, more likely, will be a burden to an unsuspecting buyer or roaster.

Fortunately, these risks are not enough to deter exploration. When asked why Pavaraga Coffee plays with processing, Leo Javar, the farm's operations manager, replied, "In essence, we are coffee treasure hunters. We love to seek the best way or find the potential of our coffees." Their treasure hunting has amassed 12 different types of processing styles, most of which are hybrids of processes on the continuum from fully washed to full naturals.

Pavaraga Coffee originated out of the Javar family farms. While the Javars have a long history of farming, their coffee operation is a fairly recent addition. Although their coffee farming in Hawaii began in the Ka'u region of the Big Island, they now operate farms in Kona and on Oahu.

Another Ka'u coffee farm known for experimentation and passion is Rusty's Hawaiian Coffee. Lauded with awards (2010 Hawaii Coffee Association Cupping Contest first-place winner, 2010 Outstanding Producer of the Year by the Speciality Coffee Association of Europe, and several 92+ scores from *The Coffee Review*), Rusty's is a paradigm of meticulous processing. Owner Lorie Obra works tirelessly to process her coffee to perfection. The pulped naturals can require raking every 20 minutes the entire day after pulping whereas the full naturals need the most attention three to five days after being laid out.

"Non-washed coffees must be raked very frequently so they will dry faster and avoid getting moldy," Obra explains. The level of attention necessary to dry the coffee properly requires a great deal of time and energy. This translates into higher labor costs as someone (Obra, usually, or her daughter, Joan) needs to babysit the coffee and monitor the weather once drying begins until the critical periods have passed.

These labor costs, of course, show up in the final cost of the coffee, making non-washed coffee significantly more expensive than its washed counterparts (though this isn't true for the mechanically harvested farms; their coffees cost the same). Considering the already relatively high cost of Hawaii-grown coffees and the resistance some consumers have to them, offering coffees that are seemingly even more outrageously priced is a significant risk. Fortunately, as the specialty coffee market persistently demonstrates, consumers are willing to pay almost any price for coffees they find to be extraordinary. Both Hula Daddy and Rusty's Hawaiian consistently sell out of non-washed coffees priced as high as $60 per roasted pound.

Risks and Rewards

Even though nontraditional processing methods are new to Hawaii, they have been a remarkable and nearly instant success. They've not only contributed to new, exciting Hawaii cup profiles, but they've also garnered accolades and respect for the mavericks who've risked product and reputation to try something new.

Admittedly, consumers get to experience only the successes of this experimentation. Every farm has produced failures unfit for general consumption, resulting in the loss of coffee that could otherwise have been produced under the relative safety of the washed process. There is no guidebook for how to process coffees. At best, farmers can glean what they can from others who've discovered success. Ultimately, with the limited scientific understanding of cherry processing available, farmers must experiment as the conditions on their farm present unique

Coffee Processing Terms Are Evolving

WHILE THE PROCESSING TERMS discussed in this article are still the most widely used in the industry, new terms have been introduced that may be more accessible for consumers and increase the potential for market differentiation. In January 2015, under the leadership of Flàvio Borém, Ph.D., of the University of Lavras in Brazil, the Specialty Coffee Association of America (now the Specialty Coffee Association [SCA]) released new terminology to describe variations in coffee processing.

Focusing on how coffee is dried rather than how the fruit is removed from the bean (i.e., wet versus dry), these new categories include:

- **Fruit-dried,** for coffees dried with the skin and fruit intact

- **Pulp-dried,** for those dried with the skin removed, but with some pulp intact

- **Parchment-dried,** for coffees that are dried after the skin and pulp are removed but with the parchment intact

- **Seed-dried,** for coffees that have the skin, pulp and parchment removed before drying

challenges to be overcome. It is up to consumers to encourage them, work with them, and reward them for their successes. ∎

SHAWN STEIMAN, PH.D., *is a coffee scientist, consultant and entrepreneur. His coffee research has included coffee production, entomology, ecology, physiology, biochemistry, organoleptic quality and brewing. He owns Coffea Consulting, a coffee-centric consulting firm, and Daylight Mind Coffee Company, a multifaceted business that includes a coffee roastery, coffee house, coffee school and restaurant. Steiman regularly presents seminars, workshops and tastings for both public and private events. He has authored numerous articles in scientific journals, trade magazines, newsletters and newspapers. He is the author of The Hawai'i Coffee Book: A Gourmet's Guide from Kona to Kaua'i, Coffee- A Comprehensive Guide to the Bean, the Beverage, and the Industry, and The Little Coffee Know-It-All: A Miscellany for Growing, Roasting, and Brewing, Uncompromising and Unapologetic. Steiman has also modeled for advertisements in South Korea.*

A portion of this article was reproduced in The Little Coffee Know-It-All, *Quarto Publishing Group USA, Inc., 2015.*

Photo by Mark Shimahara

Making Sense of Certifications

A Guide to Green Coffee Certifications

by Kelsey Klebba

As a roaster, there are many opportunities to expand your social responsibility efforts. Purchasing certified coffee can be beneficial for the earth, the farmers and their communities, and it can increase the perceived value of your coffee for consumers. The following provides basic information on some of the most prominent certifications available for coffee producers to help guide you in your purchasing decisions.

(Benefits listed are in addition to product differentiation, which is inherent in every certification and labeling system.)

**LABEL ›› ** 4C Association

**FOCUS ›› ** Uniting all relevant coffee stakeholders in improving the economic, social and environmental conditions of coffee production and processing

**CERTIFIER ›› ** Accredited independent third-party verifiers

BASIC COMPONENTS ››
- Promote sustainable standards
- Focus on critical issues that threaten the coffee sector
- Create and foster a collaborative platform to address overarching sustainability issues in the coffee sector
- Cooperation with other sustainability standards

**INSPECTIONS ›› ** Every three years, with self-assessment annually

**ORIGINS ›› ** Worldwide

**PRODUCERS ›› ** Approximately 444,500

**COST TO PRODUCERS ›› ** Fees vary based on total volume of green coffee produced.

**BENEFITS TO PRODUCERS ›› ** Meets demand for sustainably grown coffee. Increased income with the application of improved and more sustainable practices. Free access to information and training tools.

**COSTS TO ROASTERS ›› ** Fees vary based on total volume of green coffee roasted.

**BENEFITS TO ROASTERS ›› ** Assurance of appropriate supply chain management. Appeal to consumers who value sustainably produced and processed coffee. Opportunities for collaboration and dialogue with other stakeholders.

**CONTACT INFO ›› ** 4C Association, Adenauerallee 108 53113, Bonn, Germany; P 49.0.228.85050.15; *4c-coffeeassociation.org*

Bird Friendly

LABEL ›› Bird-Friendly

FOCUS ›› Conservation of migratory birds and their habitats

CERTIFIER ›› Certification agencies with U.S. Department of Agriculture (USDA) accreditation and Smithsonian Migratory Bird Center (SMBC) training

BASIC COMPONENTS ››
- Maintenance of forest environment/characteristics, with a diversity of shade trees that includes structural diversity
- Organic certification as a prerequisite (no synthetic agrochemical use)
- Protection of waterways and other sources of drinking water

INSPECTIONS ›› Every three years

ORIGINS ›› More than 24 in Central and South America; three in Ethiopia

PRODUCERS ›› 1,200 growers

COST TO PRODUCERS ›› Approximately $250 to $800 every three years for inspection and certification fees in addition to the cost of organic certification. (Combining certifications can save money.) Additional costs related to the maintenance of shade trees.

BENEFITS TO PRODUCERS ›› Processes can improve the quality of the coffee and the environment. Additional cents per pound above the organic premium.

COSTS TO ROASTERS ›› Fees run in the pennies per pound of coffee sold. Additional costs for labor involved in submitting quarterly sales reports. Limited sourcing options.

BENEFITS TO ROASTERS ›› Much bird-friendly coffee is also Fairtrade-certified, providing a "triple certified" product (organic/Fairtrade/bird friendly). Promotional support provided by SMBC.

CONTACT INFO ›› National Zoological Park, Washington, D.C., 20008; P: 202.633.4209; *nationalzoo.si.edu/scbi/migratorybirds/coffee*

Certified Organic– OCIA

LABEL ›› Certified Organic—OCIA

FOCUS ›› Minimizing deforestation of coffee ecosystems

CERTIFIER ›› Organic Crop Improvement Association (OCIA)

BASIC COMPONENTS ››
- Encourage biodiversity in tree species
- Track progress of improvements through a written plan
- Acquired in addition to organic certification

INSPECTIONS ›› Annually

ORIGINS ›› North America, Central and South America, Africa, Europe and the Pacific Rim

PRODUCERS ›› More than 9,000

COST TO PRODUCERS ›› Inspection fee varies depending on the location of the farm and time required to complete inspection, plus an additional fee based on projected organic sales.

BENEFITS TO PRODUCERS ›› Market access. Increased quality of coffee and the environment resulting from organic practices.

COSTS TO ROASTERS ›› Inspection fee varies depending on location and time required to complete inspection, plus an additional fee based on the projected organic sales.

BENEFITS TO ROASTERS ›› Many consumers equate certification with improved quality.

CONTACT INFO ›› 1340 N. Cotner Blvd., Lincoln, Nebraska, 68505; P: 402.477.2323; F: 402.477.4325; info@ocia.org; *ocia.org*

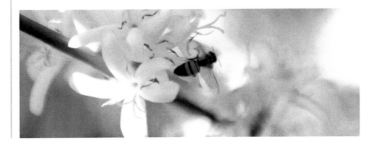

Fair Trade USA

LABEL ›› Fair Trade USA

FOCUS ›› Developing sustainable and resilient coffee supply chains through producer-buyer relationships that result in improved farmer livelihoods while strengthening coffee organizations and protecting the environment.

CERTIFIER ›› SCS Global Services and collaboration with FLO-Cert

BASIC COMPONENTS ››
• Minimum price and market access
• Direct relationships with buyers
• Social and community development incentives
• Democratic organization of producer groups
• Labor and environmental protections
• Stewardship, including training standards around water use and water treatment

INSPECTIONS ›› Annual audits, with reduced frequency contingent on past compliance

ORIGINS ›› Central America, South America, Africa, Asia and the Caribbean

PRODUCERS ›› 1.3 million

COST TO PRODUCERS ›› Fees vary based on the size of the co-op or producer.

BENEFITS TO PRODUCERS ›› Training in key areas of agronomy, farm management and business management. Access to market and direct relationships with buyers. Premiums paid for community development projects.

COSTS TO ROASTERS ›› A Community Development Premium is paid to producers through the supply chain, as outlined in each contract, and nominal service fees are paid to Fair Trade USA (no fee on the first 20,000 pounds) for supply chain services, impact reporting, consumer education and marketing support.

BENEFITS TO ROASTERS ›› Secure and sustainable supply of traceable coffee from all farm types. Increased visibility and consumer recognition. Measurable impact. Consumer marketing support.

CONTACT INFO ›› Fair Trade USA, 1500 Broadway, #400, Oakland, California, 94612; P: 510-663-5260; *fairtradeusa.org.*

Fairtrade International

LABEL ›› Fairtrade

FOCUS ›› Environmental, organizational and labor components intended to promote small-farm sustainability

CERTIFIER ›› FLO-Cert (owned by Fairtrade International)

BASIC COMPONENTS ››
• Minimum price to protect producer when market prices fall
• Additional financing for farmers to invest in community and business projects
• Long-term contracts with buyers
• Democratic organization of cooperatives
• Labor and environmental protections

INSPECTIONS ›› Annually

ORIGINS ›› Latin America, Caribbean, Africa and Asia

PRODUCERS ›› 1.2 million

COST TO PRODUCERS ›› Fees vary based on size of co-op, determined by the number of workers. Pre-harvest financing is available to cover fees. Additional costs associated with record-keeping requirements.

BENEFITS TO PRODUCERS ›› Access to market. Higher selling price. Organized management for members. Long-term producer-buyer relationships.

COSTS TO ROASTERS ›› Twenty cents per pound purchased, plus additional costs to complete reports and ensure certification of all partners in sourcing chain.

BENEFITS TO ROASTERS ›› Access to marketing campaign with high-profile labels and consumer recognition.

CONTACT INFO ›› Fairtrade International, 1145 Carling Ave., #7500, Ottawa, Ontario, K122K4, Canada; P: 613.563.3351; communications@ fairtrade.ca; *fairtrade.ca.* FLO International, Bonner Talweg, 177 53129, Bonn, Germany; P: 49.228.949.230; info@fairtrade.net; *fairtrade.net.*

Rainforest Alliance Certified

LABEL ›› Rainforest Alliance

FOCUS ›› Environmental and social components

CERTIFIER ›› Rainforest Alliance inspectors in Costa Rica. Many producing countries have affiliated organizations that can conduct local inspections.

BASIC COMPONENTS ››
- Protection and conservation of ecosystem using low-impact agricultural methods
- Shade-grown where applicable
- Minimum-wage benefits for employees
- Specific contribution to community is expected
- No premiums built in for farmers; market-based pricing
- Monitoring plan and continual improvement
- Open to private farmers and cooperatives

INSPECTIONS ›› Annually

ORIGINS ›› Latin America

PRODUCERS ›› 50,000

COST TO PRODUCERS ›› Fees based on hectares of cultivated land. Daily fees for inspectors, plus travel expenses. Additional costs related to initial compliance.

BENEFITS TO PRODUCERS ›› Improved farm management. Increased product quality. Coffee earns up to 25 cents above market value.

COSTS TO ROASTERS ›› No cost required to register.

BENEFITS TO ROASTERS ›› Appeal to consumers who are socially and environmentally conscious. Market-based pricing. Publicity for being involved in program.

CONTACT INFO ›› Rainforest Alliance, 223 Broadway, 28th Floor, New York, New York, 10279; P 212.677.1900; F 212.677.2187; *ra.org*

 USDA Organic

 Utz Certified

LABEL ›› USDA Organic

FOCUS ›› Environmental

CERTIFIER ›› The U.S. Department of Agriculture (USDA) has registered multiple entities to certify organic imports.

BASIC COMPONENTS ››
- Reduce use of toxic pesticides or fertilizers
- Continuous improvement of soil and water quality
- Crop management
- Renewable resources
- Reduction of waste, recycling
- Focus on management, documentation of activities, clear traceability, separation of organic product from non-organic product

INSPECTIONS ›› Annually

ORIGINS ›› Latin America, Caribbean, Africa and Asia

PRODUCERS ›› More than 650,000

COST TO PRODUCERS ›› $3,000 to $5,000 in annual renewal and inspection fees.

BENEFITS TO PRODUCERS ›› At least 15 cents per pound above the "C" market price, plus regional premiums. No risk of exposure to improperly applied chemicals. Reduces pollution.

COSTS TO ROASTERS ›› Approximately $1,000 annually for onsite inspections and detailed record keeping. Labor involved in maintaining a clear division between organic and conventional products and operations.

BENEFITS TO ROASTERS ›› Appeal to consumers who are socially and environmentally conscious. Consumer recognition.

CONTACT INFO ›› A list of USDA-registered certifiers is available at *ams.usda.gov/nop*

LABEL ›› Utz Certified

FOCUS ›› Sustainable farming and production practices, and social, labor and environmental traceability

CERTIFIER ›› Multiple third-party certification bodies

BASIC COMPONENTS ››
- Minimal pesticide use
- Minimum wage for workers, labor protection
- Livable housing and education for farm communities
- Continuous farm improvements
- Tracking for chain-of-custody available online

INSPECTIONS ›› Annually

ORIGINS ›› Latin America, Asia and Africa

PRODUCERS ›› More than 160,000

COST TO PRODUCERS ›› Audit costs depend on certifying body; no fee is paid to UTZ.

BENEFITS TO PRODUCERS ›› Market access. Improved trade terms, farming and management practices, and living and working conditions. Producers receive a premium negotiated directly with the buyer.

COSTS TO ROASTERS ›› Audit costs depend on certifying body, plus program fee of $0.012 per pound.

BENEFITS TO ROASTERS ›› Inclusive approach benefits smallholders and estates, cooperatives and individual farmers. Variety of blends, origins and quality. Real-time traceability.

CONTACT INFO ›› De Ruyterkade 6 1013 AA, The Netherlands; P: 31.20.530.8000; F: 31.20.427.8099; info@utzcertified.org; *utzcertified.org*

GREEN COFFEE BUYING

Signed, Sealed, Delivered

A Guide to Green Buying Parts 1 & 2

By Andi Trindle Mersch

• FROM THE SEPTEMBER/OCTOBER 2009 ISSUE OF *ROAST* •

PART ONE

Simply put, green buying is the act of securing raw coffee beans from a producing country, shipper, importer, trader or broker, so that they can be roasted and distributed in a consuming country. Of course, nothing in specialty coffee is simple. Many changes in the industry over recent years, such as roaster-direct sourcing and auction and certification programs, have altered the green buying process significantly. Nonetheless, even with a constantly evolving industry, the knowledge required to understand and successfully manage a green buying program remains largely the same.

Part One of this series looks at green coffee purchasing at origin and explains market pricing. Part Two will review green coffee buying from within consuming countries, while clarifying what a successful green buyer should know about securing the right coffee at the right time and at a preferable price.

The Sellers at Origin

Like any type of purchasing, green buying involves a buyer and seller. But in the coffee industry many different types of people play these two roles, and most often there is more than one of each between the original seller (coffee grower) and the final buyer (coffee roaster).

In all cases, coffee producers/farmers are involved in the original sale because they provide the product: ripe cherries. Coffee producers may run large private estates or, on the other end of the spectrum, they may be farmers who tend to small plots of land and later pool their harvest with other smallholders who have joined into a cooperative. Beginning coffee's journey from farm to cup, producers first sell their crop to millers, exporters or any number of additional folks in between, generically labeled "middlemen" or "coyotes."

The number of middlemen that exist between a producer and an exporter is determined by the location, education level and economic situation of producers, which dictate whether they can fully process their own coffee and whether they have direct access to buyers. Larger producers or cooperatives may run their own processing mills, and some may even have an export license, so they have the ability to manage cherry-to-seed processing from start to finish and sell green beans directly to importers.

The smallest producers, on the other hand, likely have no capability to handle processing, so they sell their unprocessed coffee cherries directly to a mill when possible or, when necessary, to a middleman, who facilitates the movement of coffee from the farm (or nearby roadside) to a processing mill. Middlemen offer credit and transportation in places where often neither is available.

Upon delivery, the mill will generally purchase the cherries in full. Payment is typically a dollar amount per quintal (100 pounds) of cherry; mills that produce the best quality will purchase only

fully ripe cherries and ideally pay a premium for them. In some cases, if a coffee lot will remain separate and sell under the name of a particular farm or mark, partial payment may be issued at the time of cherry delivery, with full payment being made after the coffee is sold to a buyer.

Next, the mill processes the coffee by the wet or dry method, or various semi-washed methods in between. Depending upon the mill's size, capabilities and connection to buyers, the mill may or may not keep the coffee through the dry milling and export process. If the facility does not have a dry mill, the coffee may change hands again before reaching an exporter, who will sell the coffee to the buyer.

The Buyers at Origin

The green buyer at origin is typically an importer who takes physical possession of and pays for the coffee while it is still in the producing country. The importer then has the responsibility to ship the coffee from the producing country to a consuming country warehouse or directly to their buyer's plant. Importers incur costs over and above the FOB (free on board) per pound price, including ocean freight, insurance, interest, duty and all fees until the coffee arrives at its destination. (Under FOB terms, the seller maintains fiscal and practical liability for the coffee until it passes over the ship's rails. At this point, the buyer generally issues payment in full and takes over fiscal and practical liability from there on out.)

The Offer and Contract

Regardless of who is serving as the buyer or seller in a particular transaction, the final paperwork between the end-point seller at origin and the consuming-country buyer remains largely the same.

◆ The buyer and the seller connect (either one contacting the other first) and the buyer makes an inquiry to the seller communicating what they need, specifying coffee quality, total quantity, shipment or delivery timing and, perhaps, a price indication. Alternatively, the sellers provide regular offers of available coffees.

◆ The seller reviews their availability (either within their own inventory or by contacting a grower or miller to arrange a purchase) and uses the information to prepare an offer for the buyer. A typical offer quote looks something like the sample on the following page; these are the same details that will ultimately be recorded on a contract if the offer is accepted.

◆ Assuming a buyer accepts a quote, the buyer and seller sign a contract to finalize the purchase. (See sample on page 72.)

◆ After both parties sign the contract, the seller arranges for a pre-shipment sample (PSS) for buyer approval, assuming a PSS is required for the contract. In some cases, a sample is available immediately and, in other cases, it may be weeks or even months before a contracted coffee becomes available. (Many coffees are sold in advance of processing and even harvesting in the interest of securing particular farms/grades/etc. as soon as they are available. This is why sample approval designations are especially important on contracts.) Whenever the sample is available, the next step is for the buyer to approve a sample before shipment. Ideally, this is a straightforward process with a single sample submitted and approved; however, if a sample does not match the buyer's expectations based on the contracted quality, they will reject the sample and request an alternative lot if the contract is "Replace" and not "No Approval No Sale" (NANS). This process continues until the buyer approves a sample.

◆ Next, the exporter prepares the coffee for shipment. At this point, the coffee is most likely still in parchment and will need to go through hulling and grading before it is ready for movement to the port of departure. Simultaneously, the buyer books space on a vessel and sends shipping instructions to the seller.

◆ The coffee ships. After arrival at the receiving country's pier, the coffee is then transported by land to the ultimate destination, which is typically the importer's warehouse, although sometimes it will go directly to a roaster buyer's plant. Customs and other inspections may slow the process, but generally a coffee reaches its ultimate destination within five to seven days from arrival at the port.

SAMPLE OFFER

Date	08/01/09
Contract No.	85459
Your Reference	roastreader

Subject to confirmation, we offer: **1**

Quality	El Salvador SHG Finca Apaneca-Ilamatepec **2**
Quantity	250 bags **3**
Approval Terms	SAPSS, SAAS **4**
Shipped by	Ship FH May **5**
Transfer	FOB Acajutla **6**
Price	+ 44 May NYC **7** OR $1.75 **8**

1 Subject to confirmation is a critical designation as availability and producer-side pricing can change rapidly. Alternatively, an offer can be made "firm," which guarantees that the product and price are held through an agreed-upon time frame (usually no more than 24 hours).

2 The coffee description includes a country of origin (El Salvador), almost always a grade (SHG), and optionally a specific region and/or farm (Apaneca-Ilamatepec). Coffee specifications may include defect count and screen size.

3 Containers ship with 250, 275, 300 or 320 bags, depending upon the country and preference, so the bag quantity must be specified. The weight per bag generally varies between 60-70 kg., depending upon protocols within the producing country.

4 This seemingly obscure coding refers to a buyer's opportunity for approval or rejection of the coffee based on quality and/or grade specifications. In this case, the buyer is approving a sample before shipment (SAPSS, or Subject to Approval of Pre-Shipment Sample) and again after arrival (SAAS, or Subject to Approval of Arrival Sample). These codes may also be followed by "NANS" (No Approval No Sale) or "Replace," which indicates whether the contract is void if the sample does not meet specifications or whether an alternative lot is provided for approval.

5 This designates the time frame for departure from the producing country. FH indicates first half of the month; in this case, the coffee will leave El Salvador between May 1 and May 15. Often in commercial trade, only whole month periods are designated as there are too many variables to control and it is preferable to broaden the time frame. The month designated for shipment also dictates the NYC contract month used for pricing.

6 FOB (Free on Board), discussed earlier, indicates where transfer of ownership occurs. FOB is the most common, although other options for transfer of ownership exist. For example, CIF (Cash, Insurance and Freight) designates that the seller covers these charges and releases liability for the coffee after freight services.

7 +44 May NYC indicates a differential price over the coffee market; the buyer will pay 44 cents per pound (U.S. currency) above the May market price settled upon when the contract is fixed.

8 Alternatively, coffee may sell at an outright price per pound. The buyer and seller are locked in at the designated per-pound price regardless of activity on the coffee market.

◆ Upon arrival at the plant or warehouse, the coffee is sampled again and, provided there are no major problems or discrepancies between the approved PSS and the arrival sample, the business between this particular buyer and seller is complete.

Rarely, an arrival sample is defective or substantially different from its PSS, and the importer and exporter must work through the situation. In worst cases, buyers may reject the entire lot and demand their money back. In best cases, the buyer can still resell or use the coffee, and they will work out a discount with the exporter. If the two parties fail to negotiate a solution, the dispute may result in arbitration.

Pricing: Differential and Outright

Understanding the green coffee pricing process requires a familiarity with a number of factors, including world economic markets, currencies, the oil market and, more recently, hedge funds. Pricing is complicated enough that it easily requires its own explanatory book. Nonetheless, here's a simple pricing primer, covering the basic terminology needed to navigate a contract.

Differential Pricing

Green coffee is initially priced by the seller (usually the exporter) at origin and sold in full container loads, for the most part. This price is frequently a differential price based on the New York "C" Market for arabica and London LIFFE Market for robusta.

Differentials are often consistent for a particular coffee origin of a particular grade. So, for example, all Guatemala SHB lots will likely have a similar differential regardless of the seller. In specialty coffee, however, notable above-average quality will likely command a higher differential based on the buyer and seller's agreed-upon value for the coffee, which can vary substantially.

For example, a producing country seller may offer a Guatemala Huehuetenango at +40 May NYC. This means the buyer will pay 40 cents per pound above the New York "C" Market price for May on the day the contract is price-fixed. (A fix may be called in a number of different ways: at the literal time to the second of fixation, at the market closing price on the day of fixation, or automatically when the market reaches a particular price specified in advance.) The producer or importer—whomever is designated to select the fix (indicated by the terms buyers call or sellers call)—then scrupulously follows the coffee market and, at any time prior to the first notice day for May-designated contracts, fixes the contract. When a fix is called in (which occurs only when the market is open and trading), the final contract price is confirmed by adding the differential to the market price. If the Guatemala contract is fixed by the seller when the market is at $1.2880, for example, then the final contract price becomes $1.69 per pound ($1.29 + $0.40).

Logically, in a sellers-call contract, the producer-side seller waits for the coffee market to reach what they hope is the highest level before they call in the fix, so that they are receiving the highest possible ultimate price on their contract. On the other side, the buyer waits for the coffee market to reach what they hope is the lowest level before they fix. Traditionally, origin contracts are sellers call and domestic contracts are buyers call. Exporters wait to price-fix (buy the market) at a high level, and roasters seek to price-fix (sell the market) at the lowest levels. These transactions are not related and can take place at any time between contract creation and first notice day, or date or transfer of ownership of the coffee, whichever comes first.

This scenario of trying to predict the market to maximize final price on the sell side and minimize final price on the buy side is an educated guessing game at best. As we all have learned, the market is not always predictable. And, even more frustrating, this process does not guarantee adequate coverage of the cost of production or coffee quality. Coffee is initially sold at a differential that is intended to support everyone's costs, plus a reasonable profit attached to service and quality provided. But depending on changes in the unpredictable coffee market, a producer using this method may not even cover production costs. Green coffee buyers and sellers can really only make the best decision possible using all of the available information and learn from successes and mistakes.

Outright Pricing

When coffee is sold at a flat price, like $1.85 per pound, it is called outright pricing. Unlike differential pricing, outright pricing allows for predictability of final sell and purchase pricing at the time of the sale. The clear advantage here is that origin-side sellers can be certain they are covering costs and, ideally, earning a suitable profit; buyers also have certainty of their cost of goods, so they can ensure profitability when selling to the final buyer—whether it is an importer selling to a roaster, or a roaster selling to its customer.

So far in this series, we've covered how coffee begins its journey from the farm at origin and who plays a part in transporting the coffee from place to place. And we've discussed offers, contracts and green pricing. Next up, part two of this series—which will explore how green buying works from the perspective of those in consuming countries, and explain the best times to buy.

SAMPLE CONTRACT

PART TWO

I n part one of this series, we examined green coffee purchasing from within a producing country. In this second installment, we will cross many miles of land and sea to look at how green coffee ultimately gets to a coffee roaster.

For any roaster—from the smallest microroaster to the largest commercial operation—sourcing green beans is arguably *the* most important task on the schedule; roasters must have green coffee or they'd have nothing to roast and sell. Furthermore, green coffee is often the single largest cost for a roasting operation.

Roasters need to understand how and when to purchase green coffee so they are never without the essential raw product, and they need to purchase at the right price to stay in business. When working with specialty coffee, a roaster has the added challenge of sourcing high-quality, fresh beans—and, like any great chef will tell you, the final product is only as good and consistent as the ingredients used.

Buyers and Sellers in Consuming Countries

In consuming country transactions, green coffee may be sold through a number of different channels before reaching a roaster buyer. Here's a rundown of the various roles in the coffee buying and selling business:

◆ Importers buy coffee from the producing country, maintain ownership during transportation, and then either deliver directly to a roaster buyer's plant or into a warehouse for sale to single or multiple clients. If all or part of the lot is unsold, it goes into the importer's spot position for future sales.

◆ Traders (not to be confused with commodity market traders in this scenario) buy coffee from an importer within a consuming country and then sell the coffee from their inventory; like importers, traders may have a buyer in advance or they may keep coffee in their inventory to sell at a later date.

◆ Brokers sell coffee from an importer's or trader's inventory and make a commission (usually a number of cents per pound) when they find a buyer; brokers never take physical possession of coffee and therefore have the least financial risk, whereas importers have the most and traders are somewhere in between.

After its domestic arrival, green coffee is sold (or sampled and released if pre-sold) to a coffee roasting company. Depending on the company size, the responsibility for coffee buying lands on various players. For example, coffee buyers may hold several job functions and spend minimal time on purchasing, or they may focus solely on securing the right coffees at the right time and price.

In small companies, the buyer is often the owner or the owner/roaster, so they are performing multiple functions within the business. In medium-sized businesses, production roasters may hold responsibility for purchasing green coffee. In larger companies, one or more people may be dedicated exclusively to green buying. The sourcing function is a full-time position, which may include sample roasting and cupping work in a green coffee lab.

Whatever the ultimate scope of responsibilities, a green buyer's essential task is to "source the best green coffee while managing the risk," according to Thomas Hodges, director of coffee at La Mill in Los Angeles. Hodges seeks to balance his "desire and passion to source the most interesting coffees with actual demand, and contracting the ideal amount of coffee that will remain at the peak of freshness until it has been exhausted." And let's not forget that buyers aim to purchase coffee at the right price. Green buying is not a simple job when put like that.

The Offer and Contract

Similar to origin buying, green coffee transactions remain largely the same regardless of the type of buyer and seller. To keep things simple, we'll use the example of sales between direct importers and roasters.

While purchasing at origin often involves full container loads (250 to 320 bags of coffee, equaling 37,500 to 45,000 pounds), the quantity of coffee exchanged between an importer and a roaster varies. Coffee may be purchased in full container loads or in smaller quantities by the bag. Generally, larger (macro) roasters purchase most of their coffee in container quantities, while midsized and microroasters purchase in significantly smaller LTL (Less than Container Load) amounts.

However, the large roaster Coffee Bean International (CBI) in Portland, Oregon, buys through "all of the above," says Paul Thornton, the company's former green buyer. CBI, says Thornton, undertakes smaller "spot buys to fill holes and smaller specialty coffee needs," in addition to container volume purchasing. Clearly, it's useful for roasters to understand the unique processes for both full-container purchasing and smaller LTL-volume purchasing.

LTL (less than container load) Transactions

Smaller roasters frequently buy beans on the spot market, which

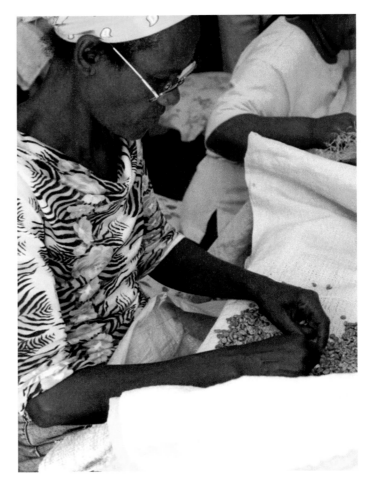

means they buy coffee that is already stored in a regionally located warehouse. Typically, these transactions range from one to 100 bags. The process for this type of purchasing goes something like this:

◆ The roaster and the importer connect to discuss the buyer's needs, which may include a particular coffee origin, region, farm, price or cup profile. The seller often initiates this process by sending an offer list.

◆ The importer makes an offer—an informal verbal bid, a formal written quote or both. Please see part one for a review of a typical formal quote from a producer to an importer, which is similar to a quote from an importer to a roaster. The contract between importers and roasters details a delivery time frame to the roaster, rather than a shipment time frame from origin.

◆ The roaster then purchases the coffee based on its price and description alone or, ideally, requests a sample. If sampling before buying, the roaster may choose to purchase the coffee on an SAS (Subject to Approval of Sample) basis or wait to cup the sample

before deciding whether to purchase. Roasters should book an SAS contract only when they are committed to purchasing the coffee and plan to reject solely based on quality parameters (it is not appropriate for buyers to use an SAS contract system to protect coffee supply and pricing while they evaluate coffees from different suppliers). However, roasters may ask the importer to informally reserve a certain coffee while they have opportunity to evaluate their options. It is common practice for an importer to protect its customers in this way. Ideally, the roaster will make a timely decision to prevent the importer from losing a potential sale elsewhere. An SAS contract does not allow for canceling if the buyer finds a better or less expensive coffee. Buyers who manage their inventory by rejecting coffee often lose suppliers or pay higher prices due to the financial risk on the seller's part.

◆ After sample approval or verbal description, the roaster and importer finalize the number of bags, the price and the delivery schedule. Delivery for many smaller-volume roasters is immediate, but it is also possible to purchase coffee on a forward delivery spread. A delivery spread allows a roaster to lock in pricing and availability of a particular coffee over a given number of months. For example, a roaster may require 60 bags of a particular coffee over four months. Based on limited warehouse/cafe space and lack of cash flow, the roaster may prefer to receive the coffee on a monthly basis. In this case, for an additional carry charge fee (importers charge different rates—usually a small percentage of the coffee's value per month, plus the cost of warehouse storage) the importer agrees to hold the coffee and release 15 bags per month to the buyer. The roaster will pay for the coffee as it is released, not when it is booked.

◆ When the roaster is ready for the coffee—whether in total immediately, or in part on a spread—they contact the seller and request that the seller issue a delivery order, which is a negotiable document that transfers ownership of the coffee from the seller to the buyer at a specific location. A delivery order details the coffee type (identified very specifically with bag markings and warehouse location coding), number of bags, destination and carrier (trucking company or client pickup). Most delivery orders also include one of the following terms, which designate exactly where the coffee changes ownership and who pays for what charges:

XW or EX-W (EX Warehouse): The buyer takes ownership of the coffee where it is stored at the warehouse and assumes responsibility for all charges thereafter. Buyers must have their own account with the warehouse in this scenario, as the warehouse will apply out-loading charges when the coffee is picked up, which may or may not include palletizing, shrink-wrapping and strapping. (Coffee often leaves the warehouse on a wooden pallet, which typically fits a maximum of 10 bags. Small roasters purchasing less than five bags at a time may take the coffee "floor

loaded," which reduces out-loading charges but may increase risk of product loss or damage in transportation.)

FOT-D (Free on Truck-Delivered): The seller pays out-loading charges through to loading on the truck (these costs are usually incorporated into the original offer price), and the buyer pays all charges after coffee is loaded on a truck.

Delivered: The seller pays all charges through delivery to the client's location. This method is often used in full container load purchasing, direct from origin.

◆ The roaster receives the shipment and carefully inspects the load to ensure receipt of the right coffee in the right quantity, devoid of damage. If there are any issues, a buyer must note the problem or discrepancy on the bill of lading (BL) before the truck driver leaves.

John Gozbekian, director of coffee for Cult Coffee Roaster in Phoenix, Arizona, is insistent about this process. "Always write it [any discrepancy] down," he says. "You can't push a claim forward without doing so, but you can always back off." He notes that "concealed damage," which is not visible upon reasonable initial inspection, is technically still recoverable even if not noted at the time of delivery. However, concealed damage can be difficult to prove, so it is worth the time and effort to ask a driver to wait for a thorough inspection.

For most mistakes, like a torn but mostly full bag, the buyer will accept the delivery and use the documented evidence to hold either the trucking company or the seller responsible for managing the solution. In this case, the buyer should weigh the coffee before the driver leaves and note the difference in shipped versus delivered pounds on the BL. This provides the proper evidence to submit to the trucking company or importer to receive credit for missing coffee.

In cases of extreme error or damage, like delivery of the wrong coffee—or, as Gozbekian once experienced, delivery of coffee contaminated by garlic—the buyer may reject the shipment completely, requiring the trucker to return the coffee to the original warehouse. From here, the roaster should promptly call the trucking company office and the importer to begin tracking the root of the problem, and work toward resolution and a replacement delivery.

◆ After the roaster has the coffee safely in hand (as in most cases, fortunately), the final stages in the buying transaction are arrival sample evaluation (as possible) and payment. A buyer compensates the seller based on agreed-upon payment terms, such as immediately, net 10, net 15 or net 30 days after issue of delivery order; new clients are frequently required to pay before the coffee can be released.

Payment may be withheld or postponed, however, if there is a problem with the arrival sample. Arrival sample rejections are rare, but they can occur if the arrival coffee possesses major defects or substantial quality variance from the PSS sample. If this happens, the roaster may reject the entire lot outright, in which case the ownership reverts back to the importer, and the roaster does not pay. Or the roaster may negotiate a price reduction based on the significance of the quality difference (this is the same negotiation that may occur between the exporter and importer).

FTL (full container load) Transactions

Larger-volume specialty and commercial roasters often buy their coffee in full container loads, which are frequently booked (purchased on paper) before coffee is shipped and sometimes prior to harvest. This type of purchase transaction is called forward contracting. Though volumes are much higher, the transaction details and contract between a roaster and importer in this buying scenario are similar to spot purchasing.

A contract confirming the transaction still designates the same details about coffee type, quantity, pricing, delivery schedule and payment terms. One possible difference, however, is additional sampling of the coffee before it ships from origin, which is referenced on a contract as SAPSS approval (Subject to Approval of Pre-Shipment Sample). In this scenario, the roaster buyer and the importer have the opportunity to evaluate and approve (or reject) a sample of the specific coffee lot before it ships from origin. After arrival, they will have another opportunity to approve the coffee, which is referenced as SAAS (Subject to Approval of Arrival Sample). Sometimes the acronyms are combined and read something like this: "Subject PSSAS." Additionally, orders may stipulate "Delivered" (to buyer's plant), rather than XW or FOT-D.

When to Buy

Regardless of volume purchased and delivery scenarios, determining *when* to buy is key. Availability is of utmost importance, as roasters need their core ingredient in order to produce their core product. This may sound easy to manage, but it

can become complicated due to conditions in producing countries that influence supply and demand. For example, if there is a predicted or reduced harvest and a buyer is not protected through a forward contract, they may not be able to buy the specific coffee.

Roasters should book forward when they can and pay attention to news from producing countries that may significantly affect future supply. Keep in mind that an upcoming shortage of new-crop coffee can rapidly affect the supply of spot current crop as aware buyers purchase existing spot inventory to cover anticipated shortages.

In addition, price is critical for roasters—especially for those purchasing containers. Based on supply-and-demand cycles, roaster buyers generally attempt to purchase when the differential price is low. These buyers must also fix their contracts at a favorable level, but this is generally a consideration for down the road. (See Part One for more on fixations.)

For all buyers, purchasing with awareness of harvest seasons is necessary to anticipate availability and manage coffee freshness. (Harvest cycles vary depending on the producing country's distance from the equator, which impacts temperature and other climatic conditions. Importers should be able to assist their customers in determining appropriate buying times based on harvest seasons.) Toward the end of a harvest cycle, availability of coffee frequently becomes scarce. Regardless of shortages, buyers must foresee the need for fresh coffee before they run out of current stocks. Buyers must weigh these needs and make the smartest decision for their business. According to Hodges, "Booking too much coffee is much worse, in my opinion, than running short because quality always suffers, and it unnecessarily ties up cash flow."

Specialty coffee buyers also use knowledge of harvest seasons to manage coffee freshness. Green coffee has a shelf life of roughly nine to 12 months with ideal storage conditions, so buyers should be aware when they are buying coffee within a harvest cycle. Unless buyers rotate their coffees seasonally, it is difficult to avoid purchasing old or past-crop coffee at times. (Fortunately, properly processed and stored green beans do not lose quality dramatically. Usually it is a slow progression—first with the subtle loss of flavor attributes and acidity, followed by the increase and eventual dominance of dry cocoa and baggy [like the jute bag] flavors, deemed "past croppish.")

Forward container load buyers may try to time shipment from origin so coffee stays in parchment until the last minute to maintain freshness. However, the coffee should be shipped before periods of high heat and humidity, both of which can significantly deteriorate quality. Some buyers purchase coffee from particular pickings within a harvest cycle. For example, many consider coffee from the second or third picking of a harvest to maximize flavor, since cherries sweeten when they ripen more slowly; these buyers may request their preferred picking in their contract.

Building Relationships

To close our series, it's worth highlighting that successful green buying relies on relationships. All participants in green coffee buying and selling—both in producing and consuming countries—must communicate openly, understand each other's business on some level, and respect each other's right and desire to earn a living. Developing and maintaining strong relationships is arguably the most important part of green buying and selling. Producers and importers have no business without roasters to buy coffee, and green business grows when a roaster's volume grows. Wise sellers truly want their roasting clients to succeed and will work with them to make that happen. Smart roaster buyers emphasize the same priority.

Thornton emphasizes the critical nature of the importer/roaster relationship when addressing management of difficult situations like the arrival of lesser-quality coffee than that approved before shipment. Considering this scenario, Thornton says he will do what he can to salvage the coffee, believing "it is in my best interest to make sure my importers are in a lucrative business, so we do what we can to make our business a good business for importers."

Hodges goes even further, saying that his relationship with an importer/green broker "is like a marriage ... and partners understand that my success is their success, and we are in this together at all times." ∎

. . . .

ANDI TRINDLE MERSCH *has a varied background within her specialty coffee career, which began behind the espresso bar in 1989 and, since then, includes cupping, training, consulting, green coffee trading and buying, quality control, sales and writing. Mersch currently serves as director of coffee for Philz Coffee. She was elected to the Roasters Guild Executive Council for a two-year term in March 2015, and she volunteers with the Specialty Coffee Association (SCA) developing coffee business curriculum. She is a past board member of the SCA and the International Women's Coffee Alliance.*

Talk the Talk

Understanding Commodity Market Lingo

by Matt Daks

• FROM THE SEPTEMBER/OCTOBER 2016 ISSUE OF *ROAST* •

Coffee is a people business, and working with people requires good communication. We value communication so highly that we have multiple industry-funded organizations working to create a standardized global sensory lexicon to describe how we experience our beloved brew. And yet, although the commodity market factors heavily into our daily work, important aspects of communication surrounding it are not well understood by many specialty coffee professionals. Without getting bogged down in the intricacies of market pricing and how it relates to quality and supply—how a frost in Brazil can affect the price of a microlot in Tanzania, for example—suffice it to say, we are all inextricably tied to the commodity market, and our ability to communicate around that, like our ability to communicate about cup profiles, is paramount to our success.

Specialty coffee is still very much an old-world business. Deals often are sealed with the shake of a hand and the honor of one's word. Not many industries remain in which business can be handled in this manner. To be able to maintain this trust among peers, it is essential that we all understand what it is we are hearing and saying.

Not only is coffee an old-world business, but in fact, so is the commodity—or futures—market. The Chicago Board of Trade opened its doors in the mid 1800s, while the Amsterdam Stock Exchange was established in the early 1600s. The earliest futures contracts are believed to have been executed around 4000 B.C. in Sumer, Mesopotamia, or modern-day Iraq.

These early markets were used to protect both producer and buyer from wild changes in price due to weather conditions, national conflicts or supply shortages. By establishing "futures" contracts that detailed the specific quality and quantity of a product for delivery at a precise time in the future, at a designated place, and for a negotiated price, farmers were able to sell their goods before the harvest, and buyers could pay for goods before they needed to take possession. To ensure the integrity of this system, boards and exchanges were established to collect and transfer payment, store goods and provide a mechanism for contract settlement. This also created the need for a standard commodity market vocabulary.

To provide an introduction to this vocabulary, we asked several experts to explain some of the most common commodity market terms coffee professionals will encounter. I have provided further explanation and, in some cases, examples, in the sections titled "In other words."

Futures

Jennifer Roberts, director of trading,
Atlas Coffee Importers, Seattle

A future is an agreement to buy or sell a commodity at some point in the future. Futures contracts are standardized according to the quality, quantity, and delivery time and location for each commodity. For coffee traders, futures typically are used to mitigate exposure to the ups and downs of the commodity market by offsetting physical purchases or sales. For example, an importer will sell a future (short) when he purchases physical coffee and buy a future (long) when he sells the coffee later. If the commodity price has gone up between the first and second transaction, the importer

Jennifer Roberts of Atlas Coffee Importers.

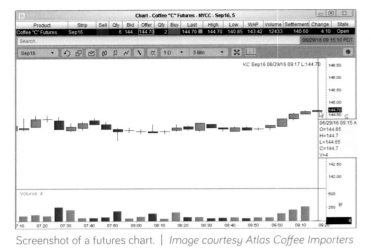

Screenshot of a futures chart. | *Image courtesy Atlas Coffee Importers*

Screenshot of an options quote board. | *Image courtesy Atlas Coffee Importers*

loses money on the futures transaction (sold low, bought high), but gains money on the physical transaction. Conversely, if the price has gone down, the importer will gain money on the futures transaction to offset the loss on the value of the physical.

IN OTHER WORDS (Matt Daks): It is interesting to note that physical coffee is rarely traded via the futures market. Futures are used as a mechanism for participants to lock in pricing so they are able to plan accordingly. To expand upon the example above, consider this scenario: An importer buys a Colombian supremo from an exporter FOB (free on board) after all import costs are calculated, at a differential of +.50 (50 cents over market price), EXW Oakland (meaning the seller will make the goods available to the buyer at an Oakland, California, warehouse). When the importer purchases the physical coffee, she also will sell a futures contract at the price fixed with the exporter, say $1.50. The invoiced price for that contract then is $2.00 ($1.50 + 50 cents). Now let's say the importer sells that coffee two weeks later at a differential of +.65 EXW Oakland, but the market has dropped to $1.25. The invoice to the buyer, then, is $1.90 ($1.25 + .65 cents), 10 cents lower than the invoice from the exporter. However, the importer sold the futures contract at $1.50 and bought it back two weeks later at $1.25, making 25 cents per pound. So, the importer loses 10 cents per pound on the physical trade, but makes 25 cents per pound on the futures trade, netting 15 cents per pound.

Options

Jennifer Roberts

A type of security that gives the buyer the right, but not the obligation, to buy or sell an asset—such as a coffee future—at a specific price on or before a specific date. Buyers of options are primarily trying to limit risk of a rising or falling market.

IN OTHER WORDS (MD): Options can be complicated, but one way to describe them is like insurance. You pay a premium to make sure you are covered on a rainy day. Although certain types of options can act like insurance, others hold unlimited risk, so this is not the type of tool you want to use without trusted, professional guidance. Few roasters actually use options, and more often than not, those who do work closely with their finance departments to make sure they limit their risk.

Hedge

Tina Berard, vice president and senior trader, Atlantic Specialty Coffee, Hayward, California

Tina Berard of Atlantic Specialty Coffee.

Hedging is a process for buyers of physical coffee to use the futures and/or options markets to transfer some of the price risk. Hedging is a strategy tool to protect users of physical coffee in the rising and falling New York Intercontinental Exchange (ICE) market by locking in a price or by establishing a minimum and/or maximum price level. This can be useful for long-term planning.

IN OTHER WORDS (MD): Hedging is not a means of guaranteeing the lowest or highest price possible, but rather of establishing an amount of risk with which one is comfortable. When farmers hedge their crops, they secure, or lock in, a futures price at which they are comfortable selling their coffee.

Bid / Offer

Jennifer Roberts

A bid is a price a buyer agrees to pay for something—a bag of coffee, a lot of coffee, a delivery spread on a lot or lots of coffee, a coffee future or option, or maybe a pony. If a seller agrees to the bid, the transaction is concluded, the pony is yours. An offer is a price at which a seller agrees to sell something. If a buyer agrees to the offer, the transaction is concluded.

. . . .

IN OTHER WORDS (MD): These are some of the most important words for coffee buyers and sellers to understand, as they get to the root of the industry's ability to exist on a participant's word. Both words imply a commitment to adhere to the agreed-upon terms. Generally, either a bid or an offer should come with information regarding the quality of the coffee, the dates of delivery or shipment, the place of delivery or shipment, expected payment terms and price. Additionally, a bid or an offer should include a length of validity. For example, "I am able to offer you 320 bags of Kenyan AB for August delivery plus 75 cents per pound EXW New Jersey, NSW (net shipped weights), Net 30 (payment due within 30 days). The offer is valid until this Friday." If the potential buyer agrees by the stated deadline, the seller (the person who made the offer) is obligated to sell the coffee per the stated terms. The same holds for a bid. If a buyer made that same bid, and a seller accepted the terms, the buyer is obligated to buy as laid out in the bid. There is another common clause, however, that sort of acts as an escape clause for an offer, which is "subject final confirmation." This stipulates that, though it is an offer, it needs to be reconfirmed by the seller before the transaction is completed. If you want to express a price idea without a commitment, do not use the terms bid or offer.

Open, Close, Last & Settlement

Julio Sera, senior risk management consultant, INTL FC Stone Latin America, Miami

These terms refer to the behavior of coffee futures prices (or any other exchange-traded financial derivative) on any given trading day.

- **OPEN:** The first price at which at least one buyer and one seller agree to trade a coffee futures contract on the ICE at the beginning (or "open") of each day.

- **LAST/CLOSE:** The last price at which at least one buyer and one seller agree to trade a coffee futures contract on the ICE at 1:30 p.m. Eastern Standard Time (EST).

- **SETTLEMENT:** The official price used by the ICE to settle all coffee futures contracts on each trading day. This represents the volume-weighted arithmetic average of all trades during the settlement window (between 1:23 and 1:25 p.m. EST).

. . . .

IN OTHER WORDS (MD): Interestingly, the open doesn't always correlate to the previous day's close. With the electronic trading platform,

Julio Sera of INTL FC Stone Latin America.

additional trading takes place in the five minutes after the official close. The close is typically used to evaluate market performance. When you hear people talking about the New York ICE market reaching new five-year highs, it most likely refers to the price at the close of the day's trading. The settlement is critically important because it affects individual accounts. To put it simply, if the market settles a penny higher than the previous day's trading, you have an extra penny in your account. This is overly simplistic, but it helps to demonstrate the importance of the settlement. Because of this, trading into the closing minutes of a day's session can sometimes get quite lively.

Long & Short

Tina Berard

Long means one owns a position in the market. In trading lingo, "going long" means to buy futures. A long position is at risk of a falling market forcing the owner to sell lower.

Short means one needs a position in the market. In trading lingo, "going short" means to sell futures. A short position is at risk of a rising market forcing the one in need to buy higher.

. . . .

IN OTHER WORDS (MD): Going long essentially means you buy a futures contract, with the expectation that the market will rise. If the market falls, you lose money when you sell. Going short means you sell a futures contract. In this case, you are betting the market is going to fall. Someone who "goes long" may be referred to as being "bullish." Someone who "goes short" is referred to as being "bearish."

Moving Averages

Julio Sera

A moving average is a technical analysis indicator applied by market participants to "smooth out" the price action or volatility of financial contracts. It is a so-called lagging indicator because it is constructed using a body of data that has already been observed. In the most basic example, a simple moving average is the arithmetic mean (average) of a body of data; the 10-day simple moving average of coffee futures contracts takes the last 10 daily settlements and averages them to smooth out any random price fluctuations. The intent is to view the underlying trend of how coffee futures prices are behaving with respect to their overall direction, and whether any current trend is about to reverse itself. It is one of the tools market participants use for the purpose of timing entry and exit decisions (when to buy or sell). There are variations on this theme, including simple linear weighted and exponentially smoothed moving averages. Each implementation processes the relevant body of data differently depending on what the subjective trader is focusing on within the numbers.

IN OTHER WORDS (MD): The moving average is a great tool for observing market tendencies. When the moving average is higher than the current market price, it may act as a magnet, drawing the price up to the average. If the market crosses over the moving average to a higher price, that is an indicator that the market may be trending upward. Trends in the coffee market—as with all trends—are fueled by expectations, human behavior, time and perspective, so there are different moving averages to consider. The nine-day moving average gives near-term indications, for example, while the 100- and 200-day moving averages provide longer-term market guidance.

Open Interest

Julio Sera

Open interest is the sum total of all buyers and sellers who hold "open" positions at the end of each business day in all available contracts of an exchange-traded financial derivative. One contract of open interest consists of one buyer and one seller. The daily increases/decreases of total open interest in a particular contract provide insight into how price fluctuations should be interpreted from trading session to trading session. For example, a price increase combined with an increase in open interest for a specific trading day most likely represents new buying coming into the market. Conversely a price decline together with an increase in open interest would constitute new selling filtering into the market. Two other possible scenarios are: (1) a price increase with an open interest decrease, which is defined as "short covering," or participants buying back "short sales" in anticipation of additional upside potential; and (2) a price decrease with an open interest decline, which would be characteristic of "long liquidation," or traders "selling their longs" expecting prices to head lower still.

IN OTHER WORDS (MD): Open interest is like the number of

people still at a party. Who is still interested in seeing what happens next? Did people leave to go somewhere else? If the party is swinging and people are still showing up, this thing's going to go on for a while.

Volumes

Mark Williams, partner, Cape Horn Coffees, Denver

In financial markets, volume refers to the frequency at which a particular holding is traded throughout the day. Higher volumes indicate that there are more investors buying and selling a particular security, which means it is easier for an investor to

Mark Williams of Cape Horn Coffees.

transact in that given security. Thin volumes bring a risk that an investor will have to pay a large premium to buy or sell a security in order to convince new counterparties to enter the market.

IN OTHER WORDS (MD): Volumes are important because it determines how easily you are able to get into or out of a position. In order to execute a trade, there has to be a party to take the opposite side of the trade. If you want to buy but there are no sellers, you will have to wait until volume picks up and your trade can be executed. On the opposite side, when volumes are high, prices can move quickly.

Commitment of Traders

Keith Flury, head of coffee research, Volcafe Ltd., Zurich, Switzerland

Commitment of Traders (COT) reports help us assess how different market players are positioned in the futures and options markets. The reports are released every Friday by the Commodity Futures Trading

Keith Flury of Volcafe Ltd.

Commission (CFTC) and are an important tool for understanding price movements on U.S. commodity exchanges.

IN OTHER WORDS (MD): Similar to open interest, the COT report gives us insight into market participants. It does not tell us exactly how many people are at the party, but it does provide insight into the mood of the partygoers. The COT report breaks down the partygoers into the following descriptions:

● **Commercials** (Keith Flury): The commercial position represents the entities along the supply chain who deal with physical coffee. The net position represents the balance of hedging by producers and traders holding coffee, generally with short contracts, and hedging by users (roasters) using long contracts.

IN OTHER WORDS (MD): These are our people. The coffee folk.

● **Non Commercials** (KF): Generally considered the main part of the speculative position as reported, this includes funds that are trading coffee not for hedging purposes but to anticipate price moves and realize profit and those using commodities as a way to diversify portfolios.

IN OTHER WORDS (MD): These could be the hedge funds, the index funds, etc. This demonstrates how folks outside the coffee world view coffee markets for investment purposes. It is useful in the sense that it shows how people who aren't emotionally tied to the industry think about coffee.

● **Non Reportable** (KF): The COT uses this category for the residue, the total reported traders minus the open interest. These are participants who do not fall under the classical definitions of traders. Generally, this includes small traders who have small open positions and are not required to report to the CFTC but are speculating on prices.

IN OTHER WORDS (MD): These are the day traders, typically trading in small volumes.

Managed Money

Mark Williams

Managed money refers to a pool of assets where the investor, rather than buying and selling his own securities, delegates a third-party investment manager to make investing decisions for

a fee. Examples of managed money include mutual funds, hedge funds and retirement plans. Managed money can have a dramatic impact on commodity markets as managers decide to invest in or divest of commodity holdings. When commodity funds invest large sums of money into commodity markets, it can push prices higher in a short period of time.

IN OTHER WORDS (MD): Managed money can sometimes be seen as outsiders meddling in our business. They can move the market quickly, in directions that don't seem to make sense. They may bully the market a bit to ensure the profitability of their positions. However, they play an immensely important role by providing liquidity to the market. In order to buy or sell a contract on the futures market, you need to have someone to take the opposite side of that contract. Managed money helps provide that other side.

These explanations cover only a small segment of the terms commodities traders must understand in order to do business, but for the typical specialty coffee professional, this should provide a good foundation on which to build. To develop your knowledge further, explore the free educational resources available through Investopedia (*investopedia.com*) and the Khan Academy (*khanacademy.org*), and speak with your trading partners, particularly the importers with whom you work.

We are all coffee lovers, and one thing coffee lovers love to do, maybe as much as we love to drink coffee, is talk about coffee. ◼

MATT DAKS *has worked in the coffee industry since 1999, in numerous roles from seed to cup. He is currently the senior category manager for coffee at National DCP, the $2 billion supply chain management cooperative serving Dunkin' Donuts franchisees.*

GREEN COFFEE STORAGE & TRANSPORTION

Banking Your Green

Proper Storage and Handling of Green Beans

By Karen Foley

• FROM THE JANUARY/FEBRUARY 2006 ISSUE OF *ROAST* •

IN THE SEED-TO-CUP CHAIN of events, maintaining coffee quality can amount to a small miracle. From growing and processing to roasting and preparation, coffee must endure an incredibly involved series of steps, all of which can irreparably impact its final character. Chief among these tenuous steps is green coffee storage. One pest infestation, one natural disaster, one pungent aroma or one sweltering summer day and what began as a special coffee can quickly become anything but. Choosing the right storage facility can dramatically affect your coffee's quality, so it's imperative to know what to look for and what questions to ask.

To begin, temperature, humidity and light are critical factors. Coffee professionals often debate the exact ideal storage temperature, espousing anywhere from 50 to 70 degrees F, but Jennifer Roberts, director of trading for Atlas Coffee, an importer in Seattle, uses a simpler gauge. "Our rule of thumb is that if people are comfortable where your coffee is being stored, it will be too."

In areas with low humidity, coffee can lose moisture, and in areas with muggy summer months, humidity control is crucial in preventing beans from absorbing too much moisture and, thus, molding. The general rule is below 65 percent humidity, allowing beans to retain a 12 percent moisture content prior to roasting. In ports along the East Coast and in coffee importing hubs like New Orleans, humidity is of paramount concern, and warehouse facilities often integrate climate control technology into their operations to ensure environmental stability.

Some roasters in hot, humid regions have even taken matters into their own hands. In St. Louis, Ronnoco Specialty Coffee built its own climate control room for storage of certain coffees during the steamy summer months. The room, which is kept at 70 degrees F and holds around 800 bags of coffee, is especially useful for storing beans that are not fast movers. "It makes a huge difference," says Robert Carpenter, Ronnoco's green coffee buyer. "In areas with hot, humid summers, coffee can deteriorate so quickly that in one month it tastes like it's been sitting around for a year."

Stockton Graham & Co., a wholesale roaster in North Carolina, has employed a similar strategy. "North Carolina generally has high humidity levels, so we condition our coffees in climate-controlled storage before roasting them," says Jeff Vojta, Stockton Graham's president. "Thus, we generally maintain a few weeks' supply in an air-conditioned/heated space. By keeping them in our air-conditioned facility a few days to a week or so before roasting them, we have found that the moisture levels, shrinkage, roast times and overall cup quality tend to be more consistent."

Stockton Graham tries to keep no more than three to five weeks' worth of coffee on hand in the climate-controlled facility, and Vojta says they typically store the balance of their coffees in warehouses at the ports. In choosing a facility to warehouse green coffee stocks, Vojta says it's critical to look at a company's overall coffee experience and general reputation. He also advises asking the following questions:

• Is the storage facility secure?

• Is the coffee secured from the elements, especially water and humidity?

• Does the facility meet organic handling and storage requirements?

• Can they keep the different lots of coffee accounted for and maintain proper lot tracking and inventory records?

• Are they responsive to normal inquiries about the coffee or its handling?

• Do they have good overall customer service for processing load tickets?

Indeed, as with any other aspect of the coffee business, experience matters when it comes to the business of coffee storage. That is, in fact, what led to the formation of The Green Room, a green coffee storage and handling facility in Auburn, Washington. "We had certain frustrations related to the lack of understanding of how to handle green coffee," says Green Room co-owner Pat Perkins. "My partner had experience working at Starbucks in warehousing and distribution, and my background is importing, which gave me experience with other warehouses that were handling green coffee. We wanted to start a green coffee warehouse that was based on knowledge of the product. We want all of our staff to be people who really know coffee and are trained to know how to recognize coffee that's damaged in any way."

The Green Room stores around 100,000 bags in 113,000 square feet of storage space for about 40 clients around the United States. Even though humidity is not usually an issue in the Pacific Northwest, the warehouse has devices on hand that measure humidity levels, and the company goes to great lengths to preserve the integrity of the coffee it stores. Pest control, for one, is critical. "You want to have people who are trained for the inbound to identify infestations," says Perkins. "Our primary pest control is having a professional come in and trap and monitor and write reports. If anything does appear, they'll come in and do what needs to be done to fix the problem."

In terms of storage specifications, The Green Room uses kiln-dried pallets to prevent moisture damage; inserts a protective

> "You want to have people who are trained for the inbound to identify infestations. Our primary pest control is having a professional come in and trap and monitor and write reports. If anything does appear, they'll come in and do what needs to be done to fix the problem."
>
> —Pat Perkins, The Green Room

layer between the coffee and the skid to keep bags from sagging; and maintains adequate spacing between coffee stacks to allow for proper airflow and inspection. To prevent foreign odors from contaminating the coffee, The Green Room does not handle any items that could damage the beans, and the warehouse takes pains to communicate with customers and maintain organized systems and records for tracking coffees. "If you're a smaller roaster or importer, that takes its own set of procedures and ways of

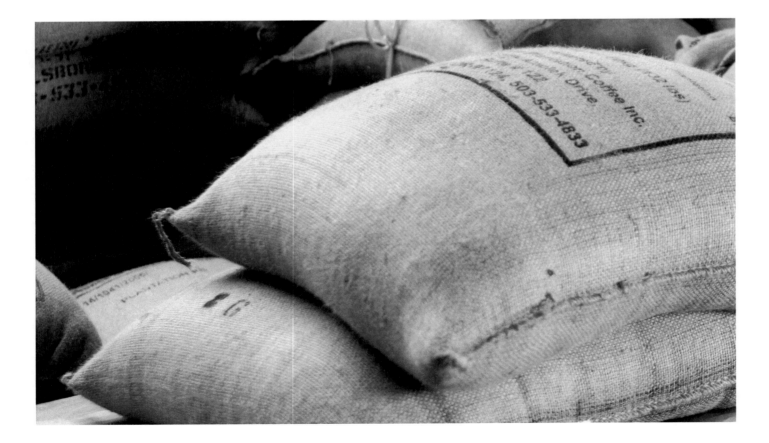

managing small batches so you don't mis-ship and get them mixed up," says Perkins. "We send so many pallets out with different coffees on them, so it's important for our people to be able to identify coffees correctly."

And that leads to staff education, something Perkins takes very seriously. He says teaching employees what to look for when shipments arrive and how to handle any problems that arise is key to ensuring quality. "You want them there when you crack the container to first look for moisture, and second, any kind of grassy or moldy smell."

When they run into something alarming, Perkins says he or his partner will take a look and send their customer digital photos if necessary, alerting them of the problem and deciding what steps to take. He says that 95 percent of the time when there's a problem it only affects a few bags, in which case they simply separate out the questionable beans and then send the customer a report of the inventory.

Of course, once a coffee clears the checkpoints at a warehouse, it is still susceptible, and Vojta says there are some red flags to look for, indicating that beans have suffered damage in storage. "We look for water stains or damage on the bags, appearance of mold and off smells for signs of water damage or mold," he says. "We also look to see if the marks on the bag are faded as evidence of age or UV/sunlight exposure. We try to see if the bags have been torn and re-sewn to verify weight of the bags or other holes and damage to indicate rough handling."

Roberts advises roasters and importers to visit warehouses to check out the operations in person. "If that's not possible, ask if the warehouse has organic certification, since you'd expect that their practices are good, and a few other leading questions like what their pest control procedures are," she says. "Another good (but not absolute) indicator is the condition your shipped beans arrive in. A good warehouse will use sturdy pallets and slip-sheets as well as stretch wrapping. Of course, accidents occasionally happen in transit that are out of the warehouse's control, but you can get a general sense over several shipments of the level of care with which your coffee is prepared."

In the overall scheme of the coffee chain, green coffee storage should be taken as seriously as every other step in the road to the final cup. Granted, it may not be as romantic as sourcing, cupping, roasting or blending, but it's certainly as important. Choose wisely and you're much more likely to safeguard the exceptional coffees you've put so much time, passion and energy into sourcing. ■

• •

KAREN FOLEY *is the publisher of* Imbibe, *a consumer beverage magazine. For information visit* imbibemagazine.com. *Karen can be reached via email at* karen@imbibemagazine.com.

Pier pallets can support up to 25 bags. This creates a slightly larger footprint, but allows you to stack more bags than a standard pallet, says Caribou Coffee's Brian Aliffi, of the company's in-house storage techniques. | *photo by Brian Aliffi, Caribou Coffee*

Storage Woes

The Pros and Cons of Third-Party Warehousing

By Andi Trindle Mersch

• FROM THE MAY/JUNE 2015 ISSUE OF *ROAST* •

Coffee roasters have a multitude of responsibilities beyond the obvious and mammoth task of producing a perfectly profiled, consistent roast with each and every variant green bean batch. Innumerable, seemingly mundane but highly impactful matters require our careful consideration—matters such as green coffee storage.

For example, how much green coffee can we store at our roasting plant—and how much do we want to store there? Even if we have enough room to store our raw goods, which most of us don't, is it the best use of our production space? Is it the best use of cash to pay for all our coffee outright if our importers are willing to offer delivery spreads, allowing us to shorten the timeline from cash out for green goods to cash in for roasted coffee sales?

For many roasters, deciding when to use third-party warehousing is based generally on two things: space and cash. As Michael Rogers, executive vice president at Apffels Fine Coffees in Santa Fe Springs, California, says, "If we have the space and cash, we will keep our green coffee internally to save on storage costs. If we don't have the need for the coffee yet and we don't have the extra cash and/or space, we will store it in a warehouse under an importer account."

Brian Aliffi, senior manager of green coffee sourcing at Caribou Coffee, headquartered in Minneapolis, agrees. While Aliffi works in a large production facility with minimal space constraints, he says storing inventory offsite frees up capital for investment in other areas of the business. By leaving a portion of its green coffee in its importer's "position" at a third-party warehouse, Caribou avoids paying for the coffee until it requests a delivery order from the importer. In this common scenario, importers finance the coffee for some set percentage of the coffee's value—generally 1.5 percent, including storage fees—and a roaster isn't invoiced until the time a delivery order is placed.

For many small roasters, it's not a matter of freeing up capital but an overall lack of working capital. After overhead costs for labor, rent, taxes and other necessities are met, there often isn't enough cash left to purchase green coffee too far in advance of roasting. However, many specialty roasters want to secure their supply of specific lots of coffee for an entire season or longer. In this case, warehousing offers not only the needed storage space, but the necessary assistance of third-party financing.

Warehousing Pros

In addition to space and cash constraints that mandate external storage, roasters and importers cite numerous reasons to opt for outside warehousing. During his many years on the roasting side at Mountanos Family Coffee and Tea of Petaluma, California, Dave Weber, now senior vice president at Annex Consolidation Center, a San Leandro, California-based green coffee warehouse, often had what appeared to his mangers to be ample space for holding green coffee. Nonetheless, he insisted on using offsite storage.

"A roaster's income comes from roasting and packaging coffee, and available space should be dedicated for income-generating production activities," Weber says. "Storage of raw goods isn't a best use of space."

Michael Giudice is coffee operations manager at Costco Wholesale in Monroe Township, New Jersey. While his operations-based view is "you can't have too much coffee in-house," he respects the demands of the company's inventory control team, so when floor space gets squeezed for various seasonal non-coffee items, he moves more green coffee offsite.

Like Weber, George Vukasin, Jr., president of Peerless Coffee & Tea, based in Oakland, California, believes in dedicating as much space as possible to the core business tasks of roasting and packing, but Vukasin also cites another reason he prefers to store the majority of his company's green coffee offsite: disaster planning.

"The main reason (we store offsite) is we always want to have duplicate inventory in case a disaster hits our roastery," he explains. While this strategy mainly protects a company from disaster in close proximity to its roasting facility (a regional or wider-spread catastrophe likely would wipe out offsite inventory as well), it does constitute a smart and relatively simple-to-employ contingency plan. Furthermore, in companies fueling expansion efforts with outside investors—a phenomenon growing as steadily as geisha tree plantings—this type of exigency planning often is mandated. At Philz Coffee, for example, offsite storage to protect some portion of our green coffee supply is required by our venture capital partners.

For Giudice, it's the additional services East Coast warehouses such as Continental Terminals and All Jays provide that add real value. As a multi-product food facility, Costco has many unique demands, including a requirement to fumigate all green coffee before receipt at its plant, and the need to receive all coffee delivered direct to its door in sealed containers post-fumigation. Giudice relies on his warehouse partners to provide these services and has found them "very nimble and accommodating of many different special needs of the company." Furthermore, these warehouse partners have been "fantastic in reminding new brokers of how we need our coffee delivered, which ends up expediting delivery," he adds.

Importers don't realize any financial benefit from holding their green beans in a third-party facility, but they do recognize other benefits. While many think of importers principally as physical movers and owners of green inventory, Dane Loraas, a relationship coffee manager at Sustainable Harvest Coffee Importers, based in Portland, Oregon, notes that importers "provide many services and trainings such as cupping, financial risk management, agronomy and marketing, so having a warehouse perform the heavy lifting allows us to focus on our strengths." Specifically, he says, "most warehouses have staff that are accustomed to dealing with coffee and have become experts in managing problems such as stains, damaged coffees, reconditioning bags, etc."

Warehouses provide a variety of services beyond simple storage, ranging from sampling, re-bagging, re-sorting, delivery and inventory tracking to blending, gravity tables, color sorting machines, fully equipped quality labs and more. | *photo courtesy of Annex Consolidation Center*

Along with expertise in noting and handling problems, warehouse crews literally "perform the heavy lifting" by unloading containers, moving bags and pallets around, and driving forklifts. From Loraas' perspective, there's a definite advantage to allowing warehouses to provide this expertise and manpower. As a roaster, I, too, would rather my importers focus their energy and expertise on sourcing, specifically securing and managing consistent, high-quality, traceable coffee sources. And just as importers can focus on their areas of expertise, warehousing allows roasters to focus on the core activities at a roasting plant—cupping, roasting, blending, packaging and shipping—without worrying about all the nuances of storing and moving green coffee.

Beyond the arguments for focusing on core expertise areas, John Visbal, president of San Leandro, California-based East Bay Logistics—a friendly competitor warehouse to the Annex—points out an additional value add: "By keeping their coffee in a third-party warehouse, the roaster has the advantage of being able to sell the coffee to another importer or roaster if their needs change. In the warehouse, the transaction is completed without physical movement or extra costs and is seamless for the roaster."

Warehouses can provide a variety of services beyond simple storage, including sampling, re-bagging, re-sorting, delivery, inventory tracking, general storage expertise and more. Janet Colley Morse, business development director at Dupuy Storage & Forwarding in New Orleans, says her company provides a variety of value-added services in each of its five locations across the southeast United States, including blending, gravity tables, color sorting machines, and fully equipped quality labs. Find out what your warehouse offers beyond the obvious floor space to maximize the benefits of your partnership.

Warehousing Cons

Clearly, there are many benefits associated with using an external warehousing service.

WHAT WILL WAREHOUSING *Cost* YOU?

With so many variables playing into the total cost a roaster will pay for warehousing, it's difficult to generalize about costs, but here we offer some ballpark figures. These ranges refer to basic warehousing services using traditional burlap bags; additional services also are available. The figures below were provided by several warehouses across the United States in 2016; however, it's important to note that rates vary depending on overall volume, services required and payment history. Some rates also vary based on bag/box weight, and most warehouses charge extra for processing certified-organic lots and coffees bagged in GrainPro.

Inbound Unloading
$0.65 to $1 per bag

Outbound Floor Load-out
$0.68 to $0.82 per bag

Forklift Load-out
$0.30 to $0.31 per bag; minimum $25

Palletizing (includes shrink-wrapping and strapping)
$16 to $21.50 per pallet

Monthly Storage
$0.53 to $0.60 per bag

Minimum Monthly (per lot)
$15 average

KNOW *Your* WAREHOUSE

H ere are some key questions to ask when choosing a third-party warehouse or evaluating a current warehouse.

- What are your rates for storage, including minimums?

- What are your rates for inbound and outbound loading?

- What additional services do you provide (sampling, re-bagging, local delivery, etc.)?

- What is your cutoff time for delivery order processing? If we have an emergency need, can you help?

- Can you consolidate with multiple shippers?

- What storage conditions do you maintain (temperature, humidity, etc.)?

- Do you store products other than green coffee? If so, what products, and how are they isolated from your green coffee storage area?

- What are your pest-control practices?

- Are you organic certified?

- Are you food safety certified?

- What inventory management tracking can you provide?

- When do you recommend a roaster open his or her own account with you versus keeping their coffee under an importer's account?

- When can we visit (how frequently and during what hours)?

Nonetheless, there are almost an equal number of reasons many roasters lament the need to do so. For starters, warehousing is expensive.

Joel Edwards, head roaster at San Francisco-based Ritual Roasters, says the cost of maintaining offsite storage was a primary motivator for his company to explore the possibility of storing as much of its green coffee in-house as possible. According to Edwards, after realizing the company was paying an enormous amount of money for carrying costs in the form of finance fees to importers and warehouse storage fees, he was tasked with finding a way to reduce these expenses. After a careful analysis of carry costs, separating out the finance charges from warehouse fees and comparing finance fees charged by the bank versus those charged by the importer, Edwards achieved significant savings—"in the thousands of dollars annually," he says—by bringing more of the company's storage in-house.

Ultimately, the cost savings came through a combination of borrowing money from the bank at lower rates than the importers were charging and eliminating outside storage fees where possible. And while the savings are substantial, it's important to note that space limitations still come into play and a significant percentage of the company's green coffee remains offsite—whether financed by banks or importers.

In addition to the expense of offsite storage, Mark Stell, president and owner of Oregon-based Portland Roasting Coffee, notes some frustration with billing. Because invoices are processed by the warehouse months after shipping, Stell says, he and his staff spend extensive time reviewing each bill to verify the amounts are correct. Giudice also expresses vexation over invoicing, reporting a "mind-boggling" array of charges associated with every delivery. Line items for load-out, palletizing, stretch-wrapping, banding, drayage, use of hooks or not, and the differentiation by bag weight per line item make it a dizzying task to reconcile invoices, he says.

Fortunately, invoicing nightmares weren't a standard complaint among the roasters interviewed for this article. However, another grievance of Stell's—that the warehouse is "slow to get the product out when in a jam"—does seem to be a common one.

Regardless of planning acumen—and as a former importer, I can attest that many roasters lack forecasting expertise, or at least the time to focus on it—a roaster inevitably will experience the occasional last-minute need. An unexpected burst in demand, a

If you're thinking about in-house storage, says Brian Aliffi of Caribou Coffee, consider silos to open up floor space and provide an automated system to replace manual blending or forming loads by hand. | *photo by Brian Aliffi, Caribou Coffee*

photo by Brian Aliffi, Caribou Coffee

Some companies rely on third-party warehousing as a safeguard against potential inventory loss caused by disaster at the roastery. | *photo courtesy of Annex Consolidation Center*

problem with a green or roast batch, or generally poor planning between sales and production can cause a roaster to request a rush release. The best case in this scenario is that the warehouse helps you (though often they simply cannot), but even so, it may come with additional "rush" processing fees and could lead to mistakes.

Even notwithstanding these hopefully rare last-minute needs, lead time between requesting a release and receiving coffee is an ongoing struggle for many roasters. From receipt of a delivery order request from the account holder (usually your importer, which means additional processing time), most warehouses require a minimum of 24 hours (some up to 48) to prepare an outbound release—and this is just the time to get your green coffee from the warehouse floor to the warehouse door. From here, additional time typically is required for inland transportation. For St. Louis-based Kaldi's Coffee Roasting Co., that's three to five days for inland transit after release from either an East Coast or West Coast warehouse. Furthermore, as Kaldi's co-owner and green coffee buyer Tyler Zimmer laments, "If a big snowstorm comes through the Midwest or Northeast, we can be without some coffees for two to three additional days."

For many roasters, reducing the time between a request for green beans and loading the roast hopper is almost as desirable as eliminating the considerable expense of outside warehousing. Realistically, however, a company's options are limited to expanding its physical space, which requires a considerable expansion of working capital, or incorporating the appropriate lead time, including a cushion for the unexpected, into the planning process. Clearly, the latter is far more viable, and fortunately it's fairly easily mastered with fundamentals of supply chain planning. Courses offered through the Specialty Coffee Association can help.

Other grievances related to third-party warehousing include mistakes and a lack of care in physical handling of the green beans. Most roasters interviewed reported few mistakes, especially when working within ample lead times, but because even infrequent mistakes can be costly, it's a significant problem. Mistakes such as torn bags from moving them around too quickly

The FOOD SAFETY MODERNIZATION ACT

CONSIDER YOURSELF WARNED

The Food Safety Modernization Act (FSMA), signed into law by President Obama on Jan. 4, 2011, will almost assuredly change your production plant processes on some level and most likely will change your relationship with your warehouses, too. The first major change to domestic food safety laws in more than 70 years, FSMA requires food facilities, under authority of the Food and Drug Administration (FDA), to implement and document control plans for food safety. Additionally, importers of food products have "an explicit responsibility to verify that their foreign suppliers have adequate preventive controls in place to ensure that the food they produce is safe."

Parts of the law already have taken effect, but there are still many unknowns within the coffee industry in terms of how these rules will impact both green and roasted coffee handlers and manufacturers, and even the laws themselves are still being interpreted and fine-tuned. It's critical for roasters to stay abreast of the law, and it's recommended you work with knowledgeable warehouses and importers who can ensure your compliance if/as the requirements develop to include third-party raw goods storage facilities. The National Coffee Association also is a good source for information as it has been heavily involved in advocating with the FDA on behalf of the coffee industry.

At the very least, says Bob Forcillo, managing director at Continental Terminals in Jersey City, New Jersey, costs for facility upgrades and compliance with these expanding food safety laws inevitably will drive warehousing costs up over time. Smart roasters will start budgeting for these increases.

For more information, visit:
fda.gov/Food/GuidanceRegulation/FSMA/

For more details on the FSMA, read "The Food Safety Modernization Act" on page 448.

or too roughly, or the misreading of bag marks, can cause a substantial burden. Pulling the wrong lot of coffee is particularly troublesome because, even if caught immediately upon delivery and returned to the warehouse before a mistaken roast (which does happen!), the order-to-delivery timeline starts over upon return and even the best supply chain planner can't always allow enough of a window to cover it.

Maximizing the Warehouse Experience

To gain the most benefit from third-party storage, it's important to maintain an active relationship with your warehouse partners.

"Don't be a stranger," advises Vukasin. "Visit your warehouses and make sure they are professional, clean and organized."

In addition to welcoming occasional site visits, warehouses invite and even recommend you maintain close communication with them. Weber and his colleague, Hugo De La Roca, general manager at the Annex Consolidation Center, insist they appreciate direct, early communication from roasters, whether they have their own accounts with the warehouse or their inventory is held under importer accounts.

"Having an ongoing, open dialogue with roasters and importers alike is essential to ensuring the best quality and service available," agrees Colley Morse.

As a bonus, if you get to know your warehouse team through regular communication, you're more likely to get a better response to those rare last-minute requests—as long as they remain rare.

Of course, communication is a two-way street. If port shutdowns have created a backlog and 50 containers are likely to be released at once for inbound drayage and unloading, for example, a good warehouse will keep you apprised of the situation, enabling you to incorporate delays into your planning. Ensuring this type of communication happens is another important reason to reach out to your warehousing partners directly, as they can be more likely to communicate with larger importing customers about these matters than with the smaller roasters on their client lists.

"Complaints and confusion are almost always directly linked to poor communication," Visbal notes. "That can be either through the warehouse not listening and paying attention or the roaster/importer not providing enough pertinent information."

Either way, a lack of communication inevitably leads to frustration, while regular dialogue provides the opportunity for a rewarding partnership. Best yet, you're likely to be pleasantly surprised (as I have been) by the expertise and depth of knowledge your warehouse partners can share on a variety of subjects when you think to ask them. ◼

Relying on warehouse partners to handle storage, inventory control, physical moving of green coffee and other tasks allows importers and roasters to focus on their own areas of expertise. | *photos by Bryan Moran, East Bay Logistics*

ANDI TRINDLE MERSCH *has a varied background within her specialty coffee career, which began behind the espresso bar in 1989 and, since then, includes cupping, training, consulting, green coffee trading and buying, quality control, sales and writing. Mersch currently serves as director of coffee for Philz Coffee. She was elected to the Roasters Guild Executive Council for a two-year term in March 2015, and she volunteers with the Specialty Coffee Association (SCA) developing coffee business curriculum. She is a past board member of the SCA and the International Women's Coffee Alliance.*

PART II

ORIGIN & GREEN COFFEE

GREEN COFFEE DEFECTS

Detecting Defects

Plants & Quakers

by Andi Trindle Mersch

• FROM THE JANUARY/FEBRUARY 2008 ISSUE OF *ROAST* •

A Guatemalan coffee cherry attacked by a coffee borer beetle. | *Photo courtesy of Jeff Taylor, PT's Coffee*

Roasters in the specialty coffee industry are fortunate to work with the very best coffees in the world—coffees layered with fruit, spice, floral, citrus, chocolate, and a multitude of other beautiful aromatic notes, which are divinely interspersed with refreshing acidity, silky body, and natural sweetness. You all know what I'm talking about; likely your mind has already wandered to that last beautiful cup you had. In the specialty coffee roaster's world, even the most average coffees on the cupping table tend to be of good quality, with at least one notable positive attribute.

Given this privileged position, many roasters newer to the specialty coffee industry have never experienced a truly bad sample, much less an actual defect. Coincidentally to working on this article, I had a conversation about defects with 2003 and 2006 U.S. Barista Champion, Heather Perry, who cups coffees with her family's business, Coffee Klatch, in Southern California. Perry lamented that she had never tasted a defect, so she would not know how to identify one should it show up on someone else's cupping table or in an international cupping competition. You can hardly call this a sad state of affairs (who *really* wants defects showing up on their cupping table anyway?), but, nonetheless, as Perry believes, it's important that roasters understand and learn how to identify defects. Defects will inevitably occur and there is

Within the general category of plant-based defects, it is possible to identify a few smaller categories based upon the core (not necessarily exclusive) cause of the defect. For example, field defects can be caused by genetics (something within the coffee tree itself), soil and climactic conditions, pests, and poor crop management. Each of these root problems/conditions can lead to specific defects, which may be visually noticeable and/or manifested as a mild or severe off-flavor in the cup. I'll briefly overview a few examples of the different types of field defects and then focus in-depth on one particular egregious defect: quakers.

Roasters are probably most familiar with insect-related plant defects. In these cases, an insect, like the coffee berry borer (*Hypothenemus hampei*), attacks the coffee cherries on the tree. As expected, the coffee seeds within the coffee cherries are damaged as the pests eat away at the bean tissue. With this particular pest, the defective beans are visually identifiable by small insect holes, generally no bigger than 1.5 mm in diameter. They are also identified in the cup by mild to severe off-flavors and a general loss of aroma, acidity and flavor.

Elephant beans, triangular beans and peaberries (yes, the peaberry beans we all know and love) are examples of genetic plant defects. In each of these cases, the coffee seeds develop

Yirgacheffe region sun-dried naturals on elevated drying patios. Example of under- and over-ripe selections. | *Photo by Darrin Daniel*

Yirgacheffe cherries, partially dried using a sun-dried process. Example of primarily overripe picking. | *Photo by Darrin Daniel*

Yirgacheffe cherries at washing station, an example of underripe picking. | *Photo by Darrin Daniel*

educational value for all of us in learning more about them—how to identify them visually and in the cup and how they are caused and prevented. Hence, this new series, Detecting Defects, which will look at various defects in detail and give you additional insight on how they occur, what they look and taste like, and how to make sure they're not showing up in your coffees.

This first article in the series focuses on plant-based defects generally and then more specifically on quakers. Plant-based defects, also called field-damaged defects, are exactly as they sound: defects that occur in the coffee plant, while coffee cherries are growing *before* the coffee seeds are processed. Generally speaking, plant-based defects cannot be repaired in the processing, roasting or brewing once they have manifested themselves. If we're lucky, they can be detected before the coffee is processed, sold and shipped, but this is not always the case.

differently than usual due to genetic variance. Fortunately, these particular defects, although identifiable visually, are not known to cause significant deterioration in cup quality. In fact, in the case of peaberry beans, which form when only one seed develops within the coffee cherry, creating a single rounded bean, many contend that the flavor is improved due to an increased intensity. The unproven theory here is that the single seed receives all the nutrients that would usually go to two beans, so the single peaberry bean is richer in nutrients and, therefore, more intensely flavored. Whether or not this is true, peaberries are commonly selectively sorted and sold at a premium.

Soil and climactic condition defects, as expected, vary from country to country, region to region, and year to year. Climactic conditions, such as temperature, rainfall, humidity and sunlight, are all critical components of producing good coffee. Generally speaking, coffee is only grown in areas where the appropriate environmental conditions exist, however, major climactic events, such as the infamous frosts of Brazil, hurricanes and tsunamis, inevitably affect and sometimes seriously damage coffee crops. Farms affected by frost damage, for example, will suffer particular defects, which can include the generically named frost-damaged beans, as well as brown and foxy beans. All of these defects are detectable in the appearance due to distinctive brown and black coloring. They also all have some impact on the taste, though the degree will vary based upon the specific defect and the severity of it. At the very least, aroma, flavor and acidity are diminished and, in severe cases, actual off-tastes may develop.

Defects caused by poor soil conditions, such as amber beans and immatures among others, develop when the soil lacks certain critical nutrients or has an abundance of particular nutrients. To remain healthy and productive, coffee trees require a careful balance of macro and micronutrients, which come from the soil. Macronutrients like nitrogen, potassium, phosphorus, calcium and magnesium contribute essential elements to aid in the development of healthy trees and fruit. Micronutrients like zinc, copper, iron and others, at particular levels, similarly provide important elements to maintain the health and productivity of coffee trees. Not surprisingly, when the soil has a lack or an abundance of certain nutrients, the coffee trees are affected and the coffee beans may develop improperly, ultimately lacking necessary sugars, starches and cell structure.

The final category of plant-based defects encompasses those defects caused by poor crop management. Poor farm management overlaps our discussion of poor soil conditions, since it is within the farmer's control to compensate for soil deficiencies through fertilization and other crop management techniques. When farmers do not fertilize their soil properly, manage water supply, control weeds, and implement other important practices in the field, coffee cherries and the coffee beans within them are at risk for developing defects—defects like quakers, for example. (Yes, we are finally here.)

QUAKERS

I've chosen to focus on quakers as the primary defect for this first article because, in asking some casual questions to prepare for writing this series, I discovered that many people don't have a clear understanding of this particular defect, even though it poses a serious problem for many roasters. According to Peter Giuliano, former director of coffee and co-owner of Counter Culture Coffee in Durham, North Carolina, "The number-one culprit for rejections has always been quakeriness … The impact of quakers on coffee quality is profound."

There is a good side to quakers however: they can be prevented. Here's some further information about this pervasive, but preventable, defect.

Defect Name: Quaker

Quakers are more generically called immature beans, but the term quaker is used to identify immature beans that reveal themselves very specifically after roasting. According to David Roche, executive director of the Coffee Quality Institute in White Salmon, Washington, the term quakers is only used in the cupping room, since they are not identifiable until after roasting.

Causes

Quakers are a specific manifestation of immature beans. Most commonly, immature beans are caused by underripe picking (the picking of green, not yet fully developed, coffee cherries). And, according to Ensei Uejo Neto, chemical engineer and food technologist at the Specialty Coffee Bureau in Patrocinio, Minas Gerais, Brazil, "The main cause of quakers is the picking of unripe beans." All sources agree that underripe picking is the principal cause, however, climactic and/or soil conditions and poor field care may also result in quakers.

In Nicaragua, according to Lexania Marín Grádiz, Star Cupper and consultant working throughout Nicaragua, immature beans—which may or may not result in quakers—are a frequent problem of poor fertilization. When soil is not properly nourished, necessary nutrients are not available for the growing coffee seeds. Roche agrees with this theory and states, "When coffee trees are stressed [lacking adequate nutrition], it is difficult for the nutrients, carbohydrates, and essential components to fully ripen the bean. … This is true of any fruit in the world. If you don't provide enough nutrients, water, or anything essential, then plants go into survival mode and will not have enough to ripen the fruit." In the case of coffee, when this happens, the cell structure of the green beans within the coffee fruit is not well defined and the seeds will lack the starches and sugars necessary for good flavor.

It is interesting to note that, although quakers can certainly be caused by soil nutritional problems and not exclusively by picking underripe cherries, Giuliano has never experienced quaker problems in countries like El Salvador, where his experience shows that cherries are consistently allowed to ripen fully before picking. (Note to producers: Pick ripe cherries to avoid quakers and, ultimately, rejections.)

Although quakers are created in the field, processing customs within a country may influence the likelihood that quakers show up in the final roasted product. According to Roche, the prevalence of quakers can be influenced by the processing method that is most common to a country. This is not to suggest that quakers are caused by processing (they aren't), but that Roche has found that quakers are more commonly allowed to pass through the processing cycle to the final product in countries where natural processing is more common. This may be true because countries producing more naturals or semi-washed coffees do not generally utilize gravity separation methods that assist in eliminating underripe beans. In the washed coffee processing method, coffee cherries go through a gravity separation process, where floaters (cherries that float, rather than sink in water) are removed. Although removing floaters does not guarantee the removal of potential quakers, it reduces the number of overall immature beans, which logically will reduce the likelihood of quakers. Important note: Floaters and quakers are not synonymous. Floaters are caused by a number of different problems, including overripe beans in some cases.

Commonly Found

Quakers can occur anywhere, but some roasters and importers find this particular defect more common in deliveries from certain countries. Counter Culture has historically experienced the most problems with quakers in deliveries from Mexico, Costa Rica and Brazil. Ian Kluse, senior coffee trader at Olam Coffee, agrees that Brazil and much of Central America have regular problems with quakers; he also finds significant problems with quakers in Sumatra. In spite of these patterns, there is no clear indication that quakers are consistently more common from one producing country to another, and they can certainly be found in coffee lots from every origin at times.

How to Identify Quakers

Quakers can be identified visually after roasting and in the cup. Visually, quaker beans are distinctly lighter/pale in color after roasting; regardless of the degree of roast, quakers will stand out obviously among roasted coffee beans. Unfortunately, though, quakers cannot be detected by examining green coffee and they may manifest sporadically in a coffee lot, which can create serious problems for roasters even when they are scrupulously cupping their arrival and spot samples. Grádiz agrees that quakers cannot be identified when examining green coffee, but, she states that she can sometimes predict the likelihood that quakers will exist when she notices a problem with immature beans in general. Immature beans can be visually identified by a smaller size, by a wrinkled surface, and when the silver skin adheres very strongly. It's important to be clear, however, that the term "quakers" is reserved for immature coffee beans that show up as distinctly pale colored beans *after* roasting. And, because it is not possible to determine how many quakers there may be in a bag of green coffee until roasting, they are a particularly insidious defect.

In the cup, quakers have a distinctly peanutty/peanut butter taste, with the possible addition of woody, grassy and papery notes—not exactly the profile of specialty coffee. Quakers will also lack full flavor and sweetness—no surprise, since the sugars and carbohydrates are not there. According to Steven Diaz, quality director at Expocafe S.A in Colombia, "Just one quaker bean among the beans that go into one cup can affect the flavor dramatically." Diaz, co-author of the Specialty Coffee Association's *Arabica Green Coffee Defect Handbook*, emphasizes, "That is why in specialty coffees the standard is so strict concerning quakers." For the record, according to the green coffee defect handbook, in evaluating a roasted sample (100-gram sample size) for specialty grade classification, no quakers (that's right: zero) are allowed. However, when evaluating a green coffee sample (350 grams), immature beans, which may result in quakers when roasted, are a secondary defect and five are allowed before they are considered a full defect equivalent.

The best way to learn how to identify the taste of quakers in the cup is to find them in a roasted sample (you really can't miss them), hand sort them out, and taste them on their own. It won't be fun, but it will be educational.

Prevention /Fixes

Quakers cannot be fixed once they have occurred (besides being painstakingly removed by hand from the roasted product), but they can be prevented at the farm level. Giuliano said it best in his interview by stating emphatically, "Producers can prevent quakers by picking ripe and caring for their soil. I will repeat: Pick ripe, care for your soil. Pick ripe, care for your soil. Repeat until you win the Cup of Excellence." Even if a producer is not out to win Cup of Excellence competitions, surely avoiding rejections and eliminating the potential for a serious taste defect is worth a renewed effort to pick ripe cherries and focus on soil nutrition.

Why roasters should care: As I started this article off stating, there is educational opportunity and value for roasters in understanding defects because they inevitably occur. Quakers are particularly worth understanding as a roaster because they are a preventable and prevalent defect. If you experience a high level of quakers from a particular origin, region or farm, it is possible to communicate with the producer about the problem and encourage the farmers to, once again: "Pick ripe, care for your soil." ■

. . . .

ANDI TRINDLE MERSCH *has a varied background within her specialty coffee career, which began behind the espresso bar in 1989 and, since then, includes cupping, training, consulting, green coffee trading and buying, quality control, sales and writing. Mersch currently serves as director of coffee for Philz Coffee. She was elected to the Roasters Guild Executive Council for a two-year term in March 2015, and she volunteers with the Specialty Coffee Association (SCA) developing coffee business curriculum. She is a past board member of the SCA and the International Women's Coffee Alliance.*

Detecting Defects

Overferment / Sour and Stinker Beans

By Andi Trindle Mersch

photos by Ensei Neto, Specialty Coffee Bureau

• FROM THE MARCH/APRIL 2008 ISSUE OF *ROAST* •

Black, fermented and broken beans.

I HOPE EVERYONE has now experienced the wondrous peanut-buttery taste of quakers (flashback to the first article in our Detecting Defects series), and I invite you to move forward along the coffee production chain to experience the tastes of rotted fruit, vinegar and even rotten fish. I know, these are not the descriptors we like to find at the cupping table, but in the interest of education, we are going to look at some defects that produce these particularly unpleasant profiles. For those of you following along in our series, in the interest of logic, I'm moving us forward in a linear fashion along the coffee production chain. We started with plant-based and harvesting defects, and we're now going to examine defects generated in the next stage of coffee production: coffee processing.

Processing coffee is the phase in coffee production where the coffee seeds are removed from within the freshly harvested cherries, then dried and prepared for export as green coffee. Processing defects occur during this phase. With numerous steps and many different methods utilized (depending upon the origin country, region and/or buyer specifications), coffee processing is a critical and expansive phase in coffee production. As Robert Barker, vice president of quality assurance at Growers Direct Coffee in Berkeley, California, states, "Coffee processing can substantially remove defective beans or contribute to them." In some cases, mistakes made in processing can ruin coffee, rendering it totally undrinkable. In better scenarios, defects developed during the coffee growing and harvesting phases can be mitigated or eliminated. With the employment of proper processing practices, producers can ensure that well-grown coffee seeds leave the country as top-grade green coffee suitable for the discriminating specialty market.

Categories of Processing Defects

The category of processing defects includes damage caused by incorrect or inadequate methods in pulping, washing, fermenting, drying, cleaning and hulling. Specific defects that can occur within these phases include bruised beans, stinker beans, soft beans, over-dried beans, overfermented beans, sour beans and many others.

To better understand defects created during processing, it's helpful to first review the methods and steps in coffee processing. We will do this very briefly.

The **methods** of coffee processing are washed (or wet process), dry (or natural process), semi-washed and pulped natural. Each of these methods produces unique flavor profiles and all must be skillfully managed. Farmers/millers generally employ one of the particular methods above based upon the climactic conditions of their region, the availability of water resources, and the traditions of their region. For example, in countries where clean water is more available, specialty coffee producers most often utilize the washed process, and in countries where water resources are limited, the dry process is most often utilized. However, in the modern world of specialty coffee, where coffee buyers choose coffee based upon the cup profile and its particular place in their coffee lineup, many producers are choosing nontraditional methods for their region in order to experiment with taste profiles and to satisfy the requests of buyers. This newer development of experimenting with processing methods is, in part, responsible for the growth in the usage of in-between methods, known as semi-washed and pulped natural.

The *broad* **steps** in coffee processing, which do vary depending upon the method used, include the following:

- 1) Pulping: removal of coffee seeds from within the coffee cherry (wet processing)
- 2) Fermentation and washing (wet processing)
- 3) Drying of fermented green beans still in parchment skin (in the dry method, coffee seeds are still within cherries and dried on patios before the cherry skins are removed)
- 4) Storage of coffee parchment
- 5) Cleaning/sorting of coffee parchment prior to hulling
- 6) Hulling (removal of green beans from within parchment)
- 7) Grading/sorting
- 8) Bagging for export

Clearly, an expansive range of activities during the processing phase makes the topic of processing defects a large one. To add to the challenge, many of these steps incorporate a variety of sub-steps and decisions in which a coffee mill has the opportunity to maintain and contribute to coffee quality or to destroy it.

FUNGUS

Bean showing mold. The black color means that the fungus is dead and probably consumed the sugars from the pulp through the skin. In this cherry phase, the external skin changes with the atmosphere.

The mold turned green, which means a new kind of fungus is working. This can lead to phenolic fermentation because the bean is partially dry.

UNRIPE AND IMMATURE

The lighter beans are quakers or unripe; the darker are immatures. These beans have some particular features like the absence of sugar (it dries on the plant without passing through the cherry phase), which explains why it roasts faster than the cherry (without sugar it's faster, but the oils go to surface faster, too) and is very bitter, rancid and smells like rubber.

FERMENTATION

Beans with high moisture + pilling + heat - oxygen = fermentation (acetic if cherry, phenolic if raisin).

Some origins pick the coffee after the cherry turns to raisin. If these beans gain humidity, the phenolic fermentation starts.

Before they go to the dry mill, these beans should pass through a cleaner.

For the purposes of this series, we're going to divide the above steps into two major phases. Phase one incorporates just the first two steps, which are components of the washed-process method. The second phase, which we will discuss in the next article, incorporates steps three through eight, which are components of all processing methods.

Coffee Processing: Phase One

After ripe cherries are harvested, the seeds (soon to be called green beans) must be removed from the cherries. In washed coffee processing, this is done by pulping, washing and fermenting the beans; this is our arbitrarily defined Phase One. There are a number of different steps within each of these main activities that require scrupulous attention to ensure quality in the final product. One of the most critical areas is fermentation.

Fermentation is a natural process that occurs to some extent in all methods (more on this later), but in the washed process, fermentation is a controlled process that requires, well, good control because, when fermentation is not well managed, we may end up with the aforementioned rotted fruit, vinegar and rotten fish flavors. (I'm all for education at the cupping table, but seriously, who wants rotten fruit and vinegar in their cup of Joe?)

Overferment

Although there are many potential defects developed during processing—many just within our designated Phase One—I've chosen to focus on overferment because it remains a common problem and it can contribute to a number of different specific defects, including stinker, sour and black beans—all of which produce notable visual and taste defects. (Note: Black beans are often the result of plant-based problems prior to fermentation, but they can stem from overfermentation as well, so they are included here as an example of overferment-produced defects.)

Causes

First off, it's good to know that fermentation is a naturally occurring chain reaction of chemical responses that transforms organic compounds. *The American Heritage Dictionary of the English Language, Fourth Edition* defines fermentation as "a group of chemical reactions induced by living or nonliving ferments that split complex organic compounds into relatively simple substances." Although occurring naturally in many cases, fermentation is often deliberately induced and carefully controlled in the production of wine, beer, and, yes: coffee. Whether deliberately induced and tightly controlled, whether occurring naturally, or whether occurring by some combination of both, the fermentation process generates a number of incidental byproducts that affect the taste and aroma of the final green beans.

In washed coffee processing, fermentation is used to describe the managed process utilized to transform and ultimately remove the sticky mucilage surrounding the parchment skin (the parchment skin houses the green beans until hulling). Up to a point, fermentation creates positive flavor transformations, but the process must be tightly controlled in order to prevent overfermentation. "Overfermentation," according to Ensei Uejo Neto, chemical engineer and food technologist at the Specialty Coffee Bureau in Patrocinio, Minas Gerais, Brazil, "causes defects by biochemical transformations that end up punishing the cup strongly."

There are many different stages in coffee processing where naturally occurring fermentation can spiral out of control, leading to the risk of overfermentation. High temperatures, high humidity, interactions with other organic compounds through shared and unclean equipment, and a number of other conditions can expedite the fermentation process of newly harvested cherries.

According to Mané Alves, president of Coffee Lab International in Waterbury, Vermont, fermentation varies significantly depending on several factors, including the following: time from harvesting to processing; ambient temperature; time of fermentation; mass of coffee in the tank; water being used; controlled environment in the tank; and cleanliness of equipment. In each of these stages, controls implemented by the producers and millers can mitigate factors that impact fermentation negatively. The principal challenge for producers/millers is to ensure that the fermentation process is stopped before the mucilage begins to overferment.

Commonly Found

Overfermented beans, which generally yield an overly fruity (rotten fruit) cup and sometimes specific defects like black, sour and stinker beans are found everywhere. Certain conditions that increase the rate and minimize the manageability of fermentation, including temperature, rainfall and even infrastructure (ability of small coffee producers to transport coffee cherries to the nearest mill quickly enough after harvesting, for example), will impact the

DEFECT IDENTIFICATION CHART

Defect Name	Causes	Visual Identification	Taste Identification	SCA Classification
Sour	Overfermentation due to picking of overripe cherries, processing cherries that have fallen from the trees, water contamination, humid conditions whereby fermentation begins while the cherries are on the tree	Full or partial yellow or yellow-brown to red-brown coloring	Sour, vinegar-like flavor Note: according to the SCA Arabica Green Coffee Defect Handbook, "one single full sour bean can contaminate an entire pot of coffee"	Full sour= primary defect; 1 sour bean= 1 full defect Partial sour= secondary defect; 3 sour beans= 1 full defect
Black	Overfermentation due to picking of overripe cherries and/or improper management of conditions during processing	Full or partial black opaque coloring	Fermented/rotted fruit, dirty, moldy, sour	Full black= primary defect; 1 black bean= 1 full defect Partial black= secondary defect; 3 black beans= 1 full defect
Stinker	Overfermentation due to extended/repeated fermentation, polluted water, delay in pulping after picking	Light-brown, brownish, or grayish coloring and dull appearance	Fermented/rotted fruit, foul, rotten fish flavor	Unknown

likelihood of overfermentation occurring. However, fermentation problems can and will occur in every producing country.

Identification

Overfermented beans, used as a general defect here, are primarily identified by the taste of rotted fruit in the cup, and they are not visually recognizable. Deciding when a coffee has positive fruity characteristics versus when it has crossed to a rotted, overfermented quality can be a very individual decision, however. I have served on a number of cupping juries where half of the panel finds a coffee overfermented and half finds the coffee "pleasantly and wildly fruity." Identifying overfermented coffees that have manifested into specific defects is less controversial, though, because the negative flavors intensify and, as Alves states, "detection happens in the cup and also visually."

The defect identification chart (page 107) provides information on the causes and identification methods for the three distinct defects mentioned earlier that can be caused by issues of overferment; potential causes included here are only those stemming from fermentation issues. Note that these defects, unlike the more general term "overfermented," are identifiable visually, as well as on the palate.

Prevention

Overfermentation and the defects it produces can only be prevented by a firm command of the fermentation process as stated earlier. Natural fermentation often begins as soon as the coffee cherries are picked from the coffee trees (and in very humid conditions, sometimes while the cherries are still on the tree), so prevention strategies to avoid overfermentation must occur as soon as the coffee cherries are harvested.

There are many places in which fermentation varies (read: places in which fermentation can spiral out of control), so it makes sense that there are many strategies that farmers and millers must employ to avoid problems created by uncontrolled fermentation. Prevention strategies include processing coffees promptly after harvesting, adapting for temperature and other climatic conditions, carefully monitoring fermentation time, utilizing clean equipment and fresh water, and closely watching the process. One particular strategy to avoid the challenges of controlled fermentation used in washed processing is the use of mechanical demucilaging.

Whether or not a miller goes so far as to modify their processing method to better control fermentation, conscientious and knowledgeable farmers and millers can often successfully control the conditions that can lead to overfermentation. Nonetheless, it is not always possible and certainly not always done, so it is important to find opportunities to eliminate visual and taste defects produced by overfermentation before export.

Fixes

To be crystal clear: Overfermentation cannot be reversed. However, careful sorting and grading can eliminate some of the resulting defects of overfermentation before green coffee is exported. According to Rob Stephen, president of Coffee Solutions in Hopedale, Massachusetts, "More attention to incoming coffee at the mill level, including cupping and solid grading, will discover defects like immature beans, sour and ferment." Responsible millers should be able to visually identify and catch blacks, sours and stinker beans before samples reach specialty roasters, and specialty importers and roasters should reject samples that do not follow the clearly defined visual standards for specialty coffee. However, general overferment, which is not identifiable by sight alone, is frequently not caught before export. Although more producers and millers are gaining skills in cupping analysis, there is still a steep learning curve in many countries.

What does this all mean for the specialty coffee roaster? You can probably guess what I'm going to say: Cup carefully! And remember that the best way to learn how to identify taste defects is to taste them, so I send everyone off with the task of tasting some rotted fruit, vinegar and rotted fish. ■

. . . .

ANDI TRINDLE MERSCH *has a varied background within her specialty coffee career, which began behind the espresso bar in 1989 and, since then, includes cupping, training, consulting, green coffee trading and buying, quality control, sales and writing. Mersch currently serves as director of coffee for Philz Coffee. She was elected to the Roasters Guild Executive Council for a two-year term in March 2015, and she volunteers with the Specialty Coffee Association (SCA) developing coffee business curriculum. She is a past board member of the SCA and the International Women's Coffee Alliance.*

Detecting Defects

Defects Created in the Dry Mill

By Andi Trindle Mersch

photos courtesy of Steven Diaz, Expocafé & Jeff Taylor, PT's Coffee

• FROM THE MAY/JUNE 2008 ISSUE OF *ROAST* •

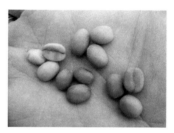

If you've been following along in our detecting defects series, you may remember that we are moving forward in the coffee production chain to investigate defects occurring in Processing Phase Two. (You may also be a little annoyed with me if you've been following along, since I've recommended that you taste some pretty awful cups.) Nonetheless, if you appreciate the end goal is to understand defects better and are still reading along, as a reminder, "Processing Phase Two" (admittedly arbitrarily defined) includes the following activities, which generally occur at a dry mill (which includes the stages of coffee processing *after* pulping and washing in wet processing, or the full processing of dry processed coffees):

■ Drying of pulped (possibly fermented) coffee beans still in parchment *or* drying of coffee cherries with seeds still inside

■ Storage of coffee parchment

■ Cleaning/sorting of coffee parchment prior to hulling

■ Hulling (removal of parchment *or* removal of dried cherry husks depending upon method)

■ Grading/sorting

■ Bagging for export

Looking at the list above, you may think that I've made a mistake in including all of these activities in one phase and, frankly, you're probably right. After undertaking my research and talking with millers in Colombia, El Salvador and Brazil, I've realized that I should have broken processing into about 20

DEFECTS

Full black

Partial black

Full sour

Partial sour

Fungus damage

Foreign matter

Cherry pods

Insect damage

phases—or at least one or two more. Certainly, I could.

Many activities take place at the dry mill and these activities, if not carefully managed, can cause serious defects—even though, as Steven Diaz, quality director for Expocafé, S.A. Colombia states, "The mill is designed for the sole purpose of removing physical defects by different means." By means, Diaz is referring to various activities that take place in the dry mill, which, in theory, improve coffee quality by eliminating defects.

CATEGORIES OF DRY MILL DEFECTS

Indeed, Diaz is correct in stating that the milling process is, at least in part, designed for the purpose of removing defects that have occurred prior to reaching the dry mill. For example, equipment such as density, size and color sorters, and hand sorting are utilized specifically to remove defects. Nonetheless, activities in a dry mill also include drying of parchment coffee or cherries (the latter in natural processing) and de-hulling coffee seeds from within parchment or from within the dried cherry husks. It is during these drying and hulling activities in particular that a dry mill may induce, rather than reduce, defects.

Defects Created at the Dry Mill

According to Jeff Holman, president of El Volcan S.A. de C.V. in San Salvador, El Salvador, "Among the defects caused during the milling process are the following: stained beans, smashed beans, black and semi-black beans." To this list, we can add sour, stinker, overfermented, and fungus-damaged beans, dried cherries/pods, and parchment. (See why I wanted to turn this into a 20-part series?)

Causes/Identification

With such a long list of potential defects within a long list of activities at the dry mill, it's not very practical to focus on a specific defect. Instead, it makes sense to review a number of defects that have a lot in common despite having distinctly different visual and taste identification points. As we'll see, even though a variety of defects can occur in poor dry milling conditions, many of them share root causes.

DRY MILL DEFECT CHART

Defect Name	Causes	Visual Identification	Taste Identification	SCA Classification
Smashed, broken, chipped, cut beans	Poorly calibrated hulling machine; excessive friction	Green and roasted beans that are broken, chipped and/or cut. Green beans may have dark red or blackish marks	Potential for dirty, fermented and other off flavors created by the oxidation of broken beans and the resulting bacterial activity	5 broken beans = 1 full defect
Stained / discolored beans	Over-drying; moisture below 9%)	Off-color, dull, yellowish	Diminished attributes; greenish flavor; possible grassy and woody flavors	Unknown
Black/ partial black	Inconsistencies or delays in drying that result in overfermentation	Full or partial black opaque coloring	Fermented/rotten fruit, dirt, mold, sour flavors	Full black = primary defect; 1 full black = 1 full defect Partial black = secondary defect; 3 black beans = 1 full defect
Sour	Inconsistencies or delays in drying	Full or partial yellow or yellow-brown to red-brown	Sour and vinegar flavors	Full sour = primary defect; 1 full sour = 1 full defect Partial sour = secondary defect; 3 sour beans = 1 full defect
Stinker	Inconsistencies or delays in drying	Light brown, brownish or grayish coloring and dull appearance	Fermented/rotted fruit, foul, rotten fish flavor	Unknown
Fungus damaged	Cut and chipped beans during pulping that allow fungus growth; inconsistencies or delays in drying; improper storage of parchment in high temperatures/humidity	Yellow, reddish-brown spots/spores	Ferment, mold, earth, dirt, and phenolic flavors	1 fungus damaged bean = 1 full defect
Cherry pods	At the dry mill, dried cherries/pods (natural coffees) show up in green coffee when hulling machines are not properly calibrated and maintained	Dried cherry pods	Potential for ferment, mold, loss of acidity and aroma	1 cherry or pod = 1 full defect
Parchment	Poorly calibrated hulling machine; lack of density sorting	Coffee in parchment	Diminished positive attributes and potential woody characteristics	5 parchment beans = 1 full defect

NOTES

■ Some defects in the chart above can also be developed on the farm or in the wet mill, but we're including only causes associated with problems at the dry mill here.

■ Although discussed in Processing Phase One as potential defects from overfermentation, sour, black and stinker beans are included again here with causes associated with mistakes at the dry mill.

DEFECTS

Broken, chipped, cut

Withered

Floater

Hull

Immature

Shells

Parchment

Husk

In fact, in general, according to Luis Pascoal, director of Daterra Coffee in Brazil, all defects that occur at the dry mill can be attributed to "lack of education/proper training, a mindset for productivity and not for quality, lack of infrastructure, and, in times of high production, too much coffee." (Too much coffee moving through a dry mill taxes the equipment, potentially causing equipment to shift out of calibration, potentially causing excessive heat and friction, which may damage beans. Furthermore, if a mill is overloaded, the chance for inconsistent or improper drying increases.)

Ultimately, it seems true that these general conditions are the root cause of all defects occurring in the dry mill, which, on the plus side, makes prevention methods more focused. Nonetheless, in spite of common general causes for dry mill-induced defects, we can still separate out a number of distinct defects, isolate their particular causes, and give you some tips on how to identify them visually and in the cup. (See the defect chart on page 111.)

Before moving on to look at some prevention methods, I think it is worth noting that a surprising number of defects are caused by inconsistent and improper drying. Many of us probably understand that the moisture content of the exported green bean is critical, but have we realized how important the *process* of drying coffee is to the ultimate quality of green coffee? As Jorge Pacas, an agronomist in El Borbollon, El Salvador, reveals, "The worst problem we have ever had was fermentation or overheating of the bean in the patios or mechanical dryers." Pacas works with his uncle Eduardo Alvarez at a quality-driven mill in El Salvador known for processing award-winning coffees. Even with their experience and understanding of the critical nature of drying, they can experience challenges. For example, when coffee is not moved correctly on the patio or when excessive heat builds up either on the patio or in mechanical dryers, then inconsistencies in drying yield defects like blacks, sours, stinkers and others.

Pacas emphasizes, "The most common problem is the stinkers, where wet coffees are trapped in the machine layers." Stinkers, as we see in the chart on page 111 and perhaps remember from our previous discussion on overfermentation defects, have severe ramifications in the cup. Clearly, it is not enough for a mill to simply deliver a green coffee with the proper end moisture content; a dry mill must pay close attention to *how* parchment reaches the appropriate moisture level.

Prevention

The good news for defects caused at the dry mill is that, unlike other categories of defects we've discussed in this series, these are almost always preventable. Pascoal broadly identifies prevention methods, such as training, discipline and infrastructure. By examining each one of these a bit further, we uncover some specific prevention methodologies.

TRAINING

The benefits of proper training at the dry mill are fairly obvious. We all know that in every area of specialty coffee production—from growing all the way to the final shot pulled by a barista at a retail store—proper training is the key to quality. When talking about training at the mill level, Pascoal and others are referring to the knowledge of mill managers and employees in drying coffee on patios (and/or in dryers) and in calibrating, monitoring and maintaining equipment. When coffee is carefully dried and hulling and sorting equipment is properly maintained by knowledgeable operators, the dry mill doesn't create new defects and, better yet, defects caused by activities or circumstances on the farm and in the wet mill process are removed.

DISCIPLINE

Discipline comes into play by paying careful attention during the drying and milling process. As Diaz reports, "Usually mill operators take periodic samples in order to make adjustments on the go before it is too late." More than just *knowing* how to implement proper drying procedures and how to calibrate and maintain equipment, mill managers must take responsibility for monitoring the process and making adjustments regularly. "If they do not perform this activity," states Diaz, "they will end up with a finished lot which will probably be rejected by the QC [quality control] person who buys the coffee."

INFRASTRUCTURE

At the mill, infrastructure refers to the patios used for drying, mechanical dryers (if used), equipment used for hulling, grading and sorting, and the overall facilities. When the infrastructure is clean, calibrated, and well maintained, a dry mill serves its purpose to remove pre-existing defects while avoiding the creation of any new ones. To give a couple of specific examples around drying patios (since, as we discussed, improper drying is a significant issue), Pascal mentions the need for a "very good concrete patio/terrace with water drains for mold control and proper equipment to turn over the cherries without walking over them because it breaks the outer skin and increases the risk of mold or fermentation." In addition, he adds, the size of the patio is important as producers with patios that are "too small tend to increase the layers and damage the coffee cherries."

Fixes

Ironically, many defects occurring at the dry mill can be fixed or, perhaps, more accurately stated, removed by other activities at the dry mill. For example, equipment utilized in the final stages of dry mill processing—the size sorters, density sorters, color sorters—are precisely designed to remove many of the defects mentioned previously, assuming, of course, the machines are calibrated correctly. In addition, hand sorting, which occurs in most mills producing specialty coffee, serves to remove defects that have passed through earlier sorting stages.

Parting Comments

In the first couple of articles in this series, we homed in on one or at least a fewer number of total defects, which have had some very specific manifestations in the cup. Nicely, this has left me with an easy job of recommending some, uh, interesting cupping assignments. This time, however, a longer list of defects prevents me from pushing a specific tasting task. Instead, I recommend that roasters revisit the role of green coffee grading and sorting as an important aspect of green coffee buying. This is not to say that defects caused in the mill don't have negative impact in cup quality (we can see in the chart that they certainly do), however, solid grading at the mill level and the demand of specialty coffee buyers in insisting that they receive properly graded coffees will likely prevent many of these defects from ever showing up in your roasting plant.

If you really want another cupping project, though, here you go: Source out some fungus-damaged beans and let me know how you find the flavors of ferment, mold, earth, dirt and phenol in the cup. If you're really lucky, maybe they will all show up at one time. ◼

· ·

ANDI TRINDLE MERSCH *has a varied background within her specialty coffee career, which began behind the espresso bar in 1989 and, since then, includes cupping, training, consulting, green coffee trading and buying, quality control, sales and writing. Mersch currently serves as director of coffee for Philz Coffee. She was elected to the Roasters Guild Executive Council for a two-year term in March 2015, and she volunteers with the Specialty Coffee Association (SCA) developing coffee business curriculum. She is a past board member of the SCA and the International Women's Coffee Alliance.*

Detecting Defects

Storage and Transportation Defects

by Andi Trindle Mersch

• FROM THE JULY/AUGUST 2008 ISSUE OF *ROAST* •

What's the worst phone call an importer can receive? It's that dreaded phone call from a roasting client letting you know that the arrival sample of a full container shipment (we are talking somewhere between 33,000 to 45,000 pounds of coffee) is defective and that they can't accept the delivery. I recently received one of these phone calls so the experience is fresh—painfully fresh—in my mind.

In cases like this, what usually happens is a coffee lot has been approved as a pre-shipment sample (PSS) by the importer and by its roasting client (if the coffee is pre-sold) and a full container of the coffee lot is shipped based upon this approved PSS sample. When the coffee arrives, both the importer and roaster are also going to approve an arrival sample and, in *most* cases, this is a formality. Of course, there can be subtle changes to a coffee lot between approval of the PSS sample and arrival of the container, but most often coffees arrive as expected. In fact, sometimes green coffee may actually improve as the coffee receives more resting time during transit where flavors further develop and even out amongst the lot. However, when a coffee lot does not arrive as expected and is in fact rejected as either fully defective or even just different enough to be classified as "not to specification," everyone begins scrambling and nobody ever wins.

So, what happens in these circumstances between approval of a coffee lot before shipment and delivery? How can a coffee that has made it all the way through growing, harvesting and processing as a top-grade specialty coffee transform from specialty to defective post processing? If you've been reading previous articles in this series, you will recall that there are many different problems that can occur during the vast and complicated stages of growing, harvesting and processing and that it takes tremendous skill, dedication and even some luck to get quality coffee through this long, labor-intensive chain. So, truly, it is heartbreaking when something goes wrong so late in the game.

As Martin Diedrich, owner of Kéan Coffee in Los Angeles, stated when discussing his experience in receiving delivery of a drastically diminished Zimbabwe coffee, "It was a huge loss for us and a blow to the farmer as well." In this circumstance, Diedrich reported that he had been buying this top-quality coffee from the same farm for many years with excellent deliveries every time, but that this time, something happened between his approval of the PSS sample and arrival of the coffee into the states. Having worked with the farm for nearly 14 years, Diedrich had no doubts that the right coffee was shipped to him and that the producer followed quality protocols diligently to the final points of influence; but, nonetheless, the coffee was drastically diminished. Although not technically fully defective—in this article, we are going to include coffee that experiences a significant loss or change in flavor even if the coffee is not ultimately classified as fully defective; in these cases, a noticeable transformation of the green coffee from pre-delivery approval to arrival certainly warrants investigation and better understanding by roasters—it was "a shadow of its former self," according to Diedrich and unusable as a specialty grade single-origin coffee. This type of tragedy—or worse—is what we are going to examine in this last article in our series on green coffee defects.

CATEGORIES OF POST-PROCESSING DEFECTS

Defects created post processing are best categorized by their root causes. First, there are those defects caused by naturally occurring latent internal changes in the green bean likely due to problems during drying. (If you recall from part three in our series, proper drying of green coffee is extremely important.) Second, external conditions after processing, such as heat, moisture, and humidity, grouped together as the "general climatic conditions during the resting process" by Stefan Wille, general manager of Coricafe in Costa Rica, can degrade or even drastically transform green coffee during storage or shipping. Third, external contaminants, including pests and highly odorous substances, can destroy coffee quality.

To better understand post processing defects and their ramifications on green coffee quality, we're going to take a closer look at each one of the categories above.

Internal Changes Post Processing

The first category—latent naturally occurring internal changes— is probably the most challenging of post-processing defects to understand and trace because something has gone wrong earlier in processing that causes degradation of the green coffee later even when the climatic and environmental conditions post processing are controlled properly. In these cases, the green coffee was improperly dried—either not dried enough or inconsistently dried—so the green coffee retains too much internal moisture. Green coffee with high internal moisture may develop fungus damage, leading to "mold and earthy tastes," according to Wille. In extreme cases, the green beans will grow mold on the exterior, so they are easily identified visually even before tasting. In addition,

green coffee retaining high moisture may continue to ferment, which will lead to, yes, you've got it: overfermentation. Remember the glorious flavors of rotten fruit we've talked about throughout this series? They can develop this late in the game even if carefully avoided at all other stages.

External Climatic Conditions

Because of a highly hygroscopic (absorbent) nature, even properly dried green coffee can develop a variety of defects after processing if climatic conditions are not managed properly. At all times, green coffee must be stored in appropriate conditions that control temperature and humidity or the same defects that occur from improper initial drying can develop. (We'll review proper storage conditions under prevention strategies.) Both too much and too little moisture can contribute to significant deterioration in quality.

In addition to the possibility for overfermentation, fungus, and mold, conditions in storage and transit that create excessive moisture may cause spongy/faded/whitish beans and white beans.

Spongy/faded/whitish beans are, unsurprisingly, whitish in color and have a consistency like cork, caused by enzymatic activity due to excessive moisture; they may pick up woody or cereal notes in the cup. White beans, caused by bacteria developed in high moisture, range in color from pale green to white, but maintain a normal density. According to Jorge Pacas, an agronomist in El Borbollon, El Salvador, "In the cup, they will have baggy flavor or old crop flavor."

On the other side of the moisture equation, environmental circumstances that cause coffee beans to lose moisture can be equally detrimental to quality. If warehouse temperatures become too hot, for example, internal moisture within the green bean may reduce below an acceptable level (absolute minimum 9 percent; ideal 12 percent), causing the beans to "lose all of their flavor and aroma due to evaporation of the oils," states Pacas, or in more extreme cases, to develop "woody and oldish [flavors]," according to Wille.

Contamination

Some of the most dramatic post-processing defects occur by contamination. For example, green coffee that is stored near or exposed to contaminants like "oil, diesel, gas, pesticides and smoke," as identified by Pacas, can infect green coffee due to the highly absorbent nature of green beans, which easily pick up odors from surrounding materials and products.

One of the most dramatic examples of a contamination problem occurred with coffees from the Honduras 2006 Cup of Excellence (COE). As most of us know, COE coffees are some of the best in the world, having been scrupulously selected through a national and international jury process to reflect the very best coffee in a given country each year. Unfortunately, in Honduras in 2006, the winning coffees were contaminated and largely destroyed after processing. According to Susie Spindler, with the Alliance for Coffee Excellence, "The jute bags were made with a petroleum substance that permeated the jute and tainted the coffee," in some cases so significantly that the coffee was "god-awful."

It may seem obvious to most of us that no food product—let alone one as absorbent as green coffee—should be packaged in materials containing petroleum or other harmful chemicals, but it is not an exclusive case. Diedrich also recalled a situation in Kenya a number of years back where the paint used on the coffee bags contaminated the green beans. In this case, fortunately, the paint was not ultimately significantly harmful to the taste profile and most of the damage was visual.

Another external contamination defect transpires when pests invade beans in storage. Typically, the guilty party is the coffee bean weevil (*Araecerus fasciculatus*). Beans that are subjected to the weevil will exhibit uneven holes larger than 1.5 mm. The extent of this damage can vary from slight to heavy and, in worst cases, a full infestation can occur and live and dead insects may still be

found with the beans. Impact on the cup can include noticeable off-flavors and diminishment of aromatics and acidity.

Fixes

Undoubtedly, everyone managing green coffee will agree that post processing defects/quality loss are very unfortunate. Certainly, producers, millers, importers, shipping lines and warehouse managers should do everything possible to prevent situations where these defects can develop and, in most cases, they do. Nonetheless, it is not always possible and, unfortunately, like many other defects we've discussed throughout this series, post-processing defects generally cannot be reversed or fixed after they've occurred. On the financial side, producers and importers are likely insured for some of the direct financial loss in these situations; but, depending upon the circumstances, this is not always the case, so serious financial loss can occur. Even more challenging than financial losses, however, is the challenge faced by importers trying to ensure that their roasting clients still get the coffee they need when they need it.

Fortunately, in some less severe quality loss cases, it may be possible for a roaster to still use a diminished coffee. In the best-case scenarios, where the problem is minor to notable flavor degradation but not an actual defect, producers, importers and roasters often try to work together to come up with a solution that will work for all parties, a solution that hopefully doesn't result in a full container being rejected back to the importer or, even worse, the producer. For example, if a roaster can utilize the coffee in another capacity, perhaps in a blend, then the importer may offer a discount off of the original price to reflect the quality difference. Depending upon when and how the problem occurred, the importer may or may not go back to the producer and request a similar price adjustment. In most of these cases, this loss cannot be recovered by an insurance company, so the financial adjustment loss is covered by the importer/exporter or the producer out of pocket, which is part of the risk that exporters and importers manage.

In more difficult circumstances where a coffee cannot be used by the roaster, the importer has the responsibility to replace the coffee, which is never an easy process and can sometimes lead to a mad and even impossible scramble if the particular coffee is in short supply. In worst-case scenarios, an importer may not be able to find a replacement, so the entire sale is canceled, which is certainly a financial loss for the importer and potentially a disaster for the roaster, who does not have the coffee they need to meet their sales.

In the case of the Honduras COE coffees contaminated by petroleum-laced bags, there was great variability. As Spindler recalls, "Even within one lot, one whole bag was perfect, one was god-awful, and another one may have been off, but not completely tainted." Due to this inconsistency, there was no single solution to managing the problem. In Europe and Japan, buyers were willing to sample and test each bag individually, which yielded the best possible results for producers, who were able to get full price on some bags and discounted pricing on others where possible. Interestingly, Spindler reports that the U.S. market was apparently not willing to go to the same lengths, so the U.S. lots were rejected in full.

Given the extensive challenges in replacing defective coffee after shipment and the barely adequate fixes that exist, it seems most important for efforts to be focused on prevention methods.

Prevention/Proper Storage Conditions

Prevention of post-processing defects requires protection from contaminants, proper initial drying, and maintenance of ideal conditions at all times during storage and shipping. We reviewed proper drying in the last article in this series and avoiding contaminants is fairly self-explanatory (not to presume always easy or possible), but what are ideal conditions for green coffee during storage and transit?

According to Douglas Martocci Jr., vice president of Continental Terminals, Inc., in Kearny, New Jersey, "warehouses should maintain an ideal green coffee storage temperature of 45 to 85 degrees F and a relative humidity of 50 to 55 percent. When held at the ideal storage temperature and humidity levels (45 to 85 degrees F and relative humidity of 50 to 55 percent), the green coffee should not experience more than a 1 percent variation in moisture levels." When these conditions are maintained, green coffee is generally protected from quality degradation beyond the gradual and natural decline of green coffee post processing. Green coffee warehouses are also generally devoted strictly to green coffee, so risk of contamination from other products is minimized and warehouse managers, like Martocci, are experts at managing green coffee storage conditions.

These same conditions applied at Continental and other coffee warehouses should *ideally* be applied to green coffee at all times after processing, which means that export warehouses should strive for similar conditions before shipment (often difficult for poor producing countries) and shipping vessels ideally provide similar conditions.

Interestingly, according to Ming Chen, operations manager for Marco Polo Enterprises, a freight forwarding company in California that manages coffee cargo by ocean and air freight, green coffee is not shipped under such strict conditions. "We ship coffee beans as general cargo since it is not required to have temperature control," Chen states, adding that their company has not yet had any claims for loss of quality in transit. So perhaps the conditions of the average vessel are sufficient for protecting green coffee, but uncontrolled shipping conditions certainly risk harm and, in some cases, are assuredly the cause of containers of high-quality coffee arriving significantly reduced in quality or outright defective.

One newer idea to protect against variants and uncontrollability in export warehouse and shipping environments is the use of valve/vacuum packaging. Daterra, producers of specialty coffee in Brazil, have been successfully packaging their top-end green coffee in valve packaging for a number of years and it is now becoming an option in a number of other producing countries as well. This type of packaging protects coffee against contaminants and creates an environment where there is "less moisture variance," as Spindler puts it when revealing that COE is moving to this type of packaging where possible. Roasters are catching on to the concept and some roasters, like 49th Parallel in

Canada, are starting to request that their importers move toward providing valve packaging for all of their top-quality specialty coffees. Although I have concerns about the environmental ramifications of packaging coffee this way across the board, it does seem to be a logical and worthwhile option for expensive auction and microlot coffees in particular.

Wrapping Up

For those of you who have been reading along in my Detecting Defects series, this is it. This is the end of defects. OK, that's not true—I can't actually do anything to end the defects in the world of green coffee, but I do hope that this series of articles has illuminated some prevention, identification and, in rare cases, repair strategies useful to roasters. Though I've tried to get in-depth where possible, in many places I've just managed to scratch the surface. I encourage roasters (and importers and producers) to continue learning about defects. If you find a defect on your cupping table, beyond just rejecting and replacing the coffee and covering losses, try to track down where and how the problem occurred. Dialogue with your importers and their producer partners openly about the visual and taste ramifications, the possible causes, and preventative measures for future shipments. Only through knowledge and open communication can we hope to prevent more defects over time. For your final tasting assignment, I recommend brewing up a perfect cup of your current favorite NON-defective coffee to remind you why understanding and ultimately preventing defects is important to you as a roaster. I mean, what if my beautiful El Salvador bourbon coffee were to taste like rotten fish, vinegar or peanut butter? That's just no good. ■

. . . .

ANDI TRINDLE MERSCH *has a varied background within her specialty coffee career, which began behind the espresso bar in 1989 and, since then, includes cupping, training, consulting, green coffee trading and buying, quality control, sales and writing. Mersch currently serves as director of coffee for Philz Coffee. She was elected to the Roasters Guild Executive Council for a two-year term in March 2015, and she volunteers with the Specialty Coffee Association (SCA) developing coffee business curriculum. She is a past board member of the SCA and the International Women's Coffee Alliance.*

Detecting Defects & Celebrating Gems

The Search for the Perfect Green Bean

by Timothy J. Castle

• FROM THE MARCH/APRIL 2006 ISSUE OF *ROAST* •

As the specialty coffee industry matures, the subject of defects becomes increasingly important, and increasingly controversial. Understanding green defects—those visual and gustatory signs that something has gone wrong—is a vital skill for coffee roasters, and yet is one of the most difficult to learn. Defects are like mythical creatures: hard to discern, difficult to describe and occasionally subject to great debates over the very nature of their existence in a particular cup.

Ironically, the specialty industry, with its focus on creating defect-free coffee, is more vulnerable to the impact of these defects than larger coffee companies. The big companies often have the resources, experience and layers of administration to address each and every documentable defect.

Smaller companies, with their passionate yet less experienced buyers (and with less financial leverage over their suppliers) may be willing to cup a slightly fermented coffee and accept it on the grounds that it's interesting and might work in a particular blend. The "ferment" might even add to the coffee's "sweetness" after all. And who's to say there is anything wrong with that?

In fact, there is nothing wrong with that philosophy; it's just that once you start tinkering with the idea of adding defects in your coffees, your ability to keep your coffees consistent decreases markedly. Consistency may be one of the best reasons not to even *think* about having a more open mind about defects. Large roasters can't even "go there" but small roasters, for better or worse, have the ability to do so.

Defining a Defect

Clearly, a defect is something we don't like, something that detracts from a taste we would otherwise find desirable. In terms of coffee, we can look at defects in two very different ways: the defects we can taste and the defects we can see. (The purpose of this article is how to approach the issue of defects generally, and how to approach the subject of defects specifically, not only at the cupping table but with suppliers as well. For a comprehensive catalog of green coffee defects, I suggest the Specialty Coffee Association's (SCA) *Arabica Green Coffee Defect Handbook*, which describes and illustrates the impact of the most important and troublesome defects that plague the taste of coffee.)

These two types of defects often go hand in hand. With defects we can taste, we often find a particular taste that we must then

attempt to narrowly identify and work backward to find the cause. While working backward, we often find a number of funny-looking beans that, serendipitously for the search, prove to be the cause of many of the flavors we don't like. Thus, the defects we can taste are often caused by the ones we can see. For instance, cup a coffee with a sour, acetic acid taste. Then go back to the green sample and find a few orangeish/reddish beans and scratch them—you may get the same distinct aroma. An amazing consilience emerges.

It's fortunate for us that so many taste defects can be traced back to beans that *appear* to be different—it didn't necessarily have to work out that way. Indeed, there are some defects in the cup, taints, for example, from foreign aromas present during storage or transport of coffee, that do not manifest themselves in any sort of unusual physical appearance in the bean. Much more difficult is when a coffee looks fine but tastes a little earthy, inscrutably gritty and somehow flat. We can argue amongst ourselves about this sort of thing, but when you can't *see* the defect, it's hard to gain traction with farmers, exporters, importers or dealers.

Another way to look at it is to call those defects we can see active defects and those we cannot, but can only taste, passive. Both kinds can arise from neglect, for example allowing insect infestations to overrun one's farm (an *active* defect for purposes of this comparison because they leave visible damage), or simply not maintaining the soil, which may lead not to one particular defect per se, but to flat, flavorless and/or unbalanced coffee (thus, a more *passive* defect). All practices that allow defects to occur, passive or active, visible or not, chip away at a stellar coffee to turn it into just one more earthbound cup.

All this said, if you can eliminate the visible, physical defects in a coffee, you would probably eliminate nearly all defects in the cup. This is because undamaged coffee tastes better than coffee that's been physically disrupted. The green coffee bean is pretty tough and designed to resist damage by mold, bacteria and insects (even the caffeine in coffee is said to be there in order to discourage insects). But once its physical integrity has been disrupted (by damage from processing or from the chomping of a hardy insect), then anything goes. Fungi, especially, run riot, and the bad-tasting possibilities are endless. This is one reason careful processing is so important to producing specialty coffees, even though many farmers and exporters complain that "defect-free" standards are onerous and unproductive, leading only to coffee that looks pretty but tastes no better than a delivery with chipped and cut beans in it.

The Visible World

There is, then, a sort of struggle between visible (active) and invisible (passive) defects. The origins of both are complex, and eliminating them is sometimes impossible due to the facilities available at a farm or co-op, or because of the intransigence of the people involved in producing the coffee. Gaining the ability to differentiate situations that can be improved and those that cannot is one of the greatest skills an aspiring specialty coffee roaster can develop. This skill can best be developed by jumping in and asking for farms to improve their practices, asking questions, understanding the reasons things are done a certain way, etc.

Of those that are referred to here as active defects—black beans, sours, fungal damage, foreign matter, dried cherries/pods, insect damage, broken/chipped/cut, immature, withered, shells, floaters, parchment and hulls/husks—seven of the 13 result primarily from failure to process correctly, and five are from agricultural deficiencies (see *Bean Defects: A Handy Reference Chart*, pages 124–125). The final is from a random genetic occurrence that might be more common among certain varieties.

Processing defects—those of fungal damage, foreign matter, dried cherries/pods, broken/chipped beans, floaters, parchment and hulls/husks—are either the result of sloppy practices that leave stuff in that should not be there, or practices that damage beans and thereby allow microbial damage. Agricultural defects—namely black beans, sours, immature beans, withered beans and those damaged by insects during growth—usually result from inadequate water, poor practices or microbial infection during bean development.

Unseen and Poorly Understood Defects of Monumental Proportions

Eliminating visible defects won't necessarily get you out of the woods. While, for instance, seven of the 13 visible defects can lead to ferment, it is also possible to have a coffee that's free of physical defects but nonetheless throws fermented cups. This is why it is so important for farmers aspiring to produce specialty coffee to understand that great coffees start from the seedling and that *every* step in production is important and you can't create specialty coffee at the mill if you don't grow it to begin with. This is also why dedicated specialty roasters need to be so concerned about the physical appearance of the coffee. Sure, one little misshapen bean may have no effect on cup quality, but if a farmer is unconcerned about what you *can* see, how careful is that farmer going to be with things you *can't* see?

Unfortunately, you also have farmers, processors and exporters who've figured out that a great appearance sells coffee, at least to some of us, so you will also find defect-free lots that taste insipid (and worse) while they look and roast beautifully. Obviously, exhaustive cupping is the only way to escape this trap. Finally, it is important to remember that defects must be removed at the source, as much as possible at the point they occur, rather than sorted out after the fact. There will always be a few defects at the end of the production cycle that need to be physically removed, but this should not be relied upon. The *origin* of each defect needs to be addressed.

Hard and rioy coffees are seldom identifiable visually, yet they are some of the most strikingly defective coffees. Hard coffees can be very sour and sometimes unacceptably bitter. Rioy coffees are usually described as having an iodine-like quality.

Coffees that are phenolic are found increasingly in many producing countries and are sometimes associated with the sensations experienced in hard and rioy coffees. While once thought to have one particular cause (and theories have changed over the years), phenolic coffees are now viewed by many scientists and cuppers as having several causes and several distinct manifestations. Some researchers postulate as many as 50 distinct phenolic tastes or compounds, and this is aside from the phenolic compounds generated during the roasting process, particularly with dark roasts. Some of these phenolic compounds are said to result from airborne microbial infections and others from the coffee plant's reaction to excessive sunlight. The jury, as they say, is still out.

When Is a Defect NOT a Defect?

Is there ever an instance where a defect is NOT a defect but desirable or at least acceptable? According to many passionate specialty coffee professionals, the answer is a resounding "no."

But the fact is, many people are used to drinking coffee that would be considered patently defective by others. The example of hardness and/or rioy coffees that are, plainly, intensely phenolic is one example. In many markets, including those in Brazil and throughout the Mediterranean coast of southern Europe, these coffees are expected, if not preferred. Likewise, some Ethiopian, Yemeni, Brazilian and the coffees of Coban, Guatemala, are expected by some buyers to be fruity—while many cuppers would simply term them fermented and call it a day. Finally, many Indonesian coffees are found to be "dirty" at the cupping table and given the heave-ho. Other buyers will ask, "If a Sumatra doesn't have a little earthiness, what's the point?"

As with so many things in the specialty industry, there are many sides to this particular debate. Roasters and cuppers can discuss for hours whether a particular taste is a ferment, and yet, in the end, two things are certain: Those debatable flavors and tastes are present in many coffees, and someone somewhere wants just that flavor and taste in a particular delivery.

A Culture of Defects, or a Culture of Perfection?

The process of correcting active defects, and reducing them throughout the growth and processing of a particular crop, usually results in a reduction of passive defects as well. One of the things that people who study the agriculture of coffee (and other crops as well) will find, is that the human factor is of paramount importance. Sometimes a more effective route to changing a coffee is in helping the people, usually a family, change their entire approach to growing coffee. Changing the culture of a farm can reduce defects often faster than attacking each and every defect separately. For instance, establishing an incentive program, wherein family members and employees can initiate improvements and benefit from the results, can reduce or eliminate several defects at once. Similarly, working with communities to help groups of farmers understand problems inherent to their areas can help them work together to eliminate defects that plague them all. Most farmers want to produce the best coffee they can as long as they believe that there are sincere roasters with consistent, predictable requirements that they can strive to meet in order to obtain a premium.

What's essential is that the farmer/processor/exporter and buyer understand the expectations and deliver to them, or you can end up with the bizarre but not unheard of scenario where customers attempt to reject coffees for not being hard, for lacking ferment or being too clean. Clarifying expectations is essential not only for the parties involved but for the industry at large. When roasters ask for particular coffees that might normally be considered defective, it can lead producers to think that these coffees are generally acceptable, and they aren't. Producers can therefore maximize the value of their production overall by knowing what their customers want and tailoring their production to suit each of their needs—perhaps even charging premiums for coffees that otherwise are considered defective. Again, this is not so simple. Often with a coffee like a Yemeni, when you sort out all the defects you end up with a cleaner, more uniform cup of coffee, but nothing recognizable as a Yemeni coffee. Some argue that that's what a Yemeni coffee *should* look and taste like (i.e., what it tastes like when it is defect-free). Others will tell you that their customers are expecting a certain *wildness* and will be disappointed without it.

What should be made very clear is that unless a particular defect is specifically requested, then it should not be there and the delivery can be rejected if it is present. We call them, after all, defects, not "things we love to see in our coffees," or "especially delicious taste attributes." So, bottom line, work with your suppliers, and if what you're looking for is the least bit idiosyncratic, let your suppliers *know* that you know this so they can be clear as to what you're looking for and not that you're simply a sloppy coffee buyer. It will also ensure that your suppliers are more careful with *all* their deliveries. For instance, if you like your Sumatran coffee a tad earthy, make that clear *and* that you know earthy Sumatran coffee is not, technically, defect-free.

What to Do?

Except in cases where the defect represents a fluke occurrence, and this can happen in the finest, most pristine coffees once in a while, the presence of defects is often something that must be managed and minimized rather than eliminated. That process is often best addressed with as much communication with your suppliers as possible, whether you work with importers, exporters or directly with producers.

Sometimes producers may place too little emphasis on certain problems and too much on others. This is especially true for coffees that are used in blends, where the roaster may be looking for certain strengths but is not concerned with weaknesses or attributes that might be considered desirable. If you are looking to eliminate defects in particular coffees, communicate this clearly to your supplier chain and also determine if the expectation is realistic in the first place. Are there other examples of defect-free coffee coming from the area where you're buying? Is the infrastructure in place? Are there farmers who have the management and leadership skills to effect change? Do they want to? Many farmers still don't cup their own coffee and believe, nonetheless, that their coffee leaves no room for improvement. You are not likely to effect much change in such a situation.

This is not to say, on the other hand, that the active defects we've addressed here are in any way acceptable. Generally, a specialty roaster should be able to put down three to five cups of each coffee in their inventory on a cupping table and not find a single defective cup. Once in a while there might be a piece of dried cherry, especially in a natural coffee, and sometimes some parchment in a washed coffee. Nonetheless, as the demand for high grown coffees increases, the available expertise to produce these coffees is not keeping pace. Many roasters are responding to this by turning to coffees they believe have potential and working with their suppliers/exporters/processors and farmers to improve them. But it takes a lot of dedication, persistence and the ability to identify situations that can be improved and those that cannot.

Smaller roasters do not always have the same opportunities to pick and choose which farmers they work with, but they can provide feedback to importers/dealers about what they like and what they don't. It's important, though, that they really understand the impact that various visible defects have on cup quality and what the prevailing standards are for a given coffee before wading into a long commentary about a particular coffee. For instance, complaining about a few defects in a Genuine Antigua, SHB EP is different than commenting that a certain Yemeni coffee has one or two defects. In the former case, *any* defects are unacceptable, but in a Yemeni coffee, only one or two defects might constitute an exceptional lot.

Then there's the question of exactly what sort of defects are present and in what amount. What impact does each and every defect have, and how serious are they? Can the buyer accurately identify each one? It is critical that buyers new to the game check and recheck their facts and conclusions before making the case that a certain coffee has a certain defect. The SCA's *Arabica Green Coffee Defect Handbook* is a good place to start. But after studying it, make sure you also get a hold of some physical examples so you can familiarize yourself with them and know the difference, for example, between a "sour" and a bean that has perhaps absorbed some coloration from the water it was processed in, (and is thus not sour at all). Even for the best cuppers, it is good to approach the serious subject of defects with humility and inquiry rather than categorical surety.

Finally, focusing on what can go wrong with coffee production and processing is important in order to protect oneself and know what is acceptable and what isn't. But looking for what's wrong should not be the job of the specialty coffee roaster. Rather, finding coffees that are truly special and identifying what has gone right is far more important. No one is going to rush back to your store (or your bag of coffee on the grocery store shelf) because there is nothing wrong with it. Asking what's wrong with a coffee is the easy question after all; much more difficult is asking yourself what's *right* about it. ∎

. . . .

TIMOTHY J. CASTLE *is co-author of* The Great Coffee Book *and the author of* The Perfect Cup. *Castle is president of Castle Communications, an international consultation, public relations and marketing firm servicing the food and beverage trades. He can be reached at* tim@castleandcompany.com.

Bean Defects

A Handy Reference Chart

Defect	Black Beans	Sours	Immature	Withered	Insect Damage	Shells
Bean Appearance	Black beans	Yellow, brown or red beans	Smallish malformed beans, tightly attached silverskin	Withered, smallish beans	Evidence of insect boring, nibbling or chomping	Seashell-shaped beans
Cause	Infection during bean development	Opportunistic microbial attack resulting from bad agricultural and processing technique	Poor picking practices	Lack of adequate water to tree during bean development	Agricultural and processing techniques that allow insect/bean interaction (the bean always loses)	Genetic. Bean develops with one-half wrapping around other, resulting in seashell-shaped beans (other half usually is screened out due to small size)
Basic Origin of Defect	Agriculture	Agriculture	Agriculture	Agriculture	Agriculture and processing	Inherent
Taste	Various badness, including ferment, dirty, moldy and phenolic	Sour, fermented or stinker taste, depending on degree of fermentation	Astringent to grassy	Grassy, strawlike, can also be astringent	The insect isn't the problem so much as the mold and bacteria that attack once the insect has cause damage and disrupted the bean's integrity	Doesn't roast evenly with regular beans. Somewhat thins the taste in high enough percentage

Photos and information courtesy of Arabica Green Coffee Defect Handbook, *available from the SCA.*

Fungus	Foreign Matter	Dried Cherries/ Pods	Broken/ Chipped/Cut	Floaters	Parchment	Hulls/Husks
Yellow, red to brown, sometimes blackened	Self-explanatory	Whole dried coffee cherries with bean inside	Self-explanatory	Faded to bleached appearance, beans lack original hard, green appearance	Parchment husk still attached to bean	Pieces of dried cherry with no bean inside
Opportunistic, usually the result of bean damage during bad processing	Sloppy practices	Sloppy processing, inadequate use of sorting equipment	Bad processing with rough equipment or equipment settings that cause damage	Exposure to swings in humidity cause beans to dry out and reabsorb moisture, lowering their density. Over-drying	Inadequate processing techniques	Sloppy processing
Processing	Processing	Processing	Processing	Processing	Processing	Processing
Primarily phenolic tastes, bitter, dirty, earthy and sometimes ferment notes	Whatever the foreign matter tastes like when roasted and brewed	Ferment, moldy (bitter, dusty/dirty) and phenolic	Again, once bean integrity is damaged, microbial attack ensues	Various flavors including strawlike, thin, fermented and bitter	Can introduce annoyingly foreign cinnamon/ clove, generic spice notes	Various flavors, see dried cherries/ pods

Cracking the Phenol Code

Uncovering the Mystery Behind This Taste Defect

by Beth Ann Caspersen

• FROM THE JULY/AUGUST 2007 ISSUE OF *ROAST* •

Coffee is good for you. Studies suggest that some of the phenolic compounds found in coffee may play a protective role against human chronic degenerative disease, cancer and cardiovascular disease. In addition, the antioxidants contained in coffee berry pulp are believed to be more powerful then those contained in pomegranates or blueberries, and coffee berry extract is now being used in skin care products.

In fact, there are 16 phenols in coffee. One member of this group and a primary contributor to the smell and flavor of roasted coffee are chlorogenic acids (CGA). Evidence suggests that the level of CGA in coffees—based on species, cultivar and maturation of coffee cherries, as well as the roasting process—influence the quality of coffee flavor found in the cup.

However, one of the phenols found in coffee—named 2,4,6-trichloroanisole (TCA)—has also been identified as a flavor taint known as phenol. The term "phenolic" is not universal and is sometimes used interchangeably or confused with coffee tasting terms such as astringent, rioy, ferment, medicinal, chlorine, inky, sulphurous or even rotten shrimp. Science suggests that the flavor is identifiable, but the cause of phenolic flavors appear to be theoretical and a bit controversial.

Different coffee experts have different ways of describing the flavor. Paul Songer of the Alliance for Coffee Excellence says, "From a flavor standpoint, my experience of phenolic is like over-chlorinated swimming pool water that just got hit with an organic load that is oxidizing."

However, many believe the previously mentioned terms refer to different defects. Craig Holt, president of Atlas Coffee Importers, says that phenol and rio are distinct from one another, "Phenolic is a chlorine-based taste," he says, "while rio is iodine."

What Does It Look Like?

According to the Specialty Coffee Association's (SCA) *Arabica Green Coffee Defect Handbook*, the flavor of phenolic can be identified as one of many possible flavors resulting from poor harvesting or processing. Defects such as blacks, fungus, insect damage and dried cherry pods or coffee husks are seen as the causes. However, there is no isolated definition for phenolic in the handbook, and earthy, moldy, ferment and sour flavors are also associated with these defects. Basically the SCA is saying that there are a number of possible flavor defects presented by the aforementioned imperfections. Although it is not stated in the book, a number of coffee professionals mentioned that they noticed a phenolic flavor when they observed green coffee beans that were light to dark red in the crevice, on the belly of the beans themselves.

What Are the Causes?

As mentioned previously, there are a number of possible causes, including climate, fertilizer use and processing methods. While much research is still being conducted, there is not yet conclusive evidence as to what causes the phenol flavor.

Climate

According to a study done by Adriana Farah and Carmen Marino Donagelo of the Universidade Federal de Rio de Janeiro, Brazil, in 2006, "Severe weather conditions such as cold, high visible light and water stress conditions tend to increase the content of phenolic compounds" in coffee. At high altitudes, coffee cherries may be subjected to very low temperature and freezing rain. This freezing rain can burn the coffee cherries during development and produce an imperfection known as a *quemados* (burns). These physical imperfections appear to be partial blacks, but depending on the level of severity, they may not be classified as such.

An example of these conditions was present during the 2005/2006 harvest in Chiapas, Mexico. In that harvest, there was a high concentration of burned beans. After isolating the beans and testing them for cup flavor, Marilec Sevilla, the head cupper for COMPRAS in Chiapas, determined that this was a possible cause for the phenolic flavor. Severely burned beans, which would be classified as partial and/or full blacks, seemed to have produced the flavor in this case.

Along with climate changes from hot to cold, overexposure to sun during the ripening process may also increase the amount of CGA in the coffee cherries. Songer theorizes, "Since some branches

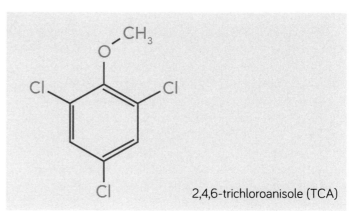

2,4,6-trichloroanisole (TCA)

get more sun than others, this explains why the defect is so non-homogeneous. Makes sense since major changes and stress in the plant can cause changes in the makeup of CGA. There are compounds of this type in the fruit and possibly there is some interaction when the cherry is still on the tree. There are also a lot of changes in CGA structures as the coffee matures."

Fertilizers and Insecticides

Various studies from Brazil and Kenya suggest that nitrogen-rich fertilizers and situations of boron deficiency can increase the chlorogenic acid content. Other studies have suggested that TCA, the phenol thought to produce the phenolic flavor, is caused by a chlorophenol and fungicide known as Prochloraz. Steven Diaz, quality manager of EXPOCAFE in Colombia and a member of the SCA Technical Standards Committee, says that, "the use of insecticides to control Broca" is another possible cause. "This has been largely debated here [in Colombia] among cuppers and the flavor attributed to this problem is a strong chemical-like flavor and it is not phenolic; it is basically a contaminated flavor," says Diaz. "It is important to distinguish between phenolic and chemical flavors, which are different."

Coffee Cherry Selection

No matter how many times I say it and hear it—"only pick the red ripe cherries"—I know this is not always being done. If the coffee cherry is green and under-ripe, the flavor can be astringent and hard with a high content of chlorogenic acids. On the contrary, cherries that exhibit a deep black over-ripe color will taste like rotten fruit and have a low CGA content. Imagine that the cherries are selected when they are perfectly ripe but are not processed immediately. Songer suggests that a possible cause for the phenolic flavor could be that "the fruit or mucilage remains in contact with the seed too long or at high temperatures after pulping, before drying."

Many coffee professionals I spoke with, including Julio Obregón, cupper at CECOCAFEN in Nicaragua, thinks that another fault in the process of selection could be in "retrieving coffee cherries that had fallen during the harvesting process onto the soil below the trees." This may be happening all over the world. Some producers line the bottom of the trees to save the cherries that fall during the harvesting. The farmers' livelihood is dependent on the amount of coffee they process and the red ripe cherry on the ground will contribute to that end. Whether they are seasonal pickers or farm owners, the choice is the same: The cherry is there and it is red and ripe—does this really affect the flavor? My instinct says yes, but the flavor would seem to be dirty, soil-y or perhaps rotten or unripe, and not necessarily the cause of phenolic.

Washed Coffees

Depulping

Regardless of what make or model the depulper, the objective is the same: to strip the fleshy pulp off of each coffee cherry without cutting, scratching or chipping the surface of the seeds inside. Some depulpers are more efficient then others due to age, design and maintenance.

Carmen Vallejos, lead cupper at CECOCAFEN in Nicaragua, believes that an unclean depulper can result in the phenolic flavor. It is commonly recommended to use clean water to rinse

How to IDENTIFY the defect known as phenolic

COFFEE SHOULD BE roasted to a light cupping roast, 90–120 seconds past the first crack. The cupping should be prepared by weight as opposed to volume. Measure 10 grams of whole-bean roasted coffee into each 6 ounce (180 ml.) cup. It is important to measure out each cup of whole-bean roasted coffee individually and grind them separately to isolate possible problems. Be sure to use clean, filtered water that is between 195 and 198 degrees.

Observe the differences in fragrance and flavor from cup to cup and as the cups cool. Inconsistent smells and flavors from cup to cup are key indicators of defects, and phenolic flavors may be light in their intensity or slap you in the face with their stomach-turning power.

Remember the descriptions of phenol earlier? Well, now is your chance to put them to the test. You're looking for flavors of chlorine, sulphur, iodine and bad shrimp. Yum.

However, some cuppers aren't as able to smell and taste phenol as others. "It is a real sensorial problem in panels because in my experience, individual sensitivity to this varies widely," Songer says. "Some cuppers cannot detect it unless it is quite strong, while a number of cuppers I have met are extremely sensitive to it. One could smell it on the break in some cases."

the depulper at the end of each use. During the depulping process, water is added to aid in the removal of the coffee cherry. However, the thick sweet juices are crushed into the crevices of the machinery and the depulper needs to be scrubbed thoroughly to reduce the growth of bacteria. If proper maintenance is not performed, the depulper may become bacteria ridden and could be the cause of the phenolic flavor.

Fermentation Tanks and Washing Canals

I have seen many kinds of tanks to ferment coffee: wood baskets, wood boxes, cement boxes and cement boxes lined with ceramic tile. In recent years, I have seen Roto Plas containers that were originally used to capture rain water for consumption and irrigation being used as tanks for fermentation.

Most coffee professionals believe that a fermentation tank, like a depulper, should be cleaned out after each use and scrubbed, no matter what kind of tank it is, to reduce the growth of bacteria. However, each vessel used to ferment coffee may require a different cleaning procedure and some will function better then others. Diaz says, "The use of disinfectants and bleach during the cleaning of the fermentation tanks has also been attributed to the phenolic flavor; if it is not washed off properly, the pulped coffee can get contaminated during fermentation."

Washing the Beans

In order to stop the fermentation process, coffees are often washed with water. As mentioned in the fermentation section, the cleanliness of the water is vital in making this step a success as is the cleanliness of the washing canals used to sort quality beans.

Fatima Lopez, lead cupper and quality manager of PRODECOOP, theorizes that if the coffee is not washed well enough before it is put out to dry, this could cause the coffee to continue fermenting and impart a phenolic flavor.

Water Cleanliness and Source

The cleanliness of the water will certainly play a role in how clean any of the previously mentioned equipment is after the maintenance has taken place. If the amount of water used to clean the equipment is not adequate or the water is dirty, residue could be left behind.

Water is sourced in a variety of ways, from neighboring streams to centralized water facilities. Diaz reminds us that, "as small coffee-producing towns grow and gain access to running water, the natural mountain waters may be replaced. Utilizing this water may result in a high concentration of chlorine, a common ingredient in treated water. Fermenting the coffee in chlorine-rich water or using it to clean processing equipment may result in the chlorine flavor found in coffee."

But what if the phenolic flavor you find is only in one cup? Shouldn't the entire sample taste like chlorine? Is it the fault of the water source as opposed to the process step?

All of the aforementioned defects may produce the phenolic flavor, however, what if you find a phenolic cup on the table, but your green coffee sample is perfectly clean? It makes sense that primary defects like blacks or sours could impart the phenolic flavor, but many cuppers have found that clean green coffee can produce this flavor defect as well.

Coffee Drying

One theory is that the phenolic flavor is caused by mold growing inside the bean due to improper drying, a situation that is prevalent in mechanical dryers.

According to Diaz, the phenolic flavor in Colombia started to appear in the late 1980s when there was a shift from sun drying to mechanical drying. "It isn't the mechanical dryers themselves that cause the problem," he says. "It is how they are used. The layer of wet parchment in the dryer has to be less than 16 inches and temperatures at a constant 40 degrees C. Operators try to speed up the drying by using 32 inches of parchment and cranking up the temperature of the dryers to 60 degrees C. The bacterial activity starts to build up in the middle part of the bean that is not drying and mold and fungus start to affect the bean inside, which is apparent on the inside but not on the outside and can only be found in the cup. You cannot pick up on the phenolic flavor based on the appearance unless it is so seriously contaminated that it smells."

He goes on to add, "One important thing, and for this no one has the answer yet, is that for some reason only some beans actually produce the compound 2,4,6-trichloroanisole (TCA), and not the whole mass that has been subjected to mold due to improper drying. This is why it is so random during cupping and usually does not repeat in the second cupping and can come back very strong on a third or fourth cupping."

Still a Mystery

As we all know, processing coffee requires a tremendous amount of work, and each step in the process will affect the outcome of the final product. If one step is poorly executed, the results could ruin an entire lot of coffee for a coffee producer. Care and attention to detail are important aspects of processing coffee, but education and sharing information are also vital in producing excellent quality coffee.

The goal in writing this article is to improve our understanding as a coffee community that the defect phenolic can be caused by any of a number of steps in processing coffee. Perhaps the flavor of phenolic is caused in a variety of ways, but it would behoove the coffee industry to put more time and energy into the subject.

What do you do when you find a phenolic sample?

IN THE EVENT that you find a defective cup, ask a colleague to taste the coffee with you. If both of you notice a problem, cup the coffee again. Holt says, "When we hit phenolic in a five-cup set, we re-cup with 10 cups. If we hit it again, we reject the pre-ship. If you, as the roaster, hit phenolic cups on a first pass of a pre-ship, follow the process above. If it's in an arrival sample, then set up a 10-cup set of the pre-ship and a 10-cup of the arrival. If both have the phenolic problem … you approved a phenolic coffee. You can negotiate with the vendor on it, but the shame is your own for not cupping carefully on the first pass."

If you end up in this situation and you think you have a real problem, be sure to double-check your water source by boiling and smelling the water before you use it for cupping. Another possible way to identify the extent of the problem is to evaluate the green coffees in question. Take green coffee samples from various bags of the lot you have purchased (be sure to mark the bags) and a control sample from a green coffee that smells normal to you. Smell the green coffee samples. Is there a difference? Much like the smell of the roasted coffee sample you cupped, green coffee can have the same chlorine-like smell.

Roast and cup the sample again to determine if there is a possible problem in one or many of the samples. If you don't know what green coffee should smell like, start smelling all of your green coffee from this day forward to understand the fresh characteristics of your coffees and how they perform over time. Once you have determined the extent of the problem, isolate the questionable bags as far away from the good coffee as possible.

We need to support more research into this phenomenon that continues to mystify the most seasoned coffee professionals. I can conclude that the specialty coffee industry still needs to work on improving the growing need for a common vocabulary by sharing information and experiences. My hope was to put some of these theories to rest, but in any good process for sharing information, it is important that you draw your own conclusions and continue the conversation. ∎

BETH ANN CASPERSEN *is coffee quality control manager at the Equal Exchange Cooperative in West Bridgewater, Massachusetts. Equal Exchange is a specialty food cooperative that sources coffee, chocolate, tea and other products from small farmer cooperatives all over the world. She is a specialized instructor for the SCA, a member of the Coffee Tasters Pathway Committee, a Q instructor, co-founder of Java Jog for a Cause and an advocate for women's rights. Contact her at bacaspersen@equalexchange.coop.*

A Focus on Flaws

Do You Use the SCA's Green Arabica Coffee Classification System?

by Beth Ann Caspersen | *photos courtesy of Equal Exchange*

• FROM THE MAY/JUNE 2016 ISSUE OF *ROAST* •

T he term "specialty coffee" has grown and changed over the past several decades. Today, when a buyer considers the options for purchasing coffee, he or she probably takes a variety of things into account: quality, cost, social and/or environmental impact, and more. As a specialty coffee professional, what is your definition?

The Specialty Coffee Association (SCA) has created standards for a number of activities over the years—including the Green Arabica Coffee Classification System (GACCS) discussed in this article—all aimed at producing a quality product. Today, the SCA defines specialty coffee based on whether specific physical and sensorial attributes—in other words, how the coffee looks and tastes—meet clearly defined standards.

The physical attributes include size, weight, number of defects and moisture content of green coffee, and the number of quakers (immature beans that do not darken when roasted) in a roasted sample. The sensory evaluation scores roasted coffee in 10 categories encompassing all aspects of flavor, from acidity to cleanliness; a coffee must achieve a score of 80 points or higher to be considered specialty. To eliminate any variables other than the coffee itself, the SCA has established protocols for evaluating the sensory attributes of roasted coffee (cupping protocols).

Clearly, the system is designed to consider both defects and cup quality. After all, the two go hand in hand—or do they? Does your decision to buy a coffee take defects into account, or is the emphasis solely on cup score?

Green Coffee Standards

There are dozens of green coffee grading systems around the world. Most countries that produce coffee have their own internal systems to evaluate their exportable crop, and many are detailed and provide clear guidance to evaluate the physical attributes of green coffee (size, defects, moisture) and the flavor of roasted coffee, as well as altitude and regional characteristics. They use terms like fancy, extra, AA, SHG (strictly high grown) and SHB (strictly hard bean), among others, to describe levels of quality. Each country is different, but all appear to have a shared goal of grading quality. With so many green grading systems available, why did the SCA create its own?

In 1998, I began learning about different types of defects and their causes from my first mentor in the industry, George Howell, one of the pioneers of specialty coffee in the United States. We looked at pulper damage, blacks, triangles, insect damage and the elusive foxy. We didn't have a list or chart to reference, but Howell shared his knowledge about where the defects might have come from and what they were called.

At the time, while many green coffee standards existed, they were geared toward commercial grades. Specialty coffee was gaining traction, but it did not have a clear set of standards that differentiated it from commodity grade. Without a system, how could you identify great coffee? Clearly, there were cuppers and buyers who already knew the difference, but the SCA (then the Specialty Coffee Association of America [SCAA]) worked to develop a definition and provide a clear way forward, to create a common vocabulary and define the parameters for extraordinary coffee.

In the 1990s, the SCAA introduced the first Coffee Tasters' Flavor Wheel, and we saw the development of the cupping form and a green grading system—one that would evaluate the physical characteristics of green coffee and set standards for specialty grade. It appears there were a variety of influences, including organizations in producing countries, like the Brazilian and Colombian coffee federations, and the "C" contract.

According to Ted Lingle, executive director of the SCAA at the time the standards were developed and a key architect in the process, the GACCS was created in 2001 as a follow-up to the SCAA cupping protocol and form. From there, green defects were displayed on a poster with defect names and pictures.

In 2001, when I became coffee quality manager at Equal Exchange, I implemented a rigorous set of standards for the coffee we were importing. At the time, it was common to describe European Preparation (EP) in coffee contracts (and still is, in many cases). I discovered that EP meant clean coffee, but lacked a detailed definition. The GACCS had just been published in poster form, so I began with that. It was a good way to start conversations in our supply chain, but I wanted more definition to fully adopt the SCAA standards as our own.

Fortunately, in 2004, the SCAA Technical Standards Committee published a booklet to accompany the defect poster. It was a welcome and necessary addendum to the poster. The booklet provided a tool to support the SCAA and the Coffee Quality Institute (CQI) in developing what would become the Q grader program.

Using the GACCS

The GACCS is a detailed approach to identifying and grading green coffee, often referred to as the physical analysis of coffee. A 350-gram sample of green coffee is put through a series of tests to analyze the moisture content, bean size and imperfections, which are categorized into two groups: category 1 and category 2 defects. One full category 1 defect typically eliminates a sample from receiving specialty status. A cumulative score of five full category 2 defects does the same. (See chart on page 137 for more details.)

The defect assignment is based on appearance and categorized according to how the defect affects flavor. Once the coffee is roasted, there is an additional step to count the number of quakers. This system is detailed in the SCA's *Arabica Green Coffee Defect Handbook*, with a shortened version available in colorful poster form. The poster includes pictures and descriptions for each defect, as well as the possible cause, remedy and effect on the cup.

Despite the pictures and definitions, a lot of education still was needed. We were speaking a different dialect within the language of coffee that was not just theoretical, it was intended to be the standard for specialty coffee. Over the years, I have spent hours learning to use this clear tool and teaching it to everyone in our supply chain, including wet and dry mill managers, farmers, cuppers, export managers—anyone who touches the coffee.

Then something changed for me. At a specialty coffee seminar a few years ago, I heard one of my colleagues describe the GACCS as an "ideal," implying that it wasn't being used as a regular unit of measure for quality. I'm fairly certain my jaw dropped to the floor. Shouldn't a standard be a firm set of rules that guides business decisions? In order to build and maintain a common vocabulary, shouldn't we as importers and roasters be holistic in our approach to analysis? In theory, the defect count affects the cup flavor—or does it?

The Creation of the GACCS

There's a lot of overlap throughout the world of green coffee grading systems, with different equivalency tables and defects that are country-specific. The SCAA set out to develop a universal system, one that could work for many countries while differentiating

Farmers in Uganda learn about the importance of harvesting ripe cherries.

Beth Ann Caspersen of Equal Exchange (right) and the quality team from the Gumutindo co-op in Uganda introduce farmers to the SCA green coffee defect system.

specialty coffee from commercial grades. So how did the association choose the specific defects included in its system?

"The idea was to identify the most common defects that occur during processing," says Steven Diaz, commercial and quality director for Expocafe—an exporter for coffee grower cooperatives in Colombia—and a member of the SCAA Technical Standards Committee at the time the standards were developed.

"From a scientific perspective," adds Joseph Rivera, a coffee scientist with coffeechemistry.com and the SCAA coffee science manager at the time the system was developed, "those defects that are currently considered category 1 defects are typically those with objectionable compounds—dimethyl sulfide, butyric acid, acetic acid, etc.—and extremely low sensory thresholds."

Insect damage can be particularly mysterious. The GACCS divides it into two classifications: severe and slight. Severe insect damage is defined as three or more perforations in a single bean. Five beans with severe insect damage in one sample equals one full category 1 defect. If a bean has fewer than three perforations, it is considered to have slight insect damage. Ten beans with slight insect damage equals one full category 2 defect.

Why are insect-damaged beans divided into two categories? Aside from their appearance, what is it about severe-insect-damaged beans that places them as a category 1 defect while many other systems place them in category 2?

"Severe-insect-damaged beans carry adults, larvae and, most likely, mold development within the bean that affect cup quality,"

A sample of coffee drying on raised beds in Uganda.

Caspersen works with farmers at a washing station in Uganda.

Raised beds for coffee drying in Uganda.

Women sort coffee for defects on raised drying beds in Uganda.

Overripe cherries on a coffee tree.

Diaz says. "Slight-insect-damaged beans are usually in the initial stages of attack."

Flavor Blame

If a coffee tastes bad, shouldn't there be a green defect that correlates to that flavor?

The vast majority of defects can have more than one cause, and to make matters more complex, many defects can produce multiple defective flavors in the cup. For example, a full-black coffee bean (a category 1 defect) could produce any of the following defective flavors in the cup: ferment, stinker, dirty, moldy, sour or phenolic. However, an insect-damaged bean also could produce dirty, sour, moldy or rioy flavors. How do we know these defects produce these flavors? Is there science to support our assertions?

Most of the flavor descriptors for these defects are based on deep and entrenched knowledge within the coffee industry. Coffee tasting in some form has existed for more than 100 years. Becoming a coffee taster historically involved an apprenticeship, with detailed information passed from one generation to the next. The descriptions for defective flavors are based on this information, along with the experiences of the SCAA Technical Standards Committee members at the time the standards were developed.

There appears to be some science that correlates the physical defects with the flavor descriptions in the GACCS; however, it's relatively limited and difficult to access. Many coffee professionals have done their own testing—spiking cups and roasting specific defects to observe the taste attributes. Experiments in my own lab over the past 10 years have yielded inconclusive results.

Interestingly, one cannot assume that because you taste a defect in the cup, it will correlate to a defective bean. For example, I have cupped samples with phenolic flavors from green samples that were perfectly clean—no trace of black, fungus or hulls as the system might suggest. It's clear we still have a lot to learn and share about the correlation between green coffee defects and their impacts on cup quality, but this in itself provides a strong argument for counting defects and scoring sensory attributes of every coffee one is evaluating.

Who Uses the GACCS?

I have long believed in the power of a common vocabulary, so it made sense to me to adopt the GACCS, but I wondered if others use it consistently for contracts or purchasing decisions.

"When both the seller and buyer agree to a green coffee classification system, as well as the allowable defects for a green coffee contract, both sides of the transaction are fully aware of the quantitative measurement to define quality," says Spencer

Turer, chair of the SCA Technical Standards Committee and vice president at Coffee Analysts in Burlington, Vermont. "The system, or any system that is agreed to, removes any guessing and misunderstanding for the acceptable quality to execute a green coffee contract. Without a measurable standard or classification schedule, quality rating would be vague and ambiguous, quality could not be controlled, and consistency to the consumer would be impacted."

At Equal Exchange, as an importer and roaster, we include "SCA preparation" in our green contracts, which includes the physical and sensorial evaluations. We analyze both pre-shipment and arrival samples based on the GACCS and write detailed reports about our findings. Our goal is to be transparent and fair with our analysis, and to hold our suppliers accountable.

For years, I have thought this is what specialty coffee professionals are supposed to do—if it's considered specialty, it should adhere to these standards—but time and again I hear colleagues emphasize cup quality, sometimes without even analyzing green coffee defects. After numerous conversations with our suppliers about a holistic approach to specialty coffee quality, meaning both physical and sensorial, I wondered if my experience reflected the reality in the market. I was astounded by what I learned.

While I did not do a widespread industry survey, I did speak with about a dozen industry professionals, including exporters, importers and roasters. None of these professionals includes

Washing station managers in Uganda attend a green coffee sorting workshop presented by Equal Exchange in 2012.

SOME COMMON DEFECTS

Full Sour

Immature/Unripe

Full Black

Shell

Partial Black

Fungus

Washing station managers get hands-on experience sorting green coffee at a 2012 workshop at Nasufwa primary society in Uganda.

A density sorting machine in Colombia.

Clean green coffee (right) compared with defects removed by a green coffee sorting machine.

Caspersen sorts green coffee and discusses defects with women at the Gumutindo co-op in Uganda.

SCA specifications in green coffee contracts, though all say they include quality scores, sometimes noted as SCA points.

One importer told me, "Nobody grades specialty coffee (in the United States)."

I was baffled to learn that specialty quality for many people is one-sided, focusing only on cup quality. A few told me defects aren't a problem in their purchases because they buy such high-grade coffees, but they also admitted they never grade their coffee.

The standards are in place to provide clear guidance based on data and evaluation. Sorting coffee to specialty standards costs more—how much more depends on the quality of the cherry or parchment that arrives at the buying station. If the coffee is especially clean before it is put through the dry mill process, the cost may be minimal. Several professionals who sort based on the GACCS estimate it can cost from 5 to 30 cents more per pound to do so. If given the choice, are you willing to pay for it?

What's Next?

A lot has happened since the GACCS was established, and some wonder if the system needs to be updated. How will climate change affect the level and intensity of defects? Is this system truly universal for washed arabicas?

Diaz hopes for an expanded version of the defect booklet, "with more description of the defects and their variations," he says, and "more technical and detailed information of the causes and occurrences during processing."

Rivera would like to see a system developed for alternatively processed coffees, such as naturals, pulped naturals, semi-washed, double-fermented and others.

But as Turer notes, "Any changes to the SCA quality classification system for cup or grade will impact the determination of specialty quality and Q certification, and will financially impact the stakeholders of the green coffee supply chain. Changes of this magnitude are very serious, and are not being considered by the Technical Standards Committee."

While I would like to see the system updated to reflect the science currently available, first I would encourage industry professionals to use the existing system consistently.

If you don't use it, why not? ∎

. . . .

BETH ANN CASPERSEN *is coffee quality control manager at the Equal Exchange Cooperative in West Bridgewater, Massachusetts. Equal Exchange is a specialty food cooperative that sources coffee, chocolate, tea and other products from small farmer cooperatives all over the world. She is a specialized instructor for the SCA, a member of the Coffee Tasters Pathway Committee, a Q instructor, co-founder of Java Jog for a Cause and an advocate for women's rights. Contact her at bacaspersen@equalexchange.coop.*

AN OVERVIEW OF DEFECTS *in the* GACCS

The SCA Green Arabica Coffee Classification System divides defects into two categories. Category 1 defects are the most severe; one bean showing any of these defects (except in the case of severe insect damage, where five damaged beans are required) excludes a sample from achieving specialty status. Category 2 defects are less severe; these are counted and given a cumulative score, with a sample showing the equivalent of five full defects or more being excluded from specialty status. If a bean has more than one defect, such as the bean shown in the photo to the right (partial sour and slight insect damage), the sorter can count only one, so he or she counts the defect with the most adverse effect on flavor (in this case, partial sour).

The following brief explanation of common defects has been compiled from information in the *SCA Defect Handbook*. Find the official handbook at *sca.coffee*. See page 135 for photos of some common defects.

CATEGORY 1 DEFECTS

DEFECT NAME	# OF BEANS EQUAL TO 1 FULL DEFECT	DESCRIPTION
Full Black	1	Opaque in color.
Full Sour	1	Yellowish or yellowish-brown to reddish-brown in color. The embryo inside the bean (see photo, page 135) typically is dark or black. If the bean is cut or scratched, a sour or vinegar-like smell is released.
Dried Cherry/Pod	1	The dried pulp usually covers part or all of the parchment, sometimes with the presence of white spots or powdery residue.
Fungus Damaged	1	Yellow to reddish-brown powdery spots (spores), which can cover part or all of the bean.
Foreign Matter	1	All non-coffee items such as sticks, stones, nails, etc.
Severe Insect Damage	5	Broca beans, as they are commonly called, are distinguished by small (0.3 to 1.5 millimeters in diameter), dark holes, often on opposite sides of the bean. Three or more perforations = severe damage; five or more severe damaged beans = one full category 1 defect.

CATEGORY 2 DEFECTS

DEFECT NAME	# OF BEANS EQUAL TO 1 FULL DEFECT	DESCRIPTION
Partial Black	3	Less than half of the bean is opaque.
Partial Sour	3	Less than half of the bean appears sour. (See "Full Sour" under category 1 for description.)
Parchment/ Pergamino	5	Partially or fully enclosed in a thick, papery, white or tan husk.
Floater	5	Distinctively white and faded, giving the sample a mottled appearance. Will float when placed in water.
Immature/Unripe	5	Pallid, yellow-greenish color of the silver skin. The silver skin is tightly attached to the bean. Often smaller than normal beans, curved inward in a concave shape with sharp edges.
Slight Insect Damage	10	See description under category 1, above. Fewer than three perforations = slight damage; 10 or more slight damaged beans = one full category 2 defect.
Shell	5	Malformed beans consisting of an inner or outer part. One or both may be found; in some cases they will still be together. The outer section has a seashell shape. The inner section can be conical or cylindrical.
Broken/Chipped/Cut	5	Usually dark reddish in color due to the oxidation of the area where the cut/chip took place during pulping.
Hull/Husk	5	Shows fragments of dried pulp with a dark red color.
Withered	5	Usually smaller than normal beans and malformed, with wrinkles that resemble those of a raisin.

ROASTING EQUIPMENT

In Hot Pursuit

What Every Business Owner Needs to Know Before Purchasing a Coffee Roaster

By Willem Boot

• FROM THE SEPTEMBER/OCTOBER 2010 ISSUE OF *ROAST* •

PURCHASING A ROASTER is one of the largest investments you will make in your coffee business. If planned well, the roaster acquisition can give you a longtime, loyal friend with countless shifts of valuable production hours. The reliability of a production machine is priceless.

Yet businesses still tend to make common mistakes during the roaster selection process because they don't ask the right questions. If you don't prepare for the purchase with a proper plan, the consequences can be disastrous—such as purchasing a roaster and shipping it to your coffeehouse, only to discover that it's too big to fit through the door.

We all recognize the importance of doing due diligence prior to purchasing a house or a car, or deciding on an ideal location for a cafe. So why not set aside the time and resources to find the coffee roaster that will work best for your business and your budget?

Planning the Purchase

Those looking to buy a roaster must diligently prepare for the purchase by devoting sufficient time to inspecting different machines, using specific qualification criteria. If you want to prevent major post-purchase surprises, develop your own checklist of questions and issues that need to be addressed during the selection and procurement of a machine.

It's a daunting task to compare the specifications of all of the roasting systems on the market. This article doesn't contain recommendations for certain machine brands or models. Instead, it outlines some clear guidelines and tips that can be indispensable during the process of buying a new or used roasting machine so you can develop your own requirements for the purchase.

For the sake of keeping this article brief enough to fit in these pages, the article is geared toward those who are considering the purchase of a drum roaster. However, roasters who are looking into air- or wood-burning roasters can use many of the same tips to help make an educated decision.

To discover which roaster is right for you, be prepared to ask lots of questions. Take the time to quiz roaster manufacturers, other roasters and, most importantly, yourself. Your questions will fall into three general categories: business, technical and practical.

Know Thy Own Business

Buying a roaster is a major investment. Unlike a t-shirt, you can't take it back if you change your mind. Take a realistic look at your business and ask yourself some key questions.

What size roaster will you require, and what is your budget? One roaster can be five times the cost of another. Once the roaster arrives, what is the cost to install it, and who will install it? Closer tech support means that you'll have easier access to manufacturers.

Investigate additional equipment that you may need to buy to complement your roaster. A powerful roaster may require an equally impressive afterburner. Figure out how you will handle (and budget for) extra equipment before making a purchase.

When budgeting, figure in the cost of maintenance and labor. If you need to replace a part on the roaster, procuring a spare part requires not only cash but also a slowdown (or worse, a complete standstill) in production. The length of time you can wait between ordering and receiving a spare part may steer you toward certain manufacturers.

The answers to these questions will be unique to your situation, so take your time and make sure you are comfortable with your budget before you get serious about your hunt for a machine.

Get Technical

Next, you'll need to consider the technical aspects of the machine.

As a first step, ask the machine vendor for a technical diagram of the roaster. Make sure you're talking to the right person. With smaller manufacturers, the chief engineer of the company often owns the business, and this would be the ideal person to speak with. The technical diagram generally shows the combined product flow and airflow of the roaster. It should list which motors are part of the system and how all parts are mechanically interconnected. Once you have the technical schematics, you're ready to start asking about the specifics.

BUSINESS QUESTIONS TO ASK

- What size and type of a roaster do I need?
- How much does the roaster cost?
- If I outgrow it, what are my options?
- How much will it cost to crate and ship the roaster?
- How much will it cost to install?
- Does the manufacturer have a warranty? If so, what is it?
- Does the manufacturer have a reference list with roasters of a similar size?
- Will I need any other equipment to operate this roaster (afterburner, loader, etc.)?
- How much will it cost me to roast a batch of coffee (energy and labor)?
- What are my options for financing the purchase?
- What is my time frame? Some manufacturers take up to a year to fabricate a roaster.

Those considering purchasing a roaster should talk to other roasters—not only those who have dealt with certain manufacturers, but also those who roast or have roasted on similar machines. Roasters generally are all too willing to discuss what delights and irritates them about certain machines, reveal modifications they have made (or been forced to make to overcome shortcomings or achieve desired results), talk about maintenance issues and discuss the difficulty or ease in repair or finding replacement parts. Ask them what they would do differently if they could do it over again.

Some roasters may even be willing to let you run a few batches on their machines. Rather than relying solely on the testimony of a manufacturer, use other roasters as additional references to help make an informed decision.

Let's review a few key technical questions:

■ Describe the unique benefits of this machine. Why did you choose this specific design?

The best manufacturers know exactly how to answer this question. This doesn't necessarily mean that their system is superior, but at least it provides proof of their knowledge of the roasting system. A good engineer will have a plausible explanation for the design choices that were made in the development of the machine. In addition to speaking with the manufacturer, the buyer should also seek out another roaster who is using one of the company's machines. What are the pros and cons of the machine, from another roaster's standpoint?

■ How does the process of heat transfer differ from other brands?

The issue of heat transfer is at the core of fundamental roasting discussions. Most roasting machines use three different types of heat transfer: convection, conduction and radiation.

Convective heat is transferred by a continuous flow of preheated air. In order to make this work, the roaster must have a roaster fan that moves the air along the burners and subsequently through the bed of coffee. Increasing the speed of the airflow can significantly shorten roasting times.

The second type is conductive heat, which is transferred through the contact between the beans and the hot parts of the machine (the wall of the roaster drum and the veins of the roasting chamber). Some conductive heat also travels from bean to bean.

The third type is radiant heat. The radiation is emitted by the heavy, hot parts of the machine, like the face plate. To accomplish a more gentle radiant heat, some manufacturers make these face plates from cast iron.

Machines with relatively low airflow use more conductive heat transfer, though a roaster operator can increase conductivity by using slower relative drum speeds. Low-airflow roasters have the tendency to respond more slowly to changes in the applied heat. Simply stated, in this case it takes more time for the beans to register and react to the changed heat conditions. It's important to test drive your candidate roasting machine to determine the roasting style you prefer.

What is the maximum rated batch capacity?

This is often a tricky question because batch capacity can hinge on several variables, including installation and roast level. Potential buyers should verify the actual required roasting time and actual capacity with someone who currently uses one of the roasters.

What is the maximum roasting time per batch?

Roasting times longer than 20 minutes may produce baked flavors with a suppressed brightness and, at times, leathery aftertaste. Ideally, your candidate machine should have no problem completing a batch to the start of the second crack in 15 minutes or less. Most roasters can easily produce a faster roast, but keep in mind that defects such as scorching and tipping can occur when roasting beans too quickly.

What is the airflow of the system?

The airflow is generally expressed in cubic feet per minute (cfm). Airflow is important in a roaster for several reasons. Convective heat transfer occurs when hot air flows through the roaster. But after the beans have been roasted, good airflow enables the beans to stop roasting quickly once they're emptied into the cooling tray. Without proper airflow in the cooling system, beans will not stop roasting immediately and can reach a darker roast level than the operator intended. Poor airflow can be caused by dirty machinery, installation problems or other machinery that creates a pressure problem in the roastery.

The absolute rating of airflow is necessary to calculate the appropriate dimensions and design of an afterburner or other device for the cleaning of smoke and odors. Afterburner choice will also affect airflow. Additional homework may be required to be certain of your airflow rates after final installation of the afterburner.

How can I produce and repeat consistent roasting profiles?

Ideally, the roaster should have two temperature-measurement points—one for the bean temperature and a second to measure the environmental temperature. On top of that, roasters should have some way of measuring the actual applied energy during the roasting process. Nowadays, various brands include a gas pressure gauge that measures the actual pressure between the main gas throttle and the burners. In this configuration, this gauge is a good indication for the level of heat you're using to roast.

TECHNICAL QUESTIONS TO ASK

- How do I control the roaster?
- Can I roast and cool at the same time (separate blowers)?
- Why and how is your roaster different from your competitors'?
- Do I want a drum roaster or an air roaster? Can you explain the difference?
- What are the different control options for your machine?
- What is your drum made from, and why?
- What type of burner do you use, and why? What are the differences in the types of burners?
- Is there a difference between natural gas and propane (LPG) in the quality of the coffee?

Creating consistent roasting profiles can be an arduous task if you have to manage without these tools. Make sure that your machine supplier provides detailed information on the merits of automated profiling data loggers as well as full profile control systems. Data loggers are used to compile the time and temperature data during the roasting process to assist the roaster operator in profile roasting, while a profile control system uses electronic process control hardware to manipulate the burner, airflow and drum rotation speed to produce consistent, repeatable roasts. Again, your best validation is to ask someone who uses the brand you're looking into.

What are the unique features of the drum design?

Double-walled drums can help prevent scorching and tipping. Both of these roasting defects are undesirable as they can produce "off" flavors in the cup.

The drum's interior design and how the air moves through the drum can also impact the beans' heat absorption process. Some designs prohibit the beans from moving evenly throughout the drum, which can hinder the consistent development of flavor profiles. Ideally, the drum includes a set of mixing veins, which allow for a consistent multi-directional movement of the beans.

◼ Does the roaster have separate roasting and cooling blowers?

If the roaster works with only one blower, then it's generally impossible to roast and cool at the same time, which will definitely extend the cycle time per roast. Obviously, a dedicated fan will get the cooling task done much faster. For the sake of maintaining a consistent roasting performance, it's important to clean your machine's interior system regularly. Roasters are prone to developing residues of roasting particles, oils, tar and dust. Over time, these residues will alter the performance of your machine, specifically due to the fact that the roasting fan gets clogged bit by bit, which will reduce its output and—as a consequence—the airflow though the roasting system. Verify what types of blowers

are used and find out whether they, and other parts, can be replaced locally. Also, find out how you can get access to the roaster and cooler fans, and learn how to properly clean them.

◼ How long does the cooling take?

Forget about how long it takes to cool the coffee to room temperature. The most important job of the cooling system is to halt the roasting process (see the question on airflow on page 143). Extended cooling times may produce unnecessary loss of sweetness and undesirable bitter flavor notes.

◼ Is the machine UL-approved? If not, are the parts UL- and AGA-listed?

Buyers should ask this question to protect themselves from unforeseen surprises during the startup phase.

There are numerous cases of roaster operators who have been hurt by their own machines. Most common are "normal" occupational hazards like first-degree burns, which belong to the least serious category of accidents. Usually, there is enough time to respond if you accidentally touch the hot plate of the roaster, and more serious burns can easily be avoided.

Other reported cases are much more serious; for example, when a finger or arm gets stuck near the moving parts of the cooler stirrer arm. If the machine isn't equipped with an accessible emergency safety switch or clutch, this can potentially cause serious injury.

Inspectors can put your startup on hold if there is insufficient proof that your roaster complies with the electrical and gas certifications that may be required by local authorities.

Also take into consideration your state's regulated emission guidelines. If your machine does not meet the guidelines, you will not be allowed to install it.

Lastly, talk with other roasters to determine what machines work best based on the cup profile that you would like for your coffee. Those buying a new roaster should ensure that the burner has the capacity to produce their desired roast style. If you already own a machine and are looking to purchase a second roaster, make sure your new one will produce a similar taste style.

The Practical Perspective

Admit it—you've impulsively purchased a cool new gadget just because you liked the color or design. Avoid making a rash choice on a roaster by sticking to your budget and your list of priorities. And ask a level-headed friend to help talk through your options before you make a decision.

Remember the adage "measure twice, cut once" when shopping for a roaster. Figure out whether you'll be able to fit the roaster through the door of your coffeehouse or warehouse. Many otherwise intelligent roasters have neglected this step and suffered the embarrassing consequences. If you have a tight space, draw a map to show to manufacturers all of the hallways, turns and stairs that the machine will have to navigate to reach its new home.

How about the ergonomics? Roasting sessions can continue for many hours. During a production day, you and your machine should be able to collaborate in harmony. Ideally, the temperature displays and operational switches and handles should be located on one side. Preferably, the sampler should be mounted on this same side, and the sampler itself should be designed for a right- or left-handed operator.

Did the manufacturer address the risk of back stress as a result of lifting heavy machine parts and green beans? How many times does the operator have to bend over during the operation cycle?

Also consider how your machine will interact with its surroundings. Will the roaster interfere with traffic at your cafe or warehouse? Measure where you'd like to situate the roaster, and then compare those numbers with the measurements of the roaster itself—do the math once, twice, even three times to make sure you've got it right. Don't forget to consider the placement of your gas pipe. If it extends into the room, then your machine's position will need to shift as well.

PRACTICAL QUESTIONS TO ASK

▶ Can I install it myself?

▶ If I can't install it, who can?

▶ Do I need permits? From whom?

▶ What is the impact of a roaster on my fire and liability insurance coverage and costs?

▶ If renting a space, how will adding a roaster impact the rent? If my lease will be up soon, will I be able to find another space that will accommodate the roaster?

▶ Do I need to season the drum?

▶ How long will it take for me to feel confident in my finished product?

▶ How long will it take for me to be consistent?

▶ Do you offer training?

▶ Do you offer startup support?

▶ Is the roaster difficult to maintain?

▶ How do I get the roaster off the truck?

▶ Will it fit through my cafe door?

Looking at the big picture, adding a roaster may involve a permitting process to make sure your system is set up to code. Talk with your insurance broker about any changes to the business's fire and liability insurance, and discuss the roaster addition with your landlord—adding a machine may increase the landlord's liability and could impact your rent.

Create the Purchase Protocol

Once you have done your initial homework, it's time to get really serious by putting it all in writing. Establish a clear agreement with your supplier on the technical specifications of the roasting machine to minimize the chance of miscommunication.

When it's finally time to take delivery, inspect the machine at the supplier's shop if you have the budget to visit the manufacturer. While you're there, review step by step that all delivery criteria have been met. At this stage, it's still relatively easy to make

modifications on the machine. Once your machine has been installed in your shop, making technical changes will be much more challenging.

Used and Rebuilt Roasting Systems

Let's briefly discuss the selection and purchase criteria for a used or rebuilt roaster. Both options are usually, but not always, less expensive than purchasing a new roaster. Most new roasters come with a warranty and technical support, but you'll probably be on your own if you buy used.

Rebuilt roasters are typically older machines that have been disassembled, inspected and cleaned. Worn or faulty parts may have been replaced. Used roasters, on the other hand, are put up for sale in varying conditions. As with any fixer-upper projects, many used roasters will need some elbow grease to get them looking and working their best.

Purchasing a used or reconditioned roaster can be just as tricky as buying a used car. Never buy a machine that hasn't been tested thoroughly before purchase, and always inquire with other roasting companies about the reputation of the vendor. Ideally, you should talk to the previous owner of the used machine. Those looking at a refurbished model should find and speak with the person who worked on the roaster to learn about what repairs were made.

In the business of used roasters, not all vendors are knowledgeable about the actual process of coffee roasting or about developing roasting profiles. The better you do your homework, the less chance there is of getting your hands burned on the purchase of a mediocre machine that was either improperly rebuilt or that is operationally unsafe.

Buying Used or Rebuilt— Generic Roaster Checklist

The following checklist was specifically developed for production roasters, though most questions can also be used for the majority of sample roasters.

• Who is the seller? Did they actually roast with this machine?

• What's the history of the roaster? What year was it manufactured? (This can usually be found on the serial plate.)

• Are there any signs of roaster fires? Check for a warped cooling screen or for other signs of charred components. In general,

replacing a cooling screen can be a costly affair.

• When was the last time this machine was serviced? Who did the work? Can this person be reached to discuss what repairs were made?

• How is the general machine performance? Turn the machine on and listen for any unusual sounds. Locate the position of the roaster fan and the cooling fan. If you can inspect the fans, then open them and check the cleanliness of the fan housing. Does the roaster fan make a rattling sound? If so, then the bearings might be ready for replacement. Are the motors noisier than normal? If yes, then the bearings of the motor might need replacement, or the motor might need to be rewound. In most large cities, you can find shops that rebuild electric motors, but keep in mind it can often cost more to rebuild an electric motor than to purchase a new one.

• Check the electrical specifications of the machine. European machines usually come as 220 volt at 50 cycles, while the conditions in the United States normally allow for 110 or 208 volt at 60 cycles. Due to the difference in cycles, the European motor will run 20 percent faster if used in the United States. Obviously, this will have an impact on the airflow and the drum's revolutions per minute, which can affect the process of heat transfer and may even cause scorching and tipping. In addition, it can have a negative effect on the life of the motors and make parts more difficult to replace, as the mountings and shafts are metric, not standard.

• Check the gas system of the machine. Does the gas installation have a safety valve? Under normal conditions, the machine must have a thermocouple that registers the presence of a flame after the burner is turned on. If for any reason the flame blows out, the sensor will immediately register the change in temperature and send a signal to the valve to turn off the gas flow.

• Does the roaster have a safe electrical system?

• Most importantly, can you test-roast with the machine? In general, it's risky to purchase a machine that you cannot test

adequately. Visit the manufacturer or a nearby business that roasts with a similar machine, and roast at least two or three batches.

Final Words

Whether this roaster purchase is your first or your tenth, be assured that you will gain knowledge and become a more sophisticated buyer with each experience. Just remember to also use your palate while researching a roaster. Your roaster will likely become a longtime companion in your exciting quest for creating great-tasting coffees. With this concept in mind, it's essential to make the final choice for your machine on the cupping table. ■

• •

WILLEM BOOT *is president of Boot Coffee Consulting & Training, a company specializing in hands-on training courses for specialty coffee roasters. He can be reached at* willemboot@bootcoffee.com.

Grounds Maintenance

Care and Feeding of Your Roasters

by Boyd Guildner | photos by Cheryl Guildner

• FROM THE MAY/JUNE 2005 ISSUE OF *ROAST* •

IN THE COFFEE ROASTING WORLD, one of the most overlooked areas is roaster maintenance. Many roasters don't realize the benefits of taking pride in their roasting equipment the way they take pride in the proper way to roast a particular bean. Proper roaster maintenance creates consistent roast profiles, ensures coffee quality and prevents some of the most common roasting problems, including roaster fires. The lack of regular cleaning is also one of the biggest reasons for roast inconsistencies.

As a maintenance person, I often hear roasters say, "I don't have time to work on the roaster. I have a business to run." I am always amazed by this comment since without well-running roasters, there is little chance you're going to have customers to buy your coffee. And if you let your roaster go for too long, you run the risk of a roaster fire where you are not only compromising your livelihood, but other people in your building. As with most things, a little prevention goes a long way.

Maintaining a roaster is not difficult; it just takes a solid plan and someone who is willing to get the work done. A solid maintenance plan should include removing creosote from ducting and cooling trays, greasing the ball bearings, and cleaning motors, gearboxes and any other moving parts. The chaff should be cleaned out of the chaff collector every three to five roasts, and the whole roaster should be cleaned approximately every 150 roasts. The frequency of roaster cleaning depends on the darkness of your roasts, since darker roasts can create more oils.

Ducting & Cooling Trays

You might notice greasiness when you touch different parts of the machine; this is creosote, and over time, it can be your biggest enemy. Creosote buildup happens two different ways: when the beans are hot in the roaster drum and when they are cooling down in the cooling tray. Motors, gearboxes and cooling trays are affected by the oils in the coffee as the beans transition from hot to cold.

It is important to keep your airflow (ducting) clean. If ducting isn't cleaned regularly, creosote will begin to adhere to the sides of ducting, motors and cooling trays. This creosote buildup will not only cause your pipes to shrink (much like arteries with cholesterol buildup), it can also increase the risk of fires. In addition, airflow issues can be seen in increased cooling times. Imagine it as the difference between breathing air normally through your mouth and then trying to breath through a straw—not only do you have to work twice as hard, you're probably not going to get as much air in through the straw.

Ducting is composed of two parts: one that runs the exhaust from the roaster to the cyclone to the afterburner or out of the building, and one that runs from the cooling tray to the afterburner out the building. Some roasters utilize the same duct for both processes, while others have the processes separated. Creosote buildup in the ducting happens in two ways as well: hard and heavy creosote buildup from the roasting process and sticky, gummy, oily buildup from the cooling tray. The creosote in the pipes of the roaster is caused by the smoke generated by the mass of the coffee as it reaches its drop temperature. The environment temperature bakes this oil onto the sides of the pipe.

The oils in the cooling tray pipes are from the thermal mass of the coffee beans transitioning from hot to cold. Since there is no maintained heat associated with the smoke, there is no baking on the pipes. Consequently, you get the sticky oily residue buildup.

The creosote in the cooling tray appears softer than its counterpart in the flue pipe but is equally dangerous. In the cooling tray, airflow can be compromised by beans that get stuck in the cooling tray during the cooling period as well as the oils from the coffee as it cools. By keeping the holes on the cooling tray clean, you minimize the amount of airflow restriction.

It is also important to clean the fan on the motors (blow them out with air) to get rid of any oily buildup on them. When the motors are dirty, they have to work harder and hotter, which shortens their life expectancy.

The stir flex motor is another place to keep on eye on. It is prone to creosote buildup, since the beans are dropped into the cooling tray hot and have a greater time and closer contact with the stir flex motor as the beans cool.

There are many products available to keep your roaster clean. You need some type of cleaner that can be washed off of the cooling tray, motors and gearboxes.

The tubing (steel pipe part of the roaster) or flue pipe (insulated) should be cleaned with brushes to keep the creosote out of the pipe. If you have stainless steel tubing, you should use a stainless steel brush. Likewise, mild steel tubing requires a mild steel brush.

For complete cleaning for your ducting, you can buy rods or chains, depending on how your ducting is run. The rods attach to your brush and you take all the ducting apart and clean each piece and reattach with either silicone or clamps, depending on your tubing. On the brush with chains, you can have one person on the top of the tube and one on the bottom with the brush in the middle of two pieces of the chain. Each person pulls the brush from one end to the other. This allows for thorough cleaning without having to take everything apart. While cleaning, you should also look for any compromises in the ducting to make sure that there are no places where carbon monoxide could leak.

Bearings

It is important to clean the ducting and cooling tray and to grease the bearings. By greasing the bearings both front and back, you will keep them from seizing to the shaft that runs through the drum of the roaster. While bearings get worn and need to be replaced as the roaster ages, greasing will help prolong their life.

Grease is also where a lot of people get confused. You should always use the roaster manufacturer's suggested grease in your roaster. The higher the temperature rating on the grease, the more protection you have in the bearing. If the temperature rating is lower, then your greasing intervals need to be increased because of the loss of the grease in the bearing.

If you hear a grinding noise, you already have a problem. In this case, the bearings may be welded to the shaft, and you will most likely need to buy both new bearings and a new shaft.

Chaff Collectors

Another important cleaning issue is the chaff collector. Chaff is like burning paper, which can quickly exceed the 520-degree barrier and start a chain effect.

You need to keep the chaff cleaned out of the bottom of the chaff collector after every few roasts. The safest way to do this is to cool the roaster completely down and empty the chaff collector. You should always follow the manufacturer's recommendations for this procedure, as it may vary from roaster to roaster.

What a lot of people don't realize when it comes to the chaff collector is that the side walls of the chaff collector also get an oil buildup that needs to be chipped off and kept clean. A lot of the fires that start in a chaff collector are caused by a burning ember getting in there and starting the creosote on fire. Cleaning this out takes a putty knife or something similar that you can scrape the sides of the chaff collector with.

Burners

Burners also need some attention occasionally to make sure the burner orifices don't become clogged. Burners collect ash and particulate that block the jets and air holes, which consequently reduces efficiency. An indication that this is an issue would be longer roast times and varied cupping results.

If the burner has ceramic on the burner cups, it's a good idea to check them occasionally to make sure the ceramic is not cracked or broken. The problem that occurs with radiant heat systems is the ceramic plates can become cracked or clogged with ash just like the regular burners. An indication would be backfiring.

When cleaning and inspecting the ceramics, it is imperative that you are careful, as they are very delicate, and any mishandling can cause you more problems than you started with. If in doubt, call the roaster manufacturer for specific help.

The bottom line is that you should never discount the importance of keeping your roaster in the best shape possible. This will keep your costs down by preventing fires and decreasing unexpected maintenance problems, and it will keep your coffee quality high because you won't have any airflow or burner issues.

When it comes to your roaster, try to think of it as a classic car: A little knowledge, elbow grease and TLC is all it takes to keep you on the road to the best possible roast. ■

- -

BOYD GUILDNER *has been in the equipment maintenance field since 1972. In 1989 he chose a new career path, entering the world of coffee. He started as a maintenance mechanic with Allegro Coffee in Colorado and later started his own coffee maintenance company, Ponderosa Roasting Maintenance & Manufacturing in 1990. Guildner can be reached at boyd@ponderosamaintenance.com.*

PLAYING WITH FIRE

ROASTER AND CYCLONE FIRES can be a roaster's worse nightmare. The good news is that most fires can be prevented with a diligent maintenance schedule and the correct equipment. If a fire does occur, these two things, combined with proper staff training, can also decrease the severity of the damage.

FOILING THE FIRE

When it comes to proper ducting, people sometimes don't realize the importance of having a roaster maintenance person or roaster manufacturer help them buy the tubing and ducting for their roasters. While it's temping to take the cheaper way out, say by going to the hardware store or having an HVAC person spec the venting, you may not end up with the correct ducting for roasting.

There is something called "B" pipe which is used in furnace systems and which is rated at 450 degrees plus ambient. Inspectors or installers will ask you what your operating temperature is, and while it's true that your roaster operates in a normal environment in that temperature range, that doesn't mean B pipe is the answer. First off, B pipe is not designed for a dirty roasting environment, and, thus, has an aluminum lining that is not easy to clean. In addition, if you were to have a fire in that pipe, it could exceed temperatures of 3,000 degrees F, which is much higher than the pipe's rating system.

Stove venting might seem good enough for roasting applications—after all, you are just venting smoke out of it—but stove venting is not rated for positive pressure (positive pressure is created by a blower fan that pushes the air out of the ducting). Often, people don't understand this difference until they have had a severe fire that melts, ruptures or collapses the ducting and damages the building. The problem is that it is too late by then to do anything about it.

Many people think that just because an inspector signs off on their B pipe that they are okay and that people who are always spouting off about positive pressure pipe and insulated ducting just want to spend more of their hard-earned money. But in the long run, there is a right way and a way that will possibly get you by. You can either hope that it won't happen to you or you can pray to the roasting gods daily. Pay the extra money up front, and chances are you'll be glad in the long run.

DOUSING THE FLAME

If you do have a fire somewhere in the roaster, it's important that you—and your staff—know the proper way to put it out.

As mentioned, fires often start in the ducting. If the fire is in the ducting, use water on it externally to keep the temperature from exceeding the pipe's rated capacity.

Fires can also start in the roasting drum. Roasting beans can flash and start a fire when they reach approximately 505 degrees. If you do experience a fire in the drum, you want to keep the fire contained in the drum. Do not think that by dropping the roast in the cooling tray to quench that you will have less of a problem. This will actually add oxygen to the fire and make it worse. Instead, remove the trier from the roaster and put a water hose to the hole of the trier and allow the water to put out the fire in the drum. This will create less damage to your roaster and to your roasting environment since the fire will be contained in one place. That's not to say that you won't make a mess and that you won't have roaster damage that will need to be inspected. But it is safer than having the fire in the cooling tray.

If you have a fire in your cyclone, it is probably caused by lack of cleaning the walls of the cyclone. If you leave the chaff cleaning until the end of each day, you may be waiting too long in between cleanings and run more of a risk of starting a chaff fire. Once the fire is started, it then generates enough heat to soften the creosote buildup on the sides of the cyclone and you will have a very hot fire, sometimes in excess of 3,000 degrees. These fires can be put out by quenching with water, which will drop the temperature below the flash point.

In addition, make sure you know what your roaster manufacturer recommends to put out a possible fire. Some manufacturers recommend nitrogen or carbon dioxide. The idea is to remove the oxygen from the environment, thereby suffocating the fire.

As part of a maintenance routine, it is a good idea to train staff on both potential fire hazards and the appropriate response should a fire occur. Proper training and guidelines for everyone working in the roasting environment will ensure that these steps can be implemented quickly in the event of a fire in any area of the roaster.

Roaster Maintenance Checklist

This checklist is a general guideline to help keep your roaster properly cleaned and maintained. You should also check the roaster manufacturer's recommendations for maintaining your equipment and follow those guidelines.

Daily

- ☐ Clean out the chaff collector frequently during the day to decrease the chance of fire
- ☐ Keep cooling tray holes cleaned out so that airflow is not blocked

Weekly

- ☐ Scrape the walls of the chaff collector and vacuum out
- ☐ Clean all pipes and inspect for compromises that could allow carbon monoxide or smoke to escape
- ☐ Clean the cooling tray with cleaner to keep the screen free of oily buildup
- ☐ Grease the bearings if needed (see manufacturer's recommendations)
- ☐ If your roaster has belts or chains, inspect them for cleanliness and signs of wear

Monthly

- ☐ Clean motors and gear boxes with cleaner to remove creosote buildup
- ☐ Inspect burners for ash buildup on the jets or ceramic
- ☐ Check ceramic burners for cracks
- ☐ Clean the fans on the motors if needed

The Book of Roast **151**

PART III

ROASTING

THE SCIENCE OF COFFEE & COFFEE ROASTING

The Science of Coffee Roasting

A Brief Overview of Chemical Changes

By Joseph A. Rivera

• FROM THE MAY/JUNE 2008 ISSUE OF *ROAST* •

Inside the Bean

Ah, yes, coffee. To millions, it marks the start of a fresh day or the beginning of a stressful night. For many drinkers, coffee is simply a means of delivering caffeine into our biological system, while to others who savor every last drop, it represents the ultimate source of sensory pleasure. Comparing coffee's makeup with that of other agricultural products shows that it is perhaps one of the most complex food matrices in existence. Chocolate, for example, has an estimated 350 compounds, while wine contains a mere 150. According to researchers, the latest findings suggest that coffee contains an estimated 1,000 to 1,200 compounds. So what are all of these compounds they're talking about? Well, they are compounds such as carbohydrates, lipids, proteins, caffeine and many others that, through the roasting process, combine to create coffee's unique flavor.

Caffeine

Ok, so let's cut to the chase and discuss what first comes to mind when most people think of coffee: caffeine. Caffeine (1,3,7-trimethylxanthine) is an alkaloid that makes up an estimated 1.2 percent of arabica and 2.2 percent in robusta coffee. As with most alkaloids, caffeine is a bitter compound produced by more than 60 plant species, and believed to act as a defense mechanism against insects during cultivation. This primitive defense system has functioned well over the centuries and is part of the reason robusta coffee is so much more "robust." As insects attack the coffee cherry, they are deterred by the bitter taste of caffeine and move to the next crop. Since arabica is typically grown at higher altitudes where the risk of insect attack is reduced, arabica coffee has evolved to produce less caffeine that its robusta counterpart.

From a physical perspective, caffeine exists as a white powder with a relatively high melting point. As such, model studies have shown that caffeine readily survives the roasting process with miniscule amounts lost through sublimation. Though this may surprise many roasters, it is something that has been proven time and time again within the scientific community. But there is another source of inconsistency when dealing with caffeine, and that is the belief that darker roasted coffee always contains more caffeine than lighter roasts. Hmm, interesting, but which one is right? Well, actually both.

The belief that darker-roasted coffee has more caffeine makes perfect sense and stems from the fact that as coffee is roasted darker, more and more of the bitter compounds are generated during roasting. Since caffeine is also bitter, there is the assumption that darker roasts have *more* caffeine. But careful inspection of the bean shows otherwise. Let's take a closer look.

If we have 100 grams of green arabica coffee, we can estimate on a dry basis that the caffeine content would be approximately 1.2 grams or 1.2 percent caffeine (1.2g caffeine/100g coffee x 100). Now, let's assume we take this very same coffee and roast it to a light roast, thereby losing 10 percent of its initial mass in the process. Now we no longer have 100 grams of coffee, but rather we have 90 grams. Since the caffeine content has remained the same per bean, our total caffeine content now is 1.33 percent (1.2g caffeine / 90g coffee x 100). So in reality, although the caffeine content has remained the same in each bean, from a weight perspective, we see a slight increase. It just depends on how you look at the issue.

Lipids

Lipids play an important role in the overall coffee experience. Generally, most of the coffee oil is located within the endosperm of the bean with only a small amount deposited within the coffee wax on the outer side of the bean. Coincidentally, much of the chemical makeup of these oils is found in proportions similar to what we would find in vegetable oils. Arabica coffee has about 60 percent more lipid content than its robusta counterpart. Through a combination of genetics and differences in cultivation, this higher lipid content plays an important role in creating mouthfeel and delivering aroma in brewed coffee. Why? Well, turns out that most aromatic compounds are oil soluble.

Surprisingly, much of the lipid concentration in coffee remains stable and relatively unchanged during the roasting process. It sounds strange, but let's think about it. What do we use to cook fries, steaks and other foods? That's right—oils. And not just any oils, but often some kind of vegetable oil. As it turns out, many of these oils have a staggeringly high melting point, which allows them to act as a great medium. It also explains why the lipids in coffee may be so stable. Though lipid concentrations may drop, it typically occurs during the improper storage of green coffee whereby enzymatic activity and/or auto-oxidation of the lipid itself leads to off flavors.

Carbohydrates

Carbohydrates make up a significant portion of coffee's composition and are estimated at roughly 50 percent of coffee's total dry weight. Sucrose, otherwise known as table sugar, makes

> There is the belief that darker-roasted coffee always contains more caffeine than lighter roasts.

up a mere portion of this, at 6 to 9 percent and 3 to 7 percent for arabica and robusta, respectively. But besides sucrose, small amounts of monosaccharides such as fructose, glucose and mannose are present as well. As with all agricultural products, variations in the sugar concentration occur for several reasons, including the degree of ripening of the bean prior to harvesting. But typically, we can expect sucrose levels to increase as the degree of ripening progresses.

Carbohydrates are also commonly known collectively as "sugars," though not all of these sugars may impart a sweet taste. For example, fructose, which is one building block of sucrose, is

Table 1. Chart of Coffee Components

Component	C. Arabica (%)	C. Canephora (%)
Caffeine	0.9–1.2	1.6–24
Minerals	3.0–4.2	4.0–4.5
Lipids	12.0–18.0	9.0–13.00
Proteins	11.0–13.0	11.0–13.0
Chlorogenic Acids	5.5–8.0	7.0–10.0

Table 2. Carbohydrate Content in Green Coffee (% dry base)

Compound	Arabica	Robusta
Polysaccharides	0.2-0.5	0.2-0.5
Sucrose	6-9	3-7
Monosaccharides	43-45	46.9-48.3
arabinose	3.4-4.0	3.8-4.1
mannose	21.3-22.5	21.7-22.4
glucose	6.7-7.8	7.8-8.7
galactose	10.4-11.9	12.4-14.0
rhamnose	0.3	0.3
xylose	0-0.2	0-0.2

Source: Illy, A. Espresso Coffee, 2nd ed., p.151

actually twice as sweet as sucrose itself, while sugars such as arabinose and mannose have virtually no sweetness whatsoever.

In recent years, researchers have observed a correlation between the level of sugar contained in the bean and coffee quality. Generally, the higher the sucrose levels, the better the cup profile. So what might you guess happens to carbohydrates during the roasting process? Would you expect a rise or drop? Hopefully, by now, you should have it engrained in your mind that carbohydrates participate in yet another reaction. Any ideas?

That's right, the Maillard reaction. As such, we can expect carbohydrate concentrations to drop significantly after roasting. Even at light roasts, up to 90 percent of the initial sucrose concentration is destroyed, with some of the fragments producing weak acids such as acetic and formic acids.

Proteins

When combined, coffee contains both free and bound protein concentrations in the range of 10 to 13 percent for both arabica and robusta coffee. Although actual figures may vary, due to the degree of ripening and method of analysis used, we generally see a slightly higher concentration of protein in robusta. During roasting, proteins play an important role in the development of flavor since they're also involved in the Maillard reaction. Because of the high temperatures typically associated with roasting, a significant portion of the proteins is destroyed with very little carried through to the cup. As seen in Table 3 (page 159), all the arginine is destroyed, while substantial amounts of cysteine, lysine, methionine, serine and theorine are lost.

Interestingly, according to researchers the bulk of coffee's "bitterness" is not due to caffeine, but rather to compounds produced during the Maillard reaction. Caffeine, it turns out, only contributes to 10 to 15 percent of coffee's bitterness.

Chlorogenic Acid

Discovered in 1932, chlorogenic acids (CGA) represent a family of important organic acids found in both in green and roasted coffee. Coffee has by far the largest concentration of chlorogenic acid of any species in the plant kingdom, accounting for 6 to 7 percent in arabica and 7 to 10 percent in robusta. Interestingly, chlorogenic acid production in plants can be initiated by several factors including changes in environmental conditions, plant stress, and pest infestation. It is no surprise then that robusta, when grown in harsher conditions, typically has almost twice the concentration of CGA than arabica.

During roasting, 60 percent of the initial CGA is decomposed even at medium roasts, with the majority of the byproducts forming quinic and caffeic acid. So what effect would this have on the cup? More than you might think.

According to researchers, chlorogenic acids readily precipitate salivary proteins and increase overall astringency of the beverage. And this is exactly what happens when we take coffee to a darker roast. As levels of chlorogenic acid decrease during roasting, we also see a parallel increase in the level of quinic and caffeic acid—both of which contribute to astringency.

Excessive concentrations of quinic acid, as typically seen in darker roasted coffee, have also been associated with the unfavorable sourness we commonly pick up during cupping. Interestingly in coffee, CGA concentrations far exceed caffeine levels by 5 to 7 times, yet up until the past decade, much of the research on coffee has focused solely on caffeine.

Closing

For those who will embark on further study, it's worth mentioning that within the scientific community, published numbers on many of these components will vary between studies due to method of analysis and degree of ripening. We may never fully understand all the chemistry that occurs within the bean, but for now food scientists are making progress, one cup at a time. ◼

. . . .

JOSEPH A. RIVERA *holds a degree in chemistry and is the founder/ creator of coffeechemistry.com. He served as the director of science and technology for the Specialty Coffee Association of America (SCAA) and frequently travels the world lecturing on coffee science. He is involved in research and development across all sectors of the coffee industry. He can be reached at joseph@coffeechemistry.com.*

Let's Review!

> Why may some people believe that darker roasted coffee contains more caffeine? Is this indeed true?

> Why may lipids play an important role in coffee quality? What coffee species has more lipids?

> What compounds in coffee significantly decrease after roasting?

Table 3. Amino Acid Composition of Coffee (%)

Amino Acid	Arabica		Robusta	
	Green	Roasted	Green	Roasted
Alanine	4.75	4.76	4.87	6.84
Arginine	3.61	0.0	2.28	0.0
Asparagine	10.63	9.53	9.44	8.94
Cysteine	2.89	0.76	3.87	0.14
Glutamic Acid	19.88	21.11	17.88	24.01
Glycine	6.40	6.71	6.26	7.68
Histidine	2.79	2.27	1.79	2.23
Isoleucine	4.64	4.76	4.11	5.03
Leucine	8.77	10.18	9.04	9.65
Lysine	6.81	3.46	5.36	2.23
Methionine	1.44	1.08	1.29	1.68
Phenylalanine	5.78	5.95	4.67	7.26
Proline	6.60	6.82	6.46	9.35
Serine	5.88	2.60	4.97	0.14
Theorine	3.82	2.71	3.48	2.37
Tyrosine	3.61	4.11	7.45	9.49
Valine	8.05	6.93	6.95	10.47

Source: Parliment, T. Chemtech, 1995

The Science of Browning Reactions

By Joseph A. Rivera

• FROM THE MARCH/APRIL 2008 ISSUE OF *ROAST* •

Enzymatic Browning

Unlike coffee roasting, which requires high temperatures to initiate, enzymatic browning reactions occur spontaneously and at room temperature. However, like all reactions occurring in nature, a source of energy is required for initial activation. In the case of coffee, the activation energy is provided by the heat created by roasters, but enzymatic reactions require the presence of a specific catalyst, or enzyme. Simply put, an enzyme is a unique protein that accelerates specific reactions. There are literally thousands of enzymes in biological systems, and without them life would come to a grinding halt. The alcohol contained in those glasses of wine we enjoyed this weekend was metabolized by none other than alcohol dehydrogenase, while the protein in our steak was broken down into smaller, more digestible fragments by pepsin—a stomach enzyme. And the caffeine that we so religiously consume every day is metabolized by a broad range of important co-enzymes called Cytochrome P450.

Although the technical name may be elusive, enzymatic browning is a phenomenon that we've all experienced firsthand. The reaction is best illustrated by taking a fresh apple and slicing it in half. As we cut through the apple's cellulose tissue, cells rupture, thereby releasing myriad compounds into surrounding tissue. One important compound is an enzyme called polyphenol oxidase (PPO). Once exposed to air, the enzyme rapidly transforms colorless phenols present in the apple's tissue into a long chain of brown-colored polymeric compounds—and ultimately ruins our pristine white apple. Although the brownish hue may be unappealing to

the eye, contrary to popular belief, the reaction in no way creates toxins or endangers the health of those consuming it—as long as you're not bacteria.

Just like a Russian KGB agent carries a pill of lethal cyanide with him (in the event of capture by enemies), the apple senses when it's been attacked and immediately jumps into self-defense mode. But, how? By creating the very same brown polymers we discussed. According to researchers, the brown polymer created during enzymatic browning is highly toxic to bacteria. It's Mother Nature's way of protecting the plant from bacterial infection during its latter, more vulnerable stages of ripening.

Though the benefits of enzymatic browning remain limited to only a handful of products such as raisins, plums, figs and cacao, the reaction is, for the most part, a detriment and serious quality concern. Because of its spontaneous nature, enzymatic browning represents a significant economic loss within the fruit and vegetable industry. It's been estimated that at least 50 percent of all fruit and vegetable goods are damaged due to bruising/tearing

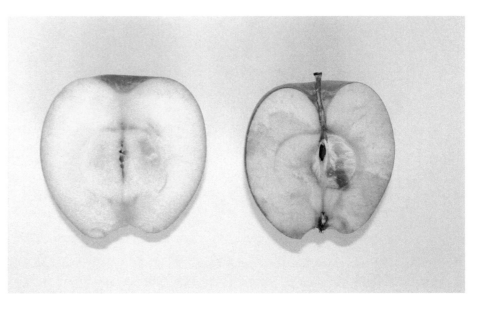

during transport to market. As such, scientists have developed relatively simple ways of inactivating enzymes and mitigating browning losses. Blanching, or essentially steaming, is useful as the heat deactivates PPO and prevents browning. Unfortunately, not all products can be subjected to this. Another method involves the addition of an acid, usually ascorbic acid, to the pre-oxidized product. Many chefs, for example, add a bit of lime juice to fresh guacamole during preparation. Turns out that the decrease in pH prevents the phenols from oxidizing and thus prevents, or at least delays, enzymatic browning.

So with all this talk about enzymatic reactions you're probably wondering at this point, "So how does this relate to coffee?" Well, it doesn't. Sorry. Enzymatic reactions are only important for products such as tea and cocoa, which during post-processing serve to create flavor changes. We only mention enzymatic reactions as a formality, since any discussion on browning reactions would be incomplete without it. For now, think of enzymatic reactions as the boring sibling of browning reactions. And for the typical caffeine-junkie roasters, that's not enough—we need more spark and complexity! This is where we begin our next discussion of nonenzymatic reactions. This next set of complex reactions will serve to explain the bulk of the chemical changes occurring in coffee during roasting.

> **Two of the most important nonenzymatic reactions in coffee are caramelization and the Maillard reaction.**

Nonenzymatic Browning

Unlike the enzymatic reactions we discussed earlier, nonenzymatic reactions are significantly different. In the latter, no enzyme is required, but the reaction does require the presence of heat, sugar and amino acids. As we'll discuss in greater detail, two of the most important nonenzymatic reactions in coffee are caramelization and the Maillard reaction.

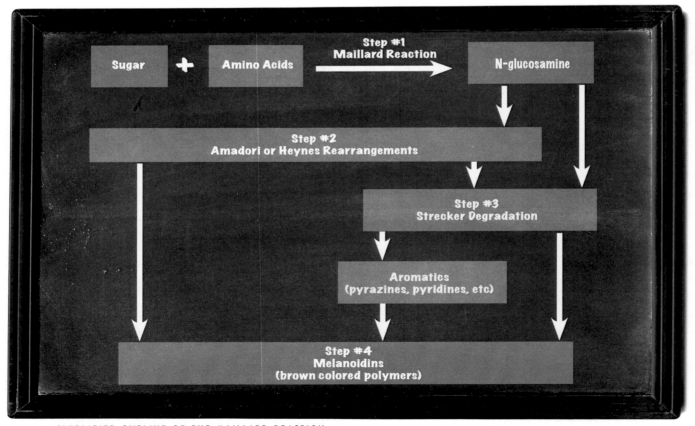

■ SIMPLIFIED OUTLINE OF THE MAILLARD REACTION   *several detailed steps omitted for simplicity*

• Caramelization

Caramelization is perhaps the easier of the two nonenzymatic browning reactions to describe. Simply put, caramelization is the oxidation or the thermal decomposition of sugars into color and flavors. Although any sugar can be caramelized, we typically see sucrose, or table sugar, as the sugar of choice for cooking applications. As sucrose is heated to 160 degrees C it slowly begins to melt, losing water molecules in the process and becoming a viscous semi-transparent liquid. As heating reaches 200 degrees C, the compounds in the molten sugar begin to rearrange, forming brown-colored caramel-like compounds and imparting its characteristic burnt caramel aroma. But this isn't your grandpa's caramel; the caramel created in this process is unlike the caramel candy we all loved as kids. This caramel is a bitter/burnt gooey compound with little to no sweetness, occasionally used as the topping on custard desserts. The caramel we eat is created by mixing sugar, milk and other flavorings, but it is produced in much the same manner as the caramel that occurs in coffee.

Depending on the heating conditions, manufacturers can shift the byproducts of caramelization to either maximize the formation of aromatic compounds or colored caramel-like compounds. In the latter condition, sugar is heated in the presence of ammonia to produce high concentrations of brown-colored compounds, typically used by the cola industry for coloring.

In addition to creating aroma and color, caramelization creates a broad range of compounds including organic acids in the process. We can clearly see this, for example, in the making of peanut brittle. In the latter stages of commercial brittle making, caramelized sugar is allowed to cool and thicken, at which time baking soda and flavorings are usually added. The baking soda then reacts with the organic acids produced during caramelization, neutralizing them to form carbon dioxide gas. This gas acts as a leavening agent, creating tunnels in the product and ultimately producing the characteristic "Swiss cheese" texture commonly found in candy brittle.

In coffee, a similar reaction occurs. As sugar is decomposed, it too produces carbon dioxide gas, which increases cell pressure within the bean, rupturing it and, ultimately, producing the audible "pop" we hear during second crack. What about first crack? Well, technically, the first crack is produced, partly, by the rapid increase in cell pressure by evaporating water—steam—during the roasting process.

Up to 90 percent of the initial sucrose is decomposed during roasting to produce a wide range of byproducts, including formic and acetic acid. Studies have shown that acetic acid concentration in model studies can increase up to 20 times its initial concentration, namely in the early part of roasting, then quickly evaporating in latter stages—due to its volatility. But acetic acid is unique in that it is a relatively weak acid, which affects perceived acidity and overall coffee quality. It's no surprise then, that with

Getting a Reaction

INTERESTINGLY, the Maillard reaction does not always require heat to initiate. To see one example of this, we need to go no further than our local beach. That's right, it turns out that much of the same chemistry that is involved in the Maillard reaction is actually used in the production of self-tanning creams. Though these creams don't produce a "real" tan, they do provide enough brown-colored pigment under the skin to impress a few beachgoers.

arabica containing almost twice the concentration of sucrose as robusta, we perceive a greater intensity of aroma and acidity in the cup.

In summary, caramelization serves to create color, aroma, acids and carbon dioxide during the roasting process. Since both caramelization and the Maillard reaction (discussed next) occur at different temperatures, what we ultimately get after roasting is a product that has byproducts of both.

• The Maillard Reaction

Of all the reactions discussed so far, the Maillard reaction is perhaps the godfather of all browning reactions. Though the reaction is typically associated with food, its true origin is actually deeply rooted in the medical field. In 1900, Dr. Louis Camille Maillard embarked on solving one of life's most complex questions: how does the human body create proteins? His early attempts to solve this involved combining isolated amino acids in vials and agitating, with no luck. When he combined reducing sugars (glucose) and subjected the same amino acid mixture to heat, he was stunned. As heat was applied to the mixture, the solution slowly changed from a clear liquid to a brown solution, giving off nutty/bready aromas—essentially marking the discovery of the Maillard reaction. Since then, hundreds of manufacturers have tweaked the reaction, and it now serves as a source for aroma development within the food industry. But it wasn't until after World War II—when soldiers complained that their powdered eggs were changing color and producing off-flavors—that the military seriously began to study the reaction in detail. Fifty years later, we're still unlocking the mystery of this complex reaction. Though the reaction still plays an important role in food, in recent years it's also become a topic of great interest in the medical field since it's believed to be involved in the aging process.

In essence, the Maillard reaction is the process whereby available amino acids and sugars combine in thermally processed food. We'll discuss details later, but it's essentially the reaction responsible for producing the aroma and flavor in products such as toasted bread, steak and coffee. Its been estimated that in steak and coffee alone, more than 600 compounds combine to create their complex aroma. And though extremely complex, what we'll discuss next is simply a layman's introduction to the Maillard reaction, as a comprehensive explanation would be outside the scope of this article.

In a nutshell, the Maillard reaction can be summarized in four major steps: In step one, amino acids combine with sugars to form several N-glucosamine compounds during roasting. Since these compounds are relatively unstable, they typically undergo a second set of reactions—Amadori or Heynes—to form several other intermediates (step two). Up until this point, all the compounds produced are colorless and lack any detectable flavor. But it's not until we reach step three, or the Strecker degradation, where a handful of N-glucosamine (those with double bonds created in

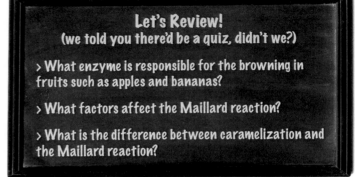

Let's Review!
(we told you there'd be a quiz, didn't we?)

> What enzyme is responsible for the browning in fruits such as apples and bananas?

> What factors affect the Maillard reaction?

> What is the difference between caramelization and the Maillard reaction?

step one) react with other amino acids to form compounds we typically associate with coffee aroma. Pyrazines and pyridines, which typically have maize/nutty/bitter aromas, and many other compounds are produced in this step. And finally, in step four, all remaining intermediates combine to form long chains of brown-colored melanoidins—the compound responsible for a coffee's color.

There are a number of factors that affect the Maillard reaction, including moisture level, pH and temperature. Since water is produced in the combination of amino acids with sugars, products with excess water activity actually impede the reaction. So for those products such as bread, powdered milk or powdered eggs, which already have a low water activity, browning occurs much more quickly. Also, the reaction accelerates in alkaline environments (pH greater than 7) and varies with the type of sugar and amino acid present. Though some of these factors may be out of our immediate control, the one thing we can control is temperature. According to

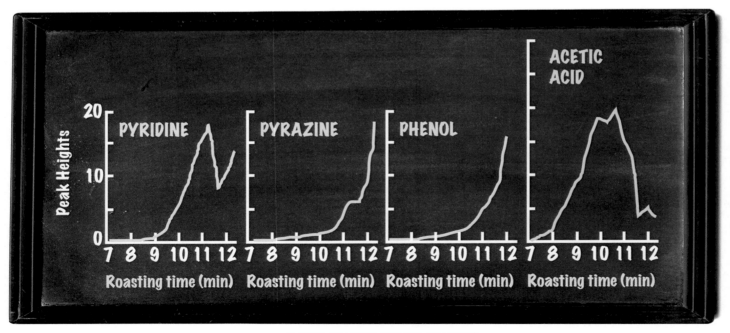

■ FLAVOR CHANGES DURING ROASTING

empirical data, it's been shown that the Maillard reaction doubles for every 10-degree increase in temperature. Interesting, but anyone who has ever taken a roast past second crack can easily attest to this. Why?

Here's the technical scoop: As the bean enters deeper roasting stages, more and more water is driven out of the bean, thereby increasing the concentration of potential reactants (much like when water evaporates in the ocean, increasing the salt concentration) and allowing more reactions to occur. Also, as temperatures elevate and changes in composition occur, several variables react to generate the flavor trends shown in the graph (page 164). We can see that as roasting progresses, a significant increase in the levels of pyrazine, phenols and pyridines is produced. Acetic acid increases in the early part of the roast, reaching a peak, then rapidly diminishing due to its volatility. There are literally hundreds of other reactions taking place simultaneously, but in the end, what does all this mean? It basically explains why we see a general increase in the level of aroma, body and astringency and a muting of acidity in darker roasted coffees.

So at this point you're probably wondering: "Is there a difference between caramelization and the Maillard reaction? They sound similar." It's true, they do sound the same, but they aren't quite. Here's a recap:

■ Caramelization does not require a nitrogen source. Remember, caramelization is simply a decomposition of sugar. This is unlike the Maillard reaction, which requires sugar and amino acid (nitrogen source).

■ Caramelization occurs at much higher temperatures than the Maillard reaction. The Maillard reaction can occur at room temperature, albeit very slowly, while caramelization typically requires much higher temperatures (over 150 degrees C).

■ Both reactions form melanoidins and flavor compounds. Although caramelization and the Maillard reaction follow different paths, we essentially end up with the same type of end products—color and flavor.

Thus far, we've only skimmed the surface in attempting to explain the chemistry behind coffee roasting. Though I'm sure many people now have more questions than answers, we hope that the material presented in this article will serve as a good starting point for further study. ■

JOSEPH A. RIVERA *holds a degree in chemistry and is the founder/ creator of coffeechemistry.com. He served as the director of science and technology for the Specialty Coffee Association of America (SCAA) and frequently travels the world lecturing on coffee science. He is actively involved in research and development across all sectors of the coffee industry. He can be reached at* joseph@coffeechemistry.com.

Roasting Science

Looking Closely at Your Curves

by Kathi Zollman

• FROM THE MAY/JUNE 2012 ISSUE OF *ROAST* •

WE, AS CONSUMERS, APPRECIATE CONSISTENCY. We like knowing that when we step to the counter and order a double scoop of mocha almond fudge ice cream on a sugar cone, we will be rewarded with the same deliciously cold, creamy treat we know and love—there are no surprises, and we're never disappointed. Our heightened anticipation is matched with the consistent flavor from the first taste to the last, and we celebrate the experience. With this in mind, why is it that when we step up to the cupping table and begin the day's sipping and slurping, the coffee we loved last week tastes dramatically different this week—not even coming close to meeting our expectations of flavor and delight?

To satisfy our curiosity about this altered flavor, we must go to the source of the difference, pinpointing the cause and correcting the variance to retrieve the much-appreciated flavor. This is a big task, but when armed with the right tools, roasters of all sizes can easily integrate a few key steps into a quality-assurance program. Diligence in record keeping and best roasting practices can assure that our favorite Yirgacheffe is predictably bright and sweet with a twist of lemon every time it drops out of the roaster.

The first step in understanding the dramatic differences in a coffee is to cup it. That may sound like a no-brainer, but many roasters never cup their coffees, or they may not cup consistently. Cupping plays a significant part in quality assurance and building consistency of product, providing information to the roaster about each nuance the coffee brings to the cup. This is especially true when the coffee is roasted to the same color, but the roast profile experienced some variance in the path from start to finish. A visual inspection reveals that all is well with the roast; look for even roast color, full bean development and no hot spots on the bean. In most cases, a cupping evaluation is the only way to identify a problem before the coffee leaves the roastery. Or, even better, routine cupping can identify the best roasting results ever. If a coffee if roasted to perfection, having documentation of how it happened is even more important.

Cupping can be a quick evaluation of the flavor character; roasters can create a cupping form that best suits their needs to

---

SAMPLE CUPPING NOTECARD

Carefully comment on the cup character as follows:

FRAGRANCE AND AROMA—Describe the smell of the ground coffee, both dry and wet. Some roasting taints can be found in the aroma and then confirmed when the coffee is slurped. Floral, spicy, sugary, medicinal, burnt, vanilla, meaty or fishy can describe the fragrance and aroma.

ACIDITY—Find words to describe the type of acidity in the sample as well as the degree of acidity. Is there a bright sparkle or harsh bite? Also note if the coffee is flat with a lack of sparkle. Describe the acidity as clearly as possible.

BODY—How does the coffee feel: thick, buttery, heavy, thin, light or watery? There are times when the acidity is so harsh that the body of a coffee can be masked.

FLAVOR—What does the coffee taste like? Is it perfect, or is there room for improvement? Does the overall flavor meet expectations? Good or bad, make easily understood notes.

record their cupping notes. Complete and thoughtful cupping notes will make it easier to find a problem if one should arise later, but cupping notes can be as simple as a pass/fail system. Although cupping protocols may vary, it is important that roasters implement a protocol that suits their needs and carefully follow the protocol during each and every cupping session to ensure integrity of the process.

After reviewing the cupping notes, we next look deeper to see where the roast profile varied. Roasters rely on records of past roasts to track many things. A well-developed roast log provides data for quality control, product development and cost controls, and can even help track down a problem with a specific roast. Roast logs can be efficiently completed by hand, by charting time and temperature along with other variables, or roasters can install software to assist with the logging of each roast. These logs will provide the information to track down the changes in the roast profile that are causing the inconsistency in cup quality.

Now, let's look at the curves and technique applied by the roaster. By reviewing roast logs and making comparisons, it is likely that there is a variance in the curve. The slightest change in the roast profile—as little as 5 degrees on either side of the desired profile—can be evident in the cup. Too fast, too slow, too hot or too cold, each change will affect the resulting flavor of the roasted coffee, positively or negatively. Chemists have identified hundreds of compounds in a single coffee bean; most of these compounds are chemically altered during the roasting process. These alterations can produce a range of flavor variables. A quick review of the Specialty Coffee Association (SCA) flavor wheel shows the colorful variety of flavors found in the roasted cup, most of which are developed during the roast process. Bright, fresh, fruity acidity; sweet honey or maple syrup; spicy, warm clove—these flavors are all there under the roaster's control. The evil cousins to these same pleasurable results are flavors described as medicinal, bitter, woody and rubber.

To illustrate the range of roasted flavors in a single coffee variety, several coffee roasters were asked to participate in a roaster challenge. This small army of roasting daredevils was asked to take their favorite roasted coffee and then perform two more roasts, intentionally risking the results. The roast profile was drastically altered to obtain the resulting changes. Roasters were challenged to roast faster, slower and longer—breaking away from the preferred roast profile. These roasting facilities do not have access to scientific analytical equipment to measure the results of the roast variations, making this a very practical hands-on type of experiment. The results, however, were so obvious that an HPLC, or high-performance liquid chromatography, wasn't required to identify the resulting chemical changes. (In a food lab setting, tools like the HPLC are used to separate the mixture for the purpose of identification and quantification of the components found in each of the liquid coffee samples.)

Simply cupping the coffees revealed both great and awful roasting results. Interestingly, when these profiles were repeated and cupped in a blind cupping, the cupping volunteers (consumers) were surprised to learn that there was only one coffee on the table. The differences in flavor, body and aftertaste were so dramatic that they assumed there were several coffees.

Technique #1
"I forgot to turn on the heat"

This is a surprisingly common technique that occurs most often when roasters are distracted and forget to turn the heat on, or up, after the green coffee is dropped into the roaster. Phone calls and texting are common causes for practicing this technique; the interruption of answering the phone takes the operator away from the task just long enough that the heat is forgotten. Then, about halfway through the roast time, full heat is applied, resulting in what is referred to as "catching up." The coffee turns the correct color and reaches the final temperature in the right amount of time. The S-curve for this profile would appear flat in the first half of the roast with little increase in bean temperature, with a sharp climb in the second half of the roast. The point of equilibrium was 150 degrees F; the slow start also produced a noticeably quiet first crack as a portion of the free moisture in the bean evaporates. The bean appeared to be well developed and had a slight oil sheen to it.

Common cupping comments: Light fragrance/aroma, little to no sweetness, flat acidity and a chalky alkaline aftertaste.

Technique #1 Roasting Curve
Time vs. Temperature

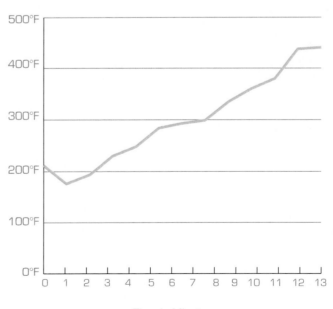

Time in Minutes

An exaggerated slow start to a roast with an extreme and aggressive finish did not produce a favorable cup result. When roasters experience a flat, chalky-tasting coffee, it could be linked to an extreme profile like the one experienced here.

Technique #2
"I have to roast a lot of coffee"

Many roasters feel the need for speed. Time is indeed money for any roasting company, and the more batches that are produced per hour, the better. Or, in some cases, the faster the work is finished, the sooner the roaster can go home. The fast-roast exercise was completed by dropping the coffee into a hot roasting environment at full heat. The application of full heat pushed the roast to completion in half the time of the control roast profile. The roasted coffee was dropped at the same temperature and looked pretty much the same as the other test roasts. A closer visual inspection revealed several scorch marks and some blowout marks from the extreme-heat environment.

The cupping results did not bode well for the hot-and-fast roast technique. The aromatics were pleasant and berry-like, more apparent than in Technique No. 1, but the attributes were less flattering as the cupping proceeded for this sample. One cupper experienced a severe case of "bitter beer face" after the first slurp, not expecting the cup to be so astringent and medicinal. The cup produced no sweetness, with harsh acidity, herbal flavor, very light body and a lasting aftertaste of dirt.

The fast roast produced an undeveloped-tasting coffee, making it difficult to identify what coffee was in the cup. The sweet

caramel notes did not appear, and the fruit acids were masked by the harshness. Though production is nearly doubled using this technique, the coffee was very bitter and unpleasant.

Technique #3
"My roaster is too hot"

This roast technique involves a highly heated drum combined with minimal heat application to slow the roast down, which makes the roast appear to be controlled. This technique employed high initial heat with a point of equilibrium of nearly 250 degrees F and low heat application to prevent the coffee from gaining momentum and roasting too quickly. The heat was maintained at about 50 percent until first crack was reached; at this time, maximum heat was required to hit the desired time and final temperature of the roast profile. First crack was light with minimal noise. As with the previous two techniques, the coffee looked fine, with no reason to assume otherwise. The profile has a bit of an S-curve to it, and the prescribed time and temperature were reached.

Cuppers' notes included a range of descriptions for this technique. Aromatics included marshmallow and toasted nuts, even warm brown sugar. Other notes: a hint of sweetness, bittersweet chocolate, moderate acidity, slightly skunky by one cupper, aftertaste was lingering and slightly ashy. The body of this coffee was considered moderate rather than light, as in the first two techniques.

This was not a perfect cup as evaluated by the panel, but this technique did develop some of the sweeter characteristics of caramel and chocolate of the Maillard reaction. There was some

Technique #2 Roasting Curve
Time vs. Temperature

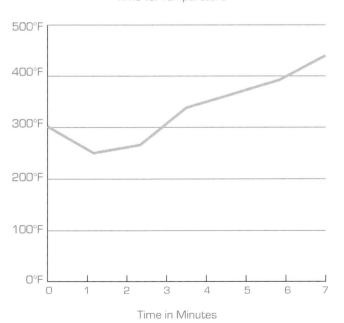

Time in Minutes

Technique #3 Roasting Curve
Time vs. Temperature

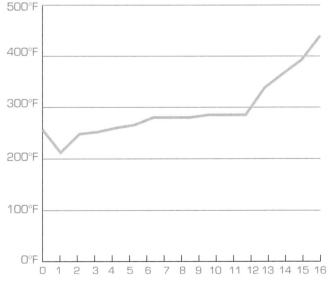

Time in Minutes

improvement over the other samples, but it was still difficult to identify the coffee in the cup and even more difficult for the panel to accept that this was the very same coffee cupped in the previous round.

Technique #4 | "Can it get any worse?"

With this technique, the roasters were challenged to roast out everything good about the coffee. Can a roaster take a remarkable sweet and bright coffee and turn it into something that even the most skilled cupper can't recognize? The answer is simple: Yes. This technique starts out very hot, and then all heat is pulled as the beans dance around in the roaster. There is enough residual heat to keep the roast moving forward and not stalling out. One-third of the way into the roast time frame, the heat is introduced at 50 percent; a very dull first crack follows. Then at two-thirds time, full heat is applied to bring the roast in on time. The roast finished at the right time and the correct temperature. Good news for the roaster: the roast log looks great, the coffee has a dull look to it but otherwise looks okay—not too bad at all. The proof will be in the cupping. The S-curve looks slightly like a stair-step.

Cuppers' comments were not positive for this technique; the notes were blunt and pulled no punches. The aroma of the coffee was compared to burnt peat moss, compost and bitter dirt. After the break, one cupper noted a hint of roasted peanuts. No sweetness was found, flavor was nutty and slight. No acidity; the coffee was scored as flat, all sparkle was roasted out. Aftertaste was lingering compost, and body was described as watery by all cuppers.

This radical S-curve technique brought out the worst in this coffee, taking a very respectable sweet, bright and hard bean and transforming it into brown water that wasn't palatable. Yes, it really was that awful. This technique produced undesirable results and should be avoided.

Roasting, or the application of energy, is what changes green coffee from a plain-looking, slightly fragrant bean to a desirable, complex, aromatic bean. The flavors are waiting to be developed and experienced. The changes the coffee goes through during roasting are both physical and chemical in nature. These changes are complex and occur at different stages along the roast path. Beyond the obvious color change from green to rich brown, other physical changes are observed. Most roasters have experienced first crack, occurring at around 385 degrees F; here, the coffee pops, sounding similarly to popcorn, and the coffee nearly doubles in volume in this phase. Other chemical changes are increasingly complex and occur within the bean. Optimum roasting conditions for these changes result in the formation of desirable coffee attributes.

Changes occurring during the roast are extremely complex and require a food chemist's knowledge to decipher. A very simplified model would identify the major changes as follows:

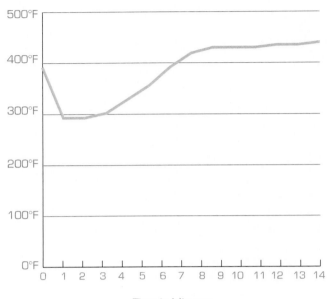

Technique #4 Roasting Curve
Time vs. Temperature

Time in Minutes

■ Loss of water content—Green coffee has a moisture content of 10 to 12 percent; water is lost in the early stage of the roast, in the Maillard reaction, and finally during the dry distillation phase of the roast.

■ Loss of weight—The darker the roast, the higher the loss of dry mass, ranging from 10 percent in medium roasts to near 20 percent in darker roasts.

■ Decomposition of chlorogenic acids—Nearly 10 percent of the coffee bean's weight is made up of chlorogenic acids, a bitter tasting group of acids. When chlorogenic acids break down during roasting, two byproducts are quinic acid and caffeic acid, both known for bitter and astringent qualities. The entire CGA group is susceptible to change during roasting; 50 percent of the CGAs are destroyed and 80 percent are decomposed by the dark roast profile.

■ Reconfiguration of sucrose—Nearly all the simple sugars are lost during the roast process, resulting in water and carbon dioxide, and flavor, aroma and color in the Maillard reaction.

■ Decreased concentrations of amino acids and proteins—Proteins, amino acids and sugar combine in the Maillard reaction, resulting in some of the most enjoyable aromas and flavors found in roasted coffee. Caramel and chocolate flavors are considered to be a result of the Maillard reaction.

Simplified, yes, but the basic premise is achieved. With the hundreds of compounds developed during coffee roasting, there are also a few compounds that remain stable and unchanged. Lipids, salts, caffeine and a group of carbohydrates escape change in roasting. There is plenty of room for error, but also room for great success for coffee-roasting enthusiasts wanting to take the rather bland green bean and roast it to something wonderful, unlocking all the secret flavors and textures hidden within the walls of the bean.

Managing roasting techniques and practicing cupping as a part of a quality-assurance program will assure the consistency we all appreciate and eliminate most of the surprises. An untested coffee shouldn't leave the roastery if there is even the slightest chance that it could vary from the best profile. If the favorite Yirgacheffe coffee from last week is not the same lemon-sweet, sparkling coffee this week, a quick review of the roast log will help isolate the potential problem. Too much heat, too large of a batch size, not enough heat—there are so many ways for trouble to brew.

Roasters need to become experts at cause and effect; if something negative is happening, what can be the cause (or causes)? Use the extreme roast techniques illustrated here as a reference point for corrective changes to the roast profile. For example:

■ If the coffee tastes flat, not quite as bright as you remembered it being, look at the first portion of the roast. If the curve is flat with little temperature increase before it starts to climb, the acidity could be flattened out and the bright sparkle will be lost. Some loss of aromatics might also be noted in this scenario.

■ If the sweet coffee has lost its sweetness and tastes bitter and harsh, look at the point of equilibrium and the application of heat. These characteristics can be associated with too much heat too soon and too fast of a roast. These beans might also appear to be unevenly roasted.

The four roasting techniques described are exaggerated but also very real, with each one taken from an actual roasting situation. Taking roasting shortcuts typically results in a variation in the final product, even when it visually appears to be identical.

Consistency in product is essential to customer satisfaction and retention, wholesale or retail. Creating a consistent product requires record keeping and a quality-control protocol that becomes the rule, not the exception. There are literally hundreds of opportunities for the coffee to be amazing, so roasters shouldn't leave it to chance. Take time to control the outcome with proven roasting techniques for each coffee and be accountable to the practices. The cupping table results will support the sound roasting practices, and you can be confident that when your customers place an order for their favorite coffee, the beans will meet or exceed their expectations. ■

KATHI ZOLLMAN, assistant director of specialty green coffee sales at Coffee Holding Company, is a frequent presenter at a variety of roaster education venues. She has shared coffee-roasting skills at Roasters Guild events, the annual SCAA Conference, Coffee Fest and multiple regional roaster gatherings. Specializing in blending, sensory skill-building, and profile roasting and manipulation, she continues to be a student of all things coffee.

The Heat is On

A Roaster's Guide to Heat Transfer

by Terry Davis

• FROM THE MAY/JUNE 2009 ISSUE OF *ROAST* •

God grant me the serenity

to accept the things I cannot change;

the courage to change the things I can;

and the wisdom to know the difference

THE SERENITY PRAYER seems tailor-made for the task of controlling and understanding the process of roasting coffee, especially when the discussion turns to heat and heat transfer. Conduction, convection and radiation—the three forms of heat transfer—are deceptively simple scientific concepts that underscore some of the more fractious debates within the coffee roasting industry. In our current age, when scientific terms are often used and misused to prove or disprove diametrically opposed points of view, these three terms are at the heart of two of modern roasting's most fundamental debates, one practical and the other very much philosophical.

The practical debate centers on how to control the rate of heat transfer in the roasting process or, more simply, how to control the roast itself. This debate is at the base of the more specific drum versus air question, as well as any number of smaller arguments about what tools are the most necessary and return the best value for the investment, which manufacturer's equipment has the perfect balance between differing types of heat, and other niggling controversies. Many of these debates do nothing more than serve to distract us from the practical task at hand—controlling the roast.

The philosophical debate is simply whether the act of coffee roasting is an art or a science. And like many modern philosophical debates, both sides tend to use science, specifically the science of heat transfer, when making their case. Furthermore, the absolutists on both sides seem to be the only ones with an opinion, making it difficult for the rest of us to find common ground, to gain a better understanding of what we need to know and, more importantly, how that knowledge pertains to our own distinctive roasting operations.

Since most of us already have our roasting equipment, let's set this debate aside and assume that what we're really attempting to do is to gain better control of the roasting process within our own operations. Better control will help us create a better and more consistent product in a much more repeatable, and hopefully in a more efficient, manner. Better control requires a basic working understanding of the three types of heat transfer—conduction, convection and radiation—and how they work within a drum roaster. In short, as roasters we are interested in the application of science, not necessarily in the science itself.

Conduction

Conduction is the transfer of heat from direct contact between the molecules of a hotter substance to a cooler one. If you were to accidently touch the end of the trier to your nose while attempting to smell your coffee, and burn your nose, this would be the result of conducted heat: the hotter molecules of your trier directly transferring heat to the cooler molecules of your skin. In drum roasters, we have three potential sources of conducted heat: the drum, the faceplate and the beans. There are those who would argue that the metal of a hot cooling tray is also a potential conductor, but for this to occur the sides and/or bottom of the tray would need to be hotter than the coffee itself. And while warm cooling trays can lengthen cooling times, they should never be hot enough to conduct heat directly to the coffee.

The rate and ratio of conduction in a drum roaster is initially affected by drum preheat temperature and load mass.

Convection

Convection is the transfer of heat through currents in a liquid or gas. In the case of coffee roasting, the transferring substance is air and the receiving substance is coffee. There are two major types of convection: natural convection and forced convection. Natural convection occurs as our air heats up, causing density changes; as air grows hotter, it gets lighter and rises, while the denser, cooler air falls. This flow then allows heat to transfer through the natural movement of buoyancy. Forced convection is heat transferred through currents that are moved by an outside force, such as a pump or fan. Forced convection is a quicker, more efficient method of heat transfer than natural convection.

In most modern drum roasters, approximately 80 percent of the heat transference is via forced convection. In air roasters, the percentage is significantly higher. Air roasters force air through the roasting chamber via positive pressure (blow), and drum roasters use negative pressure (suck). Either way, when roasting personnel discuss convection in the roasting process, it is forced convection to which they are referring.

THREE IMPORTANT THINGS TO REMEMBER REGARDING TOTAL ENERGY

1 Coffee roasting is a dynamic process that changes throughout the course of the roast.

2 There is infinitely more energy later in the process than earlier.

3 None of the forms of heat transfer is independent of the others.

The rate and ratio of convection in a drum roaster is directly affected by airflow and energy supplied by the burner. The higher the airflow and the higher the energy input from the burner, the faster the roast.

Radiation

Radiated heat is thermal radiation that is defined as electromagnetic waves, and it occurs naturally between two bodies of differing temperatures. It needs no carrying medium, unlike conduction and convection, and travels at the speed of light. A substance's ability to accept and/or throw off radiated heat is affected by its color, temperature, density, surface area, finish

and geographical orientation to other thermal-producing bodies. In short, radiated heat is the most complex type of heat transfer for laymen to understand, and in the case of coffee roasting, very difficult to measure or to control. For roaster operators, the important thing to remember about radiated heat is that it exists, period. You can neither measure it nor control it, so realize it's there and then focus on the types of heat you can both measure and control.

There is, however, some confusion over radiant heat or infrared burners in drum roaster applications. Even using infrared burners, it is still the conduction of the drum and the beans, plus the forced convection of the air, that is of primary concern to the operator.

The rate and ratio of radiation in a roaster is an unknown.

It Is About Total Energy

Drum, Air, Bean

Air, Drum, Bean

Bean, Drum, Air

These are the three sources of heat over which you, as a roaster, have some level of control. The little mantra above represents the periods of the roast at which each type of heat is at its most influential. At the beginning of the roast, the amount of stored energy in the drum—represented by drum or preheat temperature—is at its most important and potentially most damaging to the bean. Air or convection is the dominant form of heat transfer throughout the roast, but air is also the all-important driver for the body and flavor formation portion of the roast. Toward the end of the roast, the coffee beans themselves become an important source of energy and can actually become the dominant way that heat is transferred in some roasts and/or roasters. At the end of the day, however, all of the above forms of energy play their part in the process. As the roaster, it is your job to begin to gain a better understanding of each source of heat, and then exercise that knowledge of each within your own equipment to better control your roasting. This is what the concept of total energy is about.

Strategies For Gaining Control of the Roast

⬤ Conduction (Drum/Faceplate to Bean)

Many roasters believe that they have little or no control over drum-to-bean conduction. This simply is not true. What is true is that you only truly have control over this type of heat transfer at the beginning of the roast. Once a roast has begun, there is little you can do to affect this type of heat transfer. But, at the beginning of the roast, there is plenty that you can do. Controlling drum-to-bean conduction is all about preheat temperatures.

Roasters should set and follow preheat temperatures. Preheat

temperatures represent stored energy. The higher the preheat temperature, the hotter the roaster, the more energy is stored in the drum and the faceplate, and the more energy can be transferred via conduction. By being consistent in your preheating, you will be starting every roast with approximately the same amount of stored energy, allowing you to roast in a more consistent manner.

For partial batches, it is absolutely imperative that you lower your preheat temperatures if you wish to follow a similar profile as when you are roasting a full batch. Less coffee (mass) requires less preheat energy—pretty simple. Partial-batch preheat temperatures can easily be determined with a little experimentation; just take note of the lowest reading via your bean probe after the coffee is dropped in the drum. You want this point of equilibrium (sometimes called "turning point") to be the same, or nearly the same, regardless of batch size. If, when roasting partial batches, you see that the point of equilibrium is above that of a full batch, then lower your preheat temperature the next time you roast this size of batch. Eventually, you will be able to determine the correct preheat temperatures for the varying load size of your roaster. Remember this when roasting partial batches in drum roasters: It is always easier to add energy than to take it away once your roast has begun.

⬤ Conduction (Bean to Bean)

Through the majority of the roast cycle, you have two sources of heat energy—the drum and the air. Just before you hear first crack,

> **SYMPTOMS OF TOO MUCH CONDUCTIVE HEAT (DRUM TO BEAN)**
>
> - **Tipping**
> - **Uneven roasting/too fast**
> - **Mottled/scorched beans**

you have a third source of energy—the coffee beans themselves.

As the coffee approaches first crack, it begins to go exothermic and throws off heat, hence the sound associated with the cracking of the bean. Sound is a form of energy, and the cracking of the bean signifies that energy is being released. If this energy is not accounted for in the overall energy equation, then the roaster risks losing control of the profile, or the roast. There are three strategies for taking control of the roast at this point: adjust the burner down or off, increase airflow, or both. In essence, you are manipulating the rate of convection in order to control the total energy and hence the profile of the roast.

As you approach the end of the roast, you must be aware of the possible consequences of bean energy once again. The faster and harder you approach the termination of the roast, the more kinetic energy will need to be dissipated by the cooler. In other words, the more aggressive your profile curve is at this point, the harder it will

> ### SYMPTOMS OF TOO MUCH HEAT AT FIRST CRACK (BEAN TO BEAN)
>
> • **Uneven roasting/too fast**
>
> • **Unusual amounts of smoke**
>
> • **Moving almost immediately from first to second crack**

be to stop the roast at your desired termination temperature. This can become especially critical if you are operating in a building that is not climatized, in an area where there are significant swings in temperatures throughout the year. Additionally, the darker the

roast, the more energy is available to push the coffee past your desired stopping point. This potential problem can be handled in the same manner as you deal with gaining control at first crack: adjust the burner down or off, adjust the airflow, or both. By "slowing down" or reducing heat at the end of your roast, you will gain more control and use less energy as well. Once again, you are manipulating the rate of convection to lessen the impact of the energy of the beans themselves.

Note: A well-functioning cooling system is critical for gaining control of roast profiles. Many a darker-roast coffee has been, and still is being, ruined by inadequate or ill-functioning cooling systems.

Convection

Convection is the cornerstone of the roasting process for both drum and air roasters. It is the most dominant, the most easily understood, the most measurable and the most controllable. Once again, forced convection is heat carried by currents created by a fan or blower. You can change the rate of convection by changing the airflow, changing the energy output of the burner, or by a combination of the two. Unlike all forms of conduction in the roasting process, it is possible to make adjustments in the rate of convection that can have near-immediate effects on your roast profile. Although you cannot truly read convection, you can begin to get a handle on its effects by reading the drum environment temperature along with a bean probe, or through the use of a real-time data logger.

Convection is truly a modern roaster's friend. A high rate of convection means coffee is roasted more evenly, more cleanly—as most smoke and chaff is pulled away from the coffee—and each roast is more controllable and repeatable. The trick is finding the technique that works best for you in your installation.

Convection is the most dominant and the most controllable form of heat transfer and, as such, it is the place to start in gaining better control.

Working through the questions at right can help you create a better, more flavorful product in a more efficient and more consistent manner—and that is truly the hallmark of a professional roaster. ∎

TERRY DAVIS *is the founder of Ambex Roast and Control, Inc. In his coffee career, he has been a retail roaster, a wholesale roaster, a barista and cafe owner.*

10 QUESTIONS TO ANSWER TO GAIN BETTER CONTROL OVER CONVECTION AND, HENCE, THE ROAST ITSELF

1 What style of burner do I have?

2 What does the style of burner I have mean to me as a roaster?

3 How does the manufacturer recommend that I control the burner?

4 How do I change airflow in my roaster?

5 Do I need to change the airflow of my roaster?

6 What does the manufacturer of my roaster recommend as the best way to control the rate of convection in the roasting process?

7 Is my roaster equipped with the necessary tools to allow me to do what I wish to do with my roasts?

8 What tools should I consider adding to my roaster, if any?

9 Is my installation causing me to lose some level of control of my roaster?

10 Is my roaster clean and well maintained?

Heat Wave

The Way Heat Transfers Your Beans from Green to Brown

by Henry Schwartzberg and Vishwa Adluri

• FROM THE MARCH/APRIL 2007 ISSUE OF *ROAST* •

GREEN COFFEE BEANS do not have a desirable taste. It is only through roasting that we can change them into highly flavorful coffee. Roasting is a series of carefully controlled chemical reactions that occur in green bean compounds due to heat transfer. Clearly, the science behind heat transfer—what heat transfer does, how the heat should be applied, how much heat should be applied—is essential to helping us roast knowledgeably and profitably.

Application of heat causes many thermally induced reactions to occur throughout roasting. These reactions produce any number of desired flavors, aromas and colors, depending on the rates and duration. Rates for all roasting reactions increase rapidly as bean temperature increases. Rates for some reactions increase tenfold for an 18 degree F bean temperature rise.

Reaction rates also depend on reactant concentrations (a reactant is basically any component in green coffee). For this article, we are mostly interested in those compounds that participate in the chemical reactions during roasting.

This means that reaction rates depend on how much of the original compounds or reactants have been consumed thus far or on how much of a new reactant has been produced due to roasting. Thus, reactant concentrations depend on both the reaction rate and reaction duration. Some reactants break down while other reactants are produced. Therefore, the taste, aroma and color of roasted coffee depend on the bean temperature profile, or how bean temperature changes with time. To consistently reproduce the desired character and quality of a roasted coffee, one should provide the same bean temperature profile for that coffee, roast after roast.

Heat transfer to and within beans determines how bean temperature changes during roasting. Therefore, heat transfer determines how rates of coffee roasting reactions change during roasting and strongly affects the nature of coffee flavor, aroma and color generated by those reactions. Understanding heat transfer can help us understand how and why bean temperatures change with time. This involves understanding heat-transfer mechanisms and factors that drive and control rates of heat transfer during roasting. Armed with such knowledge, we can determine how to modify and control bean temperature profiles and roasting reactions. The aim of this article is to help roaster operators understand how heat transfers to coffee beans during roasting. Bean temperature changes are also affected by the thermal properties of beans. Therefore, those properties will also be discussed.

Basic Elements of Roasting: Fire and Air

Usually, the heat used for roasting is generated by burning a fuel with air. The fuel most commonly used is a hydrocarbon gas, such as natural gas (mostly methane) or propane. Electrically generated heat, which can be thermally inefficient and costly, is used in some small roasters. This article concentrates on roasters where heat is generated by burning a hydrocarbon gas. Production of heat is a delicate issue, and not as simple as just burning something to make the roaster vessel hot. There are three scenarios of what happens when fuel is burned:

1. When gas is burned with no excess air, i.e., exactly enough air to ensure complete combustion, all the carbon in the gas converts to carbon dioxide (CO_2) and all the hydrogen to water vapor (H_2O). For example, if natural gas is burned with zero percent excess air, each molecule of methane (CH_4) produces one molecule of CO_2 and two molecules of H_2O, and all the oxygen in the air is used up. Air, however, is mostly nitrogen. The nitrogen remains after burning and makes up a major part of the burned gas.

2. If too little air is used, some carbon monoxide (CO) is produced in place of part of the carbon dioxide. Carbon monoxide is poisonous. It also can burn, producing a great deal of heat as well as an explosion hazard.

3. Fuel gases are burned with some excess air, which ensures complete combustion and prevents the formation of carbon monoxide. However, if too much excess air is used, it leaves extra oxygen, which combines with nitrogen to form nitrogen oxides (NO_x), an air pollutant. To limit NO_x production, a good rule is to use 10 to 20 percent excess air.

Combustion gas produced by burning hydrocarbon gas with excess air contains carbon dioxide and water vapor generated by combustion, nitrogen from the air, oxygen from the excess air, and traces of NO_x. The temperature of such gas is very high (around 3,050 F for natural gas burned with 10 percent excess air or around 2,850 F for burning with 20 percent excess air). These temperatures are far too high for direct use in roasting. In most roasting systems, the gas that enters the roasting chamber is 550 to 900 degrees F. Combustion gas is diluted with cooler gas to provide these lower temperatures. Let us call the diluted, cooled gas, "roaster gas." Roaster gas contacts and transfers heat to roasting coffee beans.

It's Getting Hot in Here: Roaster Drum

In most roasting systems, hot roaster gas contacts coffee beans in a horizontal, rotating drum with a solid side wall. Most of the principles involved apply to all types of roasters. Roaster gas usually first flows over the outer wall of the drum, and transfers heat to that wall. The gas then enters the drum from a central opening at the drum's rear and flows axially through the drum. There the gas contacts and transfers heat to: a) the roasting beans; b) the inner drum wall and; c) other metal parts the drum contains. Roaster gas temperature drops markedly as the gas transfers heat. The partly cooled gas leaves the drum through a central opening in the drum's front wall. At the start of the roasting process, roaster gas may enter a roaster drum at 900 degrees F and leave the drum at 250 degrees F. Near the end of a roast, 700 degrees F gas may enter the drum and leave at 550 degrees F.

How combustion gas is diluted depends on whether a roaster is a single-pass roaster or roaster gas is recirculated.

1. Single-Pass Roasters

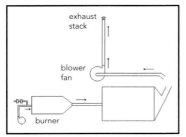

Single-pass roasters are used in most small and some medium-size roasting establishments. In these roasters, heated gas passes through the roaster system and contacts beans only once. Combustion gas mixes with room temperature air, thereby providing roaster gas cool enough to be used for roasting, but still hot enough to transfer heat rapidly to beans. A blower located downstream from the roaster drum draws the mixed gas over the drum's outer surface and then through the drum.

2. Recirculating Roasters

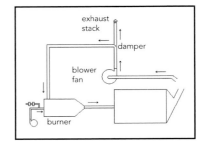

In many large roasters, combustion gas mixes with gas flowing out the roasting chamber. Then most of the mix flows back into that chamber. Thus, most outflowing roaster gas recirculates. That gas is much hotter than the fresh air used in single-pass roasters. Therefore, less combustion gas has to be mixed with it to provide gas temperatures suitable for roasting. Use of recirculation reduces fuel consumption and saves money and resources. Again, a blower draws the mixed roaster gas through the roaster drum. Roaster gas usually flows over and heats the outer wall of the drum before passing through it.

In most recirculating roasters, fuel gas combustion occurs in a burner located in a refractory-lined furnace. Combustion gas mixes with relatively hot recirculated gas but must be cooled quickly to minimize NO_x production. To accelerate cooling, the two gas streams are mixed very close to the gas burner in the furnace.

What's In It? Roaster Gas Composition

Combustion gas is diluted in different ways in single-pass and recirculating roasters, as we explained earlier. Thus, roaster gas composition differs in these two types of systems.

Water evaporates from beans during roasting. The beans also emit carbon dioxide, carbon monoxide and volatile organic compounds (VOC). The emitted water vapor and carbon dioxide significantly affect roaster gas composition. NO_x and the emitted VOC and carbon monoxide are minor constituents, but important pollutants.

Table 1 (following page) lists average weight-percent concentrations for the major components of roaster gas and gas leaving the roaster burner. Concentrations of carbon monoxide, NO_x and VOC are low and not listed.

The creation of water vapor and carbon dioxide in roaster drums causes higher concentrations in the gas leaving the drums. The difference between entering and leaving gas component concentrations is smaller in recirculating roasters, because the gas flows back into the drum.

Bean water mostly evaporates near the middle of roasts, so mid-roast water vapor concentrations are typically higher. Beans emit carbon dioxide most rapidly near the end of roasts, so the

Table 1	Average weight-percent concentrations			
Location	Nitrogen	Carbon Dioxide	Water Vapor	Oxygen
Burner Discharge	73.2	12.8	10.2	3.7
Single-Pass Roaster Drum	72.4 in 69.6 out	2.7 in 5.2 out	2.1 in 3.6 out	22.8 in 21.6 out
Recirculating Roaster Drum	50.6	16.6	30.2	2.6

end-of-roast carbon dioxide concentrations are also higher. VOC and carbon monoxide concentrations also are greatest at the end of roasts.

The composition of roaster gas is extremely crucial. Roaster gas composition affects its heat capacity (C_G). C_G indicates how much heat a unit weight of gas loses when its temperature drops 1 degree F. Roaster gas composition also affects radiation from roaster gas to beans and roaster parts.

Bring on the Heat: Heat Delivery

Heat carried by roaster gas has to be transferred to the roaster drum before it can be delivered to roasting beans. Delivery of that heat depends on the operating characteristics of the blower that circulates hot gas in the roasting system. The temperature of the delivered gas strongly affects how rapidly heat transfers to coffee beans. How the blower operates also strongly affects that temperature.

Bring on the Wind: Blower Behavior

In drum roasters, blowers draw in gas that has passed through the drum. The temperature of that gas tends to rise progressively as roasting proceeds. Drum roasters operate at very close to atmospheric pressure. Gas densities at atmospheric pressure are inversely proportional to their absolute temperature in degrees Rankine or degrees Kelvin. The Rankine temperature of drum-discharge gas is its Fahrenheit temperature + 459.7. Thus, absolute temperatures of drum-discharge gas also increase as roasting proceeds. Consequently, the density of the gas passing through the blower decreases as roasting proceeds. Roaster gas's ability to carry heat is proportional to its mass-flow rate. The mass-flow rate is proportional to the gas's volume-flow rate times the gas density. In most roasters, blowers run at constant speeds and consequently provide a nearly constant volume-rate of gas flow. But gas density

progressively decreases. Therefore, the mass flow-rate and heat-carrying capacity of roaster gas progressively decrease as roasting proceeds.

Roasting With Science

Equations describe how rapidly heat transfers by these mechanisms. These equations, some old, some recently developed, allow us to predict how roaster gas temperatures and flow rates affect bean heating in roasters. In much of the text that follows, such equations will be presented. These are basic defining equations that govern or model the main aspects of heat transfer, with roasting of coffee specifically in mind. Each aspect will be discussed in its own section, along with the associated equations that characterize that aspect. These equations are by no means easy, but they might prove very useful if you take some time to get comfortable with them and have a basic understanding of how they work.

Inlet Gas Temperature

Burner control valve settings regulate the mass-flow rate of combustion gas. If these settings are not deliberately changed, that mass-flow rate tends to remain constant. When hot combustion gas flowing at constant mass rate mixes with cooler gas flowing at a progressively decreasing mass rate, the temperature of the resultant mix of roaster gas increases. Unless corrective measures are taken to counter this phenomenon, the roaster gas temperature (i.e. $(T_G)_{in}$ as presented on the next page) can progressively increase to a point that it becomes too high. The rest of this section will discuss the primary method the operator uses to apply such corrective measures.

$(T_G)_{in}$, the temperature of gas entering a roasting chamber, depends on whether single-pass roasting or recirculation is used. For single-pass roasting, the equation looks like this:

$(T_G)_{in} = [(G - F)T_A + F T_F]/ G$

F is the mass-flow rate of combustion gas, G, the mass-flow of roaster gas, T_F, the burner flame temperature, and T_A, the temperature of fresh air.

For recirculating roasters,

$(T_G)_{in} = [G (T_G)_{out} + F T_F]/(G + F)$

$(T_G)_{out}$ is the temperature of roaster gas leaving the roaster chamber.

F is artificially reduced during roasting to prevent $(T_G)_{in}$ from becoming too high. Using practical terms, reduction in F may be referred to as "reducing burner output". F is reduced in steps in roasters with simple control systems. These F reductions cause $(T_G)_{in}$ decreases that allow roaster operators to approach desired end-of-roast bean temperatures in a slower, more controlled fashion.

Both the gas fuel flow rate and air flow rate to the roaster burner are reduced proportionately when F is reduced. Thus, the air-to-fuel ratio used for combustion remains constant. More sophisticated control systems are employed for an increasing number of roasters. These systems automatically and continuously adjust F and thereby continuously control $(T_G)_{in}$.

Roaster gas mass-flow rate reductions directly tend to reduce heat transfer from roaster gas to beans. But these flow reductions also cause $(T_G)_{in}$ to increase, which tends to increase heat-transfer from roaster gas to beans. Thus, roaster blower behavior changes heat transfer in a complex way.

Heat Transfer Mechanisms

Heat delivered by roaster gas to roasting chambers transfers to roasting beans by convection, conduction and radiation. In all cases, heat flows from a higher-temperature source (e.g., roaster gas), to a lower temperature receiving body (e.g., beans or roaster drum walls). Now let's have a look at each transfer mechanism in detail.

Conduction heat causes molecules in solids and stagnant fluids to vibrate. The higher the temperature, the more rapidly they vibrate. In solids, rapidly vibrating hotter molecules conductively transfer some of their vibratory energy to their less rapidly vibrating, cooler neighbors. This causes those molecules to vibrate more rapidly and to increase in temperature. The neighboring molecules, in turn, transfer some vibratory energy to still cooler, slightly more distant molecules. Thus, conductive heat transfer tends to be proportional to how rapidly temperature changes with distance.

With **convection**, higher temperatures cause atoms in gas molecules to both vibrate more rapidly and to move about more rapidly, i.e., have more kinetic energy. Roaster gas flow transports such hot molecules to the surfaces on roasting beans or roaster drum walls. The hot molecules in the stream convectively transfer part of their vibratory energy and kinetic energy to molecules on these surfaces. These surface molecules then conductively transfer part of the vibratory energy they pick up to neighboring molecules within beans or the roaster drum wall.

With **radiation**, hot bodies emit photons, massless packets of thermal energy. The hotter the body, the faster the rate of emission. The energy emission rate is governed by the Stefan-Boltzman law, which states that radiant energy emission is proportional to the fourth power of absolute temperature of the emitting surface, i.e., its temperature in degrees Rankine or degrees Kelvin. Emitted photons move across space until they intercept the surface of another body. There, the photons may be absorbed, reflected, or (for bodies transparent to radiation) moved through the body. If the receiving body's temperature is less than that of the original emitting body, it absorbs photons at a greater rate than it emits them and is radiantly heated. Photons emitted by a heat source may fail to intercept another body. For example, photons emitted by part of a roaster drum wall may intercept another part of the wall instead of beans and thereby fail to transfer heat to beans.

Parallel Transfer Coffee beans simultaneously receive heat by convection and radiation during roasting. They may also receive heat conductively transferred across solid contacts between the drum wall and beans and across stagnant films of gas surrounding such contact areas. The total amount of heat beans receive is the sum of all such contributions.

Now, Back to Convection

As we mentioned, during roasting, heat convectively transfers from flowing hot roaster gas directly to surfaces of coffee beans that gas contacts. Heat also transfers convectively from roaster gas to the inner and outer metal surfaces of the roaster drum and to metal parts in that drum.

G, the mass flow rate of roaster gas and C_G, its heat capacity per unit mass, determine the gas's heat-carrying capacity and strongly influence how fast heat transfers convectively from roaster gas to beans and roaster walls. The overall rate at which roaster gas transfers heat to beans, roaster drum walls, and metal parts in the drum is proportional to G times C_G and to how much roaster gas temperature drops as it flows to and through the roasting chamber.

Gas Heat-Loss Rate =
$GC_G[(T_G)_{in} - (T_G)_{out}]$

$(T_G)_{in}$ and $(T_G)_{out}$ are the respective temperatures of the entering and leaving gas. The heat loss rate consists of two parts: the rate of heat transfer directly to coffee beans, and the rate of heat transfer directly to the drum or metal parts in the drum.

Local rates of convective heat transfer to beans are

proportional to the difference between the local roaster gas temperature, T_G and to T_S, the mean surface temperature of the beans. When roaster gas traverses a small bean surface area increment, dA_B,

Local Rate of Convective Heat Transfer to Beans =
$h_B(T_G - T_S)dA_B$

h_B is the convective heat-transfer coefficient between the beans and the gas. Beans in drum roasters are well mixed. Thus, T_S does not vary much with position in drums. T_G, on the other hand, varies markedly and often is several hundred degrees higher for gas entering a roaster drum than for gas leaving the drum. As roasting proceeds, T_S increases and progressively approaches T_G. Therefore, rates of convective heat transfer to beans progressively decrease as roasting proceeds, and bean temperatures tend to rise at a progressively decreasing rate.

Heat convectively transfers to beans at different exposed bean surfaces. The overall rate of convective heat transfer to beans is the sum of the rates of heat transfer to all such surfaces. These heat-transfer contributions are proportional to the product of the exposed area of a surface times h_B, the convective heat-transfer coefficient at that surface. In rotating-drum roasters, these areas and heat-transfer coefficients depend on bean location and movement.

The Bean Shuffle: Bean Movement in Roasting Drums

During roasting, most of the bean charge lies in a tumbling pile near the drum's bottom. Two sets of spiral metal flights, or scoops, an outer set and inner set, are attached to the inside cylindrical wall of the drum. Each set may contain as many as six evenly spaced flights. The flights pass through the tumbling beans as the drum rotates. The outer set moves beans toward the front of the drum, the inner set toward its rear. Thus, flights act like ribbon blenders and mix beans well along the drum's axis. Beans heated by hot incoming roaster gas at one instant are shortly thereafter heated by cooler discharging gas. Thus, axial mixing increases uniformity of bean heating.

The flights lift portions of beans from the pile as the drum rotates. These beans move upward until the flight surface tilts downward enough to cause them to slip off the flights. The flight motion imparts upward and sideways velocity to these beans. Thus, released beans move upward slightly and sidewards until gravity acceleration counteracts the upward velocity and causes beans to move downward. Then they move downward at a progressively increasing rate. The beans still move sideways across the drum as they fall. Thus, falling beans follow a parabolic trajectory. Falling beans mix radially, which further improves uniformity of bean heating.

Though the parabolic curtain of falling beans appears dense, there actually is a great deal of space between neighboring beans. Hot roaster gas passes around and contacts beans in the curtain and transfers heat to them. In solid-wall drum roasters, falling beans usually pick up most of the heat convectively transferred from roaster gas. Gas flows over all surfaces of falling beans. Thus, convective heating of falling beans is quite uniform.

Bean motion and roaster gas flow follow different paths in other commonly used types of roasters, where bean motion causes dispersed beans to move across or through the gas stream and mix well. These roasters provide good gas-bean contacting and good convective transfer of heat from roaster gas to the beans.

Surfaces Exposed to Gas Flow

In a rotating-drum roaster, roaster gas contacts and convectively transfers heat to falling beans, the surface of the pile of beans near the drum's bottom, surfaces of the small piles of beans on ascending flights, and other exposed surfaces of metal.

The sizes of these exposed areas depend on how big a drum is, how fast it turns and how many flights it contains. In a typical 250-pound rotating drum roaster with six inner and six outer flights, bean piles at the bottom of the roaster and on flights provide roughly 23 square feet of exposed surface area. The sum of exposed areas of metal on flights and the drum's inner and outer wall is roughly 74 square feet. If the roaster drum rotates 40 times per minute, roughly 8.75 percent of the bean charge is falling through hot gas at any given time. Their exposed surface area is roughly 100 square feet. In smaller roasters and roasters with fewer flights, falling beans provide a smaller portion of the total surface area contacted by hot gas.

Equations similar to the last equation with different heat-transfer coefficients, surface temperatures and areas apply for local convective heat transfer from the hot gas to each exposed surface. The heat-transfer coefficients vary when G varies, but less markedly than G does. Typically, heat-transfer coefficients increase roughly 40 percent when G doubles. These coefficients are larger for surfaces of small size, such as individual falling beans, than for large surfaces, such as the inner wall of a drum, or the surface of a

pile of beans taken as a whole. In a typical 250-pound roaster, heat-transfer coefficients for falling beans are roughly six times as large as for exposed metal surfaces and for the surfaces of bean piles. For such roasters, I estimate that falling beans receive roughly 85 percent of the heat transferred convectively from roaster gas, drum walls receive 10.5 percent of that heat, and the surfaces of piles of beans receive 4.5 percent. In smaller roasters and roasters with fewer flights, greater proportions of heat convectively transfer to roaster drum walls and flights and to beans in piles and on flights.

Wall-to-Bean Heat Transfer

Most heat that convectively transfers to drum walls and flights subsequently transfers to beans. Roasters are pre-heated before loading. Part of the heat the drum walls pick up during preheating also transfers to beans.

Drum walls transfer heat to beans conductively and most intensely at small areas of contact between the wall and beans. Heat also transfers from walls to beans by radiation and by conduction across films of gas adjacent to bean-wall contact areas. Because beans are convex, gas film thickness is greater at distances farther from solid-solid contact points. As film thickness increases, less and less heat conductively transfers across the film. Thus, wall-to-bean heat transfer is very non-uniform. This non-uniformity can cause local overheating.

To minimize local overheating, some roaster drums have two walls, an inner and outer wall, with an air gap between them. The air gap retards transfer of heat from the drum's strongly heated outer wall to its inner wall, thereby reducing total wall-bean heat transfer.

Heat transfer from the drum wall to beans depends on the wall's heat-storing capacity. Drums with thin, double walls store relatively little heat and, after a short while, cool enough to markedly reduce wall-bean transfer of heat. Drums of small, older roasters often have thick cast iron walls. These walls store a great deal of heat during preheating and eventually transfer much of it to beans. In small roasters with thick-walled drums, wall-bean heat transfer provides a much greater fraction of the heat that beans receive than in large roasters with thin, double walls. These small roasters, when properly operated, still provide good roasted beans. They have a great deal of thermal inertia and thus are less affected than newer roasters by changes in operating and environmental conditions.

Radiation From Drum Walls

In a 250-pound drum roaster, only 7 percent as much heat transfers to beans by radiation from drum walls as transfers to them by convection from roaster gas, and 3.5 percent as much heat transfers to them by conduction from drum walls. For smaller roasters, particularly those with few flights and those with thick cast-iron drum walls, wall-bean transfer represents a larger fraction of the total heat transferred to beans.

Radiation from Roaster Gas

Roaster gas contains appreciable amounts of carbon dioxide and water vapor, both of which absorb and emit radiation. The radiating power of these gases increases as their concentration increases and as the effective length of the radiation path through the gas increases. Concentrations of carbon dioxide and water vapor are much smaller in single-pass roasters than in recirculating roasters. Radiation path lengths are short in small roasters. Therefore, radiant transfer of heat from roaster gas to roasting beans is negligible in small, single-pass roasters.

Conduction Within the Bean

Coffee beans are porous, but the gas in those pores is stagnant. Therefore, heat transfer within beans effectively can be treated as conduction. Local rates of conduction in solids are proportional to temperature gradients, i.e., how rapidly temperature changes across a distance along heat-flow paths in a body. These rates are also proportional to a property of a body called thermal conductivity. In coffee beans,

Local conductive heat transfer rate per unit area =
$- k_B (dT_B /dr)$

k_B is the thermal conductivity of beans. T_B is the local temperature within beans. dT_B/dr is the bean temperature gradient, i.e., the local rate of change of T_B with respect to distance, r, from the bean's center.

Thermal conductivities of coffee beans have been difficult to measure because beans are quite small. Researchers have guessed that the thermal conductivity of beans is the same as that of wood. Wood's thermal conductivity decreases when its density and water content decreases and varies with grain orientation. The density and water content of beans decrease markedly during roasting. Coffee beans expand less when roasted longer. Thus, for 10 to 15-minute roasts, k_B probably would decrease only roughly 21 percent.

Thermal Diffusivity

Unsteady state conduction determines how internal bean temperatures, T_B, change with time and position in roasting coffee beans. Such conduction is strongly affected by a parameter called the thermal diffusivity. Studies have found that for coffee beans, thermal diffusivity remains roughly constant as roasting progresses.

Bean Temperature Uniformity

Thermal diffusivity, bean size and roasting speed strongly influence uniformity of temperature and roasting reactions within beans. Heat flows from higher to lower temperatures. Thus, temperatures at surfaces of roasting beans are higher than in their interiors. Temperatures are still higher at bean tips. Thus, the surfaces of beans roast more darkly than bean interiors and bean tips roast even more darkly. While mixes of dark roast and lighter roast beans have flavor attributes that are desirable to some extent, excessive temperature non-uniformity will cause burning at the tips of beans and leave their centers under-roasted.

The temperature differences within roasting beans are greater for large beans than for small beans and are proportional to the time rate of bean-temperature rise. When bean temperatures rise rapidly near the start of a roast, bean surface temperature may well be 10 F higher than their mean temperatures and 25 F higher than their center temperatures. Near the end of roasting, bean temperatures rise much more slowly, and temperature differences in beans are usually small.

Temperature differences within beans mid-roast are affected by cooling caused by evaporation of the beans' water content. Later, temperature differences within beans are affected by heat generated by exothermic reactions. Nevertheless, roasting in less than three minutes has caused excessive temperature non-uniformity and tipping near the end of roasts.

Bean-to-Bean Heat Transfer

After beans contact hot roaster gas, they mix with and transfer heat to slightly cooler beans in piles near the bottom of the drum. Conductive bean-to-bean heat transfer occurs at areas of contact between beans and across gas films adjacent to those contact areas. Heat also transfers radiantly between these films. Differences between surface temperatures of individual beans are small in roasters that mix beans well.

The heat-transfer process that takes beans from undesirable green to perfect brown is complicated, to be sure. But if you take the time to understand how heat transfer works and to discover how you can utilize it in your day-to-day operations, you'll have acquired one of the most important roasting techniques out there. ◼

· ·

DR. HENRY SCHWARTZBERG *is Professor Emeritus Food Science Department, University of Massachusetts.*

VISHWA ADLURI *is vice president at Praxis International Inc. He writes on a variety of subjects from philosophy to coffee roasting technology and can be reached at va@presocratics.org.*

Turning Up The Heat On Acrylamide

By Joseph A. Rivera

• FROM THE JANUARY/FEBRUARY 2008 ISSUE OF *ROAST* •

As a child, one of my favorite memories was waking up every Saturday morning to the smell of freshly baked sweet bread and coffee from my mom's kitchen. Other times, it was the smell of handmade tortillas and the savoring aroma of *carne asada* from a mid-Saturday afternoon barbecue. In looking back at these different sensorial memories, one would immediately assume that these products share nothing in common. But probing a bit further, one would discover that they indeed *do* share a common denominator, at least in terms of flavor development, during preparation. Enter Flavor Chemistry 101.

During thermal processing, be it baking, frying or roasting, food products undergo a simple yet complex array of chemical reactions combining available amino acids with carbohydrates in a process called the Maillard reaction. Occurring at roughly 150 degrees C (302 degrees F), the Maillard reaction is what makes coffee as we know it today, as the intensely aromatic "nectar of the gods"—without it, coffee would be a dull green bean with no more than a mere handful of earthy aromas. Indeed, the Maillard reaction *is* the most critical reaction for all thermally processed foods, and it's responsible for creating hundreds of savory aromas in products such as toasted bread, steak, beer, coffee and many others. It's been estimated that in coffee alone, more than 800 aromatic compounds are formed during this reaction, many of which remain unidentified today.

But the Maillard reaction goes much further than just creating pleasant aromas, for the very color of coffee, its flavor, its complex aroma and many of the recently discovered therapeutic compounds are a direct result of this reaction. Furan, or the compound responsible for the "nutty/caramel" aroma in coffee, is also a potent antioxidant and potential anti-carcinogen. Melanoidins—the long-chained polymers responsible for creating coffee's color—are also potent antioxidants, making up 25 percent of brewed coffee's composition. Other studies suggest that coffee is a rich source of niacin (vitamin B3), potassium and soluble fiber and is ultimately believed to prevent many debilitating diseases.

Alongside these myriad beneficial compounds comes the formation of a recently discovered questionable byproduct.

According to a Swedish study, coffee, along with several other thermally processed foods, contains relatively low levels of the byproduct "acrylamide." Acrylamide, which is commonly used in manufacturing a broad range of industrial products including plastic, contact lenses and paper pulp, is classified as a "probable" carcinogen by the International Agency for Research on Cancer (IARC). Although there have been numerous animal studies conducted, there is no direct link to date correlating the consumption of acrylamide with formation of certain cancers in humans.

Acrylamide's accidental discovery in potato chips and French fries by Swedish scientists in 2002 shocked the food safety world and made it the center of headlines in recent years. Since then, the World Health Organization (WHO), the United Nations and the European Union have launched more than 200 research projects throughout the world in an effort to assess the risk and prevalence of acrylamide in other thermally processed foods.

Acrylamide Formation During Roasting

In much the same the way the Maillard reaction produces its beneficial compounds, the same reaction is also believed to be the pathway for acrylamide formation in coffee. The relatively low concentrations of the amino acid *asparagine* and free sugars in both arabica and robusta coffee provide just enough reagent to form acrylamide. Although published concentrations on acrylamide in food vary, its formation is generally dependent on a number of factors, including frying/baking time, temperature, storage conditions and exposure to UV light. As shown in Figure 1, ordinary food products such as baby food, cereals, potato chips, coffee and French fries all contain some residual level of acrylamide. Interestingly, one often overlooked factor—*surface area*—also plays a critical role in acrylamide formation during processing. It is no surprise then that potato chips, with their relatively large surface area, contain 8 to 16 times the concentration of acrylamide as coffee. French fries come in at a distant second. And although acrylamide concentrations are quite significant, one must remember that potatoes, in general, contain a much greater concentration of asparagine than what would ever be found in green coffee.

Fortunately, acrylamide formation in coffee occurs during the early stages of roasting and, due to its unstableness at high temperature, degrades progressively during the latter stages of roasting. As seen in Figure 2 (next page), during roasting acrylamide formation peaks at about 125 degrees C

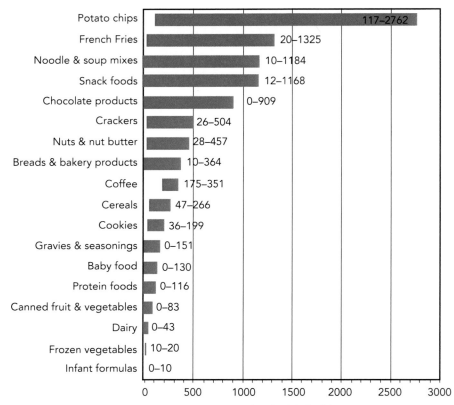

FIGURE 1

Food	Acrylamide (ppb)
Potato chips	117–2762
French Fries	20–1325
Noodle & soup mixes	10–1184
Snack foods	12–1168
Chocolate products	0–909
Crackers	26–504
Nuts & nut butter	28–457
Breads & bakery products	10–364
Coffee	175–351
Cereals	47–266
Cookies	36–199
Gravies & seasonings	0–151
Baby food	0–130
Protein foods	0–116
Canned fruit & vegetables	0–83
Dairy	0–43
Frozen vegetables	10–20
Infant formulas	0–10

Acrylamide (ppb)

(257 degrees F) then begins to degrade, up to 95 percent, with darker roasting styles. But although darker roasts may mitigate acrylamide formation, it does so at a significant price. For darker roasts styles tend to disrupt much of the delicate organoletic, therapeutic and nutritive effects contained within the bean itself. And in coffee, with roasting and the Maillard reaction playing such a critical role, it's nearly impossible to implement mitigation strategies without any effect on coffee quality. Thus, roasters electing to use darker roast style place themselves in a delicate "risk-benefit" situation between choosing a roast profile that has the desired flavor characteristics (acidity, aroma, etc.) and one without them.

These days, with the widespread use of temperature/time profilers on most commercial roasters, roasters now have greater control over acrylamide formation during roasts. One option available is the use of longer/lower-temperature roast profiles, which allow for enough flavor compounds to develop within the bean, without the risk of excess acrylamide. Another method patented by Proctor and Gamble involves the use of an enzyme, asparaginase, to reduce asparagine levels in green beans prior to roasting. Still another method recently developed involves a combination of steam roasting with high temperature/short time profiles to minimize acrylamide formation. Interestingly, according to the Swedish Institute for Food and Biotechnology, it's the duration of roast that is the greatest factor in acrylamide formation and not temperature as we would expect.

Though the options and use of technology are endless, for now researchers are continuing their quest to reduce acrylamide in food with minimal affects on flavor.

Acrylamide During Storage

With the sheer complexity that roasting plays in flavor development, it would seem almost futile to attempt any control over acrylamide formation. Fortunately, when we cannot implement roasting strategies to mitigate acrylamide formation, we can turn to the next best thing under our control: packaging. Since acrylamide is not very stable, both before and after roasting, its condition during storage plays an important role in determining residual acrylamide content in coffee.

According to one German study, coffee stored under non-vacuum conditions showed a 30 to 65 percent reduction in acrylamide during three to six months of storage. Higher levels of reduction were seen as the ambient storage temperature and exposure to light increased. Interestingly the reduction of acrylamide during storage was seen only for roasted whole-bean and ground coffee, but remained effectively stable for soluble and coffee substitute type coffees. No degradation was seen for frozen coffee at -40 degrees C.

While many would not advocate consuming six-month-old coffee, it does create a strong impetus for those consumers to switch from drinking soluble to specialty-grade coffee. As it turns out, drinking stale coffee may not be so bad after all (see Table 1.)

Interestingly, nowhere is the impact of the Swedish study felt more in the world than in California. Acrylamide is classified as a carcinogen under the Safe Drinking Water and Toxic Enforcement Act, otherwise known as Prop 65. The law requires every food product containing additives "*known to the state of California to cause cancer*" to be properly labeled. Thus far two groups have already sued fast food manufacturers for failing to comply. Though there continues to be much debate on acrylamide, the FDA's official statement on it says that "... research on acrylamide ... is neither a warning to consumers nor a finding of risk with any particular food."

Ironically, it is these same chemical reactions (responsible for creating coffee's complex flavor and numerous therapeutic compounds) that create products such as acrylamide. For now, it looks like Starbucks and others who have traditionally used darker roasts may have

FIGURE 2
Formation of acrylamide during coffee roasting.
[CTN = Color tile number]

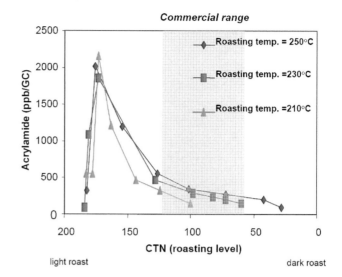

accidentally been on to something early on. Now, it's up to us to choose the best path. ∎

JOSEPH A. RIVERA *holds a degree in chemistry and is the founder/ creator of coffeechemistry.com. He served as the director of science and technology for the Specialty Coffee Association of America (SCAA) and frequently travels the world lecturing on coffee science. He is actively involved in research and development across all sectors of the coffee industry. He can be reached at* joseph@coffeechemistry.com.

TABLE 1
Acrylamide levels during storage at room temperature

Product	Storage time	Acrylamide before	Acrylamide after	% Reduction/ Increase
Coffee, roast and ground	3	305	210	- 31%
Coffee, beans	3	285	200	-29%
Coffee, soluble	3	840	850	+1.2%
Coffee, substitute	12	1300	1200	-8%

Alchemy in the Roasting Lab

Discovering Organic Acids | Parts 1 & 2

By Joseph A. Rivera

• FROM THE MARCH/APRIL 2005 AND MAY/JUNE 2005 ISSUES OF *ROAST* •

PART ONE

Mention the word "alchemy" and most people will automatically think of long-bearded Medieval men mixing magical potions in their never-ending quest to convert lead to gold. Although the fruits of the early alchemists were never actually realized, the quest to instill greater value into something as common as lead continues to fascinate us.

Roasters are no different. Who else, on a daily basis, converts ordinary green beans into something consisting of more than 1,000 complex compounds and an aroma "as sweet as honey?"

But the idea of turning lead into gold is not so far-fetched, since, according to the First Law of Thermodynamics, *"matter is neither created nor destroyed, but simply changes form."* In this article, we'll explore the basics of coffee chemistry and discover some of the wonderful magic that occurs within those tiny beans and in the laboratories of thousands of roasters every day.

Raw Materials

Coffee plants, much like humans, produce hundreds of byproducts through their metabolic life, each terminating in the formation of organic acids and other intermediate compounds. (In layman's terms, "organic acids" are any acids that contain a carbon in their molecular structure.)

Coffee plants, via the Calvin cycle, produce more than a dozen different acid intermediates, all of which remain locked inside the bean at harvest. Variables such as genetics, varieties and species ultimately determine the sugar production that is "locked inside" the beans. For example, the species *Coffea arabica* contains almost twice the concentration of sucrose as its *Coffea robusta* counterpart. As we'll discuss later, these sugars play a critical role to the development of acidity in the cup. Sugars, being heat-labile, decompose during the roasting process to create more than 30 organic acids and hundreds of volatile compounds.

Though genetics play a key role in what sugars are ultimately produced, it would be premature to conclude that this is the only variable that affects quality. To fully explore the magic that occurs in the bean, one must look at altitude and microclimate, yet another example of the classic nature vs. nurture paradox.

On the physical level, altitude has the effect of increasing both bean size and bean density. With the help of a screen sorter, you can quickly confirm this, such that many countries rate coffee quality based on screen size. The effect makes sense, since at cooler temperatures reaction rates decrease and the plant effectively has more *"time"* to pack nutrients and sugars into the beans.

Altitude also has the effect of changing not only physical parameters, but of altering chemical composition as well. At higher altitudes we tend to produce coffees higher in perceived acidity, such that for every 100 meters gained in altitude we can expect a 0.60 degree C drop in temperature, and for every 300 meters, a 10 percent increase sugar production, namely sucrose. What does all this mean? Higher acidity!

But the puzzle doesn't end here. For if altitude determines *how much* acidity is produced, then regional humidity determines the *type* of acid produced. It is not just how much acid is produced, but what type, that effectively defines the acidity profile of a certain coffee. This is easy to see when cupping any one of the seven regional coffees in Guatemala. Anyone who has ever cupped an

Antigua or Huhuetenango alongside a Coban can attest to a pronounced difference. To those not familiar with Coban, it is one of the most humid regions in Guatemala, at times resembling a rainforest. In the cup, many would say the Coban cups with a delicate fruitiness or wineyness as compared to the other regions in Guatemala. As it turns out, the regional humidity has the effect of increasing the "fruity acids" in the bean, much like the fruitiness of chardonnay wines. This would suggest that humidity increases the level of malic acid, though I have not seen published studies on this.

For countries that lack the topographical elevation necessary to maximize the beans' potential, shade plays an ever-important role, for what is not achieved through altitude can be made up, within reasonable limits, by proper shading. The goal is to slow down the metabolic rate of the plant, increase sugar production and, ultimately, improve cup quality.

Although there are more than 1,000 compounds produced during roasting, by far the most important when dealing with cup profile are the organic acids. As we embark on this brief journey, we'll explore the science behind the scenes.

Let's begin the journey...

Chlorogenic Acids (CGA)

No explanation of organic acids would be complete without a

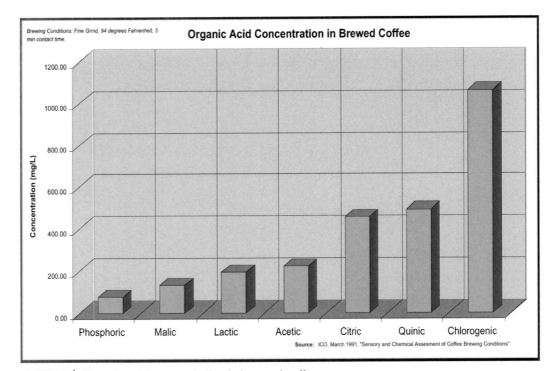

FIGURE 1 | Organic acid concentration in brewed coffee.

thorough discussion of chlorogenic acids (CGA). As seen from Figure 1, CGA accounts for the majority of the organic acid concentration in coffee, accounting for 6 to 7 percent for arabica and up to 10 percent in robusta on a dry basis. Although it may not appear to be much, the relative content of CGA compared to that of caffeine is seven to eight times higher. And in a typical 8-ounce cup of coffee, CGA represents roughly 2 ounces, or an estimated 30 percent by volume.

During roasting, CGA plays an important role in the development of coffee flavors. Almost half of the CGA content is decomposed in a medium roast, whereas French roasts can exhibit up to an 80 percent loss. The portion that does decompose is used in the production of quinic acid and flavor precursors.

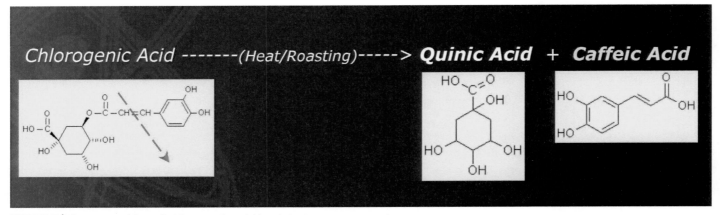

FIGURE 2 | Decomposition of chlorogenic acid leads to two components.

It should be mentioned that chlorogenic acid does not refer to a single compound, but rather a family of more than six different isomers of the acids, each with different flavor attributes. Without getting too technical, there are basically two families of these acids; mono-caffeoyl and di-caffeoyl. While mono-caffeoyl acids readily decompose during roasting, those of the di-caffeoyl family remain almost unchanged and have been reported to impart a metallic-bitter taste. It's no surprise then that robustas, which exhibit a similar metallic taste, contain a larger concentration of these acids than their arabica counterparts. It has even been suggested that due to their undesirable taste, CGAs have effectively been used by plants for protection from animal and insect infestation. Perhaps those pesty bugs do know a thing or two about specialty-grade coffee!

At just past the second crack, these di-caffeoyl acids decompose and the metallic-bitter taste slowly diminishes, though a few savvy chemists at soluble factories have effectively been able to slightly alter the levels of these acids through steam treatment of lower quality green beans. Who would have ever thought of such a thing? I guess necessity is truly the mother of invention.

Decomposition of CGA leads to the production of two very important components. As seen in Figure 2 (page 192), the decomposition of CGA causes a steady increase in caffeic and quinic acid, both of which are classified as phenolic compounds. Such compounds are often astringent in nature, thus darker roasts tend to produce coffees higher in astringency and body. The same principle is seen when we compare the body and astringency of a red wine, such as a cabernet, to that of a chardonnay. As a rule of thumb, any naturally occurring substance that exhibits color will

always contain a large concentration of chromophores, a class of colored phenolic compounds.

Recently, CGA has also been suggested as the main culprit for people suffering from acid reflux. It's been estimated that as little as 200 mg. of CGA can increase levels of HCL in the stomach. A typical cup of coffee yields anywhere between 15 and 325 mg. of CGA, well within the suggested range. Those drinking decaffeinated do benefit, as the decaffeination process results in a slight decrease of CGA content. But it should be noted that the initial increase in stomach acidity is due solely to CGA and not caffeine as many are led to believe.

CGAs: Quinic and Caffeic

Before the first crack, CGA continues to decompose, while quinic acid progressively increases in concentration. Being a phenolic compound, quinic acid also proportionately increases body and astringency and forms colored compounds, namely *melanoidins*.

Interestingly, increases in quinic acid concentration have been documented in cases where green coffee is stored for an extended period of time in warehouses, at times up to 1.5 percent dry basis. Luckily, one does not need to wait months to see the immediate affects on acidity, as it can be demonstrated in any cupping lab. As most of us have experienced while cupping, the longer we leave out a coffee liqueur while cooling, the greater its perceived acidity. Why this happens is only one part of the fascinating chemistry that occurs in our morning cup of joe.

At roast levels exceeding 6.5 percent dry basis—roughly cinnamon roast—we begin to see the formation of *quinide*, the same compound commonly found in tonic water. As this compound remains in the hot infusion, it slowly hydrolyzes back to quinic acid and serves to increase the level of perceived sourness. Thus, with dozens of reactions invisibly taking place in the cup, it truly makes cupping an extremely difficult time-dependent exercise. Away from the cupping lab, the effect is also seen when coffee has been left sitting on a heating element for an extended period of time. This is all too common during long road trips, when we're welcomed at the nearest highway coffee shop with sour coffee, and when we hear stories of unscrupulous coffee shop managers leaving their coffee on the heating pan for up to eight hours on end, only to serve it "fresh" to you. Unfortunately, there is no magic potion to prevent this reaction, and we're once again reminded of the importance of coffee freshness.

Another one of CGA's byproducts is caffeic acid. It is also a phenolic compound and one that will contribute slightly to cup astringency. Recently, caffeic acid has been documented to be a potent antioxidant and is believed to prevent the onset of several human cancers.

into a unripe orange? Describe its taste? During early maturation, fruits tend to produce a large concentration of organic acids, but as maturation continues, these same acids are converted into sugars. Wait a couple days and that same unripe orange will taste significantly sweeter.

Any roaster who has ever received a shipment of green coffee only to find it cup sour has experienced this firsthand. Fortunately, roasters can use this bit of information to verify the quality of post-harvest separation at origin. Being a process-controlled defect, poor separation of unripe beans will always elevate levels of this citric acid along with a corresponding sourness. So what should a roaster do if he's unable to return a sour lot of coffee? Quite simply, roast darker! This will drive off as much citric acid as possible.

While this article only offers a glimpse into the magic that occurs in the roasting lab, I hope it expanded your mind and introduced you to the wonderful world of chemistry that occurs within those tiny beans.

In Part 2, we'll look at the role of the rest of the important organic acids: acetic, malic and phosphoric. We'll discuss how these acids are formed, how they are affected by wet processing and how they ultimately change during roasting.

Citric Acid

Second on our list is citric acid. Occurring naturally as part of the plant's metabolism, citric acid follows CGA in concentration levels. Unlike many other acids, citric acid is not produced during the roasting process, but it is slowly decomposed. At 9 percent weight loss, we begin to see the concentration slowly diminish. A medium-roasted coffee will contain 50 percent less citric acid as compared to its green bean state. Citric acid's effect on perceived acidity is significant, as it is one of the major acids contributing to cup profile. However, citric acid is not an acid you would like to have in high concentrations, as most people describe its taste as acerbic and intensely sour. So intense is its characteristic sourness that many candy manufacturers use it in the production of gelatin-based confections.

But one needs to look a little further to understand why this is so. Ever bitten

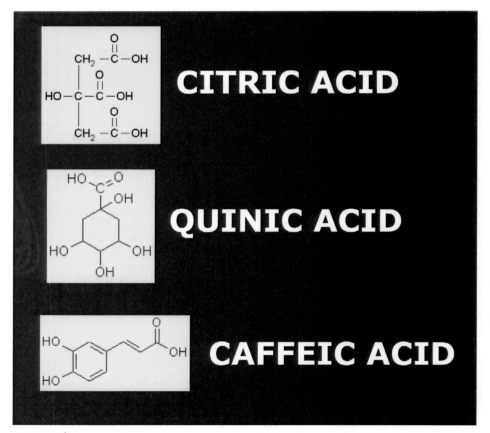

FIGURE 3 | Composition of citric, quinic and caffeic acid.

PART TWO

W ELCOME BACK as we continue our journey into the mystical world of coffee chemistry. In part one, we discussed the roasting process, the thermal decomposition of compounds and the formation of more than 30 organic acids, half of which are volatile. We discussed three acids at length, namely, chlorogenic, quinic and citric.

To review, both chlorogenic and citric acids decrease in concentration due to thermal decomposition and have an inverse relationship with degree of roast, whereas quinic and caffeic acids actually increase in concentration due to the breakdown of chlorogenic acids.

During the roasting process, more than 800 compounds are created, 60 of which are key coffee odorants and many of which remain unidentified by scientists, making coffee a truly complex beverage. What we do know is that the contribution of organic acids to coffee flavor is of paramount importance. Besides acidity, organic acids play an important role in the development of flavor precursors and aroma elucidation. In this article, we will probe further and investigate some of the other minor acids in coffee and their major impacts in the cup.

Malic Acid

Found in high concentration in apples, malic acid commonly goes by alias of "apple acid." Malic acid has a greater perceived sourness than citric acid and is commonly detected by the foliate papillae on the side of the tongue. As such, it is frequently used in the food industry to impart sour/fruity characteristics commonly found in chewing gums, ciders and low-calorie beverages. After phosphoric acid, malic acid is the most common acidulant used in food.

In a coffee plant, malic acid serves as a key compound in several important metabolic processes. As such, its final production within the bean is invariably affected by environmental conditions. As we mentioned in part one, regional humidity tends to raise the level of the fruity acids in coffee, such as coffees from the highly humid Coban region of Guatemala. What exactly causes this increase in "fruitiness" remains to be determined, but my guess is that it is an increase in the level of malic acid in the bean. This guess may hold merit; for example, in wine chemistry, wines that typically exhibit the most fruitiness, such as chardonnays, tend to have higher levels of malic acid.

During the roasting process, malic acid's fate closely resembles that of citric acid. With a melting point of 130 degrees C (268 degrees F), slightly below that of sucrose, malic acid rapidly decreases in concentration as the degree of roast increases. While green beans contain anywhere from 0.30 to 0.70 percent malic acid, a typical medium roast will lose roughly 30 percent of that due to thermal decomposition.

Acetic Acid

Acetic acid, most commonly known as the active ingredient in vinegar, is for the most part created during the roasting process. During roasting, carbohydrates composed of six to 10 carbons in length are broken into smaller fragments. These fragments give rise to a number of different products, including acetic acid and others, which simply dissolve in the coffee infusion to increase the level of soluble solids.

Depending on roasting conditions, levels of acetic acid in roasted coffee can increase up to 25 times from its initial green bean form. Because its production originates from the breakdown of carbohydrates, arabica beans with almost double the concentration of sugar than robusta will always contain more acetic acid after roasting. But as we'll discuss later, acetic acid is quickly lost once you roast past a medium roast, at times exhibiting up to 90 percent loss.

Unlike some of the other acids we discussed, acetic acid is a weak acid that dissociates only 7 percent in the coffee brew. But don't be fooled into dismissing this acid as unimportant. For although its contribution of protons (hydrogen) in the cup may not be significant, it is what it does not do that is most important. It has been known for more than 75 years that perceived acidity is not only a function of free protons in solution, but also of the "reserved acidity" due to undissociated acids. That is, acids that do not readily break down and contribute to any great extent to pH; this property is common in weak acids such as acetic. Furthermore, research has confirmed that even minor changes in pH due to undissociated acids can significantly alter aroma, flavor and overall character. Trained cuppers, with their sensitive palates, have been known to detect a change in beverage pH as small as 0.10 pH units.

Another important quality of acetic acid is that it is a volatile molecule that our olfactory system readily detects. How can you test that? Simply open a bottle of vinegar. As the acetic acid molecules in vinegar begin to absorb heat due to ambient room temperature, they begin to vibrate. These vibrations occur by the thousands with many simultaneously

colliding and eventually gaining enough energy to escape the liquid and pass into the surrounding air. The room soon fills with thousands of acetic molecules and a nasty vinegar smell permeates the air.

Because acetic acid is so volatile, it plays an important role in coffee aroma. Since most identified aromatic compounds are oil-based, many remain dissolved inside oil droplets within coffee. Interestingly, arabica has an estimated 60 percent more lipid content than robusta, perhaps explaining why arabicas have so much more aroma complexity.

During roasting, the level of acetic acid will peak during light roasts, then rapidly decrease as roasting progresses due to loss by evaporation. For roasters wishing to capitalize on this, roasting technology has an answer. Enter pressure roasters. These roasters minimize the loss of volatile acids and maintain higher levels of acidity than traditional roasting by taking advantage of simple physics. Perhaps one of the best known is the

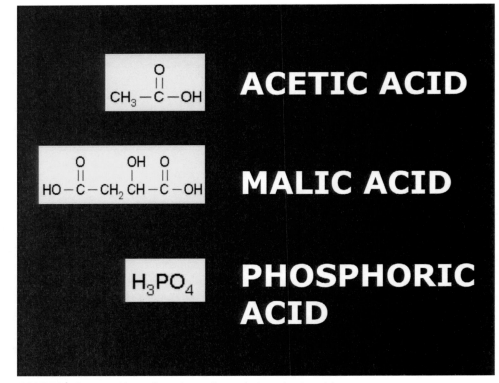

FIGURE 1 | Composition of acetic, malic and phosphoric acids.

Smitherm Continuous Pressure Roaster, into which Michael Sivetz put much research. At times, pressure roasting can gain as much as 0.20 units in beverage pH. That is, it will decrease the pH in coffees from 5.20 to 5.00 simply by using pressure versus conventional roasting. Although 0.20 units may not seem like much, it represents almost double the level of acidity based on the logarithmic scale. Unfortunately, pressure roasting has mainly been suited for use with lower-quality robusta coffee, where an increase in acidity is always desirable.

Another minor source of acetic acid is post harvest processing. During wet processing, acetic acid is produced as a byproduct of fermentation. Depending on regional temperature, fermentation time can range between 12 and 36 hours. Fermentation time in excess of 48 hours typically leads to the formation of "stinkers" as a result of excess production of undesirable volatile acids, such as acetic, proprionic and butyric acids. During processing, fermentation comes to an end when the sticky mucilage is removed from the bean, followed by thorough washing with clean water. But even with proper washing, trace amounts of acetic acid remain in the bean. In these trace amounts, the acid is a desirable trait, for it contributes to a noticeable cleanliness and brightness as compared to other dry-processed coffees.

Phosphoric Acid

Unlike the other acids discussed so far, phosphoric acid is not an organic acid, but rather an inorganic acid. How do we know this? Its lack of available carbon in its structure classifies it as such (Figure 1, page 196). Although there are many conflicting views on the origin and role of phosphoric acid in coffee, it is currently believed that phosphoric acid stems from the coffee plant's uptake of inositol hexaphosphate or phytic acid, an organic acid.

During roasting, phytic acid decomposes to form phosphoric acid, an acid that is 100 times more potent than most of the organic acids discussed so far. As such, many researchers believe that phosphoric acid significantly contributes to beverage acidity due to its strength and ability to readily dissociate. In a 1999 study by the Coffee Quality Institute, formerly the Specialty Coffee Institute, a significant amount of phosphoric acid was found in specific lots of Kenya AA and SL28 as compared to a Colombian Supremo. Furthermore, experiments in which this acid was added to other coffee origin brews significantly altered acid profiles to levels almost identical to Kenyan coffees.

As an inorganic acid, much of this acid survives the roasting process, and it is believed that phosphoric acid is better extracted from darker roasts, which is quite contrary to what we may expect. But the puzzle still remains open, as many researchers on one side claim that phosphoric acid, due to its potency, significantly contributes to perceived acidity; whereas others claim that the acid is neutralized by an equivalent amount of potassium in the coffee brew.

The good news is that, as with all branches of science, coffee chemistry is a continuously evolving field that every day brings new answers to old questions. But there is still much more to explore on our road to truly understanding the complexity of coffee. With its myriad compounds formed and its physiological and psychological effects on the brain, coffee is by far the most radical drink ever introduced to mankind. Fortunately, through modern technology and advances in chemistry, we are closer now to truly understanding this "nectar of the gods" than we have ever been. ■

JOSEPH A. RIVERA *holds a degree in chemistry and is the founder/ creator of coffeechemistry.com. He served as the director of science and technology for the Specialty Coffee Association of America (SCAA) and frequently travels the world lecturing on coffee science. He is actively involved in research and development across all sectors of the coffee industry. He can be reached at* joseph@coffeechemistry.com.

Coffee Taster's Flavor Wheel

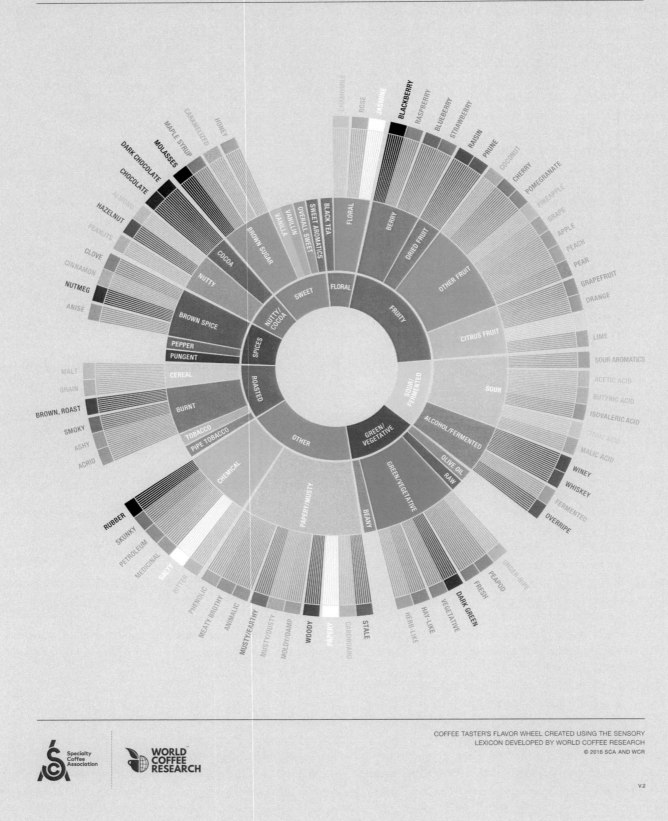

COFFEE TASTER'S FLAVOR WHEEL CREATED USING THE SENSORY
LEXICON DEVELOPED BY WORLD COFFEE RESEARCH

© 2016 SCA AND WCR

V.2

Specialty Coffee Association

WORLD COFFEE RESEARCH

The Science Behind Coffee Aroma

By Joseph A. Rivera

• FROM THE JULY/AUGUST 2008 ISSUE OF *ROAST* •

Our Senses

Humans perceive the world through a combination of our five senses—namely hearing, seeing, tasting, feeling and smelling. Although man has walked the earth for 6 million years, we are still far from understanding how each of these senses truly functions. Today, we know much more about hearing and seeing than we do about taste, and even less about smell. Why is this? Well, much of the complexity lies in the number of receptors each of these senses requires. Take, for example, hearing—the simplest of them all, with two receptors essentially detecting both the frequency and amplitude of a sound wave. Vision, slightly more complex, has three types of receptors located at the back of retina and designed to detect colors on the RGB (red, green, blue) scale. Taste, even more complex, has five receptors designed to detect sweet, salt, sour, bitter and umami (savory). Simple enough, right?

But then we have smell—the Godfather, the Einstein, of all senses. It has not two, not three, not five, but more than 1,000 receptors. This remarkable number of receptors allow humans to detect over 10,000 different aromas, or 10 times the "built-in" capacity. But don't be so amazed; that's roughly the same number as a mouse. And in the grand scheme of things, animals are far superior. That's right, rabbits have about 1 million receptors, while dogs such as bloodhounds have an estimated 100 million.

Since the sense of smell is tied directly to the limbic system, or the "primitive" section of the brain, smelling almost always elicits an emotional response. How often have you walked past a bakery only to be reminded of grandma's apple pie, or dabbed on an old cologne only to have it precipitate memories of that long-lost college love? We've all experienced something similar. Smell, more than any other sense, is an emotional sense.

But our ability to detect an odor is far simpler than our ability to identify it. We can easily detect an odor, but many times the ability to place a word with that odor can at times be "on the tip of our tongue." And in the world of coffee, it's imperative that

coffee professionals be able to associate unique words with flavor characteristics.

The Flavor Wheel

Although we're barely at the tip of the iceberg in understanding how coffee aroma works, the industry has made some significant attempts at systemizing the puzzle. Enter the flavor wheel. Created by the Specialty Coffee Association, the flavor wheel is a systematic attempt at classifying some of the most common flavors found in specialty coffee.

Perhaps the most striking aspect of the wheel is the clear separation between taste and aroma. At every level of the wheel we can drill down two levels to pinpoint other descriptors. Take for example, sour. This base modality can be broken down into two other types: soury and winey. These terms can, again, be drilled even further to describe a sour with *acrid, hard, tart* or *tangy* notes.

Simple enough for taste, but when compared to other half of the wheel (aroma), we can see that things get much more complicated. And that's exactly what we see. On the aroma side, we see not only two levels, but at least three, owing to the true complexity of smell.

When both of these attributes—taste and aroma—are combined we get what's called "flavor," which is essentially the sum of both attributes. In coffee, aroma plays such an important role that it's been estimated that 75 percent of coffee's "taste" is not taste at all, but rather smell. But how these aromatics develop during roasting is still something scientists are trying to unlock.

The Players

Although coffee has more than 1,000 compounds, only about 80 percent of them are volatile (see Figure 2, page 201). And even then, not all of them serve as important coffee flavor constituents. According to researchers, we can approximate the smell of coffee by simply using a mere handful of compounds. Based on model reaction studies, it only takes about 20 to 30 compounds, when combined properly, to create an aroma that we would identify as coffee-like.

Ask any coffee drinker what the best part of drinking coffee is for them, and many would say it's the sweet aroma you get when brewing a fresh pot. Interestingly, many of the aromatic compounds in coffee actually represent some of the most foul-smelling compounds known to man. One class in particular is the sulfur-based mercaptans. These components smell so bad, that they are occasionally used to "odorize" the natural gas in our homes, thereby alerting us of a dangerous gas leak, and preventing it from inadvertently causing a house explosion. Though in coffee, there is one mercaptan in particular—*furfurylmercaptan* (FFT)—which has, by far, been associated with the most coffee-like aromatics. However, like all potential odorants found in food, its characteristic sensorial notes depend largely on its relative concentration. At very high concentrations, FFT can impart a pungent garlic-like smell, while at low concentrations, such as those found in coffee, it can create the perfect mix of volatiles we identify as "coffee."

Other disagreeable compounds include *methanethiol*, commonly found during decomposition of organic matter, such as rotten cabbage, and which is also the same compound found in halitosis (bad breath). Acetaldehyde, or the compound responsible for hangovers after a long night of drinking, is a potent neurotoxin, also found in small concentrations in coffee aroma. And B-Damascenone, or the rose-smelling compound commonly used in perfumes and responsible for imparting red wine's bouquet, is also a player in coffee's aroma.

On a quantitative basis, furans represent the single largest class of compounds found in coffee aroma. These compounds, which typically impart caramel-like notes, are due mainly to caramelization of sugars during roasting. While pyrazine and thiazoles, with their roasty/toasty notes, are the third most abundant, they play a particularly important role due to their low-odor threshold.

Development During Roasting

With so many reactions taking place within the bean, how's a roaster to know what's going on inside the bean? That is the $64,000 question and one that scientists around the world are still trying to solve. In looking at model studies, data strongly suggests that the formation of coffee aroma during roasting begins at roughly 170 degrees C, initially with the development of peanut-like notes. At 180 to 190 degrees C minute notes of coffee can be detected; while at 230 to 240 degrees C, we see a sharp increase in the levels of furans and caramel-like compounds. Around 250 degrees C, we see a corresponding increase in the level of pyrazines.

As any roaster would attest, progressive roasting leads to beans with higher levels of aromatics along with muted acidity. Even at temperatures as high as 260 degrees C, where many compounds begin to decompose, studies have shown that those aromas with sulfury/roasty notes continue to increase due to the formation of FFT and *guaiacol*.

So what's the driving force behind all these aromatic compounds? That's right, the Maillard reaction! Although a

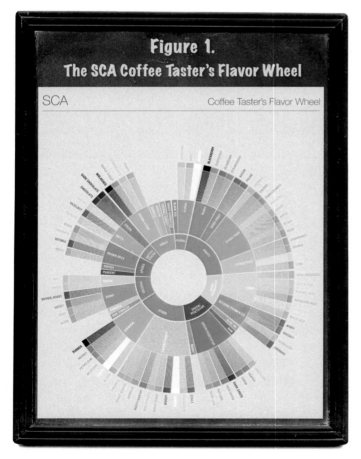

Figure 1.
The SCA Coffee Taster's Flavor Wheel

SCA   Coffee Taster's Flavor Wheel

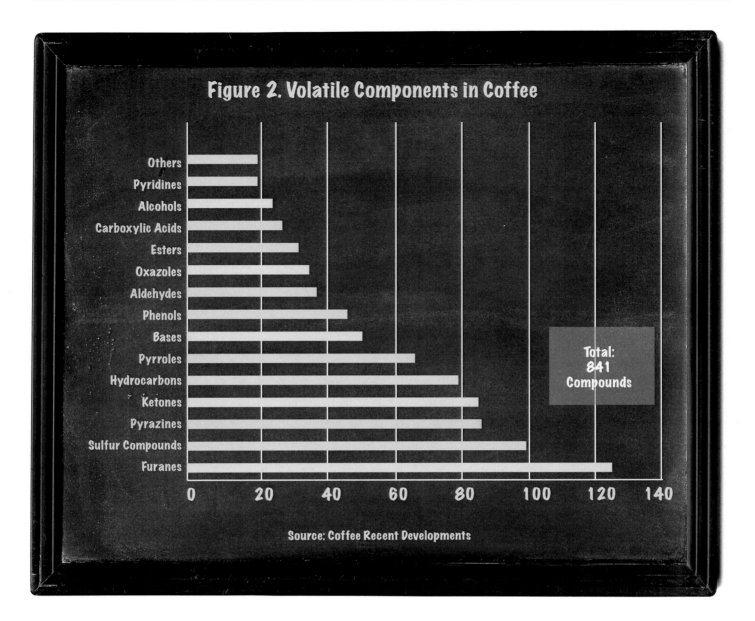

Figure 2. Volatile Components in Coffee

Total: 841 Compounds

Source: Coffee Recent Developments

comprehensive discussion on the mechanics of this reaction is outside the scope of this article, it's important to at least have a basic understanding. (For additional information, see "The Science of Browning Reactions" on page 160).

And if the science wasn't complicated enough already, we must also look at real-world factors that affect the production of these flavor compounds. Take, for example, fluctuations in lot production from year to year. Changes in bean density, moisture level, level of maturation, etc., will have a significant effect on the development of flavor during roasting, essentially making the role of the green coffee buyer, roaster or quality control personnel so important if consistency is to be maintained. ■

JOSEPH A. RIVERA *holds a degree in chemistry and is the founder/ creator of coffeechemistry.com. He served as the director of science and technology for the Specialty Coffee Association of America (SCAA)* *and frequently travels the world lecturing on coffee science. He is actively involved in research and development across all sectors of the coffee industry. He can be reached at joseph@coffeechemistry.com.*

Let's Review!

>What single compound is most associated with coffee aroma?

>What is the technical term for the combination of taste and smell?

>What class of compounds make up the largest portion of coffee aroma?

The Chemistry of Brewing

How Coffee Transforms, from Bean to Brew

By Joseph A. Rivera

• FROM THE MAY/JUNE 2012 ISSUE OF *ROAST* •

For coffee professionals, brewing is a critical step in completing the coffee chain from bean to cup. Although brewing is a relatively simple procedure, over the years there has been no shortage of technological innovations developed in an effort to extract the best cup. From the ancient ibrik used in boiled Turkish coffee to the hippest pour-over at the local cafe and everything in between—they all share the same principles of brewing extraction. In this article, we'll briefly discuss a few important factors involved in brewing and provide additional insight into the chemistry involved in achieving that ultimate cup.

Water

Of all the hundreds of chemical constituents making up coffee, water is by far the most critical when it comes to the brewing chemistry. This simple yet universal liquid serves not only as an effective extraction medium, but also as an integral element into which flavor solubles can dissolve. When one considers that coffee contains myriad compounds, each of various chemical structures and complexity, it is amazing how a single compound—water—can achieve so much. To date, approximately 1,000 compounds have been identified in roasted coffee, each consisting of various forms of carbohydrates, acids, alkaloids, proteins, lipids and numerous minerals. So with all these different types of molecules, how is it that this simple water molecule can extract them all? The answer begins with a study of water's chemical structure.

Water (H_2O) consists of two hydrogen atoms attached to a single oxygen atom, which allows it to achieve unique structural properties. Because the oxygen atom has a much greater attraction for electrons, this creates an unbalanced electron density around

the oxygen atom, giving it a slightly negative charge, while leaving both hydrogen atoms with a slightly positive one. Under such conditions, we say that water is *polar*—namely due to its charged properties across its structure. It is this "unbalanced" nature of water, or polarity, that allows for hundreds of flavor molecules to interact with it and ultimately dissolve.

Of course, not all molecules dissolve to the same extent, since the ability of any molecule to dissolve depends greatly on its medium. But as any physical chemist will tell you, the degree to which a compound dissolves in solution is directly proportional to the temperature of that solution. At higher temperatures, we will always get more material dissolving in solution than at lower temperatures. In the case of drip coffee brewing, where temperatures range between 92 to 96 degrees C (197.6 to 204.8 degrees F), we can assume that those compounds that *are* water soluble will readily dissolve into solution with little to no effort, while those compounds with lower solubility will significantly increase.

Fortunately for us, coffee is a strong flavoring agent, such that at concentrations of only about 1.25 percent we can effectively create an acceptable coffee beverage in spite of water's high concentration of about 99 percent in solution. Fortunately coffee is a strong flavoring agent, such that at concentrations of only about 1.25 percent the infusion is sufficiently strong enough to produce an acceptable beverage for most consumers. In addition, the physical properties of the water used for extraction have a huge impact on its ability to extract flavor. That's why the Specialty Coffee Association (SCA) recommends water to have no more than 150 mg/L (+/- 20mg/L) of total dissolved minerals, 17–85mg/L of calcium and a target pH between 6.5–7.5 for superior brewing. Refer to the SCA Standard: Water for Brewing Specialty Coffee document for more details on water quality standards.

Contact time, or the time water is spent in contact with the coffee, also plays an important role in the overall extractability of coffee. Since extraction levels are directly proportional to the amount of time that coffee and water are in contact, it is no surprise that extractions made via the drip method will always have corresponding higher levels of extractions than those made of espresso with a fraction of the brew time. Although we can certainly achieve higher rates of extraction simply by adjusting physical parameters—grind size, contact time, water temperature, etc.—in coffee, more isn't necessarily better.

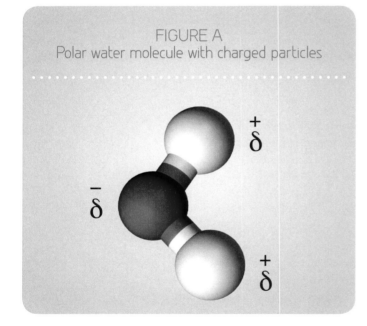

FIGURE A
Polar water molecule with charged particles

According to studies conducted by the Coffee Brewing Center in the early 1960s, the "best" cup of coffee is achieved when 18 to 22 percent of the total coffee flavoring material is extracted from the grounds. In looking at the SCA Brewing Control Chart, this translates into a coffee brew strength level of 1.15 to 1.35 percent total dissolved solids (TDS) or what is termed the coveted "Golden Cup." For more information on the Brewing Control Chart, see *The Coffee Brewing Handbook* by Ted Lingle.

Now that we've briefly discussed some basic physiochemical factors in brewing, we'll carry on and discuss what these soluble solids actually consist of.

Carbohydrates

Carbohydrates are a collective term used to classify compounds containing carbon, hydrogen and oxygen. They include everything from simple sugars to complex compounds containing thousands of smaller, linked components. Sucrose, or table sugar, is a relatively simple carbohydrate consisting of only two sugar molecules—glucose and fructose—while others such as hemicellulose are made up of several thousand. Although these compounds appear very different, they both fall under the same general classification of carbohydrates. Biochemically, carbohydrates are also involved in numerous physiological functions, serving as a plant's primary energy source as well as a reservoir for building more complex molecules. Since a significant portion of the coffee bean's structure is made up of hemicellulose, it is no surprise that carbohydrates will also make up a significant portion of the brew itself.

Although carbohydrate levels vary depending on the species, variety, maturity and growing conditions, it's been estimated that 40 to 50 percent of coffee's dry composition is composed of various forms of carbohydrates. But take a green bean, grind it and brew it, and you'll find that only a small fraction of this carbohydrate-like material will actually extract into the cup. So what gives?

Well, it turns out that even though we may expect these "sugars" to readily dissolve in solution, a large portion of this carbohydrate material in green coffee is actually insoluble. Fortunately, before we can brew a cup of coffee, green coffee must undergo the major transformation of roasting, thus saving us from this issue. During roasting, large chains of carbohydrates are progressively broken down into smaller, more water-soluble units that increase in solubility and readily extract into the cup. It is these smaller "sugar" molecules derived from hemicellulose that are partly responsible for the development of mouthfeel or body we perceive in the cup. As these solubilized molecules extract from the grounds, they remain suspended in solution and effectively serve to coat our tongues and create the light body of a filtered coffee or the heavier texture of a French press.

Carbohydrates also play a particularly important role not only in sensorial appreciation but visual appreciation as well. During roasting, many carbohydrate fragments recombine to form longer chains of brown-colored polymers called melanoidins. The formation of these melanoidins ultimately provides for the opaqueness of coffee and its characteristic brown color. Chemical analysis on melanoidins has confirmed that they consist of an extremely complex structure of tens of thousands of smaller units, each with pronounced bitter properties. Since they are readily soluble in hot water, it's easy to see why darker-colored coffee solutions typically contain more soluble solids than those brews

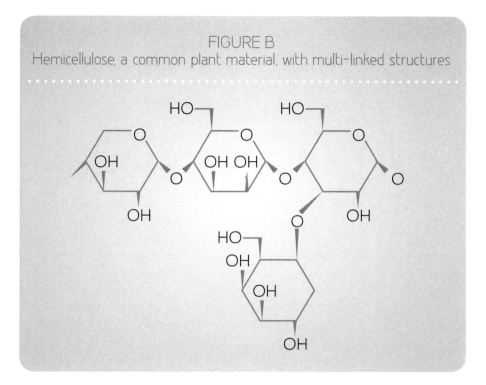

FIGURE B
Hemicellulose, a common plant material, with multi-linked structures

with lighter color. But what is perhaps more surprising is that melanoidins can make up to 25 to 30 percent (dry basis, or db) of the total soluble solids in brewed coffee and have considerable impact on health. In the past few years, research on melanoidins has suggested that in addition to playing an important role in taste, they also have significant antioxidant potential at levels possibly higher than those found in green tea.

Caffeine

Unlike carbohydrates, which readily decompose to form numerous other compounds, caffeine is unique. Its physical properties include the ability to transform from a solid to a gaseous phase without undergoing an intermediate phase (i.e., liquid) in a process called sublimation. Over the years there have been numerous studies suggesting that even when coffee is exposed to roasting temperatures well above its sublimation point of 350 degrees F (178 degrees C), only negligible amounts of caffeine are lost.

Interestingly, of all the hundreds of compounds contained in the coffee matrix, it's fair to say that caffeine—or 1,3,7-trimethylxanthine—is perhaps the sole reason people choose to drink coffee over numerous other beverages. For green arabica, caffeine levels average 1.2 percent dry basis (db) with almost double the concentration in robusta. Since caffeine is stable, its

concentration per bean remains the same, such that brews made from darker roasts may contain higher levels of caffeine than those made from lighter ones, all things being equal. Why? Because darker roasts result in larger beans with greater surface area and less weight, it takes more "mass" of coffee to achieve the same throw weight. As such, this greater increase in "mass" results in higher overall extraction and, ultimately, greater extraction of caffeine when compared to an equally portioned lighter roast.

But with caffeine playing such an important role in why people drink coffee, it is amazing that caffeine is even in solution to begin with. Although not immediately apparent, caffeine has a relatively low solubility in water at room temperature (25 degrees C or 77 degrees F) and is marginally more soluble at 50 degrees C (122 degrees F). But at typical brewing temperatures near 100 degrees C (212 degrees F), there is a 30-fold increase in solubility, which allows caffeine to readily dissolve into solution. As such, it is quite common to achieve extraction rates exceeding 90 to 95 percent, even during the first minute of drip brewing. For espresso, the rate of extraction is slightly lower at about 75 to 85 percent, due to the coffee's significantly shorter contact time with water than in other traditional brewing methods. But what about cold-brew coffee?

Unfortunately, there have not been any published studies on cold-brew coffee, so the verdict is still out. In looking at the chemistry of caffeine, however, one can speculate that cold-brew may have significantly less caffeine than traditionally hot-brewed coffee. On the other hand, if one considers that cold-brew has an

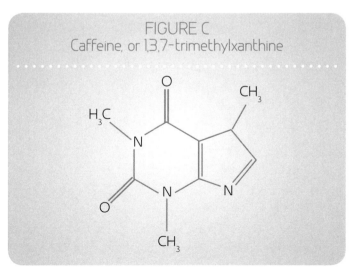

FIGURE C
Caffeine, or 1,3,7-trimethylxanthine

exponentially longer duration of extraction (12 to 48 hours versus four to six minutes), this may offset the relatively low solubility at lower temperature.

[UPDATE 2017: At the 2016 Specialty Coffee Association of America Expo, I presented the first Cold-Brew Chemistry seminar and confirmed that, when using identical brewing ratios, cold-brew does indeed have lower concentrations of caffeine than hot. In addition, there were qualitative and quantitative differences in aroma, acidity and organic acid concentrations on this preliminary study. A more comprehensive study on cold-brew versus hot is scheduled for 2017.]

Regardless of how much caffeine is actually in solution, when one considers its overall impact on taste, caffeine—sad to say—falls rather flat. According to taste researchers, caffeine contributes only 10 to 15 percent of coffee's total bitterness in solution; coffee's bitterness is more a function of melanoidin and other bitter components. What role caffeine *does* have in terms of overall taste has yet to be determined, but it may play a hidden role in possibly synergizing with other taste molecules in solution.

Chlorogenic Acids

When compared to caffeine, chlorogenic acids make up a significantly greater portion of the dissolvable material present in coffee. Although the term chlorogenic acid (CGA) may seem to refer to a single compound, CGAs actually represent a broad class of acids, each with varying forms of structural similarities.

In coffee, CGA concentration can make up anywhere between 7 to 10 percent of the bean's total composition, with higher concentrations found in robusta than in arabica. During the roasting process, CGAs readily break down to form quinic and caffeic acid to levels about half their initial concentration. Both quinic and caffeic acid can undergo even further decomposition, leading to the formation of harsh/bitter phenols commonly found in darker roast styles.

Since a large portion of CGAs survive the roasting process, they readily extract into solution by all types of brewing methods and contribute significantly to overall cup flavor. Compositionally, they make up about 19 percent of the total dissolved solids on a dry basis (db), or almost as much as the soluble carbohydrate portion in the brew. As such, CGAs serve important sensorial functions including the development of body, astringency and overall acidity in the cup. In addition, when compared to the other series of organic acids in coffee, CGAs are at the very top, exceeding concentrations of even citric or malic acid. But unlike citric/malic acids, which have a predominantly sour taste, CGAs have a slightly bitter edge to them when dissolved in solution. It is the balance of these CGAs along with other organic acids and carbohydrates that

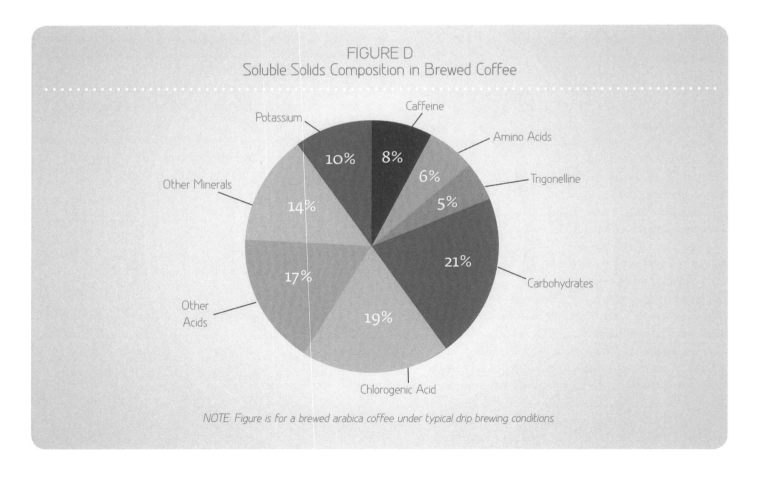

FIGURE D
Soluble Solids Composition in Brewed Coffee

Potassium 10%
Caffeine 8%
Amino Acids 6%
Trigonelline 5%
Other Minerals 14%
Carbohydrates 21%
Other Acids 17%
Chlorogenic Acid 19%

NOTE: Figure is for a brewed arabica coffee under typical drip brewing conditions.

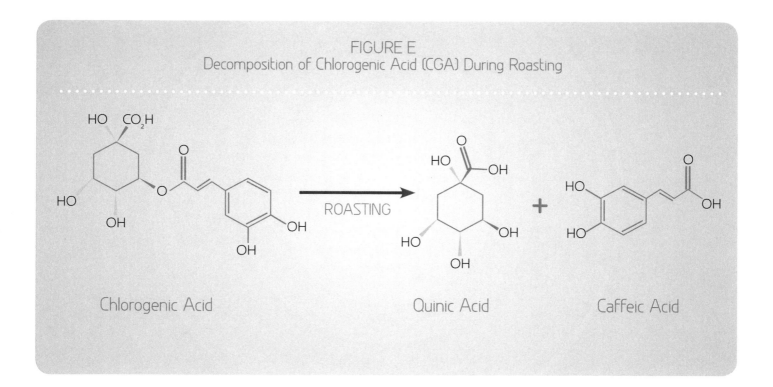

FIGURE E
Decomposition of Chlorogenic Acid (CGA) During Roasting

Chlorogenic Acid   ROASTING   Quinic Acid   +   Caffeic Acid

ultimately give balance to the cup. Over-extract one brew, and the pronounced bitterness can easily overpower the coffee and ruin it—but exactly how?

All CGAs are water soluble to varying extents and readily extract during the early phases of brewing, but as brewing time increases so does the extraction of other less-desirable compounds. In darker roasts where quinic and caffeic acid have undergone further decomposition, bitter phenols form. These phenolic compounds, which are relatively small in structure, remain tightly bound to coffee grounds. But as brewing times are prolonged, these phenolic compounds slowly dissolve and ultimately accumulate, giving rise to an unbalanced, bitter cup. What, then, is the proper brew time?

According to the SCA, the recommended brew time for drip coffee is 4 to 6 minutes, and 6 to 8 minutes for coarser grinds. But prolonged brew times not only bring about issues of bitterness but degrade overall aromatic quality as well. When one considers that coffee is a complex mixture of both taste and smell, any reduction in one attribute will greatly affect the other. As prolonged brews in open-air systems are carried out, there is also an increased loss of volatile aromatics due to volatilization, and an overall decrease in beverage quality.

Conclusion

We've only touched on many of the physical and chemical factors involved in brewing chemistry. Factors such as the brewing method, chemical composition of water, temperature and type

of coffee all play a significant role in the quality of extraction. Fortunately, many of these parameters are under our control, and we can use the fundamentals of brewing to maximize the potential of each and every cup we brew. ■

JOSEPH A. RIVERA *holds a degree in chemistry and is the founder/creator of coffeechemistry.com. He served as the director of science and technology for the Specialty Coffee Association of America (SCAA) and frequently travels the world lecturing on coffee science. He is actively involved in research and development across all sectors of the coffee industry. He can be reached at joseph@coffeechemistry.com.*

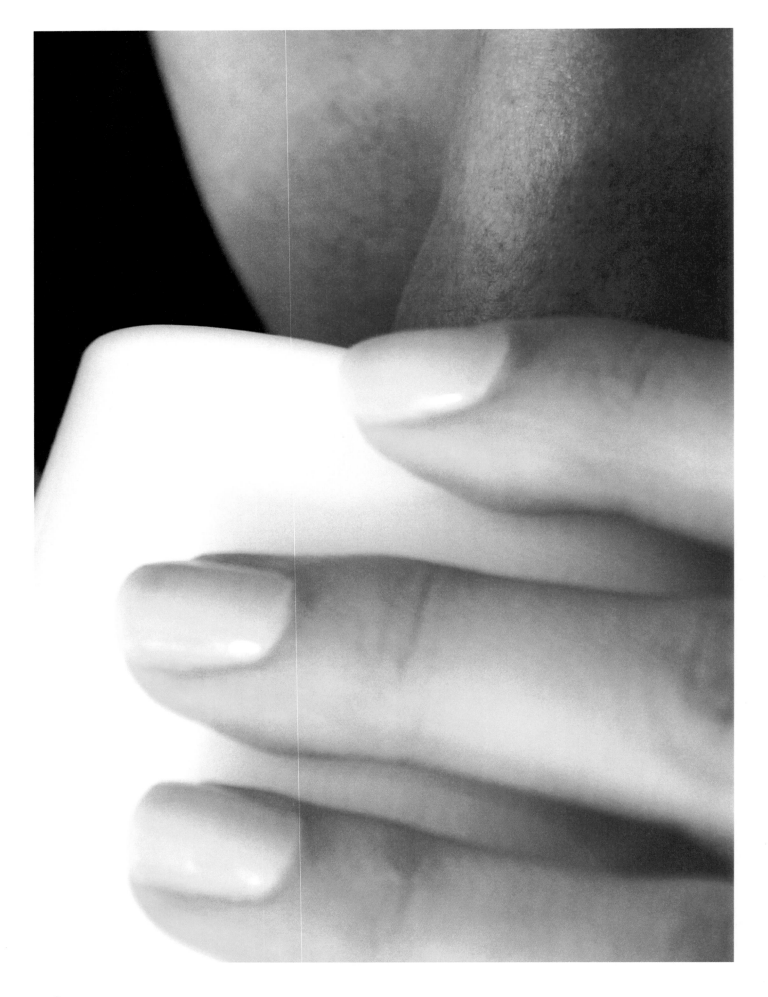

The Bitter End

Making a Case for Chlorogenic Acid

by R. Luke Harris and Christian Axen

• FROM THE MAY/JUNE 2014 ISSUE OF *ROAST* •

C affeine is bitter. Yet the vast majority of coffee fanatics and professionals would be loath to deny themselves the caffeine buzz that is, arguably, the only reason coffee was popularized by Kaldi and his goats in the first place.

In other words, we accept the bitterness of caffeine in our coffee because it presents us with something stimulating. But caffeine is not the only biologically active bittering agent present in the delightful elixir that is your passion and your livelihood.

In their paper, "Correlation Between Cup Quality and Chemical Attributes of Brazilian Coffee," published in the scientific journal *Food Chemistry*, Adriana Farah and colleagues present their analytical chemistry investigation of the Rio off-flavor. According to Farah, the unpleasantness of Rio-like coffee is "usually described as a pungent, medicinal, phenolic or iodine-like flavor associated with a musty, cellar-like odor," which at its extreme, is characterized as an "intolerable taste and smell." Farah and colleagues' data show that with increasing abundance of chlorogenic acids—or CGAs—in light and medium roast coffee, the cup quality decreases markedly, including a much more prominent Rio off-flavor. Higher caffeine levels were also associated with lower cup quality, but these negative flavor associations of caffeine were only observed in medium roast coffee, not in light roast, and to a lesser extent than for CGAs.

For better or for worse, the role of CGAs and caffeine in coffee flavor is unavoidable. As roasters already know, it is possible to influence the amounts of these compounds in the cup because levels of such chemicals decline with longer heat application for darker roasts. But there are so many other aspects of coffee flavor and aroma—sweetness and sourness to name only two—so isolating these two compounds and attributing flavor characteristics to them is an oversimplification. That said, when it comes to caffeine and CGAs, is bitter better?

CGAs, Caffeine and Oxidative Stress in Plants and Animals

Dr. Terry Graham, a professor of human health and nutritional sciences at the University of Guelph in Ontario, Canada, spoke with us about the biological importance of caffeine and CGAs in the human diet. Dr. Graham's message is that chronic coffee intake over a lifespan has largely beneficial effects for human health. "Most scientists attribute these positive effects to antioxidant content of coffee, and one particular group are the derivatives of chlorogenic acid," he says. What is the basis for this antioxidant benefit of CGAs?

Oxidative stress is a chemical process that occurs in plants and animals, promoting damage to key biochemical constituents of cells and tissues, including DNA. Damaged DNA speeds up aging and can lead to mutations. In coffee trees and other plants, environmental stressors, such as excess direct exposure to sun or extreme cold, impair the plants' metabolic functions, resulting in oxidative stress. CGAs are a major component of plant antioxidant defenses, which protect them against the resulting biochemical damage. Many plants produce CGAs and related chemicals for this reason, but green coffee beans contain more CGAs than any other edible plant product, except perhaps for the leaves of Ilex paraguariensis, from which maté teas are made.

In 2010, Ana Fortunato and colleagues published a report about the important antioxidant role of CGAs in protecting coffee plants from cold stress, found in the *Journal of Plant Physiology*. In their study, titled "Biochemical and Molecular Characterization of the Antioxidative system of Coffea sp. Under Cold Conditions in Genotypes with Contrasting Tolerance," Fortunato and colleagues analyzed the contents of CGAs in 1.5-year-old trees from five coffee varieties, including catuai, which had been grown at a range of temperatures decreasing from 25 degrees C/77 degrees F down to as low as 4 degrees C/39 degrees F. In response to this cold stress, the catuai trees increased their production of CGAs by around 30 percent, and increased their production of caffeic acid by around 39 percent. In general, plants produce considerably more CGAs when exposed to sun and cold, with combined exposure to sun and cold resulting in the most dramatic increases—so shade helps to reduce cold-induced increases in CGAs.

As mentioned by Dr. Graham, some of the major effects of CGAs on our bodies are related to the same antioxidant functions for which plants produce them. In our bodies, the parallels to cold and sun exposure are things such as eating the wrong foods (think transfats or saturated fats), smoking cigarettes, suffering traumatic injury or suffering an infection. We also experience oxidative stress all of the time, just by living and breathing, as

a byproduct of natural metabolic processes. Just like plants, our bodies produce antioxidant compounds to combat oxidative stress, thereby slowing our aging and providing us with some protection against the effects of our sometimes-lacking diets and sedentary lifestyles. For even better protection we have to supplement our own antioxidant supply through the foods we consume.

"In the average North American diet, coffee is responsible for 50 to 60 percent of daily antioxidant consumption," says Dr. Jane Shearer, an associate professor of kinesiology and medicine at the University of Calgary. "A cup of blueberries has more antioxidants

Table 1.

Chlorogenic acid (CGA) and caffeine contents in freshly roasted coffee brews prepared using machine drip, pour-over and press pot methods.

Method	CGA mg/mL	Caffeine mg/mL	CGA per 240-mL cup	Caffeine per 240-mL cup
Technivorm	0.773	0.522	185.5	125.3
Technivorm	0.890	0.518	213.7	124.2
Technivorm	0.604	0.512	145.0	122.9
Technivorm	0.588	0.479	141.0	115.0
Technivorm	0.427	0.463	102.5	111.2
Pour-over	0.400	0.444	96.1	106.5
Pour-over	0.399	0.449	95.8	107.9
Pour-over	0.483	0.442	115.8	106.1
Pour-over	0.508	0.462	122.0	110.8
Pour-over	0.449	0.441	107.7	105.9
Press Pot	0.458	0.489	109.9	117.4
Press Pot	0.449	0.428	107.8	102.6
Press Pot	0.441	0.421	105.8	101.0
Press Pot	0.422	0.416	101.2	99.8
Press Pot	0.366	0.372	87.9	89.2
AVERAGE	0.510	0.457	122.5	109.7
Standard Deviation	0.15	0.04	35	10

than [the same volume of] coffee. The problem is that most individuals don't consume enough fruits and vegetables on a daily basis. On the other hand," and fortunately for coffee professionals, "individuals readily consume multiple servings of coffee per day."

The Better of Bitter

Previously, in 2007, Dr. Graham had humorously concluded a visiting lecture at the University of Alberta with the phrase, "Caffeine bad, coffee good," implying that CGAs are primarily responsible for counteracting the negative effects of caffeine in human health. Seven years later, we asked him if he would still say the same thing. "Caffeine pushes the metabolism toward a Type 2 diabetic state for hours," says Graham. With this negative effect in mind, he says, "With regards to caffeine, I would now have to modify this a little and say, 'Caffeine mainly bad.' " However, he adds "There are likely some positive neural health effects [of caffeine]." Dr. Graham refers to "evidence that chronic caffeine consumption may have positive health effects on some aspects of brain function, such as memory and aging."

"With coffee, I would now say 'damn good,' as there is strong evidence for not only reduced risk for Type 2 diabetes, but also some cancers and neurological conditions." Actually, the story with Type 2 diabetes is

photo by Mark Shimahara

not so straightforward. Says Graham, "It is impossible to compare caffeine and caffeinated coffee. Caffeine is obviously biologically active, but coffee contains many other bioactive substances." Just as these thousands of bioactive substances complicate coffee flavor and aroma, they affect its physiological effects, too.

"A clear example of how one could draw the completely incorrect conclusion about coffee consumption is that caffeine leads to insulin resistance," thereby promoting a diabetic state, "and [the logical] extension of this finding to coffee would be that coffee increases the risk for Type 2 diabetes. However, many excellent studies demonstrate the opposite: Chronic consumption of caffeinated coffee decreases the risk for Type 2 diabetes in a dose-dependent manner," Dr. Graham says.

Dr. Shearer elaborates on this argument: "The more coffee consumed, the lower the risk [of developing Type 2 diabetes]. This has been shown in various populations worldwide."

One of the reasons caffeinated coffee doesn't pose a serious long-term risk for developing diabetes and related conditions is that CGAs protect us against the negative effects of caffeine. CGAs slow the movement of sugars from our gut into the blood, and also promote the uptake of sugar from the blood into the liver, thereby reducing glucose levels in the blood. The net effect of CGAs, then, is to counteract the pro-diabetes effects of caffeine; compare this

Figure 1a.

CGA Concentrations Classified by
Brew Method (mg per 8-ounce cup)

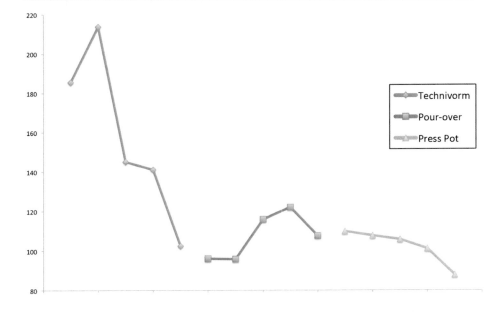

Figure 1b.

Caffeine Concentrations Classified by
Brew Method (mg per 8-ounce cup)

to non-diet colas that deliver high levels of glucose and caffeine simultaneously. Over many years, daily consumption of colas poses a huge risk for developing metabolic diseases because there are no CGAs in cola to blunt the effects of caffeine. We'll take CGAs in our coffee any day, thank you very much.

Caffeine and CGAs in Coffee Brews: Our Experiment

Caffeine and CGAs work alongside each other in our bodies, sometimes collaborating and sometimes competing. Their benefits for the coffee trees, their influence on coffee flavor, and this metabolic dance they perform in the human body got us thinking about how we brew our coffee.

We performed an experiment to compare the levels of caffeine and CGAs in coffee brews, prepared using different methods: machine drip, manual pour-over and press pot. Previous studies have already quantified the concentrations of caffeine and CGAs in coffee. However, they have mostly focused on the total amount of caffeine and CGAs found in coffee beans, and the extractions have been performed using conditions that do not yield drinkable coffee, such as organic extraction with methanol, the use of very high coffee-to-water ratios, and dwell times of up to a few hours in duration. Our goal was to measure these compounds in coffees that had been freshly roasted, ground and brewed with human consumption in mind.

We performed our experiment onsite at the Prince George campus of the University of Northern British Columbia (UNBC). Coffee (Ethiopia wet process Guji Oromo) was purchased green from Sweet Maria's in Oakland, California, and roasted within two months of receipt. Specifically, we used a Behmor 1600 counter-top roaster on a P4D program with appropriate adjustments, 1/4-, 1/2- or

1-pound. Green coffee batches were roasted to a city level, with the cooling cycle started at the end of first crack.

First crack start and end times were consistent within a few seconds across batches of the same size. Coffee samples were brewed in 650-mL volumes according to SCA standards using a coffee-to-water ratio of 0.068, with freshly ground coffee that had been roasted one to two days before brewing.

Using a Technivorm Moccamaster for machine drip, a Hario V60 Buono kettle for pour-over, or a stainless steel Frieling press pot, each brew was prepared with a four-minute extraction in filtered and freshly boiled water at 90.5 to 95.6 degrees C/195 to 204 degrees F. Once brewed, the samples were cooled immediately in an ice bath, and then 3 mL of each brew sample was transferred to a separate plastic tube. We drank the rest.

Our analytical chemistry methods were a modification of the methods described previously by Luiz C. Trugo and Robert Macrae in their paper "Chlorogenic Acid Composition of Instant Coffees," published in the journal *Analyst* (1984), as well as JK Moon and colleagues in their article "Role of Roasting Conditions in the Level of Chlorogenic Acid Content in Coffee Beans: Correlation with Coffee Acidity," published in the *Journal of Agricultural and Food Chemistry* (2009). We carried out a number of chemical steps to isolate and purify the CGA and caffeine from our brew samples. Alan Esler, the analytical chemistry support specialist in UNBC's central equipment laboratory, then determined the CGA and caffeine contents of the samples using an Agilent Liquid Chromatograph 1100 high-performance system. Each sample was analyzed twice, using different ultraviolet light detection wavelengths: once to quantify CGA (at 325 nm) and once to quantify caffeine (at 275 nm). The

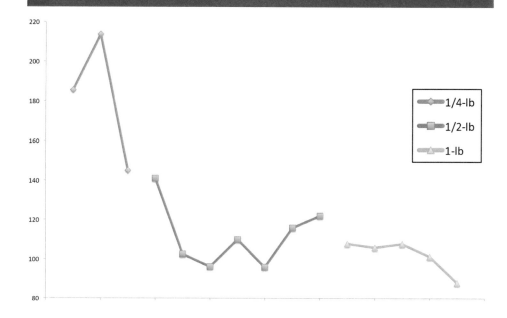

Figure 2a.

CGA Concentrations Classified by Batch Size (mg per 8-ounce cup)

1/4-lb
1/2-lb
1-lb

Figure 2b.

Caffeine Concentrations Classified by Batch Size (mg per 8-ounce cup)

1/4-lb
1/2-lb
1-lb

quantifications of CGA and caffeine, respectively, were performed using the linear regression equation of the concentration and peak area of standard CGA and caffeine solutions prepared using pure standards of these chemicals purchased from Sigma-Aldrich—a life science and high technology company. All measurements were performed in triplicate.

Experimental Data

CGA and caffeine concentrations of our Technivorm, pour-over and press pot brews are shown in Table 1 on page 210. Overall, across all three brew methods, the CGA concentration in the brew samples varied from 0.366 to 0.733 mg/mL brewed coffee, with an average of 0.510 mg/mL. The caffeine concentration in the brew samples varied over a slightly narrower range, from 0.372 to 0.522 mg/mL of brewed coffee, with an average of 0.457 mg/mL. According to Dr. Shearer's 2008 work, "Coffee, Glucose Homeostasis, and Insulin Resistance: Physiological Mechanisms and Mediators,"

published in the journal *Applied Physiology, Nutrition, and Metabolism*, a standard 8-ounce cup of coffee (240 mL) contains CGAs in the range of 88 to 250 mg, and an average of 130 plus or minus 20 mg of caffeine. Based on the same coffee "cup" size, our data is remarkably similar, with CGAs in a range from 87.9 to 213.7 mg per 8-ounce cup, and caffeine at an average of 109.7 plus or minus 10 mg per cup.

Finding Meaning in the Data

We plotted the data found in Table 1 as graphs of CGA or caffeine contents according to brew method. As shown in Figures 1a and 1b on page 212, it seems that brew method might actually affect the amount of CGA and caffeine in the cup, with machine drip resulting in the highest levels of CGA and caffeine, manual pour-over resulting in intermediate levels, and press pot resulting in the lowest levels.

Even though our data are remarkably close to that reported by Dr. Shearer, we were curious as to why our values were so variable despite our efforts to achieve consistency across roasts, brews and HPLC analyses. Caffeine exhibited a relatively tighter range of values, regardless of brew method, which might mean that caffeine content is more dependent on the coffee beans themselves, rather than the roast or brew method. With CGAs, on the other hand, the effect of roasting on variations in CGA levels is well established in the scientific literature, with longer heat application times leading to the breakdown of CGAs into different molecular structures.

Consequently, we thought that perhaps the variation in CGA content could be due to variations in the roasting conditions. We plotted the data from Table 1 again, this time according to the 1/4-pound, 1/2-pound or 1-pound size of the roast batch. As seen in Figures 2a and 2b on page 213, as we expected, cup contents of CGA and caffeine also appear to vary with roast batch size. Thus, an alternative explanation for the CGA and caffeine contents we measured is that their levels decreased with the longer heat application required for larger batches in the Behmor roaster.

The most direct implication of our experiment for roasters is that larger batches and longer roast times will probably result in lower CGA and caffeine contents in brewed coffee. Of more general interest to coffee professionals, fanatics and consumers may be the possibility that different brew methods can affect the cup contents of these biologically important compounds.

"CGA does not appear to have one action in the body, but many. One very surprising role may be to feed the millions of bacteria living in our gut."

—Dr. Jane Shearer, University of Calgary

photo by Mark Shimahara

The Bitter End

Coffee is a "mess" of chemicals, and in this sense, it is probably a bit of a mistake to think too hard about the role of caffeine and CGAs as bittering agents in our coffee. Rather, for the final word on CGAs and caffeine, let's switch from the mouth to the, um, other end.

Not long ago, a friend contacted one of the authors to ask, "You know about chlorogenic acid, right? I just read that it induces recto-sigmoid motility. What does that mean?" Well, to put it delicately, recto-sigmoid refers to the "end" of the human digestive system, and motility refers to movement, so CGA is one of the reasons many coffee drinkers experience some degree of—shall we say—regularity associated with their morning cup.

This brings us back to the question of coffee and human health. On this point, Dr. Shearer also explains that CGA "does not appear to have one action in the body, but many. One very surprising role may be to feed the millions of bacteria living in our gut. Gut bacteria break down and metabolize many of the phenolic compounds found in coffee. Having 'healthy' gut bacteria has been shown to prevent disease and maintain health."

So, thanks in large part to CGAs, and perhaps to caffeine, coffee is good for you, but most definitely—to borrow from Dr. Graham—because it tastes so "damn good." ■

. . . .

JOSEPH A. RIVERA *holds a degree in chemistry and is the founder/creator of coffeechemistry.com. He served as the director of science and technology for the Specialty Coffee Association of America (SCAA) and frequently travels the world lecturing on coffee science. He is actively involved in research and development across all sectors of the coffee industry. He can be reached via email at* joseph@coffeechemistry.com.

R. LUKE HARRIS *is an assistant professor at the School of Health Sciences and an adjunct professor in the Northern Medical Program at the University of Northern British Columbia. Reach him at* cafe.luke@gmail.com.

CHRISTIAN AXEN *is an analytical chemist in Calgary with a Bachelor of Science in chemistry from the University of Northern British Columbia. He can be reached via email at* chris.axen@gmail.com.

ROASTING STYLES & TECHNIQUES

photo taken at Ristretto Roasters, Portland, Oregon

Coffee Roasting

Fine-Tuning Your Technique

by Kathi Zollman

• EXCLUSIVE TO *THE BOOK OF ROAST* •

Y OU ARE A COFFEE ROASTER. Can you describe what you do in 10 words or less?

It's difficult to create a description for the title of coffee roaster. There's a hint of mystery surrounding the coffee roaster vocation. This mostly results from the consumer's lack of exposure to and understanding of what it really means to roast coffee.

Customers might ask, *"Oh, you grind it yourself?"* And yes, roasters might grind it themselves, but that is a small fraction of what a roaster does. A roaster performs myriad tasks each day, some related to roasting coffee, others not.

It's Complicated

You are a scientist. Some roasters describe roasting as a strict scientific exercise. The process and thought behind it are based on basic parameters defined by science. A roaster makes use of strong scientific knowledge to turn coffee from green to brown, following a structured series of steps. The scientist is organized and completes each step methodically, without wavering from the formula.

You are an artist. At the other end of the spectrum is the artist, the roaster who approaches the process with more flair and flexibility. The artist runs the risk of inconsistent results because of this more fluid process. The artist's roast log and cupping notes might reflect a lack of discipline in standardizing the process while allowing room for colorful interpretation of the final results. The outcome can be a great coffee, but there is no data to support replicating the roast profile.

The key to creating the optimal roast style and an amazing cup of coffee is balancing the science with the art.

Many art forms rely on heat to transform raw materials into glistening creations. Glass artists understand the melting point of sand, metalsmiths pour molten metals into new shapes, and ceramicists use heat to harden clay and transform earth elements in glazes into colorful finishes. Each requires a specific set of skills and a strong understanding of the science behind the art. Once the basic skills are mastered, the artist within the scientist can explore the limits to create his or her own artistic style. Coffee roasters use scientific knowledge to define the parameters of artistry in their own roast style.

Explore the Science

In its most simple form, coffee roasting is a process of transferring heat to green coffee beans. The heat source is the roasting equipment. Roasting equipment varies widely, from simple to extremely complex. The common thread that ties the diversity of equipment together is the fact that they provide the heat exchange to transform the green coffee.

Green coffee in a cast iron skillet over an open flame receives enough energy to change from green to brown. The results are a pan full of fresh roast ready to brew. This pan method does require some agitation of the skillet to avoid scorching, so be prepared with a safe way to hold the skillet handle.

The barbecue grill is another roasting method for the backyard thrill-seeker; the dense smoke that billows from the grill is a small price to pay for the freshly roasted coffee. Roasters often can convince their neighbors to ignore the smoke by sharing their fresh, barbecued coffee.

There is also an enclosed drum-type roaster that works well over a campfire or a charcoal or gas grill. It is a form of rotisserie. The coffee is secured in the drum and then turned on the spit as it roasts. These primitive drum-style roasters vary in both size and materials. Sometimes they are called "cowboy coffee roasters," easy to carry in a chuck wagon and requiring only fire and someone

Roasting at San Francisco's Sightglass Coffee.
Photo by Mark Shimahara

to turn the crank to power them. A slightly tweaked version of a hot-air popcorn popper is another successful small-batch coffee roaster. Again, be warned that coffee creates a lot of smoke during this roast process.

Although the methodology of these techniques varies, typically there are similar versions available for home and commercial roasters. The heat source varies—from wood or charcoal to natural gas, propane or electricity—as does the heat exchange method, be it a fluid-bed air roaster, or a solid or perforated drum. Because there are so many choices available to today's coffee professional, it's worthwhile to study the similarities and differences in technologies prior to selecting roasting equipment. Personal preference will dictate the choice of roasting equipment.

• HEAT EXCHANGE

Radiant, conductive and convective forms of heat exchange play a role in coffee roasting. How much of a role depends greatly on the type of roaster and the level of technology used in the roaster's design. Working in tandem, two different types of heat exchange can be controlled with modern roasting systems to achieve a consistent, evenly roasted product. Radiant heat is generated directly by a flame (produced by gas fuel or burning wood) or by an electrical element. Heat is radiated from the source. The heat can be felt radiating from the source without physical contact or a fan to create airflow. Standing next to a campfire and enjoying the warmth is a form of radiant heat transfer. If there is physical contact with a heat source, the transfer becomes conductive. Coffee beans that come in contact with the heated surface of a roasting cylinder (the drum or other parts of the roasting equipment) are undergoing conductive heat transfer. Once the beans become heated, bean-to-bean conductivity also occurs.

The frying-pan roaster relies on conduction for heat exchange; the beans that spend the longest amount of time in direct contact with the heated surface run the risk of scorching and tipping. Modern roasting machines implement the principles of convective heat exchange for the roast process. Convection is the transfer of heat through hot air. Convective heat transfer relies on a constant supply of heated air being circulated through the roasting environment. Convective roasters rely on a blower or fan to create the airflow through the roaster cylinder. Convection creates an efficient roast environment as each bean is consistently surrounded by hot air.

• WEIGHTS AND BALANCES

In coffee roasting, the scientist is called upon to perform the weight and balance measurements in the roastery. Most small roasting businesses don't have a coffee lab with high-tech equipment, but there are simple measurements you can use to assure quality. There are many weights and balances to be measured before, during and after each batch of coffee is roasted. A roaster must confirm the capacity of the roasting equipment and the maximum green weight the cylinder will accommodate. Many commercial roasters are most efficient when roasting at a percentage of capacity rather that maxed out. Comparing green weight in to green weight out is necessary for calculating the shrinkage of each roast, which is extremely important for factoring price and profitability of the finished product.

Ambient conditions also should be noted prior to the start of the roast. What are the temperature, barometric pressure and current wind conditions? All of these can affect the airflow in the roasting environment. Note the gas pressure coming into the building. Is there enough pressure to sustain a consistent flame? At what altitude is the roaster? There are many things to consider and note before dropping the green coffee into the roaster. Once the coffee is in the roaster, more measurements are required to complete the roast log for each batch. Roast log measurements vary according to the specific needs of the business, but they often include a time/temperature plot and notations for airflow changes.

The roaster warms up at San Francisco's Sightglass Coffee. | *Photo by Mark Shimahara*

• THE BEAN PATH

Consider the coffee bean and the path it takes from the hopper to the cooling tray. The light green bean changes from a rock hard pellet to a larger, more fragile brown version of itself. The green coffee has little aroma and a lackluster taste. The hard bean is impossible to chew or even break open with a hammer. The green coffee usually will enter the pre-heated roasting environment at room temperature. Once the bean temperature and the temperature of the roasting environment become equal, the beans begin a predetermined path (profile) created by the roastmaster specifically for the variety of coffee being roasted. The coffee takes on energy and the bean temperature increases. The rate of rise is directly dependent on the roast profile desired.

Continuing along the path, the coffee bean loses up to 25 percent of its weight as the visual and chemical changes take place. By the time the coffee enters the cooling tray, the bean has nearly doubled in size, changed from green to brown, and might have developed an oily sheen. The once non-remarkable green

bean has developed a unique fragrance and is fragile enough to be broken in half and tasted for a first glimpse of the coffee's final flavor.

• VISUAL CHANGES AND CHECKPOINTS

Stand beside a coffee roaster with a clear view of the sight glass and observe the many changes that occur to the green coffee bean while it tumbles around in the super-heated air. First it's green, though the color can range from a blue-green hue to a more faded sage green. Watch closely as the coffee starts to warm up and the green gets brighter and brighter—for a short time it nears apple-green and smells like grass. The green fades to a yellow shade that in turn becomes light brown. Take time at this point to smell the roasting coffee; it's at this stage that it starts to smell like cookies baking. There might be a bit of steam on the sight glass as water vapor builds. The brown gets richer and darker as the Maillard reaction transforms the sugars and amino acids into browned goodness. This reaction also occurs in other browned foods, such as meats, toast and cookies.

Another significant change in the bean occurs near 385 degrees F—first crack. First crack is the popping of the bean, the result of water vapor being converted to steam within the bean. When the coffee cracks, it breaks out of its skin and becomes larger, similar to popcorn popping. The sound is similar, too. From this point on, the bean continues to darken in color, but the physical changes are less obvious visually. If the coffee is taken to second crack, it's quite likely that surface oils will begin to appear.

•HIDDEN CHANGES

A food scientist could describe in great detail the multitude of hidden chemical changes that happen to the bean during roasting. While there are many chemical reactions that result in visible changes, the hidden changes that occur within the bean remain a mystery to roasters. These unseen chemical changes include, but are not limited to, transformation of sugars in the Maillard reaction, development of water vapor, decomposition of organic acids, and reduction and management of chlorogenic acids. Chlorogenic acids make up the largest group of compounds in green coffee, even more than caffeine. The breakdown of these acids occurs at different temperatures. Studies show that at a medium roast level, about 60 percent of the chlorogenic acids are decomposed. The formation of oxides (salts) and the development of carbon dioxide also are results of the roast process.

As the roast progresses beyond first crack, water vapor is completely depleted and a pyrolysis reaction begins as the bean starts to produce energy. The cell walls of the bean begin to fracture and oil starts to appear. There is also a dramatic increase in aromatic compounds in the roasted coffee.

• CAUSE AND EFFECT

Learning to identify changes in the roast process and the effect these changes have on the outcome of the roast is what makes a roaster a master of science and art. Once the roaster starts to ask "what if" and then finds the answer, his or her success begins to soar. This is also true of problem solving. For example, if the coffee is sharp or flat or presents another unexpected and undesired characteristic in the cup, the roastmaster must solve the problem.

Each day, coffees underperform on the cupping table—not because of the quality of the bean, but rather the quality of the roast. Learning to first identify the problem then correct it is a skill that takes time and practice. There are many opportunities for the roast to get off track and once that happens, it's nearly impossible

to fix. It's important to learn to prevent the same problem from occurring again.

What happens if the roasting environment is too hot when the green coffee is charged? In a drum roaster, the coffee can scorch and roast too quickly and unevenly, resulting in a bitter cup. Roasters should learn to identify the difference in coffee that is roasted too quickly versus the same coffee roasted too slowly. The cup quality is indeed different. In a side-by-side comparative cupping of these two extreme styles, it's hard to believe it's the same coffee. One is harsh and green tasting while the other is flat with no sparkle.

Roasters get inconsistent results when too much coffee is loaded into the roaster. In this overcrowded space, the inability of air to reach the beans evenly will cause an inconsistent and sluggish roast progression. Beans trapped on the outside of the roasting cylinder become over-roasted while the beans stuck in the middle don't roast or develop as they should. Finding the ideal ratio of green coffee to air space in the roaster will aid in creating consistency and an evenly roasted product.

Roasters also can expect to face challenges related to the moisture content of the green coffee. Fresh, moist coffee is going to require a much different roast profile than an aged bean that has lost moisture. These coffees require special attention and some tweaking of the profile to keep the roast on track. A super-moist, fresh green coffee might be more successful with fewer pounds in the cylinder while a drier bean could perform with a higher mass.

Replicating success is a benchmark for all coffee roasters to achieve. This means the roaster is able to identify the positive cup qualities of a freshly roasted coffee and attribute the results to the perfect balance of science and art. The ability to produce the same product each and every time has its rewards. Consumers reward consistency with repeat business. Coffee drinkers expect coffees to exhibit specific flavors in the cup. A Yirgacheffe should taste like a Yirgacheffe and a Sumatra should feel like a Sumatra—no surprises or artistic interpretation accepted. Replicating the roast results requires a level of understanding of the roast process, and there are tools available to make certain each coffee's cup attributes are as close to perfect as possible every time.

Enter the roast log and cupping forms, two means by which roasters can record each roast in order to replicate specific results while standardizing practices for consistency in roasting. The data collected in the roast log provides the road map for each roast, though the data included varies based on specific needs and equipment. The important element here is that each roast follows the guide exactly for each specific coffee roasted. No artistic license is allowed; variance of the profile proves to be costly if the cup quality does not meet the criteria.

There a numerous examples of roast logs, and each one can be adapted to the specific roastery. Collect as much information as possible so the roast can be repeated each and every time. Consider recording weather conditions, temperature of the roastery, green weight, and numerical sequence of the roast for the day, as well as time and temperature, airflow changes and any other information that could affect the outcome. Roast logs can also aid in inventory control and help you determine overall product shrinkage. The roast log is a tool, so use it as such. Make it user friendly—this is vital to standardizing the process—and keep a roast log for every roast.

The companion to the roast log is the cupping form, an often overlooked tool for success. Too many roasters neglect to take the time to cup their coffee or have anyone else cup their coffee before it is packaged. Roast results can vary. The only way to identify a problem, or a success, is by tasting the coffee. Here again, the data collected is vital to the success of each coffee. Cupping forms can be complex, but even a simple cupping form that collects minimal data can help you assure quality attributes are met. If a roast problem is identified in cupping, it can be remedied by cross-referencing the cupping form. For example, if a typically bright-acidity coffee seems flat and without sparkle, go back to the roasting log. Look to see if the roast progressed too slowly, or the overall degree of roast was not correct for this coffee. The same steps can be taken for other cup problems such as sharpness, or lack of aromatics or sweetness.

Sightglass roaster Joe Garambone roasts on a 1961 Probat UG22. | *Photo by Mark Shimahara*

Explore the Art

• USE YOUR SENSES

Developing sensory skills improves roasting skills. There is an art involved in learning to use the flavor wheel and recognizing flavor attributes of the various coffees and roast styles. Discover how the taste and aromatics of coffee combine to create flavor. Explore flavor modulation and how the roast profile can enhance specific coffee flavor. A visual evaluation of the coffee tells about origin, variety, processing method and even, to some extent, the age of the green bean. Continue to scan the coffee throughout the roast. Watch for color changes and the evenness and degree of the roast. Listen to the roast. The cracking should be a cacophony of sound, not a few soft pops.

Smell also is a guide along the roast profile. Learn the grassy smell of the early stages, then note the change to a cookie-type aroma as the sugars in the coffee start to decompose. Smell the sample trowel as the coffee develops to the desired roast level. The sense of smell also can reveal trouble—a scorched roast, a fire, even defects of fermentation, mold and mildew. The nose is usually the first responder to trouble. When something smells "off," we look for the source.

Record what the coffee looks like, smells like, sounds like and feels like. Describe the sensory observations throughout the entire roast. Use the sense of touch. Note the coolness of the moisture-laden green coffee compared to the lighter, more fragile roasted bean. Complete a visual inspection of the roasted beans. Are beans evenly developed? Any "hot spots?" Anything else out of the ordinary?

Identify problems before the coffee gets to the cupping table. Note any concerns on the roast log. The results also may be evident on the cupping table, where the senses again work together to complete the evaluation of the brewed coffee. Try to go beyond simply tasting the coffee. Does it meet all expectations? If not, use sensory perception to identify how the roast could be improved.

• THE ART OF CUPPING

Learn and master the art of cupping. It is an important part of becoming a true artist. Both quality assurance and product development rely on the cupping protocol. Learning what each coffee can do and how to roast to optimize the attributes of each are valuable tools for roasters. There is also a language specific to coffee cupping. It takes time to become comfortable choosing the descriptor for each attribute discovered in the cup. "Tastes like" or "feels like" are common phrases at the cupping table. Becoming fluent in this language will increase the roaster's ability to communicate with other coffee professionals as well as consumers.

Recording cupping results is another tool roasters rely on for consistency. There are hundreds of cupping forms available. Some are vertical, some horizontal. Some are simple, some overly complicated. The attributes to evaluate during cupping include fragrance/aroma, acidity, flavor, sweetness, balance, body, and finish, with variations between forms. Choose a comfortable format and stick with it. Practice does push us closer to perfection. Standardize the process and complete the task while the senses are fresh and there are few distractions. The Specialty Coffee Association (SCA) cupping protocol is an excellent road map to a successful cupping practice.

Once the results from cupping are recorded, don't file them away immediately. Take time to review the cupping notes in

Photo by Mark Shimahara

comparison to the roast log. Look for opportunities to improve the coffee's overall performance. After the corrections have been noted, consider and discuss possibilities for future application. How can the coffee be used for other applications? If a coffee has great sparkle or heavy body, a super-sweet or chocolate finish, how can that coffee be used in other ways? Would it make a great iced coffee or toddy extraction? Pour-over? Espresso? Blend contributor? It is here on the cupping form that complete notes and discussion can open the door to artistic exploration.

Improve Your Roast Results

Now comes the opportunity to improve the results of the roast, fine tuning the profile for a more favorable coffee flavor. Critical review of each roast will serve as a tool to raise the overall quality and assure consistency for the coffee roaster. Identify points on the roast log where the profile might have gone off track. Also note those points where changes made the results even more spectacular. It is disappointing to create a wonderful cupping coffee and not be able to remember the details of the roast process. Check pre-heat temperature, point of equilibrium, green coffee load size, airflow, roast time and temperature rise, then make corrections where needed.

• ROAST RESULTS AND EXPECTATIONS

The moment of truth. Does the fresh-roasted coffee meet the expectations? If yes, congratulations. If the Harrar is not quite blueberry enough, the Sumatra not syrupy, no fruity wine in the Kenya or spicy sparkle in the Guatemala, it's time to use the information in the roast logs and cupping notes to identify how and where to correct the shortfall. Thoroughly understanding the cause and effect of each step of the roast process and cupping results allows the roaster to correct and improve, combining science and art to create the perfect cup.

A scientist. An artist. A coffee roaster. By blending the structure of science with an artful flair, each coffee roaster can explore and define an individual style that is uniquely his or her own. Use technology to enhance the art of the roast, then artfully explore the science of turning the coffee from green to brown. Explore the parameters and always strive to improve the style of the roast as it is defined by the perfect cup of coffee. ■

KATHI ZOLLMAN, *assistant director of specialty green coffee sales at Coffee Holding Company, is a frequent presenter at a variety of roaster education venues. She has shared coffee-roasting skills at Roasters Guild events, the SCA Expo, Coffee Fest and multiple regional roaster gatherings. Specializing in blending, sensory skill-building, and profile roasting and manipulation, she continues to be a student of all things coffee.*

Blending Art and Science to Define Your Individual Roast Style

A roaster can develop specific roast styles to highlight the attributes of a particular growing region or variety. Find the style to showcase each coffee—don't let the roast style decrease the multitude of flavors and characteristics in the cup.

Note that some roast styles—including espresso, French, Italian and others—can refer to different roasts depending on the roaster or the geographic region. (French roast can vary by degree of darkness, as can other styles, for example.) That's precisely the reason each roaster needs to define his or her own style.

WHITE COFFEE: A barely roasted coffee style. White coffee is roasted just long enough to turn the coffee to a slightly brighter green. The aroma is very grass-like. White coffee is still very hard and requires super-sharp burrs in the grinder. It's often used as an espresso shot for milk-based beverages. The flavor is similar to a grassy green tea. This style is cyclical in popularity, most often seen in the Northwest.

CINNAMON: A very lightly roasted coffee style. At this roast level, there is very little aroma development. The body is thin and the flavor has a fleeting grassiness and slight sourness. The bean is not yet developed and remains dry on the surface. This coffee is completed prior to first crack and is still rock hard.

LIGHT: Coffees roasted just through first crack are called light roast, reaching a maximum temperature of around 400 degrees F. The acidity is bright, the body is more developed than at lighter roast levels, and the surface remains dry and a bit sponge-like.

LIGHT MEDIUM: This roast style has gained popularity, roasted just far enough through first crack that the sour acidity has been converted to a more desirable fruit acidity. Sweetness is more pronounced, and the body has become substantial. The complex cup profile of the light medium roast has been the norm in the Northeast for years.

MEDIUM: This style was once popular primarily in the western regions of the United States but is now found throughout the country. Sometimes called city roast, this is a dry coffee with no surface oils. At this roast level, the aromatics are at their peak, and the cup is charged with complexity. The acidity may not be as bright as it would be at a lighter roast; the flavor of the variety is still recognizable. Medium-style coffees do not reach second crack.

FULL CITY ROAST: This is a medium to dark brown roast. In appearance, the surface is dry with droplets of flavor oils. This style is slightly sweeter than both lighter and very dark roasts, and the aroma has reached peak levels. Body, mouthfeel and a more pronounced finish also are evident. This style is used for a variety of applications; other names include Viennese, light espresso and light French.

ESPRESSO: This style refers to the degree of roast, dark brown in color with an oily surface. The acidity is low at this roast level. The advantage is maximum body, texture and sweetness, creating a balanced cup. Some of the dark roast character is starting to appear in the cup, too. Many coffees roast well at this level and remain complex.

FRENCH, ITALIAN, TURKISH, ESPRESSO: These terms describe very dark brown, oily coffee styles. Acidity is flat while body and sweetness are still full. Smoky undertones start to appear in the cup. This style is very common in the espresso culture and with roasters who have a following for a dark roast. This coffee is dropped at about 465 degrees F. The roast moves very quickly at this level and is extremely smoky.

HEAVY: This very dark brown style is also called dark French, Spanish, and Italian. The bean temperature reached is around 475 degrees F. The cup quality has changed dramatically, with burnt undertones masking the remaining cup attributes. Aroma, sweetness, body and acidity fade as the pungent smokiness dominates the cupping notes. There is a following for this style of dark roast among U.S. coffee drinkers.

Reflections on Roasting Fundamentals

Story and photos by Willem Boot

• FROM THE MAY/JUNE 2005 ISSUE OF *ROAST* •

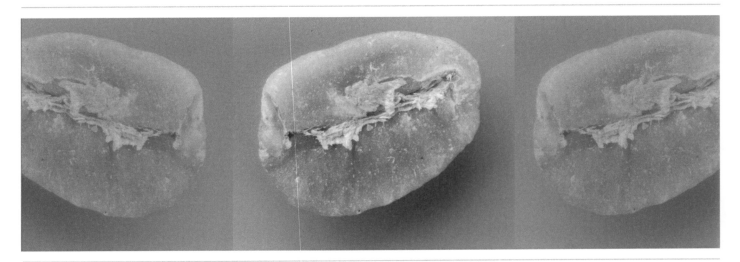

Who could have imagined the meteoric rise in the number of North American coffee roasting companies since the mid-1990s? Amazingly, almost every week a new roasting company or roasting machine is added to our family of coffee aficionados, and we can expect this trend to continue.

With this ongoing expansion, I also see an increasing need for practical, hands-on information about relevant coffee roasting issues. In this article, I have summarized a few ideas and opinions about the craft of roasting that I've learned along the way. This article only touches on a few of the myriad things that need to be learned on the way to becoming a specialty coffee roaster, but this information offers a good starting point, and will perhaps save new and growing roasters from having to learn via the ever-popular "trial and error" method.

ONE

Machine Selection: Try Before You Buy

There are more than a handful of reliable manufacturers of roasting machines, and it can be difficult to know where to begin. When shopping for a new machine, all manufacturers will claim that their product offers the ideal answer to all your coffee desires. And, indeed, manufacturers generally know their stuff. A good manufacturer will know the exact ins and outs of their specific machine. This makes sense, as most roasting machines are assembled 100 percent manually, making the construction of roasters a labor of love by itself.

However, I can testify that while most manufacturers are excellent technicians and engineers, few are coffee roasters by trade. This is part of the reason that it's oh-so-important that you "try before you buy." Remember, the roasting machine might be the most important asset of your emerging coffee emporium.

By test roasting with the prospective machine, using your own trusted green coffee beans, you, the roaster, can develop a perfect feel for the handling and operation of the machine. Most importantly, this offers the opportunity to taste the flavor of your coffee beans on each of the machines and decide which one works best for your particular beans.

In general, the roasting machine should at least have the following gadgets, which will also enable you to execute some of the protocols that are described later in this article:

➤ Digital bean temperature probe, which accurately measures the temperature of the beans being roasted. Remember, the probe only provides an indication of the bean temperature, since it is impossible to display the true internal bean temperature.

➤ Digital or analog environmental temperature probe, which displays the temperature conditions inside the drum. The read-out of this probe generally reacts immediately on changes in the BTU output of the burners.

➤ Analog gas pressure gauge, placed between the gas throttle and the burners. As a result, this gauge will provide a true indication of the BTU output of the burners.

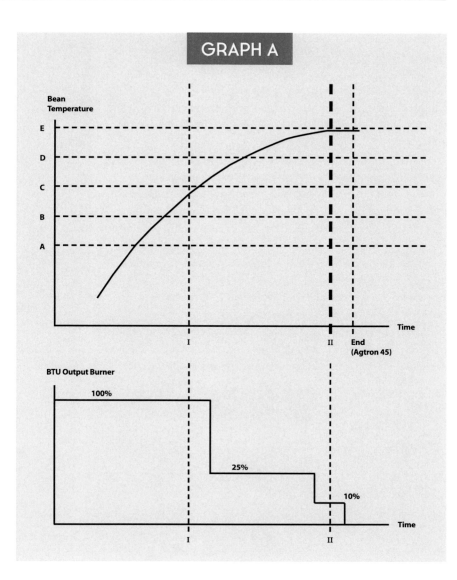

GRAPH A

TWO

Roasting Profiles: Roast Flavor Versus Bean Characteristics

The fundamental objective of roasting should be to reveal the best possible flavor profile of the bean while developing a balance between roast flavor and bean characteristics. The roast flavor develops as a result of the caramelization of sugars, while the bean flavor represents the *terroir* of the coffee. (Terroir, a French term, literally means "soil" and, as a concept, it is mainly used in the wine industry, but can also reflect all the relevant parameters that determine coffee quality: coffee variety, microclimates, processing practices and soil conditions.)

Some roasting companies apply fundamental beliefs to their roasting practice and insist on roasting light enough to reveal the characteristics of the beans only, without developing any of the bittersweet flavors that generally go hand in hand with darker roasting styles.

In general, the best choice for choosing roasting profiles is the path of taste differentiation. For that reason, it is wise to offer coffee varieties in various roast profiles so that your customers can decide. Graph A (page 227) and Graph B (below) illustrate possible strategies.

Graph A shows a roasting curve for a Kenya AA, roasted to a degree of Agtron 45 (M-basic standard). Most coffee in Kenya is grown higher than 5,500 feet, which can have a tremendous influence on the density of the beans. Picture A (right) shows an example of Kenyan coffee; look at the center cut which seems to be floating on the outside of the bean. Now look at Graph A again; notice the steep slope of the bean temperature curve throughout the roast, which is a roasting profile that generally only can be used for the hardest coffee beans. The events during the roasting process are described in Table A on page 229.

Now look at the diagram below the roasting curve in Graph A, which displays the BTU output of the burner. To establish the steep roasting curve, the operator in this scenario keeps the gas

Picture A. *Kenyan Bean*

throttle 100 percent open until the first crack is in full swing. Toward the end of the first crack, the flame is reduced to 25 percent energy output. Despite this sharp reduction in energy supply, the beans have developed sufficient internal, endothermic heat to facilitate the steep roasting curve. At the beginning of the second crack, the gas is reduced to 10 percent and the roast comes to an end. This example illustrates how we can develop a steep roasting curve with very dense coffee beans, without over-roasting or burning the product.

Graph B shows a roasting curve for the same Kenya AA coffee, roasted to a much lighter degree of Agtron 56. Many coffee professionals believe that it is impossible to create a palatable product with this light roast degree, and I firmly disagree! The trick is in the speed of the process; if roasting is done slowly enough, allowing enough time between the first crack and the end of the roast, then I guarantee you that there is true balance between roast flavor and bean characteristics. The objective in this case is to effectively slow down the roasting process right at the start of the first crack, which is shown in the lower section of Graph B. The operator anticipates the first crack by reducing the energy supply of the burners at least 15 seconds before the first crack starts. As a result, there are at least three minutes between the start of the first crack and the end of the roast, which comes at an Agtron bean color of 56 (M-basic standard). One word of caution: Always prevent the coffee from baking, which would occur if the bean temperature stalls or decreases. Provided that you selected an exemplary Kenya bean, the resulting flavor will be very balanced and rich in citrus fruit

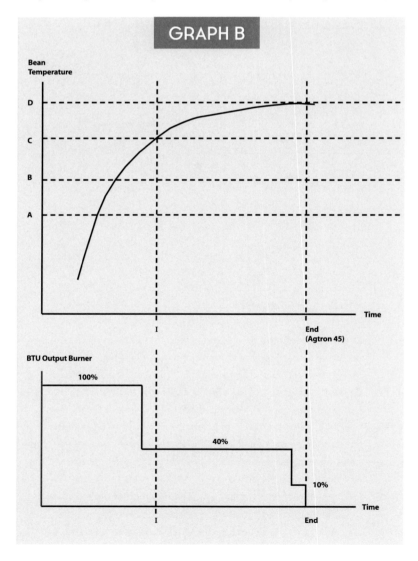

GRAPH B

Bean
Temperature

D

C

B

A

Time

End
(Agtron 45)

BTU Output Burner

100%

40%

10%

Time

End

flavors with a refreshing aftertaste, resembling a well-ripened sweet tangerine.

THREE

Roasting Profiles: Don't Be A Copycat

New companies that are just about to inaugurate their roasting machine should always devote sufficient time and energy to product development and market testing. Unfortunately, few companies invest ample resources in the important protocol of testing coffee products and recipes. Instead, they end up copying the roasting profiles of established roasting companies.

With the huge number of specialty roasters in North America, one should expect diversity in roasting recipes and flavors. Wouldn't it be great if the consumer had abundant choice between various degrees of roast, from light—for the supporters of bright acidity and refreshing flavors—to medium-dark to darker roast colors?

Being unique means additional work, but in most cases, this additional work is well worth the effort. In general, it works well to include a group of loyal customers in a process of re-engineering your roast profiles, and don't forget the next important step:

educating your customer base about the benefits of your newly developed roasting styles.

Now, let's come to the million-dollar question: Why would you go through all this hassle of differentiating your company and products from the others? Let me answer with a short anecdote. I once assisted a client with the creation of special roasting profiles for a potential customer who operates more than 10 coffeehouses at the local university campus. At least nine roasting companies were invited to bid on this mega-account by sending in samples of their roasted coffee products. Beforehand, we surveyed the roast degrees of some of the local and regional specialty roasters, and we found that the roast levels were all darker than Agtron 40. So we decided to differentiate our bid by developing some roasting profiles with a lighter roast degree but with enough complexity in the flavor of the product. We won the bid! The moral of the story: Don't be a copycat, and dare to be different with your roasting profiles. ■

WILLEM BOOT *is the president of Boot Coffee Consulting, a training and consulting firm for coffee companies. He can be reached via email at* willemboot@bootcoffee.com *or visit* bootcoffee.com.

Table A — COFFEE ROASTING EVENTS

REFERENCE POINT	EVENT	DESCRIPTION
A	Beans are releasing free moisture	Bean color rapidly changes from yellow to light brown
B	Free moisture is evaporated	Bean color is cinnamon brown; some coffee aroma becomes noticeable
C	First crack starts	The bean expands and breaks at the center cut, which causes the first "pop"
D	Ongoing bean development	Caramelization of sugars causes major developments in flavor; color changes from light to darker brown
E	Second crack starts	Carbon dioxide (CO_2) builds up within the cell structure of the beans and causes cell walls to snap, thus the second "pop"
I	First crack	
II	Second crack	

Three-barrel sample roaster.
Photo by Clay Enos

Unwinding the Sample Roasting Thread

How Roasters Manage Quality in Small Doses

by Phil Beattie

• FROM THE JANUARY/FEBRUARY 2013 ISSUE OF *ROAST* •

It's Saturday morning in the sleepy town of Sumner, Washington, and the fog has yet to lift from the green valley. Across town, children are watching brightly colored cartoons as they drink sweet milk from the bottom of their cereal bowls. Parents sit in their kitchens and breakfast nooks, gently sipping their first cup of the morning as they ponder the weekend's activities.

On the far side of town, if you listen closely, you may hear the soothing whir of a vintage three-barrel Probat sample roaster. Tucked away in a sea of warehouses, this roaster gently tosses a handful of beans over a small blue flame, coaxing and coercing the sweet flavors into fruition. And there I stand, custom-carved spoon in hand, diligently peeking at the beans. Under the bright spotlight, these beans show their true colors.

This sample roast is an urgent matter because it spells the immediate future of this coffee. This particular 100 grams is representative of nearly 20,000 pounds of coffee and carries its history to the table for scrutiny under the spoon. I appreciate and understand the gravity of the situation and put my sole focus on the development of this roast.

It's not the first time this coffee has been critiqued. This coffee's journey follows a line through many sample roasters and across many cupping tables to reach this point. It has run the gauntlet of particular palates, showing its merits. And here, once more, it will serve to impress with vibrancy, complexity and notability.

Around the globe, coffees such as this one find their way from sample roaster to sample roaster. Their destinations vary from giant automated factories where each step is monitored by computers and sensors, to small cafes with a table-top roaster being tended to by an artisan.

A Delicate Balance

With so much weight riding on this 100-gram roast, the importance of quality control at the sample roaster is self evident. Yet managing these small, seemingly simple roasts can be a challenge.

Chris Schooley, who previously roasted samples and assessed all coffees for boutique importer Coffee Shrub, has been meeting this challenge head-on for more than 10 years. His first experiences on the sample roaster were under the tutelage of Geoff Watts on Intelligentsia's 1950s three-barrel Gothot. Schooley has been preaching the wisdom of process control at the sample roaster for many years. It was under his watch as chair of the Roasters Guild that the first-of-its-kind sample roasting curriculum was developed.

The Roasters Guild sample roasting class gives students, both experienced and not, an immersion into the theories and practices behind a good sample roast. This course includes guidelines for roast duration, degree of roast, and bean development. Also addressed is calibrating oneself to the roasting equipment.

As with production roasting, some roasters tend to point to the numbers when tracking bean development while others focus on the sensory aspects. Of course, a balance is needed. The numbers to track are similar to those to watch when roasting full-size batches: charge temperature, time of roast, gas pressure and airflow settings. But the same parameters will not guarantee the proper development of each type of coffee.

"Aroma—roast aroma—is incredibly important in sample roasting," explains Schooley. Aroma is a crucial indicator of bean development; roaster operators can assess this and the surface texture and color of the beans throughout the roast. Sweet, pungent aromas, a smooth surface texture, and even coloring can be good indicators of a proper roast.

Timing is also crucial to the bean development. Schooley points to this as an important, yet frequently missed, assessment of the roast. "The most common [mistake] I see is just improper development, usually from too quick of a roast," he says. "Everything is condensed at the front of the palate and you don't get a clear picture of the sweetness and body."

Schooley currently roasts samples in his garage in Fort Collins, Colorado. His current equipment is a Probat Pre 1Z and a Quest

Each barrel of a sample roaster has its own personality. | *photo by Phil Beattie*

M3 roaster. He proves that a fancy cupping lab and roasting room are not requirements for proper assessment of a coffee—just knowledge and dedication.

Chabela Cerqueda Garcia, quality control manager for Sustainable Harvest's office in Oaxaca, Mexico, has been sample

Using a spoon to check on roast development. | *photo by Clay Enos*

Phil Beattie sample roasting. | *photo by Clay Enos*

roasting for seven years on a two-barrel Probat and demonstrates plenty of knowledge and dedication. Being closer to the source means that her sample roasts will determine a coffee's destination market and can even have an impact on the quality premium that a grower will be paid. She teaches sample roasting fundamentals to producer groups throughout Mexico and other producing countries.

Garcia points to the time and temperature, as well as color assessment, as the most important factors in sample roasting. "I use the Agtron color disks" to measure roast levels, she says. "However, it's not too common to find producers who have the Agtron disks, so when we give cupping courses to suppliers, we always include a section where we talk about roast level. We also do a cupping that is like the Q grader course test, where we taste dark, light and baked roasts, so producers know what an off roast tastes like in the cup."

General recommendations on time and degree of roast are 7 to 10 minutes per batch, with a finish point of just past first crack and not quite to the beginning of second crack. But these are broad parameters. Being comfortable with your equipment will help you narrow down those parameters to your exacting standards.

A Question of Calibration

Most experienced sample roasters will tell you that each roaster has its own personality, and quite a few test batches will allow you to get acquainted with the workings of a particular roaster. Even different barrels on one piece of equipment can behave very differently.

Mike Strumpf, who has managed quality control for a number of coffee roasters in the United States, references this learning curve when he discusses the first piece of equipment he worked on more than seven years ago. "On that roaster, as with most, each barrel had its own character, so I had to learn three roasters at once," Strumpf says. "The learning process was a lot of trial and error. First roasting the same coffee over and over, and then starting to roast actual PSS [pre-shipment samples] and arrival samples."

With Schooley, Garcia and Strumpf representing importing, exporting and decaffeination businesses in the United States, Mexico and Canada, respectively, the question of calibration has to come up. How do they know that others in the supply chain will duplicate the roast that they have sample roasted? Roast calibration can be a tricky thing when people are using different equipment in different locations.

Says Strumpf: "In-person cupping calibration is the best way to calibrate our sample roasts. I find it really useful to have suppliers and customers come to my cupping room, and [for me] to go to their cupping rooms. This works better for me than mailing pre-roasted samples."

Strumpf makes a good point regarding pre-roasted samples. With time from roast playing such a large role in the flavor of a particular coffee, sending pre-roasted samples through the supply chain does not create a foundation for educated buying decisions. Although much can be learned regarding degree of roast through the exchange of expedited roasted samples, it is not entirely conducive to answering questions about flavor development.

For the best calibration of sample roasting protocol in different labs, side-by-side roasting and cupping yields the most success. However, much can also be achieved through online, real-time cupping. Roast profiles can be discussed in conjunction with cupping notes and scores.

Discussion points on sample roast protocol largely parallel those of production roasting. However, the language and measurement tools can be different due to the simple fact that most sample roasters lack the bells and whistles of the average production roaster.

Chabela Cerqueda Garcia sample roasting in Honduras. | *photo courtesy of Sustainable Harvest*

Newer-model sample roasters often have exhaust temperature readings but many older model sample roasters lack any type of temperature readouts at all. This lack of accurate bean temperature readouts means that the sample roaster must speak in terms of bean color versus time, flame control positioning, time to first crack, and time from first crack to finish degree of roast.

Mike Strumpf sample roasts on a six-barrel Jabez Burns. | *photo courtesy of Swiss Water Decaffeinated Coffee Company*

Of course, installation of temperature readouts is possible even with older sample roasters, but it is not a prerequisite for achieving roasting consistency. The numbers and statistics of the roast are the platform for diagnosing differences in roasts. But the numbers must always be balanced by the cupping and analysis of flavor development in the particular sample.

When looking for flavor development, Schooley zeroes in on the balance. "I think that we've been pushing the idea that acidity is a positive aspect in coffee for so long that folks think that it's the only positive thing in a coffee, and they don't focus on developing the body and sweetness," he says.

I find that a routine can lend itself to more sample roasting consistency. Always prepare samples ahead of time, gathering density measurements and weighing samples during warm-up. Then space the timing of the batches in multiple drums, the same each time.

Strumpf references this practice as well. "I fully prepare all of my samples in advance of roasting so that when I am roasting all I am paying attention to is the coffees," he says. "I also stagger my barrels by a fixed time, always going from left to right, so that I can compare roast progression across barrels."

The rhythm of the process can be soothing and reminds you that you are a coffee roaster when you get into the groove. It is this blending of the use of the senses that can make sample roasting feel like a harkening back to days when the nose, ears and eyes were more important to roasting than flame settings, airflow measurements and temperature probes.

A Shared Vision

Our three sample roasters— Schooley, Strumpf and Garcia—share a common thread. Whether in a garage in Colorado, a high-tech lab in Vancouver, British Columbia, or the coffeelands of Oaxaca, they share a dedication to data gathering and sensory analysis. Although the batches are smaller, they still must possess the same passion and attention to detail that is required to roast in production settings.

I find great joy in the fact that every coffee—even the ones destined for giant automated monsters that chew up green and spew out roasted in a mechanical dance—still gets to be passionately handcrafted, even if it's just 100 grams at a time. ■

. . . .

PHIL BEATTIE *is the director of coffee for Dillanos Coffee Roasters in Sumner, Washington. Beattie is a veteran roaster, cupper and an all around coffee enthusiast. He has been an integral piece of the Dillanos success story through his coffee sourcing and relationships across the globe. He has also served as chair of the Roasters Guild Executive Council and a member of many cupping juries. You can find photos of his coffee travels under the alias @justroaster on Instagram.*

The key to sample roasting is finding the right balance in flavor development. *photos by Clay Enos*

Logged In

How to Use a Roast Log to Improve Your Coffee and Streamline Your Business

by Kathi Zollman

• FROM THE SEPTEMBER/OCTOBER 2009 ISSUE OF *ROAST* •

ON THE SURFACE, it appears to be such an easy question: "Why is it important to keep a roast log?"

Yet a closer look reveals that it is, in fact, a complex question with a multitude of answers. In short, the roast log is one of the best business tools a roasting operation can use. In addition to using the logs simply to record roasting data, operators can go beyond the obvious and put roast logs to use in other facets of the business, such as inventory control and management, quality control, new product development and profitability, as well as tracking productivity and labor efficiencies. Roast logs are also useful, and often required, for organic certification.

Many coffee roasters currently use a roast log in their roasting operations to record an array of data in a variety of methods. Some roasters log with handwritten notes on yellow tablets or preprinted forms, while some use "elephant-like" memory skills to record the data mentally. Yet another group uses real-time data loggers to plot a graph, while more complex profile systems record real-time data plus other predetermined roast parameters. The challenge is to take the information gleaned from the data and extrapolate the results into usable information. Once the information is put to work, the value of data collection in a roast log multiplies dramatically.

The specific data collected on a roast log varies by roasting operation and its perceived needs (see sidebar on page 239). Using a log, roasters can record the actual roast profile data, tracking the time and temperature path of the roast from start to finish. The inclusion of cupping notes provides a complete evaluation of the success of each specific roast. When this varied information is recorded regularly, it provides insight into the overall process and can be used as a reference guide for future roast successes.

Producing accurate and detailed roast logs requires a commitment of time and energy, so it is important for businesses to use the logs for maximum return on time and energy. Recording the data and then simply filing it away is a small portion of the overall process. Regular analysis of the completed logs is an invaluable tool for operation management. Operators can review and unlock seemingly limitless information for a coffee roasting business. This practice encourages roasters to take the note-taking process beyond "I log because someone told me to" and start using roast logs as a professional business tool.

Inventory Control and Management

Typically, roast logs contain basic information like roast date, coffee type and green weight. This information can be manipulated to create efficient inventory management tools, track trends, and forecast future raw material needs. Using the green weight numbers and coffee names recorded in the roast log, it is easy to create weekly green coffee usage reports. These reports give roasters an accurate view of the volume of each specific bean being roasted and a clearer idea of how the next period might trend, preventing overages or shortages of green. Usage reports work in tandem with physical inventories to eliminate errors and oversights.

Adding the coffee's lot number to the roast log simplifies the traceability of each coffee and eases the task of creating a legitimate paper trail. Should a situation arise in which roasted coffee product has to be recalled or traced through the distribution system, roasters can retrieve the data easily by turning to their files of completed roast logs. Tracking the coffee by name and lot number also serves as a basis for report preparation for certified coffees such as organic coffee. Logs put the vital information at the preparer's fingertips, allowing your business to efficiently summarize a coffee's roasting date, total pounds, and identifying marks. Many busy roasters put off report filing until the deadline looms near, making the process more stressful than it needs to be. If the roast logs are completed and filed in a timely manner, the raw data has been collected already, and all that remains is pulling it together. Culling data from a roast log is much simpler than digging through stacks of empty coffee bags to estimate the total amount roasted.

Quality Control

Achieving and maintaining a high level of consistency in roasted product without keeping good records is not easy. The roast log provides assurance of consistency from roast to roast, and it offers a basis for comparison and troubleshooting should a quality issue arise. The quality control portion of the roast log employs a range of data; some roasters keep the records very simple and others more complex.

Some variables to consider:

✓ Preheat temperature
✓ Point of equilibrium
✓ Progression of time and temperature
✓ Airflow in roasting chamber
✓ Energy output/heat application
✓ First crack time
✓ Roast finish time and temperature

This information creates a specific profile for each roast that can then be reviewed in conjunction with the cupping notes to further ensure the quality of the finished roasted product. The data used to create the profile varies by roaster operation, but a roast profile is still defined as the path the roast follows from start to finish.

If you are facing a quality concern, the roast log can reveal the probable answer. For example, was the roast too fast or too slow? Was there too much green coffee for the size of roaster? Did the roast stall or run? Was the point of equilibrium too high? Any of these incidents can contribute to a negative result in the cup, but they can be quickly identified and corrected by cupping the coffee and then comparing completed roast logs of the same coffee. Weather conditions can also affect the roast process; extreme air pressure changes, wind, or temperature can be noted on the roast log as a reference for comparison.

Consistency issues are multiplied in roasting operations with more than one roaster operator. The opportunity for error is greater each time a different operator clocks in for a shift. Roast logs will assure that the process remains the same for each roast and each roaster. When paired with cupping notes, the roast log can pinpoint a problem—be it machine or operator trouble.

Of course, logs are not meant only for larger operations. Single-operator roasteries can also benefit from the data compiled in the logs. Many smaller roasters operate their entire business single-handedly, carrying out each and every production job while keeping huge amounts of vital information in their heads and failing to document their tasks. What if the roaster was unable to work due to an unforeseen emergency? Most small businesses would screech to a halt without the roaster. Completed roasting logs act as a guide for another employee to step in and work through the roast process in the absence of the primary roaster. At the minimum, roasters should consider logging roast details that include the profile information necessary to produce a consistent roasted product.

The logs provide a point of reference for comparative review and assure consistency and quality in each roast. When used effectively, these tracking devices become professional tools for roasters seeking the highest levels of quality and consistency.

New Product Development

Roasters often comment on a roast that was amazing, but they cannot recall the specific path to perfection. Here, your roast logs can be invaluable tools for new product development. Whether your business is thinking about adding a new coffee to your lineup or you need to create a specific coffee for a customer, roast logs are vital to creating and replicating the preferred roast results. Recording the results of roasting to variable degrees of roast and later performing a comparative cupping is a productive use of roast logs. When developing a profile for a new coffee, expect that it will take multiple variable roasts to achieve the most favorable results for a specific coffee. Record the tweaking of a profile on the log so that once the perfect roast is achieved, it can be repeated.

But what if a coffee isn't performing as well as expected? Maybe the chocolate finish isn't there, or the promised fruit notes are overpowered by the acidity. Cupping your coffees regularly and tracking the results can enhance your understanding of how the coffees can perform. A review of roast logs can reveal opportunities to improve the overall cup quality. Which cup was sweeter, brighter, harsher or smoother? A trained eye can compare cupping results to roast logs and pinpoint where the roast can be improved or corrected. Once the new product is perfected, it can be duplicated easily. Roast logs can expedite positive results and greatly reduce frustration for the roaster operator.

Profitability

Roast logs can also lead to profitability for a coffee roasting operation. Most logs contain information regarding green weight in, roasted weight out, total number of batches and the resulting roasted product at the end of the business day. Roastery owners can analyze the logged numbers quickly and glean valuable information about the bottom line of the roasting operation.

A primary calculation derived from the roast log is "percent of shrink," or the amount of weight loss occurring in the roast process. This number should be considered in the cost factoring of the roasted product. Calculating the percentage of shrink is an ongoing process in profit management. The shrink ratio can vary as much as 10 percentage points depending on the coffee and the degree of roast—a considerable amount of weight loss and cost when pricing out a pound of roasted coffee. For example, 20 pounds of green that results in 16 pounds of roasted coffee works out to a ratio of 0.8 shrink, or a 20 percent loss in weight. Roasters can rely on this information when calculating how many pounds of green to roast to reach a specific weight of roasted coffee.

Another revealing calculation is roast production capacity. Is the roastery performing at maximum capacity, or is there room for growth? Roasters need to be aware of the total number of pounds that can be roasted per shift per day to evaluate growth potential. Roast logs provide insight into the actual number of

roasts completed per hour, production hours per shift, and total number of pounds produced per shift. These evaluations create a benchmark for efficiency in growth and total output for the roasting operation. Roasters can review the numbers to decide whether to take on additional work as well as determine if there is capacity at the current level to handle additional production demands.

Productivity/Labor Efficiencies

Reviewing daily roast logs can clue management into the productivity of each roaster operator on the team. This is most effective if the roast log indicates the operator's name and the actual time that each roast starts. The time-of-day data reveals the operator's efficiencies as well as opportunities to adhere to production schedules. If there is a large time span between roasts, what is occupying the operator's time: weighing out the next batch, waiting for the roaster to cool or heat, or texting friends?

Requiring roasting employees to keep accurate roast logs helps to identify any labor concerns within the production facility. Why does one employee struggle to get the required batches completed

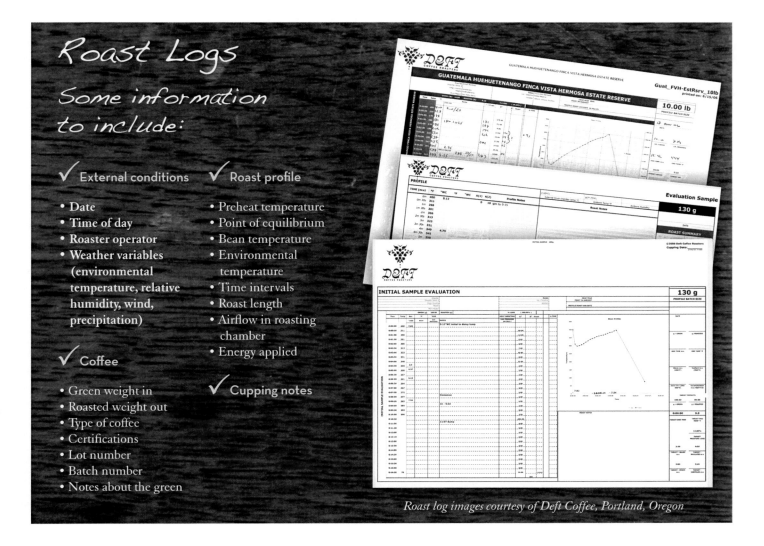

Roast log images courtesy of Deft Coffee, Portland, Oregon

while another seems to breeze through the workday? The logs will help your business recognize problems in employee efficiencies and identify specific steps to alleviate future problems.

Employee Training

Roast logs also provide an outstanding training tool for new and current employees, because they inspire a high level of performance and consistency from the start. Recording the data encourages accountability and responsibility while introducing the employee to the roast process. The trainee learns by participating, and entering data in a roast log exposes employees to commonly used coffee terminology and definitions. At the same time, employers benefit from a consistent training format for single or multiple new hires.

By keeping a roast log, operators gain a better understanding of roasting dynamics. They come to learn how a roaster works while documenting the process—and, ultimately, recording the overall flavor profile of each specific coffee. Logs provide a snapshot of the parameters of the roast and external forces that can affect the results. Roaster operators can gain an appreciation of the relationship between such variables as the preheat temperature and the size of the load, air temperature versus bean temperature, environmental effects on roasting and cooling time, differences in various coffees, seasonal changes in roasting, and basic principles of heat transfer. These dynamics are reinforced at the cupping table when roasts are reviewed for consistency.

Maintenance Schedules

Using a roast log to implement roaster maintenance schedules is simple: Just add a batch number for each roast. Maintenance activities can be noted and tracked on the log, proving beneficial for action items that need to be completed after a certain number of roasts.

Daily routine activities like cleaning the chaff collector or wiping out the cooling tray can be noted as completed at the end of the shift. Logging these activities creates a daily cleaning and maintenance report and provides information for repairs that might be required.

Operators can answer questions regarding time of use with accuracy, supported by the paper trail in the roast log. Other subtle physical changes can serve as an alert to a possible maintenance concern. Good time and temperature records for each roast serve as indicators of changes in the roast profile that could be caused by a maintenance issue. A proactive maintenance program will help reduce downtime and expenses caused by unforeseen problems or roaster emergencies. Regularly scheduled exhaust cleaning on drum roasters is much more manageable than a roastery full of smoke.

Safety Log

Keeping a roast log requires focus and diligence on the part of the operator, forcing roasters to tune in to the process in front of them. When compiling a steady stream of data, there isn't time to talk on the phone, check email or send text messages. Many roaster fire stories sound like this: "Everything was just fine. Then, when I got off the phone and turned around, flames were shooting from the roaster and smoke was rolling out."

Many safety problems occur because of lack of attention on the part of the operator. Staying hands-on increases the focus and awareness of all aspects of the roast and greatly reduces the chance of problems. An employee training program and a sound maintenance schedule work together to make the roastery a safe work environment. The roast log increases awareness of potential problems, possibly eliminating them before they have a chance to develop. Many roasters practice safety shutdowns so their employees can be as prepared as possible if an emergency happens. Preparedness exercises like these should also be documented on the roast log.

Continuing Professional Development

Roast logs provide an infinite amount of information for roaster operators. Beyond the basic mechanics of the roast, those wanting to glean more knowledge and understanding of what goes on inside the roaster can use the logs to start answering their questions. Roasters can attain a clearer understanding of the entire roast process and the cause and effect of changing the variables of that process. Numerous external influences affect the roast process, but with a solid understanding of the procedure, roasters can learn to predict and react to avoid problems well in advance.

Roasting is an ongoing educational journey, and roast logs are valuable tools to better understanding. By recording as much data as possible, roasters can study and extract information, increasing their knowledge while creating a consistently improved cup of coffee. The return on the investment for the owner, roaster and industry as a whole could be extremely rewarding indeed. ■

KATHI ZOLLMAN, *assistant director of specialty green coffee sales at Coffee Holding Company, is a frequent presenter at a variety of roaster education venues. She has shared coffee roasting skills at Roasters Guild events, the SCA Expo, Coffee Fest and multiple regional roaster gatherings. Providing quality training and skill-building at a local level has been a focus for several years as Zollman has been involved in the grassroots regional movement. Specializing in blending, sensory skill-building, and profile roasting and manipulation, she continues to be a student of all things coffee.*

A Sample Roast Log

For a PDF of this roast log, go to
roastmagazine.com/roastlog

Date: _____

Date: _____
Coffee: _____
Profile: _____
Batch Weight: _____
Pre-Heat T

Weather:

Weather:

OAT _____

IAT _____   Gen. Cond. _____

Date: _____

Coffee: _____

Profile: _____

Batch Weight: _____

Pre-Heat Temp: _____

Weather:

OAT _____ _____   Gen. Cond. _____

IAT _____   _____

Rel. Hum. _____   _____

Bar. Pres. _____   _____

500°		500°
475°		475°
450°		450°
425°		425°
400°		400°
375°		375°
350°		350°
325°		325°
300°	CUPPING NOTES	300°
275°		275°
250°		250°
225°		225°
200°		200°
175°		175°
150°		150°
125°		125°
100°F		100°F

0 min. 1 2 3 4 5 6 7 8 9 10 11 12 13 14 15 16 17 18 19 20 21 22 23 24 min.

Total Roast Time _____   Total Cool Time _____

Ambex ROAST TRUE!   **www.AmbexRoasters.com**

By recording as much data as possible, roasters can study and extract information, increasing their knowledge while creating a consistently improved cup of coffee.

The Naked Bean

Roasting to Perfection

Story and photos by Willem Boot

• FROM THE MARCH/APRIL 2004 ISSUE OF *ROAST* •

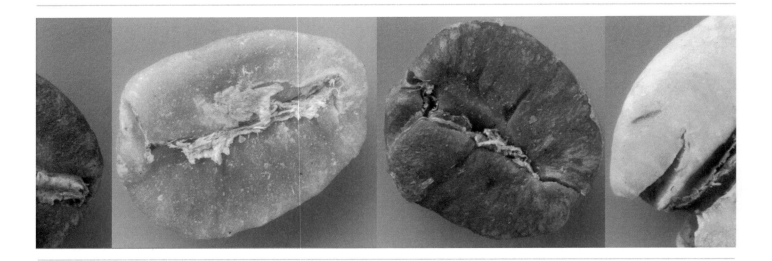

For me, roasting coffee is as meaningful for my personal fulfillment as it is critical to the creation of an aromatic cup of coffee. My personal journey with roasting started at the age of 14 when my father built the prototypes of his "Golden Coffee Box" home coffee roaster. A few years later, I learned roasting on a vintage L12 batch roaster, which required the use of the most sophisticated and valuable measuring tools a human being has: sight, sound and smell. The many hours I spent roasting coffee in the artisan way were inspirational and challenging at the same time.

The inspiration comes from the satisfaction of creating a final product, from turning a tasteless green bean into a lively aromatic roasted coffee. In my experience, the challenge with roasting has always been connected to the intricate desire for perfection, from the quest of roasting the beans just right to that defining point of maximum flavor in the cup. A colleague described the challenge of roasting in an interesting way: "Imagine sailing a yacht in 8-knot winds, and instead of lowering your sails, you steer the boat right at full speed past the entry buoys, into the harbor, just left of the main pier. When you arrive at your dock, you steer the yacht 180 degrees into the wind, which stops the boat completely and brings you home safely."

Coffee roasting is just like this scenario. In the roasting process, coffee beans are first loaded with energy until the heat-absorption capacity of the beans is nearly exhausted. Right before spontaneous combustion becomes inevitable, the roaster operator reduces heat input and allows for a gradual increase in bean temperature. Finally, at the end of the roasting process, the bean temperature needs to drop about 350 degrees as quickly as possible during the cooling process.

For understandable reasons, outsiders might think that roasting is like the ultimate balancing act: risky and hazardous. However, with the proper amount of control, coffee roasting can be as safe as toasting bread or barbecuing a burger.

Despite all these modern controls, many roasters are still confused about how to use their roaster with different bean types and how to design time-temperature profiles to get the best possible outcome in the cup. To develop the proper skills of controlling your roaster consistently, it is important to understand how parameters like moisture content and bean density influence the roasting process.

How Green Coffee Quality Affects Roasting

MOISTURE CONTENT

In roasting, the moisture content of the green bean plays an important role. Under normal conditions, green coffee beans have a moisture content of 10 to 12 percent. The moisture content will fluctuate freely with the relative humidity content of the ambient air. In cities like Amsterdam and San Francisco, relative humidity levels throughout the year are nearly perfect for storing green beans over a length of time, and for slowing down the aging process of green coffee. This also reduces the likelihood that the roaster operator has to change roast profiles to compensate for possible variances in green coffee moisture. The moisture inside the green beans is partially free or is present as bound moisture and contained in the carbohydrate molecules.

We can summarize the roasting process as a three-stage cycle:

The drying phase is when the moisture content of the coffee is reduced to about 2 percent. During this phase, the "free" moisture—the residue of the process from cherry to green bean—evaporates. Free moisture also plays a role in the heat transfer during roasting. As soon as the beans are energized with heat, the bean's moisture conducts this heat throughout the bean. When the internal bean temperature approaches 212 degrees F, the free moisture starts evaporating.

In the second phase, from the first crack to the second crack, coffee beans develop their specific aromas and flavors, which as coffee tasters know, can produce a very complex taste profile. At the end of the second phase, all free moisture has evaporated. The length of the second phase depends on the roasting degree, which can vary from region to region and from product to product.

With very dark roasts, there is also a third phase which starts when the second crack is almost completed. During this phase, carbonization takes place and the bound moisture is destroyed.

Picture A.
Kenya coffee bean: hard bean structure

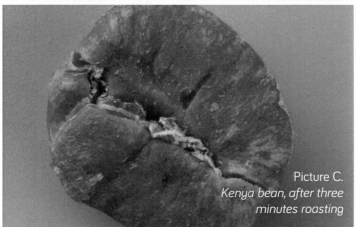

Picture B.
Robusta coffee bean (Indonesia): soft bean structure

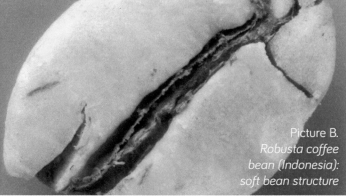

Picture C.
Kenya bean, after three minutes roasting

Picture D.
Kenya bean, after six minutes roasting

Picture E.
Kenya bean, after 11 minutes roasting (after the first crack)

Picture F.
Kenya, half bean, after three minutes roasting

Picture G.
Kenya half bean, after six minutes roasting

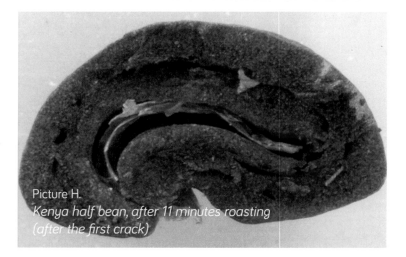

Picture H.
Kenya half bean, after 11 minutes roasting (after the first crack)

Beans with a moisture content of less than 10 percent have a sharply reduced free moisture level and will tend to roast much faster, especially in the first phase. In this case, the roaster operator needs to change the roasting profile by initiating the roasting process at a lower heat level and by maintaining a lower amount of energy supply (less BTUs) during the first roasting phase.

Beans with a high moisture content (fresh crop coffees can have a moisture content in excess of 14 percent) often require that the roaster operator includes a pre-drying phase before starting the first phase of the process. During pre-drying, it is recommended that the roaster maintains a drum temperature of 300 degrees F with the objective to slowly remove the excess free moisture. The actual phase one of the roasting process can begin as soon as the beans start losing their deep green color.

CELL STRUCTURE DENSITY

Lower grown beans generally have a less solid bean structure than higher grown beans. The density of the bean structure is revealed by the shape and the position of the center cut. Picture A (page 243) shows a bean from Kenya, which was grown at an altitude of at least 5,500 feet. The center cut is tightly closed and almost seems to be floating in the upper layer of the bean. In sharp contrast, Picture B (page 243) displays a robusta bean, grown at almost sea level. In this case, the center cut is widely opened and draws like a deep crevasse through the coffee bean.

What is the relationship between bean density and roasting? High-density beans have a denser cell structure and more cells per cubic millimeter than low-density beans. As a result, high-density beans are more resistant to heat, which will be especially noticeable during the first phase of roasting.

After the evaporation of free moisture, the color of the coffee beans starts changing from (light) green to yellow to light brown. During this color change, the bean starts expanding. With lower-density beans, the center cut will open more quickly, allowing for a faster transfer of heat, which will accelerate the process even further.

Green Bean Types and Time Temperature Profiles

To develop an effective roast protocol, I recommend dividing green coffee beans into the following four categories:

I). Hard bean types: Roast these coffees with high initial heat and moderate heat in the final stage of the roast process.

Examples: Kenya AA, Guatemala SHB and almost any coffee grown higher than 5,000 feet.

II). Medium hard bean types: Roast these coffees with moderate initial heat and moderate heat in the final stage. Examples: Brazil, Sumatra, Java and most Latin American coffees grown lower then 5,000 feet.

III). Soft bean types: These coffees should be roasted with low to moderate heat during the entire process. Example: Hawaiian coffees, Caribbean types and beans grown lower than 3,500 feet.

IV). Fresh-crop coffees: These coffees normally have a bean structure that is not settled or hardened yet, especially if the coffee did not have its required resting or curing time. During the first 3–5 minutes, the operator should maintain a moderate roasting temperature, after which the roasting cycle can be continued according to the category indication that was described before.

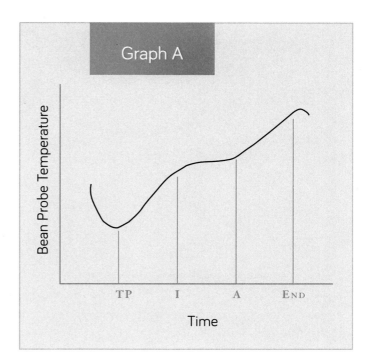

Following a normal roasting pattern for medium-hard beans, pictures C (page 243), D (page 243) and E (page 244) show the external development of the coffee beans during the roasting process.

The next three pictures F, G and H (page 244) display the internal development of the same coffee beans. In this case, the roaster operator should attempt to obtain an almost linear roasting curve, with the internal bean temperature increasing proportionally with the roasting time. Notice the remarkable bean expansion shown in picture H. During roasting, coffee beans expand dramatically, and their volume can increase by more than 75 percent.

Roasting Profile for Hard Bean Coffee

For hard beans, especially when roasted beyond the second crack, I recommend an "S-curve" for the roasting process. (This is based on endless cupping trials and comparison of different roast profiles). Graph A (this page) illustrates the corresponding roasting protocol for a hard bean.

After loading the beans into the drum, the bean probe will display a drop in temperature, which will bottom out at the turning point (TP). Hard beans will now be roasted with high initial heat. Until the start of the first crack, the heat inside the beans is endothermic; the beans are absorbing the supplied heat.

Right before the start of the first crack, the heat inside the beans becomes exothermic and the beans start generating heat. At this point the operator has to reduce energy supply in order to gain control of the roast process (point I).

After about two minutes of controlling the roast with low energy supply (less BTUs), the operator can again increase heat (endothermic heat; the beans are again absorbing heat) to prepare

for the finish of the roast. The start of energy increase can be seen at the point where the temperature curve is rising again (point A).

During numerous cupping trials, I have found that the ideal time between the start of the first crack and the end of the roast (points I and End) is at least three minutes.

The ideal roast time for solid drum roasters with convection heat (airflow heat passing through the drum) is 12 to 15 minutes. With these roasters, roast times longer than 20 minutes will produce baked flavors; roast times shorter than eight minutes will enhance sour notes. For solid drum sample roasters, the roast time can be done in 8 to 10 minutes.

Drum roasters using infrared heat usually allow longer roasting times without affecting the quality of the roasted coffee. Fluid-bed roasting machines, which use the concept of transferring heat through a high-velocity airflow at a reduced temperature, usually allow faster roasting times.

After learning roasting the hard way—by using sight, sound and smell—I later discovered the important value of proper measuring tools, such as probes for exhaust, environmental and bean temperature. Anyone who operates a coffee roaster can replicate the experiments I've completed over the past years. Learning how to roast each green bean to perfection is just the first step in creating that perfect cup of coffee. In all cases, a stringent cupping protocol should determine the optimal roasting profile of your coffee. ■

. . . .

WILLEM BOOT *is the president of Boot Coffee Consulting, a training and consulting firm for coffee companies. He can be reached via email at* willemboot@bootcoffee.com *or visit* bootcoffee.com.

Picture A | Sample Roast

Washed Beans | Green beans before roasting

Picture B | Sample Roast Stages 1–2

272° F | 4'10" | Freshly cut grass

Picture C | Sample Roast Stages 3–4

327° F | 7' | Bread

300° F | 5'30" | Hay

Picture D | Sample Roast Stages 5–6

365° F | 9'00" | Just before first crack

354° F | 7'50" | "A" point

Picture E | Sample Roast Stages 7–8

387° F | 10'15" | First crack almost done

Picture F | Sample Roast Stage 9

393° F | 11'20" | Finish Roast

Washed Coffee Beans.

To Have and Have Not

The Struggle With Sample Roasting

Story and photos by Willem Boot

• FROM THE MAY/JUNE 2011 ISSUE OF *ROAST* •

With the expansion of international specialty coffee communities, coffee roasters around the world have been making significant progress in developing and applying sophisticated protocols for the roasting of samples.

One example of this has been playing out in San Francisco's Mission District, an area traditionally known for its vibrant Latino community. The Mission has developed into an epicenter for artisan coffee-roasting cafes where the concept of single-origin coffee has become popular. Traditionally, roasting styles in Northern California have been pitch dark, to the point where unique and distinct tastes created by Mother Nature are hidden under a veil of flavors that are most reminiscent of caramelized sugars, tobacco and simplistic carbon.

Innovative artisan companies have become the catalysts of a new specialty roasting surge that will lead specialty consumers around the world to a brighter, more complex roasting style. With this ongoing coffee renaissance, operators have become much more aware of the basic quality parameters of sample roasting protocols. Voilà: Sample Roasting 2.0.

In 2004, I wrote an article for *Roast* titled "Ruling the Roast: The Struggle with Sample Roasting," about the inherent flaws and shortcomings in the professionalism of roaster operators, specifically pertaining to the process of roasting small quantities of green beans prior to the cupping of coffee samples. At that time, I estimated that less than half of the coffee roasting companies in North America actually employed a machine for the roasting of samples—although plenty of regional and larger roasters had invested in these machines, very few local and microroasters had done so. This percentage has, unfortunately, hardly increased. As a result, there is the division between the Haves and Have-Nots of sample roasters.

The Haves coughed up significant funds for the hefty price tag of a professional sample roasting machine, which generally costs well over $5,000 and up to $15,000 for a top-of-the-line two-barrel gas model. The Have-Nots endure ongoing challenges in the selection and purchasing process of green beans, and often they face the difficult task of investing in green bean inventory without actually knowing for sure what type of flavor profile their purchase will entail. It almost feels like shooting an arrow in the dark with your eyes closed.

Buying green coffee sight unseen, solely on the recommendation of your importer, or contracting green beans because of the attractive name and description of the product, is dangerous in the coffee trade, and trusting the quality and the reputation of your business on someone else's opinion is not recommended. Besides that, lack of skill when sample roasting jeopardizes the entire purpose of the machine and creates the risk of producing the wrong test results. In short, it's a ridiculous proposition to run a quality-focused specialty roasting operation without a sample roaster.

Key Requirements

Why do we roast samples? Generally, there are two compelling reasons. First, and most important, sample roasting is used to qualify green bean samples for the process of purchasing coffee. Second, businesses roast samples for the sake of product development, which enables a company to craft alternative profiles for the larger-volume batch-roasting process.

Assuming that your business is classified as one of the Haves, and for the sake of repeatability a gas-fired machine was purchased, which basic requirements must be observed? Your machine should at least contain the following components: a gauge for bean temperature and ideally also for the drum air temperature; a gauge for the gas pressure; a gas control valve, ideally with a needle valve; and an efficient cooling section. On top of that, the machine should be equipped with an efficient external chaff cyclone and an optional hood system for air exhaust, plus a fire suppression system. Additionally, the machine should have a gas-safety valve that automatically shuts off the gas supply if there's no working flame. This last feature is a basic UL-required (Underwriter Laboratories) safety precaution, and it is strongly recommended that roasters not install a machine without this valve.

For the purpose of green bean buying, the sample roaster's objective is to roast the beans during a time frame of 11 to 13 minutes, regardless of the quantity roasted, to a stage that corresponds with a color close to Agtron 58. Please see pictures A through F on page 246 (washed coffee beans) and pictures G, H and I on page 251 (honey process coffee) for the separate stages during the roast cycle of these different bean types.

Let's review some essential milestones during the roasting process. First, pre-weigh the sample to an exact consistent weight. Various manufacturers overestimate the capacity of their roasting machines, and inefficient airflow and heat transfer can result if too many beans are loaded into the roasting drum. The density of the coffee also plays a role here. Ideally, roasters should also

Central Liquoring Unit (CLU)—*Addis Ababa, Ethiopia*

Coffee Board—*Santo Domingo, Dominican Republic*

Dorman Ltd. coffee laboratory—*Nairobi, Kenya*

Norberto Mendoza of Kotowa Estate Coffee—*Boquete, Panama*

measure the bulk density and moisture content of the beans in order to get a better idea of what they are dealing with. Then, preheat the roasting drum for at least 15 minutes to a final heat level that doesn't exceed 400 degrees F (drum air temperature) or 350 degrees F (bean temperature). Add the beans to the roasting drum, and off you go. From here on, you must put your senses to work while you diligently observe time and temperature. For a useful model based on my sample roasting experience, see Table A on page 250 for a comprehensive overview of the essential stages of development and what to look and smell for.

Sample Roasting Protocols

Many third wave coffee roasters in North America have been inspired by the Slow Food movement, which proclaims to "stand at the crossroads of ecology and gastronomy, ethics and pleasure" by "opposing the standardization of taste and culture." Roasters' renewed focus on quality and on specific roasting protocols is slowly filtering through to the mainstream specialty roasting community. Various third wave roasters have been able to save enough money to afford a sample roaster, or their business has matured to the point where sample roasting is required.

Despite these positive developments, many roaster operators lack adequate training and instruction to operate their sample roaster successfully and, as a result, the flavors of the roasted samples aren't necessarily representative of the *real* flavor profile of the coffee lot being tested during the quality review. In general, if a roaster operator can't get around operating a sample roaster, his or her bigger issue would be operating a production-size roaster. For this reason, it is essential that sample roasting protocols form an integral part of the curriculum taught by organizations like the Roasters Guild and the Coffee Quality Institute. Training sessions should include how to match time versus temperature profiles during the roasting of samples for cupping as recommended by the Specialty Coffee Association (SCA). The current SCA standard requires roasting levels of Agtron 58 for beans and 62 for ground coffee. Realizing these colors requires an adequate skill level on behalf of the operator as well as the proper controls for monitoring temperatures and controlling the energy supply to the beans. It is also apparent that manufacturers should professionalize their instruction manuals and provide clients with clearly written guidelines describing the recommended roasting strategies and tools to determine proper roast color, such as Agtron or color tiles.

Upon review of the recommended protocols of a well-known roaster manufacturer, I noticed that the protocol itself was written for a different era, where it was acceptable to roast samples in a time frame of about six minutes. Some still consider the six-to-eight-minute sample roast as a suitable time frame to identify defects or to evaluate the coffee's cleanness. However, other professionals consider this roast time too short, and I agree with their reasoning.

Antique Coffee Roaster—*Private Collection of Jacob and Marianne Boot*

Golden Coffee Box roaster—*designed and produced by Jacob Boot*

QuantiK two-barrel, gas-fired roaster

Table A provides an overview of the separate stages during the sample roasting process and which milestones to aim for during the roasting cycle. Here is my key recommendation to all roasters out there: Use your senses while roasting! Discover the fragrance of freshly cut grass, followed by the smell of hay and the smell of baking bread. Right before the first crack, oils and specifically gases are migrating as a result of the escalating pressure inside the bean's cell structure. With the right pressure and with the ongoing expansion of the bean, the gases pass through the plesmodesmata (tiny channels that traverse the bean's cell walls) as if a valve suddenly opens. The result: an important sensory milestone, which I call the "A" point. In essence, the bean starts revealing its inner secrets for a limited time frame of about 20 seconds.

From the perspective of flavor development, most chemical reactions inside the bean occur from the onset of the "A" point. For that specific reason, I recommend maintaining a roast development time of preferably two minutes when roasting samples. With short roasting times, the operator creates the inherent risk of rushing through this window of flavor development with the possible consequence of under-developing the bean, which can cause acidic and/or acetic flavors. An inexperienced cupper could easily get confused by these tastes and might conclude that the coffee is grassy. In this case, the blame could fall on the farmer/producer while the real culprit was the roaster operator!

Besides that, I have noticed that it's much more challenging to roast consistently with a six-to-eight-minute roast. When roasting colors are progressing too fast, even the most experienced professionals can be misguided with the consequence of sample colors being incongruous. Times have changed, and manufacturers should make their best possible effort to establish protocols that have proven to work with their machines. Although it is not up to the machine manufacturer to establish how to roast, the operator's manual should be a contemporary guide with safety instructions and some basic description of the instrumentation that comes

Table A | Roasting Stages

Stage	Desired Milestone	Recommended Action	
		Roasters without airflow control	Roasters with separate airflow control
Start	Charge green beans at 325 to 375 degrees F (bean temperature).	Apply moderate heat levels to prevent scorching or tipping.	Low to medium airflow through the drum.
2 to 3 min.	Greenish/yellow color. The beans emit a crisp fragrance reminiscent of freshly cut grass.	Maintain heat levels to ensure ongoing bean development.	Low to medium airflow through the drum.
4 to 5 min.	Yellow color. The onset of the Maillard reaction produces the smell of hay.	Maintain heat levels to ensure ongoing bean development	Gradually increase airflow through the drum and keep heat at consistent level.
5 to 6 min.	Cinnamon color. Initial caramelization of sugars creates the fragrance of baking bread.	Carefully reduce heat to ensure ongoing gradual bean development.	Gradually increase airflow through the drum and keep heat at consistent level.
7 to 8 min.	Cinnamon/brownish color. Exothermic heat expels coffee-specific aromas: the "A" point. This is an exciting milestone; the beans will reveal some of their hidden aromas.	Carefully reduce heat to ensure ongoing gradual bean development.	Gradually increase airflow through the drum and keep heat at consistent level.
8 to 9 min.	Brown spotted color. First crack will start, driving out coffee aromas and remaining water vapors; exterior layers of bean break open.	Carefully reduce heat to ensure ongoing gradual bean development.	Increase airflow through the drum and reduce heat if necessary.
10 to 11 min.	First crack finishes. Heat becomes endothermic and the beans absorb more heat, which leads to ongoing bean development.	Maintain low heat application to ensure roast development time of at least two minutes.	Maintain increased airflow to ensure roast development time of at least two minutes.
11 to 13 min.	Finish the roast and complete cooling process within three to four minutes.	Maintain lowest possible heat level to prevent overheating of the drum.	Maximum airflow through the cooler and maintain lowest possible heat level to prevent overheating of the drum.

with the equipment. Additionally, technical personnel of manufacturers might help roasters with their personal input and experience if a roaster is having trouble. Roasting with a high-airflow Probat versus a lower-airflow San Franciscan requires two distinctly different protocols that recognize the different parameters of each machine. In the end, the flavor profiles of the different systems will not be exactly the same, but at least the samples will be representative of what the coffee delivers from cup to cup once roasted in larger batches.

Budgeting for the Machine

Let's cut to the chase: What budget should you prepare for with your new sample roaster? Fortunately, there are various options, and the higher your budget, the more features your machine will have.

[Editor's Note: This list of prices and models was compiled in 2011. For a more recent list of small roasters, read "The Quest for Quality at Home" in Roast's September/October 2016 issue (roastmagazine.com/education/roasting101/homeroasters).]

$1,000 OR LESS
In this category there are various higher-end consumer units like the Behmor, Hottop and Gene Cafe. During the 2010 Cupping Caravan in the Sidama and Yirgacheffe regions of Ethiopia, Gene Cafe roasters were hooked up to car batteries, allowing roasters to cup samples from various cooperatives right at the spot where the coffees were produced.

AROUND $1,500
QuantiK manufactures a compact, one-barrel, electrically heated roaster that has proven to produce acceptable results due to adequate airflow, which also benefits the cooling function of the machine. In rural southern Ethiopia and in other origins where electricity is the only available energy source, the QuantiK is the sample roaster of choice. This small roaster cannot handle full-time production, as the machine tends to overheat after an hour of continuous use.

$1,500 TO $5,000
At the time of writing this article I wasn't aware of any acceptable professional sample roaster in this price range. Roaster manufacturers, take note—there is an opportunity here.

AT LEAST $6,000
This category includes the single-barrel Ambex, Diedrich, Probat, San Franciscan, US Roaster and Primo. With these machines, a roasting business will purchase a range of

Honey Process Beans

Picture G | Sample Roast Stages 1–2

308° F | 8'40" | Bread

275° F | 6'10" | Hay

Picture H | Sample Roast Stages 3–4

367° F | 10'40" | First crack

345° F | 9'50" | "A" Point

Picture I | Sample Roast Stage 5

390° F | 12'10" | Finish Roast

features and controls. When comparing these machines, it will take some training and many trial roasting sessions to become proficient in their operation. The calibration between heat supply and airflow can be quite challenging, though rewarding at the same time. During the roasting process, beans continue to develop as long as the air supply temperature exceeds the bean temperature. The airflow damper, a feature on all of these more expensive machines, allows roasters to gradually increase the bean temperature instead of roasting too fast or too slowly.

Allowing more air through the roasting drum will slow down the roasting process, and the opposite will lock more heat inside the roaster, which speeds up the roasting cycle.

MORE THAN $10,000

Only a small group of Haves can confess to owning one of these machines. This category includes the multi-barrel versions of any of the aforementioned models. An additional option is the more expensive configure-it-yourself option. I found a three-barrel vintage (1952) Gothot machine, which had been reconditioned by a local technician, who also configured it with thermostat-controlled burners.

Final Advice

Roasters who can't afford to be a Have at the moment may be able to work more closely with their dealers to get roasted samples of coffee they are interested in. The broker can match roasted samples to a submitted sample, which allows roasters to play around with a coffee to see if it is what they are looking for. A good, close supplier will go the extra mile for their roaster clients.

If you're planning to become a Have by purchasing a sample roaster in the near future, here are some helpful final pointers for the purchasing process: First, always insist on performing multiple test roasts on the actual machine you are purchasing prior to releasing the final payment. Second, establish superior lighting around the machine using full-spectrum light. Third, make sure to document your roasting results in a dedicated roasting log. Finally, clean your machine thoroughly every week, as the slightest buildup of coffee oils and dust will affect the flavor profiles of your samples. ■

San Franciscan 1-lb. roaster—*Boot Coffee Lab*   Cafe Verde Peru—*designed by K.C. O'Keefe*

1952 Gothot three-barrel sample roaster—*Boot Coffee Lab*

WILLEM BOOT *is the president of Boot Coffee Consulting, a training and consulting firm for coffee companies. He can be reached at* willemboot@bootcoffee.com *or visit* bootcoffee.com.

Roast Right the First Time

How to Prevent Inconsistencies, Deficiencies and Errors

Story and photos by Willem Boot

• FROM THE JULY/AUGUST 2005 ISSUE OF *ROAST* •

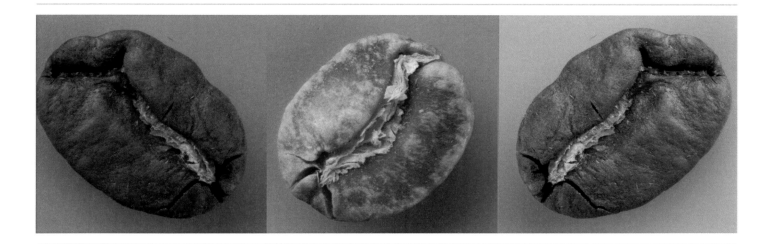

ONE OF MY PREVIOUS ARTICLES described various examples of roasting defects and how to deal with them in your coffee roasting business. In the past year, I have received a lot of feedback from roasters in and outside the United States who, after reading my articles, confessed that they had noticed many opportunities for change in their own roasting practice. Over the last year, I've also noticed that many roasters find it easy to take small errors and defects for granted. Most likely, this attitude stems from the fact that in the majority of specialty businesses, roasting is done very frequently; as a result, the roaster might easily fall into the habit of thinking that the consumer won't notice a slight variation in the roast degree or roast profile. Thus, it seemed like a good time to look at some additional common examples of roasting defects and explore simple strategies to help prevent them.

In the art and practice of coffee roasting, we deal with a number of factors that affect the outcome of the process. Some, such as the mechanical design of the machine or the airflow capacity of the roaster, cannot be controlled by the roaster operator. However, other factors can be directly controlled, including the time-temperature roasting profile, the applied cleaning procedures, and the facilities and conditions around the roasting machine. Generally, there is a greater likelihood for roasting defects to occur when any of these factors is not adequately managed.

Roasting defects fall into three main categories:
- Roasting inconsistencies, the most common type and the easiest to prevent
- Roasting deficiencies caused by ignorance of process or market requirements
- Roasting errors that actually damage the bean, like tipping, scorching, baking or bean cracks

Picture A. Fluorescent Light Conditions

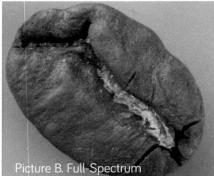

Picture B. Full-Spectrum Incandescent Light Conditions

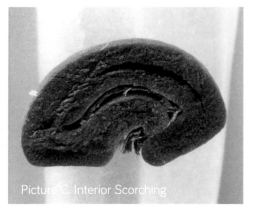

Picture C. Interior Scorching

Roasting Inconsistencies

Roasting inconsistencies are the most common form of defect, and I see them more often than you might imagine. A perfect example: I recently visited a roasting company in Europe. The company has been in business for nearly 30 years and their roastmaster, a self-educated coffee and fine foods connoisseur, has been their coffee specialist for almost 25 years, a period during which the company grew steadily to an annual production of 220,000 pounds of roasted coffee. To prepare for further expansion, the company recently hired a coffee-roasting apprentice who is being trained under the watchful guidance of the senior roastmaster.

While I was visiting the company, I had the great pleasure not only of observing the roasting process, but of completing some hands-on roasting with the roastmaster and his apprentice. All the coffee is roasted on a beautiful vintage Gothot roasting machine and the time-temperature roasting profiles are maintained in the artisan way, by utilizing the senses of sight, smell and sound. While the Gothot was slowly developing roast after roast, I followed both roaster operators in their roasting rituals. Every 90 seconds or so, they would smell the beans being roasted by pulling samples with the trier, evaluate the color of the beans and listen to the emerging sound of a first or second crack. Toward the end of the roasting cycle, the roastmaster or his apprentice would frantically take samples, quickly smell them and then, finally, finish the roast by starting the cooling cycle.

Despite my admiration for their genuine artisan approach to the roasting process, I quickly developed some doubt about the effective consistency of their protocols. In the late afternoon, I invited the roastmaster and his apprentice to join me in a basic quality inspection procedure by comparing whole-bean and ground samples of several batches of roasted coffee against the master color sample for each product type. The outcome was stunning. By using a special light I had purchased for the occasion, a full-spectrum 75-watt Verilux incandescent floodlight, we could immediately distinguish the inconsistencies between the roasts which, under optimal conditions, should have been the same.

To help them increase the consistency of the roast color, I suggested they improve the lighting conditions around the roasting machine. This can easily be accomplished by installing one or more full-spectrum incandescent light bulbs. These bulbs, often marketed as full-spectrum or "daylight" bulbs, mimic the color of the light from the sky, not the direct beam of the sun.

Pictures A and B (above) show two identical coffee beans under different conditions of light. Picture A illustrates the quality of illumination produced by fluorescent lights and picture B shows the clear light spectrum created by the incandescent bulbs.

In addition, I suggested they develop a logbook for their roasting operation so they could register at least the roasting times and temperatures at several intervals during the roasting process.

Roasting Deficiencies

These errors are either market- or process-related and are mostly caused by the ignorance of the business owner and his roaster about the basic requirements of the market or about the fundamental criteria for the preparation of the coffee.

A typical process-related roasting deficiency is espresso coffee roasted so dark that the aromatic qualities and the sugars of the beans are decomposed, resulting in a bitter, burnt and bland cup of espresso with very little crema.

Another example of a roasting error—in this case a market deficiency—occurs when the owner or roaster doesn't understand basic market requirements. For example, my current hometown is situated in the Bay Area. Here, consumers like their coffee dark; the credo is "the darker the better." Now, imagine you are a Northern European roaster and, after having freshly moved to San Francisco, you decide to open a small wholesale coffee roastery utilizing the traditional roasting recipes and protocols you have applied in your hometown in Europe. Knowing that roast degrees are much darker in your new domicile, you still are convinced that things will work out as planned and you brand yourself as the European "Roast It Light" alternative.

What is the likelihood for success of this courageous roaster?

Picture D. Interior Scorching

Picture E. First Signs Of Internal Scorching

throughout the cell structure of the coffee bean. As a result, there are groups of cells that contain less moisture and groups of cells (where the drying process did not evolve efficiently) that contain more moisture.

So, what is the impact of the uneven drying on the roasting process? Improperly dried coffee beans will most likely develop unevenly and inconsistently during roasting; the interior bean sections with more moisture will roast slower and the areas with less moisture will easily roast too fast, resulting in internal scorching.

Now we come to the key question. How do you know that the green beans you're roasting were properly dried? The answer: You can't! At least, it is nearly impossible to deduct this from the green coffee beans before roasting. However, during the first part of the roasting process (before the first crack), you can check if there are any major inconsistencies in the exterior development of the bean color. Picture E (above) shows a coffee bean after three minutes of roasting. You can already see darker and lighter spots on the surface of the bean; this could be a first sign of internal scorching.

The best prevention for internal scorching is to ensure a very slow roasting process in the first stage, followed by a moderately fast process in the second stage. Make sure there are at least three minutes between the start of the first crack and the second crack or, if you roast relatively light, keep at least three minutes between the start of the first crack and the end of the roast.

In addition, there are a few other simple techniques to establish a quality assurance protocol in your roasting department:

- Schedule roasting plans at the beginning of each production day
- Fill out roasting logs with temperature profiles, roasting time, shrinkage and color for each batch
- Perform (Agtron) color tests of each individual roast
- Review roast profiles with the roastmaster
- Maintain a preventive maintenance schedule for your roasting equipment
- Perform quarterly cleanings of the entire roasting system

Last but not least, a stringent cupping routine will help you to improve the consistency of your roasted coffee. I recommend documenting the target flavor profile for each coffee type, which should be compared against the production results using effective cupping protocols. ■

Despite my personal preference for lighter coffee, I do not expect that this roaster will succeed, simply because he is ignoring prevailing market conditions.

To prevent roasting deficiencies—either market- or process-related—I suggest frequently applying product and market research to your own products. A small company or coffeehouse can begin product research by forming a small team of tasters and inviting these folks to taste the coffee products in a somewhat controlled setting, after which you can ask them for their honest feedback and opinions.

Scorching

There are numerous types of roasting errors, but I receive many questions by roasters about the interior scorching and its proper prevention, so I would like to focus on that here.

Scorching is a defect that is easy to see in the beans. Pictures C (previous page) and D (above) show coffee beans that appear to be scorched inside. On top of that, the interior development of the coffee bean is very inconsistent, resulting in an internal bean color darker than the outside color. Now, compare the internal roast colors on picture A (previous page), in which the left half of the bean appears to be roasted darker than the right half. As we concluded during our cupping evaluation, the outcome in the cup was bitter with a slightly burnt aftertaste.

After more in-depth research into the causes of this type of defect, I concluded that interior scorching might be related to improper drying techniques of the green coffee bean. The drying process of parchment coffee (the green bean with the parchment husk) has the objective to lower the moisture content of the bean to 12 to 13 percent.

Summarized, there are two basic approaches to drying: mechanical (in large revolving cylinders with hot air moving through) or static (in the open air by utilizing the radiation heat of the sun). If the drying process is completed too fast for any reason, then this can result in an uneven internal moisture content of the green beans. In this case, the free moisture is dispersed unevenly

WILLEM BOOT *is the president of Boot Coffee Consulting, a training and consulting firm for coffee companies. He can be reached at* willemboot@bootcoffee.com *or visit* bootcoffee.com.

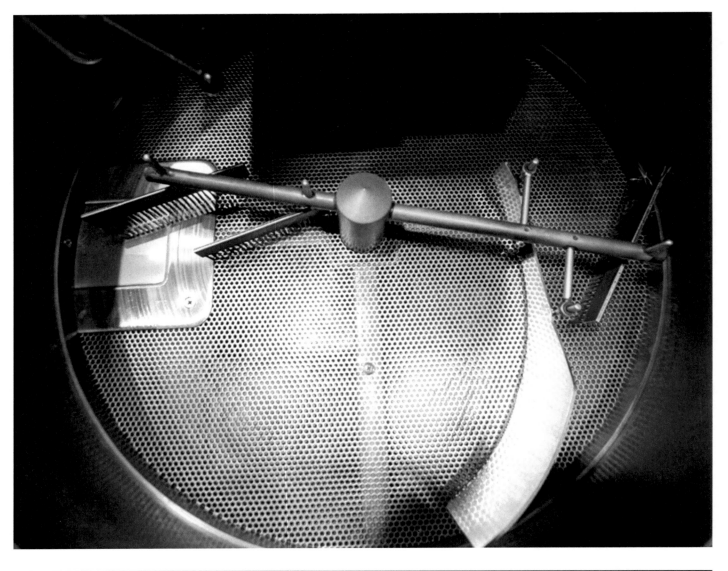

How to Be Cool

Cooling Methods and Their Impact from Roast to Cup

by Christopher Schooley | *photos by Nolan Dutton of Ozo Coffee*

• FROM THE JULY/AUGUST 2014 ISSUE OF *ROAST* •

The roasting process has many stages: drying, browning reactions, caramelization, first crack and cell expansion, to name a few. Each stage plays an important part in the development of the flavor profile of the coffee—the whole roasting process is development. The stage that begins with the first crack and includes the beginning of caramelization is referred to as the "development stage" by some roasters, but this can be misleading as it diminishes the importance and the impact of the other stages during roasting.

One such stage that can be easily overlooked is the cooling stage. While it doesn't happen in the roaster itself, properly cooling the roast has a dramatic impact on the cup.

The roasting process is an exchange of momentum. Energy is built inside the roasting chamber and then transferred to the coffee as it progresses through the roast. With that thought in mind, at the end of the roast, the coffee has quite a bit of energy and momentum itself, so much so that even when removed from the roasting chamber it's still changing, only now it's doing that in an uncontrolled environment—that is, if the core temperature of the beans is not actively being brought down.

In cooking, this is called carry-over. The food item continues to cook and adds as much as 10 to 15 degrees of internal temperature after being removed from the heat. This may change the development and degree of doneness past the point desired.

Without continuing to add energy to the coffee, it will eventually cool; however, the longer it takes to cool to room temperature, the more the coffee will continue to change from when the roast was initially stopped. Delayed cooling may result in an undesirable baked or dried-out character, but generally, sweetness is the most notable difference. This is a common roasting anecdote, but one that has been demonstrated time and again through various trials conducted by roasters and roaster manufacturers.

In a lecture on cooling at the Specialty Coffee Association of America (SCAA) Expo in 2002, Agtron managing partner Carl Staub spoke about the impact of proper cooling on sugar development during the roasting and cooling process:

"The primary sugar in coffee is sucrose. During the roasting process you fracture the sucrose, and you want to caramelize it or polymerize it in the scientific term. But, you also have to maintain solubility. If it doesn't come out when you put water into it, it is not going to be a sweet cup. Having the sugar there is one issue, and being able to get it out with hot water is another issue. If you cool it too slowly, the long series chain polymers, sugars, fructose and glucose will find other constituents to link up with in the coffee, and they are not as soluble."

Staub is saying that if a coffee takes too long to cool, there's not as much soluble sweetness to draw from when brewed. Through extensive testing done by Staub, as documented in that 2002 lecture, by me, and by a number of other roasters and roaster manufacturers that I spoke with for this article, it has been duly noted that getting post-roast cooling times down to four minutes or less provides a noticeable difference in the sweetness of the cup.

The difference in cooling from between five minutes and four minutes is so dramatic that the panel that tasted the coffees in the experiments Staub created felt the sweetness had increased by at least double by shortening the cooling to less than four minutes.

Joseph A. Rivera, founder of the online coffee science resource *coffeechemistry.com*, says that because the soluble/insoluble chemistry described above happened during roasting at temperatures greater than 400 degrees F, and not during cooling,

cooling itself might not be the cause of this greater perception of sweetness.

He adds that if rapidly cooled coffees do possess more sweetness, it is more likely due to certain aromatics being preserved by the quicker cooling process. "Aromatics are temperature dependent, meaning that when beans are exposed to higher temperatures they will also release more aromatics, some of which may be sweet in character and ultimately lost in the cup," Rivera says.

One concern about cooling is fracturing the cells. According to Stephan Diedrich of Diedrich Manufacturing, in order to fracture the cells the coffee would have to be cooled almost instantly, which would take a great deal of resources to remove the energy in the beans and bring the temperature down at that required speed. So, the bigger issue is still cooling in time.

Cooling with Air

The most common cooling method used by small, craft coffee roasters is cooling with air. Although some fluid-bed roasters do include a water quench as well as a cooling tray, most drum roasters purely use a cooling tray with a perforated bottom. This is connected to a blower that pulls air from the room through the just-roasted coffee as a pivot arm stirs the coffee to create a more even cooling for the whole charge.

Most roasters view the blower (motor-driven impeller to suck or blow large volumes of air) as the key component in this cooling setup, and in many ways, it is. As much air as possible has to be moved through a cooling tray full of coffee freshly released from the roasting drum at more than 400 degrees F. There are a number of roaster models that use a single blower for both the roasting drum and the cooling tray, and include a damper for switching the function between the two. Many of these roaster models are capable of cooling the coffee to room temperature in less than four minutes, but one of the most commonly cited issues, if cooling times are not below the four-minute mark, is whether or not the roaster has a cooling-specific blower.

Beyond the blower, though, there could be a number of other impacts on cooling times, such as ambient air temperature. The ambient temperature in a non-climate-controlled warehouse may vary by as much as 30 degrees F between summer and winter. The pivot arm stirring the roasted coffee in the cooling bin can also be considered. If this arm is spinning too fast, it could actually slow down cooling times. Diedrich sometimes recommends stopping the stirring arms after the coffee has been evenly distributed, about a minute, in order to pull more air more quickly through more coffee.

In Staub's 2002 SCAA lecture, he talks about using a frequency drive on the stirring arm and adjusting the speed of the armature throughout the cooling process for optimal results, starting faster and slowing down as the coffee cools. The most important

consideration in this regard is the even distribution of the batch. This is one of the reasons a more rapidly spinning arm slows down cooling; it collects greater amounts of coffee in certain areas while also creating areas where the bed is much shallower—where more air will move through faster. Air always wants to take the path of least resistance.

Mark Loring Ludwig of Loring Smart Roast says his company designs its cooling trays to cool coffee faster by using a relatively smaller-diameter cooling tray with a strong blower. He says, "In the smaller tray the air velocity is much higher for better wind chill factor. It travels through a deeper bed of beans, so there's more exposure, and there are no open screen areas behind the sweeps on the stirring arms where the air can take a shortcut. It works very well; cooling times can actually be under three minutes." (He cites a 450-degree-F start point on a 65-degree-F day in low humidity.)

Truly the biggest impact on cooling performance is maintenance, and the health and condition of the airflow systems. Diedrich stresses the idea that the entirety of the roaster is all one system, and regular maintenance throughout that system is the key to proper cooling times. At each step of the cooling process there is the opportunity for particulate buildup from the smoke, steam and broken bits of coffee.

Loring mentions that his cooling tray design also played into his desire for ease of maintenance. The smaller diameter and design adjustments to the paddle assembly allow the screen of the cooling tray to be easily lifted out for direct access and quick cleaning.

Daily, weekly and monthly maintenance on a cooling system is vital for performance. The perforated bottom of the tray can easily become blocked as those perforations fill with bits of coffee or oil. Scrubbing and wiping down the tray regularly will go a long way to maintaining cooling performance, and cleaning under the tray each time it's brushed, scrubbed or wiped down is important to make sure any particulate freed during the process doesn't travel further down along the system.

Removing any residual oil should be part of safety procedures, as well as quality control to prevent oil from turning rancid and contaminating other batches. Cleaning the impeller on the blower and every point in the exhaust is key. Diedrich says it's important to clean the exhaust up to the roof regularly and to check that the exhaust cap isn't too restrictive, which could lead to greater buildup.

Water Quenching

In many specialty roasting circles, water quenching, the other common cooling method, is looked down upon and generally completely disregarded. Its dismissal has become one of those specialty coffee tales that gets passed on from roaster to roaster without any exposure to, or understanding of, the actual practice.

One of the reasons for this dismissal of water quenching is the misconception that it adds moisture back into the coffee. While some roasters may have used, or currently use, quenching to add weight back to the roasted coffee, properly water quenching coffee for cooling purposes may not involve any absorption. One roaster who uses water quenching in cooling (and who chooses to remain anonymous for proprietary reasons) says he noticed when using a quench with darker roasts where the coffee did absorb some measurable moisture, the harsher flavors of the darker roast were reduced while the sweetness was more pronounced.

To clarify, water quenching is really just a step in the cooling process, and a water-quenched coffee generally finishes its cooling cycle in a cooling tray. The purpose of the quench, usually in the roasting chamber or just at the door at the drop, is simply to halt the increase in internal temperature. It takes further cooling with air to actually bring coffee down to the prescribed (room) temperature.

In water quenching, the coffee is not soaking to bring the temperature down. Most commonly, the water is sprayed toward the charge as a mist for 30 to 90 seconds. This generally evaporates immediately, given the high temperature of the beans and the environment.

Water quenching is much more of an issue with larger roasters and darker roasts, yet Diedrich recommends it in any machine with more than a 25-kilo capacity.

Another roaster I spoke to who declined to give his name for proprietary reasons says he began experimenting with water quenching in order to control his darker roasts at the final stage. Following success with the darker roasts, he started looking at his others and was impressed with the cup results at all roast levels after using water quenching to lower cooling times across the board.

Quenching is carefully monitored and compared to non-quenched batches to ensure there is no moisture being absorbed in the process. This roaster found all of his roasts sweeter while water quenching helped to shorten cooling times. He also noted there was no noticeable impact on the shelf life of the coffee—another of the oft-cited concerns with quenching.

Another question that has come up in trials and in a 2007 study by the Institute of Food Science and Nutrition at the Swiss Federal Institute of Technology (ETH) in Zurich, Switzerland (titled, "Influence of Water Quench Cooling on Degassing and Aroma Stability of Roasted Coffee"), is the impact of water quenching on degassing and shelf life. While quenching seems to perhaps lead to quicker degassing, it may not be directly linked to shelf life of roasted beans. Even so, the roaster who spoke to me about water quenching lessening the harshness of darker-roasted coffee said his research had shown that degassing was longer with water-quenched coffees.

He says, "Higher moisture slows degassing times as water inhibits the flow of gasses in coffee beans. If quenching results in higher moisture in coffee, then it does indeed shorten shelf life.

Water is a medium for reactions, and if there is more water in coffee then it will encourage those reactions."

That said, proper and timely cooling does have a noticeable impact on shelf life, as longer cooling times lead to more rapid oil expression, which then leads to quicker degradation. There are a number of other factors at play here, including the moisture content of the green coffee to begin with, as well as the actual roast profile.

Blower unit for a Diedrich IR12.

Diedrich says another positive impact of water quenching is that air-quality restrictions become more stringent. Water quenching can help reduce the workload of the thermal oxidizer (afterburner), along with gas consumption. Remembering that the air and any smoke from the cooling tray also has to go through the exhaust and afterburner, in some cases, a water quench system can help reduce smoke present in the cooling tray.

Cool Out

Like almost everything in coffee roasting, the true quality impact of cooling is ripe for further research. Though the four-minute magic number seems to be consistent for all of the roasters I spoke with for this article, there are other matters to regard. Everything from the age and density of the green coffee to differences in roast profiles could have a dramatic impact on whether or not that cooling time is truly ideal.

That said, experientially, a quicker cooling time results in a sweeter cup. We've been unfairly dismissive of water quenching, and it warrants further consideration. It could be cooler than we thought. ■

• •

CHRIS SCHOOLEY'S *coffee odyssey began in 1997 at Margie's Java Joint in Greeley, Colorado. In 1999, he joined Intelligentsia in Chicago, where he managed the company's first retail location, working his way into production and roasting. He then moved to Metropolis Coffee in Chicago where he became director of coffee purchasing and roasting. In 2009, he moved back to Colorado, where he started working with Sweet Maria's to create Coffee Shrub, a service to act as a conduit between coffee farmers and small roasters. After collaborating with craft brewers, he saw an opportunity to be a conduit between Colorado farmers and brewers, and started Troubadour Maltings with Steve Clark in Fort Collins. Troubadour is in full production providing Colorado-grown and -malted grains to craft brewers throughout the country. Schooley was elected to the Roasters Guild Executive Council in 2008 and served as chair from 2011 to 2012. He has been a regular contributor to* Roast *and the* Specialty Coffee Chronicle.

Fire Fighters

Prevent Your Beans from Going Up in Smoke

by John Larkin

• FROM THE MAY/JUNE 2007 ISSUE OF *ROAST* •

SUDDENLY THE ROASTERY is filled with smoke, and flames jet out from parts of the roaster where you've never seen them before. Fire happens—and it could happen to you. If it does, it can destroy equipment, inventory and buildings, and it might cause personal injury. How can you minimize the possibility and protect your people and your investment? What do you do if it does happen to you?

Roaster-related fires tend to have three typical causes: installation issues, maintenance issues or double batching/operator errors. The risks can be substantially minimized through proper installation, good maintenance practices, training in roaster operation and emergency procedures, and attentive operation.

Proper Installation

The first rule of minimizing fire risk in coffee roasting is to make sure that the roaster is installed according to the manufacturer's instructions. Pay special attention to selecting the material and grade of ducting or piping that the manufacturer recommends for the temperatures and buildup associated with coffee roasting. Do not be enticed by less-expensive piping even if recommended by contractors or inspectors. Roaster manufacturers are acutely aware of the heat curves and byproducts associated with coffee roasting, and they know that inferior piping may not withstand this over time, resulting in meltdown and/or fires that could have been avoided.

Maintenance

Once up and running, the roasting process naturally generates two major types of byproducts that need to be controlled through cleaning. These byproducts are hydrocarbon residue and chaff. In order to ensure roaster efficiency, safety and a good product, these byproducts need to be removed on a regular basis.

Hydrocarbon Concerns
Successful coffee roasting is a balance of flame and airflow. The byproduct of this aspect of the process is hydrocarbon residue, which adheres to the walls of ductwork and piping, restricting the airflow in the circulatory system. Left unchecked, this buildup tips the flame/air balance and impedes roaster performance, which can eventually affect your cup.

Hydrocarbon buildup is dangerous because it creates traps that can become catch points for sparks and embers in the piping. In addition, the residue is very flammable.

Removing hydrocarbon buildup means regularly taking pipes apart and scraping them down to bare metal—while wearing safety

FIRE DRILL
10 STEPS TO MINIMIZE FIRE DAMAGE RISK

1   Install equipment correctly

2   Clean equipment regularly and often

3   Train operators to pay special attention to feed and discharge

4   Train operators to watch for smoke, equipment color changes (hot spots) or flames

5   Train operators to listen for laboring equipment—scraping, rattles, grunts, speed changes

6   Train operators to note burning smells

7   Train operators to turn off the gas if fire is suspected

8   Train operators to leave the drum turning but turn off the air (fan) if it is a separate motor

9   Train operators to use water and fire extinguishers sparingly if possible

10   Train operators to call 911 as necessary

goggles, gloves, and a fire retardant smock or apron. Follow your roaster manufacturer's recommendations for cleaning frequency and clean at least twice as often if you're doing dark roasts.

Proper pipe maintenance can help reduce your fire risk, but it doesn't eradicate it. You'll also need to pay attention to early warning signs of fire issues. Urgent warning signs of trouble in your pipes include more obvious symptoms such as smoke puffing out of places where it shouldn't, or even flames at joints or elbows. Hot spots on pipes—perhaps visible by discoloration—are another warning sign. More subtle warnings that require attention are changes in roast times, unexpected changes in the cup or color, and difficulty starting the roaster.

If the worst happens, and smoking or flaming occurs, always be ready to call 911 and to exit the building for safety. If at all possible, turn off the gas to shut down the roaster flame. If your roaster has separate motors for the drum and the fan, turn off the fan. If the removal of airflow smothers the fire (flame no longer visible, smoke dissipates), check the roof also to be sure that sparks going up the stack have not ignited it.

The removal of fuel (gas/flame and oxygen/airflow) will often starve a fire if caught early. Water and fire extinguishers may be necessary and should, of course, be used as required, but sparingly if possible. Ironically, they can cause more damage than the fire in some cases. Try to avoid spraying the controls and other electrical components with water or fire extinguishers.

■ Chaff Considerations Another byproduct of coffee roasting is chaff from the bean itself. This collects under the screen in the cooler and the chaff collector and can cause a smoky, often smoldering fire if a spark from the roaster ignites it. If this type of fire becomes hot enough, it can burn off paint and warp the cooler—not to mention damage other pieces of equipment and possibly the building if left unchecked.

To prevent chaff fires, the most important step is to regularly and frequently remove chaff from the equipment. This usually requires both scraping and sweeping. Always follow manufacturer's instructions for removing chaff, and observe or exceed recommendations for cleaning frequency.

If you do have a fire and smoke is detected coming from the bottom of the cooler, as always, be ready to call 911 and exit the building. If the fire is caught early, you can open the access hatch and carefully remove smoldering embers to a metal pail where you can smother them.

Again, use water and fire extinguishers as required, but sparingly if possible. It is especially important not to blast a chaff fire with water or a fire extinguisher as that can send sparks flying. Be sure to observe the cooler and the surrounding area for any sign of sparks or smoke. Once you're sure that the fire is out, scrape the chamber clean, start up and roast.

Double-batching

Double-batching is an operator error in a manual roast and an equipment malfunction in an automated roast. Double-batching is a major cause of roaster fires. The weight and volume of a double batch of bean is more than the equipment was designed to handle. The natural expansion of the bean—now times two—results in reduced airflow and leads to extreme hot spots that can flash and burn.

Operator training and attentive operation—especially during feed and discharge—can greatly minimize this risk in a manual operation. It is especially important for an operator to verify that a roaster drum is empty prior to feeding beans into it from the hopper, and not to leave the roaster during feeding until the batch has been fed and the gate has been closed.

Fire is also possible if a roaster fails to discharge even a single batch roast in a timely manner and it starts to burn within the drum.

Warning signs of a roaster fire usually include seeing smoke where it shouldn't be, such as on the roaster front, side or around the fan; seeing paint discoloration, a visible sign of excess heat; or smelling a stronger than normal odor that may include the smell of burning paint or an electrical fire (like an overheated toaster). Listen for changes in the sound of your roaster, such as speed changes, motors laboring, scraping sounds, rattles and grunts.

If you notice any of these warning signs, it is important to turn off the gas if at all possible, thereby shutting off the flame. If your roaster has separate motors for the drum and the fan, turn off the fan only. It is important to keep the drum turning in order to minimize damage. Don't open any vents.

Once again, be ready to call 911 and to exit the building for safety. If the gas is off and flames are still visible at a seam of a pipe, a joint of the roaster body cladding, the damper, or the fan inlet, you can spray them lightly with a squirt bottle or with short bursts from a hose. Look for hot spots on the roaster and on the outside of the stack.

Try to resist dousing with water if you can avoid it—just spray lightly, as roasters are built to take a great deal of heat, and water can cause more damage to the equipment than the fire. Especially try to keep water and fire extinguishers away from controls and other electrical components if possible. It is also very important to keep fresh air away from the area where you think that the fire is burning.

Once the smoke has diminished, it is possible to carefully open the trier door, holding a water bottle or hose

CONTROLLED BURN— A FIRE PARABLE

IT STARTED like any other work day in the storefront roastery. The 15-kilo roaster was roasting its fifth batch of the day. An apprentice operator was in charge as the roastmaster was down the street at the post office. A surge of customers arrived from the nearby manufacturing plant. The operator walked away from the roaster to multitask for a bit too long and lost track of an already dark roast.

Suddenly the storefront was filling with smoke. Flames licked out from around the burner chamber. The dark roast was burning inside the drum, but the fire had already spread to oils and chaff that had built up in the burner chamber.

The apprentice operator ran to call the fire department and everyone else ran outside. Noticing the commotion, the roastmaster also ran—down the street from the post office and into the smoky storefront where he turned off the gas fueling the roaster.

By the time the fire department screamed into position a few moments later and burst into the roastery hoses readied, the fire was burning itself out inside the drum. The operators and fire department worked together to lightly spray water around the burner chamber and around the trier door as they checked out the progress inside the drum.

Within an hour the fire was completely out, the roaster was cooling down, the charred bean was soaking in a metal pail, and the smoke was dissipating. The roastery closed for business for the rest of the day, overwhelmed by how fast the fire happened, how bad it might have been, and how fortunate they were that no one was hurt and the equipment and building were still intact. The roaster checked out and fired up that afternoon. They aired out the storefront and opened the next day as usual. ■

ready to lightly spray. Wear fire-retardant gloves and an apron along with safety glasses when doing this, as the introduction of oxygen may still cause flame at the trier door.

Do not discharge the coffee right away, as the heat will warp the cooler bottom in roasters with attached coolers. Instead, spray the cooling tray lightly with water and intermittently discharge small amounts of coffee followed by a quick spray from a hose with a spray nozzle. Alternatively, discharge the coffee into a metal bucket and be prepared to spray the discharge with water. If at all possible, keep the fan off and the drum turning during discharge.

After a Fire

If a roaster looks intact after a fire, you can check it out further before restarting. First, make sure the power is off to the machine. Check all chambers—the cooler, roaster, fan housings, and the ducting at the clean-out spots and access hatches—for residual or puddled water. Remove any water with a sponge or wet vacuum. Be sure that anywhere that air passes is dry. Scrape pipes to bare metal and scrape and sweep out any chaff.

Next, verify that all electrical components are dry. This includes controls, switches, push buttons and motors.

Then, try moving parts by hand if possible. Check drive belts, chains and shafts to see if they are stuck or frozen. If they are moving freely, restore power to the machine. Once powered up,

bump the motors to see if they work and check for bad fuses. Stop immediately and check out components if you notice any rubbing or scraping, or if the roaster locks up.

If all of the previous steps check out, see if the startup sequence works. Put everything back together if it's not already, and introduce a small batch of your lowest-grade coffee. Try starting the roaster again, this time with the coffee in the drum, and stay with the roaster at all times as it heats up and cycles. Listen for any unusual noise and mark and seal any leaks before resuming normal roasting.

Fires are a risk when roasting coffee, but you can minimize the risk with proper installation, maintenance and training. Encourage your operators to get to know their machine and how it normally operates, so that they're alert to unusual smoke, hot spots, smells and sounds. Teach them the mantra that if the worst happens and there is a fire, they should "turn off the gas; stop the flame." Addressing a fire in its early stages can mean the difference between just one really dark roast and a complete roaster failure and expensive downtime. ∎

- -

JOHN LARKIN *is president of John Larkin and Co., Inc., which services, troubleshoots, rebuilds and installs production-scale coffee equipment and provides optimization layouts for coffee plants. He can be reached at* john.larkin@verizon.net.

HOME ROASTING SAFETY

by Emily Puro

• FROM THE SEPTEMBER/OCTOBER 2016 ISSUE OF *ROAST* •

Home roasters also need to be cognizant of safety procedures to minimize the risk of fire. To provide some important home roasting safety tips, we spoke with Chris Wade, roasting manager at McMenamins Coffee Roasters in Portland, Oregon, and an avid home roaster.

Wade roasted professionally for about a decade before he began roasting at home. He started with a frying pan while camping, then experimented with a popcorn popper. He now uses a more powerful, gas-powered Huky.

Whether you use a small air roaster or a larger, electric or propane-powered machine, it's important to make safety a priority.

PLAN YOUR SPACE

● Home roasting machines are metal and typically run at about 400 degrees F, so it's important to place your roaster away from combustible materials, and on a surface that won't be damaged by heat.

● To minimize exposure to exhaust—including gases emitted from the coffee, smoke created during roasting, and gases released from gas-powered roasting machines—make sure your space is well ventilated. Set up near a range hood, open windows, or even outside.

● Propane-powered equipment involves an even higher level of caution, Wade notes. Be sure the tank is set up in a safe area. Some manufacturers offer exhaust kits to vent gas outside, or consider running a line from an outdoor propane tank to an indoor roaster, rather than bringing the tank into your home.

Roaster Chris Wade has his Huky set up outdoors for optimal ventilation.
Photo by Chris Wade

BE PREPARED

● Before you begin roasting, make sure you know what to do if a fire breaks out. Have a plan for extinguishing the fire and keep any equipment you'll need nearby.

● If you're using a gas-powered roaster, know how to shut off the gas quickly in the event of a fire. Always make sure you close the gas valves when finished roasting, so you don't unwittingly continue to fill the space with gas.

● As you move to larger machines, especially those with electric heat sources, make sure the circuits in your home can handle the load, and don't plug in other appliances on the same circuit while your roaster is running. If you overload a circuit and the electricity shuts off, the roaster's drum will seize, which could cause a fire.

DO YOUR MAINTENANCE

● Most roasters come with clear instructions for cleaning and lubrication. Save those instructions for reference, and maintain your roaster accordingly.

● Home roasters don't require the daily cleaning commercial roasters do, although if you're doing a lot of dark roasting, oil can build up quickly. Wade—who doesn't do much dark roasting—says he cleans the fan on his roaster every few months, using a toothbrush or nylon brush. Be sure the roaster is cool before you clean it to avoid damaging the brush.

● If you use an air roaster, make sure there's no debris in the vents on the bottom, and keep chaff screens and filters free from debris. This will minimize the chance of fire and increase the quality of your coffee.

● If you're roasting several batches per day, keep the bearings inside the roaster lubricated so they don't stick, which could cause the drum to seize. Wade recommends keeping an extra set of bearings available as well.

● Be sure to use food-safe lubricant that's appropriate for high temperatures, so you don't contaminate your coffee.

● After you're finished roasting, make sure your machine has properly cooled before leaving it unattended.

A FINAL WORD OF CAUTION

● Be particularly careful when roasting in a home with children or animals. Never leave a child—or a dog or cat that might jump onto the roasting surface—unattended with a hot roaster. ■

On Good Terms—
A Roaster's Dictionary

Green Bean, Roasting and Cupping Terminology

• FROM THE NOVEMBER/DECEMBER 2006 ISSUE OF *ROAST* •

ACERBIC A taste fault in brewed coffee that leaves an acrid and sour taste. Often the result of leaving brewed coffee on heat.

ACIDITY A pleasing piquant or tangy quality characteristic of high-altitude coffees. Acidity is a perceived taste quality—it is not a measure of pH. Citric, malic and lactic acids are three of the most pleasing and predominant of the hundreds of acids found in coffee.

ACIDY A desirable taste that is nippy and sharp.

ACRID An irritating and piercing taste associated with harsh, bitter and pungent sensations. Sometimes found in over-roasted coffees.

AFRICAN BEDS Raised flat-bed structures, usually made of wood with a metal screen, on which parchment coffee is dried. Used as an alternative to patio drying, and notable for the fact that they allow more airflow to pass through the coffee during drying.

AFTERBURNER A device attached to a roaster that incinerates smoke and odor.

AFTERTASTE The mind's second opinion and lingering memory of a coffee. The nose and taste sensation after swallowing. *Also: Finish*

AGTRON SCALE A number system for characterizing degree of roast by measuring coffee's luminance on a white to black scale. *Also: Agtron Rating*

AIR ROASTER A roasting apparatus that utilizes forced hot air to simultaneously agitate and roast green coffee beans. *Also: Fluidized Bed Roaster, Fluid-Bed Roaster, Sivetz Roaster*

AIR QUENCHING The use of rapid airflow to stop the roast and cool the coffee upon the completion of roasting.

ALKALINE A secondary taste sensation related to pungent.

ALQUEIRE A traditional unit of volume and land measurement. In terms of volume, it is equivalent to about 13.8 liters or 12.5 U.S. dry quarts. One alqueire also equals a variety of land measurements ranging from 0.35 acres to 24 acres.

AMERICAN ROAST A traditional term for a medium roast characterized by a moderately brown color and dry bean surface. Generally falls between 420 and 440 degrees F when reading bean temperature.

APPELLATION A distinct term denoting a geographic growing region having noticeably distinct flavor attributes.

AQUAPULP METHOD A coffee-processing method in which the pulp or mucilage is scrubbed from the beans by machine. *Also: Demucilage, Lavado, Washed Process, Wet Process.*

ARABICA A traditional species of coffee originating in Ethiopia. There are many varieties, including typica and bourbon.

AROMA The fragrance of brewed coffee.

ARROBA A measure of volume used in Spanish-speaking countries, equal to about 25 pounds.

ASTRINGENT A drying sensation on the tongue most often caused by the presence of immature beans in the coffee.

AUTOMATION The automatic operation or control of any equipment, process or system.

BACTERIAL BLIGHT A coffee disease that can occur when wet and cold conditions prevail.

BAG A burlap sack of coffee. Bag weight differs by country of origin, but is traditionally 132 or 152 pounds. *Also: Bale*

BAGGY An off-taste or smell similar to that of burlap bags. Can be due to a storage problem or biological issue.

BAKED Bland, tasteless or flat. Often the result of coffee roasted too slowly at too low a temperature.

BALANCED Denoting a pleasing combination of two or more primary taste sensations. Containing all the basic characteristics to the right extent and aesthetically pleasing. *Also: Round*

BASIC TASTES Sweet, sour, salty and bitter.

BATCH ROASTER Apparatus that roasts a given quantity of coffee at a time. Unlike continuous roasters, batch roasters have an identifiable start and stop time to each roast. *See also: Continuous Roaster*

BEAN PROBE Any measuring probe positioned on a roaster to enable the operator to read external bean temperature.

BEAN TEMPERATURE The external temperature of the coffee bean during the roast cycle. Generally used as the control temperature for the roasting process.

BENEFICIO A Central American coffee term for a coffee-processing establishment, such as a wet mill.

BIRD FRIENDLY A certification that designates that a coffee has been grown in accordance with the Smithsonian Institution's Migratory Bird Center's guidelines, which help protect bird habitat through shade-grown coffee and other environmental focuses.

BITTER A harsh, unpleasant taste perceived at the back of the tongue. All coffees have a slight bitterness that is characteristic of the roasting process and moderate bitterness can be balanced by sweetness. Commonly found in dark roasts or overly extracted coffees.

BLACK BEAN A common physical defect of green beans, resulting in a bean which is at least 50 percent black externally or internally. Usually the result of an infection during bean development or the prolonged fermentation of cherries that have been picked up from the ground.

BLAND Lacking in positive taste characteristics. Not highly flavored. *Also: Dull, Mild, Tasteless*

BLEND A mixture of two or more coffees that differ by growing regions, districts, farms, varieties, processing methods or roasts.

BODY The tactile impression of the weight or viscosity of coffee in the mouth. *Also: Mouthfeel*

BOUQUET Usually a reference to an overall aroma impression of brewed coffee. The total aromatic profile of the initial fragrance of the dry ground coffee plus the aroma of the brewed coffee and the nose impression when drinking. *Also: Fragrance*

BOURBON A botanical variety of *Coffea arabica* that features broad leaves and small, dense fruit.

BRACKISH A taste sensation that is distasteful, bitter and salty.

BREAKING THE CRUST During cupping, the action of breaking apart the cap of coarse grounds on the top of a cup prior to tasting.

BROKENS Coffee beans that were cracked or broken during processing; considered a defect.

BURNT A bitter, smoky or tarry flavor characteristic, often found in brewed coffee that has been overroasted.

BUTTERY A full and rich flavor with an oily body or texture.

C & F Common term for Cost and Freight, which is a buying term that means the seller owns the coffee goods until they are loaded on vessel and that the selling price includes all costs so far plus cost of ocean freight.

Coffee cherries.

"C" MARKET The New York Board of Trade commodities exchange where coffee futures are bought and sold.

C.I.F. Common term for Cost, Insurance and Freight, which is a buying term similar to c & f, except that the seller absorbs the insurance premium.

CAFFEINE ($C_8H_{10}N_4O_2$) A bitter white alkaloid found in coffee beans and leaves, having certain drug-like properties.

CAFFEINE CONTENT The amount of caffeine in a product. One cup of coffee contains about 1.5 grains of caffeine.

CAFFEOL A volatile aromatic conglomerate formed during roasting.

CARAMELIZED A burnt-like flavor, as in cooked/browned sugar. A desirable taste note if complemented with a strong coffee flavor.

CARAMELLY The smell or taste of cooked sugars without any trace of burntness.

CARBON DIOXIDE PROCESS (CO_2 PROCESS) A decaffeination process involving soaking green beans in highly compressed CO_2 to extract the caffeine. The caffeine is then removed from the CO_2 using activated carbon filters and is reused to extract more caffeine from the coffee.

CATIMOR A modern variety of *Coffea arabica* that is a cross between caturra and a natural arabica-robusta hybrid. Designed to be high-yielding and disease-resistant.

CATUAI A modern variety of *Coffea arabica* that is a hybrid of mondo novo and caturra. This high-yield plant can grow in high densities and is resistant to strong winds and rains.

CATURRA A modern variety of the *Coffea arabica* species discovered in Brasil that generally matures more quickly, produces more coffee, and is more disease resistant than older, traditional arabica varieties.

CAUSTIC A burning, sour taste sensation.

CERTIFICATION A way of showing that a coffee is grown, harvested, processed and/or roasted within the guidelines of a specific set of social or environmental values. Can also be used to mean coffee that meets origin certification, national certification or other political district certifications.

CHAFF Flakes of the innermost skin of the coffee fruit that remain on the green bean after processing, and which float free during roasting.

CHAFF COLLECTOR The part of any roasting system designed to collect the chaff. Often, but not always, a cyclone configuration.

CHEMICALLY Term used to describe a taste or aroma suggesting a phenolic or hydrocarbon presence. It may be inherent in the coffee or the result of contamination.

CHERRY The fruit of the coffee tree. Each cherry contains two regular coffee beans or one peaberry.

CHOCOLATEY A positive taste or aroma reminiscent of unsweetened, semi-sweet or milk chocolate, cocoa and/or vanilla. *Also: Chocolaty*

CINNAMON An underlying spice accent sometimes detected in the aroma. Also, a flavor nuance in light roasts.

CINNAMON ROAST A traditional term for a very light roast, used mostly for cupping, with a final roast temperature around 420 degrees F. There is very little or no oil on the bean surface.

CITY ROAST A traditional term for a light to medium commercial roast.

CLEAN The term "clean cup" refers to a coffee free of taints or faults. Does not necessarily imply clarity of flavor impression.

COCOA Can be a positive attribute, when it has a sweetish chocolate smell, or a taint of completely stale roasted coffee. Not to be confused with chocolatey.

COFFEE BERRY BORER A coffee pest that eats coffee beans throughout the stages of both its and its host plant's development. Can cause defects in raw coffee. *Also: Broca*

COFFEE BERRY DISEASE A coffee disease caused by the virulent strain of *Colletotrichum coffeanum*. The fungus lives in the bark of the coffee tree and produces spores which attack the coffee cherries. Can cause defects in raw coffee.

Cupping with cupping spoons.

COFFEE BLOSSOM An aromatic scent found in ground coffee that is reminiscent of the white flowers of the coffee tree, similar to jasmine.

COFFEE CLASSIFICATION A way of sorting, or grading, coffee that looks at a number of factors including quantity and level of defects, bean size and cup quality. *Also: Coffee Grading*

COFFEE LEAF RUST A coffee disease that is spread by spores from lesions on the underside of the plant by wind and rain. Originally discovered in Brazil in 1970, it is now in most coffee-growing countries. Can cause defects in raw coffee.

COFFEE OIL The volatile coffee essence developed in a bean during roasting.

COFFEE TRIER A special pointed device for removing a sample of green coffee beans through the bag wall without opening the bag. Also, as part of a roasting machine, a metal scoop that is used to catch small samples of roasting coffee for examination during the roasting process. *Also: Trier, Tryer*

COMMERCIAL COFFEE Coffee that is bought and sold on the "C" market.

COMPLEX Describes a balance and intensity of flavor. The impression of a coffee with an interesting mix of flavors, undertones and aftertastes. *Also: Deep*

CONTAINER A volume of measurement that equals about 40,000 pounds of coffee.

CONTINUOUS ROASTER Large commercial coffee roaster that roasts coffee continuously rather than in batches.

COOLING TRAY A piece of equipment, usually circular and equipped with stirring arms, which agitates fresh-roasted coffee to cool it to room temperature and may be used to halt the roasting process in roasters not equipped with water quenching.

CREAMY A measure of body somewhat less than buttery.

CREOSOTY A taste sensation related to pungent. A bitter, burnt vegetal taste found in the aftertaste of some dark-roasted coffees. Similar to tarry.

CUP OF EXCELLENCE A coffee competition and auction, seeking the absolute highest quality single lot of coffee from a particular harvest, judged by national and international juries.

CUPPING The sensory evaluation of coffee beans for flavor and aroma profile. The beans are ground, water is poured over the grounds, and the liquid is tasted both hot and as it cools.

CUPPING SPOON A spoon, about the size of a bouillon soup spoon, but perfectly round, used to taste coffee during a cupping session. Made of silver or stainless steel so as to have no flavor or aroma impact.

CURRENT CROP Green coffee from the recent harvest available after processing. *Also: New Crop*

DATA LOGGER Equipment used to record the time and temperature data during the roast process.

DATA LOGGING The act of compiling time and temperature roast data in order to assist an operator in profile roasting. May be manual or automated.

DECAFFEINATION The process of removing the caffeine from coffee.

DEFECTS Unpleasant flavor characteristics in green beans caused by problems during picking, processing, drying, sorting, storage, transportation, roasting or packaging. *Also: Flavor Defect, Visual Defect*

DEGASSING A natural process in which recently roasted coffee releases carbon dioxide gas.

DELICATE Pleasing to taste or smell. A sensation that is mild, subtle and sometimes fleeting. *Also: Gentle, Mellow*

DEMUCILAGE A procedure in which the sticky fruit pulp, or mucilage, is removed from freshly picked coffee beans by scrubbing in machines. *Also: Aquapulp, Mechanical Demucilaging, Water Process, Wet Process*

DILUTION AND DISPERSION A process used to lessen the nuisance impact of coffee roasting emissions. This process involves mixing emissions with fresh air.

DIRECT PROCESS A decaffeination process that involves applying a solvent directly to the green beans after the caffeine has been brought to the surface by steam or hot water.

DIRTY An undesirable, unclean smell or taste. Can imply a defect, such as sourness, earthiness or mustiness.

DOUBLE-PICKED Coffee that has been hand-picked twice to remove imperfect beans, pebbles and other imperfections.

DRUM ROASTER A coffee roaster where the beans are agitated inside a metal drum. The heat is provided by a flow of hot air through the drum, as well as by the hot metal of the drum.

DRY PROCESS Coffee process that involves harvesting and drying the beans while still in cherry. Dry-processed coffees often have less acidity and heavier body than their washed counterparts.

DRYING CYCLE The first phase of the roasting process, when the temperature of the beans rises to 100 degrees C. During this phase, the beans change from a bright green color to a pale yellow.

DULL Term used to describe a coffee lacking in character. *Also: Flat, Unimpressive*

EARTHY A complex mustiness found in certain dry-processed, low-acid coffees. Often considered a taint in washed coffees. *Also: Dirty, Groundy*

EAST AFRICAN FINE COFFEE ASSOCIATION (EAFCA) An association of coffee producers, processors, marketing people and organizations in a number of East and South African countries, as well as others from outside Africa.

ENVIRONMENT TEMPERATURE/DRUM TEMPERATURE Temperature in the roasting chamber during the roast cycle. Sometimes used as the control temperature.

ETHYL ACETATE ($C_4H_8O_2$) A colorless, volatile, flammable liquid having a fragrant, fruit-like odor. Used as a decaffeinating agent.

EXHAUST TEMPERATURE Temperature of the exhaust stream of a coffee roaster.

EMISSIONS CONTROL The process of regulating roasting emissions, typically in accordance with regional environmental, smoke or odor regulations.

F.O.B. Shipping term meaning Free On Board, where the seller delivers freight to the purchaser's designated shipper.

FAIR TRADE A certification that designates a coffee has been grown in accordance with the guidelines of Fairtrade International or Fair Trade USA. These guidelines are geared toward providing a living wage to farmers in coffee cooperatives.

FERMENTATION The stage during the wet method of coffee processing when the sticky pulp is loosened from the skinned coffee beans by natural enzymes while the beans rest in tanks.

FERMENTED A sour or acrid vinegar taste or smell. Obvious and unpleasant. A common processing error.

FINCA Spanish for "estate," a specific coffee farm, either large or small. *Also: Cafetal*

FIRST CRACK The second stage of coffee roasting. Once the beans reach 160 degrees C, complex chemical reactions occur, which cause an audible cracking sound.

FLAT Coffee that has been exposed to oxygen for too long. Often tastes stale or cardboardy. Lacks intensity. Can also refer to acidity, in which case it means light or no acidity. *Also: Stale*

FLAVOR PROFILE The total impression of aroma, acidity, body, sweetness and aftertaste. Usually described with specific major taste impressions.

FLAVOR WHEEL A systematic terminology used by cuppers for describing the faults, basic tastes and unusual flavors of coffees. Developed by the SCA.

FLAVORED COFFEE Roasted coffee that has been mixed with flavoring agents or brewed coffee mixed with flavored syrup.

FLOATER Green bean defect characterized by a faded or bleached appearance. Can introduce fermented, bitter or straw-like flavors in the cup.

FLUID-BED ROASTER A roasting apparatus that utilizes forced hot air to simultaneously agitate and roast green coffee beans.

FORWARD SALE A way of purchasing green beans that allows you to specify how much coffee you will purchase from a certain buyer over a period of time in the future.

FRAGRANCE The smell of dry ground or whole bean coffee before brewing. *Also: Bouquet*

FRENCH ROAST A traditional term for a very dark roast, with a stop temperature around 460 to 465 degrees F. In this roast, the beans are the color of bittersweet chocolate and are usually covered in oil. *Also: Dark Roast*

FRESH A recent roast, often characterized by a distinctly pleasing aroma.

FRUITY Denotes the aromatic scents of citrus or berry fruit in the cup. Also, a flavor taint bordering on fermented.

FULL BAG Coffee sold in its country of origin bag weight. Generally 60 or 70 kilos.

FULL CITY ROAST A traditional term for a medium commercial roast, with a stop temperature around 440 to 445 degrees F. *Also: North Italian Roast*

FUTURES The purchase or sale of a coffee contract for delivery in the future.

GEISHA A variety of *Coffea arabica* that features large fruits and long, curvy beans.

GRADE The level of quality given to a particular coffee based on factors such as defects, bean size and moisture content. Can be seen as numbers (e.g. Grade 1), letters (e.g. Grade AA) or a combination of the two (e.g. 1AAA).

GRASSY A flavor taint indicating a slight chlorophyll or herbal taste or odor. Can be found in green coffee that has not been sufficiently dried, as well as in under-roasted coffees. *Also: Green, Hay-like*

GREEN COFFEE Unroasted coffee beans. *Also: Raw*

GREEN COFFEE ASSOCIATION An association that works in conjunction with the coffee, sugar and cocoa exchange to help benefit the coffee industry.

HACIENDA Farm, ranch or coffee plantation.

HARD BEAN (HB) A term used to describe coffees grown at relatively high altitudes, usually 4,000 to 4,500 feet.

HARRAR Dry-processed, or natural, coffees of Ethiopia. Grown in eastern Ethiopia near the city of Harrar, these coffees are usually fragrant and light-bodied with complex acidity. *Also: Harar, Harer, Mocha Harrar, Moka Harrar, Mocca Harrar*

HARSH Crude raw taste with the obvious presence of bitter and astringent compounds. Can taste caustic or medicinal.

HEAVY Quantitative term for body or mouthfeel.

HECTARE (HA) A customary metric unit of land area, equal to 100 acres. One hectare is a square hectometer, so the area of a square 100 meters on each side; exactly 10,000 square meters or approximately 2.47 acres.

HEIRLOOM A species of arabica that is more variable and genetically closer to wild coffee than other cultivars.

HERBY A taste sensation resembling the flavor or odor of herbs.

HIDY Unpleasant odor reminiscent of wet leather or wet dog. Can be caused by excessive heat during the drying process usually associated with coffees dried in mechanical dryers. *Also: Fauna, Hidey*

HIGH-GROWN Arabica coffees grown at altitudes of more than 3,000 feet.

HOME ROASTERS Any number of small coffee roasters manufactured specifically for the consumer/hobbyist market. Generally roasting 4 ounces or less, and electrically heated.

HULLING The process of removing the parchment and silver skin from washed coffees just prior to milling.

IMMATURE BEANS Small, malformed green beans with tightly attached silverskin. Can taste astringent or grassy in the cup.

IMPERFECTIONS Defects in the green beans, such as broken beans, shells, quakers, etc. Coffee is graded by the number of imperfections in the sample. *Also: Defects*

INSECT DAMAGE A green bean defect characterized by signs of insect boring, nibbling or chomping.

INTENSITY Measure of the total impression of bouquet.

INTERNATIONAL COFFEE ASSOCIATION (ICO) An intergovernmental organization for coffee that brings together producing and consuming countries to tackle the challenges facing the world coffee sector through international cooperation.

INTERNATIONAL STANDARDS OF OPERATION (ISO-1401 9000) International Organization for Standardization (ISO) An international standard-setting body composed of representatives from national standards organizations. The organization produces world-wide standards (ISO standards) for industry and commerce, including coffee.

ITALIAN ROAST A traditional term for a darker commercial roast, with a stop temperature around 450 to 455 degrees F. The beans are usually the color of milk-chocolate and are half-covered with oil droplets. *Also: Vienna Roast, South Italian*

KOSHER Fit or allowed to be eaten or used according to the dietary or ceremonial laws of Judaism. Certification for adherence to the laws governing kosher foods, including coffee.

LE NEZ DU CAFÉ A set of jarred scents formulated to train professional coffee cuppers and roasters.

LEMON The fresh zippy scent or flavor of lemon peel or zest found in coffee.

LICORICE A candy-like smell or flavor found in coffee, characteristic of licorice root.

MACHINE-DRIED A term used to describe coffee that has been mechanically dried, usually in large, rotating drums or cascading silos.

MALTY A flavor fault that produces the odor of roasted cereal grains, walnuts or maple.

MARAGOGYPE A variety of *Coffea arabica* distinguished by extremely large, porous beans and low yield. *Also: Maragogipe, Elephant Bean*

MATURE COFFEE Coffee held in a warehouse for two to three years. Mature coffee has been held longer than old crop coffee, but not as long as aged or vintage coffee.

MEDICINAL A flavor or odor, usually unpleasant, often chemically and/or astringent.

MELLOW Used to describe a sweet coffee that is well-balanced with low to medium acidity.

METALLIC Describes coffees that are metallic in flavor, usually caused by immature beans. May be accompanied by astringent or bitter tastes.

METHYLENE CHLORIDE (CH_2CL_2) A colorless, volatile liquid used as a decaffeination agent.

MILD A taste sensation associated with mellow. A smooth and soft or sweet washed coffee.

MILLING The mechanical removal of the entire dried fruit husk from dry-processed beans or the dry parchment skin from wet-processed beans.

MINI C A miniature version of the New York Board of Trade's coffee "C" contract. Designed to make the coffee futures market accessible to those who buy and sell smaller lots of coffee.

MOLDY A visual or flavor defect caused by damp storage conditions.

MONDO NOVO A modern coffee variety that is a natural hybrid between typica and bourbon. Highly productive and disease-resistant.

MONSOONED COFFEE Coffee deliberately exposed to monsoon winds in an open warehouse to increase body and reduce acidity.

MOUTHFEEL Describes the sensation in the mouth of weight or viscosity.
Also: Body

MUDDY A dull indistinct flavor. Full of sediment, possibly from grounds.

MUSTY A smell associated with earthy. As a taint, the coffee will smell of a musty cellar. Slight mustiness is not always a taint, especially in aged or monsooned coffees.

NATIONAL COFFEE ASSOCIATION (NCA) A trade association for the coffee industry.

NATURAL PROCESS Coffee processing method that involves removing the husk or fruit after the coffee fruit has been dried. By utilizing only ripe fruit and drying carefully, this method can produce coffees that are complex and fruity.

NEUTRAL Used to describe coffee that is fundamentally characterless, inoffensive or insipid, without virtue yet without defects.

NEW CROP Green coffee from the recent harvest available after processing. *Also: Current Crop*

NEW YORK BOARD OF TRADE (NYBOT) An international marketplace for agricultural and financial futures, including coffee and sugar.

NIPPY A taste sensation perceived from a very clean high-acidity coffee.

NON-LINEAR PROCESS CONTROL SYSTEM A roasting control system that uses a non-linear math function to define the roasting path. Usually more sophisticated than a linear process control system.

NOSE The combination of taste and smell when swallowing coffee. The
aroma component of aftertaste. Most commonly caramelly, nutty or malty.

NUTTY The aromatic sensation of roasted nuts, often found in brewed coffee.

OILY Term used to describe the surface of roasted coffee; denotes darker roasts.

OLD-CROP Green coffee that has been held in a warehouse and is available in the later half of the harvest cycle, but still within the harvest year.

ORGANIC A term used to describe coffee that has been certified by a third-party agency as having been grown and processed without the use of pesticides, herbicides or similar chemicals. *Also: Certified-Organic Coffee, Organic Certified*

PACAMARA A variety of *Coffea arabica* that is a cross between maragogype and pacas.

PACAS A variety of *Coffea arabica* that is a cross between caturra and bourbon; produces good yields and can perform at medium to high elevations.

PAPERY An off-taste suggesting the taste of wet paper or cardboard. Sometimes the result of paper filters or the decaffeination process.

PARCHMENT A thin, crumbly skin covering wet-processed coffee beans after they have been de-pulped and dried. *Also: Pergamino*

PARCHMENT COFFEE Wet-processed coffee with the dried parchment skin still covering the bean. The parchment is removed by milling prior to roasting. *Also: In Parchment, En Pergamino*

PAST-CROP Green coffee that has been held in a warehouse and is available from the previous harvest year.

PAST-CROPPISH Said of coffees that have deteriorated in the green state before roasting and, thus, taste weakened or toned down. Particularly with less acidity and a heavy woody or papery flavor and little body or aroma.

Peaberries.

PATIO-DRIED Coffee dried by exposing it to the heat of the sun by spreading and raking it in thin layers on open patios. *Also: Sun Dried*

PEABERRY A small, round bean formed when only one seed, rather than the usual two, develops in a coffee cherry. *Also: Caracol*

PERFORATED DRUM A type of drum roaster with a drum that is fully perforated on the sides.

PETROLEUM Off-smell or taste usually originating from contamination. Often found in coffee stored in poorly manufactured bags.

PIQUANT A pronounced and pleasant pungent acidity; slightly tart or biting.

POINTED Coffee with a fine, acidic sharpness.

POTATOEY A disagreeable and unpleasant taste of raw potato.

PROCESSING The way in which coffee is prepared at origin. The type of processing, such as washed or dry-processed, can determine the presence and strength of certain aromas and tastes in the coffee.

PROFILE An analysis of the temperature path of coffee during the roasting process, usually in the form of a time and temperature graph.

PROFILE ROASTING The science of controlling the rate of heat transfer into the coffee during the roasting process, with the goals of repeatability and optimized flavor. Also, as a verb, taking a measurable and repeatable action during the roast process to

change the taste of the coffee by changing the roast profile.

PROFILE ROASTING SYSTEM A roasting control system utilizing electronic process control hardware to manipulate the burner, airflow and/or drum rotation speed.

PROFILING The act of profile roasting; making a hard copy profile of a roast temperature path, often in the form of a graph.

PRUNY The fruit-like taste reminiscent of prune found in some dark-roast coffees.

PULP The part of the coffee cherry that is removed during processing. *Also: Mucilage*

PULPING Removing the outermost skin of the coffee cherry.

PUNGENT A primary taste sensation related to the presence of bitter compounds. Usually from phenolic compounds that range in taste from creosoty to alkaline.

PYROLYSIS During roasting, the chemical breakdown of fats and carbohydrates into the delicate oils that provide the aroma and much of the flavor of coffee.

Q AUCTION An alternative market for specialty grade green coffees defined by ratings given by qualified cuppers and online auctions.

QUAKERS Blighted and underdeveloped coffee beans.

QUAKERY A peanutty flavor caused by unripe or underdeveloped beans. They appear very light when roasted.

QUINTAL A unit of weight. When applied to coffee, it is generally around 101.4 pounds, but this varies from country to country.

RAINFOREST ALLIANCE A certification that designates that a coffee has been grown in accordance with the guidelines of Rainforest Alliance. These guidelines are geared toward ecosystem protection and conservation, as well as sustainable social practices.

RANCID Having a rank odor or taste as that of old oil. A sour and unpleasant smell.

RANK A dirty unpleasant flavor due mainly to contamination or over-fermentation.

RESONANT Descriptive term for a long, pleasing aftertaste.

RICH Mainly a descriptor for bouquet. Also used to indicate depth and complexity of flavor, big pleasing aroma and full body.

RIOY A harsh medicinal or slightly iodized, phenolic or carbolic flavor. Considered a taint by most roasters but appreciated by others for blends.

ROAST INITIATION The third stage of roasting, when beans swell to around 150 percent of their normal size. Elements within the beans begin to caramelize, giving the beans their brown color.

ROAST STYLE The way in which coffee beans are roasted. Can be described as light, medium and dark, as well as in traditional terms like cinnamon and full city.

ROASTERS GUILD A trade guild of the Specialty Coffee Association consisting of specialty roasters dedicated to the craft of roasting quality coffee.

ROBUSTA A high-bearing, disease-resistant coffee species that produces coffee with higher caffeine content than *Coffea arabica*. *Also: Coffea Canephora*

ROUGH An unpleasant taste sensation related to sharp.

ROUND Commonly used term for a balanced and rich coffee. *Also: Full*

ROUNDED A quantitative descriptor for a moderate bouquet.

RUBBERY Burnt rubber odor characteristic of some robustas and noted in some dark roasts.

SALTY One of the four basic taste sensations, yet saltiness rarely comes to the forefront in coffee taste. When it does, it is just perceptible.

SCORCHED A roasting defect resulting in an odor taint that gives

the coffee brew a slight smoky-burnt aftertaste with an overall under-developed taste. Can be seen on the surface of roasted coffee.

SECOND CRACK The stage in roasting where the beans become brittle due to dehydration. As a result, the beans crack and begin to carbonize, producing the burnt characteristics of extremely dark roasts.

SET POINT PROCESS SYSTEM A roasting control system that utilizes simple on/off logic, similar to a thermostat.

SHARP Intense flavor taint resulting in salty and soury compounds. Sharp towards salty is termed rough. Sharp towards soury is astringent. When used in reference to acidity, it can be a complimentary term relating to tangy and nippy.

SHELL Green bean defect characterized by seashell-shaped beans.

SILVERSKIN The thin, innermost skin of the coffee fruit. During roasting, any silverskin left on the bean turns into chaff.

SINGLE-ESTATE Term used to describe coffee produced by a single farm, single mill or single group of farms, and marketed separately from other coffees. *Also: Estate-Grown, Single-Farm*

SINGLE-ORIGIN Term used to describe unblended coffee from a single country, region or crop.

SIZE CLASSIFICATION A way of sorting coffee by the size of the green bean. The beans fall through screens with round holes of various dimensions. Sizes range from 13, which is the smallest, to 20, which is very large. Peaberries are sized with screens which have oval-shaped holes from 9 to 13. *Also: Screen Size*

SLURP AND SPIT The term for slurping the coffee from the spoon, tasting it and spitting it out.

SMOKY A taste sensation reminiscent of smoked food. Usually a positive descriptor, and more common in dark roasts.

SMOOTH A quantitative descriptor for moderately low-bodied coffee. Also referring to a full-bodied, low-acidity coffee.

SOAPY An off-taste similar to earthy and dirty.

SOFT Low acidity coffees that have a light or very light acidity just short of bland. A mild coffee with a dry aftertaste.

SOFT BEAN Term used to describe coffees grown at lower altitudes.

SOLID DRUM A type of drum roaster that has a drum with solid sides.

SOUR One of the four basic tastes: sweet, sour, salty and bitter.

SOURCE The place of a coffee's origin. Also used as a verb, as in "to source coffee" from a particular place.

SOURS Visual green bean defect typified by yellow, brown or red beans. Often the result of improper agricultural or processing techniques. Can result in sour or fermented flavors in the cup.

SOURY A distinctly sour, rank or rancid taste often due to improper processing. Not to be confused with acidy and acidity.

SPECIALTY COFFEE Coffee produced with care and sophistication to achieve recognized quality. Also refers to green coffee with a limited amount of allowable defects.

SPECIALTY COFFEE ASSOCIATION (SCA) A global association of specialty coffee roasters, wholesalers, retailers, importers, growers and manufacturers.

SPICY Said of aroma or flavor suggestive of spices. Sometimes associated with aromatic, piquant or pungent. Suggesting cloves, cinnamon, nutmeg, etc.

SPLIT BAG Term used define the sale of a coffee at any amount less than full bag.

SPOT SALE An on-the-spot purchase of green coffee subject to current availability and pricing.

STAGE PROCESS SYSTEM A roasting control system that follows a predefined path or program.

STALE An unpleasant taste fault found in old and deteriorated roasted coffee. Roasted coffee that has faded in quality after excessive storage or exposure to air. *Also: Flat*

STRAWY A taste taint that gives a distinct hay-like and woody flavor.

STRENGTH Usually a term quantifying brewed coffee. Strength is conveyed through concentration of soluble solids in suspension, not the prominence of any one characteristic.

STRICTLY HARD BEAN (SHB) Coffee grown above 4,500 feet.

STRONG A term indicating strength derived from greater soluble solids in the extraction or intensity of any one characteristic of

note. It is also used as an adjective to virtue or defect, as in "a strong sour taste" or "a strong fine aroma."

SUN-DRIED Term used for coffee that is dried by exposing it to the heat of the sun by spreading and raking it in thin layers on drying racks or patios.

SUN-GROWN Describes coffee that is not grown under a shade canopy.

SUPER SACK A method of selling and shipping coffee in large sacks, containing coffee already removed from the full bag.

SUSTAINABLE COFFEE A slightly vague description for coffees grown and sold in an environmentally and socially sustainable way.

SWEET One of the four basic tastes. Also the recognition of sweetness or the absence of bitterness in a coffee. Said of a smooth, palatable coffee, free of taints or harshness.

SWISS WATER PROCESS A trademarked decaffeination method that removes caffeine from coffee beans using hot water, steam and activated charcoal.

TAINT A negative taste, fragrance or aroma occurring anywhere in the coffee chain.

TANGY A somewhat sour and fruity taste sensation.

TARRY A taste fault giving a burnt character.

TART A sour taste sensation between tangy and soury.

TASTE The total sensory impression of the four combined basic tastes of sweet, sour, salty and bitter.

TERROIR The personality and character in aroma and taste represented by a coffee's origin. An overall flavor profile common to a particular growing region, district, altitude or processing style.

THICK Term to indicate an extremely heavy body.

THIN Coffee that lacks body or flavor.

TIPPED Coffee beans that are charred on the ends due to a roasting fault, usually starting the roasting process with an excessively high roaster drum temperature or simply roasting too fast for the type of coffee.

TOASTY Having the aroma of fresh toast or fresh-baked bread.

TRIANGLE CUPPING A system of cupping where the cupper tastes three cups of coffee to identify the one that is different from the other two. Used as a skill-building technique, as well as to compare and contrast coffee samples.

TURPENY A medicinal aftertaste reminiscent of turpentine, resin or camphor-like substances.

TYPICA A botanical variety of *Coffea arabica*. The trees are conical in shape and can reach heights of 15 feet. Widely considered to be the original arabica variety.

UMAMI Commonly called the "fifth taste," this word describes the flavor that is often thought of as pungent, savory, tangy or meaty.

UNDER-DEVELOPED Coffee roasted too slowly at too low a temperature.

UTZ A certification that designates that a coffee has been grown in accordance with the guidelines of Utz Certified. These guidelines are geared toward responsible coffee production and sourcing.

VAPID Lacking character and liveliness. Particularly lacking acidity, tang or briskness. *Also: Insipid, Dull, Flat*

VARIETY Traditionally refers to the genetic subspecies of coffee based on location, such as Costa Rica or Colombia. Today, more commonly used to mean varieties of arabica, such as typica and bourbon.

VELVETY Heavy in strength and body, low in acidity.

VINEGARY A sour off-taste related to ferment.

WASHED PROCESS Post-harvest process of separating the seeds from the fruit before drying. Most important is the intermediate step of controlled fermentation between the pulping and the rinsing and drying phase. Poor processing can lead to defects that can render the coffee unusable. On the other hand, properly washed coffees typically exhibit sweetness, clarity and good acidity. *Also: Aquapulp, Demucilage, Wet Process, Lavado*

WATER PROCESS A trademarked decaffeination method that is similar to the carbon dioxide method, but instead of removing the caffeine with activated carbon filters, it is washed from the CO_2 with water in a secondary tank and is then recycled to extract more caffeine from the coffee.

WATER QUENCH Using water to rapidly cool roasted coffee to prevent over-roasting and the loss of aroma.

WATERY Relating to body, it means the coffee shows signs of being thin. Relating to strength, the coffee is weak in flavor either due to the available soluble solids in the bean or to the ratio of grounds to water.

WET PROCESS A type of coffee processing that involves removing the skin and pulp from the bean while the coffee fruit is still moist. In the traditional wet process, the coffee skins are removed, the skinned beans sit in tanks where enzymes loosen the sticky fruit pulp and then are washed. In the demucilage method, the pulp is scrubbed from the beans by machine. *Also: Aquapulp, Demucilage, Wet Method, Washed Process*

WHOLE-BEAN COFFEE Coffee that has been roasted but not yet ground.

WINEY A bittersweet fruity quality characteristic of a fine red wine. A sweet soury taste, sometimes used to describe acidity.

WOODY A flavor taint characteristic of past-croppish coffees and those grown at lower altitude. Also, a desirable scent or flavor reminiscent of a fine wood such as cedar or sandalwood. ∎

CUPPING & SENSORY EVALUATION

Craft of Cupping

The Art and Science of the Silver Spoon

by Robert Barker

• FROM THE SEPTEMBER/OCTOBER 2004 ISSUE OF *ROAST* •

C upping coffee is a labor of love, one that rewards you with membership in a very special club of coffee aficionados. Even after 25 years of cupping, I confess I'm still like a kid in a candy shop when I'm at the cupping table. There is a certain excitement to the ritual sniffing and sipping. Each new cup is mysterious; each spoonful the key that can transport you to a coffee farm halfway around the world or open the door to a new origin, a new vintage or a special offering that you never knew existed.

Unlike the majority of the food and beverage industry, where tasters in white coats are sequestered in sterile laboratories, coffee cuppers seem to be a little more social. While taste assessment is essential for quality control and for determining a coffee's appeal, it is also an opportunity for cuppers to engage the public and share their enthusiasm.

Cupping is a system of classification based on a few learned skills. Once you learn these skills and have a chance to practice and become confident in your abilities, you'll find that cupping reveals the answers to many of the most important roasting questions.

Whatever your cupping level is, a good vocabulary is paramount for communicating with green coffee suppliers and for recording your impression of coffees received. Novice cuppers are encouraged to invent their own terms when first introduced to the revolving table and silver spoon. Learning a vocabulary of a hundred or so terms is daunting at first glance. It's more important to write your impression in your own words when starting out and gradually integrate the professional terms as you become more accomplished. You can modify and add to your own list—it's something you grow into. (To help you get started, check out the cupping glossary on page 289.)

Why Cup?

There are so many reasons to get out your silver spoon: sourcing new coffees, trouble-shooting problems, developing new blends, comparing your products with the competition or educating your staff. But perhaps the most important reason for cupping is a business one: If you don't cup, you're disadvantaged by everyone else who does. Cupping is quality control. Without a doubt, it is the most valuable asset to maintaining and improving the quality of your product. As a proponent of specialty coffee, it's important to assess the quality of the green coffee purchases and follow that up with an assessment of your production roast.

Here are a few discoveries a roaster or green coffee buyer can make at the cupping table:

● *What does growing altitude have to do with cup quality?* Differences in acidity will become obvious when you taste high- and low-grown coffees from the same region.

● *What decaffeination process yields the best taste?* Here I recommend using as many samples from the same national origin as possible. You may not know the quality of the unprocessed beans, but you should be all right if using reputable sources. Try samples from each of the decaffeination processes: Cup methylene chloride, also known as MC or KVW; ethyl acetate, also known as EA or natural; water-processed; and CO_2-processed. Use regular unprocessed coffee from the same origin for a control, and note any papery or cardboard taste in the decaf samples. Some processes weaken the overall flavor, and others add off tastes.

● *What is the difference in a washed coffee and a traditional dry-processed coffee?* Here you can compare washed and natural versions of coffees like Brazils, Sumatrans and Sidamos.

● *What does aging do to a coffee's taste and acidity?* Use aged and regular Sumatrans or Indian Mysore compared with Monsooned Malabar. At the same time, you can compare past-crop coffees with new-crop examples. Often, past-crop coffees are marketed as vintage or aged coffees.

● *How does tree variety contribute to taste?* You can learn this by tasting beans from typica, bourbon and caturra trees. Check with brokers and importers for coffees with known pedigrees.

● *Can a washed robusta taste as good as an average arabica?*

● *Can I taste the difference between patio-dried coffee and mechanically dried coffees?*

● *Can I taste the difference between dry-pulped coffee and traditionally washed coffee?*

Of course, tasting isn't just beneficial at the roastery. Most roaster/retailers also cup or taste their coffees at their shop to ensure the quality of the coffee from roaster to customer. Taste tests in a shop can be done with a variety of brewing methods, including French press, pouring over Melitta filters, and regular brewers.

Discoveries that can be made with retail shop testing include:

● *What contribution does the filter paper make to the taste of the coffee?*

● *What does a difference in grind do to the taste?*

● *What does a difference in water temperature do to the taste?*

● *Can I taste a difference when using tap water compared to purified water?*

● *Which milk producer delivers the best taste complement to my coffee?*

● *What is the best water-to-grounds ratio for my brewer?*

● *How does my coffee change after 30 minutes in the brewer?*

● *What does a wooden stirring stick do to the coffee flavor?*

Convenient Cupping

Cupping can be a daunting experience for newbies and old hands alike. There are a number of ways to make the process easier and more convenient.

Much like a science experiment, cupping requires foresight, a scenario and premise focusing on the question you wish to address, and the results you expect to achieve. For instance, if you are comparing 10 lots of Colombian coffees, it helps to know as much as possible about each lot. In the end, it is not just the overall ranking you will leave the table with, but also an understanding as to why the coffees came out in that order. Are they the same age, same processing, grown at the same altitude, same tree variety? Planning will help you get the most out of every cupping. Add some controls and known quantities to expand the usefulness of the exercise.

The Four Steps of Planning a Cupping

1. **Design**: The determination of purpose. What do we want to find out? What should we expect? How many coffees are going to be included? How many do we have? How many do we need? How many are manageable? Can it be broken into two if it is too large? What other coffees would be complementary and add to the experience? What would be a suitable control coffee?

2. **Setup**: The setup follows the design. First, everything should be labeled clearly and put into proper order. This means that coffees should be grouped, either by type, degree of roast, region or other category that offers some degree of order. The layout of these samples should be adequate for moving from sample to sample with convenience. Are controls in the right order? Is there room for more than one cupper?

3. **Facility**: This includes a number of components, including place, time, schedule and, ideally, an assistant. The place can

be a table or counter, but the standard is a tall, round, rotating table. The time of day may be determined for the convenience to the parties involved or the availability of the space. Samples must be weighed out and ground, so a scale and grinder must be available. The assistant will need to have hot water ready at the right time as well as a good supply of cupping spoons, napkins, paper cups, paper towels, notepads, clipboards and pens.

4. **Write-up**: Notes are best written on cupping forms that will be helpful to the process. These forms can be tailor-made to suit your purpose and include your company logo, a vocabulary list or other cupping aids. (Sample forms can be found on pages 286 and 287.) When doing the tasting, additional comments should be clear and even wordy, because it's easier to edit than to recall some nuance days later. It's useful to discuss the results afterward to see if there is agreement and a common conclusion. Sometimes it may be decided that the cupping should be repeated under different circumstances.

A Few More Tips

- The easier the process, the more fun it will be. Sometimes I highlight my cupping forms with colored markers. One color for major tastes and another for nuances. Above all, written comments are most valuable for cup-to-cup comparisons, ratings and rankings.

- The easier the cleanup the more likely you will be encouraged to do more cuppings. Here is where the trainee assistant can be very helpful.

- Many successful roasters make morning cupping an everyday practice. These daily cuppings are conducted to check the latest roast quality and consistency.

- Separate cuppings may be conducted in the afternoon to assess samples representing possible replacement stocks or special offerings.

- A daily quality-control cupping is a good opportunity to introduce a new employee to the practice. Sometimes I invite special guests or clients to join in.

- For years, I have kept my cupping reports in loose-leaf binders for reference. Now I can keep them on a computer that can be searched by country of origin, estate name, region, bag marks or just chronologically by descending dates or ratings.

Subjectivity vs. Objectivity

Cupping is an attempt at objectivity, but at every step assessments tend to become subjective. After all, no two cuppers have the same taste buds, with the possible exception of identical twins. Assessments are often skewed by preference or expectation. How

could you ever be disappointed when cupping a Jamaican Blue Mountain sample? Isn't it supposed to be the greatest coffee in the world?

So don't be discouraged if you find that your cupping responses don't seem to match everyone else's at the table. Remember, it was only a few years ago that many roasters were cupping an exemplary Kona coffee only to find out later that it was "Kona Rican." Cupping is obviously not a perfect science. But it is a useful one—and one that you're likely to enjoy each time you pick up your silver spoon. ∎

CUPPING RESOURCES

ON THE NEXT SEVERAL PAGES, *we* present a unique collection of cupping resource materials*, including cut-and-copy forms, a vocabulary sheet and a glossary.

286 Cupping Form

287 Evaluation

288 Vocabulary

289 Glossary

*These forms were developed by Robert Barker and *Roast* magazine; they are not official forms of any industry group.

roast
MAGAZINE

THE CRAFT OF CUPPING
CUPPING FORM

A AROMA

1	2	3	4	5	6	7	8	9	10

Caramelly	Big	Woody	Cedary	Malty
Floral	Chocolaty	Rich	Smoky	Resinous
Spicy	Fruity	Nutty	Slight	Pungent
Earthy	Herbal	Winey	Vanilla-like	Flat

AROMA TAINTS

Fermented	Burnt	Hidy	Rancid	Earthy
Baked	Medicinal	Strawy	Petroleum	Cardboardy
Ashy	Moldy	Fishy	Green	Stale
Rioy	Grassy	Turpeny	Papery	Rubbery
Musty	Tarry	Fauna	Cocoa	Bricky
Herby	Chemical	Woody	Creosoty	Soapy

B FLAVOR

1	2	3	4	5	6	7	8	9	10

Chocolaty	Mellow	Cereal	Berryish	Cedary
Caramelly	Earthy	Smoky	Clean	Tobaccoey
Sweet	Grainy	Citrusy	Bitter	Woody
Complex	Vanilla-like	Smooth	Leathery	
Toasty	Pruny	Musty	Winey	
Nutty	Mild	Cinnamon	Malty	
Fruit-like	Pungent	Spicy	Strong	

FLAVOR TAINTS

Fermented	Acrid	Sharp/Salty	Hay-like	Fishy
Bitter	Potatoey	Hidy	Ashy	Briny
Herby	Petroleum	Vinegary	Rancid	Cocoa
Chemical	Earthy	Fauna	Bland	Cardboardy
Rank	Edgy	Baggy	Strawy	Rubbery
Harsh	Cabbagy	Grassy	Carbony	Astringent
Oniony	Turpeny	Burnt	Alkaline	Baked
Medicinal	Groundy	Acerbic	Neutral	Creosoty
Rioy	Hard	Insipid	Woody	Pasty
Soury	Soapy	Green	Tarry	Tippy
Peasy	Moldy	Charred	Brackish	
Metallic	Rough	Caustic	Stale	
Dirty	Musty	Vapid	Papery	

ROAST TASTES

Fresh	Resonate	Rounded	Balanced	Piquant
Under-dev.	Green	Grassy	Soury	Biting
Burnt	Carbony	Cresoty	Tarry	Bitter
Pungent	Ashy	Fishy	Rubbery	Harsh
Past-crop	Scorched	Tippy	Baked	Bland

DARK ROAST ASSETS

Chocolaty	Vanilla-like	Pungent	Roasty	Powerful
Complex	Smoky	Rich	Broad	Full-
Deep	Heavy	Round	Intense	flavored
Mellow	Smooth	Hardy	Bittersweet	

C ACIDITY

1	2	3	4	5	6	7	8	9	10

Bright	Brisk	Sweet	Piquant
Fruity	Tangy	Nippy	Winey
Sharp	Smooth	Soft	Flat
Medium	Moderate	Mild	Slight
Impressive	Pronounced	Delicate	Disappointing

D BODY

1	2	3	4	5	6	7	8	9	10

Oily	Buttery	Creamy	Thick
Heavy	Full	Medium	Light
Impressive	Disappointing	Thin	Watery

E AFTERTASTE & FINISH

1	2	3	4	5	6	7	8	9	10

Strong	Moderate	Weak	Negligible
Clean	Fresh	Rounded	Resonate
Floral	Spicy	Fruity	Winey
Long	Fast-fading	Thin	Astringent

F ASSESSMENT

-5	-4	-3	-2	-1	+1	+2	+3	+4	+5

Exceptional	Exemplary	Excellent	Outstanding
Very good	Good	Above Average	Average
Fair	Poor	Defective	Foul

G CUPPING SCORE

This form is based on a 100-point scale. Combine all of the above scores and add 40 to determine the overall score.

OVERALL SCORE

H NOTES

_____

_____

_____

roast
MAGAZINE

THE CRAFT OF CUPPING

CUPPING EVALUATION

Received date_____ Sample #_____ Roast date_____

Origin_____ Region / Name_____

Green appearance_____

Vendor_____ Vendor reference #_____

Roast_____ Agtron # WB_____ Grade_____

	1	2	3	4	5	6	7	8	9	10
Fragrance/Aroma	1	2	3	4	5	6	7	8	9	10
Flavor	1	2	3	4	5	6	7	8	9	10
Strength/Intensity	1	2	3	4	5	6	7	8	9	10
Sweetness	1	2	3	4	5	6	7	8	9	10
Bitterness	1	2	3	4	5	6	7	8	9	10
Acidity	1	2	3	4	5	6	7	8	9	10
Body	1	2	3	4	5	6	7	8	9	10
Aftertaste/Finish	1	2	3	4	5	6	7	8	9	10
Balance	1	2	3	4	5	6	7	8	9	10
Terroir Distinction	1	2	3	4	5	6	7	8	9	10

100-POINT SCALE

COMMENTS

_____
_____
_____
_____

Cupper_____ Date_____

roast
MAGAZINE

THE CRAFT OF CUPPING
CUPPING VOCABULARY

FRAGRANCE

Sweetly floral	Sweetly herbal	Sweetly spicy

AROMAS & SCENTS

Caramelly	Chocolaty	Nutty	Vanilla-like
Floral	Fruit-like	Acidy	Winey
Spicy	Herbal	Cedary	Malty
Earthy	Woody	Smoky	Pungent

AROMA TAINTS

Fermented	Moldy	Fauna	Earthy
Baked	Grassy	Woody	Cardboardy
Ashy	Tarry	Rancid	Stale
Rioy	Chemical	Petroleum	Rubbery
Musty	Hidy	Green	Bricky
Herby	Strawy	Papery	Soapy
Burnt	Fishy	Cocoa	
Medicinal	Turpeny	Creosoty	

AROMA INTENSITY

Big	Rich	Full	Rounded	Flat

PRIMARY FLAVOR NOTES

Acidy	*nippy–piquant*	Pungent	*creosoty–phenolic*
Bitter	*slight–harsh*	Salty	*briny–brackish*
Bland	*soft–neutral*	Sharp	*astringent–rough*
Fruity	*soury–ferment*	Soury	*acrid–hard*
Harsh	*caustic–medicinal*	Sweet	*acidy–mellow*
Mellow	*delicate–mild*	Winey	*tangy–tart*

FLAVOR NUANCES

Caramelly	Floral	Vanilla-like	Citrusy
Smoky	Spicy	Grainy	Tobaccoey
Herbal	Chocolaty	Berryish	Cedary
Earthy	Cereal	Leathery	
Nutty	Fruit-like	Woody	
Toasty	Cinnamon	Malty	

FLAVOR TAINTS

Fermented	Earthy	Grassy	Woody
Bitter	Edgy	Burnt	Tarry
Herby	Cabbagy	Acerbic	Brackish
Chemical	Turpeny	Insipid	Stale
Rank	Groundy	Green	Papery
Harsh	Hard	Charred	Fishy
Oniony	Soapy	Caustic	Briny
Medicinal	Moldy	Vapid	Cocoa
Rioy	Rough	Hay-like	Cardboardy
Soury	Musty	Ashy	Rubbery
Peasy	Sharp/Salty	Rancid	Astringent
Metallic	Hidy	Bland	Pasty
Dirty	Vinegary	Strawy	Baked
Acrid	Fauna	Carbony	Creosoty
Potatoey	Baggy	Alkaline	
Petroleum	Tippy	Neutral	

OTHER COMPLIMENTS

Balanced	Deep	Mellow	Soft
Bright	Delicate	Resonate	Strong
Brisk	Fresh	Rich	Sweet
Clean	Gentle	Round	Velvety
Complex	Mild	Smooth	

TERMS NOT SO COMPLIMENTARY

Biting	Vapid	Edgy	Insipid
Flat	Thin	Dull	Negligible

ACIDITY

Bright	Moderate	Sweet	Piquant
Winey	Brisk	Smooth	Soft
Fruity	Tangy	Nippy	Flat

BODY

Oily	Heavy	Creamy	Medium
Buttery	Full	Thin	
Thick	Watery	Light	

FINISH

Resonate	Long	Clean	Negligible
Fresh	Weak	Astringent	
Hard	Rounded	Fast-fading	

ROAST TAINTS

Underdeveloped	Past-croppish	Baked	Stale
Grassy	Scorched	Green	Tippy

DARK ROAST TAINTS

Carbony	Rubbery	Fishy	Tarry
Pungent	Bitter	Creosoty	Burnt

BREWED ITEMS

Strong	Full	Acerbic	Watery
Insipid	Vapid	Thin	Briny
Stale	Weak	Brackish	

NOTES

_____

_____

_____

_____

_____

_____

_____

THE CRAFT OF CUPPING

Cupping Glossary

Why another cupping glossary?

Mainly because we have more novice roasters in this country than ever before, and many have limited cupping experience. It is likely that most are accustomed to using abbreviated glossaries with only the most basic terms. The assessments made at a cupping session are usually documented by a written record on a cupping form. If that record is going to serve a useful purpose when called upon in the future, it needs to be concise and clear to anyone familiar with the language. This is not to say that one needs the *Oxford International Dictionary* to cup, but even the best of us get stumped now and then for just the right word to express a thought.

These descriptions are not made up by me, but are a compilation of many glossaries that I have collected over 30 years. It is not to be considered definitive or end-all. Glossaries are just aids for clarity of thought and notation, both of which are germane to the cupping process.

In the past, only seasoned professionals were responsible for buying green coffee for large regional and national roasting companies. These people came up through the ranks and learned the language of coffee quality over a number of years. Today many small neighborhood micro-roasteries are owned by young entrepreneurs who have entered the business with little or no coffee trade experience other than ordering a Frappuccino at Starbucks. I hope this glossary will help those who have reached a plateau and wish to hone their cupping skills in order to describe the "specialty" in specialty coffee.

–Robert Barker

A

ACERBIC   A taste fault in brewed coffee that leaves an acrid and sour taste. The result of leaving brewed coffee on heat.

ACIDITY   A pleasing piquant or tangy quality characteristic of high-grown coffees. Acidity is a perceived taste quality—it is not a measure of pH, nor does it have anything to do with stomach irritation. Acidity may be high, medium, low or lacking altogether. High acidity gives a fresh, clean quality to brewed coffee. Low acidity coffees are often described as dull or flat.

ACIDY   A pleasant and sweet liveliness in the brew. Acidy toward sweet is called nippy, while acidy toward sour is termed piquant.

ACRID   A taste sensation related to soury. An irritating and piercing taste associated with harsh, bitter and pungent sensations. Typified by some Rio coffees from Brazil. Sometimes found in over-roasted coffees.

AFTERTASTE   Your mind's second opinion and lingering memory. The nose and taste sensation after swallowing. See nose and finish.

ALKALINE   A secondary taste sensation related to pungent. It can be a displeasing bitterness in dark-roast coffees.

AROMA   The odor of the prepared coffee beverage. It may be lacking, faint, delicate, moderate, strong or fragrant (also called aromatic). It may be pleasing or not, and it is not always a good indication of taste. Prominent scents are nutty, herbal, berry-like and citrus-like.

ASHY   Reminds one of a fireplace after the fire is out. Within certain limits, a positive characteristic in dark roasts.

ASTRINGENT   A pronounced and irritatingly bitter and salty taste sensation characterized by puckering. Most often noted in aftertaste. As in the taste of alum or as noted in some over-steeped teas.

B

BAGGY   An off-taste or smell similar to that of burlap bags. Either a storage problem or biological in nature. Similar to corky as it relates to some wines.

BAKED   A taste and odor description given to coffee roasted too slowly at too low a temperature. Caused by under-development of the bean during roasting due to insufficient rate of heat input. Results in an insipid taste and a flat bouquet. See underdeveloped.

BALANCED Denoting a pleasing combination of two or more primary taste sensations. Containing all the basic characteristics to the right extent and aesthetically pleasing. See round.

BERRYISH A scent or flavor reminiscent of blackberry, boysenberry, etc.

BITING Very pronounced or intense. Generally associated with acidity, sourness or bitterness.

BITTER A harsh, unpleasant taste detected on the back of the tongue. All coffees have a slight bitterness that is characteristic of the roasting process and is not always considered undesirable. Moderate bitterness can be balanced by sweetness. As a defect, it is usually associated with a green coffee defect, over-roasting or over-extraction of the brewed coffee. Sometimes associated with overly acidic coffees.

BLAND A somewhat disappointing flavor resulting from an unfortunate balance of saltiness and sweetness. Bland toward sweet=soft. Bland toward salty=neutral. Common in low-grown coffees.

BODY The impression of viscosity in the mouth. Mouthfeel of the coffee as related to the strength and chemistry of the brew. Some coffees have more or less oily constituents released into the brew. Body may be described as watery, thin, slight, light, medium, full or heavy. Extremely heavy-bodied coffees may be referred to as thick, buttery, chewy or creamy. Body cannot be assessed in weakly brewed coffee. Not a measure of actual viscosity.

BOUQUET Usually a reference to an overall aroma impression of brewed coffee. The total aromatic profile of the initial fragrance of the dry ground coffee plus the aroma of the brewed coffee and the nose impression when drinking. See aftertaste and finish.

BRACKISH A salty or alkaline taste fault found in the coffee or in the water used in the brewing. Also occurs when excessive heat is applied after brewing. Distastefully bitter and salty.

BRICKY The smell of clay bricks or concrete.

BRINY A saline taste fault associated with brewed coffee held on heat too long. See salty and brackish.

BRISK/BRIGHT Qualitative terms for acidity.

BURNT A bitter, smoky or tarry flavor characteristic common in dark-roasted coffees. Can be accompanied by fishy, rubbery, ashy or charred.

BUTTERY A full and rich flavor with an oily body or texture. Commonly used to describe espresso-style beverages. See Body.

CARAMELLY The smell or taste of sweet caramels without any trace of burntness.

CARAMELIZED Burnt-like flavor, as in caramelized sugar. A desirable taste note if complemented with a strong coffee flavor. A loss in coffee flavor enhances the caramelized flavor.

CARDBOARDY The taste or smell of wet cardboard. See papery.

CARBONY An excessive aftertaste sensation present in some dark roasted coffees. See burnt.

CAUSTIC A taste sensation related to harsh. A sour taste that increases as the brew cools.

CEDARISH An aroma scent reminiscent of cedar. A positive woody taste.

CEREAL The aroma or taste of malt or bread. See malty and toasty. A clean fresh grain smell.

CHEMICAL A taste or aroma suggesting a phenolic or hydrocarbon presence. See medicinal. It may be inherent in the coffee or the result of contamination.

CHOCOLATY A positive taste or aroma reminiscent of unsweetened chocolate and/or vanilla. An aftertaste common in Yemen Mochas and Ethiopian Harrars. A common dark roast characteristic.

CINNAMON An underlying spice accent sometimes detected in the aroma or a flavor nuance in light roasts. Also a term describing a light roast.

CITRUSY A scent or flavor note of citrus prominent in some East African coffees.

CLEAN Opposite of dirty. The term "clean cup" refers to a coffee free of taints or faults. Does not necessarily imply clarity of flavor impression. Washed coffees often taste "cleaner" than natural-processed coffees. Synonymous with clarity in taste.

COCOA A sweetish chocolate smell of completely stale roasted coffee.
Not to be confused with chocolaty.

COMPLEXITY Balance and intensity in flavor. The impression of a well-blended coffee. An interesting mix of flavors, undertones and aftertastes. Opposite of dull or one-dimensional. A hallmark of specialty coffee.

CREAMY A measure of body somewhat less than buttery.

CREOSOTY A taste sensation related to pungent. A bitter, burnt vegetal taste found in the aftertaste of some dark-roasted coffees. Similar to tarry.

DEEP Implying depth and intensity. See complexity.

DELICATE Pleasing to taste or smell. A sensation that is mild, subtle and sometimes fleeting. See mellow. Some cuppers use the term gentle.

DIRTY An undesirable, unclean smell or taste. Can imply a defect such as sourness, earthiness or mustiness. Something foul or foreign in the taste.

DRY-PROCESSED Coffees harvested and dried in cherry. Also called natural-processed coffee. Coffee processing can determine the presence and strength of certain aromas and tastes prominent in the brew. Knowing whether a coffee is washed or dry-processed will suggest different expectations in several major characteristics. Dry-processed coffees are expected to have more strength, less acidity and heavier body than their washed counterparts. There are several processes between the fully washed process and the traditional dry process. You may see terms such as semi-washed or pulped natural. Knowing the process is helpful in making a quality assessment. See washed process and natural.

DULL Lack of character. Opposite of round. May be flat or notably unimpressive. Indicates coffee that has lost its original or usual zest and character. Gives the impression of roundness but at the same time lacks character.

EDGY A taste flaw bordering on hard. See sharp.

EARTHY A complex mustiness found in certain dry-processed, low-acid coffees. Often considered a taint in washed coffees. The smell of freshly turned soil. See potatoey, dirty, groundy.

FAUNA Wet dog, animal-like smell. See Hidy.

FERMENTED A sour or acrid vinegar taste or smell. Obvious and unpleasant. The most common processing error following harvesting.

FINE CUP An ambiguous term best defined by the user. A coffee with apparently acceptable taste qualities. Commonly used as a grade descriptor from certain origins. Also "Good clean cup," "Fair average cup."

FINISH The lingering taste on the tongue. An aftertaste that can be the same as the cup flavor or evolve into nuances. Usually, heavy-bodied coffees will have a longer finish. Rated by quality and persistence.

FLAT A descriptor of a coffee's bouquet. Lacking intensity. A dull lifeless quality due to staling or age. Also, when referring to acidity it means without acidity or very slight acidity.

FLAVOR The total impression of aroma, acidity and body. Usually described with specific major taste impressions. Rated from weak to strong, poor to exceptional.

FLORAL A smell of flowers with a pleasant sense of freshness.

FRAGRANCE Odor of the dry coffee grinds prior to brewing (aroma describes the brewed coffee). See bouquet. Sweet scents can indicate acidity. Pungent scents can lead to sharp tastes. Intensity can be a measure of freshness. Ranges from sweetly floral to sweetly spicy.

FRESH Opposite of stale. A recent roast. A distinctly pleasing scent.

FRUITY Denotes the aromatic scents of citrus or berry fruit in the cup aroma. Also, a flavor taint bordering on fermented. A sharp, piquant, pungent or vinegary taste associated with over fermentation. A strong over-ripe characteristic prevalent in coffees left too long in the cherry.

GRAINY The taste sensation of toasted grain. See cereal.

GRASSY A flavor taint indicating a slight chlorophyll taste. Can be found in fresh green coffee insufficiently dried. An odor and taste taint giving the coffee a distinct herbal character similar to the odor of freshly mown alfalfa and the astringent taste of green grass. Said to be found in new crop coffees due to immature beans. More pronounced in under-roasted coffees.

GREEN A flavor tint usually associated with under-ripe coffee beans. In roasted coffee it is usually associated with under-roasting or lack of development. Also grassy, pasty.

GROUNDY Synonym for earthy.

HARD Opposite of soft, sweet or mild. Description of Brazils between soft and rioy. Considered a secondary taste sensation to soury. Also bricky or edgy.

HARSH Crude raw taste used to describe certain Brazils and robustas. An obvious presence of bitter and astringent compounds. Can be caustic or medicinal.

HAY-LIKE See strawy or grassy.

HEAVY Quantitative term for body or mouthfeel.

HERBAL Fragrance note similar to garden herbs. See spicy.

HERBY Found in cup aroma resembling the odor or flavor of herb. A cooked vegetable odor. Taints can range from oniony to cabbagy.

HIDY Unpleasant odor reminiscent of wet leather or wet dog. Can also be described as fauna. Can be caused by excessive heat during the drying process usually associated with coffees dried in mechanical dryers.

INSIPID A lifeless brew caused by staling and exposure prior to brewing.

INTENSITY Measure of the total impression of bouquet.

LEATHERY The aroma of a luggage retail shop. The smell of fine leather.

MALTY A toasted cereal grain aroma. A smell or taste of malted grain or sourdough bread. See toasty.

MEDICINAL Reminds one of a pharmacy or hospital. Obviously a negative note. A harsh flavor or smell similar to disinfectant, chlorine, iodine or some phenol compounds.

MELLOW A sweet coffee that is well-balanced with low to medium acidity. Mellow toward sweet=mild. Mellow toward salty=delicate.

METALLIC Said to be caused by immature beans due to poor grading. May be accompanied by astringent or bitter tastes.

MILD A taste sensation associated with mellow. A smooth and soft or sweet washed coffee.

MOLDY/MOULDY Fungus infected. Ruined by dampness due to poor storage. Improperly dried coffee can become moldy in storage or during shipping in containers.

MUSTY A smell associated with earthy. Slight mustiness is not always a taint especially in aged or monsooned coffees. As a taint it will have the smell of an overly musty cellar. See bricky.

NATURAL COFFEE Natural-processed or dry-processed coffees. Natural-processed coffees are usually different from wet-processed coffees in that they may lack clarity of flavor and pointed acidity. Some may have a more intense complex flavor and fuller body. See washed coffee.

NEGLIGIBLE Something less than slight or delicate. Almost none.

NEUTRAL A fundamentally characterless, inoffensive or insipid coffee without virtue yet without defects. Basically, a coffee safe for economical blending. A desirable character in robustas and in otherwise undistinguished Brazils. Boring.

NIPPY A taste sensation perceived from a very clean high-acidity coffee. Bright, brisk or biting. See acidy.

NOSE The combination of taste and smell when swallowing coffee. The aroma component of aftertaste. Most commonly caramelly, nutty or malty.

NUTTY Said of coffees that lack a bold coffee flavor or have a flavor that suggests a specific nut, such as fresh almonds, roasted nuts, etc.

ONIONY An off-taste reminiscent of onion. See herby.

PAPERY An off-taste suggesting the taste of wet paper or cardboard. Most common in decaf coffees. An obvious taste contribution from paper filters.

PAST-CROPPISH Said of coffees that have deteriorated in the green state before roasting and, thus, taste weakened or toned down. Particularly with less acidity and a heavy woody or papery flavor and little body. Aroma will also suffer in past-crop coffees. See strawy, wood and neutral.

PASTY The smell or taste of elementary school white paste. Sometimes associated with baked.

PEASY A disagreeable taste of cooked green peas. A microbiological taint similar to that causing oniony and potatoey taints. These taints are usually limited to certain origins.

PETROLEUM Smell or taste usually originating from contamination. Often found in coffee stored in poorly manufactured bags.

PIQUANT Acidy. A pronounced and pleasant pungent acidity slightly tart or biting. Synonymous with tangy and pointed.

POINT/POINTED Fine acidity sharpness. A coffee with good flavor characteristics.

POTATOEY A disagreeable and unpleasant taste of raw potato. See peasy. Sometimes associated with earthy.

PRUNY The fruit-like taste reminiscent of prune found in some dark-roast coffees.

PUNGENT A primary taste sensation related to the presence of bitter compounds. Usually from phenolic compounds that range in taste from creosoty to alkaline. Not to be confused with earthy.

RANCID Having a rank odor or taste as that of old oil. A sour and very unpleasant smell. See stale.

RANK Offensively gross or coarse. Foul or rancid. A dirty unpleasant flavor due mainly to contamination or over-fermentation. A grading term used in Brazil.

RESONANT Recurring. A long, pleasing aftertaste.

RICH Mainly a descriptor for bouquet. Also used to indicate depth and complexity of flavor, big pleasing aroma and full body. Overused.

RIOY A harsh medicinal or slightly iodized, phenolic or carbolic flavor typical to certain Brazils. Said to be a regional characteristic. Considered a taint by most roasters but appreciated by others as a blender.

ROUND Commonly used term for a balanced and rich coffee.

ROUNDED A quantitative descriptor for a moderate bouquet.

ROUGH An unpleasant taste sensation related to sharp. An unflattering description of some natural robustas.

RUBBERY Burnt rubber odor characteristic of some robustas. Noted in some dark roasts.

SALTY One of the four basic taste sensations, yet saltiness rarely comes to the forefront in coffee taste. When it does, it is just perceptible. See sharp.

SCORCHED A roasting defect resulting in an odor taint that gives the coffee brew a slight smoky-burnt aftertaste with an overall under-developed taste.

SHARP Intense flavor taint resulting in salty and soury compounds. Sharp towards salty is termed rough. Sharp towards soury is astringent. When used in reference to acidity, it can be a complimentary term relating to tangy and nippy. A moderately strong perception of acidity.

SMOKY Reminds one of smoked food. Usually a positive descriptor, and more common in dark roasts.

SMOOTH A quantitative descriptor for moderately low-bodied coffee. Also referring to a full-bodied, low-acidity coffee. See mellow. Sometimes used to describe acidity.

SOAPY An off-taste similar to earthy and dirty.

SOFT Low acidity coffees that have a light or very light acidity just short of bland. When associated with Brazils, a character that is mild and not harsh. A mild coffee with a dry aftertaste.

SOUR One of the four basic tastes. Sweet, sour, salty and bitter.

SOURY A distinctly sour, rank or rancid taste often due to improper processing. Not to be confused with acidy and acidity. Soury toward salty is acrid. Pronounced soury is hard. See sharp.

SPICY Said of aroma or flavor suggestive of spices. Sometimes associated with aromatic, piquant or pungent. Suggesting cloves, cinnamon, nutmeg, etc.

STALE An unpleasant taste fault found in old and deteriorated roasted coffee. Roasted coffee that has faded in quality after excessive storage or exposure to air. Aroma of stale coffee changes from flat to rancid and finally to cocoa-like, while the flavor of stale coffee changes from bitter to rancid and cardboardy.

STRAWY A taste taint that gives a distinct hay-like and woody flavor. See past-crop and under-developed.

STRENGTH Usually a term quantifying brewed coffee. Strength is conveyed through concentration of soluble solids in suspension not the prominence of any one characteristic.

STRONG A term indicating strength derived from greater soluble solids in the extraction or intensity of any one characteristic of note. It is also used as an adjective to virtue or defect (as in "a strong sour taste" or "a strong fine aroma").

SWEET One of the four basic tastes. Also the recognition of sweetness or the absence of bitterness in a coffee. Said of a smooth, palatable coffee, free of taints or harshness. See mild. Also used as a descriptor for acidity.

SWEETLY FLORAL Flowery scent commonly found in some fresh grinds. See fragrance.

SWEETLY SPICY Spicy scent commonly found in some fresh grinds. Reminiscent of aromatic spices, such as cardamom, cinnamon, nutmeg etc. See fragrance.

TANGY A secondary taste sensation related to winey. A somewhat sour and fruity sensation.

TARRY A taste fault giving a burnt character. See rubbery.

TART A secondary taste sensation related to winey. A sour sensation between tangy and soury.

TASTE The total sensory impression of the three combined basic tastes of sweetness, saltiness and sourness resulting in six primary tastes:
Acidy: Acids increase the sweetness of sugars. Piquant to nippy
Mellow: Salts increase the sweetness of sugars. Mild to delicate
Winey: Sugars reduce the sour taste of acids. Tangy to tart
Bland: Sugars reduce the saltiness of salts. Soft to neutral
Sharp: Acids increase the saltiness of salts. Rough to astringent
Sour: Salts reduce the sourness of acids. Hard to acrid

TERROIR The personality and character in aroma and taste represented by a coffee's origin. An overall flavor profile common to a particular growing region, district, altitude or processing style.

THICK Exaggerated term to indicate an extremely heavy body.

THIN Said of coffees that lack body or flavor. Typical of low-grown coffees.

TIPPED/TIPPY A roasting fault usually caused by starting the roasting process with an excessively high roaster drum temperature or simply roasting too fast for the type of coffee. Tipping is the charring of the ends of the coffee beans. Tippy is the recognition of a charred flavor to an otherwise good coffee.

TOASTY Aroma of fresh toast or fresh-baked bread.

TOBACCOEY An aroma scent reminiscent of a tobacco shop or aromatic pipe tobacco.

TURPENY A medicinal aftertaste reminiscent of turpentine, resin or camphor-like substances.

UNDER-DEVELOPED Coffee roasted too slowly at too low a temperature. See baked.

VAPID Lacking character and liveliness. Particularly lacking acidity, tang or briskness. Synonymous with insipid, dull, flat.

VELVETY Heavy in strength and body, low in acidity.

VINEGARY A sour off-taste related to ferment.

WASHED/WET PROCESS Post-harvest process of separating the seeds from the fruit before drying. Most important is the intermediate step of controlled fermentation between the pulping and the rinsing and drying phase. Poor processing can lead to defects that can render the coffee unusable. The most common taint is an overly strong fermented taste that cannot be removed or masked by blending. On the other hand, properly washed coffees typically exhibit sweetness, clarity and good acidity. See dry process and natural.

WATERY Relating to body, thin. Relating to strength, weak in flavor either due to the available soluble solids in the bean or to the ratio of grounds to water.

WINEY A bittersweet fruity quality characteristic of a fine red wine. A sweet soury taste. Winey toward sweet is termed tangy, while winey toward sour is described as tart. Sometimes used to describe acidity.

WOODY A flavor taint characteristic of past-croppish coffees and those grown at lower altitude. A desirable scent or flavor when reminiscent of a fine wood such as cedar or sandalwood (similar to the oaky taste of a good Chardonnay). ■

. . . .

ROBERT BARKER *has worked in the coffee industry for 25 years as a coffee producer, importer, trader, buyer and trainer. He is currently a contractor for Coffee Review and an occasional consultant. He can be reached at barker.robert@ att.net.*

Many thanks to the SCA, Ted Lingle, Michael Sivetz, Donald Schoenholt, Ernesto Illy and Kenneth Davids, who have all given much time and effort to educate us over the years.

Cupping Revisited

A Primer for Advanced Coffee Testing

by Spencer Turer

• FROM THE MARCH/APRIL 2010 ISSUE OF *ROAST* •

C UPPING, SAMPLING, TASTING, testing, analyzing. Whichever term you use, the process is generally the same. Coffee professionals and hobbyists seek to determine coffee quality and compare coffees in a process that is fun, exciting and somewhat easy to complete.

We visually inspect the coffee, smell it, sip, savor and spit—much like the sensory testing for tea, wine, beer or other beverages. Studying sensory science and learning how to determine flavor and aroma perceptions will help cuppers, quality controllers and product developers use basic sensory testing practices to enhance their operations.

The Science of Cupping

Cupping is the purest way to evaluate coffee's basic attributes—fragrance, aroma, sweetness, acidity, body, aftertaste, uniformity and cleanliness—and to experience and appreciate the individuality of each coffee. The coffee is unadulterated and unfiltered to ease the identification of defects. Before making a purchasing decision, cupping is the best way to judge quality and determine each coffee's distinctive taste and aroma profile. It can also be used as the first test for product development and quality control.

During the past generation, the coffee industry has grown considerably as hundreds of new roasters and roaster/retailers have opened for business. This is certainly an exciting time to be working in coffee, yet these new business owners, managers and employees are not always given the opportunity and time-honored tradition of learning coffee sensory testing in a controlled manner. Much of the time, the priority when operating a coffee business—while directed by quality—is efficiency, profitability and customer satisfaction, with sensory science and testing being an afterthought. However, we as an industry have a history of apprenticeship and learning from those more senior and experienced.

Cupper training at the side of our mentors and teachers is an efficient way to learn coffee evaluation and has served our industry well for decades. Recently, the coffee industry has embraced formal training for cupping and grading via coffee schools and trade conferences. Even so, learning by doing (or on-the-job training)—where cuppers design and judge their own training expertise—is often the norm. This individual process does not take advantage of calibration to standards or alignment with other cuppers and may produce unsatisfactory results.

With any training program, students must practice daily the ritual of evaluating taste and aroma and comparing coffee quality if they choose to keep their sensory abilities as keen as possible. Cupper trainings tend to focus on identifying taste and aroma attributes rather than studying the scientific principles of sensory testing. However, cuppers must also determine the best way to reach their desired conclusion about each coffee. Deciding which coffee test to use is essential. Testers must also keep strict control over the testing and data collection processes to ensure the most accurate results. Cuppers who learn about the various types of sensory testing will work more efficiently and make faster, more accurate decisions about quality and purchasing.

Embracing the principles of the scientific method will help cuppers work more efficiently and effectively. The scientific method is a process used when conducting experiments. Food scientists, chemists, biologists and other professionals use this systematic approach to investigate, test and collect data.

Think of each cupping as a mini-experiment. Only through the collection of data can a final decision be made on coffee quality—whether for commercial interests, product development or quality control.

Individual Perspective

Is your coffee cup half full or half empty? An optimistic or pessimistic personality will be the first guide, or stumbling block, to sensory testing. When you approach a new coffee, are you silently thinking, "Give me a reason to reject this coffee"? Having high standards is wonderful, and an important part of specialty coffee, but having the mindset to seek reasons for rejection is biased. On the other hand, do you think to yourself, "Give me a reason to accept this coffee"? This perspective is just as biased, as it will cloud your judgment for sensory testing.

When testing for quality, cuppers should be neutral in their opinions, striving to remove any personal bias, historical issues or prejudicial opinions for an origin, shipper, importer, region or variety. Approach each coffee with an open mind, let the coffee test be true, and judge each coffee fairly, allowing the actual flavors and aroma to guide the evaluation.

Components of a Good Test

Many pitfalls can affect the outcome of a test. Cuppers need to understand all of the variable elements and control for them to

ensure that the data collected is not compromised or inaccurate. Variable elements include anything that may change during a test, such as water temperature, coffee dose, fineness of coffee grind, coffee roast profile, air temperature of the testing room and lighting intensity. Once these elements are managed to be exactly the same for each test, they are no longer variable factors but controlled items.

Trying to judge taste, aroma, quality and character to make a purchasing decision or quality approval from memory may be challenging, even for the most skilled cuppers. Cuppers should compare the unknown coffee to a known sample (or a standard quality sample) to test for quality. Testers should aim to use a fresh sample or recent arrival of the known/standard sample so that age and green staling are not factors in determining character differences.

Cuppers should evaluate their coffee independently of other testers in the room and follow good cupping etiquette by minimizing discussion and any other distractions. They should also avoid over-analyzing a coffee sample by placing more cups than normal on the table, cupping the table an extra time "just to be sure" or asking additional cuppers to join the test. When coffee testers increase the number of cups sampled or the number of times each sample is tasted, the resulting data may change. This increases the likelihood of finding a reason to upgrade to an approval or downgrade to a rejection.

How to Create an Experiment

● DETERMINE THE QUESTION

Specifically, what are you hoping to learn? Are you testing coffees for purchase approval? Judging the acceptability of a new blend? Evaluating production samples for quality control, or testing the operation of new equipment on your coffee products? Completing descriptive analysis for retail marketing? Each question will require a unique testing protocol and process.

● DESIGN THE TEST

Once you settle on your question, you can determine the best test to reach your conclusion. Will you be testing one coffee, two coffees, comparing two or more coffees, evaluating component percentages for a blend, or evaluating brew strength options? For each question, there may be a different test that is best suited to collecting the right data (see page 301 for more on this). Before testing begins, you must determine the standard for acceptance. If you will be using the Specialty Coffee Association (SCA) cupping quality scale, what is the score necessary for an approval? When using other testing methods or scales, the criteria for success and failure must be predetermined before you begin cupping.

Next, determine who will complete the testing: a coffee expert, trained panel or consumer panel. For small to medium coffee operations, one cupper ("the expert") may make the decisions. In many coffee companies, a group or team of cuppers ("trained panel") might make purchasing decisions, and a separate group of coffee enthusiasts may be asked to emulate the consumer experience for product development tests. Consumer marketing groups may be enlisted to perform actual consumer testing.

● CONDUCT THE TEST / COLLECT THE DATA

Coffee sensory testing should use quantitative analysis for data collection, which means using measurable scales for the amount of perceived character, as opposed to qualitative analysis where subjective judgment is recorded.

To collect measurable data, use a cupping score chart or custom-created chart to indicate the perceived tastes and character intensity of each sample. For example, a scale of 1 (no character) to 10 (intense character) is often used for sensory analysis. Qualitative analysis—using one's judgment or flavor wheel lexicon to describe the coffee—is best used for descriptive analysis and may be used for purchasing or quality questions based on flavor profile.

Care must be taken when preparing coffees for sensory testing. The goal is to manage for all of the variables so that the only aspect actually tested is the quality or character and the intensity of the quality and character. Examples of variables to manage and control for include water temperature and quality; cup shape, size and composition; and waiting time before testing. For green coffee testing, a representative sample of a lot (full container) is required to be drawn from at least 10 percent of the bag count from several different locations to prevent testing of just one "pocket" of coffee. Green samples must be mixed to be sure that all beans, including defects, are randomly located within the sample before testing.

Keeping a consistent roast level for all samples is critical. Small changes in the roast profile will impact a coffee's flavor development, acidity, body and sweetness. Any differences in roast profile may cause unfounded bias for or against particular samples that bear no reflection upon the inherent quality of the cup and thus change the test results and conclusions. The date and time of roasting should also be the same for all coffees so that roasted staling is not a variable in the test.

The SCA cupping protocols recommend using a light roast (48 Agtron Commercial Scale) to provide the best opportunity to identify defects. Many roasters use a production roast level for their cuppings to allow the coffee to demonstrate its character from the consumer perspective.

Cuppers should begin by documenting all measurable variables—the external factors and unforeseen issues that may influence the outcome of the test. When repeating tests over time, it will become obvious which variables need to be measured and which factors will not affect the outcome. Noting all measurable

variables may be difficult when conducting informal testing, such as developing drinks at the barista bar or testing brewing processes. Nonetheless, cuppers must understand the details of the test to replicate it for further evaluation.

Consumer-brewing processes—drip, French press, extract or Clover—also provide valuable tools when testing for consumer acceptability. Brewing tests should follow a similar scientific method, with consideration for how the consumer would individually brew and serve the coffee, or how the retailer would prepare the beverage for sale. Testing the coffees black and also modified with sweeteners and whitener will help provide the full range of data needed to make consumer-oriented conclusions.

Using non-professional tasters in consumer tests may generate higher-value data. Regular consumers and frequent coffeehouse guests would be the best testers; non-coffee drinkers or those unfamiliar with the products may skew the results too far positive or negative. Even those who drink coffee regularly may have unforeseen biases or misunderstandings about quality. These factors should be taken into account when using these testers, as the results may be valid only for purchase preference, purchase intent or post-purchase satisfaction, without resulting in usable data for actual coffee quality.

● ANALYZE THE DATA AND MAKE YOUR CONCLUSION

When all aspects of the testing are complete, with confidence that all variables were managed and controlled for, the data can be reviewed against the predetermined success criteria to reach an ultimate conclusion. Let the coffee and the data—not personal opinion—determine the conclusion.

● TEST THE RESULTS

In an often-overlooked last step, cuppers who repeat a test should compare the data collected and the conclusion to prior tests. Are they the same? If so, this verification process allows the cupper to be confident that the correct conclusion was reached.

If there is any inconsistency in the data or conclusion, one of the following problems may be to blame: 1) serious issues with the testing method, 2) calibration/consistency issues among the cuppers, 3) improper data analysis, 4) inconsistencies in the item being tested, or 5) the inability to confirm the conclusions.

When repeating tests, the order of the items being tested may be changed, reversed or randomized to ensure that results are true, accurate and independent of the testing order. It may be necessary to repeat tests, especially when using the consumer perspective, at various times throughout the day: mid-morning when taste buds are most sensitive, after lunch to replicate interference with other flavor and aroma factors, or late afternoon when fatigue sets in. Sensory perception testing is complicated, and human fallibility should be considered, especially when a single tester is used. Cuppers should take into account emotional factors that may influence their judgment or distractions that may inhibit concentration. Again, a second testing may be necessary to verify the results and conclusions.

When conducting a series of sensory tests, the first item tested in a series sets the standard and may receive a higher rating simply because it is tested first. To protect against this, set a calibration sample to cup first before collecting any data, or repeat the first sample within the series to determine if the score is the same at both positions.

Conducting proper tests will not only help build confidence and expertise, but it will also help cuppers answer supplier and customer questions about quality evaluations. Testing will help to reject the coffee that should be rejected and to approve the coffee that should be approved, based on unbiased and scientific data collection. The opposite—approving a coffee that should be rejected because of a bad test or poor testing process—could be devastating to your business financially and your reputation among your suppliers and customers. Approving a bad coffee may set a precedent for quality that you are not proud of. This, in turn, affects the quality of future deliveries from suppliers because of inconsistent quality communications, or it may cause you to lose a customer based on what you thought was great coffee but, because of a bad test, is actually inferior. Who wants to reject great

A simple cupping form (see page 286).

coffee and allow it to be sold to a competitor because of a bad test that yielded the wrong result?

Rejecting a coffee that should be accepted could also be financially devastating for a producer, particularly in relationship/ direct trade purchases, since premiums may be lost or the coffee could ultimately go unsold. It is the duty of the tester to understand the importance of the test and its implications for the stakeholders of the coffee, and to remain true, unbiased and professional in all aspects of the evaluations.

Those new to the scientific testing method may find the process very detailed and cumbersome, but, with practice, these concepts will become as familiar to you as any other process in the roastery. Understanding the basics of sensory testing and choosing to apply these principles to cupping will advance the caliber and credibility of your quality testing. After all, specialty coffee is a matter of choice, not a beverage of chance. ■

• •

SPENCER TURER *is vice president of Coffee Analysts in Hinesburg, Vermont. He is a founding member of the Roasters Guild, a licensed Q grader, and a recipient of the SCAA's Outstanding Contribution to the Association award. Turer is an active volunteer for the SCA and the National Coffee Association USA.*

CHOOSE YOUR TEST

THE BASICS OF TESTING

■ MONADIC

When one product is tested by itself without a comparison. For example, try this coffee and provide your cup results. A cupping table set with one flight each from different origins, without comparison to a standard or baseline, provides a series of monadic tests.

■ COMPARISON

Tests two or more coffees—an unknown coffee against a known—to compare the cup character. Product development departments often use this type of testing when considering blend variations for product rationalization or new product development. Comparison will allow several different coffees to be tested next to each other. This type of test can be completed through cupping or with brewed coffee, either as an objective test by professional tasters or a subjective test by consumers.

TYPES OF PRODUCT TESTING

■ PREFERENCE

Primarily used as a consumer test. With all aspects of the test controlled, the questions are: Which coffee do you like better, and why? Preference testing is purely subjective and based on opinion. It can be used to test brew strength, hold times, blend development or roast levels.

■ PAIRED COMPARISON

Used to compare two coffee samples side by side with a specific question asked. For example, which sample has higher acidity? This test forces the taster to make a firm decision. Paired comparison tests are fast and easy to conduct, but the success or failure criteria must be determined before the test begins. For instance: How may cuppers need to score the same for the results to be conclusive, and how many times can those cuppers reach the same results each time?

■ THRESHOLD

Determines the level that one can perceive a change or detect that a flavor or aroma is present. More detailed threshold tests assess the expert tester's ability to recognize or identify the change. The SCA Sensory Skills Test uses this method. When seeking to change a coffee blend, a roaster will use a threshold test to compare two samples and identify at what level a variation in the blend can be detected.

■ SORTING

After the threshold test is complete and the cupper is able to identify variations in the coffee characters (acidity, sweetness, body), the sorting test allows cuppers to rank the intensity of each character (strong, medium, weak). In advanced sorting, cuppers must identify at least two different characters within each cup and rank them individually on the intensity scale. Again, this is part of the SCA Sensory Skills Test.

■ TRIANGLE

A powerful test when determining if two items are virtually the same or different in character, taste and aroma. Triangle tests use a defined format with a specific number of participants to statistically differentiate between guesses and perceived differences. Each participant is presented with a trial of samples in three cups; two are identical and one is different. They are required to identify which sample is different. To account for the probability of guessing, typically 24 or more participants are required to determine a high-confidence conclusion. Each participant receives the trial samples in one of six formats:

AAB BBA
ABA BAB
BAA ABB

This test provides true confidence in the data collection and conclusion.

■ DUO-TRIO

Determine which of two test samples is the same as the reference sample provided. This test gives cuppers a greater opportunity for guessing correctly than the triangle tests, making it less powerful. To ensure accuracy in duo-trio tests, some tests must be designed with three identical samples and others where both samples are different from the reference sample.

Changing the sample positions—and creating all the same or all different sample sets—is not intended to confuse the cuppers. On the contrary, this is designed to increase the confidence in the test results by providing the cupper the opportunity to accurately identify the differences and similarities in the coffees in a variety of ways.

■ DESCRIPTIVE ANALYSIS

A process used by sensory testers to communicate the specific flavor and aroma perceptions to a level where most individuals can detect the same perceptions. Descriptive analysis is intended to include flavor and aroma characteristics that most people can perceive; when they see the words written in a coffee description, it should make sense. For example, describing a particular coffee as exhibiting a "sweet fresh raspberry acidity with light caramel characters and a lingering chocolate aftertaste" is a descriptive analysis.

This test is controlled by a group of judges who first create individual lists of descriptive words to use. Next, the judges agree on a standard vocabulary list for the test. Finally, they evaluate the coffee, working in groups to reach a consensus for the coffee's profile. The group consensus is vital to create a descriptive analysis without using a single person's individual opinion for the coffee's profile.

The success of a good descriptive analysis is when the consumer is able to understand the coffee character by reading the menu description and then agrees with the description after tasting the coffee. A poor product description from this analysis includes references unknown to the consumer or flavor and aroma characteristics that are not perceived by most people, cause confusion, or reduce the purchase intent of the coffee. ■

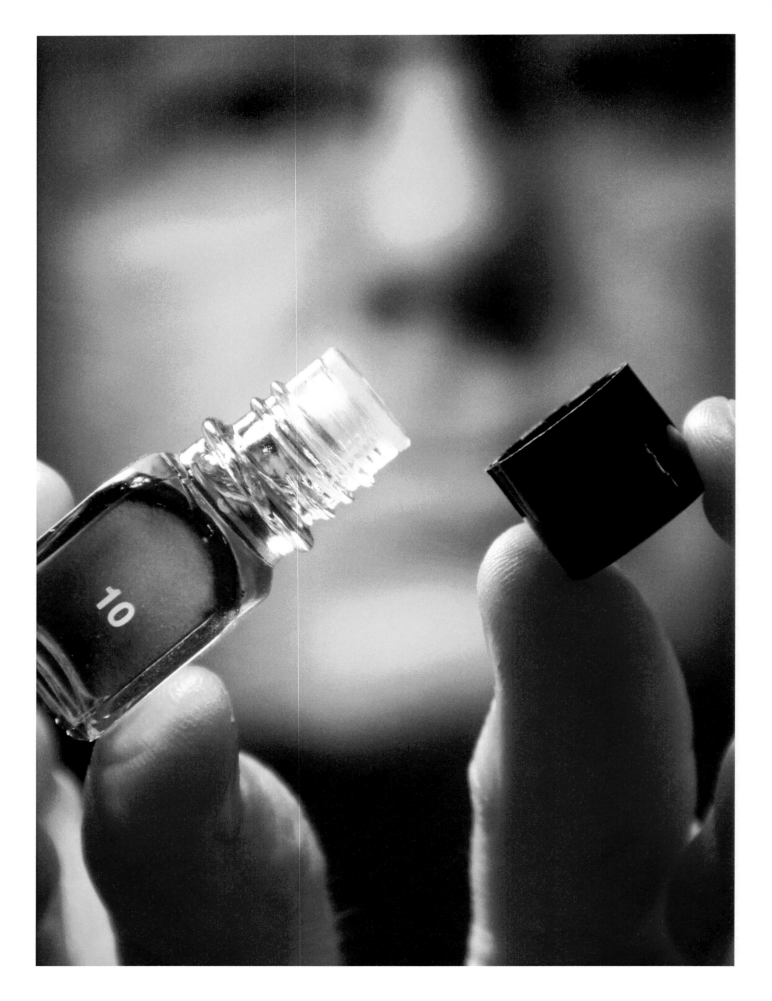

Unbottling the Aromas of Coffee

Improving Sensory Skills with Le Nez Du Café

by Paul H. Allen | *Photos by Paul H. Allen & Olivia C. Allen*

• FROM THE MAY/JUNE 2011 ISSUE OF *ROAST* •

"CARAMEL, dark chocolate, peanut, garden peas, apricot … We have all encountered these aromas at one time or another. But can we recognize them amidst the symphony of aromas in coffee?" says Jean Lenoir, the author of Le Nez du Café, the boxed coffee aroma set and guide book.

We are taught many things, but rarely are we taught to smell. And yet, there is no more sensitive detector than the human nose. Some work has been done, but coffee still remains a language waiting to be translated. For many people, the language of coffee can be like deciphering a foreign language or, at best, a problem with the dialect, where you know the language but someone else is speaking it differently.

This alphabet of coffee scents needs to be learned. If the letters are not known, then the words, paragraphs and eventually the books cannot be written. The aroma kit can be a tool that enables us to detect and identify. This allows us to talk to one another, to be on the same page when we taste a coffee and blurt out descriptors like "toast" or "basmati rice."

Scents can sometimes feel like a strange key that fits "something," but that "something" needs to be discerned. Some theorists call this shape theory, where scent shapes fit specifically into other receptor shapes, like keys into locks. There are many scent-based theories, and each seems to have its set of proponents and detractors. Weak-shape theory, known as odotope theory, suggests that different receptors detect only small pieces of molecules, and these minimal inputs are combined to form a larger olfactory perception. The vibration theory proposed by Luca Turin states that odor receptors detect frequencies of vibrations of odor molecules in the infrared range by electron tunneling. As of yet, there is no theory that explains olfactory perception completely.

All the theories have in common some sort of recognition. Take the lock-and-key theory. The odor emitting from the coffee has specific shapes (keys) that can then be learned by the brain (padlock). Le Nez du Café is, in essence, a set of keys that we can learn, unlocking many previously unknown smells.

Le Nez du Café literally means "the nose of coffee." Once this is realized, you are well on the way to understanding and recognizing coffee. In former Coffee Quality Institute Executive Director Ted Lingle's words, "The tongue can tell, but the nose knows." Less slurping and more sniffing would be the order of the day. Many experts of sensory perception say that it's when you smell a food or beverage, even before it enters the mouth, that you can be up to 80 percent sure of what it is. It is also said that people recall smells with 65 percent accuracy after a year, while visual recall sinks to about 50 percent after only three months. Between the nose and mouth, the nose is definitely the chief player. More specifically, we are talking about the olfactory bulb, defined by the folks at Merriam-Webster as either of two small round structures projecting from the lower surface of the brain above the nasal cavity that transmit stimuli from the olfactory nerves to other areas of the brain for processing.

The Beginning

As Lenoir remembers, he was asked to create Le Nez du Café via a phone call. Dr. Andres Lloreda, the communication officer of the Colombian Coffee Growers Federation, called Lenoir one day and "asked me point blank: Could you make Le Nez du Café?" Lenoir recalls. "A beautiful adventure begins for me and my team; we were really driven by the immediate confidence and enthusiasm of the federation ... The researchers and professionals led us on paths of coffee tasting and discovering their aromatic range ... we could not leave in silence!" Le Nez du Café was created with scientific analysis carried out by David Guermonprez and a taste analysis by Eric Verdier.

Smell is highly underrated in our society. We go about our activities, breathing in and out, not realizing odor receptors are constantly recognizing molecules. It is only when an odor irritates or pleases us, or reminds us of a past event, that we take notice.

That can and will change with the use of a sensory kit like Le Nez du Café. This happened in the wine industry in 1981 when Lenoir published Le Nez du Vin, a sophisticated instructive guide to the most common essences found in all types of wine, which some coffee professionals use in conjunction with Le Nez du Café to identify even more scents. The 54 aromas in the wine kit include cinnamon, strawberry and grapefruit—scents that are not found in the coffee kit.

Because coffee is complex, a few wrong definitions will enter our personal scent dictionaries. "Flavor equals taste, which should be corrected to flavor equals aroma," explains Lingle. "Generally speaking, coffee cuppers rely on a highly developed odor memory created through years of experience rather than on hypersensitivity."

Some of this is due to genetics, but it is true that you can train yourself to have an excellent sense of smell—a skill achieved in part with the olfactory epithelium you were born with, and in part with patient training. If you are in the average percentile genetically, why not move intentionally to the top of this average group?

It's all in the tiny book located in the center of the kit—you know, the one that comes with the set but is rarely opened other than to check vial numbers.

The Theory

When you look at photos, you simultaneously remember the events and your feelings at the time. As Lenoir's description in Le Nez du Café goes, "The electrical message is projected in the form of an image onto the olfactory bulb. The olfactory bulb might be said to correspond to the retina in the eye and the image of an odour on the bulb to that of an object on the retina." The converse is also true that if a picture is not taken, you will not have that memory.

This suggests that we actually learn when a picture or a sniff has been taken. These pictures reside in the temporal lobe of the brain, waiting to be pulled up and remembered. Technically, the image is processed, says Lenoir, and then reduced to an outline. This outline is compared to images already in the temporal lobe. Le Nez du Café is a deliberate act to take pictures, learn smells and store them in the brain. The bottom line is, you need to make a memory to have a memory. We need to smell, talk and collaborate—not be shy but rather speak out what comes to our minds. This is called association and helps us to retain and retrieve smells.

Andi Trindle Mersch, director of coffee at Philz Coffee, recalls training with the kit. "After I nailed each group, I then moved into taking all of [the vials] out

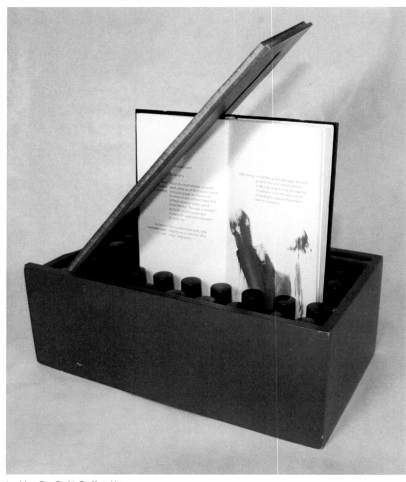

Le Nez Du Café Coffee Kit

at once and identifying them," she says. Trindle was developing good, clear pictures—as do all of us who focus on learning scents. "When someone said, during cupping, 'dirty socks,' the picture was enhanced with a flash. I now have strong emotions with this coffee, good or bad."

Good cuppers have compiled a personal coffee dictionary. They need to learn each new odor so that the next time they come to this smell, they can look in their scent dictionary and find the right word. The kit gives us a dictionary—the big picture. Stephanie Backus, the purchasing manager at Portland Roasting in Portland, Oregon, explains, "The biggest practical reasoning behind this kit is to give cuppers a better idea of the entire realm of aromas that coffee bears in every stage, from the flower and cherry through the processing and onto the cupping. I think the [scent] test is very objective and gets people on the 'same page' for what they should be looking for in the cup."

But once cuppers begin building a scent dictionary, they need to take refresher classes, as the images can fade. "I haven't been using [Le Nez du Café vials] regularly of late, but I do go back to them every once in a while and get myself back up to speed," Trindle notes. "It usually goes much quicker than the initial time."

It is important to associate a specific word with an aromatic scent, "as the word is the place in the mind where the memory of the scent is stored for future reference," Lingle says. Joseph A. Rivera, founder of the website *coffeechemistry.com*, says in the July/August 2008 issue of *Roast*: "We can easily detect an odor, but many times the ability to place a word with that odor can at times be 'on the tip of our tongue.'" The Nez goes another step in bridging the void between an odor detected and naming it.

Shakespeare's famous phrase "That which we call a rose by any other name would smell as sweet," is true, yet it would enable the specialty coffee industry to gain ground if we all used and meant the same names.

The Science

Smell is not simple; science certainly shows how we are fearfully and wonderfully made. You have just to look and marvel at the process involved when you put your nose to the vial:

Nasal Cavity: As we breathe in coffee, from the fragrance or the aroma, the air flows up into the nasal cavity. A good sniff or slurp drives these odors up the nasal cavity, bringing them into contact with the olfactory apparatus.

Cilia: These cilia, or tiny hairs, trigger nerve signals (if the scent shape is recognized) and transform them into electrical messages.

Mucus layer: Working like a chemical signal, odors are dissolved with mucus, which stimulates receptor sites on cilia.

Olfactory sensory neurons: The nerve signals pass upward from the cilia to the olfactory bulb via neurons' axons, which look like wires.

Olfactory bulb: Here, axons combine with mitral cells, becoming hundreds of glomeruli. The resulting message is sent to the olfactory area.

Olfactory area: The messages transmit to two areas in the brain. The pathway is in the limbic system, which also deals with memory and emotions.

The path that odor takes is important. There is the direct route, one that is exploited when we inhale (dry fragrance). And there is the retro-nasal route—the passage connecting the palate to the nasal cavity when we taste the coffee (wet aroma).

Odor Pathway

The olfactory system is important enough to be included in the test for Q graders. The qualifying score is 70 percent, which "seems like a relatively low qualifying score, but for many cuppers who do not have a highly developed flavor memory, these can be very challenging tests," says Lingle.

For aspiring Q graders, the kit is a good start, but there are a few missing scents. Willem Boot, president of Boot Coffee Consulting, suggested adding the following: "Blackberry and bergamot for the exotic attributes from stellar coffees in Eastern Africa. Tamarind and canteloupe for some of the El Salvadors and Nicaraguans. Notes of spice and musty soil to illustrate aromas from Sumatra."

Here we touch on foreign difficulties with the test. What happens when there is no matching word due to culture? The kit could also include scents relevant to different areas of the world. This would benefit the Ethiopian who has no access to such things as hazelnuts or the American who doesn't know the scent of tamarind.

The Keys

At some stage, whether we are experienced tasters or not, we are going to have to start practicing and learning. We do not know all smells. This will be a gradual process. Lenoir and Guermonprez suggest learning by analogy—for example, learning the smell of

straw—to bring us all onto the same sensory page. Bring straw into the cupping room to smell. Do any coffees that you have smelled have similarities to this?

Building a scent dictionary should be done progressively in order to give precise names to flavor and improve our ability to discriminate. Don't try all 36 vials at once—we know that cramming does not generate long-term memories.

Take the book out of the center of the box and then slide open the kit.

Take the vial numbered 1. Check that the cap is on securely, and gently shake the vial.

Unscrew the top and hold both the vial and cap up to your nose. Take one small sniff. Think. Does it remind you of something? Think. Take a guess. Remember, you have a possibility of at least 850. Check the number with the corresponding name in the booklet provided. Sniff again. Confirm. Which family does it belong to? Are you getting floral, fruity, vegetable, nutty, spicy or toasted?

Take out some similar aromas and compare them. Frequently checking the vials will only enhance your abilities. Screw the lid back on and place the vial back into the correct place in the box. Now sniff your elbow. That's right. This will neutralize the preceding odor so you can move onto the next one. Proceed to vial number 2 and, in the coming days, all the way to 36.

Put the lids back on immediately so as not to cross contaminate. Writing a number on the lid that corresponds to the bottle is helpful. You could also put a corresponding number in each vial space in the box. Choose a quiet room where you will be able to concentrate and, of course, where there are no inappropriate smells such as tobacco, perfume or dirty socks.

Smell is the sense in which habituation occurs most quickly. Habituation is the process by which a sense becomes accustomed to what it detects so that it is no longer perceived. Most odors can hardly be perceived just 30 seconds after they are first detected. Therefore, take a few small sniffs. Variation 1: Take five vials and proceed to test yourself as described above. Variation 2: Take any vial and proceed to test yourself as described above.

And get someone else involved to test you. This helps with personal honesty. Trindle's method is "to mix all of the vials into a grand mess of little vials and take each one, one by one, and try to identify its aroma." Start out small. After a recurring 100-percent success rate, you can make things harder.

If you are learning "honeyed," why not bring some real honey in? If you're learning the scent of peanuts, bring peanuts—or, my favorite, "cooked beef." (I have yet to find this odor in coffee.) This will also help to cement the odor into the memory as odor memories frequently have strong emotional qualities. Olfaction is handled by the same part of the brain (the limbic system) that handles memories and emotions. Therefore, we often find that we can immediately recognize and respond to smells from childhood such as the smell of Sunday lunch or your grandmother's perfume. Very often we cannot put a name to these odors, yet they have a strong emotive association. Use this to your advantage by using the memory to help yourself identify scents in coffee.

Smell a vial, like cooked beef. Mention a moment in your history that you have encountered this scent, and make the connection. Over time, this smell will also become a coffee odor.

The inverse is also true. If you don't have an emotion attached to the smell (for example, "coffee blossom"), then you will need to hunker down and repeat this vial over and over like your multiplication tables.

The vials will change over time, so they may need to be renewed. Le Nez du Café offers a smaller sample called Temptation, which includes garden peas, blackcurrant bud, butter, caramel, roasted peanuts and roasted coffee. To preserve the vials' scents longer, keep them away from light and heat.

Conclusion

I could have said all of this in just three words: "The nose knows!" A machine has not been created to know smell. There are gas chromatographers, but "we still need someone at the other end to smell the outlet gas sample to classify it," notes Rivera.

You have a nose and you may have a kit. Now complete the formula: Time (Kit + Nose) = YPFD (Your Personal Fragrance Dictionary). This is the beauty of Le Nez du Café. ■

. . . .

PAUL H. ALLEN *is roastmaster for Caravan Coffee in Newberg, Oregon, and a licensed Q grader with a Bachelor of Science degree. You can reach him via email at* paul@caravancoffee.com.

QUALITY CONTROL

Lab Report

How to Set Up an In-House Coffee Lab for Quality Control and Training

by Katie Gilmer Pon

• FROM THE MAY/JUNE 2011 ISSUE OF *ROAST* •

A coffee lab should be the crown jewel of a roaster's business. It's a special room where roasters can enjoy the sensory side of their operations while also validating and reinforcing quality claims. Roasters use a lab not only for purchasing decisions and sample evaluation, but also for confirming that roasting operations are performing as they should. The lab is a place to experiment with grind analysis, brewing techniques, roast level and blending—and to train staff in these areas and more. Some labs also serve as a place to educate customers and demonstrate just how important quality is to your business.

With so many uses, building or upgrading a lab can be a daunting task. But upgrades can be undertaken one by one as time and budgets allow. If a roasting business plans its coffee lab in advance, it can build and equip the lab to be useful for many years.

Why Build a Lab?

A coffee lab is a safe haven for a roaster to make buying decisions without distraction. Just as a scientist measures and experiments using the scientific method, coffee professionals should hold themselves to the highest standards of quality and consistency when evaluating coffee. A lab is a space for roasters to take ownership of their inner "Type A" personality and remain firm to standards and rules. A roaster needs to be able to make consistent decisions from year to year, and using cupping protocols and the scientific method will reduce variables.

Maybe a roaster gets a report from an importer that a certain coffee has intense acidity; the roaster needs to try it for herself, roasted at her altitude and climate, using her specific profile and her water. Getting an accurate sense of how the coffee performs in the roaster's unique environment and in the roaster's blends is key for purchasing decisions.

But maintaining a lab does not just benefit a roaster's business. Mike Strumpf, who has managed quality control for a number of coffee roasters in the United States, stresses a lab's importance. "I think it's all about fairness," he says. "When you make contracts that have quality bonuses attached to them, you need to make an accurate assessment so you don't hurt a farmer's livelihood. If you don't cup in a good lab, then your scores won't be valid."

Furthermore, having a trustworthy lab will help roasters share quality standards with other coffee professionals worldwide. The Specialty Coffee Association's (SCA) Laboratory Certification promotes consistent cupping standards and the objective evaluation of coffee. The lab certification is needed for holding Q grader courses in a coffee lab, and it addresses aspects such as room dimensions, lighting, ventilation, water specifications and roast color identification technology. Even if a roaster isn't prepared for official lab certification, the SCA's list of requirements is a good guide for widely accepted lab standards.

Positioning Your Lab

Maintaining the formal nature of a lab is important. The lab is a space to hold cuppings for buying decisions, and constant interruptions will sabotage an important cupping. Think first about the best location for the lab. A roasting business will need a dedicated place where employees can install machines and equipment. Is the space near your production roaster? Is it in your retail space? Is it in a spare room next to the bookkeeper's office? Will the public be invited into the lab? Is there adequate plumbing and electricity available?

When Charles Patton, owner of Bird Rock Coffee Roasters, launched his roastery in La Jolla, California, in 2002, he had a small lab in the room with his roaster and packaging operations. Patton says the setup was problematic. "It's hard to make buying decisions in the same room as production because of all the noise and commotion," he says. "We wanted our roaster to be involved in buying decisions, but right as we were about to break the crust, he would have to go fix a problem with the machines."

When Patton expanded to the retail space next door, he took advantage of the extra room to create a new lab. "When we expanded next door, we built a little room specifically for cuppings," he says. "We added a kids' zone next to the cupping lab. We found we had a lot of moms coming in with their kids, and we needed to contain them. It really helped us accommodate more people and grow business." The lab is divided from the kids' zone, but moms can peek in at lab activity through a cutout in the wall.

Bird Rock's lab is open to the public, but Patton schedules the most important cuppings after hours. When he needs the undivided attention of his staff, it's best to eliminate the possibility for interruptions, he says.

If a roasting business does not choose to hold public cuppings, the business can still hold them where the public can watch. Cuppings are a fairly new intrigue for public consumption, so customers will enjoy seeing this window into the coffee buyer's world.

If the coffee lab will be constructed in a shared workspace, build walls or a barrier around it to block distracting noise or smells that could affect cuppers' focus. Install windows or a sliding glass door so others can see when lab occupants should be left alone (and so those working in the lab can check on the situation outside the room). Think about all the functions of a lab—cupping, experimenting and testing, as well as training for both employees and customers. If the roasting business cannot dedicate several separate spaces to the lab, take that into consideration when planning the size of the lab.

An innovative idea coming from origin— where coffee professionals have become expert at devising economical solutions—is constructing a mobile lab. The Divisoria Cooperative in Tingo Maria, Peru, dispatches two mobile units to the most remote communities. The members can't often make the trek to the co-op offices to taste their own coffee, so the co-op brings the service

to them. Divisoria Quality Control Manager Julian Aucca built a lab composed of a small electric roaster, grinder, parchment dehuller and folding table. He stocked it with cups and spoons, and stored it in a portable cupboard. The whole unit fits in the back of a pickup truck.

While a roaster might use a mobile lab for customer visits, Divisoria uses it as a way to identify where problems are happening on the farm level. "The mobile lab allows us to create a culture of quality," Aucca says. "It gives our producers another resource to know what a good coffee tastes like and identify any quality problems before they get serious."

Roasters should consider the return on investment of a mobile lab. Will it be worth the cost, or is an in-house lab sufficient? Whether mobile or stationary, public or private, find the solution that works best for the company's location and business. First and foremost, the goal is to evaluate coffee.

Building Your Lab

Whether a roasting business constructs a lab from scratch or sets it up in a preexisting space, there are a few considerations to think about. Tables and storage areas, along with water and power sources, need to be addressed from the start. Is the business thinking of having sit-down cuppings or standing cuppings? If standing, the lab will need a table that is high enough so cuppers' backs don't hurt from bending over but low enough for the shorter cuppers. The table should have at least 2 feet of clearance on all sides so cuppers can move around it freely. If a wooden cupping table will be used, make sure to choose wood that is fragrance-free and invest in a fragrance-free finish to protect the table from water damage. For public cuppings, roasters will need to provide furniture that is accessible for people with disabilities.

Another useful piece of furniture for the lab is a cabinet or shelving unit for storing green coffee samples. Opaque plastic or metal canisters stack easily and block the green coffee from damage from outside light.

How many people will be using the lab on an average day? If the coffee business plans to dedicate a team of three people to cup every production roast, the requirements for furniture and countertop space will be much greater than the requirements for a lab for a solo green buyer who is evaluating the occasional offer sample. Think about how many coffees the roasting business will evaluate on an hourly basis. If the company is using SCA standards, it will need five cups for each coffee. Cup needs add up quickly at that rate. Planning the cupping frequency will also help roasters determine their hot-water requirements. It's essential to have a sufficient supply at the right temperature.

The water situation in a lab requires advance planning. If a roasting company intends to pipe in water, make sure a filtration system is in place. At Bird Rock, Patton chose to use bottled water for his lab instead of going through the plumbing hassle.

EQUIPMENT ESSENTIALS

✓ Sample roaster   ✓ Spoons

✓ Grinder   ✓ Timer

✓ Digital scale   ✓ Scoring sheets

✓ Electric water kettles   ✓ Digital thermometer

✓ Hot-water tower   ✓ Humidity meter

✓ Cups or glasses

Will the business be cupping coffees every day, multiple times per day? A hot-water tower will make the process much more efficient. Kim Bullock, former manager of sustainability and producer relations for Counter Culture Coffee and is a member of the company's quality-control team, has this piece of advice: "Plan for a lot of power—either a 220-volt, 30-amp circuit where you can hook up a hot-water tower or enough 110 outlets on dedicated circuits so you can plug in a bunch of water kettles." Water kettles are the least expensive way to boil water for cuppings, but they are infamous for tripping circuit breakers.

Lighting is another crucial consideration for a coffee lab. Nature is the best light source, but natural light can be hard to come by in the winter. If natural light is not an option or the company would like to supplement it, be sure to choose full-spectrum light bulbs. They emit a clean, white light that emulates daylight. Avoid yellow-toned light because it will change the way the coffee looks. For sample roasters with more than one barrel, make sure that the same amount of light falls over each barrel. A long tube or track lighting will ensure that the light, and consequently the sample roasting, is consistent from barrel to barrel. Some labs may install red light bulbs or red light covers for triangulation tests to homogenize the color of the coffee, both as grinds and brewed. Roasters can experiment with red light, but they can also try turning off their normal lights and performing a color test with only ambient light from outside the lab. Roasters may find the red lights still emit too much brightness and that low light is a better alternative for those special exercises.

Air circulation and temperature are important considerations for the lab, as well. An HVAC (heating, ventilation and air conditioning) system keeps the lab at a comfortable temperature. Carefully plan the vent locations to prevent an air vent from blowing on half of your cupping table but not the other, resulting in unevenly cooled cups. In addition, the airflow must not be so strong that it disturbs the coffee's aroma during cupping exercises. A programmable HVAC system also helps to maintain a comfortable room temperature and a consistent relative humidity inside the lab.

An advanced lab feature is an air-pressure stabilizer. Clean rooms, hospitals, and labs for pharmaceutical or electronics manufacturing frequently use pressure stabilization to maintain a sterile environment. In a hospital, a patient with a contagious illness will be put in a pressure-negative room, ensuring that when the patient's door is opened, air from the hallway flows into the room, keeping the illness inside the room. Conversely, air will flow out of a pressure-positive room. For a pressure-positive coffee lab, this means that outside aromas are kept out of the lab. Pressure stabilizers control room pressure differentials through the ventilation system; to create positive pressure, more air is mechanically supplied to a room than is mechanically exhausted.

Roasting businesses should stress that the lab really is a laboratory—a place to learn and experiment—by displaying educational posters. A green-coffee-defect chart is practical for decoding a funky-looking bean. The SCA's flavor wheel is a good source for cupping vocabulary. And maps are a must-have for pointing out sample origins. If extra space is available in the lab, stock a shelf with coffee reference books. A computer or tablet in the lab is useful for showing customers photos and video from coffee origins.

Le Nez du Café, a kit of 36 aroma vials representing the scents found in coffee, is another good addition to the lab. If inexperienced cuppers find it difficult to discern differences between coffees, have them practice with Le Nez du Café. This kit should be used for training but shouldn't be used in a coffee lab during cupping, as the aromas may taint a quality evaluation.

Lab Essentials

Building a coffee lab can be an expensive endeavor. Outfitting a lab to its fullest can easily cost more than $10,000. However,

sticking to the basics can cost as little as $2,000. There are a few essentials that every lab needs: a sample roaster, a grinder, cups, spoons, a digital scale, a timer, and water kettles or a hot-water tower. A sink, garbage disposal and dishwasher will make cleanup much faster.

Unless a coffee business can roast small sample batches with a production roaster, the business will need to procure a sample roaster to save energy and roast those small green samples. Whether a roasting business invests in a top-of-the-line model or a modest one, it's important to measure temperature and other variables accurately to produce the same results every time.

According to Bullock of Counter Culture, "The key [to sample roasting] is consistency. A machine purchased in the local market might not have the greatest airflow, but for sample roasters it's more about being consistent from roast to roast."

Even with a basic sample roaster, a coffee business can achieve consistent samples by understanding the principles of sample roasting and having a well-trained person at the helm. Leave a sample of the company's ideal roast level next to your roaster for comparison. Of course, a fire extinguisher is a necessity in a lab with a roaster. Make sure that employees are familiar with the building's fire code in case law requires a more sophisticated fire-suppression system.

It's ideal to dedicate a burr grinder for lab use only rather than sharing a production grinder. Devote the grinder solely to cupping and training purposes, and be sure to clean it and replace the burrs regularly. A quality grinder ensures consistency in the grind's particle size, which will enhance coffee evaluation. Ceramic bowls or rocks glasses are most commonly used for cupping. If the lab is using new cups, take measurements so employees can cup with the correct water-to-coffee ratio. A digital thermometer is useful to have on hand for measuring water temperature.

A humidity meter is also handy in a lab, as it will help roasters know what to expect when sample roasting. It's important to test samples' humidity before buying—green bean humidity lower than 10 percent or higher than 12 percent should throw up a red flag. An Agtron machine or color tiles are also helpful additions to a lab for analyzing the roast level of production roasts.

Strumpf also suggests procuring a top-of-the-line scale because the higher price will pay off over the years. He recommends a Class 3 scale. "A Class 3 scale is legal for trade and can be recalibrated," Strumpf notes. "Keep your scales on a yearly calibration schedule."

Calibration is a top lab concern for Strumpf. "This is something a lot of labs overlook—getting your grinder, moisture meter and scale on a calibration schedule," he says. Roasters can do some of this calibration themselves. Ask the moisture meter company to send a sample (usually barley) with a fixed moisture level. Then, tare the machine using this sample. To calibrate the grinder, do a grind analysis if the company has the available equipment, or send samples to companies who will perform the analysis and share the results.

Strumpf's other must-have tool for the lab is a commercial sanitizer, as normal dishwashers take too long. With a sanitizer, "a cycle is four minutes," says Strumpf. "You can put 30 cups on a tray. So with two trays, you can wash 60 cups at once." If roasters and buyers are cupping often, a sanitizer saves a substantial amount of time. Sanitizers work with either chemical cleansers or with hot water. If a roasting business chooses to use a cleanser, experiment with different types to ensure they are fragrance and residue free.

If the roastery will be holding public cuppings, the business may want to have scoring sheets on hand. Counter Culture Coffee developed its own internal scoring sheet that best fits that company's needs, but uses a modified form for outsiders. Bullock says, "For our public cuppings, we pared the form down so it's just the sensory categories and space for notes but not space for scores." It is useful to have different forms on hand, such as SCA and Cup of Excellence, to show to staff or anyone else who is interested in how they vary.

Getting the Most Out of Your Lab

Since you have put so much time and money into the coffee lab, it's up to you to harness all of its potential. Use it as much as possible, and use it wisely. If a roasting company installs a pull-down screen and projector, the lab can be an ideal place to gather staff or customers to show them presentations or videos. And, with some careful planning, a lab can serve as an office in a pinch.

Of course, sharing the lab space means that there are a few rules that need to be adhered to. Keeping the lab clean is a priority. Think of it as a sterile environment—you would never see stray powders or clutter in a chemistry lab. Stock a cupboard with cleaning supplies so they're always on hand. Make sure the machines receive regular cleaning and maintenance.

Cleanliness is just one of the elements of a fine-tuned lab. Another requirement is a set of lab rules. A Bill of Rights for the lab should express your wishes on paper and be posted on the wall. Strumpf says his No. 1 rule is "no smelly perfumes or deodorants." Other good rules: no cell phones inside the lab, no talking during cuppings, and no outside food or beverages in the lab area. If the lab will be used in a number of different ways, it might be helpful to post a schedule. See the sidebar on this page for more suggestions for lab rules.

With organization and rules, as well as lab protocol, consistency is the goal. Be consistent, even if the machines in the lab are not top of the line. This consistency in processes will

TOP 10 RULES FOR COFFEE LABS

1 No perfumes or colognes.

2 No outside food or beverages.

3 No interrupting the cuppers (talking, music or questions) during the process.

4 No cell phones/texting in the lab. Office phones should have ringers off during testing.

5 No flavored coffees.

6 Only unbiased evaluations.

7 Equipment is to be maintained in "new" condition at all times.

8 Do not roast samples during the cupping process.

9 Cup coffees light to dark roast, delicate to intense.

10 No clutter. Keep activities like shipping and packaging in other areas.

give you the most accurate results possible. Adhering to a strict quality-control regime will pay off when it comes time to upgrade equipment. For ratios, water temperature, and other measurable variants, defer to industry standards when in doubt.

Once roasters have decided on the uses of the lab, sourced the furniture and equipment, and established a code of conduct, the new coffee lab will serve many aspects of the business. Roasters will be able to make consistent and fair business decisions while enjoying a space to make quality control all their own. ■

KATIE GILMER PON *is the general manager of green coffee sales for La Minita. Pon has been working in the coffee and craft chocolate industries since 2006.*

The Color of Coffee

Using Color Analysis in Quality Control

by Paul Songer

• FROM THE JANUARY/FEBRUARY 2015 ISSUE OF *ROAST* •

FOODS AND BEVERAGES appeal to consumers through appearance, and color is an important visual cue. Coffee is not as bright or varied in color as many foods and beverages, but coffee enthusiasts do have preferences of roast degree and can observe this by the color of the coffee. While offering a variety of coffee flavor experiences is a key element in marketing specialty coffee, when customers find something they like, they purchase it again. If what they purchase doesn't provide the same experience as the previous purchase, they are likely to think less of the roaster.

For roasters, the degree of roast is an essential consideration in balancing flavor attributes. A "Nordic" light-roasted coffee has a great deal of acidity but little caramelization and body. A medium to full city roast has more complex aromatics and a balance of acidity and body. Slightly darker roasts of the type used for Northern Italian espresso emphasize sweetness and body, and the darkest roasts are dominated by "roasty" aromatics and burnt-sugar tastes. The character of the green coffee can be either emphasized or modified through the timing and final degree of roast, and this can be measured in terms of color.

But coffee often looks better than it tastes. If it is known that the green coffee is of good quality, the problem is likely in the roasting. What went wrong?

In production roasting, the goal is to produce the intended roast degree and flavor development consistently. Sensory determination is the primary method of quality control, but it is useful to have instrumental confirmation to examine the roast in greater detail. While roasters have flavor attributes on their mind when they design a coffee, measuring the roast so these attributes can be consistently reproduced is essential for quality control. There are a number of machines on the market that are capable of performing this task. This article looks at how the color of roasted coffee can be measured and what one can conclude from the results.

Instrumental measurement can give clues as to what has occurred during the roasting process, but other information is needed as well. As with all lab methods, sample preparation and instrument calibration will affect accuracy.

PART 1

The Science Behind Color Analysis

What to Measure?

There are two crucial processes that occur during roasting: (1) development of flavor attributes, mainly sugar-browning reactions, and (2) degradation of compounds. Both processes occur as the result of application of heat over time. The final degree of roast and the time in which it was produced is an indication of how much heat was absorbed by the coffee. From that, one can make a reasonable assumption about the processes that took place. Roast measurement usually seeks to quantify either development or degradation.

What is observed or measured in terms of visual cues is the result of three phenomena:

- The color of the light illuminating the subject by the light source or emitter. This is the result of all different wavelengths of light emitted by the source.

- The optical properties of what is being examined, measured or perceived (the subject). The subject will either absorb or reflect the light being emitted by the illuminant.

- The observer or, in the case of an instrumental measurement, the sensor. The observer perceives the light reflected from the subject and, if the wavelengths of the source are quantified, can conclude or measure which wavelengths have been absorbed.

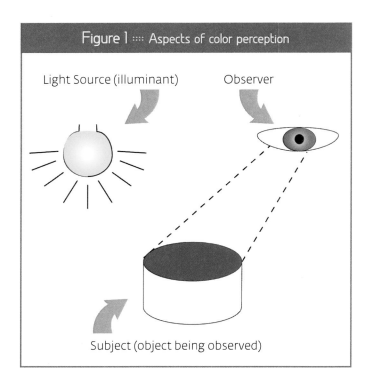

Figure 1 :::: Aspects of color perception

Light Source (illuminant)

Observer

Subject (object being observed)

What one sees or what a machine measures is the interaction between the colors of the illuminant and the color of the subject itself. The capability to perceive this combination depends on the ability of the eye or sensor to "see" the resulting wavelengths of light being reflected. With perception by eye, one's ability to perceive is limited to the visible spectrum, but some instruments are not so limited.

Instruments designed to measure degree of coffee roast differ in what they measure and how the results are reported. Instruments that measure visible color as perceived by human beings are intended to measure the degree of sugar browning produced as the result of roast; other instruments measure different roasting processes, such as the degradation of compounds, using ranges of color that cannot be perceived by the human eye. What is being measured depends on the illuminant and sensor used. How the results are reported depends on how the machinery translates those measurements into a standardized scale.

Measurement of Color

One perceives different colors because of the innate human ability to perceive light waves of specific wavelengths. A wave (Fig. 2) is a vibration with a certain wavelength; different wavelengths result in different colors. Visible color is light in the area of 400 to 700 nanometers (nm; see Fig. 3, next page), but there are other non-visible wavelengths. While there are many methods of measuring roast, they all seek to measure reflected wavelengths.

Like most sensory perceptions, not everyone sees the same wavelengths; some cannot distinguish between red and green and some cannot perceive different colors at all (color blindness). All wavelengths of light combined together are perceived as white; absence of any wavelength of light is black.

A Scale of Different Colors

A raw color measurement consists of several individual measurements of the different wavelengths of light being reflected. This is often illustrated in the form of a histogram showing the intensity of reflected light at various wavelengths. The different spectra can then be used to illustrate a "spectral curve." This measurement of the reflection depends on the wavelengths of light illuminating the sample (Figures 4–7, page 320).

As color analysis evolved, different scales for reporting colors were developed. Most of these were directly related to the graphic arts or areas where precision and consistency of visible color were important, such as in the clothing industry. However, as the technology developed and became more precise, color analysis was applied to other disciplines in ways that did not depend only on the visible spectrum.

A major challenge in the history of science has been to develop scales that are consistent enough for scientific quantification, analysis and comparison. This becomes more difficult when the scale also should correspond in a meaningful way to a sensory experience, such as taste, as one's senses do not always operate in a linear or predictable way. Developers of color measurement scales sought to simplify the complex interaction between light and the perceiver into something that was consistently measurable and corresponded to human experience.

The discovery of the spectrum of light is credited to Sir Isaac Newton (1643–1727) in his work *Opticks*. He believed different colors

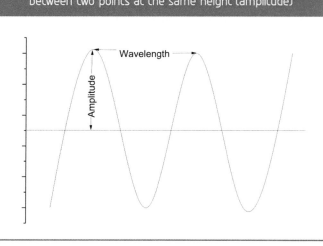

Figure 2 :::: A wave. The wavelength (λ) is the distance between two points at the same height (amplitude)

Wavelength

Amplitude

were the result of subtle particles that had mass and followed the laws of physics. J. C. Maxwell (1831–1879) theorized that color was made up of waves. Earlier, Thomas Young (1773–1829) had proposed a theory that all color was a combination of the primary colors red, yellow and blue, and Maxwell's work also focused on this theory. It was Hermann von Helmholtz (1821–1894) who concluded that the eye perceived in terms of red, green and blue, and it is now known that the eye contains individual cones that perceive these three colors.

At this point, the two major aspects of color perception were quantified: Newton had discovered that color was light (no light equals no color) and Helmholtz had determined that the observer was the final arbiter of what could be seen as the result of that light. These discoveries and the RGB (red-green-blue) scale were used to create the first "color wheels," in which a color could be quantified in terms of three aspects that could be mapped in three dimensions. The three-dimensional representations are called tristimulus color spaces.

However, these models had their limitations. Each color has the properties of hue, saturation and brightness. What has been described so far in terms of wavelength is the hue. This hue might be intensely concentrated (like scarlet red) or might have more neutral color mixed in (pink); this is saturation. Shiny surfaces are more reflective while others absorb light; this is brightness. When perceiving or measuring color, the effect of these properties must be taken into consideration.

This led to the development of other scales that corresponded well to the measures of wavelengths, but they did not correlate well with human perception of color. A group of color scientists formed the Commission Internationale de l'Éclairage (CIE), also known as the International Commission on Illumination, in 1913. They systematized the analysis of color regarding the "standard observer" (based on a person with average visual abilities), "standard illuminants" (the source of light under which the color is observed), and a model of measurement called the CIE XYZ system. A number of "standard illuminants" were defined, including incandescent light, daylight and others. The "standard observer" was represented by a set of three curves of primary colors that could be combined to produce all colors in the visible spectrum.

To get closer to the actual difference in sensory perception, the CIE L*a*b* system was developed. This scale was based

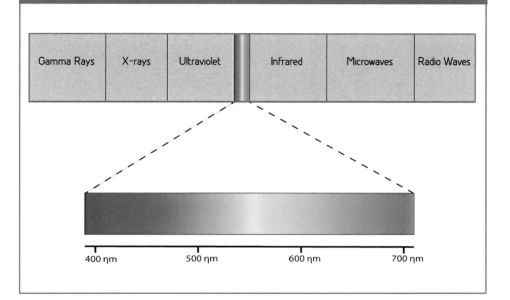

Figure 3 ⸬ Visible spectrum from infrared to ultraviolet. Wavelengths to the left and right of the infrared and ultraviolet lines cannot be seen by most humans. The spectrum shows color bands according to specific wavelengths, but in the real world colors are made up of different combinations of these wavelengths.

| Gamma Rays | X-rays | Ultraviolet | Infrared | Microwaves | Radio Waves |

400 ηm   500 ηm   600 ηm   700 ηm

on experimental data of human color matching. This allowed more precise definitions of color similarity and especially color difference, referred to in most equations as ΔE. This L*a*b* system was adopted by the food industry for various applications.

All of the tristimulus systems (RGB, XYZ, L*a*b*, etc.) are mathematically defined in such a way that they can be converted from one to another. The CIE L*a*b* system (Fig. 9, page 321) is the most-used color scale other than those specifically designed for graphics and monitors.

Other Measurements of Roast Degree

Measuring the color of roasted coffee in terms of one of the systems above corresponds to the degree of browning that has taken place. However, one may have noticed with these systems that the color brown—the one most associated with coffee—is not readily apparent. Also, the measurement of brown color does not directly indicate the type of sugar browning that took place. For example, development of furanthiol requires a temperature of at least 120 degrees C, and pyrazines also require higher temperatures. Both are important coffee aromatics.

Measurement of the visible spectrum indicates the intensity of brown (intended to reasonably correspond to sugar browning). In certain segments of the food industry, methods were devised for specific applications. For example, in the late 1970s a system was designed to determine tomato ripeness, in which a tomato was cut in half and a single "ripeness" value derived from the ratio of green reflectance to red reflectance. This ripeness ratio was referred to as the Agtron number, named after the machine that used a red neon lamp and green mercury vapor lamp to determine the green and red reflectance.

Similarly, Agtron developed two widely used scales of coffee roast degree: gourmet and commercial. On the gourmet scale—the one most widely used in specialty coffee—105 to 120 is considered the point at which the organic compounds associated with roast start to develop, and 0 indicates total reduction of organic compounds. (The scale on the machine goes from 100 for very light roast to 0 for complete degradation.)

This scale is used as a reference throughout the coffee industry, regardless of the type of instrument. However, not all instruments measure the Agtron number in the same way; most work out a correlation with the particular measurement technique they are using. In instrument specifications, the Agtron gourmet number is sometimes referred to as the SCAA number.

More recently, research performed by other companies has led to different scales based on observed changes in coffee roast degree. Most of these are based on the red or near-infrared area of the spectrum.

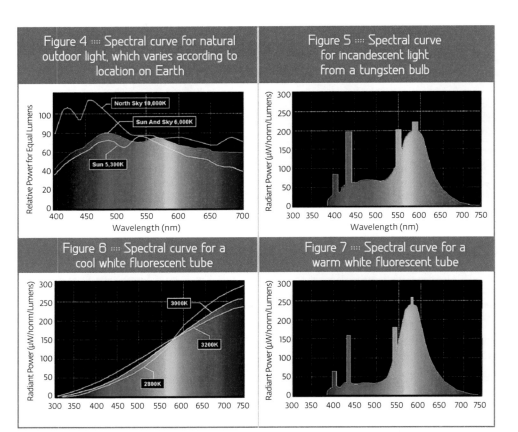

Figure 4 ⫶ Spectral curve for natural outdoor light, which varies according to location on Earth

Figure 5 ⫶ Spectral curve for incandescent light from a tungsten bulb

Figure 6 ⫶ Spectral curve for a cool white fluorescent tube

Figure 7 ⫶ Spectral curve for a warm white fluorescent tube

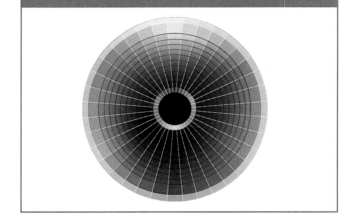

Figure 8 ⫶ A two-dimensional color wheel. Several systems use such a color space to define particular colors by degrees on such a wheel, with pure red traditionally at 0 degrees.

PART 2

Applying Color Analysis to Coffee Roasting

Using an Instrument for Quality Control

As coffee roasting businesses grow, the founding roaster typically delegates some of the responsibility for roasting to others, operates multiple roasting facilities, and/or uses a variety of roasters for production. This creates a critical challenge for a growing business—how to maintain the quality customers expect when so many variables affect production. Formal quality control procedures can ensure consistency.

In reviewing the different instruments available for measurement of color, one will notice they do not guarantee the intended flavor attributes were attained during roast. They can, however, be used as reasonably precise indicators, along with other measurements, to ensure the intended degree of roast took place.

Quality control programs start with a standard—in this case, the ideal coffee flavor profile, which is the result of the green coffee and roast parameters. To establish a standard, it is suggested that several roasted prototypes of the green coffee be roasted to the approximate desired degree and cupped. One can either select one of the prototypes or produce another prototype based on what is found at the cupping table.

Once the standard coffee is determined, the following specifications are created:

■ Measurement of degree of roast of both whole-bean and ground coffee. The whole-bean is darker than the ground and the difference between the measurements will indicate the rate of penetration of the heat and the amount and type of sugar browning that took place. The specification should include the target and the distance from the target measurement that is allowed.

■ Process measurements, or the "roast log" attributes of time and temperature, especially at what point gold, first crack, second crack (if present) and finish occur.

■ A description of the sensory aspects that should be present and their relative intensities. For example, the intensity and type of acidity, mouthfeel and finish should be detailed. This doesn't need to be overly specific, but it should indicate what makes this particular coffee unique.

With these specifications, one can use the roast degree and process measurements to indicate how close any batch is to the ideal. If measurements are too far from the standard, one can use the descriptive sensory aspects to investigate the closeness to the intended flavor balance.

To get accurate color analysis results, sample preparation procedures must be rigorous and consistent. It is common for different operators to get different measurements from the same instrument and sample because of sample preparation variability. Coffee is not homogenous in color. Small beans are darker than larger beans, and when the coffee is ground, the particles from the outside of the bean are usually darker than the particles from inside due to the progression of heat from the outside inward. Grind size, packing, density and distance from the sensor all will affect the measurement.

For most instruments, one is directed to smooth the surface without packing it, with an absence of "dimples" or low spots. If one can observe a difference, the machine likely will measure a difference. Especially when one is making comparisons, the sample must be prepared the same way each time.

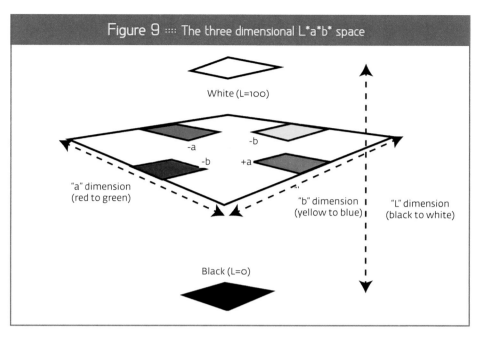

Figure 9 :::: The three dimensional L*a*b* space

White (L=100)

"a" dimension (red to green)

"b" dimension (yellow to blue)

"L" dimension (black to white)

Black (L=0)

Timing also is a factor. If the coffee is measured fresh out of the roaster, it will appear and measure lighter than if the same sample is measured several hours or days later. Part of the standard should include an approximate timing guide.

Key Elements of Color Analysis Instruments

With color, there is a chain of perception that begins with the eye sensing the wavelength, then sending a message to the brain, where one becomes conscious of and interprets the stimulus. Measuring devices have their own mechanical chain of perception, first sensing the wavelength, processing the stimulus, then converting it into a scale for output.

Instruments have been built to perceive multiple areas of the wavelength spectrum. Most instruments measure the sample in a closed, light-proof area. The sample is illuminated with a certain wavelength of light before measuring. Sensors often can be adjusted or calibrated to perceive a specific combination of wavelength bands.

When considering a machine for color measurement, one should examine the following:

■ What is the light source? If the measurement is to be taken under ambient light conditions, one should plan to use a consistent light source to minimize variability. If the machine provides its own light source but not in a sealed area, light pollution from external sources must be considered. If there is a sealed area, one must consider how the source is to be calibrated or maintained so measurements are consistent and accurate.

■ How does the sensor work? One consideration is how large an area is being measured. For most color meters, the actual area of measurement is very small. However, this small area can be amplified through the use of lenses or by taking multiple measurements and averaging them. Other considerations include the sensitivity of the sensor and in which spectra it can sense.

■ What scale is used to report the measurement? Some use the Agtron scale or another widely used color scale. Knowledge of these scales is necessary to accurately interpret the measurement.

■ How are samples prepared? What kind of sample preparation is necessary and how will (inevitable) mistakes in sample preparation affect the accuracy of the data reported?

If there are several roasting facilities involved, one also should consider inter-instrument agreement and calibration. The measurements made at each facility should reflect the same level of roast as those taken at other facilities.

Color Meters

Color instruments measure the color that corresponds to the amount of sugar browning that has taken place during the roast. However, as noted previously, the degree of sugar browning will not necessarily guarantee the intended flavor attributes are present, as the actual sugar-browning chemicals may vary according to heat applied and timing of the roast. If using a color meter for evaluation of roast, the standards must include the process aspects (time and temperature, or "roast curve") to ensure

the intended chemical changes are produced.

One advantage to using color meters is that the same instrument can be used for the evaluation of green coffee. Another is that, because the standards of color measurement are well established and precisely quantified, inter-instrument agreement can be assumed.

In general, color meters are based on two technologies, the colorimeter and the spectrophotometer. A colorimeter measures the sample by passing the reflected light through a red, green and blue filter to try to duplicate the standard observer's perception. A photodetector quantifies the amount of light passing through the filters and reports the results in terms of one of the tristimulus scales. These instruments are less expensive but may not be as accurate as more recently designed machines.

Spectrophotometers break the reflected light from the sample into a range of different colors on the spectrum. The resulting spectra then pass to a diode array that measures that wavelength of light. This method is more accurate than a colorimeter, but the instruments are more expensive.

Examples of color meters include the HunterLab ColorFlex EZ Coffee spectrophotometer and the Konica Minolta CR-410C colorimeter. Both units are capable of reporting results in terms of the SCAA number. The HunterLab ColorFlex uses an optical geometry to increase the area of measurement. The Konica Minolta has a small aperture that requires multiple measurements for accuracy. Both instruments measure the sample from the bottom of the sample dish, so the optics of the sample dish must be considered; scratches will affect the results and the dishes can get contaminated.

The HunterLab ColorFlex EZ Coffee instrument uses a xenon white light source for consistency and to approximate normal daylight color. The illumination is focused in a circle at a 45-degree incidence to the sample, allowing the light to be measured from different angles, correcting any effect resulting from sample preparation. Its diode array measures the intensity of color at every 10 nm within the visible 400 to 700 nm range, but it focuses mainly on the 640 nm measurement, which the company's research shows is the optimal measurement for coffee roast. The instrument reports the results in four ways: SCAA number, roast classification ("light", "medium", etc.), CIE L*a*b* scale, and the company's own HunterLab Coffee Color Index (HCCI).

Coffee-specific Instruments

Because of the obvious need for measurement of roast degree and its importance in quality control, several instruments have been designed especially for coffee. As noted previously, the "brown-ness" or darkness of coffee can correspond to the degree of roast, but the

Sample preparation is critical to accurate color analysis. Note the differences between the samples based on how they're ground and whether or not the sample has been smoothed/flattened. | *Photo by Paul Songer*

brown portion of the spectrum is small. One also needs to consider the process that produced the roast degree.

The Agtron is one of the first instruments to employ methodology specifically developed for coffee. Near-infrared (non-visible) light illuminates the coffee to sense a selected group of quinones (byproducts of the degradation of chlorogenic acids that occur during roasting). The sensor measures certain (proprietary) wavelengths to determine the amount of quinones developed, which directly correlates to the degree of roast. As a direct measure of the chemistry, the results correspond well with the intended flavor attributes produced.

There are two types of Agtron machines (with some differences in individual models within these types): a closed system (the M-20) and a bottom-measuring system (the M-15). With the M-20 series, the machine is calibrated each time the drawer is opened. A disk is provided for calibration of the M-15. Inter-instrument agreement can be attained with adjustments available; one must have a dead stale sample—one that has been ground and oxidized for at least 30 days without significant moisture added—to measure in each machine. (Using such a sample ensures that changes in color are no longer taking place over time.) The machine should be serviced and the infrared lamp replaced annually.

Sample preparation for the Agtron is of major importance in attaining an accurate reading. The surface of the sample must be reasonably uniform without "dimples." The particle distribution as the result of grind also is important; it was observed by one lab that eliminating the larger and smaller particles by measuring only the particles in the No. 16 screen of a standard set of particle analysis screens (particles of approximately 1.18 mm) resulted in the most replicable measurements. Whole-bean coffee can be measured, but the likelihood of voids between the beans may cause the reading to be darker than the actual sample.

Madison Instruments produces Javalytics, which uses near-infrared illuminants to measure degree of roast. The sample is prepared similar to the Agtron, leveling across the sample plate or filling a glass dish before measurement. Ambient light does not affect the result due to the use of filters. The sensor integrates the reflectance of the entire area of the sample (about 3.5 inches in diameter) and results are reported in terms of the SCAA number, with electronic temperature compensation. It has a calibration disc that should be used daily, or more often, depending on the environment. Administrator functions include the built-in RoastMatch wizard, which allows one quickly to create and store various calibrations for inter-instrument agreement. A handheld version is available as well as a laboratory bench-top model.

ColorTrack uses a laser for the light source, which rarely needs to be replaced and never needs to be recalibrated. The bench-top model has a carousel that turns the coffee sample so approximately 200,000 measurements are taken (10,000 per second over a 20-second measurement period). Because coffee color is not homogenous, the reports include standard deviation over the

What's Next?

THE GOAL OF MODERN QUALITY control programs is to prevent out-of-spec products from being produced rather than simply rejecting poorly produced products, but measurement of color in all of the cases examined in this article occurs after the roast takes place—too late to make adjustments. Out-of-spec coffee must be donated, used in another product or disposed of, often representing a loss for the roaster. Future technology could be capable of measuring color changes as the roast progresses. (There are infrared measurements for temperature, but at present these are difficult to use.)

This type of measurement is technically difficult because one would need to have a dependable light source and a quick way of reading what is reflected. However, instruments for measuring color during roasting have been investigated and currently Fresh Roast Systems (makers of the ColorTrack) is exploring the manufacture of such a system.

surface as well as the average of all measurements. Reports also include graphic representations, similar to the histograms and spectral curves discussed earlier. The ColorTrack measures the sample directly (without glass or other reflective surfaces) and the laser technology is not "surface sensitive" (does not depend upon distance, angle incidence or smoothness of surface), so sample preparation has a minimal effect on results. The measurement focuses on the 780 nm wavelength to report results in terms of the Agtron number. A handheld version also is available.

While the primary method of evaluating coffee quality is sensory analysis, the use of color measurement technology can assist in improving quality and consistency. To optimize the use of these technologies, roasters must understand the technical aspects of color measurement and integrate these measurements into a quality control program that also takes into account the roasting process and sensory parameters for each coffee roasted. ■

PAUL SONGER *has been in the specialty coffee business for more than 30 years, first at Allegro Coffee Co. in Boulder, Colorado, then Coffee Analysts in Burlington, Vermont. He holds a certificate in sensory analysis from the University of California at Davis. He currently works as a consultant on sensory and technical issues regarding coffee and serves as head judge for the Cup of Excellence coffee competition program.*

PART III

ROASTING

BLENDING

Blending the Rules

The Art and Science of Combining Coffees

by Willem Boot

• FROM THE JULY/AUGUST 2006 ISSUE OF *ROAST* •

W HETHER YOUR BUSINESS IS a small, mom-and-pop retail store, a local coffee roasting cafe or a regional roasting operation, your coffee blends create that unique edge for your business and can ultimately be an excellent tool to maintain customer loyalty.

My personal experiences with coffee blends started many years ago in the Netherlands. In my home country, like in most other northern European countries, consumers were traditionally accustomed to standardized (read "boring") blends that would have a major component from Brazil, some Central American beans, usually some Indonesian coffee, complemented by robusta beans from West Africa. My dad became our town's messiah of single-origin coffee and preached the purity of the essential flavors of single-origin coffees from countries around the world.

One day, while working in my dad's roasting retail store, I decided to experiment with some simple blending recipes. The results were fascinating. I discovered that by blending a high- and low-body coffee (like Sulawesi and Costa Rica), the blend's body became very smooth, resulting in a velvety mouthfeel. I also discovered another interesting phenomenon: Blending high-acid coffees together didn't necessarily result in a pleasant end result. It was as if the coffees, with their intense acidity, were clashing, resulting in an almost hardish sourness.

While doing my own experiments, I also started to realize the importance of proper record keeping. One day I believed I had found the ideal marriage between three coffee types: Panama, India Mysore and Tanzania AA. Each component was roasted to its own distinct degree, and after blending the beans I brewed some regular drip filter, followed by a French press preparation. The blend was delicious; the refreshing acidity of the Panama and the nutty flavor tones of the India Mysore combined beautifully with the chocolate and berry notes of the Tanzania AA. When I tried to replicate the blend, I realized that I hadn't kept any bean samples

of the individual coffees, nor had I made any detailed notes during the roast process. Despite many frantic attempts, I have not been able to successfully craft my "phantom" blend again.

To Blend or Not to Blend

Within the specialty roasting community, there is currently a rise in the popularity of single-origin coffees. That's easy to understand— single-origin coffees allow roasters and retailers to finesse a coffee into its best flavor while selling the story of the particular growing region and/or producer of the coffee. "I'm more of a fan of single-origin coffees because of the story they can tell about the roots of the coffee and the unique growing conditions of the beans," admits Michael Johnson, owner of Johnson Brothers Coffee in Madison, Wisconsin. "However, our blends have given us the opportunity to open the doors to some large accounts, like the local university."

Thus, blends are still a force to be reckoned with—in their own way, they offer the roaster a chance to test his skill, while creating a product that is in demand from consumers. "In my opinion there are really very few reasons to blend coffees," says Geoff Watts of Chicago-based Intelligentsia Coffee & Tea. "The first is if year-round consistency is a goal. Some people don't like much variability and would rather have a coffee in their store that tastes the same way in January as it does in June." All coffees are seasonal and certainly perishable, thus, creating a blend where the ingredients and proportions change during the year to keep the blend vibrant and fresh without veering away from its essential character can be a good way to achieve year-long consistency.

Beans for Blending

BRAZIL Choose a pulped natural type with full body, no musty notes and slight aftertaste of fermented fruit.

SUMATRA Select a Gayo or Mandheling region coffee with clean earthy notes, preferably double-picked.

PANAMA I recommend choosing a Volcan- or Santa Clara-grown Panama with medium to bright acidity and lingering sweetness.

GUATEMALA Find any SHB Guatemala with vibrant acidity and clean fruit notes (with lighter roast levels these attributes generally contribute to a piquant acidity; with darker roast degrees they develop attractive chocolate notes).

KENYA Source a stellar bean with multi-layered acidity and bright berry notes (these are most predominant in bourbon varieties).

ETHIOPIA For this exercise, I recommend a sun-dried Yirgacheffe or Sidamo grade 3 with well-ripened, dense fruit flavors.

NICARAGUA Prepare a Nueva Segovia or Jinotega with pleasant fruit notes and smooth mouthfeel.

COLOMBIA For this exercise, I prefer a Colombian that is of the caturra or typica variety with a bright acidity, full body and clean aftertaste. The coffee can have some fruit attributes, but if you use a Huila watch out for dominant fruity notes.

DECAF I prefer the Mountain Water Process Decaf or the Swiss Water Decaf, and I recommend trying Ethiopian decaf for the described blend.

"The second, and more compelling, reason to blend is to create a combination of taste characteristics that cannot be found in a single coffee," says Watts. "This is blending as an art form rather than as a pragmatic tool. It is fascinating to me how different sets of flavors and cup traits can interact in unexpected ways. More often than not, 1+1 does not equal 2, or 11 for that matter."

This is the benefit of proper blending, and the potential downfall of incorrect blending. This is because some coffees complement each other and, in the cup, particular traits from each coffee find a way to articulate themselves, so much so that a good cupper could clearly identify the individual constituents. Other times one coffee will dominate the other, incorporating traits from the second coffee in a way that makes them hard to discern.

Another advantage of a blend is that it has long-term retail appeal. The coffee will not just taste consistent from month to month, but also ideally from year to year. More than 10 years ago, Batdorf and Bronson Coffee Roasters in Olympia, Washington, developed its Dancing Goats Blend, and it is still one of the company's most popular sellers today. "The best blends can be used for both espresso and drip filter preparation," says Larry Challain, founder of Batdorf and Bronson, of his blend philosophy. "The blend consists of five individually roasted components which create together the popular flavor profile which is complex, rich, sweet and smooth with chocolate and blueberry-like flavor attributes. Every roast of the blend is cupped daily by the roaster operators who are rotated between our two roasting facilities."

Hands-on Blending

Over the years, I have assisted many coffee companies around the world with the development of coffee blends, and I generally follow a similar blending protocol to what I describe in this article. Without a proper strategy, it will be very challenging to develop coffee blends, and you might end up applying a "hit and miss" approach, which only in rare cases results in the creation of successful blends.

I recommend following a comprehensive five-step product development protocol that will enable you to plan and execute a program of product development that usually results in the creation of at least three successful blends for your business.

First, start planning the process of crafting your blends. In this stage it is wise to ask some fundamental questions like: What type of client is the blend for? Home consumers, restaurants, or should the blend have a versatile application? The essential task in this phase is to describe the required flavor profile of the blend with the preferred degree of roast. The roastmaster or the responsible coffee person should know which flavor attributes to look for. Will the blend be refreshing with a medium acidity or chocolate-like and nutty with a dry aftertaste? Obviously these are fundamental questions that need to be asked beforehand.

Second comes the important task of selecting the coffee components. In my opinion, the coffees should be chosen for

their individual quality attributes; each component must be able to stand on its own as a single-origin product. Some companies create blends for the wrong reasons by trying to mask mediocre coffee components in the blend. I believe this is a foolish strategy and the short-term benefits—higher profit margins—do not weigh up against the long-term consequences of losing dissatisfied clients.

CHART A | Roast Styles

Roast Style	Agtron Color	Description
LIGHT	64–68	The first crack is completed. Some coffees can now be consumed, provided that the first crack occurred slowly. To accomplish this, the roaster operator must reduce the heat supply at least one minute before the first crack.
MEDIUM LIGHT	60–64	About one to two minutes after the finish of the first crack. Color of the beans is quite even. There is a minimum of darker roast spots on the beans. To accomplish this roast style, the roaster operator must reduce the heat supply just before the start of the first crack.
MEDIUM	55–59	This is just before the start of the second crack. Beans are evenly roasted and start to expand more. At this point, the heat inside the beans almost becomes exothermic and you can notice that subtle aromas are released by the coffee.
WELL-DONE	50–54	At the beginning of the second pop and the heat inside the beans becomes exothermic.
DARK	44–49	The second crack is about 25 percent completed. There is now a rapid staccato of cracks occurring.
VERY DARK	36–43	The second crack is at least 50 percent completed and oils start showing on the beans.
FRENCH	28–35	The second crack is complete; the beans develop more oils and swell to their maximum size.

NOTE: *I strongly recommend exploring the roast styles between Agtron 40 and 60. With these roast styles you will obtain more coffee flavor with complex and potentially sweet, refreshing attributes. Try to build your market niche with this lighter roasting style!*

Third, determine the roast level for each of the coffee components that will be utilized for the design of the blend. This step is crucial and must be explored extensively for each of the components of your blend. I have noticed too many roasting companies skip this step and, as a result, companies settle too quickly for the specific roasting style for each coffee component. Remember, optimum roast levels are different for each coffee and most coffee types have more than one optimum roast degree. As a result, the roasting process and the seemingly infinite number of roasting degrees can make your job as blender an endless nightmare. For that reason I have defined seven levels of roasting, described in Chart A (page 329). Since there is so much confusion about the denominations of roast levels, I have indicated for each roast style its corresponding Agtron color range, as well as a description of the roast process.

In general, I recommend exploring the medium light, medium and well-done roast styles. Too many roasting companies are

relentlessly copying some of the well-known specialty coffee brands and, as a result, we are experiencing a glut of dark, very dark and French roast styles that thrive too much on the concept of caramelizing and baking the coffee rather than developing real flavor.

With lighter roast styles you will obtain true coffee flavor with complex and potentially sweet, refreshing attributes. Try to build your market niche with a lighter roasting style! It must be noted that roasting coffee to a lighter degree, like light or medium light, puts much more emphasis on the level of skills of your roaster operator. Fully automatic roast profiling systems are generally not capable of developing excellent tasting lighter roast profiles and as a result the roaster operator must manually ensure that the proper roasting protocol is followed.

Fourth, we get to the actual nuts and bolts of blending. Now, you must select the green coffee types for your blend and roast each type individually to the degree indicated in Chart B which

CHART B | Blend Styles

Blend Style	Brazil	Sumatra	Panama	Guatemala	Kenya	Ethiopia	Nicaragua	Colombia	Decaf
Breakfast Blend		25% Dark		50% Very Dark				25% Medium	
House Blend			50% Medium	25% Dark	12.5% Very Dark	12.5% Dark			
Espresso Blend	25% Well-Done		35% Well-Done	20% Dark		20% Well-Done			
Pacific Blend			33.3% Medium				33.3% Well-Done	33.3% Medium	
Summer Blend			25% Medium		37.5% Med. Light		37.5% Medium		
French Roast Blend		50% French						50% Very Dark	
Fifty-Fifty Blend			25% Well-Done	25% Medium					50% Medium
Vienna Roast Blend		33.3% Dark		33.3% Very Dark			33.3% Well-Done		
Exotic Blend			25% Well-Done		25% Well-Done	50% Medium			
Light Roast Blend	25% Light					25% Light		50% Med. Light	

lists 10 different blends with the recommended blend recipes and roasting styles.

Remember, along the way, it's important to take detailed notes about which greens you chose, how you roasted them and what percentage of each you used. Once you've created a blend, or blends, that are to your liking, you want to be able to replicate each element to perfection. Given the fact that coffee quality will change from season to season, I also recommend that you re-evaluate your blends at least once per quarter.

Whether blends are the mainstay of your roasting company, or something that you offer just to round out your selection, it's a good idea to remember that adage we talked about earlier: Coffee blends are always more than the sum of their parts. So the key to crafting a great blend is to make sure each of those parts is perfect before you dump them all together. Creating exemplary blends requires the utmost of your tasting skills, and even when you think you've created the perfect mix, your customers still have the final word. Good luck on your coffee blending discovery tour! ■

· ·

WILLEM BOOT *is the president of Boot Coffee Consulting, a training and consulting firm for coffee companies. He can be reached via email at* willemboot@bootcoffee.com *or* bootcoffee.com.

Types of Coffee Blends

(See Chart B, Previous Page)

· ·

BREAKFAST BLEND Usually has a slight punch (to wake up) but it should be very accessible so that the client will consume more than one cup. The described blend should be pleasantly refreshing without over-exposed acidity. Use a slightly darker roast for the Sumatra and Guatemala.

HOUSE BLEND In general, house blends should be designed for all-day enjoyment. The flavor must be accessible for most of your clients. Recently, I tasted Peet's house blend and I found that the flavor profile represented quite well the philosophy of Peet's, which advocates a deep, dark roasting style. Despite my personal preference for lighter roasting styles, I found this coffee to be well balanced with a pleasant chocolate-sweet flavor followed by a slight, refreshing aftertaste.

ESPRESSO BLEND The four components of this lighter-roasted espresso blend create a balanced flavor profile with sweet and chocolaty notes, followed by a slightly fruity finish (which is the influence of the sun-dried Ethiopia).

PACIFIC BLEND Contains three coffee types that can be found near the Pacific region. The blend is overall pleasant and can be a crowd-pleaser.

SUMMER BLEND Think of those long, warm summer days. This coffee blend will refresh your customer's palate, and hopefully make them crave a second cup. The lighter roast style accentuates the acidity.

FRENCH ROAST BLEND So you want the really dark roast? Here you go. Make sure that the Sumatra has a sweet flavor and that the bitter roast notes are not too dominant. Brace yourself for the bittersweet aftertaste.

FIFTY-FIFTY BLEND Some clients reported an increase in consumption after the introduction of this 50 percent decaf blend.

VIENNESE BLEND This blend combines a spicy and sweet flavor with a lingering aftertaste. The darker roasted Guatemala component creates the spice.

EXOTIC BLEND What can be more exotic than marrying two African coffees, one fully washed and one sun-dried natural? Look for the invigorating floral aroma with sweet, fruity flavor notes. If the fruit is over the top, then I recommend reducing the Ethiopia sun-dried component.

LIGHT ROAST BLEND Now we put your roasting skills to the test! Make sure that all coffees are roasted in a timeframe of 12 to 15 minutes.

The Art of the Blend

Channeling Inspiration Into the Cup

by Kathi Zollman

• FROM THE MARCH/APRIL 2011 ISSUE OF *ROAST* •

Some coffee blends greet us in the morning: *Sunrise Blend*

Or cleverly tell us where the coffee is from: *Two Continent Blend*

While others can create a state of mind: *Blue Jazz Java House Band*

There are regional coffee blends that, with their names alone, can take us home: *Back Porch Blend*

And some reach out to remind us of our roots: *Creole Coffee & Chicory*

Still other blend names act as a souvenir of last summer's vacation: *Glacier Centennial*

C offee drinkers wake up each morning to a fresh-brewed breakfast blend of choice. The smell is sweet and familiar and, most importantly at this early hour, the breakfast blend tastes perfect. Morning is not right without it. The fact that a skilled roaster toiled over the blend to create a perfect wake-me-up cup is usually overlooked. For those faithful coffee drinkers, there is no replacement for a favorite morning blend.

Blending is respected as an art form among coffee professionals. The process not only requires skills in cupping and flavor analysis, but also an understanding of the roasting process.

Although blended coffees make up a large portion of the specialty industry, many roasters build businesses by initially offering fresh-roasted single-origin coffees, bringing new origins and exotic coffees to the fledgling coffee consumer. But as these same coffee markets mature, blends have become a mainstay for building customer loyalty. Branding through blends is a consistently winning formula for coffee roasting companies of all sizes. Coffee blends often reflect regional variations—think about the dark blends of the West Coast, mild Midwestern blends, blends for iced coffees in the warm Southeast, and coffee and chicory of the Mississippi Delta. Blends such as these play an extremely important role in the successes of today's roasters.

Defining A Blend

In the world of specialty coffee, the definition of a blend varies for each roaster, but most agree that blending brings limitless possibilities to the roastery. Blending inspires roasters to explore new or unique flavor profiles that can be achieved only when two or more coffees are brought together. When done well, blends provide consistency with reliable flavor and quality in the cup. They are often more complex, creating more dimension and appeal than a single-origin coffee.

Roasters advise that quality green coffee and solid roasting practices are requisites for high-quality results. When a roaster creates a proprietary "house blend," it should represent an implied assurance of quality in the cup, not an assumption of low-quality blender coffee. Blends are an opportunity to showcase outstanding flavors and roasting skill by bringing coffees together for a distinct coffee experience. In addition, they create a sense of balance that may not be possible in a single-origin coffee, and blending can smooth an extreme characteristic or add dimension to round out a cup. From a business standpoint, blending can be used to achieve specific price points and maintain a desired level of profitability.

The definition of a blend may be broad or inclusive—even brewed coffees mixed together on the cupping table can be called a blend. However, simply defined, blending means skillfully bringing together coffees from different growing regions. These coffees come from either a single origin or multiple origins. A single coffee roasted to various profiles also fits the definition of blend. Great coffees are combined to create a flavor experience that is better than the independent parts. A well-constructed blend is created so adeptly that the individual components are not easily identified, but rather the cup is evaluated and enjoyed as a whole.

Several other variations on this theme come into play when defining a blend:

1 Green coffees mixed together at origin to fulfill a specific coffee flavor profile are considered a blend. This green single-origin blend—mostly from a single farm—is often referred to as a homogenous blend. Homogenous blends also result when working with small-scale farm co-ops, where green coffees from multiple farms within a geographic area are brought together as one. Another consideration: the homogenous blends created in large volume for commercial roasters.

2 Green coffees proportionately mixed together prior to roasting are considered a pre-roast blend. This is a common practice for roasters producing large quantities of a specific blend; the roasters using this method appreciate the efficiency of the technique.

3 Crafting a blend made up of roasted components is a widely used technique called post-roast blending. Purists will argue that this is the superior methodology for creating great blends, as each component is roasted perfectly and then mixed together. As with most topics in specialty coffee, there is no right or wrong answer, leaving plenty of room for lively debate.

Who Blends?

In an informal and unscientific survey of roasters around the United States, 94 percent of respondents affirmed that blends share space on their coffee menus. Microroasters and midsize regional roasters consider blends an integral part of their success. Many stated that blends have been a part of their coffee roasting business from the start, building customer loyalty with targeted brand awareness. One of these companies has celebrated 30 years in the roasting business and applauds its blend programs as an invaluable part of the company's success story.

The importance of including blend offerings also holds true with roasters who feature high-end single-origin and exclusive direct-trade coffees. It appears that these roasters have found a balance in their roasting business to feature the exquisite single-origin coffees alongside proprietary blends, finding a market and success in both revenue streams. For other roasters, blends become part of the product mix as their businesses grow, especially when creating new wholesale markets. Overall, these roasters attribute 10 percent to as much as 100 percent of their annual sales volume to sales of blended coffees. These findings support the idea that blends are an integral part of a diversified coffee menu, resulting in a wider appeal to a varied customer base.

The geographic location of these coffee companies seems to have little effect on the importance of blends for these roasters. Although blend names and styles vary from East to West, overall the blends are important to the customers wherever they drink their coffee.

BLEND STYLES

BRINGING COFFEES TOGETHER successfully comes with practice and experience. Outstanding blends are the result of careful planning and skillfully executing that plan from start to finish. And, as admitted by several roasters, skill is often combined with pure luck. The details of these great blends are considered trade secrets and are carefully guarded; don't expect a roaster to reveal the specifics of a blend. Many roasters learned their skills from a roastmaster who offered hands-on training in the art of blending. Those roasters then took the art and made it their own. While the precise details aren't shared, here are some generalities worth noting:

Harmonious blends

Harmonious blends result from selecting coffees that have common types of flavor. Think of vanilla ice cream and caramel sauce, similar flavors that combine harmoniously to create a luscious flavor. Roasters can look for coffees that have similar flavor to create a wonderful signature blend. Keep in mind the proportion of each component. After all, a bowl full of vanilla ice cream with just a dribble of caramel sauce is a different experience than a bowl full of caramel sauce with a dollop of ice cream. Roasters must successfully find the balance of the parts to produce the best flavor in the cup. Look for coffees with similar primary flavors. To achieve harmony, experiment with origins like Peru and Colombia at different degrees of roast. Or, consider coffees with similar attributes—body, for example. A heavy-bodied natural Brazil with a rich Sumatra can produce harmonious results. Look at the limitless possibilities to create overall harmony and balance in the cup.

Tension-creating blends

Tension-creating blends result when dissimilar components are mixed together. Think opposing flavors on the palate: sweet and sour, tart and buttery. Visualize a tall glass of lemonade, sour and refreshing. Take that same glass and add a few sweet strawberries to the lemonade; the bright citrus edge becomes softer with the addition of the extra sweetness, resulting in a more winey flavor than the original brew. The same is true when a fresh lemon is squeezed over a bowl of strawberries. The berries become even sweeter with a pop of tartness, resulting in another layer of dimension to the overall flavor.

To build tension-creating blends, look for contrast—for example, a super-clean Yirgacheffe is turned winey with a hint of blueberry Harrar. Consider uncommon flavor combinations for the ultimate tension-creating blends. These types of blends require more patience and an intuitive skill about flavor. Experiment with high-acid coffees paired with those that have a heavy, dense body. What happens when you add a bit of a bright Costa Rica to a rich Java? It's especially important to avoid common pairings. Once this blending skill is mastered, roasters will discover that the tension is actually a form of balance.

Why Blend?

Though roasters have different reasons for offering blended coffees, most rationales can be boiled down into three distinct categories:

 Use blends as a marketing tool to distinguish your business from the competition.

A well-prepared blend will separate a roaster from the competition, making these secret-recipe mixes a useful marketing tool for roasters of any size. Roasters have the opportunity to be the sole outlet for a specific blend or make it available through larger distribution streams; either way, the result can be profitable. "The proprietary nature of blends allows you to keep customers coming back because they can only get them from you," says Kevin Conard, the owner of Cardona Coffee Brands of Topeka, Kansas.

Other roasters find success in creating custom blends, complete with a unique flavor and name, designed for a specific wholesale customer, or by creating a private-label program. Blends are an opportunity for roasters to develop their own brands that ultimately build customer loyalty. Branded coffees also contribute to an element of mystique by presenting a great coffee product with a unique name—all created for a specific coffee consumer.

In some cases, the name of the blend is so well received that the coffee sells by the name alone, without consideration of what the blend is made of. These names might include the roaster's name (such as Bob's Best Blend from Coffee Roasters of New Orleans) or a regional landmark (Glacier Centennial by Montana Coffee Traders), creating a perception of quality and familiarity by branding alone.

 Craft a coffee that's better than each individual component.

Another important reason to blend coffees is to create a style or flavor that comes about only when uniting two or more coffees. It is human nature to combine different elements just to reveal the result. "Taking real specialty coffees and blending can create some great stuff," says Jeremy Raths, roastmaster at The Roastery in Minneapolis. "And the process is fun," he adds.

With their blending experiments, roasters aim to create a consistent, balanced cup with roundness, depth and complexity. Roasters rely on this consistency to build loyalty and repeat sales. It's important that specialty coffee customers are rewarded with the same flavor every time they make a repeat purchase of a blend, so there is no mystery as to what the coffee will taste like.

A coffee with extreme sweetness but little brightness can be sparked by blending with a more acidy coffee. A thin but tasty coffee can be given more dimension by mixing it with a more

BLEND IDEAS

CREATING A BLEND can be both time-consuming and expensive for beginners. To help roasters move into the blending fast lane, here are some ideas for a classic drip blend and an espresso blend. Both are actual blends designed and implemented successfully. Beginners can use these as suggested or draw on them as a starting point to make the blend their own. Roast all components separately; blend thoroughly.

DESSERT BLEND

Complementary to desserts and pastries, this is an elegant coffee by itself or when paired with baked goods.

Combine:

50 percent medium-dark-roast Guatemala Antigua

25 percent medium-roast Costa Rica Tarrazu

25 percent dark-roast Colombia Supremo or Excelso

KATHI Z. SIGNATURE ESPRESSO

This espresso is best when poured as a double ristretto.

Combine:

40 percent medium-dark (to second crack) Sumatra

20 percent dark-roast natural Brazil

25 percent full-city-roast Guatemala Antigua

15 percent dark-roast Colombia

---

rounded coffee. Think of creating a complete flavor dynamic that rewards the senses—taste, aroma and mouthfeel. Milk chocolate is wonderful by itself, and many enjoy peanut butter, but when combined, the taste treat becomes something very different from the components. The same process can be used in designing a blend. And discovery at the cupping table, tasting new and different flavor creations, is a great joy.

Not every blend design is a success story; there are pitfalls as the student becomes a master, learning both the art and science of creating a blend. Practice and a carefully constructed plan help determine which coffees are selected for specific attributes. But even then, there are times when great-tasting coffees don't blend well and the results are a disappointment at the cupping table.

③ Protect the company's bottom line.

"Ultimately, there has to be a business purpose for blending," says Joe Moffatt, the roaster and owner of Tupelo, Mississippi-based Joe Joe's Coffee & Tea. Pricing is increasingly important to those who rely on blends as a part of their profitability picture. Roasters are able to take advantage of less expensive, quality coffees to attain a higher margin.

Roasters use blends to expand their offerings, which may result in increased sales and profits through a larger reach. Quality blends allow roasters to enter new markets that might not have been otherwise available, ultimately increasing the overall sales volume of the business. In other markets, blends have been added to meet a competitive need or price point, and roasting businesses may be enjoying increased bean sales and profits as a result of an expanded blend portfolio.

Other roasters suggest that blends have allowed them to expand their customer base by providing more varieties and styles of coffee that appeal to more people, resulting directly in

additional income. Blends also allow roasters to maintain price stability for customers by selecting coffees within a range of price acceptability. For many roasters, blends are a profit center and contribute to the financial success of the roastery.

How Do You Blend?

Before starting the blending process, take a few minutes to review the coffees on hand. Knowing and understanding the available coffees is imperative. Mistakes and experiments can be expensive, and being well prepared helps control some of the new product development costs incurred when designing a blend.

Learn about each of the coffees. How do they perform at different roast levels? Which coffees are sweet and which are bright? Which coffees in the inventory have body? Roasters may want to create a catalog of coffees noting the outstanding cup characteristics of each coffee. This information serves as a valuable reference tool when designing a blend.

Every roaster has a unique methodology when it comes to creating a blend. The roaster uses the specific purpose of the new blend as the road map. And, although roasters do not openly share their exact processes, there are a few generalizations we can take away: First, identify the purpose of the blend. Next, plan and build the blend. And lastly, evaluate the results.

① Identify the purpose of the new blend.

What is the aim of this blend—is it a new customer-specific blend? Should it pair well with desserts, create a new flavor for a new-arrival coffee, or help with cost control? The list of possibilities is lengthy, but results are more easily evaluated if the overall objective of the blend is identified before the roaster invests time and product in the process. Be prepared to name the new blend. The name is as important as the other components and will directly drive the success of the blend.

② Develop a plan of action.

Review the coffees available for the blend and consider the degree of roast for each. Will the coffees be blended prior to roasting or afterward? Although most roasters prefer to blend post-roast, there are others who argue that blending green coffee prior to roasting contributes to efficiency when working with voluminous amounts of coffee. Even some of the staunchest supporters of the post-roast blend philosophy acknowledge that excellent-tasting results can also be achieved with pre-blending, and some roasters use a combination of the two methods successfully. Roasters should also consider continuity of the blend when creating the action plan. Are the coffees selected readily available? Is the price consistent? Are there coffees that can be substituted if necessary? All are important considerations when penciling out a new blend.

 Build the blend.

Once all of the research has been completed and the components are in place, it's time to create the blend. For research purposes, take notes on each step of the process, including profile notes and the ratios of the coffees. It is frustrating to create an outstanding blend and be unable to duplicate the results because it was created free form. Don't leave success to chance; track the blend development from start to finish. It is also imperative that the blend meets cost goals; it's upsetting to build a dynamic blend only to discover that it is too costly to produce effectively.

 Evaluate the cup.

Comment on the cup attributes of the blend; look for a balanced cup and overall pleasantness. Compare the results to the original goals of the blend. Does the blend meet the criteria set forth? List the positive attributes as well as any negative evaluations that need to be corrected. Note the changes that need to be made and repeat the process to fine-tune the blend.

As an art form, well-designed coffee blends enjoy success as a creative outlet and a business tool for the roaster. In the coffee world, a blend is a staple to coffee customers. The skill and dedication to creating the perfectly balanced cup might be overlooked but not ignored by customers. Blends are appreciated in the form of customer loyalty, a common thread among the dozens of roasters willing to discuss their blend philosophy.

Customers rely on the consistency and quality of an outstanding blend, and roasters are rewarded for their efforts with an extended customer base and increased sales. There is room for both blends and single-origin coffees in today's specialty market. And, like all skilled artists, roasters keep their blend secrets carefully under wraps. ■

KATHI ZOLLMAN, *assistant director of specialty green coffee sales at Coffee Holding Company, is a frequent presenter at a variety of roaster education venues. She has shared coffee roasting skills at Roasters Guild events, the SCA Expo, Coffee Fest and multiple regional roaster gatherings. Providing quality training and skill building at a local level has been a focus for several years as Zollman has been involved in the grassroots regional movement. Specializing in blending, sensory skill building, profile roasting and profile manipulation, she continues to be a student of all things coffee. Reach her via email at kzollman@coffeeholding.com.*

Make Your Mark

Creating a successful Signature Blend

BY SHANNA GERMAIN
AND SCOTT MERLE

Make Your Mark

Creating a Successful Signature Blend

by Shanna Germain and Scott Merle

• FROM THE JANUARY/FEBRUARY 2007 ISSUE OF *ROAST* •

IT'S CALLED MANY THINGS by many people. House blend. Signature blend. Roastmaster's blend. It's known by names like Black Cat and Hair Bender and Dancing Goats. But whatever you call it, the meaning is the same: It's that one special blend that gives your roastery an identity above all others. It's the one that customers ask for, by name or by flavor, and it is your chance to show your company's coffee prowess.

Creating and marketing a successful and enduring signature blend is a complicated, but necessary, part of any roasting business. Unlike other blends, which may come and go over the years or which may only appeal to certain customers, a signature blend must not only be high-quality, repeatable and consistent through the years, it must also be accessible to a wide number of your customers. Ideally, your blend will also have marketability, something that sets it apart and makes your customers take notice, take a sip and then take out their wallets, time and time again.

How Now, Signature Blend?

What makes a signature blend, and how a signature blend comes into being, varies almost as much as what it's called. Some roasteries set out to design their signature blend from the get-go. Others start with several blends, and then make the most popular into their signature blend.

"Our house blend is about 13 or 14 years old," says David Rier, former roastmaster for Thomas Hammer Coffee Roasters. "It was created by the owner, Thomas, who picked out his favorite coffees and blended them together to make what he thought of as his favorite blend."

Over time, that blend became the company's signature espresso blend—the taste profile of which has stayed the same since its inception—and now it is the coffee that is sold as espresso in the company's 12 retail stores, as well as to its wholesale customers.

For those who are planning to create a signature blend, it helps to have your end goal in mind before you start, suggests Richard Serpe, master roaster for Coffee Roasters of Las Vegas. "The first thing to do is to honestly understand what you're trying to do and what you want to accomplish," he says. "Once you have that down, you try to make something that's compatible. I always make a blend in my mind first and I know the tastes of the individual coffees, so it helps me start, because I can imagine what they'll taste like when we blend them together."

For Andy Newbom, former chief espresso officer for Barefoot Coffee Roasters, Inc., a signature blend is also something to plan and craft with the utmost care. "I think a roaster should develop any blend carefully, but in particular a signature blend, because it gives the roaster something to hang their hat on," he says. "We wanted our signature blend to reflect the quintessential Barefoot experience."

Newbom suggests that roasters begin by deciding what they want their blend to taste like, what they want it to represent and how they want it to be served. "You can't design a blend in a vacuum," he says. "Make sure that you know how it's going to be prepared, whether it's drip or espresso. All of those things make a difference."

For the company's signature blend, called Element 114 (after an unnamed element on the periodic table), Newbom had a desired flavor profile in mind. After about a month of roasting single-origin coffees and pulling shots, he started blending them. It took months before he had the five-bean, four-roast-level blend he wanted.

It wasn't just flavor that Newbom was looking for when creating the company's signature blend. He was also trying to create a blend that would give the best cup for Barefoot's customers. "We created a blend that is very forgiving and not as easy to screw up, so it's easier to hit for most users." Not only does the blend have few sour notes and a broad temperature range, it also has a wide range of shot times. "It has a five- to seven-second window," Newbom says. "Overall, it's easier to be more consistent with."

A Blend by Any Other Name

To make this article easier to read, we picked the term "signature blend" to describe the type of "branding blend" that we're talking about. But does it really matter what you call it?

"I think it's important to brand it and give it a name," says Tommy Thwaites, president of Coda Coffee Company. "A lot of roasters just call it a house blend, but from the consumers' standpoint, it's really easy for them to switch from one house blend to another without even realizing the difference. Branding it with a name locks them in."

Thwaites' signature blend is called Harmony, a name that's in line with Coda's music theme and, he hopes, a memorable name for a coffee. "Coda is an Italian word that means final movement in music, and we're the final movement to a meal for our customers," he says. "And we figured that Harmony said everything we wanted to say about a blend."

Ron Vaccarello, owner of Crescent Moon Coffee Roasters, felt it was important to give his company's blend a name that would not only be memorable, but useful to customers as well. Thus, the creation of Morning Blend. "It was a blend that was designed specifically for the purpose of drinking it in the morning," he says.

Photo by Dani Goot

In fact, Vaccarello takes the name so seriously that he won't allow Morning Blend to be served at any other time. "We don't serve it after 11 o'clock," he says. "We just refuse to. It's a good opportunity to introduce customers to other coffees anyway."

Of course, he admits, "we've got customers who sell it wholesale, and I can't put a gun to their heads and say, 'you can't serve it after morning,' but we do explain to them that it's really designed to be savored in the early part of the day."

However you use it, the language of coffee is important. As the awareness of customers continues to grow, so will their understanding of the language surrounding words like signature and even blend. "Language has a ton of pre-conceptions mixed into it, so we never use the word blend," says Newbom. "We usually call them mixes, because we put our coffees together after we roast them, so to us it's really more of a mix than a blend."

In for the Long Haul

The most successful signature blends are those that are maintained consistently over a number of years despite changes in coffee availability, cup profile and price. Customers perceive your blend in a very specific way, with a very specific taste profile, and it must hit it perfectly every time. Because your customers have come to expect something particular from your signature coffee, everything points to making things predictable and repeatable with a signature blend—you can't afford for your signature to be inconsistent.

With this in mind, it makes sense to begin with core components that you can buy fresh, or at least receive fresh deliveries of throughout the year. If this isn't an option, you should consider ahead of time which coffees, if any, can be substituted at different times of the year in order to keep your blend at its freshest.

Vaccarello describes an issue common to many roasters. "We choose our single-origin coffees first," he says. "And then from those coffees that we feel are up to our level for single origins, we create our blend." If a single-origin coffee isn't as good as it was last year, then they have to find another coffee that will sell not only as a single-origin, but that will also replace the missing blend component. "We try to design the blends so you can possibly switch out the coffees and still have a consistent and high-quality profile."

And it isn't just that coffee quality, cost and taste profiles change from year to year. There is always the chance that what you bought last year is no longer available. "Price has never been an issue for us," says Rier. "Availability might be though. Hopefully, you always have enough coffee booked forward from this point on. Even if you don't have it for anything else, you should have it for your house blend."

One resource that's often overlooked in the consistency chain is brokers. If a specific coffee that you use is not available or is not up to par, they may have suggestions for a temporary option. They can also help you work toward long-term relationships with growers, which will aid you in future supply and price security.

"If you have a good relationship with your exporter, he knows what you want," Rier says. "A lot of times, our exporter will say, 'I'm going to send you three or four others that might fit better with what you want to do.'"

While consistency and repeatability are key components to the longevity of your successful signature blend, it is also important to allow your blends to develop into maturity over the years. Small things contribute to important refinements, such as upgrading your green beans or advancing your roasting techniques. Success can be found in the balance you achieve between consistency and continual improvement.

"Of course, you want to be consistent, but no one is 100 percent consistent, so we let things evolve," says Thwaites. "We make very subtle changes over the years, because we might be able to do it better. Don't be afraid to change and let things evolve, because you're always learning."

Staying at the Top

After having a signature blend for one, two or even 20 years, how can you be sure that it's still not only consistent after all this time, but that it's the quality you want it to be? After all, this is the coffee that your company will be known for, the one against which all others will be compared.

Cupping seems like the obvious answer. And it's definitely part of the equation. But cupping alone isn't enough—it's just as important to make sure you're tasting your blend as you expect it to be served. "We cup our coffee all the time, but we also pull shots with it," says Rier. "A blend might be great in a cupping or as a drip, but if it's an espresso blend, you want to be tasting it in that application, just as your customers will be."

Relying on your customers' feedback is another great way to make sure your blend is staying at the top of the game. And don't just wait for them to come to you when something goes wrong—solicit feedback during deliveries, trainings and via email. If possible, try to get feedback from the coffee industry as well, from trainings, barista competitions or private consultations.

And don't overlook your company, suggests Rier. "We rely on our stores, and on our employees, as well as our customers to make sure that the flavor is where it should be," he says.

Last, but not least, taste your competitors' coffees to remind yourself what makes your own blend unique and appealing to your customers.

Whether you decide to call this coffee your house blend, your signature blend, your special mix or some other wonderfully creative name that you've come up with, it's important to remember that this is the blend that will define your company, not just for today but for years to come. So choose the best coffees you can,

Other Questions to Consider When Creating Your Signature Blend

- How important is it that your signature blend remains in a specific price target for your customers?

- How large a role does price play when purchasing components for your signature blend?

- Is there a point when you would consider trademarking the name?

Photo by Dani Goot

- Will you roast the beans individually and then blend, or will you roast the coffees already blended?

- Do the name and symbol that you've chosen for your signature blend lend themselves to secondary products, such as mugs or t-shirts? Or is there a story you can tell about your blend that will help customers remember to choose it when the time comes?

- Do you have restrictions on how customers, especially wholesalers, may use your blend? Are you willing to private label your signature blend and let someone else sell it under their name?

- Do you want to be able to offer a decaf version of your house blend? This may limit your choices of available coffees and flavors, but will garner you the favor of caffeine-free customers.

roast and blend them to your version of perfection, and repeat the process day after day after day. No one said it would be easy to make your mark with a successful house blend—but once you've mastered it, your customers are sure to love you for it. ■

SCOTT MERLE *has worked in specialty coffee since 1988 and has experience in every aspect of the value chain, from barista to roastmaster. He has extensive knowledge of green coffee sourcing, purchasing, roasting and blend development, and is proficient in various types of coffee evaluation. Merle has dedicated his career to furthering coffee quality throughout the value chain, and has emphasized and exemplified fair pricing practices to hard-working producers every step of the way.*

Blending for Italian Espresso

Parts 1 & 2

by Dr. Joseph John | *Photos by James Hoffmann*

• FROM THE JANUARY/FEBRUARY AND MARCH/APRIL 2008 ISSUES OF *ROAST* •

Part 1 | A Background and Rationale for Blending

EACH COFFEE-PRODUCING country cultivates a product that is somewhat different from that of another origin. Some display high acidity, some have high body, others are very aromatic, and still others taste of fruits, spices, chocolate and even tobacco. In each case, the coffee exhibits a flavor profile in the cup that is characteristic of its origin—the place where the coffee is grown.

Blending coffee is both an art and a science. In its noblest form, blending attempts to create a cup that does not exist in nature, by mixing two or more coffees in various proportions. When expertly done, the resulting blend displays a flavor profile that is distinctly different from those of any of the component coffees—often superior, sometimes more complete and, at other times, better balanced.

Blending for brewed coffee is relatively simple and straightforward, because brewed coffee can accommodate a wide array of physical and flavor properties. Although every such combination of two or more coffees in a wide range of relative proportions can constitute a technically acceptable blend for brewed coffee, not every one of those blends can become a commercial success, because of taste preferences. However, espresso in general, and Italian espresso in particular, is defined much more narrowly in terms of what physical and flavor characteristics it can exhibit. As a result, blending for espresso is quite different from blending for brewed coffee, because the two beverages are vastly different.

Espresso blends are not created by taking brewed coffee blends and roasting them darker and more oily; such dark roasting does not magically make it an espresso blend. However, before discussing blending for espresso, the important distinctions between ordinary brewed coffee and real espresso must be appreciated. Although this article covers the subject of blending for espresso, it is not intended to provide specific recipes for espresso blends; rather it is to elaborate on one blending philosophy and to develop a practical approach to blending for an Italian espresso.

Due to its length and the complexity of its content, this article is split into two parts. The first part develops the background information leading to the specific requirements of an espresso blend. The second part will elaborate on an approach to blending for Italian espresso.

Ordinary Coffee and How It Is Made

Ordinary brewed coffee is prepared by bringing hot water into physical contact with ground coffee at room pressure. In this process, some portion of the ground coffee, roughly 20 percent by weight, dissolves in the hot water. This is primarily a physical process. Most of the chemical reactions occur after the coffee is brewed and allowed to linger, often resulting in deterioration of its fresh brewed flavors.

There are many different ways of making coffee, but they all follow the same basic principle of bringing hot water and ground coffee into physical contact with each other. Some use steam and others use a hand piston to push water through the ground coffee, while most common techniques simply call for pouring the hot water on top of the ground coffee or dumping the ground coffee into a vessel containing the hot water. It takes about 7 grams of ground coffee to make a 6-ounce cup of coffee. Different methods of making coffee take varying amounts of time; and the contact time, during which ground coffee is in physical contact with hot water, determines the fineness to which coffee is ground. Longer contact times call for coarser grind, in order to control extraction.

Because the preparation is carried out at ordinary pressures, the water-soluble components of ground coffee are primarily extracted and account for the taste and color of the brew. The process extracts some of the water-insoluble compounds that account for the body. Much of the aroma molecules released by the ground coffee during the extraction process simply escape into the room and are lost. Only a minute fraction of this aroma stays dissolved in the liquid coffee.

The sweet, flavorful and desirable components of ground coffee are extremely soluble in water and most of them are easily extracted in a short time or by little water flowing through the ground coffee. Longer contact time, or more water flowing through the ground coffee, results in dissolving more of the undesirable components such as acids, bitters and caffeine.

Real Espresso should ooze out of the porta filter like thick, warm, honey.

What Exactly Is Espresso?

Espresso can only be made using a machine that not only heats the water and pre-measures the water volume, but also delivers the hot water under high pressure, ranging from 100 to 140 pounds per square inch. This high water pressure causes the oils in ground coffee to be extracted, formed into microscopic droplets and suspended in liquid coffee concentrate. It is this emulsification of oils that distinguishes espresso from strong coffee.

As in the case of brewed coffee, it takes about 7 grams of ground coffee to make a 1-ounce, single shot of espresso. In this process, the water-soluble components of ground coffee, roughly the same 20 percent by weight, go into solution, just as in the case of brewed coffee. But this is dissolved in only 1 ounce of water, making the espresso six times as strong as brewed coffee. The process described so far will result in producing only strong coffee, even if an espresso machine is used, unless steps are taken to ensure that oils in the ground coffee are also emulsified.

If the coffee is not ground fine enough, the pressurized water will rush through the ground coffee in less than 15 seconds extracting only the solubles and making strong, ordinary coffee. But when the coffee is ground very fine and packed very tight in the porta-filter so as to impede the flow of water, water molecules will be forced into the interior of the ground coffee particles and made to drive out the oils, with the water losing most of its energy in the process. The resulting espresso will simply ooze out of the

Cooling in the tray.

Some Statistical Considerations

WHEN AN ESPRESSO BLEND consists of two or more coffees, the exact proportion of each bean in a dose will vary from shot to shot. The extent to which these proportions vary, from dose to dose, depends on the dose size and the relative proportion of a particular bean in that blend.

It takes about 56 beans to make up 7 grams of coffee, often used to make a single shot of espresso. Thus, in making espresso, one is conducting a random sampling experiment, selecting 56 beans at random when making a single shot, or randomly selecting 112 beans to make a double. The question then becomes, if one selects 56 beans at random out of a hopper containing this blend, what is the chance that you get the correct number of each bean in that sample? Intuitively, one can see that the odds improve as the sample size expands (e.g., it takes 112 beans to make a double shot and it gets even better if the sample size is the 168 beans required for a triple.).

The same is true if the blend contains a large proportion of a particular bean, certainly when compared to the behavior of a coffee that is present in a much smaller proportion in the blend.

The table below illustrates this effect for three different doses, nominally a single shot, a double and a triple. The five rows represent the proportion of a coffee in the blend (10 percent, 20 percent, etc.). For example, if the blend has 20 percent of a particular coffee, refer to the second row of this table. If it happens to be 25 percent, one has to interpolate between the results in the second and third rows. These calculations are made and rounded to the nearest whole bean.

The columns show a measure of the "error rate" in the relative proportions of the beans when a single, double or triple shot is made. They are calculated as a set of probabilities that a particular coffee is within +/- x percent of the nominal proportion, where "x" is the heading on top of each column. For example, reading down the +/- 20 percent column, the numbers indicate the probability that the particular sample chosen has a specific coffee within +/- 20 percent of its nominal proportion.

Suppose a blend uses 40 percent of a Sumatran coffee. For a double shot, using 14 grams of coffee, the probability of that Sumatran coffee being present within +/- 10 percent of its nominal composition (between 36 and 44 percent in this case) is contained in the fourth row. Focus on the middle portion of this table, devoted to 14 grams, and look down the first column covering +/- 10 percent and read off the fourth row pertaining to 40 percent blend component, resulting in the reading of 66 percent. In other words, in selecting 112 beans at random, the Sumatran bean will be present between 36 and 44 percent concentration about 66 percent of the time. In the remaining 34 percent of the time, the concentration will be outside these limits.

If the same blend had another coffee, say a Costa Rican, at a nominal proportion of 10 percent, and we require that bean to be present within +/- 10 percent of its nominal composition (between 9 and 11 percent, in that case), in making the same double shot, we find that probability to be 39 percent. It means that in the 112-bean sample, that Costa Rican coffee will be present at concentrations between 9 and 11 percent only 39 percent of the time. In the remaining 61 percent of the time, its concentration will be outside those bounds. ■

Table 1. Shot to Shot Variation of Coffees in a Blend for Different Doses

Blend Component %	Dose = 7 grams Spread			Dose = 14 grams Spread			Dose = 21 grams Spread		
	+/- 10%	+/- 20%	+/- 40%	+/- 10%	+/- 20%	+/- 40%	+/- 10%	+/- 20%	+/- 40%
10	36	52	72	39	61	80	42	68	94
20	41	64	90	48	76	97	54	84	99
30	47	74	95	57	86	100	65	92	100
40	54	82	99	66	93	100	74	97	100
50	62	89	100	75	97	100	83	99	100

Tables courtesy of Jim Schulman of the University of Chicago.

porta-filter like warm honey without having enough energy to gush out.

These oils completely change all the physical and flavor characteristics of this coffee beverage. Its mouth feel, density, viscosity, wetting power and foam-forming ability are all different from those of strong coffee.

An example of excellent crema.

Initial pour must have the correct reddish-brown tinge.

Significance of Crema

The emulsified oils also change the flavor properties of the beverage. For example, these oils coat the taste buds and inhibit their ability to detect bitterness. This reduced bitterness will be interpreted as enhanced sweetness. Thus, if brewed coffee and espresso are made from exactly the same blend, the resulting espresso will actually taste sweeter.

Much of the enjoyment of consuming coffee comes from its flavor, consisting of taste and aroma, with a majority of the flavor sensation actually being derived from the aroma, as detected by the nose. While much of the aroma molecules escape into the room when brewed coffee is prepared, espresso preparation has a built-in mechanism to capture the aroma and keep it in the cup—the all important crema.

The emulsified oils responsible for the crema, which is a collection of tiny bubbles with a film of oil on the outside and the coffee's aroma inside, provide this mechanism to hold the aroma of fresh ground coffee in the cup. These aroma molecules, later released when the bubbles burst in the back of one's mouth, find their way to the nose through the pharynx that connects the mouth to the nasal cavity. These tiny bubbles also attach themselves to the taste buds and burst, from time to time, to release the volatile compounds long after the espresso is gone, accounting for the long aftertaste, a distinguishing feature of espresso quality. Crema, therefore, is the single most important indicator of a well-made espresso.

A Few Words About Acidity

Because espresso is six times stronger than brewed coffee, all characteristics of the coffees are exaggerated in an espresso. This is particularly true of its acidity. As the concentration of the beverage increases linearly, the acidity perceived by the tongue seems to increase much faster. As a result, high acidity, considered by many to be a virtue in brewed coffee, is not a desirable feature in a quality espresso.

This acidity has a major impact on the selection of component coffees for an espresso blend. Much of the coffees available in the United States and Canada are grown in Central and South America, many of which exhibit high acidity in the cup. Many brewed coffee blends offered in North America showcase these Central and South American coffees both for their flavors and their acidity. Because espresso does not tolerate anywhere near the acidity desired in brewed coffees, the role of these high-acid coffees in espresso blends has to be curtailed.

Single-Origin Espresso

There are some, particularly in North America, who consider espresso as just another way of making coffee. In that context, using a single-origin coffee to make espresso may be a rewarding experience. The espresso process magnifies all the good (and the bad) characteristics of that coffee, and when their good features far outweigh the negatives, this may be a way to enjoy one's favorite coffee. The single-origin espresso is favored by the home connoisseur as a way to add variety to their everyday espresso routine.

However, in a commercial environment, the single-origin espresso is best used as a "guest espresso," in addition to the house espresso staple. An additional grinder for the guest espresso is a must. This situation may change as the general quality of espresso in North America improves and the consuming public gets more conversant with espresso to the point that more than 5 percent of espresso beverages are consumed as "straight."

In a cafe or espresso bar, customers are looking for the espressos and espresso-based milk drinks to taste exactly the way they tasted the last time. In such commercial environments, the cafe is in the business of fulfilling peoples' expectations. In that situation, espresso blend stability as well as shot-to-shot consistency is of paramount importance. In that context, it is inconceivable that one single-origin espresso can fulfill that consistency objective if that is the only espresso offered in a cafe.

Roast Before Blending vs. Blend Before Roasting

As to whether it is better to roast the individual coffees separately before blending or to blend the coffees in the green and roast them all together depends on the properties of the coffees used in the blend. Both procedures are completely acceptable.

Post-roast blending, where the individual coffees are roasted separately and blended afterward, affords the luxury of being able to roast each coffee to a different degree to bring out the best flavors in that particular bean. It also offers coffee retailers who do not roast their own coffees the ability to create proprietary espresso blends out of the individual roasted coffees they get from one or more wholesale roasters.

However, this post-roast blending procedure has disadvantages, the most obvious being the need to do several batches of roasting in order to produce a blend. Also, most roasting machines have practical minima for the quantity of coffee that can be roasted in them, and it is inevitable that one has to roast more coffee than is required for a particular blending session. If one's commitment to freshness prohibits holding coffee from today's roasts for tomorrow's blending, it can lead to considerable waste of the leftover component coffees.

Blending the green beans before roasting is conceptually ideal in overcoming some of the disadvantages of the post-roast blending. Pre-roast blending is possible when the coffee beans are compatible with respect to their roast characteristics. When the beans are dissimilar in bean size, density, moisture content,

Everything coming out of the portafilter should be crema.

heat conductivity and roast development profile, blending before roasting is difficult, and in many cases, impossible.

Such is the case with the blend I have the most experience with: Malabar Gold, Josuma's premium European espresso. The coffees used in this blend cannot be more dissimilar. The Monsooned Malabar-AA Super Grade is extra large, having grown to twice the original size during the monsooning process. It is also extremely low in density. The premium washed robusta Kaapi Royale, on the other hand, is small and dense. Those beans just did not want to roast together and initial attempts at roasting them together produced disastrous results. It took me three years to perfect the blending procedures to enable the blend to be roasted properly. In that process, I learned a lot about the properties of those coffees and got a real education about the mechanics of roasting.

Thus Far

We have established the difference between brewed coffee and real espresso and laid the foundation to discuss how blending for espresso differs from blending for brewed coffee. In the second part we will cover a particular approach to blending for Italian espresso.

Part 2 | A Practical Approach to Blending

BLENDING FOR Italian espresso: It's a skill set that most roasters want to have at the ready, even if they're not using it every day. However, like so much else with roasting, blending for Italian espresso is extremely complex.

In Part 1 of this article, we developed some background information establishing the difference between brewed coffee and real espresso. In differentiating between brewed coffee and real espresso, we identified emulsification of oils in the ground coffee as the defining moment when coffee concentrate becomes an espresso and talked about the role of crema in capturing the

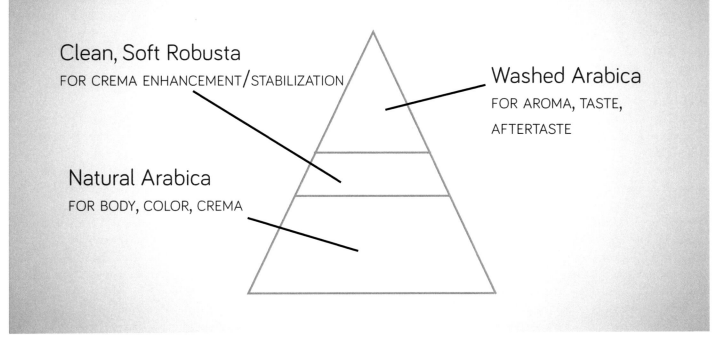

ESPRESSO BLENDING

Clean, Soft Robusta
FOR CREMA ENHANCEMENT/STABILIZATION

Natural Arabica
FOR BODY, COLOR, CREMA

Washed Arabica
FOR AROMA, TASTE,
AFTERTASTE

aroma of fresh ground coffee and holding it in the cup. We also explained the limitations in the use of high-acid coffees in a quality espresso blend.

Here, we look more closely at the specific requirements of an Italian espresso blend by further developing the concept and creating a practical approach to its creation.

A Blending Philosophy

Acidity is not the only point of departure when considering espresso blends. The experts at Istituto Nazionale Espresso Italiano, Brescia, Italy, have spent considerable effort since 1998 to establish a set of standards for producing espresso Italiano and for the sensory characteristics of the resulting product. This was triggered by their feeling that "espresso is one of the most copied products, typically with poor results." Their frustration can best be summarized in their statement, "Often the word espresso is used to evoke the Italian style and spirit and is associated to [sic] poor quality coffee blends or drinks which have nothing to share with that little cup able to offer a long lasting and superfine pleasure." Accepted descriptions of espresso, especially Italian espresso, call for low acidity; high body; ample, rich, velvety and persistent crema; reddish brown color; intense aroma and taste; and a long, pleasant aftertaste.

From these descriptions of Italian espresso, it seems clear that there is no single coffee, from any origin, that can provide all these physical and flavor characteristics in the correct balance. Thus, an acceptable espresso blend must be obtained by combining two or more coffees in the right proportions. There is a common belief that an espresso blend must comprise coffees from different origins. That is really not the case. It is more accurate to think that it takes more than one type and grade of coffee to make up a quality espresso blend. Origins such as Brazil, Indonesia and India are somewhat unique in producing different types and grades of high-quality coffee, making it possible to develop exceptional espresso blends using exclusively coffees from those respective countries. All three origins produce quality robusta and arabica that are low in acidity and high in body, as well as arabica that is flavorful to act as a highlighter in the blend.

Any blending attempt must logically start with cataloging the features of possible candidates in as detailed a fashion as practical. In the case of blending for brewed coffee, one would start with detailed "cupping notes" for each of the coffees. However, because oils have to be emulsified for it to become an espresso, and since these emulsified oils alter the physical and flavor characteristics of the beverage, conventional cupping data is of limited value for espresso blending. Instead, it is beneficial to develop corresponding data by pulling espresso shots with each candidate coffee and maintaining detailed notes regarding each of the parameters: body, color, crema (quantity, texture and persistence), acidity, aroma, taste and aftertaste.

Of these many characteristics, body, crema and color can be considered more physical in nature while others, such as acidity, aroma, taste and aftertaste can be considered attributes of flavor. If it is possible to bring the physical properties using one set of coffees, with little contribution to overall flavor, and the flavor properties can be controlled using another set of coffees that adds little to body and crema, then the blending process can be organized more simply and made more orderly. Although this is an easy principle to understand, it is much more difficult to achieve in practice. Nevertheless, one can come close with some acceptable compromises.

One side benefit of such an approach is to make it easier to balance the resulting blend. Using several coffees, all making comparable contributions to the various features used to describe the blend, results in changing many of these parameters when one component coffee is replaced or its relative proportion is altered. This makes balancing the blend a never-ending exercise, particularly if blend consistency is a high priority. Considering the physical and flavor characteristics as somewhat separable makes blend adjustment easier to manage.

Rebalancing the blend with each new coffee helps achieve consistency and quality. Not only should this occur whenever new crop coffee becomes available, but also when coffee from a different lot is added to the inventory. In addition, coffee from a given crop ages with time and changes bean characteristics, particularly acidity. In order to maintain blend consistency, it is necessary to adjust the blend, often during a crop year, to compensate for this aging effect.

Selecting a Base Coffee

A base in any espresso blend is the component that is present in the largest proportion, forming the foundation of the blend. It is best to choose the base to account for the physical properties, such

as body, color and crema; and to defer the choice of acidity, aroma, flavor and aftertaste until the base is firmly established. Thus, I find that selecting the base coffee is the first step in the espresso-blending process. This is a serious departure from conventional blending for brewed coffee where a keen eye is kept on the final aroma and taste throughout the blending process. In selecting a base coffee, it is important to screen the coffees to ensure that they do not display any unpleasant aftertaste that is very difficult to camouflage later in the process.

Color is best controlled by the degree of roast of the base coffee. To achieve the reddish brown color that is most visually appealing, in my experience, it is best to limit the roast level to full city. It also helps to keep the beans just short of oiling. Roasting the beans dark makes the resulting brew black and turns the crema dark and unattractive. And roasting them to the point of oiling causes the oils to emerge to the surface, get oxidized and cause the beans to stale quickly. It also diminishes the amount of oils retained inside the roasted beans and available to be emulsified by the pressurized water to produce the all important crema.

In choosing a base, look for coffees that are low in acidity, high in body, produce a copious amount of crema that lasts for a long time, and are relatively mute with respect to aroma and taste—or at least have aroma and taste that will not conflict with the coffees that are to be showcased in the espresso. Since natural and semi-washed coffees tend to be sweeter and to produce more crema than their washed counterparts, washed coffees are generally not prime candidates for the base of the espresso blend.

Natural and semi-washed coffees from Brazil are probably the coffees most commonly used in espresso blends, so much so that many roasters try to avoid them just to be different. Brazil is a good source of base coffees, especially when they are carefully selected for their characteristics. Indonesian coffees, particularly those from Sumatra, as well as coffees from India, provide a desirable combination of low acidity and high body. India's monsooned arabica is low in acidity, high in body, and produces a copious amount of crema, making it somewhat ideal as a candidate for the base coffee in an espresso blend. The highest grade of this class is Monsooned Malabar-AA Super Grade.

The base coffee, by definition, will be the largest component in the blend. There are no hard and fast rules that define its relative proportions. The base can be as large as 60 percent of the blend or as small as 40 percent. It is not uncommon to use two low-acid, high-body coffees together to make up the base of a blend.

Should Robusta Be Included in the Blend?

Having selected the base coffee(s), it is time to decide if a high-quality robusta would be suitable for the blend. The choice of robusta beans to be used in the blend is determined, to a large extent, by the coffee selected to be its base. This robusta selection must be made by making espresso shots using an interim blend consisting of the robusta and the base coffees. Some robustas just do not work with certain base coffees.

While quality espresso blends can be made using only arabica beans, it is not prudent to avoid using robusta based solely on prejudice. Much of this prejudice in North America is derived from the commonly available grades of robusta that have an undesirable rubbery aftertaste. The specialty coffee movement in North America, in its founding days, took a stand that the avoidance of robusta usage would be the signature difference between specialty coffee and commercial grade institutional coffee. While that position is supportable in the context of brewed coffee, it is an unnecessary and undesirable limitation to impose it upon espresso.

Superior robusta is grown at high elevations that are also well suited for the cultivation of arabica. These high-quality robusta beans are picked and processed with the same care and attention as the finest arabica. They are hard to find and expensive, often costing more than many arabica beans.

Espresso quality can be enhanced using a premium robusta that is clean, soft and mellow. First, it adds to the caffeine content of the espresso for that "extra kick" most people look for in an espresso. In addition, a quality robusta has the ability to enhance the richness and persistence of the crema without detracting from the neutral character that is so critical for a superior espresso.

Uganda, Indonesia, Mexico and India are good sources of quality robusta for use in espresso blends. If a high-quality robusta is used in an espresso blend, its concentration is usually in the 10 to 20 percent range. The higher the quality of the robusta, the higher the concentration the blend can accommodate. The goal here is to take advantage of robusta's contributions without actually being able to taste it in the cup.

Highlighter Coffee for Flavor

Having selected the base coffee and decided if a robusta is to be included in the blend, the third step is to select the highlighter coffee, whose aroma, taste and aftertaste will be showcased in the blend. Surprisingly, this is the easiest selection to make. This coffee is counted on to supply the flavor properties, and there is very little constraint placed on this coffee. It can be washed, semi-washed or natural; it can be somewhat acidic and low in body, but it has to be highly aromatic and intensely flavorful with a long and pleasant aftertaste.

The choice of flavor profile is a matter of personal preference. Only the roaster's imagination limits the use of a coffee as a highlighter coffee. Some popular coffees whose flavor and aroma are displayed in quality espresso blends include Ethiopian Harrar, Sidamo and Yirgacheffe; Guatemalan Antigua and Huehuetenango; Indonesian Sulawesi; as well as Yemen Moka and Matari.

The highlighter coffees are usually used in proportions ranging from about 20 to 40 percent of the blend. However, if highly acidic

coffees, such as those from Kenya or Costa Rica, are used as highlighter coffee, their concentration should be strictly limited, as was discussed in Part 1 of this article.

Balancing the Blend

This is the final step in the actual espresso-blending process and is probably the most demanding part of the whole procedure. It is definitely an art more than a science and calls for exceptional memory of flavor profiles of both the component coffees as well as those of past blends.

Being an agricultural product, the beans from a given coffee plant change from crop to crop. Thus, any espresso blend has to be adjusted and rebalanced at least once a year when the new crop becomes available. Actually, this process should be repeated several times a year, since all new crop coffees from all origins do not become available at the same time. In fact, this rebalancing of the blend will be performed more frequently as coffees change character as they age, with some coffees changing more rapidly than others.

The primary purpose of this step is to ensure that all the features of the blend are in perfect harmony and no particular characteristic dominates the blend. The resulting espresso should glide smoothly down one's throat like a well-balanced and properly aged cognac. Unfortunately, this is an aspect that roasters in North America seem to miss; many American espresso blends I have experienced have at least one characteristic that stands out and "hits you right between the eyes." Usually it is the acidity that is most predominant, indicating either improper choice of coffees or erroneously carrying over concepts from brewed-coffee blending into espresso blending.

Another important aspect is to ensure that today's blend is consistent in texture and taste profile with yesterday's blend. If it is not carefully planned and managed, this step can become a never-ending process. Every time a new bag of coffee is included in the blend, the whole balancing process rears its ugly head. To help neutralize this problem, I recommend purchasing coffee directly from high-quality estates in large enough homogeneous lots to minimize bag-to-bag variations.

Acidity is the characteristic that changes the most as the coffee ages. By using mostly medium- and low-acid coffees in the blend, we also minimize this aging effect as the coffee is warehoused through the crop year.

Statistical Considerations

In a cafe or espresso bar, regular customers know exactly how the espresso and espresso-based drinks should taste: exactly the way they tasted the last time they ordered them. Some customers are so particular that they will not order if their favorite barista is not staffing the counter. While that may be an indictment of the inconsistency of staff training programs, it goes to show that even with effective staff training, espresso blend stability, as well as shot-to-shot consistency, is of paramount importance.

Increasing the number of different beans used in a blend calls for more frequent blend adjustments. I have heard of espresso blends that have as many as nine different coffees in them. Except as a marketing gimmick, I do not believe such a complex blend is meaningful, since no one can really discern the effect of the last bean of the ninth coffee in the blend.

I have come across espresso blends that have three very similar coffees, e.g., three different Brazils used to make up the base of the blend. In such instance, replacing one bean of one Brazil coffee with one bean of another Brazil coffee in that blend makes little detectable difference, so why use three similar coffees in the first place? The only reason for this might be as a backup, in case one coffee becomes unavailable or there isn't enough of it; thus, one can be substituted for the other.

Besides, a complex multi-bean blend is a statistical nightmare when considering shot-to-shot consistency. We introduced the basic statistical calculations in the form of a table in Part 1 of this article (page 347), explaining in some detail, how to use that table.

Let's look at an example using the accompanying table. Suppose you make a series of double shots using a multi-bean

> Espresso preparation has a built-in mechanism to capture the aroma and keep it in the cup—the all important crema.

blend containing 20 percent of one particular coffee, say a Guatemalan Antigua. You see that the percentage of the Antigua will be between 18 and 22 (spread of +/- 10 percent about a mean composition of 20 percent) only 48 percent of the time. The other 52 percent of the time, the relative proportion is outside those limits.

So far, we have considered the effect of the variation in the bean count of only one coffee in the blend. That is the primary purpose of this set of calculations. But this table can be used to cover multi-bean blends with certain limitations. Suppose we have a two-bean blend, each at 50 percent. If we require that one of these beans be present in the 14-gram sample at a count of 56 beans with a variation of less than +/- 10 percent, the table shows that it will occur 75 percent of the time. Since the sample size is constrained to a total of 112 beans, the second coffee will automatically compensate for the variation in the bean count of the first coffee. Thus the second coffee will also be within the +/- 10 percent limit the same 75 percent of the time. However, as the bean count of one coffee is moving below the average count of 56 beans, the other coffee is moving above the average, thus doubling the ultimate effect on the blend.

We will require a different set of calculations to evaluate the impact on a three-bean blend, say with relative proportions of 50 percent : 30 percent : 20 percent (approximately 56 : 34 : 22 beans for a double shot) and those tables become more complicated. However, we can use the current table to see some of these effects. As we calculated above, the base coffee will be present within +/- 10 percent in 75 percent of the samples. Keeping the total number of beans at 112 means the other two coffees "combined" will be within +/- 6 beans (of the 56 bean total) also 75 percent of the time. However, this +/- 6 bean variation may all be in the 30 percent component (effectively 6 beans out of 34) or all be in the 20 percent component (equal to 6 beans out of 22) or somehow distributed between the two of them. In any case, the relative impact of this variation on the coffees that are smaller components of the blend will be proportionately much greater.

One simple way to overcome the statistical nightmare of a multi-bean blend is to simply grind the coffee and homogenize it soon after it is blended and take samples only from this large mass of the ground coffee. In that case, instead of dealing with 56 beans for a single shot or 112 beans for a double shot, one will be dealing with a much larger number of ground coffee particles in each sample. But there is a huge price to pay. When beans are ground, their surface area is immensely increased, by a factor of at least 100 by one estimate, greatly accelerating the staling process.

For a multi-bean blend, it really comes down to selecting between two bad choices: Accept the shot-to-shot variation but keep the beans fresher, or minimize the variations but allow the coffee to stale.

Impact of Potency?

In our statistical considerations, we have only taken into account the variations resulting from the number of beans of each coffee present in a random sample of a particular size. But all coffees do not contribute equally to any given espresso property. Some coffees affect certain characteristics of the espresso far more than another coffee in that blend.

To account for those various impacts, one has to consider the "potency" of each particular coffee. A small variation in the number of a highly "potent" bean in a random sample can have a large effect on the ultimate flavor profile of the blend. Unfortunately, highly "potent" coffees tend to be employed in smaller proportions in the blend, thereby making even small variations have a proportionately high impact on certain espresso characteristics. This is particularly true of acidity, because acidic coffees simply cannot make up a large proportion of the blend.

Help Them Get the Best Out of Your Blend

Developing an exceptional blend is not enough; the roaster must also help the end user extract the very best espresso using that blend. In addition to all elements of "best practices" that apply to all espresso production, there is information that is unique to each espresso blend that the end user must be privy to. We consider it the responsibility of the roaster to develop those bits of information and transfer them to the end user. These include, among other items, roast date, optimum extraction temperature and specific water quality requirements.

It is important for the cafe owner to know when the blend was roasted. Different blends need different post-roast rest periods until they have sufficiently out-gassed for the blend to be usable. If used before they are properly rested, copious amounts of carbon dioxide rush out of the freshly ground coffee particles as soon as the hot water hits them. This prevents water molecules from penetrating the interior of the ground coffee particles. This results in a weak brew, with little or no flavor and no oil emulsification.

Different blends also reach the peak of their flavor over different elapsed times since roasting. Blends also stale at different rates. The cafe owner can manage the coffee stock a lot better if the actual roast date is known. Any roaster who does not post the roast date on the bag is not "telling the whole truth."

The cafe owner should know the water temperature required for optimum flavor production. Some blends perform well at 195 degrees F while some others are best at 202.5 degrees F and still others require temperatures as high as 207 degrees F.

A third element that is unique to the blend is the quality of the water required for maximum flavor production. Many cafe owners are aware of the need to "condition" the water prior to its use with the espresso machine. Most of the time, this treatment is done to protect the espresso machine from excessive calcium deposits rather than to produce the best tasting espresso. Several water quality parameters affect the flavor of the espresso and our experience shows the total dissolved solids (TDS) to be one of the more critical factors.

Practical Guidelines

Based on all of the considerations discussed in this article, here are some practical guidelines to assist in blending for Italian espresso:

■ Select coffees by drawing espresso with them and making detailed notes on each coffee's behavior in an espresso environment.

■ Use as few coffees in the blend as possible. Two, three or four coffees in the blend are sufficient in most cases. Using more coffees not only complicates the blending process but also adversely affects blend stability.

■ If a coffee is to be included in the blend, use large enough proportions to make its impact felt. Using less than 15 percent of a coffee is not worth the added complication.

■ Remember that small proportions of highly potent coffee give rise to large shot-to-shot variations.

Conclusion

Although blending for espresso is very different from blending for brewed coffee, espresso blending does not have to remain a mystery. The approach described in this article is not the only way to develop a blend; hopefully it provides a good starting point to venture into producing quality espresso blends. There is really no reason the average espresso blend available in North America cannot improve to the point that an espresso prepared using that blend would in fact be drinkable as "straights." I've yet to be convinced that a poorly made espresso makes a better latte or cappuccino than a quality espresso. Happy blending! ■

• •

DR. JOSEPH JOHN *is president of Josuma Coffee Company in Menlo Park, Calif. and designer of Malabar Gold, its premium European espresso blend. He can be contacted by phone at 650.366.5453 or email at* info@josuma.com.

Flavor, Magnified

Roasting Strategies for Espresso

by Joe Marrocco

• FROM THE MAY/JUNE 2013 ISSUE OF *ROAST* •

Although roasting coffee can be fun and interesting, it certainly isn't easy. We as roasters are all too familiar with the dramatic change in taste that occurs in the cup when one moment on a roasting curve draws off course. We go running to our cupping tables to see what the flavor outcome will be. We understand the delicate hand needed to draw out just the right amount of acidity, balanced with sweetness, built onto rich body and made a bit more exciting with a touch of bitterness. We taste and taste until we find the perfect curve for the coffees we are charged with roasting— whether a delicate coffee from one specific farm or a blend of coffees from all over the globe that represents the house. At a guild retreat we burn the candle discussing at length airflow and burner tips, air roasting vs. drum, and what exactly "full-city" really means.

And then, there is espresso.

Roasting for espresso seems to be a different animal. Cupping roasts to see if we have nailed it for espresso is difficult. If cupping gives us a snapshot of the coffee and the effects of different roasts on that coffee, then tasting espresso is like we have taken that cupping snapshot and magnified it. The image is sometimes sharper in some areas and distorted in others. We work to round out the sharpness and blend in the distortion, dulling the image to a palatable tolerance. The espresso machine is like a high-powered lens that magnifies the flavors and discovers new ones, while the roaster is like a secondary lens that allows that magnified image to come into better focus.

Then, after all of our diligence, we get those dreaded calls from the barista crew that the coffee is too roasty, or too bright, or not heavy enough, or doesn't have enough crema. How do we troubleshoot and fix these issues? Let's look at strategies for not only roasting espresso, but for improving an espresso program.

Coffee Selection

If you do not have quality coffees going into your drum, you will not have quality espresso coming out of your machine. Quality does not have to mean expensive. It does, however, mean that you need to be selective in the coffees you choose. The best espressos are made with fresh green coffee. If the coffee is beginning to get old, the espresso will taste flat and papery, just as the coffee on the table tastes. Worse still, a defect in the coffee will be one of those features magnified by the espresso machine.

Conversely, if the coffee is fresh and clean, the espresso will have a deeper dimension, be more forgiving to your roast, and push through the milk that may (likely) be added to it. The espresso will be pleasant and exciting.

Many espresso blenders recommend using lower-quality coffees for features of crema and color. Don't forget the main goal: taste. Taste is the be-all and end-all. What that taste entails is where the decisions are to be made, and that decision starts in sourcing. We will discuss some strategies in a bit.

The Blend

When building a blend, consider it to be a recipe with different taste components. A good place to start is to think of a dish that you love, like pie, and try to emulate it. Pie is so delicious. Who doesn't like pie? Think about the simple parts that build the flavor profile of a great pie: sugar for sweet, fruit or berries for the acid, condensed juices and melting ice cream for body, carbohydrates in the crust for structure and texture, spice for intrigue, depth of flavor and aroma. Each of these ingredients can be added in different portions in order to create your version of the perfect pie. So it is with espresso. Build each component into the blend while thinking about the others: Will it complement or detract? Remember that this can be representative of what you enjoy. If you do not enjoy cherry-pie-flavored coffee, maybe go for something more cocoa-y, or even more savory, like a meat pie. This is where you, the roaster, can play with the flavor profile and express yourself, or express what you think your customer base will most enjoy.

It is a myth that a coffee in a blend will only add one feature. There is no such thing as a blank-canvas coffee. Low-grown coffees can add a great depth to the body/structure of a blend (like the crust or melted ice cream in our pie analogy), but that does not mean that a flavor will not also be added. If you want to add one of these to your blend, know that in order for the espresso to not taste like a low-grown coffee, you need a high-quality selection that will add to the other flavors.

Then you have the single-origin espresso debate. For the adventurer who wants to go to the place where the coffee is grown in every sip, these espressos are like mini vacations. When you find a coffee that offers all of the above, don't be afraid to flaunt it. Again, choices like this may come down to your brand more than your palate. There are balanced single-origin espressos just as there are imbalanced blends.

However, just because you have a coffee that is high in one flavor area and low in another does not mean that it is off limits. Sometimes it is lovely to have a simply sweet espresso, dynamically acidic double, or heavy/dense shot in a cap. You are the craftsperson. Have some fun.

Tasting

All of this discussion of blend versus single-origin leads us to a big issue: tasting. This is really one of the most difficult aspects of roasting for espresso. As previously mentioned, roasting typically can be sorted out on a cupping table. This is not true for espresso. You must taste the coffee as espresso in order to really dig into the roast and maximize the coffee's potential as espresso. Yet, most roasters are not baristas. Espresso extraction can be more daunting and tedious to do well than any other extraction method. Fractions of a gram in the dose, degrees in the temperature of the water, even differences in how the grounds are distributed in the portafilter can alter the flavor of that shot. In order to get a good bead on the coffee, you must first be able to extract it well, and then do that consistently over and over during the tasting session. Dialing in the espresso can be a challenge, and this is multiplied if you have more than one coffee to taste. Tasting even the best espresso is a trial in itself. Espresso is a strong beverage, and burnout can happen fast. If you taste while you are dialing in and hit a few snags, it is likely that you will reach palate fatigue before you are even able to analyze the coffee.

Do not be discouraged. If you are not a barista, it is important to find a barista to collaborate with. Having a qualified and humble barista you can trust who can offer the extractions after they have dialed in and provided input about the coffee is a huge advantage. Christopher Oppenhuis of Thou Mayest Coffee Roasters asks the baristas who use his espresso to keep a detailed cupping log. He works closely with them to continually improve their offerings. Their espresso is a constant work toward a more delicious product. If you are a wholesale roaster and have no baristas on staff, maybe it would be a good opportunity to team up with one of your flagship customers and work with their staff to remain engaged in your espresso program, such as HalfWit has done with Chicago coffee business Wormhole Coffee.

Bottom line, if you and your team do not taste the coffee as espresso, the roasts will be done in the dark. It is critical to understand how the taste is affected by the flame. You are not crafting a finished piece of art; you are creating the color scheme, and presenting the potential to another artist who will use the spectrum you give them to create the end piece.

More on Blending

Once you have settled on the coffees you will be using, you must decide on a strategy for putting the components together. Blending can be done not only with coffees of different origins, but also with coffees of different roasts. It is important to decide whether you will be blending your coffees pre-roast or post-roast.

• PRE-ROAST

Roasting blended coffees together offers a few benefits:

Brittle Factor
If all of the coffees are roasted to the same level, they will be relatively close to the same level of brittleness. This allows for a more consistent grind. Consistent grind is critical for an espresso program.

Production
Roasting a bunch of espresso components for a blend is time-consuming. If you can roast once as opposed to three times, you are cutting your costs for that coffee drastically. Skilled labor is expensive, as is keeping a roaster running.

Flavor Development
Many roasters and baristas find that when more than one coffee is roasted together, it allows more continuity to the flavor of the blend. This can supply a more consistent product, and more control over the flavor of the espresso.

However, when you roast coffees from different places with different densities, moisture levels, sizes, and flavor compounds together at one time in one roaster with one profile, well ... you can extrapolate some of the issues:

Color Inconsistencies
Each component may not color the same way as the others, giving the blend a mottled look. But, remember, the color is not the end result—the taste is. However, this can make it hard to make roasting decisions if you are using the tryer to determine when to drop a roast based on color development. As you roast a blend more and more, you will get to know the idiosyncrasies of that blend.

Flavor Development
If each coffee has an optimum profile that best suits it, or brings out the balance of that coffee in the most true to origin

STRATEGY, MAGNIFIED

Espresso Evaluation and Tracking Form
Using a form like the one here can help improve your roasting strategies. This form is courtesy of PT's Coffee Roasting Co., Topeka, Kansas.

Coffee Name:

Preparation Date:	Grinder Model:
Coffee Roast Date:	Grind Setting:
Agtron Number:	Machine Model:
Beans:	Extraction Time:
Ground:	Dose: (grams)
Varietal:	Mass: / Ratio %:
Process:	Water Temp: / Bars:

Fragrance:

Aroma Notes:

Flavor Notes:

Acidity   *Sweetness*

Bitter

Tactile Notes:

thin   creamy   syrupy

low   medium   heavy

dry   juicy

Barista Notes:

Roast Notes:

Straight Score: (1-10)

Milk Score: (1-10)

X 5

PT'S COFFEE ROASTING CO. // ptscoffee.com // 785.862.5282

and yet delicious way, then one or all of the coffees in this homogeneous roasting method will not reach that potential.

• POST-ROAST

Revisiting the pie analogy, a blend can be a gorgeous thing when done right. When you are using different features from different coffees, it is important for those features to be highlighted by the roast. Many roasters feel this is only done by roasting each coffee to its best potential individually.

Todd Arnett, the roaster and owner of Williamsburg Coffee and Tea in Williamsburg, Virginia, believes that if a roaster ascribes to profile roasting, and they are using one roast for multiple coffees at one time, this presents a conflict. "If the end consumer is deciding continually to choose a coffee experience that is more standard over one of excellence, maybe we are not creating something of excellence. I can't blame the consumer; I can only blame the links in the chain before the consumer. Compromising a profile in order to speed up production will cause some of what makes those individual coffees to be special to be lost. We call ourselves the specialty coffee industry. We need to maintain what makes us truly special."

Quantities

However you choose to blend, the process should be done delicately. Know that every coffee you add will be tasted at some level of poignancy. It is important to not over-blend, meaning: Don't use too many components. The more coffees you put into a blend, the less you will taste each individual component. This will also cause the espresso to be finicky during extraction. Due to the brittleness of different coffees, and since the ratios of components change through the burrs, so too will the extractions subtly (and sometimes not so subtly) change. Set your baristas up for success by giving them a reliable, consistent and delicious espresso to work with. (For further information on blend ratios, see Dr. Joseph John's fantastic chart on page 347.

Roasting

Once a coffee is chosen, or a blend decided upon, it is time to put the coffee to the flame. Roasters can be an opinionated group, and nowhere is this more vividly portrayed than when I hear them talk about how to roast espresso. Please keep in mind that there is no right or wrong way to present your espresso program. The important thing is that there is intention and that your choices have been made through a vision for your program. Your brand needs to be considered when you plan how you will present your coffees as espressos. Here we will highlight a few of the more widely used theories of espresso roasting (the names are my own).

• ESPRESSO CRACKALACKIN

What some in the contemporary barista community would see as a throwback way to roast for espresso is still widely used by many companies today. There is a distinct palate that loves a dark-roasted espresso and will have it no other way. If there is no oil on the beans in that hopper, they are going to walk.

Yet, just because the coffee has clearly passed through first crack and then into the deeper stages of second crack, it does not mean that love and attention was not shown it on its journey. It is important to have a gentle hand, and with the hottest fires even more so. Moving the coffee too quickly from first to second crack will cause the robust flavors of a dark roast, the burnt sugar warmth, and the sharp bitter balancing flavor of dark cocoa, black pepper and even a vintage cigar to fade into a hot, smoky mess. An espresso that tastes dark is lovely in milk. An espresso that tastes like smoke makes milk taste like smoke. When going from A to B, the journey is usually more important than the destination. If you are looking to develop those darker textures and tones, give the machine and heat time to focus on them. If you blast through, you will destroy them.

Origin is not tasted as predominantly in these blends as is the roast. This does not relinquish the responsibility of sourcing. Quality high-grown coffees will take roast more consistently than will lesser-quality coffees. More density means more sugars and other flavor compounds are present in the beans, and more will still be present in the end result, no matter how dark the coffee is roasted.

• THE WAR HEAD

There has been a movement within the past several years toward roasting everything extremely light. This roasting style seems to be filling the vacuum left by so many over-roasted, conventional espressos. The thought is that the lighter the coffee is roasted, the more origin you taste, while tasting less of the roaster. Many roasters of this train of thought focus a lot of attention on the acids in the coffee, and any sweetness that they develop is still holding tightly to its fruity lineage. These coffees can be extremely bright, exciting and fun. Many times an espresso made with a coffee sourced and roasted to highlight these features will taste like citrus candy, challenging a guest to reconsider their perceptions of coffee.

Once again, if attention is not paid to the profile of this coffee, the coffee will fall short of its potential. Just a couple of seconds too early or degrees too light, and these coffees can be categorically under-roasted. If this happens, you will find notes of straw, grass and/or malt. This is due to a lack of a Maillard reaction. It is important, once again, to give time to the reactions that bring about positive flavors and diminish off flavors. In order to get rid of the under-roasted flavors, many roasters speed up the first part of the roast, which kick-starts the reactions that build acidity, and then slow down the roast considerably once the first signs of first crack begin to show. The theory is that coasting through first crack allows the sugars to develop more while maintaining the coffee's acidity. Drop it too late, however, and the coffee is going to be baked. The acidity will have dulled due to the tardiness of the drop, and the potential sugars will

not have had time to fully develop. This style of roasting is usually reserved for single-origin coffees; however, a few blends roasted in this method do exist.

• THE POLITICIAN

This is the blend that is all things to all people. Usually this blend tastes baked when brewed, but great when pressed through a machine. The name of the game is consistency. This is the espresso that will taste great in many applications: in milk, with cocoa, in an iced drink, straight, in a smoothie, over ice cream, you name it.

Routine is of extreme importance to the human race. Many successful coffee companies have been built off this principle. When customers grow to anticipate a certain flavor, and then in the middle of their morning ritual they are faced with something different, whether good or bad, this can disrupt the routine that they have come to expect. This blend is made with this guest in mind. This espresso will almost always be a pre-roast blend roasted a bit longer, and most likely at least stepping barely into second crack. Most roasters would call this a Viennese roast. Usually the profile curve for this roast is more subtle and elongated. Many roasters will use this strategy to some degree with all coffees they are roasting for

espresso. Elongating the roast curve a bit usually results in a touch less acid (which in espresso can be almost too boisterous for some) and bring out the sweetness of a coffee.

Many barista purists do not get their kick with this espresso style. To them, this can be a boring endeavor. But, to the guest drinking it, boredom is exactly what they want. They want the same slippers in the morning, their shows in the evening, their mug in their hand, their smoke break at 10 a.m. And, they want this espresso, every day, day in, day out, and ... they pay for it.

• THE BEAR RUG

Have you ever had an espresso so comforting that you just felt like you could curl up into a ball and fall asleep? These espressos are soft, full, soothing and balanced. The aesthetic behind these goes beyond the intentions of not rocking the guest's boat, but rather encourages the guest to have a moment of comfort. I find that in specialty coffee shops, this kind of expression is the most likely goal.

Typically the approach to roasting these luxurious espressos is the same as braising a short rib. Hit it hot at first, then: Slow. It. Down. The slower development sands off the rough edges.

The major criticism with this technique is that a lot of the origin can be lost. The positive is this espresso has now taken on a whole new character of its own. This espresso is usually roasted similarly to the Politician, but with higher-grown and higher-quality coffees. However, the first part of the roast is typically a bit more aggressive. The coffee is typically roasted to just before second crack, which also works to preserve some intrinsic origin-specific characteristics. Many times this blend will be blended pre-roast, but it can also be blended post-roast, depending on the nature of the coffees used.

• THE PURIST

This is the espresso for your coffee aficionado. The intention of this espresso is not necessarily to present a delicious experience. The tastiness of the espresso is secondary and reserved for only the highest-quality coffees. The roaster's intent here is to illuminate the origin of the coffee, period. The idea is that if this coffee presents itself on the cupping table with certain flavor compounds present, then by altering that roast for espresso the compounds themselves will be altered. The Maillard reaction will continue to break down the molecular structures in the coffee, presenting new flavors. It has been said by roasters who subscribe to this methodology that "roasting for espresso" doesn't exist. One simply roasts a coffee according to its particular profile, and espresso is simply another method of brewing. When the extraction is done well, the same flavor compounds that were present on the cupping table will be present in the demitasse. If the coffee is excellent, the extraction is dialed in, and the roast is correct, the espresso has to be delicious. And, adding another dimension to this equation, most shops that use these coffees will have pressure-profiling espresso machines, which enable the barista to tailor the extraction specifically for a particular coffee.

The dangers here can be a myopic approach to the coffee, a guest left in the dust, and an opinionated way of approaching the last few links on that coffee chain. It can cause a roaster to point blame at the barista for not extracting correctly. The espresso machine can distort certain characteristics that on a cupping table may be in perfect balance and clarity.

The beauty of this approach is that the coffee is in focus. Just as a Q grader can distinguish the taste of place, processing, variety and roast level, so too can a barista embark upon that journey. When this works, it can be a really interesting and illuminating experience.

If this is ever a blend, it is a post-roast blend. When it is a blend, it is rarely more than two coffees, and the two coffees are usually very distinguishable. The blend will also point distinctly to where the coffee is grown, focusing on two differently processed coffees from one farm or region, or two microlots from one farm, for example.

Final Thoughts

It is important to approach your espresso just as you do every other segment of your business, from whom you hire to the color of your logo. People will intimately interact with it every day. In order to gauge these interactions and shape the experience, you too must engage with the espresso. A chef worth her salt would never serve a broth she had not tasted. Holly Bastin of PT's Coffee in Topeka, Kansas, has developed an excellent espresso tasting tool (see page 358). She has graciously provided it for our coffee community to use in an endeavor to better our taste understanding of espresso.

When advancing this venture, remember to have fun with it. Don't be afraid to let your customers in on the process. Intelligentsia calls its flagship espresso blend Black Cat Project. This speaks to the dynamic nature of its blend. It brings customers into the process of experiencing the flavor journey that an evolving blend goes through as seasonal coffees move in and out of the mix, roasts are altered a touch here and there, and new ideas are tried.

Scott Carey, the owner and roaster at Sump Coffee in St. Louis, Missouri, is just starting out with his roasting program. He has openly shared with his customer base that his roasts are all a work in progress. He gathers their feedback and listens to their reactions. He strives to not only continue improving his roasts with this method, but to learn to stay one step ahead of the customer's expectations, building more and more intrigue into what they will be experiencing next.

None of us roasts and extracts perfectly every time. Sometimes a mistake can be the best mode of discovery. Allow yourself the freedom to change approaches. If you are having fun, your guests will have fun too. ■

JOE MARROCCO *is a green coffee sales representative and roaster with Café Imports. He has a lot of experience in this industry: roasting, cafe, cupping, teaching classes, competing—the list goes on. However, his most meaningful experiences have simply been time spent with real people. He is a member of the Roasters Guild Executive Council and hopes to enhance connectivity within the larger coffee community. Contact him via email at joe@cafeimports.com.*

Finding Beauty in the Blend

What's the Appeal for Today's Specialty Roasters?

by Mike Ebert | *photos by Mark Shimahara*

• FROM THE JULY/AUGUST 2015 ISSUE OF *ROAST* •

Roasters have been blending coffee from different origins for centuries. Perhaps the earliest blend on record is the still popular Mocha Java, a combination of beans from Yemen and the Indonesian island of Java, which by many accounts dates back to the 17th century. In more recent times, availability and cost concerns have been the primary driving forces behind commercial coffee blending. During World War II, for example, coffee manufacturers in the United States used blending as a way to combat green coffee shortages caused by wartime shipping constraints, blending dry soy—up to about 20 percent of the total volume—with coffee beans. And when a "black frost" hit Brazil during the summer of 1975, significantly reducing production and increasing the price of green coffee for several years following, many major roasters started blending lower-quality and less-expensive coffee to maintain their margins while delivering a consistent cup profile year-round.

Flash forward to the late 1990s and early 2000s, when the specialty coffee industry began showcasing single-origin and single-lot coffees, and blending seemed to fall out of favor. But blending quality coffee is an art that many specialty coffee roasters still embrace, not merely to control cost and consistency—though those remain important factors—but also to create a taste profile that can't be obtained from a single-origin, or to create a proprietary flavor to help build and retain a loyal consumer following.

Consistency and Cost Remain Key

"Roasters blend for quality and consistency," says Spencer Turer, vice president of Coffee Analysts, a coffee testing and consulting firm based in Burlington, Vermont, "to prevent flavor fluctuations throughout the harvest year, create a proprietary flavor different than competitors, and design a flavor that can be consistent throughout the harvest and from year to year."

Blending provides flexibility for the green coffee buyer, as one can combine different components at different times to deliver a consistent profile.

"This concept is embraced when developing a 100 percent Colombia product," Turer offers as an example, "allowing the buyer and roaster to source coffees from the various departments and specific mills within Colombia to create a customized flavor, different than competitors, which can be maintained over the course of a harvest year."

Creating proprietary blends that differ from competitors' offerings has always been important at Orleans Coffee Exchange, just outside New Orleans, which was founded as a retail coffee store in 1985.

"Since our company was born in the second wave of coffee, we've had dozens of blends, probably for two main reasons," says Bob Arceneaux, the company's owner and green coffee buyer. "One, the original owners were bored, and creating a cute name and throwing beans together like dice in a back alley was something to do and talk about with customers. The other is just our natural inclination to put our own stamp on coffee offerings, our own 'street cred' if you will. Over the years, we chopped many blends from the offerings as they became obsolete, and added something new of our own that was blended with new and better coffees."

Blending also provides a way to deliver consistent flavor profiles to match specific consumer tastes.

"The specialty industry seems to be inspiring cafes to create variation in taste profiles by offering single-origins and blends," says Paul Thornton, former director of coffee at Coffee Bean International (CBI), a specialty division of Farmer Brothers, in Portland, Oregon. "Public Domain (CBI's cafe) has a house espresso. It's designed for the more standard espresso consumer who is looking for balance in body, acidity and overall drinkability."

Thornton also notes that blending can be a good way to manage inventory of coffees that are at risk of becoming past crop.

"We had or have blends that are designed to take certain coffees because we know once we are nearing the end of the year, we may have excessive inventory," he says.

Even roasters who focus mainly on single-origin coffees often see the value of the blend.

"Mostly we roast single-origin coffees, but we do sell one blend," says Oliver Stormshak, owner and green coffee buyer at Olympia Coffee Roasting Co. in Olympia, Washington. "The idea is to create a flavor profile that a customer can rely on every day, year after year."

Ruby Coffee Roasters, which opened in 2013 in Amherst Junction, Wisconsin, also offers only one blend year-round, although owner Jared Linzmeier says the company is considering adding one or two more to its lineup. The current offering, called Creamery, is a dual-purpose blend designed mainly for espresso.

"Creamery overall is becoming our biggest selling product, if it's not already," says Linzmeier. "People who are buying it are buying it in 5-pound bags primarily, so they're using it as their backbone espresso, so when we evaluate it, we're evaluating it with that in mind. Obviously there has to be a little more of a price-point consideration on the ingredients, and some degree of year-round consistency."

Developing a Unique Blend

Before developing a new blend, a roaster must identify his or her goal. Will it be a house blend, an espresso, or something else? Will the blend be offered year-round or seasonally? Are you aiming for body, sweetness, or both? Do you want a hint of spiciness—or a wallop?

A keen understanding of the coffees you source regularly, as well as other coffees that are available, is key. Which of your coffees is most likely to achieve the sensory attributes you've identified for your blend, at the desired roast level? Taking this concept a step further, one can explore different roast levels for various coffees, all blended to create a symphony of flavor, or several coffees roasted to the same roast level, but with such different density, moisture and processing methods that they require different roast profiles.

"We blend post-roast, treating each single-origin as a unique variable to our blend," says Heather Brisson-Lutz, head roaster for San Diego's Bird Rock Coffee Roasters. Bird Rock offers two blends, a seasonal espresso and a decaf-regular mix called 50/50.

Linzmeier and his crew developed a holiday blend last year called Cheers, combining beans from Kenya, Colombia and Ethiopia.

"We wanted a coffee that was super warming and super balanced," he says. The result was a unique flavor that could not have been realized using a single-origin, he adds.

"This was very much a case for synergy," Linzmeier says. "When they were combined and roasted together, we got the best of all of them."

When it came to roasting the blend, he adds, "We cooked it a touch deeper, a touch more development than we were doing with any of those coffees separately. I don't necessarily believe that blends need to be that, but in this case, that was part of the approach, more balance, developing more of the sugars."

Many roasters blend for specific brewing methods, typically espresso, but blending can be applied to almost any device. Many have said espresso shows the heart and soul of a coffee, requiring different components to deliver a well-rounded demitasse of deliciousness. Through blending, roasters can tinker with varying degrees of sweetness, body, aromatics, spiciness, balance and more.

"Blending for espresso allows us to create an experience for our customers that would not be accessible via single-origin," says Brisson-Lutz. "I say this with reference to the pre-existing flavors that are tied to varietal characteristics of a single-origin. While single-origin and single-lot coffees bring a great experience to the cup, I aim to layer flavors in the espresso blend to facilitate more of a journey with each sip as it unfolds on the palate."

> # THROUGH BLENDING, ROASTERS CAN TINKER WITH VARYING DEGREES OF SWEETNESS, BODY, AROMATICS, SPICINESS, BALANCE AND MORE.

"We find ourselves creating espresso blends for customers who recognize the importance of quality offerings," adds Arceneaux. "It is more fun and more challenging to work on a blend and roast profile for espresso. What is the goal? It's not blending for cost control. It's blending for the perfect cup, and blending for customers who demand a signature espresso that is unique to themselves. It's fun to see how a honey-processed coffee from Guatemala or a fully washed coffee from Nicaragua will work in an espresso with other components, such as a semi-washed Brazil and a washed Ethiopian Yirgacheffe Kochere."

Even so, cost and consistency remain compelling reasons to embrace blending. While some achieve success focusing on single-origin coffees, many specialty coffee roasters find it wise from a business perspective to offer a core set of two or three coffees year-round, with a reliable flavor profile and a relatively stable price. Blending can be the key to this type of consistency.

"The consumer demands a product that is uniform and consistent," says Turer. "Consumers do not always equate coffee to an agricultural product that will vary in flavor during the harvest and throughout the year, or even from year to year. Also, retailers and cafes do not always want to change their menu and retrain their staff due to product changes."

It's also important to note that for today's specialty coffee roasters, a focus on cost does not necessarily mean sourcing the least expensive beans. It's more about attempting to control the price volatility of the "C" market. By creating a blend with a specific cup profile not inherent in any single-origin, you open the door for substitutions if the price of a particular coffee increases significantly or the volume you need is not available. This is something larger specialty roasters have done well for quite some time—creating signature blends to ensure they maintain a core selection of coffees with unique cup profiles year-round.

Blending for Today's Specialty Market

As the specialty coffee industry has grown, differentiating specialty from commercial coffee has been a core marketing strategy. This began simply enough, with most "gourmet roasters" touting such qualities as "100 percent arabica," hinting that this was a rarity, regardless of the fact that arabica comprises between 65 and 70 percent of the world's coffee production. As consumers became more

> "WHILE SINGLE-ORIGIN AND SINGLE-LOT COFFEES BRING A GREAT EXPERIENCE TO THE CUP, I AIM TO LAYER FLAVORS IN THE ESPRESSO BLEND TO FACILITATE MORE OF A JOURNEY WITH EACH SIP AS IT UNFOLDS ON THE PALATE."
>
> —HEATHER BRISSON-LUTZ, BIRD ROCK COFFEE ROASTERS

educated, the strategy shifted to focus on country of origin, variety, processing method, elevation, specific farm and, ultimately, cup score.

"Even in the late 1980s and early 1990s, many roasters, before the term specialty was so commonplace, segregated their offerings into five main categories: house blend, origins, exotics, decaf and flavored," says Turer. "In those days, Colombia, Kenya, Guatemala and Indonesia were the single-origins. Expensive coffees—Hawaii Kona, Jamaica Blue Mountain, and anything that was rare or farm/mill specific—were in the exotic category."

In light of this, many small specialty roasters began focusing on exceptional single-origin offerings—often from what were relatively obscure origins at the time—as a method of differentiation. Today, a significant number of specialty roasters retain this focus on single-origins, believing the true art is in bringing out the inherent characteristics of a superb coffee rather than creating new flavors or maintaining a consistent flavor profile year-round and year to year through blending.

"Our philosophy is more about highlighting and celebrating specific coffees and the producers that create them," says Linzmeier, "and celebrating everybody in the chain that makes these coffees come to life. Blending ... obscures that. In my mind, our role is not so much as masters of blending as it is bringing coffees to market. We are presenters. Our role is to best present a coffee that has been carefully produced and try not to screw it up."

Still, when high-end specialty roasters do turn to the blend, they typically approach it with a true artisan mentality.

"Our seasonal espresso blend is very much a collaborative effort between myself and our quality control team," says Brisson-Lutz. "As a seasonal roaster, our offerings are changing throughout the year, and so is our blend. Once we have potential coffees for blending, we pull single-origin shots of each, exposing the good, bad and ugly of each coffee. Over the course of the following weeks, we work together finding a baseline of what works and what doesn't when the coffees are blended."

The process is dynamic, she says, and not to be taken lightly.

"Sometimes we will even take a coffee back to the beginning stages of this process and rework the roast profile in a direction we didn't expect," Brisson-Lutz continues. "The collaboration between myself and the quality control team is really key. We provide each other feedback that helps us to construct a blend we can all be proud of and stand behind."

Linzmeier also sees the value in creating a unique blend from exceptional single-origin coffees. Plus, he's discovered it can be useful in lightening the zealotry sometimes found in high-end specialty coffee.

"I think it's fun to take a step back sometimes and say, 'What do people really want to be drinking?'" he says. Developing the company's holiday blend, he adds, "was a way for us to create a blend that, as much as it is still super-high-end specialty, we thought it would have appeal to our families and a wider, broader market. "

Some hard-core Ruby Coffee Roasters fans weren't keen on the lack of transparency and traceability of the blend—the company didn't detail the ratio of beans used, or even the specific varieties or origins of the beans, on the label—but Linzmeier and the Ruby Coffee Roasters team took a lighthearted approach to the reactions.

"People have an expectation for knowing which coffees we're putting in a blend and what percentages," he says, "so as soon as we released Cheers, one of our approaches was to say, 'Hey everyone, let's just chill out a bit and enjoy this coffee. Don't take yourself so seriously!' ... Right away, all of these coffee geek people

were like, 'Wait, what's in it?' and I was like, 'Don't worry about it. It's delicious.'"

"At certain times, in certain parts of the country and abroad, I believe (blending) was frowned upon," says Brisson-Lutz. "The push for purity and simplifying many aspects in specialty coffee retailers and cafes led us down this road. At the end of this road, we found ourselves overcomplicating things and have started to journey back to things like a solid espresso blend."

And while Stormshak does not believe blending can provide a path to innovation in roasting, he does believe the blend is here to stay.

"I think there will always be a need and a desire for blending," he says. "In fact, the majority of specialty coffee drinkers will most likely choose an easy-to-pronounce blend over a foreign country that could push the customer out of the comfort zone—the last thing most people want first thing in the morning." ■

MIKE EBERT *is founder of Firedancer Coffee Consultants, dedicated to helping clients create a personalized strategy to ensure long-term success. He works primarily with roasters, producers and retailers, drawing from his extensive experience in all facets of the specialty coffee supply chain to guide clients in reaching their potential. Ebert is a specialized lead instructor for Specialty Coffee Association (SCA) certification programs and is chair of the SCA Coffee Buyer Educational Pathway Committee, which develops new educational experiences for the specialty coffee community.*

DECAFFEINATED COFFEE

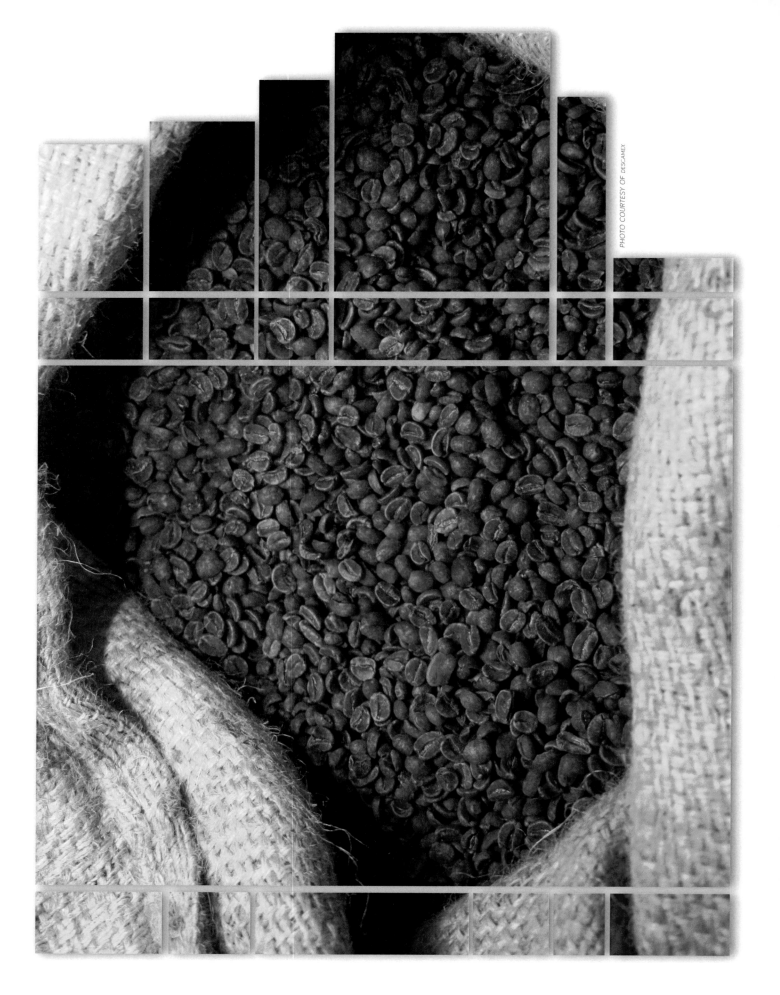

Deconstructing Decaf

Decaffeination Processes Explained

by Kelly Stewart

• FROM THE MARCH/APRIL 2011 ISSUE OF *ROAST* •

A S WE ALL KNOW, roasters love to talk about the intricacies of specialty coffee. Whether the subject is favorite origins, roasting techniques or extraction methods, conversations can go on for hours. But mention decaffeinated coffee, and roasters suddenly begin to qualify their comments with statements like, "I'm no expert, but ..." Or they discuss decaf as a necessary evil. Or even clam up entirely.

Why the reticence to confidently discuss decaf? For one, decaf often makes up less than 10 percent of roasters' offerings, so they may not feel as well versed in selecting and roasting decaffeinated beans. For another, decaf has weathered a fair amount of flak over the years due to a perception of poor flavor or the old rumor that coffee was decaffeinated using formaldehyde—and the view that it's the drink of choice of the older generation or people on medication. Simply put, decaf is "not where the sex appeal is," says Jacob Bodden, owner of Bica Coffeehouse in Oakland, California, where decaf coffee totals only about 3 percent of sales. Most roasters offer several blends and a selection of single-origins, but only one decaf coffee.

At the same time, the market for decaf is projected to increase in the coming years as the population ages. As *The New York Times* recently reported, the oldest baby boomers will turn 65 this year [2011]. And, as more coffee drinkers get hooked on decaf for health reasons, "unleaded" coffee seems poised for a reawakening, but if—and only if—roasters offer quality decaf coffee that tastes good.

"Throughout the years, many roasters offered their regular coffee at the same price as decaf, and they were using lower-quality [beans]," explains Demetrio Arandia Muguira, president of Descamex, which operates two decaffeination plants in Veracruz, Mexico. "We are strong believers that good-quality decaf will end up increasing consumption ... and benefit all the different parts of the supply chain."

Consumers who drink both regular and decaffeinated coffee are driving the push toward better-quality decaf, says David Kastle, vice president for trading at Swiss Water Decaffeinated Coffee Company, based in Burnaby, British Columbia. "As specialty coffee has matured, and quality coffee and roasting and preparation of coffee have improved, 'dual drinkers' are drinking regular coffee and they're drinking decaf," Kastle says. "They're very cognizant of times when the decaf is not up to the caliber of the regular coffee."

So it behooves roasters and retailers to learn more about decaffeination processes and sourcing quality decaf coffee—not only to increase their own coffee knowledge and confidence, but also to market decaf to an ever-expanding customer base (see sidebar on pages 376–377 for more on strategies for selling decaf). Here's a primer covering the methods available for decaffeinating beans, followed by tips from roasters on selecting and roasting decaffeinated coffee.

Conventional, Direct-extraction Processes: Methylene Chloride and Ethyl Acetate

Methylene chloride and ethyl acetate are the two solvents traditionally used to extract caffeine from coffee beans. Worldwide, methylene chloride is the most commonly used decaffeination process, says Muguira of Descamex, which offers methylene chloride-based decaffeination at one of its plants.

Both solvent-based extraction methods use similar steps to achieve decaffeination, says Joseph A. Rivera, founder of *coffeechemistry.com*. "The first step, regardless of what method you use, is you soak the beans in hot water or steam them, which swells up the beans and increases the surface area," he explains. "That way, the chemical can penetrate the bean."

Next, the coffee goes into a solvent-filled vat, which Rivera likens to a washing machine. "You just stir it up for a few hours," says Rivera, a frequent conference presenter about decaf methods and the former director of science and technology for the Specialty Coffee Association of America.

Because methylene chloride and ethyl acetate are selective compounds, they will bond with the caffeine molecules and leave the flavor compounds inside the beans alone, Rivera says. According to U.S. guidelines, 97.5 percent of the beans' caffeine must be removed to label the coffee as decaffeinated.

Though methylene chloride is the more popular solvent-based decaf process, ethyl acetate is also available as a decaffeinating agent. Sweet-smelling ethyl acetate is a naturally occurring compound, but "there are no scientists going out and collecting little bits of it from flowers. They buy 50-gallon drums of it," Rivera says. "The driving factor" for using ethyl acetate, he adds, "is that you can say it's all natural."

Once the solvent has been siphoned away, the last step is to remove the solvent from the beans themselves. "Methylene chloride is volatile like acetone, [which] you use to remove nail polish," Rivera says. To evaporate either solvent from the batch of beans, the coffee is steamed. "The boiling point of methylene chloride is 104 degrees F, and ethyl acetate is 171 degrees," Rivera continues. "So in the final stage when you dry it off, you may have to steam [beans decaffeinated with ethyl acetate] a little longer because it boils at a little higher temperature."

The end result? Decaffeinated, green coffee with a solvent residue of only about 1 part per million. The U.S. Food and Drug Administration, Rivera notes, allows for a residue of 10 parts per million, which means that the decaffeinated coffee contains about one-tenth of the legal limit.

As a second revenue stream, the decaffeination plants using these traditional methods can separate the caffeine from the solvents and sell the caffeine to other businesses (pharmaceutical and soft drink manufacturers, for example), making these processes less expensive.

Water-based Processes

Water-based processes rely on the principle that coffee is only 24 to 26 percent soluble in water. To prepare to decaffeinate coffee via a water-based method, a solution is created by soaking a huge quantity of arabica beans in water until all of the soluble components, including caffeine, seep out of the beans. The spent beans are then discarded, and the fluid passes through carbon filters that extract the caffeine. The resulting fluid is saturated with water-soluble solids, minus the caffeine.

Swiss Water Decaffeinated Coffee Company calls this fluid "green coffee extract," or GCE. Descamex has also developed a fluid saturated with coffee components to use in its Mountain Water Process.

To prepare coffee for either of these water-based decaffeination processes, coffee is first rehydrated in water. Decaffeination companies then soak batches of beans in the concentrated fluid. "The extraction takes place under special conditions of flow, pressure, temperature and vacuum," says Muguira of Descamex.

When decaffeinating with water-based methods, caffeine is the only substance preventing the beans and fluid from reaching equilibrium—so the beans do not release their flavor, but the caffeine migrates into the water. At the same time, carbon filters pull the caffeine out of the solution. The process continues until the beans reach the targeted caffeine content.

At Swiss Water Decaf, the coffee mingles with the green coffee extract for eight to 10 hours during which a proprietary carbon filtering system removes the caffeine, says Kastle.

After drying and a phase for resting, the coffee is now ready to be bagged and shipped. But what happens to the caffeine? Extracting the caffeine from the carbon filters and selling it would require applying a chemical such as methylene chloride, Kastle explains, but as Swiss Water Process is 100 percent chemical-free and organic, the company uses a furnace to burn off the caffeine.

Interior of decaffeination plant. | *photo courtesy of Descamex*

Super-critical Carbon Dioxide Process

PHOTO COURTESY OF DESCAMEX

Though we typically think of carbon dioxide as a gas, it turns into a liquid when it's compressed. To decaffeinate with this super-critical carbon dioxide, the beans are first soaked in hot water. Then, inside a compression tower, the beans are added to a mixture of water and carbon dioxide at a pressure of more than 3,500 psig, or pound-force per square inch gauge. (By comparison, car tires are inflated to a pressure of about 35 psig, and a standard air compressor for household use operates at less than 100 psig.) This tremendous amount of pressure transforms the carbon dioxide into a super-critical state, in which it's partly a gas and partly a liquid.

Inside the pressurized tower, the carbon dioxide bonds to the caffeine, while leaving the flavor compounds inside the beans. After the beans have been decaffeinated, the coffee is moved from the compression tower to a dryer, and then on to be packaged and shipped.

When the carbon dioxide/water mixture is depressurized, the carbon dioxide returns to a gaseous state and discharges the caffeine into the water. The carbon dioxide is reused to decaffeinate later batches of coffee, while the water is filtered to remove the caffeine for resale.

Carbon dioxide decaffeination is a higher-cost process because it requires an investment in heavy-duty equipment for pressurization and monitoring, as well as high energy expenditures to operate the decaffeination tanks at the forces needed to compress the gas.

Views on Decaf from the Roastery

Now that we've examined the technical side of decaf processing, let's look at the perspectives of roasters and retailers who work with decaffeinated coffee every day. What are their thoughts on the price and roasting challenges inherent to decaf coffee? And, most importantly, what are the results in the cup?

PRICE

Coffees travel from origin to a warehouse before being shipped to the roaster. Many decaffeinated coffees take an additional journey to the decaffeination plant, where they undergo an extra process before being shipped to an importer's warehouse or direct to a roaster. Decaffeination plants are scattered across the globe, with most located outside the United States. Due to the added shipping, handling and processing, decaffeinated coffee may very well be the most expensive beans that roasters purchase.

Adding to the overall cost is the fact that decaffeinators work with large batches of coffee—at least 50 to 100 bags of coffee—so only high-volume national and regional roasters can afford to

deal directly with decaffeination companies. Importers typically place decaffeination orders and offer the coffee for sale to roasters in need of smaller quantities. Of course, whenever coffee is segmented into smaller portions, the price per pound increases.

"Coffee prices are going crazy these days, but generally we have found decaf to cost us at least 50 percent more than our regular beans," says roaster Matt Hensley of 35 North Coffee Co. in Franklin, Tennessee, which purchases mainly water-processed decafs. For 35 North, however, quality is the driving factor in choosing a decaf coffee.

Coffees decaffeinated with water-based and carbon dioxide processes fetch a higher price due to their exclusivity, says Donald Schoenholt, president of Gillies Coffee Company in New York. "Methylene chloride decaffeinated is produced in quantity by many, providing a market that keeps the price competitively value oriented," Schoenholt says. Many methylene chloride decafs are designated for the mass market and blended to be price-competitive.

However, roasters who offer organic coffee cannot use the traditional methylene chloride or ethyl acetate methods if they seek to comply with USDA organic standards for their decaf. Coffees decaffeinated with a water-based process or via carbon dioxide retain organic certification because chemicals are not used.

"Generally, the water-processed coffees are significantly more expensive than the other methods, and as a result we tend to offer these at a premium. The main reason for me to purchase these is to maintain organic status on certain blends," adds buyer and roaster Caleb Mayhall of Chicago's Metropolis Coffee Company.

ROASTING

The conventional wisdom is that decafs are more challenging to roast. To start out with, the coffee comes to the roastery tinted a darker shade than regular green coffee.

"Some people find it more difficult to roast decaf if they are roasting based on bean color," says Hensley. "We profile based on how far after the first or second crack we pull a bean. For decaf, this eliminates the bean color issue altogether."

Decaf coffee is sometimes over- or under-roasted because the darker original color of the green coffee changes the roaster operator's perception of bean development through first crack, says Mayhall. "Overall, I have found a lower [roasting] temperature is required, especially on water-process coffee," Mayhall adds. "Less reliance on visual landmarks and more attention to the environment temperature, as well as a keen sense of the intensity and frequency of the first crack, are key."

But Kastle of Swiss Water Decaf says he doesn't "baby" his decaf coffee during the roasting process. "I don't change profiles anymore because I want to see if there's any performance difference between the pre- and post-decaffeination," he says. "In most cases, for washed Latin coffees, I'm seeing a variation so slight that it could be minor airflow differences."

Schoenholt says he doesn't find roasting decafs as challenging as single-origins such as Ethiopian Harrar. "Decaffeinating changes the color of the beans and removes some waxes and other material, so decaffeinated beans need a little practice to get used to," Schoenholt says, "but once you roast them up a few times, you have learned what to expect from the beans, and you are prepared to coax them through the process to where you want them to be."

Roasters shouldn't confuse roasting difficulty with simply paying attention to their beans, adds Terry V. Patano, roaster and owner of DOMA Coffee Roasting Company in Post Falls, Idaho. "If roasters put the same attention into their decaf as they do their other coffees, the world would have a lot more better-tasting decafs," Patano says.

RESULTS IN THE CUP

In many ways, decaf coffee is still saddled with baggage from years ago, when only poor-quality coffee was decaffeinated and it was nearly impossible to find a decaf that tasted good. Today, those perceptions are changing, but those who roast decaf that's past its prime or purchase coffee that didn't taste good *before* decaffeination are asking for disappointment.

"For our plant, we're at a point that I'm very confident that if you get a good coffee in, you'll get a good decaf out," says Kastle, who recommends roasting decaf beans within a month or two, just like regular coffee, to maintain peak freshness. "If you send us a really old, tired, baggy coffee, it's not going to magically turn into brand-new coffee. ... You take a not-great coffee in the door, and that's what you get out." Many importers and larger roasters take advantage of toll decaffeination services, allowing them to send their own quality coffee beans to be processed rather than buying a pre-blended decaf.

Even so, roasters say that their decafs do not exhibit the same flavors that they taste in the caffeinated version of the bean. For one, caffeine is an acidic compound, so removing caffeine from the beans affects the acidity in the cup.

"From a cupper's perspective, all decaffeinated coffees knock a bit of coffee's natural acidity away, along with some other natural ingredients, which explains why decaffeinated produces a duller roast, and sometimes a duller cup than its nondecaffeinated brethren," Schoenholt says. "Still, decaffeinated has come a long way from the insipid, uninspiring and sometimes medicinal-tasting stuff that passed for decaffeinated 40 years ago."

Hensley, who confesses to trying decaf coffee for the first time after he started roasting it, enlisted his parents to give feedback on his roasts. Flavors are not as prominent in decaf coffees, he notes. "You can make decaf very smooth," Hensley says, "but you also lose a lot of those accent flavors that other coffees tend to have, like citrus, or nut flavors, or berry, or other fruity flavors that come out in a lot of regular coffees." However, manipulation of roast, grind and dosage can counteract the milder flavor of the beans.

Bodden of Bica has been drinking decaf for years and points to two other factors that affect his perception of decaf. "First of all, it's usually roasted quite dark, and we prefer much lighter roasts," he says. "Second of all, there just is not the selection from which to choose. [The roasters I purchase from] ... oftentimes have two decaf blends, and sometimes have a single-origin decaf; I will always opt for the single-origin because it becomes more than just 'decaf.'"

When selecting decaf coffees for their lineup, some roasters prefer to stick with coffees processed via a single method, while others experiment with all types. Bica, DOMA and 35 North are loyal to water-based processes due to a combination of taste, organic certification and health reasons. Gillies and Metropolis, on the other hand, work with coffees decaffeinated with a variety of methods.

"Each method of decaffeination has a unique effect on the flavor of the coffee, and I don't generally seek out one in particular," says Mayhall of Metropolis, who says he purchases based on results in the cup. "Personally, I have found that the methylene chloride typically affects the flavor of the coffee less than other methods but can leave a slight chemical odor," he adds. "Water-process coffees tend to exhibit a unique sourness and can be tricky to roast, and the ethyl acetate process sometimes completely changes the balance of sweetness, amplifying it or giving it an artificial quality."

Early this year, Mayhall took his decaf experimentation one step further: He approved a nondecaffeinated green sample of a Kenya prior to decaffeination.

In addition to the quality of the coffee, Mayhall says the lower freight costs for decaffeination at a plant in the United States played into his choice. The decision was "a big change for me in recent years, approving the coffee before decaffeination," he says. "Really, I don't think that would have happened for a small company 10 years ago."

Mayhall's decision reflects a growing comfort with decaf coffee—from purchasing to roasting to serving the coffee to the consumer—and maybe even a shot of confidence.

"I think we could fool a lot of 'core' espresso drinkers with our decaf—and on occasion I do!" says Patano of DOMA. "There are some really good decafs out there. Don't give up if you haven't found one. Roasters [should] take the time and care you would with your other coffees—you have a lot of customers who will appreciate it."

DECAF AS A PRODUCT CATEGORY

Decaffeinated Coffee As A Product Category
(not a necessary evil)

by Ruth Ann Church

"HOW MANY of your customers buy decaf?" It seems like an obvious question, but some roasters are surprised by their answer. They begin by saying, "Hardly any; it's a very small part of our business." They're right, of course. Decaf usually comprises only 5 to 25 percent of any roaster's volume. But the question, stated more specifically, is, "Thinking about your wholesale business, what percent of your customers are buying decaf from you?" After a pause, the answer is usually, "Well, it's 100 percent."

The realization that decaf is the only other product after regular coffee that nearly every customer needs at some point can drive a whole new perspective on decaffeinated coffee. It's a unique product category in the roaster's product mix. Let's look at what it means to consider decaf coffee as just that—a product category, not a "necessary evil." Like other product categories, one of the most important aspects to evaluate is whether it's making money for you.

Product Category Review

Savvy business owners know which product categories are making money and which aren't, and they have sound reasons for each case. So the roaster's initial step with decaf is to evaluate its current status among all of the product categories. With this baseline, the roaster can decide if the status quo is acceptable (and it may very well be), or the roaster may determine that there's a missed opportunity to add profits, improve quality consistency and retain loyal customers. It's hard to find good decaf coffee, so when a consumer finds good decaf, they typically become loyal.

Tables 1 and 2 show an example lineup of product categories and the types of work one would do for the product categories that are driving profits. Replace the numbers in Table 1 with your own. For each line, consider whether that category is profitable or not, and how confident you are about your answer. If decaf isn't making money, or you're not sure if it is, you get to decide if it's worth doing anything about it.

To help you decide, you could review the items in Table 2 and determine whether any of them have resulted in improved sales for other categories. For example, what actions have helped sales of your highest-margin coffees? Have cuppings or other means of educating customers ever boosted revenue for a small category that was lagging?

TABLE 1

PRODUCT CATEGORIES

ROASTER	% of sales
Regular coffee and regular espresso	80%
Decaf coffee and decaf espresso	10%
Syrups	5%
Teas	5%
Total	**100%**
Fair-trade coffees	3%
Organic coffees	5%

TABLE 2

WHAT VALUED PRODUCT SEGMENTS GET

- Careful sourcing
- Quality checks
- Sales team educated about the product
- A place on the menu
- Promotional marketing
- Prime placement (on shelf, in store, etc.)
- Sustainable pricing

Quality Compromised for Price

All of the items in Table 2 are important, but the last one, pricing, is particularly critical and too often ignored when it comes to decaf. What appears to happen commonly is a "not thinking about it" pricing method. There's a pervasive assumption that the per-pound or per-cup price to customers must match the regular coffee price.

This assumption almost always forces a quality compromise. Decaffeination is an added cost requiring additional transportation. Plus, decaf is purchased in smaller quantities than regular coffee. If the end user is asked to pay the same price they pay for regular, the business owner can maintain margins only by buying a quality level of decaf that is significantly lower than that of the regular coffee the business serves.

Enlightened Decaf Pricing Model

This quality compromise is avoided by pricing decaf separately from regular coffee and applying a cost-plus-margin approach to both. In this model, a high-quality regular coffee might cost $3.50 per pound and a decaf of equal quality might cost $4 per pound. By adding the business's required margin of 40 percent to each base cost, the resulting prices are $4.90 per pound for regular and $5.60 per pound for decaf (see Table 3).

With this model, quality and those who value it win. "Decaffeinated coffee costs more," says Brett Struwe, director of coffee operations at Caribou Coffee in Minneapolis. "We believe Caribou customers care about quality and taste, so we put it out there." About six years ago, Caribou made the bold move of shifting its entire decaf coffee line to water-processed decaf coffees. At the same time, the company implemented a plus-$.10 per cup and a plus-$1 per pound price markup that's plainly listed on every menu board.

"It's successful," Struwe says, "or we wouldn't still be doing it. We may not be getting as much of the overall decaf market, but our decaf customers are the high end. We communicate with them, and they understand the added value we offer."

What Caribou and others have done is use marketing muscle to support the transition to higher-priced decaf coffees. At Caribou, customer service reps are trained to share colorful in-store booklets that describe the decaffeination process and how Caribou is paying attention to quality for the decaf segment. Other roasters use blind cuppings and store intercepts to promote the quality and taste of their decaf line up. One roaster/retailer welcomed a "moms' club" to his coffeehouse. It was an opportunity to share how good his decaf coffee is while also improving sales during an otherwise slow part of the day.

TABLE 3

ENLIGHTENED DECAF PRICING

	Base cost per lb.	40% margin	Customer price per lb.
Regular coffee (meeting high-quality standard X)	$3.50	+$1.40	$4.90
Decaf (meeting high-quality standard X)	$4.00	+$1.60	$5.60

The Decaf Consumer

Marketing efforts raise the question, "Who is the decaf consumer?" There is a wealth of information about them available through industry associations, although it's harder to find than one might think. The most striking demographic on decaf consumers is age. Decaf drinkers start to become a significant share of the coffee-drinking population in the over-35 range and take another noticeable step up to 25 percent market share in the 60-years-and-older range. According to the National Coffee Association, growth of the gourmet coffee market so far has been focused on the younger demographics, "a huge missed opportunity for the industry."

Other industry professionals also lament the current overall lack of attention to the possibilities in decaf coffee. In the July 2010 edition of *Coffee Review*, Kenneth Davids wrote, "Perhaps some ... innovative roasting company needs to raise the bar for the specialty industry by putting more focus on decaffeinated coffees and in the process making some waves and some money with them."

To give credit where credit is due, many roasters *are* offering high-quality decafs. They're charging for it, and increasing numbers of decaf consumers are thanking them for their efforts with extra change at the cash register. These roasters refuse to compromise on their brand promise of "high-quality coffee"—especially when they know the product is one of only two items that 100 percent of their customers buy from them. ■

. . . .

RUTH ANN CHURCH *drinks decaf coffee daily and is president and chief relationship officer of Artisan Coffee Imports, which specializes in providing great-tasting decaffeinated green coffee from all of the decaffeination processes. She can be reached via email at* rachurch@artisancoffeeimports.com.

PART III

ROASTING

PACKAGING

Coffee packaging equipment at Boyd's Coffee in Portland, Oregon.

Only the Essentials

Advances in Coffee Packaging Equipment

by Allyson Marrs

• FROM THE MAY/JUNE 2014 ISSUE OF *ROAST* •

P recious cargo, every step of the way. Beans have been harvested, carefully shipped, even more prudently roasted and then packaged—the final step in a meticulous practice, all for the simple purpose of creating the perfect cup. Yet, simplicity really doesn't have much to do with it.

At the packaging level, it's the last opportunity to put a personal finish on the product before customers get their hands (and brewing equipment) on it. Packaging is a branding opportunity; it's a growth opportunity; it's a vital financial decision. Packaging is more than just signing, sealing and delivering.

Packaging Trends: Then And Now

Like every aspect of the process, there has been substantial growth in options and variables, both for the manufacturers and the roasters. Glenn Sacco, president of PBi, says that in terms of manufacturing, there's been a burst of availability for more affordable, efficient equipment. He adds that automatic machines can now be found for less than $100,000, whereas before they cost upward of $250,000. "These simple, yet sturdy machines allow smaller roasters with high-volume items to take advantage of increased line speeds and decreased packaging material costs," he says.

For roasters, specifically small to midsize, Sacco says that many have realized automated equipment is the best investment when dedicated to one format and one or two sizes; however, manual is preferable to maintain capital and to "invest in the business you have and not the business you hope to have."

For packaging options, packages that protect beans from oxygen are becoming more of a requirement, whereas packages that make less of an environmental impact are becoming more of a popular preference. "Technology is finally catching up, and the increased desire to be responsible suppliers is bridging the gap between hope and reality," says Sacco. The final goal is for the package to completely protect the beans while also being completely biodegradable. Advances and popularity of single-serve cup brewers are also changing the scene, all of which will be discussed.

These trends are, of course, heavily influenced by the consumers and what they want out of their coffee. Tom Martin of POD Pack International says that in reality, a consumer's wants are the first variable to be considered, followed by investment plans and realities in packing equipment, floor space, ancillary systems needed (such as air, power and nitrogen supplies), machine speeds, capacity and minimum economical production volume run sizes. Flexibility, ease of training and operation, and changeover and cleanout time required are also all factors.

Jeffrey Teich of North Atlantic Specialty Bag reiterates that consumers are driving the trends, as packaging options have grown from traditional cans to flexible multilayer structures to side gussets to pouches with zipper closers and, to the newest comer, the ever-present pods.

All agree the changes are exciting and allow for creativity, both on the roasting and manufacturing sides, but with so much to consider, choosing a packaging option can prove rather difficult.

On Brand

Financials, consumers and branding push packaging decisions, and priorities can shift quickly. "This starts with what the end user wants," says Martin. "Roasters must be ready to respond to what the consumer wants before their competitor does. This can be in terms of convenience, sustainable packaging and cost/value per serving."

The primary goals always take precedence, though—preserving quality and communicating to the customer. Sacco says that roasters must then decide on a method that keeps up with demand, and while order of importance varies, quality, consumer-friendly features, graphics and branding are all to be considered as well.

"The package is the final salesperson for your coffee," says Sacco. "How effectively you convey your message and appeal to a consumer's desire for luxury, convenience and a great cup of coffee through the package is vital."

Whether a roaster opts for handcrafted appeal through labeling and bag choice, or for svelte, stylish bags with polished custom printing, it's a business decision that can dictate target market and, really, success. "There is a fine line between an innovative package and one that separates you from the consumer's concept of what a coffee package 'should be,'" says Sacco.

Teich adds that packaging is a way to reel the customer in so you can then tell your story and focus on education and coffee knowledge. After devoting so much time to roasting the perfect batch, the overall goal is to grab the customers so they, too, can enjoy your hard work.

This may indeed vary for microroasters versus macroroasters, as microroasters may have more flexibility to maximize on customization, whereas macroroasters are able to take advantage of volume and save money on large production costs (and time with automated production). This will undoubtedly affect packaging choices for both types of roasters. After all, it's about finding the right fit for the company.

Making the Decision

With so much to take into account, how can you choose? While a more traditional approach can spell success for one roaster, an on-trend option will mean big business for another.

Below, consider the trade-offs to popular packaging options, as variety isn't only the spice of life, it's also the price of growth.

◯ Form-Fill-and-Seal

Form-fill-and-seal is an automated assembly-line product packaging system that constructs bags, fills and then seals them. This option is preferred for packaging material savings and efficient production speed with a large output.

Roll-fed materials become fully formed units before being filled and then properly weighed and marked for retail. Machines often offer closure options, and add-on stations perform labeling. The machine ultimately limits control, but efficiency is impressive. Because of the large output capacity, these machines are recommended for roasters who need to get a lot of product to market quickly.

However, the challenges are the high cost of entry, as the machines are expensive, and limited flexibility of production, since they're automated. Also worth taking into consideration is the machine's size, which makes this option better suited for a larger, possibly more established roaster.

In speaking to contamination, there are some risks involved when seals are made at the roasting facility. Weak or incomplete seals will allow oxygen to damage the beans, so one must be diligent in the assembly and the seal/leak tests.

◯ Valve Bags

Possibly the most easily recognized form of coffee packaging (especially for the consumer), valve bags are favored for their ability to keep coffee fresh. But, as Sacco says, the fact that the consumer can glance at the package and instantly know what's being sold is also a prominent advantage. In addition, it's an established method for both packaging and promoting the product that has proven successful, yet it is still vulnerable to the latest trend.

One-way valves are reliable barriers to maintain freshness, specifically for a longer period of time. While cost can be greater, quality will be, too. Although there are many options on the market, one-way degassing valves allow freshly roasted coffee to degas while maintaining a barrier from oxygen. Martin says the market for

Coffee packaging equipment at Boyd's Coffee in Portland, Oregon.

atmospheric bags with degassing valves has grown immensely over the years.

Information regarding the valve's performance from a third party should always be available, and Sacco recommends reading as much information as you can about the performance before purchasing.

○ Canisters

The canister's design and function has been durable over the years; it's been around for quite some time. To many, it's a "classic." It combines durability and stackability with a traditional look, although time has altered that a bit, too.

Canisters sealed with a peelable top foil help ensure freshness. Because barrier materials are the best protection against oxygen, materials that are dense in molecular structure, such as foils, are safe bets to guarantee freshness quality, says Sacco. Some canister designs also allow for a resealable foil top, so consumers can seal the can shut after each use, which will extend the life of the coffee.

Valve-Pak canisters are a way for roasters to pack and seal immediately after roasting, without long hold times for degassing, vacuuming or sacrificing flavor and aroma. Many cans can now be made biodegradable, answering the demand for more sustainable packaging.

Conscious Coffees has been packaging in steel cans for the last five years, after only selling in bulk wholesale for the first 12 years of business. Co-owner Mark Glenn says the most positive aspect of choosing cans is that theirs are constructed using approximately 50 percent recycled steel and are completely reusable and recyclable.

"I find this packaging to be superior to flexible, vapor-barrier, heat-seal packages for a couple more reasons," he says, noting that he's referencing whole beans only, not ground coffee. "With heat-sealed packages, there exists the risk that the package was not completely sealed, and thus will perish faster due to oxygen exposure. The seaming process each can goes through is far superior, eliminating the possibility of incomplete sealing."

Glenn adds that the one-way valve technology incorporated in the top of each can maintains structural integrity, so the potential for malfunction is nearly eliminated. The rigid, steel can package also protects the cell structure of the bean in transport and handling, he says. "We continue testing shelf life of beans packaged in cans, and [as long as] they were seamed within 20 minutes out of the roaster, the shelf life continues to be several months."

Some potential downsides to this packaging option include the cost for smaller companies. Glenn says that for Conscious Coffees, cans are at least five times the cost of flexible packaging. Shipping and storing the empty cans adds to the cost, too. "For us, the additional cost is justified simply because we can continue to remain accountable for our packaging when considering environmental impact," he says.

So while cans may be a "classic" option, advances in customization and sealing, as well as the reduced environmental impact, have helped them stand the test of time.

Packaging conveyor at Longbottom Coffee and Tea, Inc. in Hillsboro, Oregon.

Coffee packaging equipment at Boyd's Coffee in Portland, Oregon.

Coffee packaging equipment at Boyd's Coffee in Portland, Oregon.

Packaging at Longbottom Coffee and Tea, Inc. in Hillsboro, Oregon.

The packaging island at Boyd's Coffee in Portland, Oregon.

Pods

One of the largest-growing packaging options, pods have become increasingly popular. "We think the single cup coffee packaging will continue to grow because more and more consumers are using single-cup brewing systems," says Martin. "This requires additional packaging materials to package smaller, individual, 10-gram units of coffee for single-cup brewing, as opposed to putting 12 ounces of coffee to brew by the pot."

Sacco agrees that this prevalent trend will dictate new methods of production and packaging as the rest of the coffee roasting industry tries to find a place in this market. "The segment is dominated by large players and co-packers right now, but the specialty coffee industry is experimenting and dipping its toe in the market," Sacco says. "This will spur innovation and advancements as small to mid-size specialty roasters try to introduce better cup quality and scale down production costs and complexity to get in the game."

Gene Kakaulin, co-founder of HiLine Coffee Company, which manufactures Nespresso-compatible coffee capsules, says a complication of single-serve cups is the added production. "After roasting, we also grind, weigh, tamp and seal the coffee so that it's ready to extract. Transferring those responsibilities from barista to packaging increases the complexity of the product, as does maintaining freshness for as long as possible after capsules have been packed."

Kakaulin emphasizes that one-way valve technology isn't yet practical for single-serve application, so coffees are more aggressively degassed before packing, as compared to typical form-fill-and-seal machinery. "Precise timing is essential to maintain a balance of optimal freshness without rupturing the capsule."

To maintain freshness, Martin says that, most importantly, each unit must be individually wrapped; however, to save costs, some single cups are sold in bulk (think 12 cups in one bag), and when this happens, the first few units that are brewed may taste fresh, but after a day, the others will stale. "Individually wrapping units also reduces the packing machine capacity as compared to bulk bag packaging because the bottleneck is waiting for each pouch to be sealed as compared to sealing fewer bulk bags," Martin adds.

Andrew Hetzel, coffee quality consultant and adviser to HiLine Coffee Company, says that recycling is another challenge. "Like most coffee packaging, the materials used in a Nespresso-compatible capsule are individually recyclable but with one caveat: The coffee, plastic and foil must be separated in order to be accepted by recycling programs. There are some 100-percent biodegradable materials available for manufacturing, but these tend to fail during storage or use, which ruins the coffee."

Sacco echoes the sentiment, asserting that the biggest concern is cup quality, but that specialty roasters are focusing their attention and skills on this issue, so changes may be happening soon. "Single-serve pods offer the ultimate in consumer convenience and allow the roaster to charge more per pound than was ever dreamed of for mass-market coffee," he says.

So, while some kinks may still be getting straightened, the demand for pods is there, and roasters of all backgrounds are working to meet it.

Sustainable Packaging

Possibly the current industry darling, sustainable packaging is gaining a lot of momentum. Consumers want biodegradable bags, and roasters want to deliver. Sustainable materials are always on the mind as many continue to research ways to make it happen while still maintaining budgets and timelines. Finding these biodegradable, compostable or recyclable packing materials that still protect against oxygen at a reasonable cost is challenging, but there have been breakthroughs. Plus, it never hurts to have the public on your side.

However, Sacco notes that each eco-friendly solution has its disadvantages. For example, "at one time, corn-based plastics were considered the best solution; however, some argued that the cradle-to-grave carbon footprint was actually more detrimental than more traditional packages, and it drove up the cost of corn," he says. "Others complained that the corn was better used to feed the population. We have yet to find a sustainable packaging option that satisfies all audiences."

It is again a situation where a roaster must weigh consumer wants against cost and output. But if current times are any indication, sustainable packaging is not only becoming more of a reality for all packaging forms, it's also becoming more of a necessity among consumers.

Wrapping Up

As with most things, time has a great influence on how coffee roasters do, and will, package their coffee. Now, more than ever, options are available in every facet, along every step of the way, and packing is no different. With each choice comes a consequence and a reward—in terms of branding, quality control and cost. Most importantly, it's a decision that requires thought and time.

The specialty coffee industry is continually growing, and this growth is visibly tangible in the packaging options. With them, you can find tried-and-true favorites, such as canisters, and the latest developments, such as pods. It's hard to say where the industry is headed in the coming years, and what else will be available, or dismissed, in the next five to 10 years. But if time has given any hint, it's that the demand for coffee has only grown, and with it, so has coffee with a personality, coffee with a voice, and a package that provides it all—especially one that provides great flavor. ▪

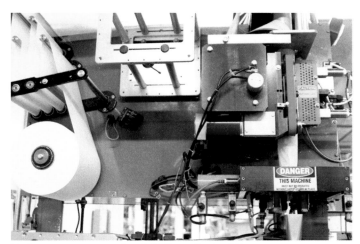

Packaging equipment at Boyd's Coffee in Portland, Oregon.

Coffee loader at Longbottom Coffee and Tea, Inc. in Hillsboro, Oregon.

Coffee packaging at Longbottom Coffee and Tea, Inc. in Hillsboro, Oregon.

PART IV

OPERATING A SPECIALTY COFFEE ROASTING BUSINESS

BUSINESS BASICS

The Importance of a Business Plan and Business Planning

By Bruce Milletto and Matt Milletto

photos by Mark Shimahara

• EXCLUSIVE TO *THE BOOK OF ROAST* •

W hen you are in the early planning stages of opening a coffee roasting operation, the attention you pay to strategic planning will influence and impact your results as you move forward. Taking the time to develop a business plan can make the difference between success and failure for a new business.

As founders and owners of The American Barista & Coffee School, we have one-on-one discussions with every student about how to move forward to attain their dream of entering the specialty coffee industry. A vast majority of our students lack critical information about the business planning process.

Planning is confusing and, at times, overwhelming. This is true even for people with many years of business experience, especially if they have no entrepreneurial background. With so many variables, it can be a challenge to prioritize all the necessary tasks and manage your time effectively. This chapter will help you determine what those tasks are, create a plan and stay focused on your path to success.

Where to Begin

The best place to start the planning process is by looking at all the tasks involved and deciding which require your attention tomorrow and which can be tackled down the line. Begin by making a list of everything you need to do to get your business started. Once you've created the list, categorize each item according to when it needs to be accomplished—before you open, the first week, the first month, etc. This will help you create a roadmap to guide your work, identify important milestones, and evaluate your progress along the way.

But what are the tasks you need to accomplish?

Creating a Business Model

Before you invest any money in your project, look at your competition and decide if there truly is a market for your coffee operation, and what exactly will make yours different. As business advisors, our clients often tell us there are no microroasters in their area. This can be an opportunity to be a true pioneer, but it also comes with the challenges of educating your potential customers about why your product is superior. In Portland, Oregon, for example, there are no less than 50 specialty coffee roasters, both large and small. When we opened Water Avenue Coffee, we knew we would be competing with some of the best roasters in the industry, but we were able to open in an up-and-coming industrial area where the business can stand out.

If you do have direct competition in your local area, you'll need to decide how your business will be different, and if, in fact, your business will fit the local market. Will you sell wholesale, mainly

to independent coffee bars and cafes? Will you also set up a grocery program? Do you live in an area where there are numerous restaurants that might want to take their coffee programs to the next level? If these types of operations are in your plan, how will you deliver your coffee to your customers?

If you decide to have a retail coffee bar to showcase your coffee, you will have even more variables to consider and processes to implement. It's easy to get overwhelmed starting a roasting operation and a retail business at the same time, so we generally suggest roasters focus on the roasting business first, adding retail once they have developed the confidence and consistency to take on another large-scale project. Using this

model, retail could be part of your three- or five-year plan. You might want to open a small tasting and cupping area in your roasting plant to start, then add a larger retail shop—possibly in a different location—when your business can support it.

Creating a Budget

Establishing a budget for your project will be at the top of your initial to-do list. Be realistic. There are many factors that influence the startup costs of your proposed business, and having a realistic plan is important in outlining how much capital you can invest, as well as how much you intend to borrow.

Research standard rents on commercial properties in your area to estimate location costs. What equipment will you need to sustain your business initially and allow room for growth over the first five years? How much will you need for marketing? Will you be hiring employees immediately, and if so, what will your personnel costs be? And finally, will you want to open a retail operation in addition to your roasting business to showcase your product for your local audience? If so, your location will be paramount to your ability to support both roasting and retail.

Finding a Location

Location dynamics may or may not be of huge importance. If you have no retail component, you likely will want to find space in one of the least expensive industrial districts. Consider the cost of exhaust and ventilation for your roasting equipment, and the zoning necessary to be a wholesale business. A one-story building may save you anywhere from $10,000 to $40,000 in initial startup costs, and taller buildings without an adequate chase or ability to vent may be impractical for your proposed business. Rent will be one of your largest initial expenses, so location matters greatly when it comes to profitability.

The easiest way to begin researching locations is simply by driving around and calling for more information when you see "for rent" or "for lease" signs. When you're ready to move forward, you might want to enlist a commercial real estate agent to assist you. A professional will have an understanding of the current market and where it is headed, and he or she often will know of sites that are not yet listed but will become available in the near future.

Equipment Needs

Your roasting equipment is the heart of your business. In addition to finding a great roaster, whether new or used, you will want to investigate the need for destoners, roast logging software, afterburners and packaging equipment. What type of tables, shelving and other furniture will you need to outfit your roasting operation? Thoroughly think through your entire operation and start factoring a cost for each item on the list.

Marketing

Some experts recommend setting aside at least 5 to 10 percent of your total startup budget—if not more—for initial marketing efforts. These costs begin as soon as you establish a name and brand and continue throughout the build-out phase. The focus is on getting your name out into the community.

You will need to devote both dollars and time to marketing and branding in order to be successful, but it doesn't have to cost a fortune or overwhelm your schedule. The following are just a few examples of simple, low-cost and no-cost ideas for promoting your coffee and your business.

• **Hand out coupons:** If you have a service bar in your roastery, create two-for-one cards and carry them with you wherever you go. The goal is to get as many people as possible into your shop to taste your coffee. If your business doesn't have a retail component, print up small cards offering $2 off any 12-ounce or 1-pound bag of coffee. The key is to get people into your roastery and make a connection. When you meet someone in person, they're far more likely to visit your business than if they receive something in the mail or see a flyer posted around town.

• **Build your web presence:** This is extremely important, so create a website as soon as possible. You can use a simple commercial Wordpress site or something more elaborate. Showcase information about your philosophy, your background, your product and what makes you unique. Keep it fresh and dynamic by updating it regularly with news of new coffees, events and more. Be sure the information you include is understandable and educational, and also heartfelt—show your passion for quality coffee! In addition to your own website, set up profiles on Facebook, Twitter, Instagram and other social media outlets to establish your brand and raise awareness of your business and your coffee.

• **Get out into the community:** Seize every opportunity to serve your coffee in a public setting—at grocery stores, street fairs, holiday bazaars, etc. This one-on-one contact with potential customers is extremely effective. Bring marketing materials with you (the two-for-one or discount cards, for example) as well as a flyer or brochure about your coffee.

• **Visit potential wholesale accounts:** Taking time out of your normal week to visit potential wholesale accounts should be key to your growth plan. Most of the companies you visit likely will already have a relationship with another roaster, so tread lightly and focus on establishing a friendship. Trying to flip a potential account from another vendor will take time, but your constant kind, friendly and persistent visits may in time lead to new business.

• **Approach grocery outlets:** Once you are prepared to set up a system of delivery and upkeep on larger accounts, try to get your coffee into grocery stores. This makes your name visible to a larger market and allows you to sell in larger volumes. Try to get your coffee into upscale specialty markets and bypass the large chains where you have little chance of getting shelf space.

Remember, when you're trying to create brand awareness for your coffee, you must have a story to tell, so create one that is real and compelling. You need to let potential customers know why your coffee is unique and why they should try it.

Labor Costs

Most small roasting operations without a retail component begin with no employees, or possibly one. During the first few months, it is important to keep your costs down. In most cases, you will be the one roasting the coffee, bagging it and delivering it. You

will look for new accounts. You will maintain your roasting equipment as well as espresso and coffee equipment for your clients. In addition to minimizing costs during your initial startup period, working all aspects of the business will allow you to train employees when the time comes.

Once your business is established, labor likely will become one of your biggest expenses, and while having employees can be one of the most rewarding aspects of owning a small business, it can also be one of the most challenging. Outline a sales growth path defining key trigger points that will allow you to bring on extra help.

Two Types of Business Plans: The Presentation Plan and The Financial Plan

When we talk about developing a business plan, we are actually talking about two types of plans: a presentation plan and a financial plan. They can be combined to create a master plan, but each has its own distinct purpose, and it's important to develop both.

• The Presentation Plan

The presentation plan is essentially your conceptual plan, articulating in writing what you intend to create with your new business. This can be useful when approaching potential landlords, investors, lenders and others. The presentation plan describes the coffee you plan to roast and sell and explains the overall logistics of success in microroasting. This plan also will include details about your proposed customers and why they will select your business over your competition. It's also important to include data on the specialty coffee industry as a whole, and to show consumer trends and examples of growth within the specialty market.

Another key element of the presentation plan is your marketing strategy. You can include some case study examples of successful businesses that represent a similar concept to your proposed business, especially in areas where there are not an abundance of progressive coffee roasters or retail shops. Finally, in this plan you will want to dust off your resume and showcase why you will succeed as a small business owner, how you have educated yourself in the specialty coffee industry, and how you have prepared yourself to succeed and grow professionally with your business concept.

A typical table of contents for a presentation plan will include:

- **Executive Summary:** Mission statement and overview of the plan.

- **Details of the Business:** Where, when, why and how.

- **Your Product(s):** Green buying, roasting, brewing, certification, etc.

- **Location:** Include details about how your business will benefit the community and why you will succeed in your selected location.

- **Company Principals and Staffing Plan:** Strategic staffing plan and plans for growth.

- **Additional Expertise**: Fees for professional services and assistance, such as consultants, trainers, attorneys, accountants, architects, and others.

- **Target Market**: Who are your proposed customers?

- **Competition:** Who are they, what have they done well, and why will you do better?

- **Marketing Techniques:** Your initial and ongoing marketing plan.

- **Market Trend Analysis:** Include examples of industry growth and trends.

- **Sample Equipment Plan & Layout:** Mainly for discussions with prospective landlords about tenant improvements.

- **Sample Menu and List of Offerings:** This is especially important if you plan to do retail.

Keep your presentation plan concise and easy to read. It is not necessary to include dozens of pages of information if it can be summarized clearly and concisely in a couple of paragraphs. Also, remember to have your contact information on the front to make it easy for landlords and investors to reach you.

• The Financial Plan

A good financial plan will provide you with a projected total cost for your project, including a list of startup expenses, so you can budget accordingly. This plan also will provide you with insights and goals for your proposed operation, including a projected profit-and-loss statement that will allow you to assess the risk of the business before making major decisions or large investments. Finally, a thorough financial plan will provide you with the data necessary to attract investors and obtain financing.

A comprehensive financial business plan should include:

- **Estimated Startup Costs:** These costs often are categorized into equipment needs, miscellaneous expenses, build-out costs, professional services, initial inventory, operating capital, and so on.

•**Projected Labor:** Outline a labor schedule for your initial business as well as a growth plan for future expansion. Determine roles and responsibilities, hours of operation and other logistics to project labor expenses.

• **Sales Assumptions:** For roasting operations, project an average sale per customer or an average price per pound or retail bag. If you plan to open a coffee bar, project an average beverage/food/retail sale per customer.

• **Estimated Sales Growth:** Determine a realistic sales growth, either by pounds per week for your wholesale program or customers per day for retail.

• **Estimated Cost of Goods:** Your cost of goods should NOT be a variable percentage based on volume. Set a realistic cost of goods on your end product so you can estimate gross and net profits by category.

• **Profit and Loss Projections:** Essentially, you will multiply sales assumptions by sales growth monthly for year one, and annually for years two and three. From gross sales, subtract your cost of goods, labor and other expenses. Be conservative and realistic about how fast you can grow. Once your business is open, compare your actual profit and loss against your projections to see if you are on track.

A well-thought-out and well-written business plan is essential for overall success and can be the key to landing your desired location and investments. Do as much research as you can on all aspects of your proposed business and do not be afraid to ask for help.

Don't become overwhelmed by the numerous tasks ahead of you—it's simply a matter of developing systems. Remember, it's relatively easy to control an established set of systems, but impossible to control countless variables. By taking the time to develop your business plan, you will set yourself up for success from the beginning.

Above all, be patient. The more time you spend planning, the more prepared you will be once your business plans come to fruition. ∎

. . . .

BRUCE MILLETTO *is recognized internationally by the press and the coffee industry as the voice of the specialty coffee industry. He has been interviewed by or quoted in The New York Times, the Wall Street Journal, Time Magazine, Newsweek, 60 Minutes, Kiplinger's, Starbucks Annual Report, Forbes, the Economist, Harvard Management Update, Crain's Business Review, the Seattle Times, The Washington Post, Business Week and Entrepreneur. He is the founder of Bellissimo Coffee InfoGroup and The American Barista & Coffee School. He and his son Matt also founded and presently operate Water Avenue Coffee in Portland, Oregon.*

MATT MILLETTO *has extensive experience in nearly every aspect of the specialty coffee industry. Over the past 20 years, he has trained more than 2,500 new coffee retail business owners and barista trainers/managers. He regularly speaks at industry tradeshows and has been quoted in numerous newspapers and magazines, including the Wall Street Journal. Milletto is the current president of the Oregon Coffee Board and a head judge for Coffee Fest latte art competitions. He is the founder of baristaexchange.com, director and developer of onlinebaristatraining.com, and coordinates consulting services with Bellissimo Coffee InfoGroup clients and American Barista & Coffee School graduates.*

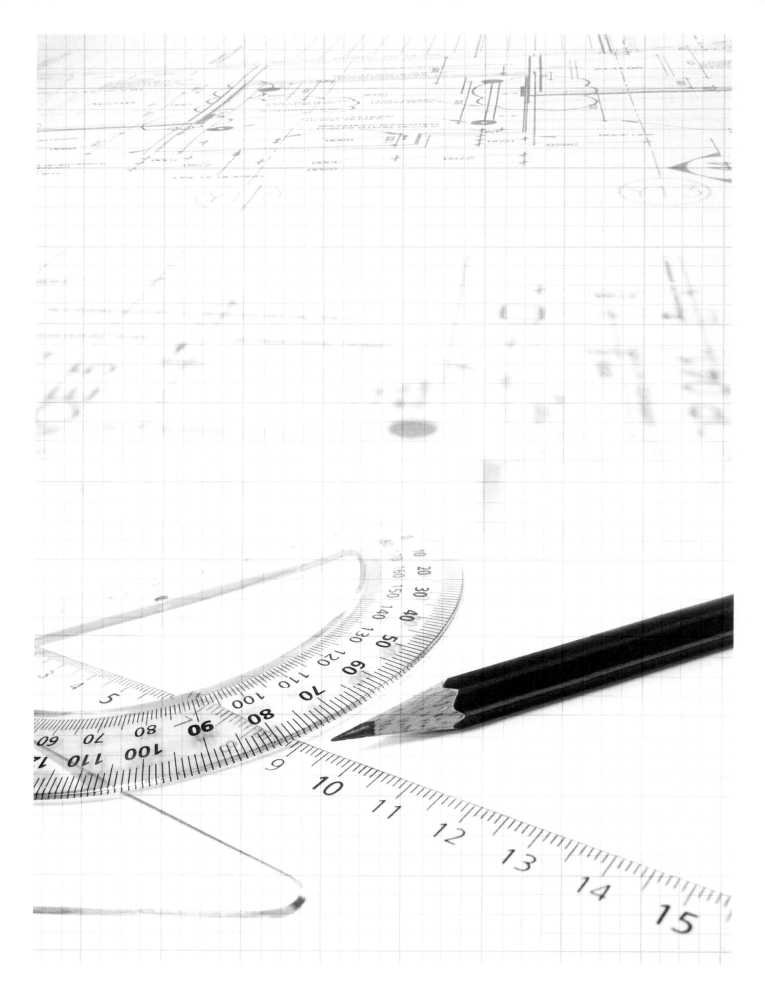

Flow Chart

How to Plan an Efficient Layout in a Small Production Plant

by John Larkin

• FROM THE JANUARY/FEBRUARY 2012 ISSUE OF *ROAST* •

Whether it's your first foray into production roasting or you are growing to the next level, careful upfront planning can help you lay out a manufacturing plant that meets your goals and efficiently delivers to your expectations. This well-designed plant will have equipment sized to your needs and matched in terms of throughput capability, space large enough to accommodate the equipment and maintenance zones around it, storage areas for green and roasted bean plus consumables and supplies, a loading/unloading area, and (for efficiency) a layout that to the extent possible flows in one general direction. Depending on your budget, this well-designed roasting plant may also position you to accommodate additional growth further down the road.

What Are Your Goals?

When starting to plan a production facility, it's important to define your immediate and long-term goals. Will your business be whole-bean, ground, flavored or a combination of these? How much green bean, and how many types, will you be storing? How much coffee do you need to roast, degas, quality check and package (and perhaps blend, grind and/or flavor) in what time frame? How long will you need to store your roasted product? Will you deliver or ship roasted coffee daily, weekly or on some other time schedule? The answers to these questions will help determine equipment needs (see "One-Roaster Plant Equipment Requirement" on page 400) and space requirements, and will have a direct impact on the project budget.

What Kind of Space Should You Consider?

The adage of "location, location, location" is true even in coffee. Make sure that the space you choose is in an industrially friendly location, or you may have to move again sooner than you'd planned. You need to factor in traffic, parking, hours of operation and emissions—all of which can become issues with neighbors, particularly in neighborhoods that are being reinvigorated with new or updated housing. For ease of your operations, good highway access is a plus, and an accessible loading dock for receiving and shipping is an important feature for efficiency and growth.

The ideal space for your manufacturing facility fits the scale of your equipment, material handling and storage needs with some additional room for growth. For example, you may want to start production roasting by offering roasted whole-bean and ground coffee, although down the road you'd like to introduce flavored beans as well. Later, you may want to add a larger grinder or even a second roaster. If you can afford extra floor space with future goals in mind, it might help you postpone a subsequent move.

An often overlooked but significant factor in space selection is ceiling height, with 25 to 45 feet being optimum with the roof directly above that. You want as much as possible to have a straight vertical run for stacks required by the roaster, cooler, destoner and pollution control (afterburner). Before signing anything, be sure that codes and landlords permit the roof penetrations required for these stacks. Then, always have roof penetrations performed by qualified roofers to be sure that stacks and flashings are correctly installed, which will help to prevent problems in the future.

A high ceiling means you can let gravity work for you, necessitating fewer pieces of conveying equipment and resulting in lower energy costs. One vertical conveying system with well-planned distribution, for example, can feed several pieces of equipment (blending, storage, flavoring, grinding and/or packaging). Vertical space can also allow for future growth—codes, construction and landlord permitting—with opportunities for mezzanines that can become platforms for production, storage and/or office space. Finally, from an installation and maintenance perspective, a high ceiling permits access, which can help minimize costs.

The floor of the space is another extremely important consideration. It must have a per-square-inch weight capacity to accommodate all of the pieces of equipment and storage that you intend to place on it. You will want to look at whether the floor construction is acceptable for food manufacturing and if there are enough restrooms for employees, plus first-aid stations and equipment cleaning/maintenance locations.

Be sure, too, that the space you're considering has enough gas/oil/propane, electric, water, compressed air and drainage to meet the combined requirements of the equipment you're installing. More than one roasting plant has added thousands of dollars to a budget by having to get gas pressure boosted or electric service changed to meet equipment needs. Also review HVAC (heating, ventilation and air conditioning) requirements and light levels. Remember noise when planning your office and conference spaces as roasters, afterburners and compressors can be loud when operating. Knowing your requirements is the first step. Some of these improvements can then be negotiated with the building owner, preferably before signing the lease.

Finally, be sure to factor into your budget the ingress and egress of the building. If your equipment will not fit through existing doors, loading docks, stairwells or elevators, there will be additional expenses to break it down and reassemble it.

The Flow Starts Here

The keys to successful equipment selection and layout planning are (1) defining and quantifying your process flow goals, (2) trying to arrange the process flow as much as possible in one general direction to minimize production floor traffic jams and redundant motion, and (3) keeping the individual pieces of equipment that implement the flow in balance with each other in terms of their capacities. For example, it doesn't usually make sense to pair a single roaster that produces up to 500 pounds of coffee per batch

with a packaging machine that handles 5,000 pounds per hour. While it may sound as if you're anticipating growth to do so, you either won't have enough product to keep the packaging machine running in an efficient way or you will need to buy expensive bin space to store enough roasted coffee to operate the packaging machine efficiently.

The roaster, of course, is the heart of everything, and it is a good place to start your planning and layout for the following reasons. To save money, time and trouble, plan to locate it as close as possible to utilities such as gas/propane, electric and water, and place it where you can make a straight vertical run through the roof for the stack. Additionally, a fire-suppression system may be required by the local authorities.

The product flow starts with the unloading of green coffee at the loading dock and the transport of the green bean through the plant to the green storage area. Be sure to allow aisle space for this material handling, which may even necessitate room for a forklift to navigate with a skid of green beans. Refer to Current Good Manufacturing Practices (CGMP) for specifics about how much space is required between product and walls, how much space is required for aisles, incorporating pest control programs into the physical space, appropriate product conveyance methods, and storage of potential contaminants such as chemicals, tools and glass away from product. Your business insurance company may provide free advice on safety considerations such as forklift training, proper lifting techniques, fire evacuation routes, first aid kits and other safety equipment.

The work flow then follows the direction of the green bean as it moves from the storage area to the roaster and cooler.

A one-roaster production plant is typically a batch type facility with a 60- to 250-kilo (120- to 500-pound) roaster that can do one to four bags of coffee per batch, and roughly three batches per hour. In one shift a day, five days a week, a one-roaster plant using a 250-kilo machine at three batches an hour can potentially roast about 3 million pounds of coffee a year. The two principal roasting technologies on the market are drum and fluidized bed, and there are a number of good roasters that offer these technologies. Starting with the technology that you already know and like—the one that has gotten you where you are—means a shorter learning curve and a seamless transition when growing to the next level.

The capacity of these production roasters means they have larger footprints that need to be factored in when selecting a production space. They will also have a proportionately larger cooler. As batches get above 25 pounds, additional equipment will also be required to load the coffee into the roaster. This might be a

John Larkin (left) and Morning Star Coffee Master Roaster Antonio Sordi discuss coffee equipment in Morning Star's West Chester, Penn., conference room. | *Photo courtesy of John Larkin and Co., Inc.*

motorized lift, an eductor or an airveyor, any of which need to be factored into the throughput balance and spatial considerations. When choosing a coffee transfer mechanism, be sure to bear in mind your final product. If it is roasted whole-bean, you will want a gentler transfer mechanism, and you always want to keep runs as straight and short as possible for any type of bean to minimize hang up and breakage.

After the cooler, you will need a destoner to remove foreign debris. The possible types of debris are remarkable and may range from stones, slag metal and jewelry to anything else that is not roasted coffee. This debris may get overlooked as you process larger batches and can wreak havoc with grinders and/or customers if it is not removed.

In a system that includes a destoner, the cooler discharges into a destoner boot. Vertically moving air raises only the beans through the destoner riser (tube) on up to the destoner hopper, leaving debris behind for removal via a cleanout door. The air is adjustable for speed and volume, making the system appropriate for whole-bean or ground coffee purveyors. We recommend as short a riser as possible for manufacturers doing dark roasts. In all cases, a smooth, unobstructed surface inside the riser is best.

Additionally, we recommend using magnets at various stages in the production flow, starting at the dump station all the way through to packaged coffee, to capture metal debris. Clean-out access to remove the debris should be provided. In fact, throughout the plant, emphasis should be on short pipe runs, as few angles as possible and frequent clean-out access.

Pollution control is also an important consideration in this day and age. We recommend addressing it upfront, even if it doesn't seem to be an immediate issue with your locality, because eventually it will become one. As hard as it is for us coffee lovers to believe, just one complaint about the aroma of coffee in the air, even in an industrial area, can lead to expensive repercussions in terms of time, money and public relations.

The type of pollution control device needs to be matched to your roaster and will probably be some sort of afterburner/thermal control. These are easier and less expensive to install and integrate when first setting up a plant than to retrofit later (although that can certainly be done). Addressing the issue upfront also shows a sense of responsibility, which can win points down the road.

When selecting and combining the roaster, cooler, destoner and pollution control, it is always best to follow the roaster manufacturer's recommendations. Using a spreadsheet to compare information on various packages can help you make an educated choice about the best dollar value that meets your needs. Expanding the spreadsheet to include footprint dimensions of the various pieces of equipment helps to define spatial requirements. Be sure to allow extra space—usually 3 to 5 feet—around the various pieces of equipment for maintenance activities. Also, allow space for cleaning pipes. This is critical work to minimize the chance of fire.

Morning Star Coffee is a one-roaster plant that has maximized space with work stations and shelving. | *Photo courtesy of John Larkin and Co, Inc.*

What happens next depends on your business focus, but all roasting plants will need to address conveying and storage (before and after packaging) and packaging. Whole-bean suppliers will flow their product on to temporary storage and then packaging via gentler conveying mechanisms (tubular conveying systems, continuous bucket elevators, totes or sacks), so as not to damage it. Ground and/or flavored coffee purveyors will need to factor in additional equipment, such as grinders, ribbon blenders and centrifugal mixers, and will direct their flow, or a percentage of their flow, to those areas prior to packaging. Flavoring presents an additional challenge of cross-contamination and may best be located in a separate room and performed on dedicated equipment. Flavorings and flavored product may also require special storage depending on fire codes.

Storage space before packaging will depend on your packing schedule and should factor in the volume of coffee that must be stored prior to packing and whether this will be required overnight or over weekends. If you're storing only for hours or days, you can probably skip pricey, big bins or silos and opt instead for mobile plastic or metal totes or fabric bulk sacks. Totes tend to be more expensive and take up more space than bulk sacks (which can be folded up when not in use). On the other hand, bulk sacks need to be replaced more often. CGMPs and Hazard Analysis and Critical Control Points (HACCP) need to be addressed for conveying and packaging equipment and stations.

The packaging process again is a function of what you're selling—whole-bean, ground, pillow pouch, square-bottom bag. Packing whole-bean can still be most economical with a weigh scale and hand bagger. For ground coffee, a single tube machine will form, fill and seal, and degassing of ground coffee can be accomplished in the totes or bulk sacks. State licenses may be required for scales used to measure items sold by weight.

Dedicated packaging equipment can become a consideration when your product line features more than one product, such as whole-bean, ground and/or flavored coffees, as the changeover between types can be time consuming and labor intensive as you

One-Roaster Plant Equipment Requirements

For Whole-Bean Roasting

- Green bean storage
- Roaster
- Cooler
- Destoner
- Pollution control
- Gentle transfer mechanisms between pieces of equipment (so as not to break beans)
- Blending area (if combining beans into custom blends)
- Packaging equipment
- Finished product storage/warehousing

For Ground Coffee

- All of "Whole-Bean Roasting" (except transfer mechanisms may not have to be as gentle because breakage is less of a concern)
- Grinder
- Dedicated packaging equipment (if also doing whole-bean, because changeover time from one to the other can be a consideration)

For Flavored Coffee

- All of "Whole-Bean Roasting"
- If flavored coffee is ground also, all of "Ground Coffee" too
- Ribbon blender and/or centrifugal mixer (maybe even a separate room and/or a ventilation system to minimize cross-contamination)
- Dedicated packaging equipment (can be even more important here so that non-flavored varieties don't end up accidentally flavored)
- Equipment for clean-out (wash station or chemical cleaners prior to changing flavors)

Other Considerations

- Current Good Manufacturing Practices
- Integrated pest control
- HVAC airflow requirements
- HACCP requirements
- OSHA requirements for employees (including first-aid stations)
- Storage for packaging: master cartons, film, labels, tape, etc.
- Storage for chemicals, glass and flavoring, and materials safety data sheets
- Space for palletizing and staging orders for shipments (including shrink wrap, if required)
- Incorporating quality control/quality assurance into plant plans
- Shipping stations by the case, pallet or truckload

Morning Star's mezzanine level. | *Photo courtesy of John Larkin and Co, Inc.*

work to remove all residue to prevent cross-contamination. For the same reason, store coffee and other products away from packaging materials to avoid contamination from aromas.

Ground coffee suppliers moving into a production mode will sooner or later want to step up from a plate mill to a roll mill to support business growth. When you get to the higher production end of a one-roaster plant and consider a larger grinder, you should also consider an exchange head program with the manufacturer, in which a worn grinder head is swapped out for a sharpened one as required.

Once the coffee is packed, the next stage in the flow is after-packing storage (warehousing), which is a separate area from green coffee storage in order to prevent flavor/aroma contamination. After-packing storage can just be shelving, except possibly in the case of flavored coffees. The amount of storage area required is also estimated, this time based on delivery schedules. The key question here is, how much packed coffee do you need to store and for how much time? Allow space to rotate inventory for stock management as well as enough space for current CGMPs/pest control.

From this final storage area, the process flow will take this roasted and packaged bean on to the shipping or loading area. Once again, be sure to allow enough aisle space in your planning for the material handling to occur, perhaps even accommodating a forklift.

Bringing Your Layout to Life

Once the planning is done, the space procured, and the equipment arriving, it is time to bring the layout to life. Equipment placement and installation involves rigging and re-assembling, and is more economically accomplished when the site is ready. While this might sound obvious ahead of time, it is easy to get caught between honoring leases, meeting production demands and dealing with site issues. You may be up against a move deadline and have a loading dock in the new facility that isn't finished or a parking lot that's a sea of mud, or utilities—like electricity—that aren't available but are necessary to operate the power tools required to assemble the equipment. An experienced project manager can be a worthwhile investment so that you can run the business you have while the new location is coming together.

Actual placing and assembling of equipment involves the following:

(1) Verifying space allocation and layout flow

(2) Placing larger pieces of equipment in the desired locations (roaster, cooler, destoner, pollution control, airveyor or tube conveyor [if applicable], grinder [if applicable], packaging machine [if applicable])

(3) Re-assembling pieces of equipment that have arrived partially assembled for shipping purposes

(4) Connecting pieces of equipment and running process piping as required

(5) Running vent and outlet piping to meet roof penetrations

(6) Hiring professionals to configure and hook up utilities

(7) Performing startup to be sure that everything has been integrated correctly and is functioning properly (and fine-tuning it if it isn't)

The amount of time that it takes to bring an efficient new roasting plant online depends on planning, coordination and budget. Help and advice are available along the way from manufacturers, plant layout and installation specialists, and project managers. Once the space is ready and the equipment is all on site, with good advance planning, you can be roasting in four to six weeks or less. ■

· ·

JOHN LARKIN *is president of John Larkin and Company, Inc., which installs, troubleshoots and rebuilds production-scale coffee-processing equipment and provides production optimization layouts for coffee plants. His company website is* johnlarkinandcompany.com.

Morning Star's Master Roaster Antonio Sordi at work. | *Photo courtesy of John Larkin and Co, Inc.*

New Equipment vs. Used

Whether to buy new or used equipment is always a question, and the answer is new equipment is usually desirable if you can afford it. New equipment first and foremost is a warranted, known quantity. It is in top condition, it is state of the art, and it comes with manufacturer's support in the form of manuals, wiring diagrams, instructions and replacement parts. New equipment may also be more energy-efficient, which can help honor both the bottom line and green initiatives.

Buying used equipment can be a viable option for incremental growth. But it can also be like buying an uncertified used car—will it include all the components you're expecting and will they be in working order when they get to your place? Moving used equipment and correcting unexpected deficiencies (missing equipment, non-working components, mismatched equipment) can end up being nearly as expensive as buying new. Also, you may not have access to manufacturer's support—including manuals, wiring diagrams, instructions and replacement parts—particularly with dated technologies.

Our advice before buying used equipment is to watch it in operation if at all possible, know your seller and/or check references, and get a second opinion on exactly what it will take to make the equipment operational in your particular facility. In the used equipment world as in the used car world, if the deal sounds too good to be true, it probably is, so buyer be careful.

Know the Regulations

· ·

IT IS IMPORTANT to remember that you will be producing a product for human consumption, so you will need to select a space that is or can be made appropriate for this type of manufacturing. You will need to meet requirements set by the federal Food Safety Modernization Act (FSMA), as well as requirements specific to your municipality.

Read "The Food Safety Modernization Act" beginning on page 448 to learn more.

Leasing 101 for Roasters

by Marshall R. Fuss

• FROM THE JANUARY/FEBRUARY 2005 ISSUE OF *ROAST* •

MONTHS OF SEARCHING HAVE FINALLY PAID OFF. There it is: your beautiful new roastery. Well, maybe not so beautiful yet. But you know what it will look like when you are done with it. The neighborhood is good, the rent's not bad and the owner is willing to give you a long rental term. Just one little detail to attend to before you start moving in: that lease form your broker brought over this morning.

If you are like many roasters, you will find that lease form is 15 pages or more of eye-straining, sleep-inducing fine print. It surely would simplify things to just sign it and get on with the build-out and move-in. But before you do that, it is worth taking a closer look at this tome to find out what you are getting and what you are giving up. As with many things, when it comes to leasing, an ounce of prevention is worth a pound of cure.

So, let's take a look at some of the clauses you might expect to see on a typical industrial lease form for a coffee roastery in the United States. This article assumes the space is not in a retail location and will be used only for roasting and related purposes, such as storage, business offices, a show room, cupping space, repair facilities and parking. While I have tried to highlight a few of the issues that commonly are raised by the more popular lease forms and what their significance is, this article is not, of course, a comprehensive review of industrial leasing. If it were, it would be many times longer than a lease. Please do not consider this legal advice, which should only be given by the lawyer who is actually reviewing or writing your lease.

Before You Sign

Ideally, you will have completed your due diligence, or your inspection of the property and of the rules and regulations surrounding the property, before you even make an offer (see "Your Due Diligence" on the next page). But what more can you do when your proposal is accepted and you are presented with a lease form?

If you were purchasing the building, the agreement would normally allow you a period of time after signing to do inspections, gather information and rescind the contract if you were not satisfied. These due diligence periods are less common in leasing. Industrial leases often contain language in which you assume all responsibility for determining that the premises meet the physical and legal requirements for your roastery. "But she told me I could ..." will not carry much weight if it is not written into the lease. Leases normally contain a clause saying they replace any oral promises made during negotiations.

If the owner will not allow you a post-signing due diligence period, you may be wise to delay signing until you complete your investigations. You might also be able to negotiate a period of time to apply for permits and variances, and still have the right to terminate the lease if you fail to obtain them. This is more likely to be granted where there are known problems and the landlord is having difficulty finding a tenant.

Don't be afraid to negotiate for what you want. Major tenants normally have more leverage than smaller ones, and bad real estate markets favor tenants generally. A landlord with a free-standing building may be more flexible than the owner of a multi-tenant project who prefers some uniformity among his leases. Remember that what starts as a standard form may be full of strikeouts, insertions and addenda by the time a tenant and his or her lawyer are finished with negotiations.

Triple Net, Net and Gross Leases

The meanings of these words are not as clearcut as tenants (and even owners) may assume. Generally speaking, the "gross lease" resembles an apartment lease in that the landlord is typically responsible for repairs, taxes, insurance, and some or all utilities. At the other extreme, the "triple net" landlord is responsible for very little other than collecting the rent. Under a triple net lease, the tenant may even be responsible for rebuilding the premises at his own expense if they burn down. For a variety of financial and building management reasons, true net leases are normally limited to single-tenant properties, and gross leases to multi-tenant properties. But there are exceptions, and very few leases are pure versions of either category.

The lesson here is not to assume from the title of the lease which expenses will be yours and which ones will be the landlord's. For example, many gross leases make tenants responsible for any increases in the owner's taxes, utilities or insurance premiums over the first year, and net leases may include

limited warranties for the utility and mechanical systems.

Lease Term and Renewal Options

Did you enjoy looking for new space? Probably not. Do you find moving equipment and building out space a distraction from your real business: buying, roasting and selling? Of course. Your landlord knows this. When your lease comes up for renewal, this knowledge gives your landlord bargaining leverage. Minimize that leverage with renewal options. You might, for example, request the right to extend the lease for two periods of five years each. Normally, some rent adjustment language will go with the options. But, even if the rent is adjusted to market rate, at least you won't end up paying *above market* rent to avoid moving.

Tenant Improvements

Unless you are buying out an existing roaster and assuming their lease, it is very unlikely you will be able to move in without some work on the premises. These tenant improvements (TIs in industry jargon) may be paid by the landlord, by you or be shared using some creative formula. Even if the landlord is initially unwilling to assume the cost, he may agree to advance the money and add it to your rent. This may be advantageous to a roaster who does not want to borrow any more money from the bank than is necessary.

The "put it in writing" rule applies to the TIs as much as any part of the lease. This is normally accomplished by both parties signing off on a "work letter" detailing the plans, specifications and cost caps, which then becomes part of the lease. The landlord may prefer to have his own designers and contractors do the work, but this is sometimes negotiable. Be careful of "change orders," or changes you approve while work is underway. It can be tempting to add more features or upgrade fixtures, but they will most likely come directly out of your pocket. Sometimes change orders are unavoidable, as when the existing improvements do not quite match the "as built" drawings, a common occurrence. Be sure you understand who will be responsible for those changes.

The tenant will usually enjoy an abatement of rent while the design and construction are in progress. This, too, should be spelled out in the lease. Try to negotiate an abatement until all permits and the "certificate of occupancy" (local terminology may vary) have been granted.

Maintenance of the Premises

This is a frequent subject of conflict between landlord and tenant after the lease is signed. Clarity is often lacking in maintenance clauses. The lease may distinguish between "maintenance" and

---

Your Due Diligence: Before You Make an Offer

Before you make an offer or sign a lease, ideally you should complete your due diligence, which means making an inspection of both the property you hope to rent and the area in which you'll be renting, as well as learning about any rules and regulations that may affect you.

Roasters may be governed by a variety of general and local air quality laws, zoning codes, "nuisance" laws, building codes, and a host of government agencies that enforce them and who may or may not be sympathetic to your requirements. You will need at least a basic understanding of how these laws and agencies will impact you before you commit your company to the space. If you do not, be sure you have a lawyer or consultant who does.

Before signing a lease, you should also be sure to get a physical inspection of the premises from top to bottom. A professional inspector can be helpful for this. Even though you are not buying the property, a title report may disclose potential problems, such as a neighbor's recorded easement that permits his trucks to cross your property, or benefits, such as your right to cross his property. A title report is usually available from local title companies, and your broker, if you use one, can help to obtain one.

Other questions to consider include: Will you be happy with the space for the roaster(s)? Will it be close by your greens? Will you have to punch through any upper floors for venting? Are the loading docks the right height and size? Can delivery trucks easily reach them? Are all the utility connections in place or will the landlord put them in place? Are they the right size and capacity?

Don't limit your inspection to the building itself. Take a walk around the block and check out the neighborhood. Many so-called "mixed use" neighborhoods in urban areas are attractive places to work, but they can present special challenges. Residents may not appreciate the noise your deliveries and pickups make, particularly when those back-up warnings wake them from their sleep. In one infamous case in New York City, a venerable roaster in an industrial/residential neighborhood has been cited for the aroma its beans emit *after* roasting (*Environmental Control Board v. Gillies Coffee Co.*, # 00152932K [2003]).

If the premises are in a multi-tenant building, speak with the other tenants about both problems and good experiences they may have had with the landlord, government inspectors and the neighbors.

"replacement," with the owner only paying for the latter. The landlord may be responsible for maintaining utility conduits up to the stub at the tenant's wall, but not beyond. The landlord may be responsible for the roof, but not the ceiling below it. Again, the lease should spell out your respective responsibilities.

Common Area Maintenance

Occupants of multi-tenant buildings and occupants of single-tenant buildings in industrial parks will normally be charged for maintenance of the common areas. These common area maintenance charges (CAMs) typically include such obvious things as landscaping, janitorial services, outside lighting and driveway repair. CAMs may also include the landlord's own office overhead, legal and accounting fees, and even major capital expenses such as building code upgrades. The lease should be carefully scrutinized for the scope of the CAMs.

Your share of the CAMs will typically match your share of the entire building or park. Watch out for language that calculates your share as a percentage of the rented space. Such a clause will automatically increase your percentage if vacancies increase.

You should insist on a right to audit all CAM charges. In practice, even the most scrupulous landlords may have a difficult time calculating CAMs accurately, especially if they have negotiated different terms with each tenant.

Up on the Roof

The roof can be valuable, too, and not simply to keep the rain out. If the location is right and local law allows, it might be the site for a cell phone relay or a billboard. You might be able to sublet for such installations and collect the rent, or you might think they are unsightly and want to prevent the landlord from doing so. The language of the lease will control this.

The lease is likely to include restrictions on your own signage, whether on the roof or outer walls. Be sure you are comfortable with them.

Insurance

The lease will almost certainly have insurance requirements. These are likely to include fire and other first-party loss, third-party liability and business interruption (so your rent keeps flowing to the landlord in the event of a casualty). The owner will normally insist on being added as an insured on your policy. Carefully review these requirements with your insurance broker before signing. You may be able to negotiate the amount of the coverage or permitted deductibles to save on your premiums. Pay particular attention to coverage requirements for natural disasters, such as floods and earthquakes, as you will want to weigh the costs—which can be significant—against the risks and benefits.

Assignment and Subletting

Your lease form will probably include a clause that restricts or entirely prohibits your right to assign it to a new tenant. It is, of course, to your advantage to have the right to assign the lease. There are many reasons you might want to assign the lease in the future. They could include estate planning, selling the business, changing your form of business organization (such as from a partnership to a corporation), wanting to move to bigger quarters or suffering a disability.

A "flexible" assignment clause may enhance the value of your business to a potential buyer, as the landlord will not be able to demand unreasonable terms from the new tenant Although astute landlords will not normally allow unrestricted assignments or subletting, they will often agree to language that requires them to act reasonably in approving assignments. You may even be able to insert a provision that automatically allows an assignment to a trust you set up or to a new tenant of equal or greater creditworthiness.

Rules

Many landlords have published "Rules and Regulations" for their tenants, which may have the force of lease provisions. Be sure to review them before signing.

"It's a Standard Form"

Your broker may tell you "it's a standard form" and urge you to sign the lease as presented. However, a good broker will look out for your interests and honestly advise you whether the changes you or your lawyer request are reasonable or not. Other brokers may see every request for a change in the lease as a threat to their commission. They will strongly discourage you from any negotiation. Avoid such brokers. Some lawyers treat every transaction as a fight to the death or as a law school exam and are known as "deal killers." Avoid them, too. You are looking for advisers who are smart, have business sense and, above all, put your interests above their own.

Now, you are either ready to sign and start making your dream come true or have decided to dream somewhere else. It may be a few days (or a few weeks) since you first laid eyes on that annoying form. If you do sign, you probably will not get everything you asked for, but you will know that you went into the deal with your eyes wide open. ■

· ·

MARSHALL R. FUSS *practices business and marketing law in Pasadena, Calif. He is a member of SCA and has been a panelist at its annual conferences. He can be reached at coffeelaw@earthlink.net.*

The Devil Is in the Details

Production Control and Inventory Management

by Mike Ebert

• FROM THE MAY/JUNE 2013 ISSUE OF *ROAST* •

Early in my coffee career, the term "inventory management" brought only one thing to mind: the dreaded physical inventory.

This was usually the equivalent of a five-alarm fire—our company would have to notify customers that we were shutting down, we'd roast late into the evening on the days prior to the closure, and then we'd shutter the plant for a few days. During that time, we would meticulously count and hang little individual inventory tags from each and every item in the warehouse.

As my career progressed, I discovered that painstaking process was the easy part. For after all of that work was done, I would spend the next week meeting with upper management and outside bank auditors, explaining the big dollar fluctuations, why green coffee loses weight during roasting (shrink), and, best of all, how a company could possibly "lose" so much inventory. The mere thought of inventory would bring me to my knees in fear.

Production control was a term that I wasn't even familiar with; was it a schedule, a management style, or merely cages for my employees? All I did know was, tasks that were scheduled on any given day rarely were completed on time, in the right way, or even finished at all.

The good news is, the story gets better. All those years ago, I had no knowledge of how large a subject production control is, or all of the aspects that were really involved in proper managing of inventory. Flash forward a few years, and not only had our company completely eliminated the need for a yearly physical inventory, but our average inventory accuracy percentage was in the high nineties, and we stuck at 98 percent inventory accuracy for the final few years I ran that plant. The most astounding thing was everything else that improved along the way—there were virtually no out-of-stocks, and orders were being shipped accurately, even with lower inventory levels. But the No. 1 improvement: Never again did we hear, "Oh, it must have been the warehouse; they are a bunch of dummies back there." Yes, we became the model for the rest of the company. In other words, we became professionals.

A Brief History of Inventory Control

Before I explain how we achieved those results, let's talk a little about the history of this movement. Today, production and inventory control is part of a much wider field known as supply chain management. The term "supply chain management," or SCM, is a fairly recent development. It started in the early '80s but did not really gain traction until the late '90s, when it became a management buzzword and was used frequently in business books and magazines that dubbed it the savior of American manufacturing.

According to the worldwide professional association Council of Supply Chain Management Professionals (CSCMP), supply chain management encompasses the planning and management of all activities involved in sourcing, procurement, conversion and logistics management. It also includes crucial components of coordination and collaboration with partners, consisting of suppliers, intermediaries and customers.

The precursor to all of this, production and inventory control (PIC), started much earlier. There is no founding father or key point in time, but PIC is widely accepted to have developed into a professional field in the 1920s, when all of its various functions were assigned to a single manager. The automobile industry brought this on as a necessary outgrowth of the assembly line, and by the 1930s it had extended beyond autos into other industries. But as a whole, PIC functions were still spread out across a company's organizational chart, with lots of crossover, or worse, some key functions not assigned to anyone.

Finally, techniques used to attack PIC issues and problems started to advance dramatically. During World War II, the British and the Americans developed operations research techniques, many of which have developed into names that are quite commonplace in the business world today—Monte Carlo, queueing and linear programming are a few examples. These developed into PIC aspects being studied, taught and developed further, which brought about models and project management tools such as economic order quantities, Gantt charts and sophisticated inventory cycle count systems.

Flash forward to 1957, when about two dozen PIC professionals met in Cleveland, Ohio. Their purpose was to discuss the possibility of creating a national society to grow their knowledge and show the manufacturing world that they were serious professionals who were an essential part of the manufacturing process.

Today, that organization is the American Production and Inventory Control Society (APICS), which serves more than 100,000 members. Half of those members have achieved CPIM, or Certified in Production and Inventory Management, which is their top certification. CPIM is now the gold standard—very similar to being a certified public accountant, or, dare I say, a master roaster?

PIC has three major objectives: to achieve the best possible customer service, the lowest possible inventory, and very efficient plant operations. Herein lies the problem I am sure we have all faced—these three objectives contradict, conflict or challenge each other. Customers want their "stuff" exactly when they need it, in the quantities they want, with little or no warning or advance planning. Obviously, this will conflict with a low inventory, because you can't run out of items, which then conflicts with running a good plant. For best efficiencies, you want big runs, with minimal equipment changeovers and maintenance. PIC systems show managers how to grapple with these conflicts, and more.

In-House PIC Essentials

What are the elements of a great in-house PIC system? There are many, but here are a few of the most important aspects:

✓ Accurate and well-laid-out bills of materials:
A bill of materials is essentially a recipe—every item that goes into a finished product. It includes the coffee, bag, shipping box, tape, labels, and even the shrink of the green bean.

✓ Good forecasting:
This is a bit like being a good card player, but it can be achieved. It's really about establishing good communication between customer, sales, customer service and the plant.

✓ Material requirements planning:
Typically this is wound into your manufacturing software but can be done manually in a smaller company. It takes into account everything needed, lead times, waste factors, etc.

✓ Good purchasing habits and documentation:
This may sound silly, but it's ultra important—knowing what you bought, at what price, when it arrives, etc., *all the time*.

✓ Accurate lead times:
It's a guarantee that if you write down what you think your lead times are and then track them, you will be much farther off than expected. In addition, accurate lead times include time at customs, downtime for preventive maintenance (PM) on equipment, lunch breaks, etc. Again, it sounds silly, but it all matters.

✓ Customer order tracking:
Ensuring that all the details are accurate, including ship-to addresses and proper quantities, is crucial.

✓ Capacity restraints:
Knowing what your plant is really capable of producing—not what you wish or dream, but what you actually produce—is also essential. This concept is tied to accurate lead times.

✓ Production scheduling and tracking:
This is a comprehensive system for telling your employees what to roast, how much and when, and then telling your software what you did.

✓ Accurate costs:
This cannot be understated: Make sure you are capturing true costs on everything you sell. Tracking and understanding details, such as waste factors, labor and shipping, PM and cleaning costs, are essential to a well-run plant.

✓ Quality control (QC) built into everything:
This essential step made my job easier. At my first company, we grew quickly and began roasting a few million pounds of coffee a year. While I was plant manager and director of coffee, I was

constantly fighting for things like freshness, cleaning, etc. with "upper management" bean counters. Utilizing PIC systems allowed me to build my QC into our procedures and bills of materials, and so it was sold as not only a quality parameter but a cost-saving driver. Sold my case every time!

✓ Cycle count program:

Regular cycle counts are the core of a PIC system. Yes, earlier I mentioned eliminating the annual complete physical inventory, but performing cycle counts is far easier. A good cycle count program is simple—count 10 different items every day. The goal is not to "correct" inventory counts daily; it's to find out what went wrong and correct the reason the count is wrong. For example, it could be that your plant doesn't have the right shrink percentage for a new coffee roast. Perhaps your order pickers didn't realize you have a Colombian Supremo *and* a Colombian Supremo Estate in the warehouse, or maybe someone tore open a bag of green on the dock and didn't report it.

When I started my first cycle count program, we picked 10 high-volume items from all different types of inventory—two green coffees; two roasted, packaged coffees; one type of carton; and a handful of distributed items. We counted the same 10 items every day for weeks. The first few weeks, we only achieved a 50 percent accuracy; five out of the 10 items were right. After about a month, we got up to 90 percent, at which point, we changed the 10 items every week. That beginning phase made it easier to find what went wrong; you only had to look at the last 24 hours, which made finding the errors much easier. We also did not keep the same people on the cycle count team. Every week, someone new came on, and one dropped off.

✓ Proper software and hardware:

Ultimately, it's ideal to connect all aspects of your business with a software program—including accounting, customer service, manufacturing, shipping and QC. But having great software is only as good as the people who use it and how well they know how to use it. It's important to set it up correctly in the first place, input accurate data and have proper information technology (IT) support along the way. If you think about the volumes of data a roasting company (even a small business) produces and needs to track, it's downright impossible to do it well without the proper IT.

How to Get There

So how does one proceed on the path to enlightened PIC? It requires dedication and commitment, and, most importantly, support from the top down. For starters, most local community colleges offer PIC classes, and some even offer certificate programs. The American Production and Inventory Control Society (APICS), the worldwide association, offers classes, articles, conferences and the like, as well as the CPIM certification.

The key to building a great PIC program is support from the owners on down, but it should be easy to explain the benefits of a successful PIC program. Here are just a few:

- Quality improvements
- Customer service improvements
- Trimmed labor costs
- A tight inventory—lower or less out-of-stocks, less obsolescence
- Improved morale—people understand what they do and how it "fits"

The last one cannot be understated—a proper PIC program is not a top-down-only program; if it is, it will fail. The key to success is an open-loop system of communication, where information flows from the top-down, down-up and in between. What a PIC system does is give everyone a common language and platform that will help your plant achieve greatness.

There is no better time to get started than right now. It may seem overwhelming, confusing and downright maddening at times. But as you begin to work at it, you will find yourself focusing on how to grow your business more often than just maintaining what you have and trying to eliminate problems. Will it solve all problems? Of course not, but it can end the days of fixing problems that your business has attempted to fix multiple times before. But most significantly, it allows you to focus on what's really important: producing great coffee. ■

• •

MIKE EBERT is founder of Firedancer Coffee Consultants, dedicated to helping clients create a personalized strategy to ensure long-term success. He works primarily with roasters, producers and retailers, drawing from his extensive experience in all facets of the specialty coffee supply chain to guide clients in reaching their potential. Ebert is a specialized lead instructor for Specialty Coffee Association (SCA) certification programs and is chair of the SCA Coffee Buyer Educational Pathway Committee, which develops new educational experiences for the specialty coffee community.

Photo by Mark Shimahara

Write It Up

A Practical Guide to Documenting Business Procedures

by Robin White

• FROM THE MAY/JUNE 2016 ISSUE OF *ROAST* •

Who has time to stop and write down all the steps involved in doing their job? What we do is way too complex for that. There are too many moving parts—it would be impossible to document all the variables. Procedures are for robots.

Most of us have either said or heard something similar. The reality is that most people like their autonomy, and the idea of being ruled by documented instructions isn't appealing. Besides, writing up procedures is not only time-consuming, it's tedious. For anyone interested in championing the project of documenting procedures, it's best to face reality—this is probably the least glamorous and least popular project you will ever tackle.

So, why do it?

Documentation Breeds Success

Think about your morning commute. Unless you're one of the fortunate few, you probably battle at least some traffic on the way to work each morning. Picture the same commute, but all traffic lights are out, road signs have been removed, and the police are on strike. While you're at it, take away the roads and give everyone 4x4s. No rules to follow! No roads to restrict your route! Now throw a few hundred thousand other commuters into the mix and this slow, frustrating, white-knuckle commute becomes more aggravating than liberating.

Many entrepreneurs and their employees have acclimatized themselves to a business environment that resembles this scenario. Every day is a new roller coaster. Adrenaline fuels the team and the company is generously referred to as "dynamic."

One major risk with this kind of chaos is staff/management burnout. Even with a steady supply of adrenaline junkies to keep the boat afloat, improvised procedures tend to create multiple financial leaks that are tough to spot and fix. For most companies with profitability issues, there's no silver-bullet solution. Excess labor, inventory surpluses, wasted materials, rush shipments, returns and quality issues all take a toll on the bottom line.

In the May 2013 *Harvard Business Journal* article "Define Your Organization's Habits to Work More Efficiently," consultant and process innovation researcher Brad Power explains, "Our ability to improve the ways we do things depends on defining and shaping our daily habits of mind and practice—'our standard work.'"

Increasing regulatory oversight in the food industry—including the ongoing implementation of the Food Safety Modernization Act (FSMA) in the United States—means that having well-documented standard operating procedures (SOPs) is more important than ever. Clear and thorough SOPs are critical to compliance with this type of regulatory oversight, as well as formal certification through third-party organizations such as the Safe Quality Food Institute (SQF), and many wholesale clients now require third-party food safety certification for coffee roasters.

Roast's 2015 Macro Roaster of the Year, Reunion Island Coffee Roasters, is one of the industry's poster children for process-driven

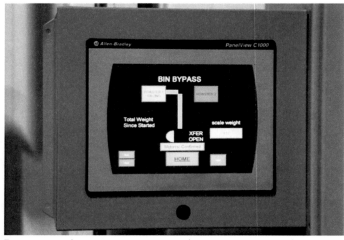

Every step in the roasting process—in this case, "Enter green bypass weight target on silo PLC"—is included on Reunion Island's roasting process flowchart (see page 413). | *Photo courtesy of Reunion Island Coffee Roasters*

culture. The Toronto-based company's vice president of operations, Greg Rusciolelli, is a vocal process advocate.

"The written procedures are the foundation that our operations run on," says Rusciolelli, "both in administration and production."

The company recently completed certification through SQF in just nine months. It passed two levels of audits, both on the first attempt. Rusciolelli attributes the success in completing this stringent certification so quickly to the years spent honing Reunion Island's company culture.

Founded by specialty coffee pioneer Peter Pesce, Reunion Island recognized that lack of definition around procedures meant missing profits and quality and customer satisfaction opportunities, and company management sought to correct this.

"Our structured procedures have been the key to continuous improvement," Rusciolelli says. "When quality, customer satisfaction and efficiency improve, the bottom line naturally follows suit."

The company is now more than five times the size it was in 2005 and has been able to maintain a healthy bottom line while achieving the goals of the Pesce family, including certification as a B Corporation and extensive quality and environmental initiatives.

Where to Start?

Have your goals clearly in mind. The following tangible deliverables will give you a good foundation on which to build:

1 Processes: flowcharts mapping out steps for core processes

2 Work Instructions: detailed instructions for each step of every process

3 Forms: one library of forms, linked to relevant work instructions

4 References: one library of reference material, linked to relevant work instructions

Before you begin mapping out your processes, it's important to decide how you'll organize your document library. It generally works well to break the company into numbered departments. Sound stuffy and corporate? It is. Remember, this is the least glamorous project you'll ever tackle. Think of it as an opportunity to release your inner organization freak.

Consider the following as a sample organization structure:

100	Administration
200	Customer Service
300	Operations
310	Production
350	Quality & Food Safety
370	Logistics
380	Material Handling
400	Sales
500	Marketing
600	Finance
700	Human Resources
900	Emergency

Using this system, make an index of the company's core processes. Here are a few examples across various departments:

P205	Processing an Order (Start with P for "process," then assign a number in the 200s for the customer service department.)
P210	Processing a Return
P405	Opening a New Wholesale Account (In this case, a number in the 400s indicates the sales department.)
P505	Event Planning
P605	Month-end
P705	Hiring a New Employee
P905	Responding to a Fire

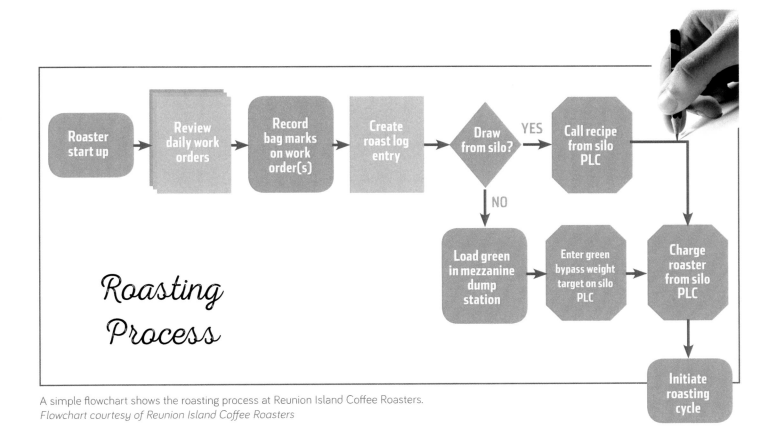

A simple flowchart shows the roasting process at Reunion Island Coffee Roasters.
Flowchart courtesy of Reunion Island Coffee Roasters

As you're listing processes, be sure to leave room in your numbering system so you can add more in the future in logical order. Create a folder in a shared area of your server called *SOP* and save the file there in HTML format as *index.htm*. Once you have your list of processes, you're ready to tackle phase one of the project: mapping out your processes.

Phase One : Fun with Flowcharts

The goal here is to create a visual map showing the broad steps involved in making things happen at your company. If you're unfamiliar with flowcharts, a little online research will get you going; you can also find samples on page 414 and above, and in the "Process" folder of the SOP template kit at *bit.ly/SOPExample*.

Process flowcharts are not overly detailed. For example, one step might be *Enter Order Into Quickbooks*. This step will be explained in detail in the work instructions you'll tackle in phase two. The chart should clearly indicate the person/role responsible

To access templates you can use for your own company, download a sample documentation folder at *bit.ly/SOPExample*.

for the step. It's a good idea to set out abbreviations in advance for consistency (e.g., CS = Customer Service).

Pick a process such as *P205 Processing an Order*, and map out how it's happening now. To do that, go see the person you think is the expert on this process. (Get into the habit of bringing treats with you to these meetings.) Let the expert walk you through the process while you map it out in flowchart format.

Once you're done, you'll have the first draft of the process. Next, walk that around to each person who is responsible for a step on the process. Let him or her confirm or deny that your map is accurate. Go back to your expert to vet any suggested changes. As a bonus, this often will expose misunderstandings between departments about the way things work.

After you're satisfied that you have an accurate picture, start looking for room for improvement. Focus on areas on the map where the same person repeatedly gets involved. When Reunion Island first tackled this project, some flowcharts looked like wagon wheels, with the work being bounced back to the same central person after almost every step. The more your flowchart looks like a linear set of steps, the better.

Next, look at the return on investment (ROI) from each step. Every step costs money. That value needs to flow through to customers in some way, as ultimately you need them to pay for it. Steps to look at eliminating might be unnecessary document

Process Flow — Grinding

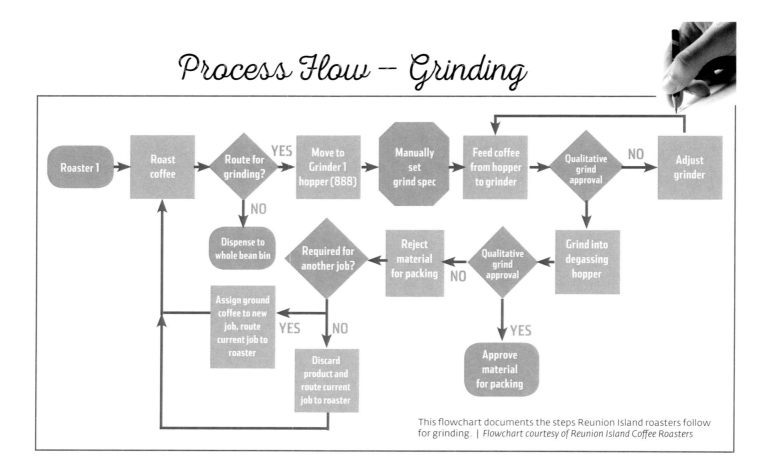

This flowchart documents the steps Reunion Island roasters follow for grinding. | *Flowchart courtesy of Reunion Island Coffee Roasters*

copies/filing, unnecessary sign-offs or redundant communication with customers or between departments. If in doubt, leave the step in, but flag it for review after new processes have been running for a few months.

Follow this procedure with each process on your master list. You should end up with a clean set of process flowcharts saved to a *Process* folder inside your *SOP* directory. Improvements should be noticeable almost immediately, even at this stage.

Phase One is done (for now).

Phase Two : The Devil

Whoever coined the phrase "the devil is in the details" was probably documenting procedures. The devil in this case is not only the level of complication, but the time involved.

Rusciolelli recalls, "The biggest mistake we made when we started out on this project was not allocating enough resources to get the job done. It took far more time than we anticipated."

To maintain momentum at this stage, be prepared to dedicate serious time to the project and make it someone's top priority. Unless you are a very small company, you need two main people: a senior person who will be the cheerleader, and a coordinator who will relentlessly push the project forward every day with a

combination of nagging, begging and bribery (more on that later). The best possible cheerleader is the owner or president.

With your core processes mapped out, it's time to list your work instructions (WI). Go through each process and list each step that will require a WI. Number them logically, beginning each with the letter W and following the same numbering system as processes, but adding a three-digit code to define each step. The easiest way to record them is to list them below *Processes* in your master file (*index.htm*).

For example, *P205 Processing an Order* might include WIs such as *W205-110 Enter Order into Quickbooks* and *W205-120 Print Invoice*. The same process may also include steps that start with a different three-digit code, if they fall under a different department (e.g., *W370-110A Ship an Order—Local*).

Once your to-do list is ready, you need to select your method for housing and sharing the documents you prepare. The key to your entire system of documentation is to make it easy. Easy to find. Easy to read. Easy to update. To reach this goal, your documentation needs to be maintained in electronic format of some kind.

Reunion Island's documentation resides on the company's server in a folder all employees can access. WIs are prepared in Word and saved in HTML format to allow hyperlinking between documents. No HTML experience is needed; simply choose "html" as the format when you save the document in Word. Once it's saved in HTML, the document can be opened with any web browser, which makes the experience familiar for team members and prevents any accidental changes.

The first step is to create a Word document that will be your directory to all WIs. The easiest way to do this is simply to put your logo in the header of your WI to-do list and save as *index.htm*. As the individual WIs are completed, you can select them on this index page and create a hyperlink to each WI. Bookmark the index page just as you would any external website for quick access.

Next, create a template for your WI files. Spending excessive time making your procedures look pretty is like trying to market a "Sport Edition" minivan—you're not fooling anyone. Clean and simple is the goal. Add your logo in the header and some basic, standard information, such as:

- WI: W370-110 Shipping an order
- Who: Shipper/Receiver
- Frequency: Daily
- Third-party Inputs: R370-110A OCIA memo —April 2, 2013 ("R" indicates a reference document.)
- Documentation: F370-110A Packing Slip ("F" indicates a form.)

> **Be prepared to dedicate serious time to the project and make it someone's top priority.**

Below this header, list the steps in the order they will be performed. At the bottom of the page, add a hyperlink to go back to the index. Below that, enter the date the WI was updated and the initials of the person who updated it. If you introduce a formal approval process, the approval notes and dates can go at the bottom of the page.

Once you're ready to start creating your first WI, open the template and use the "Save As" option to save it in HTML format, using the WI number as the file name (e.g., *W370-110.htm*).

Write instructions in the imperative tense with little to no explanation. For example, you might want to write: "In order to send the order to the shipping department, you'll need to print a copy of the packing slip and place it in their inbox. If it doesn't go in the tray by 3 p.m., then the order will not ship out until tomorrow. If that ever happens, please call the customer to explain."

This is a sloppy WI. It should be much crisper, such as: "Print packing slips for orders as they arrive and place in the shipping inbox before 3 p.m. for next-day delivery."

Processes and work instructions—in this case, "Create roast log" (see flowchart on page 413)—should be reviewed regularly to keep your company's documentation up to date with current practices. | *Photo courtesy of Reunion Island Coffee Roasters*

"Record bag marks on work orders" is another step in Reunion Island's roasting process flowchart (see page 413). The specific details of how this process is completed are included in the associated work instructions. | *Photo courtesy of Reunion Island Coffee Roasters*

In this sample, there is a third-party input from OCIA (Organic Crop Improvement Association). It is important to note where regulatory or other third-party inputs—including FSMA regulations—have an impact on WIs, so these steps do not get adjusted. For example, one step on this WI might be "Indicate lot number on invoice (per R370-110A OCIA memo April 2, 2013)." There is also a form that will be used for this WI—the packing slip. Both forms and references can be hyperlinked to the WIs in HTML, PDF or Excel format.

The person documenting a company's processes and work instructions should observe and speak with the people doing the work to ensure that every step in each process is documented accurately. | *Photo courtesy of Reunion Island Coffee Roasters*

> **"Our structured procedures have been the key to continuous improvement. When quality, customer satisfaction and efficiency improve, the bottom line naturally follows suit."**
>
> **—Greg Rusciolelli, Reunion Island Coffee Roasters**

Ideally, the best person to write each WI is the one performing the work. The coordinator can help with editing. During this process, add "DRAFT" to the title. Once a WI draft is reviewed and approved, the coordinator can add the approval initials/date and remove "DRAFT" from the title. Adjust the approval process as needed to ensure that no unauthorized procedures are introduced that could create risk for you or your employees.

Rules of Engagement

To make a success of your documentation project, it is critical to engage your entire team in the process. Ultimately, it is about changing the culture within an organization. Introducing the project in the right way will help.

To get buy-in, find an early success story to hold up as an example. As you review your company's processes, look for redundant work that has been eliminated and share that with your team. Your cheerleader needs to speak about these successes regularly to maintain good momentum.

Another way to effectively engage your team is to reward them. In addition to motivating the key documentation team, offer small perks for everyone who participates. It could be a movie pass for two for every completed WI or a small gift card for every suggestion that makes an existing WI better. In the end, rewarding your staff is far more effective than hiring the project out to a consulting firm—your instructions will be of higher quality and your team will take ownership of them.

Next Steps

Once you have built out a set of process flowcharts and the corresponding WIs, references and forms, you have a solid foundation on which to build. For example, to make new employee training faster and simpler, job descriptions can be revised to use the same terminology as the WIs. Often there is a second tier of less frequently used procedures that can be reviewed after the core work is done.

Documenting procedures is a project that is never truly complete. As a company evolves and the business environment changes, procedures must be updated.

As Rusciolelli notes, "In the throes of the moment, people make small tweaks to the way they're doing things but forget that it's important to report it."

While Reunion Island has made a lot of headway in building a process-driven culture, Rusciolelli still finds that ongoing auditing to check every process and WI at least once a year is important to capture the natural evolution that happens on the company's path to continuous improvement.

"Our team has done a wonderful job embracing the work involved in process documentation and SQF certification," he says. "It's an achievement that the whole organization can celebrate. Based on our experience, I believe every company, no matter the size, will see dramatic improvements in its business by documenting its standard operating procedures." ■

Since 1995, ROBIN WHITE has worked on marketing, product development and operational projects for hundreds of roasters and specialty coffee businesses, ranging from boutique startups to multinationals. He has developed marketing strategies for growth in the retail, office coffee, food service and hospitality channels. He is currently vice president of strategic development for Single Cup Coffee.

Photo by Mark Shimahara

Coffee Counts

Accounting and Finance for Coffee Roasters

by Andi Trindle Mersch | *photos by Bruce Mullins*

• FROM THE JULY/AUGUST 2014 ISSUE OF *ROAST* •

Our industry is constantly evolving. In producing and consuming countries both, ceaseless change and innovation offer industry members endless inspiration and provide opportunity for us all to continually learn.

At origin, we see new hybrids, improved practices on the farm, experimental processing techniques and innovations in sustainability. At home, we simultaneously see innovations in brewing and equipment manufacturing, the rebirth and expansion of artistry behind the bar, competitions to recognize these artisans, and the introduction of new business practices and products, among so many others. All of these changes are magnified by general technological, agricultural and other advances in the world. With this opportunity to learn more about what's exciting, new and different in the specialty coffee world, it can be easy to ignore or postpone the basic responsibilities of running and managing our businesses.

Not only do we too often under-prioritize the essentials, but many of us still lack a solid understanding of business basics—fundamentals such as accounting and finance.

Understanding the principles of accounting and finance and the underlying details of inventory management, cash-flow projections, tax management and market basics is essential to ensuring the sustainability of any business.

Defining the Terms

The basics of accounting and finance begin with understanding what business activities are covered under these broad categories. The terms are certainly familiar to everybody, but I'd bet a pound of Panamanian geisha that many to most don't precisely understand them or what tasks fall within them.

In order to break down some of the basics, I went to my best source for general business and financial information—my husband, Eric L. Mersch, a Harvard MBA and current CFO of Burkland Associates.

Accounting

"Accounting is a bookkeeping function designed to produce and maintain accurate records of your business," Mersch says. "These records fall into three categories: the income statement, balance sheet and cash flow statement. The income statement records revenue and expenses for a given period of time (usually one month). The balance sheet shows the working capital accounts—assets, such as your cash balance, inventory and amounts owed to you by customers—and liabilities, such as money due to your employees and vendors at a precise and specific time. Also shown are loans you've taken and a record of total profits generated by the business since inception.

"The cash flow statement shows the profit after investments, such as property and equipment needed to support the business.

The accounting function also includes internal controls, which are designed to prevent theft and fraud," explains Mersch. "To protect against theft and embezzlement, one of the best practices is to ensure that the person who pays the bills is different from the person who processes the invoices."

Finance

"Finance is a planning and analysis function, which is undertaken to understand trends in the business and the planning required for sustaining and growing the business in the future," Mersch says. "Trends you are looking for are changes in costs and revenue. (This is also an important function for detecting theft inside the company and vendors who are not paying you.) Some planning examples include sales and inventory need projections, cash flow needs, analyzing future impact of investments and the expected increase in profits from these investments.

"Most companies maintain forecasts of their business and update them as time progresses. Lenders will require your forecast before making loans," Mersch adds.

The Roles in Specialty Coffee

Following Mersch's general breakdown of the responsibilities within accounting and finance functions of an organization, the next step is to home in on how these responsibilities, and how the

control, or lack thereof, come into play for the average specialty coffee roasting business. For this, I pulled from some of my own experience, spoke with experienced roasters, and consulted Michael Menzies of Braeside Farms, who specializes in advising food and food-related businesses.

Menzies has extensive experience guiding roasters specifically through their financial accountabilities, though he is careful to point out that Braeside Farms does not provide financial adviser or tax-preparation services.

The primary and essential functions of a specialty coffee roaster are to buy green coffee beans, get these beans to their roasting plant, roast them, package them and sell them. That's it ... at least the general gist of it. Specialty coffee roasters buy a specialized raw product, add value to it and sell it. Looking just at the straightforward tasks, it becomes easy to see the primary accounting and financial functions needed to make the business model work.

First, let's start with the premise that a roasting business needs money—money to buy, run and maintain equipment; money to

"C" Market Controversy

THIS ARTICLE doesn't cover "C" market buying strategies or hedging, and as Oregon-based food business consultant Michael Menzies says, "Small roasters/green buyers should worry about their customers ... much more than they should worry about the price of a coffee hedging contract. The profit of the roasting company is likely made from selling to customers, not from fretting about purchase and hedging techniques."

While I ultimately agree with this sentiment for specialty coffee roasters, nonetheless, I strongly encourage that all green buyers get knowledgeable about the coffee market, as attention paid (or not paid) here can substantially impact your bottom line.

At bare minimum, take a look at the daily settlement price on the Intercontinental Exchange at *theice.com* and recognize that, as a specialty roaster, on any given day you will be paying a differential (almost always) above the current base market price for your beans. The differential per coffee type will vary

significantly depending upon origin, quality and a host of other factors (inquire with your importers to secure quotes), but you can expect some relative comparative stability with differentials.

There is no stability or predictability with the market base price, which is why a quick daily check is extremely useful. Additionally, the Specialty Coffee Association (SCA) has been developing an expanded coffee business curriculum (CB courses) that is extremely useful for introducing buyers to the basics of coffee market buying and a host of other critical need-to-knows for making smart purchasing decisions.

acquire raw product and packaging supplies; money to pay for labor; and, a little bit more money still to promote and distribute the final product. Money is clearly essential, and a good amount of it is needed.

When Menzies states, "most businesses fail from undercapitalization," we should perk up and pay close attention to avoid this fate. Startup costs for a roasting business alone are substantial. On the lower-volume side, excluding a facility purchase or leasing costs and any supplemental equipment, these costs could run around $20,000 for a smartly refurbished, 12-kg. Probat roaster, according to Hiver van Geenhoven, roastmaster and green buyer at Chromatic Coffee of San Jose, California.

For larger capacity machines, according to my own recent explorations, think upwards of $200,000 for a midsize, 120-kg. machine, or well into the millions for larger, four-bag-plus machines, with hundreds of thousands of dollars in additional costs for ancillary equipment necessary for efficient operation of these mid- to larger-sized roasters.

Different manufacturers and setups vary greatly, offering greater discounts or even higher startup costs, but these numbers give some rough indication of the cash flow required just for the basic equipment needed to get started. These costs, along with many other startup costs, are often taken on as a long-term liability of a new business with regular payments required to banks or other lenders. Inadequate cash flow to pay lenders can be fatal for a business.

Additionally, the base cost of the raw input product is also a variable cost. Our core input, green coffee, is traded versus a commodity market (see sidebar on "C" market, previous page) and, therefore, subject to sudden pricing fluctuations due to external market and world conditions that often have nothing to do with what's happening in our business, or even the broader specialty coffee industry.

With this unpredictability, it becomes necessary to have not just sufficient but abundant capital available in short order to replenish inventory. Roasters have to be prepared with adequate funds to keep buying green coffee even if the market price skyrockets (wholly possible per a recent example when the "C" market price jumped from an average of $1.06 in December 2013 to an average of $1.65 in March 2014, with multiple days in between and since seeing closes more than $2). If roasters can't keep buying green coffee, they can't keep roasting and selling it. While it should go without saying that ordering and receiving green coffee on payment terms without actually paying within those terms isn't a good strategy, experientially, it's worth saying. At some point, if you don't pay your green coffee bills, you will be cut off from your most critical input supply.

In my years as a green coffee importer, I witnessed many roasters from the smallest microroasters to the largest volume players struggling with their cash flow, which almost always resulted in high stress and a distracted focus at best, and

frequently resulted in more serious long-term problems. For James Freeman, chief executive and founder of California's Blue Bottle Coffee, fortunately, these challenges, while experienced "every other Friday" in the early years, never resulted in any actual problems with his import partners. Freeman quickly learned to "think months ahead to cover [bills]," recognizing that "great relationships with vendors" would be essential to his long-term success.

For others, serious problems with vendors have been painful. Mike Ebert, founder of Firedancer Coffee Consultants in Chicago, recalls all too well times with a former roasting company where "a few years of rapidly declining sales resulted in abysmal cash flow," which led to an inability to pay vendors on time. In a better practice than some in similar situations, Ebert learned to communicate very well with his vendors. "I called each on a regular basis, even if I had nothing new to report," he says. This practice and his already established good name in the industry allowed him and the company to keep operating a few extra years.

However, Ebert cautions that while he temporarily extended his sourcing ability through good and open communication with his importers, ultimately "this prevented the reality of our situation from really setting in, and most importantly, making real changes in how and what we were doing," he says. For Ebert, this resulted in an earlier-than-expected departure from the company.

Functions Needed to Manage a Roasting Business

Accounting Functions

Maintaining your books, the basic accounting function, is key. You have to have accurate knowledge of your revenue and expenses (income statement), your available working capital (see following page for more) versus your liabilities (balance sheet), and the movement of capital through your business (cash flow statement). With this information, not only do you know what you have to

spend now, you can also determine what you may need to borrow in order to be prepared for future buying.

If you determine that borrowing is necessary, you can assume that you will not find any willing public or private investors without accurate bookkeeping. While larger and more established businesses likely have solid bookkeeping practices in place, many smaller and newer specialty coffee operations are remiss. So, how does a business start managing bookkeeping?

Mersch states, "Small businesses typically employ a bookkeeper or use an outside service. The outside service is often preferable because costs are cheaper and, because it's a third party not associated with your business, potential lenders and investors will have more trust in the accounting books."

As Menzies advises, "If you don't already use QuickBooks or a similar accounting software for your accounting system, you should probably start."

Accounting is another area where Freeman benefited by thinking ahead. Recognizing that he was "better at doing other things," he hired a part-time bookkeeper early and later added an internal staff accountant, as soon as the business had grown sufficiently to pay for one.

Taxes are another component managed within the accounting function of your organization. "Accurate bookkeeping supports efficient tax preparation," says Mersch. In case you are at all inclined to ignore (consciously or unconsciously) your tax liabilities, don't risk it.

"Improper tax filings cost you," says Menzies. On the other hand, "proper tax filing, depending on the stage of your business, can save you big time."

Successful business owners pay attention to taxes. Tax liabilities are often substantial for any size business. The risks of fines, temporary shutdowns or worse if payments are neglected, should encourage every business owner to predict his or her liabilities and save sufficiently. Freeman has always been appropriately worried about meeting tax payment deadlines and, after realizing the substantial liabilities for his business, learned to prepare for taxes, frugally saving "six months in advance."

While taxation is essential to pay attention to, don't feel as if you need to become an expert to get this under control. As Menzies recommends, hire someone for this specific, critical function. "You will likely save money, time, energy and resources by hiring professionals."

Finance Functions

In addition to maintaining accurate accounting records, planning and analysis (functions within the scope of finance management) work to ensure sufficient capitalization. Two primary components of planning and analysis include projecting sales and managing inventory.

Let's look first at sales forecasting. While a roaster can sometimes be nicely surprised by rapid growth in sales or shockingly disappointed by a drastic drop in sales, more often, sales variations are predictable with careful analysis of external and internal factors, such as competitor activities, seasonal fluctuations, sales and marketing campaigns, the general economic marketplace, etc.

Make sure you have someone in your organization paying attention to happenings that can impact sales, both within and outside of your organization, and that this person is providing your buyer with accurate and timely forecast information to make smart purchasing decisions. For example, if a competitor is aggressively taking business, you may need to make some adjustments in your purchasing until you can replace that business. On the other hand, if your wholesale sales manager is about to sign 10 new accounts, make sure you're prepared with cash flow to meet quickly expanding purchasing needs.

If you're in the position of buying additional green inventory on short notice, you are likely subject to spot market pricing. In the current market situation mentioned earlier, this means your green buyer needs increased cash flow not only to support a general surge in purchasing quantities, but sufficient capital to purchase what may be the same beans at prices upwards of $0.80 more per pound than the coffee cost just a few months ago.

Purchasing decisions can make or break a roasting business. Smart purchasing decisions not only include buying sufficient inventory in growing businesses, but also buying conservatively enough that you are only purchasing the amount of coffee you can realistically sell while still fresh, within the terms you've arranged, and pricing your beans at a level at which you can make money.

A successful business requires that you turn a profit on your coffee, and not just that you roast the very best coffee you can find to its ideal roast.

Working Capital

IT'S WORTH A NOTE to distinguish working capital from profitability and assets. A profitable company with generous assets can still suffer and even fail if it doesn't maintain sufficient working capital. Working capital can essentially be boiled down to the ability to turn assets into the cash needed in order to go out and buy more product, make business investments and meet liabilities. A specialty coffee roasting company, like any other business, needs to maintain a positive working capital basis by managing inventory, receivables, payables and cash in hand.

Rest assured, though, you can do both!

Specialty coffee buyers, including myself, are notorious for what I deem "romantic purchasing decisions"—decisions based on an exquisite coffee, a personal relationship with the producer or a life-changing experience on the farm—that aren't supported by real, or even likely, potential sales volume and/or a price that your customers will realistically pay.

One way for roasting companies to quickly find themselves underwater is to overcommit and find themselves with excess inventory that starts accumulating high carrying costs—charges over your original green coffee contract price to cover financing and warehouse storage.

Ebert openly confesses to learning "the hard way" that committing to coffee "just because I love coffee, or just because we sold so many pounds the prior year" wasn't a wise or sustainable purchasing strategy. "At the end of the day I was buying coffee for a market we didn't have and was selling that green coffee way past its prime," he says. This unfortunately common and potentially disastrous practice can be avoided with accurate sales forecasting combined with proper management of existing inventory—key components of a successful organization's financial controls.

injected a dismal attitude among all staff, which to me was our Achilles heel."

Growing Pains

Another principal piece of the finance function within an organization is the analysis of investment opportunities. Upgrades or expansion are often desirable and sometimes even necessary to sustain a business. Forecasting and critical analysis skills (as well as diligent accounting) are essential to making wise decisions about potential investments.

Furthermore, "lenders will require your forecast before making loans," says Mersch. There is a good chance you will need outside money at some point via bankers, private investors or both to capitalize on the opportunities that make sense for your business.

By managing his finances well and attracting investors, Freeman has been able to do exactly that, most recently with the acquisitions of Los Angeles-based Handsome Coffee Roasters and Tonx, Inc. Freeman says when he first opened Blue Bottle he "never really had a vision" for aggressive expansion, but nonetheless, when opportunities like the recent purchases began presenting themselves to the company, he's been fortunate to have the ability to make nimble decisions.

Clean and well-managed accounting books allowed Freeman to secure substantial private investment in 2012, as well as additional investments in 2014.

On the other hand, Ebert's former company, which didn't pay adequate attention to the accuracy of its financial statements and forecasts was "never able to take the proper risks," he says. "We weren't able to stretch ourselves as the markets we sold to changed." Not only were opportunities diminished, but essentially the business was always "just keeping our heads above water, and

Privilege of Proper Business

The ramifications of not managing the basic financials of your business are too high. At best, opportunities are lost and you may find yourself in stressful, unpleasant working environments. At worst, businesses fail. Like every other business professional, coffee professionals have financial accountabilities and responsibilities first and foremost.

While the topic of accounting and finance will never be quite as stimulating as a pour-over crafted by a passionate barista, ultimately, if you can't meet your financial liabilities or create enough cash flow to buy the products that you need to sustain and grow your business, you will struggle and possibly fail, regardless of the caliber of your product or the quality of your service.

As in all things, the fun only comes, and often is only recognized, by the counterbalance of hard work. At least in our industry, we never have to tackle the hard work without the pairing of a perfect cup of coffee. ■

. . . .

ANDI TRINDLE MERSCH has a varied background within her specialty coffee career, which began behind the espresso bar in 1989 and, since then, includes cupping, training, consulting, green coffee trading and buying, quality control, sales and writing. Mersch currently serves as director of coffee for Philz Coffee. She was elected to the Roasters Guild Executive Council for a two-year term in March 2015, and she volunteers with the Specialty Coffee Association (SCA) developing coffee business curriculum. She is a past board member of the SCA and the International Women's Coffee Alliance.

Business owners can take many cues from the lemonade stand model—demonstrated here by *Roast* publisher Connie Blumhardt's daughters, Laney and Elle Fadden (from left), with customer Scarlet Hayes—which relies on product, place, price and promotion for success.

Marketing Deconstructed

A Guide for Specialty Coffee Roasters and Retailers

by Robin White

• FROM THE SEPTEMBER/OCTOBER 2015 ISSUE OF *ROAST* •

The concept of "deconstruction" has its roots in French literary criticism, but we're most likely to come across the word today on a menu or food blog. Deconstructed food involves taking the ingredients of a familiar recipe apart and reassembling them in a new and unique way. The method allows chefs to create new culinary experiences based on tried-and-true flavor combinations.

By deconstructing the traditional recipe for marketing, this article will outline how the basic elements can be reconstructed in practical ways to allow specialty coffee roasters and retailers to achieve their vision—even when their goals include more than pure profit-driven corporate objectives.

While most people have a rough idea of what marketing is, the actual blend of ingredients, and why and how they work together, can seem a little vague. This mystique is the reason we sometimes hear a successful marketing person referred to as a "marketing guru"—like Yoda with an MBA.

While marketers may appreciate the attention—who doesn't want to be known as a guru?—their efforts are most efficient and productive when the senior management team thoroughly understands what they are trying to accomplish. In many small businesses, the founders *are* the marketing department, making it even more important to demystify marketing.

Marketing Basics

"Marketing is telling your story to attract like-minded new customers and build loyalty with existing customers," says Colby Barr, co-founder of Verve Coffee Roasters in Santa Cruz, California. "One misconception about marketing in the specialty coffee business is that it's only about the coffee."

Many coffee enthusiasts who have started roasting and/or retailing businesses think of themselves primarily as artisans, focused solely on the product. They are passionate about sourcing beans with rare characteristics and developing the roast profiles and brewing methods that will showcase each bean's character. Marketing is sometimes perceived as a necessary evil, but the reality is that the marketing process is fundamental to the success of every business—even those without marketing staff.

"Coffee is absolutely a core value and central to why we do what we do at Verve," explains Barr, "but for some of our customers, it may only be part of what draws them to us. Everything from design and branding to culture and store locations may also connect them to our brand, so these are other elements that we can highlight."

Think about the most basic business: the lemonade stand. When an entrepreneurial child starts a lemonade stand, he or she considers the four fundamental aspects of marketing—product, place, price and promotion.

As these children make decisions about those aspects of their businesses, they naturally think about alignment with their target customers' wants. They start with a product they feel people will want to buy, set up shop at a place that is convenient for their customers, choose a price their customers will be willing to pay, and post a sign to promote the business. When a business' goods, location and pricing align with what a target audience wants and needs, and the enterprise uses promotion to make that audience aware of its existence, the business will have customers.

Consider a few ways that poor marketing decisions could result in a wasted Saturday for the budding entrepreneur. What if the lemonade were replaced with lukewarm prune juice? What if the stand were located in the backyard, or the price set at $19.99 per glass? What if the signage posted were illegible, or there were no sign at all? Each of these would be a major marketing error, likely dooming the business to failure.

Simple, right?

In the lemonade stand example, achieving alignment (i.e., successful marketing) is easy because the business is based on copying a proven model. On the flip side, copying success with no innovation rarely leads to long-term viability—there are not too many career lemonade stand owners.

Modern Marketing Realities

The complexities of business today require that entrepreneurs be marketers first, even if they do not like to think of themselves in that light. Business has evolved dramatically over the past 50 years, and change continues to accelerate.

Management consultant Peter Drucker, the person *Forbes* calls "the founder of 21st century management," notes one of these changes: "The customer now has the information. ... The manufacturer will cease to be a seller and instead become a buyer for the customer."

In decades past, consumers typically would walk into a shop, browse the available merchandise and choose an item based on the options in stock. Retailers wielded significant control and, working together with manufacturers, could effectively drive trends with a combination of advertising and selective distribution.

Today, we often know what we are looking for before leaving home. Our wants and preferences are shaped by reviews and

Verve Coffee Roasters' Santa Cruz, California, cafe is located on Pacific Avenue, a popular destination for tourists and locals. | *Photo by Ted Holladay*

comments by our peers as much or more than any traditional advertising. We shop at retailers that bring us the products we want in a convenient place (virtual or physical) at the best value. More and more, we also choose to purchase from businesses we feel are trustworthy and operate in a way that reflects our values.

Drucker also notes, "The aim of marketing is to know and understand the customer so well the product or service fits him and sells itself."

With a little research, anyone can understand what customers have wanted in the past. A good marketing person can identify trends and make decisions around product, price and place to keep a company's offerings in step with consumer demand. The great marketer goes a step further and makes decisions based on where consumer wants and needs will be in the future. Brilliant marketers go even further by helping to shape future consumer demand, so the supply of innovative products and demand for those products stay aligned as the company evolves.

The key is to think about marketing not as advertising, but as alignment of a company's offerings with consumer expectations in each of the four fundamental elements of business: product, place, price and promotion. (These are the traditional four Ps of marketing. While the list has been debated and appended over the years, we're sticking with the original four for this article.)

Product

When making product decisions, a business can take a variety of approaches. At one extreme, a company can offer only products with proven consumer demand. Businesses that take this approach tend to compete based on offering a lower price or more convenient access. At the other extreme, companies that are innovation-driven develop novel products, then work to find or create demand for them.

The first route tends to be a faster and less expensive path to volume, while the second is slower and more expensive. The right approach will depend on the company's goals and resources.

Many entrepreneurs who have taken the second approach have gone to market with an innovative product, but without the financial resources to stick it out long enough to see a return. Others that follow the first route have opened businesses based on immediate opportunity and have seen their quick success burn out when competition with lower prices or more convenient locations appear.

Long-term success for new and growing businesses often is found in the middle—balancing familiar, proven products with innovation. This is especially important for new businesses with limited funding. Sales of familiar products will pay the bills while demand is developed for the unique products that differentiate the company in the long run.

For example, assume there is broad consumer demand for medium-roast, 100 percent Colombian coffee. Offering a microlot

"Marketing is telling your story to attract like-minded new customers and build loyalty with existing customers," says Colby Barr (right), who co-founded Verve Coffee Roasters with Ryan O'Donovan (left). *Photo by Josh Telles*

Colombian under a proprietary brand name would be a balanced middle ground. On the one hand, this product capitalizes on existing demand while the unique innovative aspects—brand name and roast color—help secure longer-term customer loyalty. A unique roast profile, consistency between roasts and the skill of the barista also provide opportunities for differentiation, even when other retailers are using coffee from the same farm.

On the other hand, the first retailers to introduce little-known products will find more promotion is needed to align customer demand with their products. For example, if a retailer chooses to offer cascara, the coffee cherry tea, the company likely will find that adding "Cascara" to its chalkboard menu will not be enough to make it successful. By training its team, educating its customers, offering samples and so on, the retailer can use innovative products to build brand loyalists who will support the business over the long term.

Place

Location, location, location. The old wisdom around retail success is as true as ever for specialty coffee retailers. For most roaster/retailers, an online location is a critical complement to a brick-and-mortar location. Choosing a retail location is a more complex decision than can be covered in full here, but we'll focus on the choice from the perspective of alignment.

"You can't do business in a brick-and-mortar store without the presence of customers," says Mark Cohen, professor of marketing at Columbia University.

That's a simple statement with a catch. Common sense tells us that the higher the concentration of customers around our business, the more successful we'll be. The challenge becomes identifying our customers. It's crucial to truly understand which customers make up our target market before evaluating any retail location. (It's also important to avoid signing a 10-year lease simply because of the cool vintage ceiling.)

For most roaster/retailers, the target market is much narrower than "coffee drinkers." Higher-priced specialty products and the unique atmosphere of a shop likely will align only with a smaller group within the larger population of people who drink coffee. One good exercise is to create half a dozen profiles representing the customers whose expectations align with what the cafe will offer.

For example, one profile might be Audrey, a 30-something mother of two who lives within three blocks of the cafe. She works full-time and has been going to a chain cafe around the corner for years. She's looking for a fresh space for a quick coffee on her morning commute and to hang out on weekend mornings, when she will pick up a bag of whole-bean coffee to take home. She wants the baristas to be unpretentious and engaging, coffee to be lighter, and the selection of origins always varying. Audrey represents 25 percent of our customers.

Once these profiles are created, they will help us analyze potential locations more objectively as we try to determine if the community truly is aligned with our target market. It's also important to think about how the neighborhood is likely to evolve over the next 10 to 25 years. If the demographic is changing, is the retailer prepared to adapt to stay aligned?

In a world of perfect alignment, the location will be on the route customers already are taking. In this situation, the need for promotion is minimized. Choosing a less-convenient or less-visible location means the business will need to rely on promotions to create awareness and motivate customers to veer off their normal route.

The same basic principles apply to a company's online location. Visibility via unpaid search engine results and social media mentions will translate into traffic if the company's online presence aligns with its customers Internet activity. Creating awareness through organic visibility will minimize the need

"Everything from design and branding to culture and store locations may also connect [customers] to our brand," says Verve Coffee Roasters co-founder Colby Barr, "so these are other elements that we can highlight." | *Photo by Ted Holladay*

for paid online advertising, but that doesn't mean it happens automatically. Content creation, social media activity and traditional media outreach are important tools to point traffic toward an online location.

Under the general heading of place, it's important to consider more than just the geographic location. Place can include all the factors that combine to create an experience that will keep customers coming back, including customer service. Service standards also should be aligned with expectations. Do customers expect quick, no-nonsense service from a uniformed cashier, or a more casual interaction with a coffee artisan? Either way, clear direction and training for all employees is needed. Poor customer service is the fastest way to undermine all the other hard work that goes into building a retail business.

Price

Price is the least romantic of the marketing levers, but it is no less important than other aspects of marketing. Ultimately, businesses can succeed or fail based solely on their pricing strategy, so building alignment with consumer expectations is critical.

Because people like saving money, logic tells us the lower our prices, the more popular our products will be. Accepting this premise would be a huge mistake for most specialty coffee businesses.

Competing on price creates two major issues. First, lowering prices forces a business to cut corners to stay in the black. As a result, customers may receive exactly the same product, but be far less satisfied with their overall experience (grumpy underpaid barista, dirty restroom, etc.). Also, because coffee is (technically) a non-essential item, the experience of purchasing and consuming the product needs to be enjoyable or customers will look elsewhere.

Second, consumers generally anticipate a cost before they purchase an item. If a customer orders a brewed coffee at an unfamiliar cafe and the price is much higher or much lower than expected, the customer will form a judgment about the coffee. If the price is much lower, the assumption could be that the product is inferior. If the price is higher than expected, customers tend to infer the product is better than what they anticipated. In this way, a higher price is not necessarily a bad thing, especially if customer service is extraordinary and the experience offers value beyond the coffee itself, in the form of tasting, education, a unique ambience or other value-added service.

The key to a good pricing strategy is alignment. Aligning the prices you charge with how you want your customers to perceive your product is critical. Offering customers a bargain at a boutique shop with a super-premium image may actually disappoint customers. Great coffee is an affordable luxury and customers feel a distinct satisfaction in treating themselves to something truly exceptional.

Promotion

While many associate marketing primarily with advertising and promotion, the truth is that solid marketing decisions early in the business planning process reduce the need for spending on advertising and promotion later. Promotion is a broad term that includes any activity that will close the gap in alignment between customer expectations/wants and the business's offerings. Promotions that are directly tied to creating alignment will provide a good return on investment for business owners.

A good promotional plan begins by setting specific goals, then spells out how each promotional activity will help achieve those goals. Sometimes the plan seems so obvious that putting it into writing may seem unnecessary; however, that can be an expensive mistake. Putting a plan in writing prompts the kind of deep consideration of details that can make the difference between promotions costing money and earning money.

Once a goal is established, it should identify a current gap in alignment. For example, the goal for a new business might simply be, "Attract more customers." The question, then, should be, "Why don't we have the customers we would like to have?" The answer might fall under the product, place or price category. The promotional solution needs to be based on where the actual gap exists.

For example, eager to attract more customers, the busy entrepreneur might make a snap decision to invest in a larger sign, distribute coupons, or place ads in the community weekly to create more awareness. If the local community is used to dark-roast coffees and this business is offering lighter roasts, creating awareness may not help the business owner achieve his or her goal. The gap in this case lies in the product. Using those funds to offer tasting sessions to build appreciation for lighter roasts likely would be a more effective way of attracting new customers.

Promotions can be an endless money pit if they have no direct connection to specific results. A strategic approach to promotions that focuses on building alignment will help business owners reach their goals more quickly and with lower investment.

This brief deconstruction of the key elements of marketing is intended to demystify marketing and help owners take a pragmatic, hands-on approach to the process. Successful reconstruction happens when everyone within a company is engaged in applying marketing principles to achieve a common vision. ■

· ·

ROBIN WHITE *has worked on marketing, product development and strategic operational projects for hundreds of roasters and specialty coffee businesses, ranging from startups to multinationals, for the past 20 years. He has developed marketing strategies for growth in the retail, office coffee, foodservice and hospitality channels. White currently serves as vice president of marketing for Single Cup Coffee.*

Weak Link

Balancing the Synergy Between Product Development, Quality Control and Supply Chain Management

by Kate LaPoint

• FROM THE MAY/JUNE 2014 ISSUE OF *ROAST* •

The highly volatile nature of the coffee business requires adaptability—not to mention an iron stomach and the ability to assure oneself that prematurely gray hair looks distinguished rather than haggard. If you frequently wake up in the middle of the night, panic stricken, wondering what tomorrow will bring, you're probably in the coffee roasting business. Welcome to the roller coaster.

The comforting idea of predictability cannot even be entertained with regard to green coffee. There are variables none of us can control, including weather and other naturally occurring events, such as pests and disease. There are also transportation cost increases and unanticipated delivery delays.

"Flexibility is extremely important in the current market climate. Not only is the "C" price rising quickly, but also the Central American crop has been very disappointing in terms of volume. There is less high-scoring coffee available, and it is coming at a much higher price," explains Scott Reed, a former trader with Houston-based Walker Coffee Trading. Luckily, Reed assures, "There are any number of strategies on which smaller roasters can get assistance from their importers."

Product development, quality control and the supply chain all work symbiotically. Whether a microroaster with just a few employees, or a large corporation with multiple employees working in specific departments, a deep understanding of the process coupled with solid relationships are the keys to the successful management of each equally important function.

In large roasting companies, the roles of product development, supply chain management and quality control are typically separate, explains Spencer Turer, vice president of Burlington, Vermont-based Coffee Analysts. "Product development designs products that meet the needs of sales and marketing, finance and operation; supply chain manages physical risk and financial risk; and quality control evaluates product for adherence to product specifications."

In small roasting companies, like my own, these functions are performed by just one or two people. "However, the responsibility and authority remain the same," Turer advises. "To be successful, that person must understand the dynamics of each function and maintain the integrity of each responsibility for the overall success of the company. When one person is responsible for all functions, it is tempting to sacrifice quality for availability or convenience, or to conduct product development from current inventory for convenience without searching out new and unique coffees."

In other words, don't be lazy. But laziness and a simple lack of hours in the day can have the same effect. Following is advice to help the roaster who feels, like I do, spread a little too thin.

Product Development

For coffee roasters, product development is the "artistic function of the manufacturing process," explains Turer. "Artistic skill is required for taste and aroma development; however, other business considerations exist related to green coffee sourcing, including price and availability." For any manufacturer, large or small, whether roasting coffee or brewing chai or making widgets, the initial questions that must be answered prior to developing a new product are, "What will we make, how will we make it, how and to whom will we sell it, and can we make money on it?"

Once these questions are answered satisfactorily, that's when the "art" can begin. "Roasters need to understand how their varietals taste, not only by themselves, but also at different roast levels and/or with other varietals," says Brandon Riggs, former roastmaster for Stockton Graham & Co. of Raleigh, North Carolina. "Product development in specialty coffee is trial and error, based upon what you know as the roaster. The most humbling thing about coffee is, no matter how much you think you know, you can easily learn something new every day. And if that doesn't

Photo by Mark Shimahara

happen, it shows you really don't know the intricacies of coffee and blend development."

The artistic side of product development is exciting, especially when one is experimenting with different green coffee components and roast profiles, says Turer, though he warns, "The business side of product development may not be as exciting for everyone, considering the financial requirements and budgeting for the product and the development process."

But it is equally important.

There is no reason to spend one's time on developing an outstanding product if it is not equitable and sustainable for the company. To help in determining this, Turer suggests four tenets that guide product development with direct relation to green coffee sourcing:

✔ Price
What is the desired selling price for the final product and the green coffee budget for the supply chain? Figure out your margin.

✔ Quality
What is the desired taste and aroma for the finished product? Will this be consistent or evolving, and what are the specifications needed to achieve this?

✔ Availability
Is the new item a blend, a single-origin, or a region- or farm-specific item? What is the amount of coffee required, and is this a seasonal item, a limited offering or a year-round menu item?

✔ Relationship
Whether direct trade or through brokers or importers, do you have solid relationships? Which is best suited to help with sourcing?

Let's say you are in the "smaller" roaster category, and you are that one person who is wearing all the hats. This is where a great relationship with your importer(s) shows its indispensability. Importers are part of your team—your "dedicated green coffee buyer who has access to a large amount of coffee information, and who uses their time to study the market," as Turer reminds us, a relationship that often exists in larger coffee roasting companies.

These outside team members are invaluable resources for product development and consistency. Let's say you've decided to create a new blend. At Early Bird Coffee Roasters, we begin the product development process with a very clear idea of what we want the cup to offer, and work backward from there. Reed agrees: "The important thing with blends is first deciding what you want to achieve. Do you want something that is consistent? In my mind, that is what a blend suggests. Or do you just want the best, blow-your-socks-off blend, even if it's different every time?"

If blending for consistency, Reed again advises flexibility: "I have seen so many roasters create a blend and believe that they always have to use the same coffees within the blend. That is no way to have a consistent blend. Coffee is ever-changing, and for consistency, you want to focus on cup profile over coffee origin."

Similar to green coffee sourcing, Christopher Merry, president of The Chai Company, Inc. in Delta, British Columbia, says procuring raw materials from trusted suppliers makes all the difference in product development. "We are working on a new product right now, and sourcing ingredients is a critical component to the development. Time, cost and quality are major considerations," explains Merry. "We start by developing a list of potential suppliers. We look for suppliers who are audited by independent agencies, and then we must determine whether these suppliers can meet our quality standards and delivery criteria. It takes time to develop the list, contact all the suppliers, test all the samples, have them complete documentation and get pricing."

Photo by Marlee Benefield

Quality Control

Successful product development and consistency cannot happen without solid, trusting relationships along the supply chain and agility with regard to your ingredients. The same relationships will serve you very well as you work to maintain the quality of your product—raw to roasted.

Turer suggests that roasters can gain relative security by establishing product specifications for the green coffee they buy. "It is the skill of the professional coffee buyer, product developer or roastmaster to manage the variations in sensory profile through the harvest year and during the change from old crop to new crop," he says. Coffees can, and should be, purchased "subject to approval of the sample" (SAS) so the roaster has the opportunity to evaluate the coffee based on sensory profile, expected character and physical coffee specifications. As a roaster, according to Turer, it is important to be confident that the coffee you're purchasing is the coffee you ordered, and that it is of the quality you paid for.

Green coffee cherries. | *Photo by Bruce Mullins*

Your importer is deeply connected to the market and also cups dozens of coffees a week. Without the resources of a larger company, it can be difficult to maintain consistency unless you give everyone on your "team" a clear picture of what you are trying to accomplish. "If your importers, through good communication and an understanding of your particular business, have a good idea of what you are looking for in a specific origin or blender, they can contact you when they come across one on the cupping table that would work for you," says Reed.

"Also, when you find a coffee you like, consider purchasing some under contract for future delivery with your importer," Reed says. "There are certainly quality limits to how long you want to store a specific lot of coffee, of course."

"However, with a volatile market and shrinking availability, it would serve you well to lock up a reasonable amount of a

Photo by Marlee Benefield

specific lot," Reed continues. "Your importer can help you with this and there will be a small cost for the importer to warehouse the coffee for you." This can be based on past usage combined with projections for usage over the length of a given contract.

"When making your green coffee purchases from crop cycle to crop cycle, as we do, it helps maintain consistency of price and quality for your product," Riggs explains. "That being said, it may not be possible 100 percent of the time. Due to limited availability and either increased or decreased demand for a specific coffee, roasters have to maintain a quality product without having their customers notice a difference in either price or taste." Good relationships with your importers will make it easier to source coffees that can act as substitutes when another coffee is not available.

It is also important to note that green coffee substitutions, whether from one origin to another, or even from region to region, may require adjusting roast profile and/or blend percentages to maintain the most consistent end product. "It can be challenging at times, but the extra work will create a seamless transition," Riggs says. Your importer is there to help.

Reed agrees: "Your importer wants to see you do well. Communicate what you are looking for, and ask for suggestions and for samples. Coffees change. Ten years ago, finding an 84-plus Honduras was nearly impossible. Now they are commonplace. If you don't remain open to the ever-changing possibilities that coffee presents, you will be missing out."

Also working with agricultural products, tea and spices, The Chai Company's Merry explains how his team compensates for variations in the strength and flavor of their product's ingredients from crop to crop. "We request pre-shipment samples that we evaluate before placing any order. We cup them against existing inventory to judge quality and profile," Merry says. "After delivery, we compare the delivered product to the pre-shipment sample to ensure what we thought we were getting is in fact what we received. Just as with coffee, there are times when we have to adjust recipes because of fluctuating flavor profiles."

Shawn Hamilton, vice president of operations/coffee buyer for Java City in Sacramento, California, suggests roasters develop a "value proposition" for their blends. "You should have a cup profile and a known cost," he says. "Once you have that established, you will need to maintain your cup profile consistently without sacrificing margin. If you cannot maintain your margin, then you will have to decide whether to take a price increase or sacrifice cup profile."

Finally, Turer urges, "A critical part of the development process includes testing the finished products. Internal panels, trained panels, expert panels and consumer panels are all tools that professional product developers use."

Even beyond new product development, quality control must be a routine part of a coffee roastery's operations. "We perform weekly cuppings and tastings here to ensure our roasts are consistent," Riggs explains. "We often brew a blend in the same manner a specific customer would brew it, so we can get a real 'feel' for what they experience in their shop. We also experiment with modifications on espresso blends due to roast level and always strive to make them better over time."

While expert or consumer panels may not be practical on a regular basis, Riggs says that he will include as many people in the company as possible when conducting regular cuppings. "The more people you have tasting, the more feedback you get,"

Photos by Marlee Benefield

he says. "I also encourage our customers to do a test run of a new blend or roast before they commit to buying it. The feedback from customers is a top priority, and it also gives customers a sense of ownership in the shop."

Hamilton agrees on the importance of quality control on the preparation side. "Training customers on how to properly brew the coffee and maintain their equipment is crucial. In our case, we visit customers at least every 90 days to verify they are properly preparing the product," he says.

Just as coffee shop owners and coffee roasters value feedback from their customers, so do green coffee suppliers. Sergio J. Dias, owner/partner of JC Coffee Importers, LLC, in Seattle, who is a grower as well as an importer, instructs coffee roasters to be proactive: "Stay ahead of it—if you have a problem or a question about your product, tackle it immediately. Even if it means returning the green coffee and replacing it with another—do it."

Supply Chain Management

"A stable, approved supplier program is critical to our success," Merry says. His company generally has one or two preferred suppliers for each of its products' ingredients. "In addition to buying from origin, we also have local suppliers who can provide smaller quantities if we have a gap in supply, or when we are sourcing ingredients that we don't use a lot of."

At Early Bird Coffee Roasters, we have even been known to partner with other small roasters who may use similar coffees. We are comfortable calling each other in a pinch for small quantities and at cost.

Fostering a relationship with more than one green coffee source is helpful, if not necessary. "[While a] single-source supply chain is great for relationship, transparency and building a partnership for your desired quality, how do you verify price and manage availability?" Turer asks. "Multiple-importer sourcing helps identify the true cost of your green coffee requirements, and the wider variety of coffee offerings from multiple sources will increase your choices and availability."

Hamilton says this is crucial to a roaster's success: "Really, you need to form a good relationship with *all* parts of the chain to be effective. You should know the farms or co-ops you are buying from on a personal level, the exporter and the importer." Hamilton suggests it is also important for larger roasting companies such as Java City to have diversity in the supply chain, "so if one supplier fails to meet the commitments, you have alternative sources to get product to still fulfill your needs."

Dias urges roasters: "Look for quality products; this will put you on the top. Do not try to cover too much ground; concentrate your efforts locally."

"Always have two or three coffee importers in your supply chain," advises Turer. "Know the difference between an importer, trader and broker; what each one's perspective will be; and when

Photo by Connie Blumhardt

it is best to utilize each for their specific capabilities. Know that the decisions for purchasing coffee are individual to each buyer, and what is the right decision for you—based on price, quality, availability and relationship—may not be the same or right decision for other roasters."

It is important to understand how each of these three areas—product development, quality control and supply chain management—functions on its own and how each innately affects the other. The decisions made along the way, whether by a single person or by several, must hold the other areas in high regard, yet without sacrificing the individual value of each function (don't sacrifice quality for convenience!). Though production, inventory and staffing levels are much higher in a larger roasting company, the functions of (and therefore the importance of decisions related to) product development, quality control and supply chain management are the same in a smaller roasting company. They are the functions that, if managed well, will help us all grow. ◼

. . . .

KATE LAPOINT *is currently senior communications manager in the technology organization of T-Mobile. She spent more than 20 years in the specialty coffee industry as an editor, writer, marketing consultant and entrepreneur. Most recently, she was owner of Early Bird Coffee Roasters. LaPoint lives in Seattle.*

Rowster coffee cup with logo. | *photo by Andy Madeleine*

Matter of Appearance

What Trademark Infringement Can Mean for a Brand

By Kurt Stauffer

• FROM THE MAY/JUNE 2014 ISSUE OF *ROAST* •

The 2014 performance art installation of a faux Starbucks, known as "Dumb Starbucks," was ultimately a social experiment designed to stir up debate—about trademarks, corporatism, coffee culture, the Internet and media. It also initiated a conversation around the use of an obscure legal term in trademark law called the "parody defense," which grants "fair use" of legally protected material.

In United States copyright law, "fair use" is a doctrine that permits limited use of copyrighted material without acquiring permission from the rights holders. Examples of fair use include commentary, search engines, criticism, parody, news reporting, research, teaching and library archiving. Starbucks quickly filed an injunction to stop Dumb Starbucks from operating, but not before the media and coffee community had a feeding frenzy.

Preparation and Protection

Failure to protect your trademark can quickly lead to erosion of your brand assets and provide violators the opportunity to invoke the Defense of Laches. Laches is a legal term meaning that the violated party "slept on its rights" by not pursuing a claim, further prejudicing the infringer. In other words, the longer a conflicting trademark is allowed to coexist, the weaker the argument could be against the violator and against others with conflicting marks.

My company, Rowster, had an interesting brush with, and took a crash course in, trademark law in 2013. While every case is different, our story highlights the first steps to take when creating a brand, and the cautions to take when protecting it. One should never be remiss about identity protection, and it's also imperative to take great care in avoiding infringing upon another company's intellectual property.

In 2009, after toiling away for five years in the back room of an art gallery, Rowster moved into its first retail space. Our logo was initially written on a napkin and printed on a laserjet printer onto pre-made Avery labels, which were then all manually applied to bags. Seeking a clearer brand for our first retail experience, we hired a designer and hammered out a new logo and brand application. At the time, this seemed vitally important as we were trying to break through the stereotypes cast by second-wave coffee roasters. We thought we had created a bold, vintage look that showcased our difference from the rest.

Our name and brand marks were unique and seemingly impossible to copy or imitate ... or so we thought. Then we discovered a large, well-known coffee company had begun using a logo nearly identical to our own. It felt like more than a coincidence, especially after so much time had been invested in creating the look.

Since Rowster had only filed and been granted a trademark for our name, but had not yet bothered to file for logo (a variation and embellishment of our name), we felt as if there was nothing we could do. Our concern was that if Rowster continued to grow and add locations, at some point, we would be subjected to legal action. Knowing the other company's ability to successfully squash any attempt to infringe upon its identity, and being small without any real legal team, Rowster knew it was vulnerable.

A vulnerability felt by many.

"An explosion of coffee businesses around the world has led to increased infringement problems, both accidental and intentional," says Marshall Fuss, an attorney with detailed experience in business, real estate and trademark law, who also acts as general

Rowster sign with logo. | *Photo by Andy Madeleine*

Rowster espresso cup with logo. | *Photo by Andy Madeleine*

counsel for the Specialty Coffee Association of America and Coffee Quality Institute. "Many of these problems can be avoided by doing a thorough clearance of the mark before investing any money in it. But even then, there are many who do not respect intellectual property rights and will be happy to 'borrow' your good name."

Jim Mitchell, an intellectual property attorney with a special interest in trademark law, informed Rowster that although we had not filed a trademark, we could still file and be granted pre-emptive rights based upon first use of the mark for coffee sales and services.

Companies do not necessarily need to file their trademarks with the United States Office of Trademarks and Patents to protect them. However, according to Mitchell, there are certain rights gained by doing so that make it easier to protect trademarks later, and which prevent another from acquiring concurrent rights to the same mark in geographic areas where one has not yet operated. "If you only rely on your common law rights to protect your trademark, others can, under some circumstances, acquire rights which are concurrent to yours in other parts of the country," he says. "A registered trademark prevents anyone who begins using the same mark after your trademark application filing date from obtaining concurrent rights."

By filing, businesses establish constructive use of the trademark and receive nationwide pre-emptive rights, including:

• The right to sue in federal court for trademark infringement

• Recovery of profits, damages and costs in a federal court, and the possibility of treble damages and attorneys' fees

• Evidence precedence of the validity of the registration

• Registrant's ownership of the mark and of registrant's exclusive right to use the mark in commerce—in connection with the goods or services specified in the certificate

• The ability to make the mark incontestable after five years of continuous exclusive use, which constitutes conclusive evidence of the registrant's exclusive right, allowing only limited grounds for attacking the registration

• The availability of criminal penalties, treble damages and statutory damages of up to $2 million in an action for counterfeiting a registered trademark

• A basis for filing trademark applications in foreign countries

Going for millions didn't fit Rowster's goals.

The plan to proceed began with a conversation; Mitchell examined Rowster's motives for protecting the trademark. First, there has to be damage to the business to make a large-sum claim. Proving damages is very difficult and would likely require litigation, something that Rowster could not afford. "Your trademark rights are infringed when others adopt trademarks that are likely to confuse some people into thinking that your competitor's goods or services originate with, are authorized or sponsored by you," says Mitchell. At a minimum, you're entitled to an injunction against the infringer's continuing use of your mark. You may also be entitled to an award of damages, and if the infringement has been "willful," you may be entitled to treble damages.

If the infringing mark is an intentional copy of your mark, used on goods or services identical to your own, it constitutes a counterfeit mark, and you can recover statutory damages. Statutory damages for applying or selling goods or services with a counterfeit trademark may be not less than $1,000 per counterfeit mark, and not more than $2 million.

Once, in Mitchell's opinion, it was determined that there was sufficient likeness to be classified as an infringement on Rowster's mark, the next step was to determine the date of first use. Using the searchable database Trademark Electronic Search System (TESS), found on the United States Patent and Trademark Office website, we found that the infringing company had a trademark registration and a date of first use succeeding the filing date of our trademark application.

Fortunately, we had a long trail of electronic documentation in the form of emails, Facebook posts and invoices, all with our logo. They were time-stamped, too, which provided further proof of our actual first use four months prior to the other company's. In addition, we had evidence of use going beyond our immediate geographic area.

Rowster's challenge was to prove that our date of first use was indeed first, and preferably to also prove that the second user had not acquired "concurrent rights."

Mitchell drafted a letter offering three options for the infringing party to avoid further legal actions:

1. Declare that Rowster's mark and the other company's do not conflict, and agree that both companies could use their respective marks

2. The other company could buy Rowster's mark, and we would abandon our claim to it

3. The other company could abandon its mark

Having done our due diligence, the infringing company saw that we had a legitimate claim, and its attorney made a cash offer to purchase the R-Star mark. After a little haggling, we agreed to a dollar value and an end date. It is my duty to report that the company was beyond fair. It treated Rowster with respect and courtesy, and quickly rectified the situation.

"Rowster's experience illustrates the importance of being reasonable and realistic in your expectations when enforcing your trademark rights," Mitchell says.

The mark can make the brand the longer a company exists.

Rowster bag with logo shape. | *Photo by Andy Madeleine*

Front entrance to Rowster with logo. | *Photo by Andy Madeleine*

Various coffee bags with logos—a brand's face to consumers.

Dancing Goats blend packaging.
photo courtesy of Batdorf and Bronson

Regular Coffee Co. packaging. | *photo by Andy Madeleine*

Cases such as these are "impossible to predict," Fuss adds, though, commonly, "a few strongly worded lawyers' letters may solve the problem when the infringer is a U.S. company, especially if it does not have the resources to contest the issue in court."

Rowster would have been pleased with any of the three options that were offered. Had the company chosen one of the first two options, there would have been no buyout. Mitchell had another similar case in which a prior user, after having raised an infringement position, elected to agree there was no infringement, rather than to try to either buy out his client's mark or proceed with litigation.

Fuss agrees that litigation is typically the last solution. Costs can quickly accumulate and vary enormously from state to state and federal court. "It is usually safe to say that litigation costs more than either party expects," Fuss says.

For innocent infringers, though, the costs can be quite punitive. Take the case of Everyman Espresso owner Sam Penix, who had his financial records audited by the state of New York after using an image of his knuckle tattoo, "I (coffee cup) NY" as a sign on his storefront and on mugs that he sold. It was cited as too close a

likeness to the ubiquitous "I (heart) NY" logo. It cost him more than $10,000 in legal fees and fines.

Making the Mark

Abandoning a mark is a fine solution when you receive a cash settlement to do so, as in Rowster's case. It allowed us to comfortably assess our options and invest in our operation, though we did not spend as much time on rebranding. But at the time, Rowster was a brand-new company.

"Do 'marks make the brand?'" Fuss asks. "For a single neighborhood shop, probably not. But the bigger you get, the more important the mark is."

Batdorf & Bronson Coffee Roasters, an Olympia, Washington, roaster since 1986, has faced several trademark issues over the years. It trademarked the name "Dancing Goats" in 1993 for International Class 30 for the specific class, coffee beans, and for International Class 42 for retail and wholesale shops featuring the sale of coffee beans in the United States. In other words, no one can name a coffeehouse, cart, wholesale business or website "Dancing Goats" if the primary business is coffee, and no one can name a coffee "Dancing Goats" without being in violation of Batdorf & Bronson's trademark.

Because of the roaster's longevity and reach, it pays a trademark service to search federal filings for potential violations. "Usually, though, we become aware of potential violations by searching the Internet or via industry friends who let us know someone is using the name," says Larry Challain, president of Batdorf & Bronson.

As the "big guy," the company has a bit more control over the situation. When contacting violators, it opts to make a friendly phone call or send an informative letter first. "In most every situation the violation is by a new business," Challain says. "It is our preference to catch violations while it is relatively cheap for a business to make the needed changes. If this approach does

Rowster coffee packaging. | *Photo by Andy Madeleine*

not work then we turn the issue over to our trademark attorney." If the concern makes it to the attorney, Challain says he always prefers to settle issues in a positive manner. "The process can be all of the above: frustrating, devastating, annoying. Fortunately, many of the people I have had to contact voluntarily complied once they knew the facts."

At a larger company, the mark means everything. Challain says, "It's very important to us. More people probably know us as 'Dancing Goats' than 'Batdorf & Bronson Coffee.' It would cost us quite a bit to lose the Dancing Goats mark." For this reason, Challain says his company is diligent about catching an infringement early, when the business is still relatively new. "It is much less costly to change your business name (or a coffee blend name) early in the life of your business, before you have invested a lot of time and money in building your brand."

If your company is contacted about a violation, Challain recommends remaining calm and asking questions until you're sure you understand the issue.

At the Rowster cafe. | *photo by Andy Madeleine*

"Do not turn it into an adversary relationship unless you want to incur a lot of attorney fees," he says. "Verify the trademark through your attorney or on the United States Patent and Trademark Office website. If you do not think you are in violation, contact a trademark attorney for advice." He says not to rely on your business attorney, unless the attorney is well versed in federal trademark law.

The biggest mistake a new company can make regarding trademarks is not verifying if the desired name (or mark) is already trademarked. "I often hear, 'But I registered the name with the state.' This does not matter; the state is just recording names," Challain says. "Trademarks are issued by the federal government."

Regarding company size, Challain adds that being small isn't an argument against infringement. "If we do not enforce our trademark we are subject to losing it. It is just the way it is."

On either side of trademark infringement, whether it occurs in the beginning stages of a new company, on the initial name and mark, or it violates the rights of a larger company, one party will be forced to rebrand. This could be due in part to the selling of an old logo or because of a cease and desist order.

In these cases, rely on the product; don't rely on the logo, which is how Rowster was able to proceed. While to most a brand is a powerful symbol of the meaning and philosophy of a company, in the end it does very little to sell coffee. The quality of the product is what sells. The design, the details, can be rethought and

repackaged, if that's what's ultimately necessary.

But Mitchell warns, "If you are a young company and have not invested heavily in marketing your trademark, it is easier to make a change in the event of problems. It becomes much more difficult the longer you use a particular mark."

Fuss adds, "Chalk it up to experience, and be sure to clear your new mark before you use it."

Creating a brand that communicates fidelity for one thing is important; an infringed mark can exacerbate this notion. If you make a great product, your customers will support your brand. As a company, you have an obligation to protect that, to shield your customers from any confusion. At its core, a trademark is a way to validate this relationship—a way for others to recognize your business's commitment to quality. It acts preventatively, too, so counterfeiters don't deceive customers by selling a product that doesn't achieve the high standards you've set.

Eventually, when we, as coffee professionals, have educated and converted enough customers to value and appreciate the simplicity of specialty coffee, we may no longer be pioneers, but we'll always remain craftsmen. ■

KURT STAUFFER *started roasting coffee in an air popper in 2004, then bought his first roaster (a 5-kilo Has Garanti) by accident on eBay. He started Rowster Coffee in 2007. He can be reached at* kurt@rowstercoffee.com.

PART IV

OPERATING A SPECIALTY COFFEE ROASTING BUSINESS

RULES & REGULATIONS

Smoke in the Air

An Update on Emissions and Air-Quality Regulations

By Jeff Duggan

• FROM THE JULY/AUGUST 2013 ISSUE OF *ROAST* •

WHETHER you're for, against or indifferent to the fact, we live in an era of regulation. While most will agree that regulation is necessary to ensure human health and environmental protection, there are those who believe much of the regulation in the United States amounts to nothing more than income-generating bureaucracy. Regardless of the legal, ethical or health factors substantiating the need for regulation, it is a matter we as coffee roasters cannot ignore. In other words, feelings of discontent are not exclusions from any regulation existing in this country. So, we must be compliant in order to avoid jeopardizing the businesses that we dedicate so much of our lives to on a daily basis.

The coffee industry is unique in that many of its members, for various reasons and motivations, have adopted an environmentally conscious mindset. This may be due to our realization that we cannot have an industry without an intact and healthy natural environment. But let the truth be told—coffee roasting is at odds with healthy air quality. It is not just about the air we breathe, but also an ecological cause and effect. If we contribute harmful matter to our air, there is a real possibility that it will impact our climate as well as our water. With specialty coffee production being dependent on so many environmental factors, it is illogical for someone to both care about coffee and disregard the environment.

What is all the fuss about coffee roasting anyway? There can be several causes of trouble for the coffee roaster, ranging from annoying your neighbors to violating rules and regulations. Not only do we have to be respectful to those operating or living around us, we must ensure that our roasting is compliant with both state and local regulation. Easy? Often not. Important? Without a shadow of doubt.

If you currently roast or have plans to start roasting, there are a few questions you should answer before deciding on a location and the type of equipment you will purchase. A little pre-planning will go a long way to eliminate surprises and, most importantly,

money wasted. Coffee-roasting equipment is not cheap, so having to repurchase equipment to comply with air-quality regulations is a situation you'll want to avoid. Here are the questions you should be able to answer before you select your site and purchase equipment:

1) What state and local regulations apply to you?
2) What equipment fits within the specifications of the regulations affecting you?
3) Is environmental protection a priority in your equipment-buying decision regardless of applicable regulations?
4) Aside from making the regulatory agencies happy, will you be a good neighbor?

Due to the extreme variance in air-quality regulation from region to region, it is not possible to specify here what applies to the area in which you will be roasting. While the U.S. Environmental Protection Agency sets the standards for emissions, your state and local agencies establish the enforceable rules and regulations. The first step would be to check your state government website to learn about the air-quality agency responsible for your jurisdiction. For example, in California, the Air Resource Board of the California Environmental Protection Agency oversees all of the regional air-quality management districts in the state. Their website provides a list of local district regulators to contact. A simple phone call can be invaluable. It is important to know what aspects of roasting may be subject to permitting and ongoing inspection. Here are three areas you should inquire about when researching what may apply to you in the city where you will be roasting:

Stack Emissions

This is essentially the exhaust output of your roaster at the point of discharge into the environment. This will be when your exhaust enters the environment, whether it is on the roof, side of the building or elsewhere. Stack emissions include sulphur dioxide (SO_2), carbon monoxide (CO), volatile organic compounds (VOCs), odor and particulate.

Roaster Emissions

While stack emissions get most of the attention, they are not the entire story. Every roaster will output particulate and burner nitrogen oxides (NOx). NOx will be discussed in greater detail later in this article. Chaff is an example of particulate output by the roaster that may or may not reach the stack. Most roasters are outfitted with a cyclone to collect this particulate prior to being discharged into the environment. However, if the cyclone is inefficient or not properly maintained, it could release particulate at the stack. The other method of controlling chaff, or particulate, is filtration. Typically this method is used only on industrial-sized roasting equipment. Filtration systems are more costly to both purchase and maintain.

Cooling Bin Emissions

As silly as it sounds, coffee beans discharged into a cooling bin at the end of the roast continue to emit VOCs. Depending on the batch size of your roaster, the air used to cool the beans may have to be directed through an oxidizer.

Next, let's delve a little deeper into stack emissions. Roasting coffee creates harmful airborne byproducts, period. We as roasters may not like to admit this, but roasting coffee is not good for the environment. Ensuring that you have proper emissions abatement equipment in place is not only a matter of regulatory compliance, it is also one with potential long-term environmental implications. There are four ways in which we can control air pollution on our coffee roasting equipment.

1 | Thermal Afterburners

Also referred to as thermal oxidizers, these devices are designed to eliminate VOCs in stack emissions, which include toxins such as acrolein, acetaldehyde and formaldehyde. Using a dedicated burner system, thermal afterburners are designed to elevate the roaster gas to temperatures greater than 1,400 degrees F and create a residence time in the afterburner for no less than 0.4 seconds in order to eliminate pollutants and odor.

2 | Catalytic Incinerators

Also known as catalytic oxidizers, these pollution-control systems incorporate a gas or electric heating system along with a catalyst. When the exhaust gas is heated to 750 degrees F or greater, the catalyst will react with the gas to volatize and otherwise destroy the exhaust pollutants.

3 | Low-NOx Burners

Nitrogen oxides are a byproduct of incomplete combustions. The higher the burner temperature, the more NOx is produced at the burner. Low-NOx burners can reduce NOx emissions by 50 percent or more.

4 | Recirculating Systems

There are recirculating roaster systems on the market that are worth researching. They are designed to clean and re-use heated exhaust gas to reduce stack pollutants as well as reduce the amount of energy required to operate the machine. Think of it as recycling hot air. The less gas needed, the less pollutants produced. While they have controls for stack emissions, they do still emit unfiltered/oxidized cooler smoke. In these applications, controlled quenching helps to reduce the cooler pollutants as well.

Determining what type of pollution-control system to adopt is a question of regulation, cost and your own ethical beliefs as they relate to the environment. Thermal afterburners are cheaper to purchase and maintain than catalytic incinerators, but they require a higher burner output, therefore producing more NOx and carbon monoxide than catalytic incinerators do. Low-NOx burners are expensive. There are off-the-shelf roasters with low-NOx burners available, but some of them may not comply with your local NOx regulation, so it is best to verify the specifications and not assume that the roaster will produce a low-enough NOx emission because the manufacturer said so.

The latest hot topic in air-quality compliance has to do with NOx emissions. This is creating a bit of a stir in both the coffee roasting and roaster manufacturing industries. At the moment, only one region in the country, Southern California, is subjected to über-strict NOx regulation. The South Coast Air Quality Management District (SCAQMD), which affects Los Angeles, Orange, Riverside and San Bernardino counties, was the first to create a rule of this type. Rule 1147 establishes such low NOx limits as to require a gas- or liquid-fuel-fired appliance to be outfitted with a low-NOx power burner. Traditional open-flame atmospheric burners, the type found on most roasting machines worldwide, simply will not meet the requirements of this particular rule. Now many may not be concerned with what is going on in Southern California, but regulations such as this will typically spawn in one region and quickly spread to other areas of the country. In terms of an anticipatory purchase, it may be prudent to invest in a piece of equipment that satisfies this rule so as to not have to replace the burner, or worse yet the machine, if this type of rule does get adopted in your jurisdiction.

SCAQMD Rule 1147 is proving to be quite challenging for business owners who are looking to start roasting or interested in upgrading their current machine. Machines with a 60-kilo batch size and under face a significant handicap when it comes to outfitting the roaster with a compliant burner system. Finding an off-the-shelf burner system appropriately sized for smaller roasters is an enormous challenge. This is a classic case of regulation being way ahead of industry. Over time, as demand for low-NOx roasters increase, burner manufacturers and roaster manufacturers will be forced to respond by producing models designed around low-NOx requirements.

Another difficulty for those looking to place an in-shop roaster is, simply, space. Pollution abatement equipment is large, and the amount of space required to place a 15-kilo roaster may double with the inclusion of an oxidizer. Don't get discouraged by this, though. There are many installation configurations that create possibilities for maximizing both horizontal and vertical space. It is something to keep in mind in terms of equipment options and your overall budget. Be mindful of the fact that trickier installations are pricier, so budget accordingly.

Neither the environment nor "Big Brother" is the only concern if you operate, or plan to operate, a roasting facility. Aside from the chemical composition of your emissions, your roaster can be deemed a nuisance by your neighbors if proper care is not taken in the design and implementation of your system. In other words, if your roaster stinks up the neighborhood, whether commercial or residential, you may end up with an angry mob, as well as your local air-quality regulator, at your door.

Fines vary by region and can range from $500 to $2,500 per day, depending on the violation. Typically, fines are levied daily for identified violations. In other words, once the local air-quality regulator has notified a roaster of noncompliance, the roaster will be ordered to cease operations or be subject to fines for each day of operation in violation of the code.

Roaster exhaust odor is pungent and can travel much farther than one realizes. And the fact that you may consider it an "aroma" as opposed to an "odor" is of no consideration when it comes to neighbor complaints. If you roast in close proximity to other buildings, it wouldn't be uncommon for wind to push the odor toward nearby air conditioning intakes. Bob Quinlan, CEO of Metropolis Coffee Company, believes planning is the key. "Picking a location where this type of complaint is minimized is a good part of startup planning," he says.

In business, we have all heard the adage, "location, location, location," and most of the time we are focused on aesthetics, parking, foot traffic, etc. If you are a roaster in search of a location, proximity analysis should be included. However, despite your best planning or lack thereof, if you are faced with a neighbor complaint, you have two viable options. The first option is to address the problem with a pollution-abatement device discussed earlier. The second option is to use a dispersion fan. This is the "dilution" solution to the odor nuisance problem. Emissions are not reduced; they are simply diluted by mixing in "fresh" air at the stack and forcing it straight up via a high-powered blower. This reduces the concentration of the odor and moves the exhaust air mass high enough to keep it away from other buildings. If both solutions

are options, the former is preferable. Mark Wain, the owner of Caffe Luxxe, a coffee roaster and retailer in Los Angeles, opted for prevention. "We are in an industrial area, and our afterburner is oversized, thereby completely eliminating roasting odors and smoke outside," says Wain.

There is no one-size-fits-all approach to roasting and compliance. There are just too many variables that come into play. As a roasting company owner, your philosophy on the issue will have the greatest impact on the decisions you make when it comes to equipment purchases and compliance. Air-quality-focused regulation is here to stay, and burying one's head in the sand in hopes it will go away is ill advised. Whether you do the right thing because you have to or want to is moot. The more we acknowledge the fact that our craft is detrimental to the environment if performed without adulteration, the quicker our industry will "snap to" and work toward more effective and accessible solutions.

If you ever come to a point in time where you are faced with an air-quality-related issue, know you are not alone. Attempt to establish a working relationship with the regulatory agency in your area. They make the rules, so there's no better place to get an understanding of what is required of you. Also know that you are likely *not* the first person to deal with a particular issue, and help may only be a phone call or email away. The roasting community is rather small, and more often than not, you will get advice and recommendations from your peers that will lead to the right solution. Roast hard, but tread lightly! ■

JEFF DUGGAN *is the owner and roastmaster of Portola Coffee Roasters in Costa Mesa, California, Roast's 2015 Micro Roaster of the Year. He oversees both retail and wholesale roasting operations, as well as Portola's direct trade green buying program. He can be contacted at* jeff@portolacoffee.com.

The Food Safety Modernization Act

Are You in Compliance?

By Mike Ebert

• FROM THE JANUARY/FEBRUARY 2016 ISSUE OF *ROAST* •

Coffee production, specifically roasting, has long fallen under the radar when it comes to food safety concerns at manufacturing facilities. This is true for the government agencies that regulate and inspect such facilities, and for the coffee roasters who operate them.

Anyone who has helped set up or maintain written food safety plans for a roasting operation knows that one of the key elements is a Hazard Analysis Critical Control Path (HACCP) plan. The problem is, where in coffee roasting does one uncover an actual, bona fide critical control step?

Between the high temperatures at which we roast and brew and running the coffee through some sort of filter, we eliminate most concerns. Sure, the occasional rock, which will break a grinder, makes it through, but at the end of the day, a rock in coffee will not land someone in the hospital. Even glass or metal shavings don't pose major food safety concerns, because of the filter used in brewing—though every effort should be made to minimize such impurities when developing production processes, and auditors and inspectors likely will want to see that you have protocols in place to do so.

Still, in light of all this, most coffee-related HACCP or written food safety plans focus more on quality then actual safety concerns. Certainly there are control steps, and every roaster should have a HACCP plan, but seldom does it achieve what is required for food safety.

Still, to quote Bob Dylan, "The times are a-changing," and coffee roasters need to be aware of what's ahead.

Introducing the FSMA

On Jan. 4, 2011, President Obama signed into law the Food Safety Modernization Act (FSMA). This new law is designed to ensure that the food supply in the United States is safe by shifting focus from responding to problems that have already occurred to preventing problems in the first place.

The FSMA is the first major piece of federal legislation to address food safety since 1938. Some facts that drove this decision:

- About 48 million Americans become sick every year from food-related issues.

- Of these, 128,000 require hospitalization to treat food-related illnesses, and 3,000 die.

- Infants, children and older individuals are most susceptible to food-borne illnesses.

- With increasing globalization, 12 percent of the food we consume is imported from other countries.

- Terrorism-related food tampering could pose a public health risk.

- The importance of preventing contamination and health risks throughout our food chain is a key risk management strategy.

The following list, published by the U.S. Food and Drug Administration (FDA), details the five major components of the new law:

PREVENTIVE CONTROLS: For the first time, FDA has a legislative mandate to require comprehensive, prevention-based controls across the food supply.

INSPECTION AND COMPLIANCE: The legislation recognizes that inspection is an important means of holding industry accountable for its responsibility to produce safe food; thus, the law specifies how often FDA should inspect food producers [officially every three to five years, depending on risk factor, but this seems to vary in practice]. FDA is committed to applying its inspection resources in a risk-based manner and adopting innovative inspection approaches.

IMPORTED FOOD SAFETY: FDA has new tools to ensure that those imported foods meet U.S. standards and are safe for our consumers. For example, for the first time, importers must verify that their foreign suppliers have adequate preventive controls in place to ensure safety, and FDA will be able to accredit qualified third-party auditors to certify that foreign food facilities are complying with U.S. food safety standards.

TERMS YOU SHOULD KNOW

Food Safety Modernization Act (FSMA): The most sweeping reform of U.S. food safety law in more than 70 years, the FSMA was signed into law by President Obama on Jan. 4, 2011. It aims to ensure that the food supply in the United States is safe by shifting focus from responding to contamination to preventing it. Find more information, visit *fda.gov/Food/GuidanceRegulation/FSMA*.

Foreign Supplier Verification Program (FSVP): The FDA finalized rules for foreign suppliers in November 2015. As press time, the regulations were still being clarified, but importers and roasters that import green coffee directly should stay up to date on these rules as they evolve.

Global Food Safety Initiative (GFSI): A private organization established and managed by the international trade association Consumer Goods Forum. GFSI maintains methodology to benchmark food safety standards for manufacturers as well as farm assurance standards. Find more details at *mygfsi.com*.

Good Manufacturing Practices (GMP): The practices required to conform to the guidelines recommended by agencies that control authorization and licensing for the manufacture and sale of food, drug products and active pharmaceutical products. These guidelines provide minimum requirements a pharmaceutical or food product manufacturer must meet to assure its products are of high quality and do not pose any risk to the public.

Hazard Analysis and Critical Control Points (HACCP): A systematic preventive approach to food safety from biological, chemical and physical hazards in production processes that can cause the finished product to be unsafe. A HACCP plan details measurements to reduce these risks to a safe level. A HACCP system can be used at all stages of a food-processing chain, from production and preparation to packaging and distribution.

Safe Quality Food (SQF): A food safety and certification program that links primary production certification to food manufacturing, distribution and agent/broker management certification. The program is recognized by GFSI. Learn more at *sqfi.com*.

Standard Operating Procedures (SOP): While GMPs focus on food quality, SOPs cover all aspects of your business. These are detailed, written procedures that include specific instructions on how to monitor and document a food safety program. SOPs include directions about the documentation and checklists to use, personnel training, and what materials need to be posted. It's what you are going to do and how you are going to do it.

RESPONSE: For the first time, FDA will have mandatory recall authority for all food products. FDA expects that it will only need to invoke this authority infrequently since the food industry largely honors our requests for voluntary recalls.

ENHANCED PARTNERSHIPS: The legislation recognizes the importance of strengthening existing collaboration among all food safety agencies—U.S. federal, state, local, territorial, tribal and foreign—to achieve our public health goals. For example, it directs FDA to improve training of state, local, territorial and tribal food safety officials.

You're probably wondering if roasters fall under this new law. The answer is a resounding, "Yes!"

In fact, since Dec. 12, 2003 (several years before the FSMA was enacted), all domestic and foreign facilities that manufacture, process, pack or hold food for human or animal consumption in the United States have been required to register with the FDA and be subject to inspection of their facilities, records and documentation.

Begin By Registering Your Company

As a coffee roaster, your company must register as stated above. Simply visit the FDA website (*fda.gov*) and follow the links to register. Food facility registration helps the FDA determine the location and source of a potential bioterrorism incident or an outbreak of food-borne illness, and allows the agency to notify entities and consumers who may be affected in a timely manner.

There are some exceptions: If you are a roaster/retailer and do not sell wholesale, or if you operate a nonprofit roasting entity that serves coffee directly to consumers, you might be exempt. Read the information on the FDA's website to determine if you qualify for exemption.

Because this registration requirement became effective Dec. 12, 2003, unless you qualify for exemption, your company should already be registered. If you are starting a new company, you must register before you open for business. Furthermore, you must renew your registration every two years. Registration can be completed online or by mail by the business owner or an individual authorized by the owner. Currently, there is no fee to register.

You will need the following information to register your business:

- Facility name, address, phone number and emergency contact phone number

- Parent company name, address and phone number (if applicable)

- Name, address and phone number of the owner, operator or agent in charge

- Email address for the contact person of the facility or, in the case of a foreign facility, the U.S. agent

- All trade names associated with the facility

- Applicable food product categories, as listed on the registration form

- For a foreign facility, the name, address and phone number of a U.S. agent, and the phone number of the facility's emergency contact if it is someone other than the U.S. agent

- Assurance that the FDA will be permitted to inspect the facility

WHAT ARE YOUR LIABILITIES?

THE FOOD SAFETY MODERNIZATION ACT (FSMA) has created criminal liabilities for food industry firms all along the supply chain, including retailers and wholesalers. Chief executive officers and other corporate officers can be held personally liable for misdemeanor violations of the Federal Food, Drug & Cosmetic Act (FD&C Act), regardless of whether or not they engaged in the violations or had any knowledge of them.

Specifically, FSMA has created six new types of criminal violations under the FD&C Act and has triggered a seventh, which was on the books previously but had not been implemented. These include:

1 Operating a facility not in compliance with FSMA Preventive Controls regulations

2 Failure to comply with the FSMA Produce Safety regulation

3 Failure to comply with the FSMA Food Defense regulation

4 Refusal or failure to comply with an FDA recall order

5 Knowing and willful failure to comply with consumer recall notification requirements

6 The importing or offering for importation of a food if the importer does not have a foreign supplier verification program in compliance with the FSMA Foreign Supplier Verification Program regulation

7 Failure to comply with the Sanitary Food Transportation Act regulation

Find and review the regulations at *fda.gov/Food/GuidanceRegulation/FSMA*

at the times and in the manner permitted by the Federal Food Drug & Cosmetic Act

- Certification that the information submitted is true and accurate and that the person submitting it is authorized to do so

Beyond Registration

Registration is the easy part. You are also required to have a written food safety plan, including protocols, procedures, policies and thorough documentation. This should include the following:

HAZARD ANALYSIS AND CRITICAL CONTROL POINTS (HACCP)

This is a systematic preventive approach to food safety from biological, chemical and physical hazards in production processes that can cause the finished product to be unsafe. Bottom line: HACCP details the prevention of hazards rather than finished product inspection. It will follow your product—in this case coffee—through the roasting plant, from receiving through shipping. It focuses on the hazards that are unique to your product. The concerns for a seafood processor will be different than those of a coffee roasting company.

EMPLOYEE HEALTH POLICY

A company's employee health policies should detail illness reporting requirements, under what circumstances employees must stay home from work, and personal cleanliness and hygiene, including hand-washing requirements. No bare-hand contact with ready-to-eat foods is allowed. (This is a gray area for coffee, but most inspectors look for it.) You must also show that you provide training, knowledge and supervision on all things food safety-related for all employees.

RECALLS

The main question to address here is, can you get ALL your product back if there is a problem? Your written food safety plan must include a procedure detailing what you will do in the event of a recall.

For most roasters, this is one of the most challenging components of the plan. The FDA now has the authority to issue a mandatory recall; however, it must first give you the opportunity to cease distribution and conduct a voluntary recall of the product in question. If you refuse, or do not act quickly enough, the FDA could force a mandatory recall.

The challenge for roasters is how to set up a recall procedure. For starters, you should create a protocol for tracking product complaints from customers, as well as identifying potential trends these complaints might show. The FDA's focus, however, is not on quality issues but on potential health issues. To understand this further, consider how the FDA classifies recalls, based on severity:

- **CLASS 1:** Likely to cause severe illness or death
- **CLASS 2:** Likely to cause illness
- **CLASS 3:** Likely to cause "unpleasantness" but not much more

WHAT TO EXPECT WHEN YOU'RE INSPECTED

We asked a few coffee roasters about their experiences with the Food Safety Modernization Act (FSMA) and FDA inspections. Here's what they had to say:

I have had an FDA inspection every other year for the past six or eight years. ... The key difference between FDA and USDA (separating out the things that are specific to organic and use of logo) is that the FDA wants to know you have a recall policy and USDA wants you to demonstrate the process. FDA inspections tend to increase ... after a hurricane or prolonged power outage. They want to verify that food entering the commercial food supply chain has not been compromised. Once you are in the system, you are revisited at a frequency consistent with your overall hazard potential and your report history.

—Todd Arnette, Williamsburg Coffee & Tea, Williamsburg, Virginia

I have not been inspected by FDA in probably 10 years. They show up here unannounced and do a walkthrough, so I don't know about prepping for one ... because I don't know if and when they are coming. However, everything in it seems to be covered by [third-party food safety auditor] AIB International standards. So in the event I did get inspected, we would likely have all the processes and documentation required by FDA from doing it for AIB.

—Shawn Hamilton, Java City, Sacramento, California

I recently had my first FDA inspection and the big focus was on a recall plan, which we did not have in place. The inspector was very nice and informative about it. He sent me information on how to comply, but at the end of the day, he expected a plan by the end of the week. We accomplished it, but it made the blood pressure rise.

—Bob Arceneaux, Orleans Coffee, Kenner, Louisiana

[Swing's Coffee] owner Mark Warmuth and I, as director of coffee operations, routinely talk about these issues. We have a full recall system in place. ... Having a living plan is in the interest of everyone: for the consumer's sake, the brand and trustworthiness of the company, and the government's ability of intervene on a public health issue. Sometimes, when you go to work day-to-day, potential hazards may be right beneath your eyes; you just need to see it again for the first time. As we move ahead, we are becoming more and more granular and attuned to potential hazards and risks. We are looking forward to more formal training with the FDA and hope to collaborate on a decision tree specifically for coffee.

—Neil Balkcom, Swing's Coffee Roasters, Alexandria, Virginia

In your recall plan, you need to address and document what the root cause could be and what corrective action will be or has been taken. As stated previously, your plan must be updated regularly. Inspectors will want to see what problems your company has had—whether they resulted in a recall or not—and what you did to resolve them.

What would a recall mean for a roaster? Quite simply, a company must be able to notify anyone who may have received any product that has the potential to be unsafe and have the product returned. This is where it gets tricky. If you cannot break out certain lots of items—for example, you know you roasted 30 pounds of the product in question on a certain date, all packaged with a certain lot number and shipped to specific customers—you might be required to recall all product shipped within a certain time period.

Crazy, huh?

The main message here is, your company needs written documentation that covers the basics. At this point, this is one of the areas the government seems to be focusing on with smaller companies when it performs facility inspections. This falls under the category of risk management and depends on how much risk you are willing to take—the more elaborate your recall plan is, or more specifically, the more detailed your lot tracking system is, the more it will cost you.

● A QUALIFIED PLAN WRITER

Your plan must be written by a qualified individual, though what constitutes a qualified individual is not well defined in the law. Basically, the higher risk your products are, and/or the larger your firm is, this might involve hiring a food safety consultant or third-party auditor, hiring a staff member with the proper credentials (which again, at the current time are not clearly defined, though the FDA is working on clarifications in this area), or putting one or more current employees through training.

Technically, a qualified individual has successfully completed training in the development and application of risk-based preventive controls or is otherwise qualified through job experience to develop and apply a food safety system, but again, this is not clearly defined in the regulations. This person becomes the official record keeper, assuring that all plan documentation is completed, maintained properly and available for review.

● OWNER/MANAGEMENT PARTICIPATION

One of the most important aspects of a written food safety plan is the role of owners and top executives. They can't simply put someone else in charge of it. They must be active in plan development and implementation, have full understanding of the laws and their roles, and be able to assure the company is in compliance.

It's also important to understand that this is not something you do once and forget about. The plan must be reviewed and updated every three years—and any time you discover a control or procedure is not effective. Inspectors will want to see that your plan is a living, breathing document, regularly discussed and reviewed by the entire company.

The Bottom Line

Perhaps the most important thing one can say about the new regulations is this: Take them seriously. It appears that the companies inspectors scrutinize most intently are those that claim ignorance and have done nothing—or very little—to address food safety. Take the time to register and start developing a written food safety plan today.

There are many resources available to you via the Internet, community colleges, fellow coffee roasters and food safety consulting firms. At press time, no organizations or businesses had been officially recognized or recommended by the FDA; however, this is one of the agency's top priorities as it will assist in administering and enforcing the law.

As these regulations have evolved—and continue to evolve—the National Coffee Association USA (NCA) remains a strong advocate for roasters. The association has pushed for regulation changes and clarification to protect the coffee industry, and the NCA website (*ncausa.org*) provides a wealth of information about the regulations and regulatory updates that directly affect coffee professionals.

As far as regulations for foreign suppliers, at press time the FDA had not yet released the final rules. Updates will be available on the FDA and NCA websites as regulations are clarified.

This process of coming into compliance with the FSMA is not something you will accomplish and check off your to-do list. It's about creating a culture that continuously reviews, addresses and improves operations with a focus on food safety. ■

. . . .

MIKE EBERT *is founder of Firedancer Coffee Consultants, dedicated to helping clients create a personalized strategy to ensure long-term success. He works primarily with roasters, producers and retailers, drawing from his extensive experience in all facets of the specialty coffee supply chain to guide clients in reaching their potential. Ebert is a specialized lead instructor for Specialty Coffee Association (SCA) certification programs and is chair of the SCA Coffee Buyer Educational Pathway Committee, which develops new educational experiences for the specialty coffee community.*

THE BOOK OF ROAST

INDEX

INDEX

A

Acerbic 194, 267, 286, 288-289

Acidity 37, 39, 44, 52-53, 55-56, 77, 101-102, 111, 117, 131, 163, 165, 167-171, 188, 191- 197, 200, 206, 213, 223-225, 229, 235, 238, 267, 272-279, 283-284, 286-295, 297, 299, 301, 311, 317, 321, 327, 328, 329, 331, 345, 348, 351-355, 356, 360, 364, 375

Acidy 36, 37, 56, 267, 278, 288-289, 293-294, 336

Acrid 199, 267, 272, 286, 288-289, 291, 294

Acrylamide 187-189

Afterburner 30, 141-143, 149, 259, 267, 391, 397-399, 446, 447

Aftertaste 143, 168-170, 229, 255, 267, 271-272, 275, 277, 279, 286-293, 297, 301, 328-329, 331, 348, 351-353

Agtron Scale 30, 34-35, 38, 228-229, 233, 248-249, 255, 257, 267, 287, 299, 314, 320, 322-323, 329

Air Roaster 30, 143, 174, 177, 220, 265, 267

Air Quenching 267

Airflow 35, 88, 142-144, 147, 149-151, 174, 176-177, 220-221, 223-224, 232, 235, 238-239, 245, 248, 250-253, 258, 261-263, 267, 276, 314, 356, 375, 400

Alkaline 164, 168, 267, 276, 286, 288-290, 293

Alqueire 267

American Roast 39, 267

Appellation 267

Aquapulp Method 267, 271, 279

Aroma 39, 49, 101-102, 107, 111, 117, 121, 156, 163-165, 167-171, 179, 187-188, 191, 195-196, 199-201, 206, 207, 209, 211, 221-225, 229, 232, 424, 243, 250, 254, 258-259, 267-273, 275-279, 286-294, 297-298, 300-301, 303307, 314, 317, 319, 329, 331, 337, 345-346, 348, 351-354, 357, 365, 383, 399, 400, 404, 432, 447

Arroba 267-268

Ashy 169, 286, 288-290

Astringent 34, 124, 126-127, 169-170, 193, 268, 273-274, 277, 286, 288-289, 292, 294

B

Baggy 77, 117, 268, 375

Baked 143, 233, 245, 257, 268, 289, 293, 360

Balance 36, 121, 207, 225, 235, 268, 290, 317, 321, 331, 335-336, 339, 351, 356, 360-361, 364-365, 375

Batch Roaster 31, 268

Bean Probe 175, 177, 245, 268

Bean Temperature 38, 143, 168, 179, 182-185, 221, 227-228, 234, 240, 242-243, 245, 248-250, 252, 268

Beneficio 268

Bird Friendly 62, 268

Bitter 125, 144, 155, 157, 163-164, 168-171, 193, 199, 204, 206-207, 209-215, 222, 254-255, 268, 289-295, 331, 346, 348, 356, 359

Black Bean 106-107, 110-111, 121, 124, 268

Bland 268

Blend 268, 326-367

Body 39, 44, 167-170, 193, 204, 224-225, 232, 235, 268, 268-288, 290, 297, 299, 301, 317, 327-328, 345-346, 351-353, 356-357, 364-366

Bouquet 200, 268, 273, 274, 277, 290, 292-293

Bourbon 37, 43-48, 53, 119, 267-268, 274-275, 279, 284, 328

Brackish 268, 286, 288, 290

Breaking the Crust 268

Brokens 268

Burnt 163, 167, 170, 225, 254-255, 268-269, 271, 277-278, 286, 288, 290, 291 , 293-294, 317, 259

Business Plan 289-395

Buttery 167, 268, 271, 286, 288, 290, 335

C

C & F 268-269

C Market 65, 71-72, 269, 271, 366, 420-422

Caffeine (C8H10N4O2) 155-158, 161-162, 171, 192-193, 205-206, 209-215, 269, 279, 343, 346, 353, 371-375

Caffeol 269

Caramelized 163, 247, 269, 290

Caramelly 269, 275, 286, 288, 290

Carbon Dioxide Process (CO2Process) 151, 163, 170, 179-181, 184, 222, 229, 269, 271, 279, 355, 373-374

Catimor 44-46, 48, 53, 269

Catuai 43-45, 48, 53, 210, 269

Caturra 36, 43-45, 47-48, 53, 269, 275, 284, 328

Caustic 269, 273, 286, 288, 290, 292

Certification 61-65, 69, 89, 269

Chaff 55, 149-151, 177, 240, 261-265, 269, 446

Chaff Collector 149-150, 240, 262, 269

Cherry 49, 54-59, 69-70, 100-101, 105-106, 109-111, 123, 125, 127-128, 135-137, 270, 272, 276, 291-292, 305, 427

Chlorogenic Acid 46, 126, 127, 156-158, 170, 192-193, 195, 206-207, 209-215, 222, 323

Chocolatey 270

Cinnamon 38, 125, 225, 229, 250, 277-278, 286, 288, 290, 294

Cinnamon Roast 194, 270

City Roast 225, 270, 273, 317, 337

Clean 270, 286, 288, 290

Cocoa 77, 270, 273, 286, 288, 290, 294, 357, 359-360

Coffee Berry Borer 101, 270

Coffee Berry Disease 44, 53, 270

Coffee Blossom 51, 271, 307

Coffee Classification/Green Arabica Coffee Classification System 131-137, 271

Coffee Leaf Rust 48, 271

Coffee Oil 155, 252, 271

Coffee Trier 271

Color Analysis 317-323

ColorTrack 34, 323

Commercial Coffee 33, 55, 271, 363, 366

Commodity 79-83

Complex 35, 39, 56, 58, 106, 121, 134, 155, 161-164, 170, 175, 182, 187, 189, 191, 195-197, 199-200, 203-204, 207, 225, 243, 271, 286, 288, 290, 329-330, 333, 336

Conduction 142, 173-177, 182, 184, 220

Container 271

Continuous Roaster 268, 271

Convection 35, 142, 173-177, 182, 184, 220, 245

Cooling Tray 20, 143-144, 149-151, 173-174, 221, 240, 257-259, 271

Creamy 271, 286, 288, 290

Creosoty 271, 276, 286, 288, 291, 293

Cup of Excellence 103, 117, 271, 315

Cupping 271, 282-307

Cupping Spoon 271

Current Crop 77, 271, 275

D

Data Logger/Logging 143, 177, 237, 271

Decaffeination 193, 233, 269, 271, 274-275, 278-279, 283, 371-377

Defects

    Green 100-137, 223, 270-271, 273-275, 278-279, 293, 295, 297, 299

    Roasting 143, 253

Degassing 259, 271, 282-283, 399, 414

Delicate 192, 271, 286, 288-289, 291-294, 315

Demucilage 56, 267, 271, 279

Depulp 127-128

Direct Process 271

Dirty 107, 111, 122, 124-125, 134, 272, 277, 286, 288, 290-291, 293

Double-Picked 272, 328

Drum Roaster 26, 28, 141, 143, 173-175, 180-181, 183-184, 222, 240, 245, 258, 272, 278, 328

Drum Temperature/Environment Temperature 149, 177, 244, 272, 274, 279, 294

Dry Mill 70, 106, 109-113, 132, 136

Dry Process 56, 105, 109, 197, 272-274, 276, 291, 293, 295

Drying 55-59, 101, 105, 109, 100, 111-113, 115-116, 119, 125, 127, 129, 133-134, 243-244, 255, 257, 267-268, 271, 273, 275, 278-279, 292, 295, 372

Dull 107, 111, 170, 187, 268, 272, 275, 279, 288-289, 290-291, 295

Earthy 56, 116, 121,123, 125, 127, 187, 272, 275, 277, 288, 291, 292-294, 328

Environment Temperature/Drum Temperature 149, 177, 244, 272, 274, 279, 294

Ethyl Acetate (C4H8O2) 272, 283, 371-372, 374-375

Exhaust Temperature 234, 272

Emissions Control 272, 445-447

F

F.O.B 70-71, 80, 272

Fair Trade 63, 272, 376

Fermentation 56, 105-108, 111-113, 116, 124, 128, 197, 223, 268, 272, 277, 279, 292-293, 295

Fermented 56-58, 104-105, 107-1111, 120-122, 124-125, 136, 272-273, 278, 286, 288, 291-292, 295, 328

Finca 272

First Crack 38, 128, 163, 168-170, 175-177, 193, 213, 222, 225, 228-229, 233-234, 238, 243-246, 250-251, 255, 257, 272, 321, 329, 359-360, 374

Flat 121, 167-171, 222-223, 225, 268, 272, 278-279, 286, 288-289, 291-295, 356

Flavor Profile 53, 105, 143, 227, 240, 247, 249, 251-252, 255, 257, 272, 278, 294, 299, 320, 328-329, 331, 333-334, 341, 345, 353, 355, 357, 363-367, 434

Flavor Wheel 132, 168, 198-200, 223, 272, 299, 314, 319-320

Flavored Coffee 272, 399, 400

Floater 103, 112, 121, 125, 137, 272

Fluid-Bed Roaster 30, 220, 245, 258, 267, 272

Food Safety Modernization Act 96, 401, 411, 449-453

Forward Sale 272

Fragrance 128, 167-168, 221, 224, 250, 267-268, 273, 278, 287-288, 290, 292, 294, 297, 305-307, 313, 315

French Roast 33-34, 37, 39, 192, 225, 273, 330-331

Fresh 273, 286, 288, 292

Fruity 56, 107-108, 122, 168, 192, 195, 224, 273, 275, 278, 279, 286, 288, 292, 306, 328, 331, 360, 375

Full Bag 273

Full City Roast 225, 273, 277, 317, 334

Fungus 58, 105, 110-111, 113, 116, 125, 127, 129, 134-135, 137, 292

Futures 79-83, 269, 273-275

G

Geisha 44, 49, 92, 273, 419

Grade 36-37, 70-71, 103-104, 113, 115, 131-133, 136, 189, 193, 273-274, 276, 351-353

Grassy 89, 103, 111, 124, 223, 225, 250, 273, 286, 288, 292

Green Arabica Coffee Classification System/Coffee Classification 131-137, 271

Green Coffee 42-137, 273

H

Hacienda 273

Hard Bean (HB) 36, 52, 131, 170, 221, 243-245, 273, 278

Harsh 167, 169, 171, 206, 222, 238, 267-268, 273, 277, 286, 288, 289, 290, 292-294

Heat Probe 35, 37, 175, 177, 195, 227, 235, 245, 268

Heat Transfer 23, 26, 29, 31, 142-143, 147, 173-185, 220, 240, 243, 248, 276

Heavy 33, 38, 167, 224, 225, 273, 275, 278-279, 286, 288, 290, 291, 293-294, 335, 356, 373

Hectare (Ha) 273

Heirloom 273

Herby 273, 286, 288, 292-293

Hidy 273, 286, 288, 291-292

High-Grown 273, 359

Home Roasters 27, 30-31, 265, 273

Hulling 36, 70, 105, 107, 109-111, 113, 273

I

Immature Beans 102-103, 108, 121, 131, 268, 273-274, 292

Imperfections 127, 132, 272, 274

Infrared 30, 175, 245, 303, 319-320, 323

Insect Damage 110, 121, 127, 131, 133-134, 137, 274

Intensity 56, 101, 274, 287, 288, 290-292, 294, 301

International Coffee Association (ICO) 274

International Standards of Operation (ISO-1401 9000) 274

Inventory Management 407-409

Italian Roast 32-34, 38, 225, 273, 274

K

Kosher 274

L

Le Nez Du Café 274, 302-307, 314

Lemon 274, 335

M

Machine-Dried 274

Maillard Reaction 157, 162-165, 169-170, 187-188, 200, 222, 250, 260, 361

Malty 274-275, 286, 288, 290, 292-293

Maragogype 44-45, 47, 274-275

Marketing 425-429

Mature Coffee 120-121, 124, 127, 274

Medicinal 126, 167-169, 209, 273-274, 277, 279, 286, 288, 290, 375

Mellow 271, 274, 286, 288, 291-292, 294

Metallic 1936, 274, 286, 288, 292

Methylene Chloride (CH2Cl2) Neutral 274, 283, 371-375

Mild 38, 52, 101, 268, 271, 274, 277, 286, 288, 291-292, 294

Milling 58, 70, 110, 113, 273-275

Moisture Content 55, 57, 112, 131-132, 170, 222, 243-244, 249, 255, 259, 273, 349

Moldy 58-59, 89, 107, 124-125, 127, 134, 274, 286, 288, 292

Mondo Novo 269, 274

Monsooned Coffee 275, 293

Mouthfeel 156, 204, 225, 268, 273, 275, 290, 292, 321, 327-328, 337

Musty 209, 275, 286, 288, 293, 306, 328

N

Natural Process 56-58, 102, 105-106, 110, 271, 275, 291, 293

Neutral 275, 286, 288, 290, 293-294, 253

New Crop 271, 275, 284, 292, 352-353, 433

Nippy 267, 275, 277, 286, 288, 293-294

O

Oily 38, 225, 268, 275, 286, 288, 290, 345

Old-Crop 117, 274-275, 433

Organic 62, 65, 87, 89, 93-94, 106-107, 126, 237-238, 275, 320, 372, 374-376, 416, 452

Organic Acids 126, 157, 163, 180, 191-197, 200, 206, 212, 222

P

Pacamara 44, 45, 47-48, 275

Pacas 45, 47-48, 275

Packaging 381-385

Parchment 55, 56, 59, 70, 77, 105, 107, 109-112, 121, 123, 125, 129, 136-137, 255, 273-275, 313

Past-Crop 77, 275, 279, 284, 286, 288, 293-295, 364

Patio-Dried 376, 284

Peaberry 36, 101, 270, 276

Perforated Drum 23, 29, 220, 276

Petroleum 276, 286, 288, 293

Phenol 105-106, 111, 113, 122, 124-125, 126-129, 134, 161-162, 164-165, 193-194, 201, 206-207, 209, 215, 270, 276, 290, 293

Piquant 267, 276, 278, 286, 288, 289, 292-294

Pointed 276

Pollution Control 397, 399-401, 446

Potatoey 276, 286, 288, 291, 293,

Probe, Bean 175, 177, 245, 268

Processing 42-65

Profile 36, 53, 55-59, 104-105, 117, 191-192, 194, 197, 272, 294, 328-331, 333, 341-342, 345, 353, 355, 357, 363-367, 434

Profile Roasting/System 30, 31, 34, 143-146, 149, 167-171, 175-177, 179, 188, 219, 221-225, 227-229, 234, 237-240, 243-245, 253-255, 276, 298-299, 320

Pruny 276, 286, 293

Pulp 52, 55-59, 126, 137, 187, 267, 276, 279

Pulping 56, 59, 105-107, 109, 111, 127, 137, 276, 279, 295

Pungent 267, 271, 276, 278-279, 286, 288, 289, 291-294

Purchasing (a roasting machine) 140-151, 396-401

Pyrolysis 222, 276

Q

Quakers 100-104, 106, 131-132, 274, 276

R

Rainforest Alliance 64, 276

Rioy 121-122, 126, 134, 277, 286, 288, 293

Roast Initiation 277

Roast Log 168, 170-171, 219, 221-224, 237-241, 321, 391, 413, 415

Roast Style 32-39, 218-260

Roaster Maintenance 151

Roasting Curve 168-170, 228, 245, 356

Robusta 43-49, 155-157, 159, 163, 187, 191-193, 196-197, 205-206, 243-244, 269, 277, 351-353

Rubbery 277, 286, 288, 290, 293-294, 353

S

Sample Roasting 247-252

Scorched 23, 175, 223, 255, 277, 286, 288, 294

Second Crack 33, 38, 143, 163, 165, 176, 193, 222, 225, 228-229, 233, 243, 245, 254-255, 277, 321, 329, 337, 359-361, 374

Set Point Process System 277

Shell 112, 121, 124, 135, 137, 274, 277

Silverskin 55, 124, 273, 277

Single-Estate 277

Single-Origin 247, 277, 327, 329, 333-334, 339, 341-342, 348-349, 357, 363-367, 371-377

Size Classification 277

Soapy 277, 286, 288, 294

Soft Bean 105, 243, 245, 277

Solid Drum 245, 278

Sour 104-113, 121-124, 127, 134-137194-195, 199, 206, 245, 268, 272, 277-278, 286, 288, 294

Source 278

Specialty Coffee 278

Spicy 53, 56, 167-168, 224, 278, 286, 288, 294, 306, 331

Split Bag 278

Spot Sale 278

Stale 189, 270, 272, 278, 286, 288, 294

Stinker 104-108

Storage 86-96, 115-119

Strawy 274, 286, 288, 293-294

Strength 278, 287, 293

Strictly Hard Bean (SHB) 36, 52, 131, 170, 221, 243-245, 273, 278

Sun-Dried 101, 278, 328, 331

Super Sack 278

Sustainable Coffee 278

Sweet 39, 53, 56, 58, 77, 101, 103, 156-157, 163, 167-171, 199-200, 209, 212, 223-225, 232, 235, 257-259, 278, 286-289, 294

T

Taint 57, 117-118, 121, 126, 167, 270, 272, 277-279, 286, 288, 294

Tangy 199, 267, 277-279, 286, 288, 289, 293-294

Tarry 268, 271, 278, 286, 288, 290-291, 294

Terroir 37, 227, 278, 287, 294

Tipped 278, 294

Toasty 200, 279, 286, 288, 290, 292, 294

Trademark Infringement 437-441

Triangle Cupping 279, 301

Typica 43-49, 53, 267, 274, 279, 284, 328

U

Umami 199, 279

Under-Developed 277-279, 294

Unripe 102, 106, 128, 135, 137

Utz Certified 65, 279

V

Vapid 277, 279, 286, 288, 295

W

Washed/Wet Process 36, 55-56, 59, 105-106, 108-109, 194, 194, 212, 267, 271, 275, 279, 291, 293, 295

Water Process 278-279, 283, 328, 372, 374, 377

Water Quench 258-259, 271, 279

Weight Loss (of beans) 35, 194, 239

Wet Process/Washed 36, 55-56, 59, 105-106, 108-109, 194, 194, 212, 267, 271, 275, 279, 291, 293, 295

Winey 192, 199, 279, 286, 288, 294-295, 335

Woody 103, 111, 117, 168, 275, 278-279, 286, 288, 295